British Literature

PEARSON
AGS Globe

Shoreview, Minnesota

British Literature Consultants

Jack Cassidy, Ph.D., Associate Dean, College of Education and Professor of Curriculum and Instruction, Texas A & M University—Corpus Christi, Corpus Christi, TX

Bridget Murphy, English Instructor, North Hennepin Community College, Brooklyn Park, MN

Acknowledgments appear on page 697, which constitutes an extension of this copyright page.

The publisher wishes to thank the following educators for their helpful comments during the review process for *British Literature*. Their assistance has been invaluable.

Christy Brandon, English and French Teacher, Fort Payne High School, Fort Payne, AL; **Judi Bremer,** English Teacher, Thomasville High School, Thomasville, GA; **Kimberly D. Clemons,** Teacher, Lincoln Achievement Center Day Treatment, Gary, IN; **Sharone Davis-Smith,** Reading/Literature Teacher and Title 1 Reading Specialist, Kingsley Education, Arcadia, FL; **Judy Feimster,** Resource English Teacher, James E. Taylor High School, Katy, TX; **Terri Valentine,** Coordinator/High School Correspondence, Des Moines Area Community College, Des Moines, IA; **Barney Woodward,** Teacher, Accelerated Learning Center, Buena Vista High School, Corona, CA

Publisher's Project Staff

Vice President of Curriculum and Publisher: Sari Follansbee, Ed.D.; Director of Curriculum Development: Teri Mathews; Managing Editor: Patrick Keithahn; Development Assistant: Bev Johnson; Director of Creative Services: Nancy Condon; Senior Designer: Daren Hastings; Senior Project Coordinator: Barb Drewlo; Senior Buyer: Mary Kaye Kuzma; Product Manager—Curriculum: Brian Holl

1-800-328-2560
www.agsglobe.com

Contents

How to Use This Book: A Study Guide

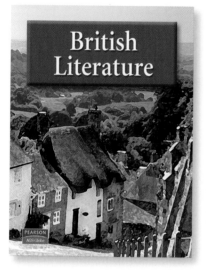

This book is an anthology of British literature. An anthology is a collection of literature written by different authors. The literature can be poems, plays, short stories, essays, parts of novels, folktales, legends, or myths. Sometimes an anthology contains selections from a certain country or continent. For example, you might have an anthology with great literature from America. Sometimes anthologies are organized around different genres, or types of literature. Then, you might have sections on poems, short stories, plays, essays, or folktales.

Reading a Literature Anthology

This anthology contains much enjoyable literature. An anthology helps you understand yourself and other people. Sometimes you will read about people from other countries. Sometimes you will read about people who lived in the past. Try to relate what the author is saying to your own life. Ask yourself: Have I ever felt this way? Have I known anyone like this person? Have I seen anything like this?

A literature anthology can also help you appreciate the beauty of language. As you read, find phrases or sentences that you particularly like. You may want to start a notebook of these phrases and sentences. You may also want to include words that are difficult.

This anthology is also important because it introduces you to great works of literature. Many times, you will find references to these works in everyday life. Sometimes you will hear a quotation on TV or read it in the newspaper. Great literature can come in many forms. On the next page are definitions of some kinds of literature genres in an anthology.

Genre Definitions

autobiography a person's life story, written by that person

biography a person's life story told by someone else (you will find biographies of many famous authors in this book)

diary a daily record of personal events, thoughts, or private feelings
- A diary is like a journal, but a diary often expresses more of the writer's feelings.

drama a story told through the words and actions of characters, written to be performed as well as read; a play

essay a written work that shows a writer's opinions on some basic or current issue

fable a short story or poem with a moral (lesson about life), often with animals who act like humans
- Aesop was a famous author of fables.

fiction writing that is imaginative and designed to entertain
- In fiction, the author creates the events and characters.
- Short stories, novels, folktales, myths, legends, and most plays are works of fiction.

folktale a story that has been handed down from one generation to another
- The characters are usually either good or bad.
- Folktales make use of rhyme and repetitive phrases.
- Sometimes they are called tall tales, particularly if they are humorous and exaggerated.
- Folktales are also called folklore.

journal writing that expresses an author's feelings or first impressions about a subject
- Students may keep journals that record thoughts about what they have read.
- People also keep travel journals to remind themselves of interesting places they have seen.

legend a traditional story that at one time was told orally and was handed down from one generation to another
- Legends are like myths, but they do not have as many supernatural forces.
- Legends usually feature characters who actually lived, or real places or events.

myth an important story, often part of a culture's religion, that explains how the world came to be or why natural events happen
- A myth usually includes gods, goddesses, or unusually powerful human beings.
- Myths were first oral stories, and most early cultures have myths.

nonfiction writing about real people and events
- Essays, speeches, diaries, journals, autobiographies, and biographies are all usually nonfiction.

novel fiction that is book-length and has more plot and character details than a short story

poem a short piece of literature that usually has rhythm and paints powerful or beautiful impressions with words
- Often, poems have sound patterns such as rhyme.
- Songs are poetry set to music.

prose all writing that is not poetry
- Short stories, novels, autobiographies, biographies, diaries, journals, and essays are examples of prose.

science fiction fiction that is based on real or imagined facts of science
- Most stories are set in the future.
- Jules Verne was one of the first science fiction authors.

short story a brief work of prose fiction that includes plot, setting, characters, point of view, and theme
- Edgar Allan Poe was a great writer of short stories.

How to Read This Book

Different works of literature should be read in different ways. However, there are some basic methods you should use to read all works of literature.

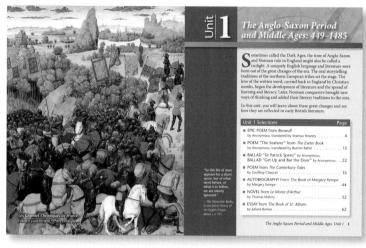

Before Beginning a Unit

- Read the unit title and selection titles.

- Read the paragraphs that introduce the unit.

- Look at the pictures and other artwork in the unit. There may be timelines or maps to help you.

- Think about what you already know about the unit.

- Think about what you might want to learn.

- Develop questions in your mind that you think will be answered in this unit.

Before Reading a Selection

- Read the selection's title.

- Look at the pictures and other artwork.

- Read the background material included in About the Author and About the Selection.

- Read the Objectives and think about what you will learn by reading the selection.

- Read the Literary Terms and their definitions.

- Complete the Before Reading the Selection activities. These activities will help you read the selection, understand vocabulary, and prepare for the reading.

As You Read a Selection

■ Read the notes in the side margins. These
will help you understand and think about
the main ideas.

■ Think of people or events in your own life
that are similar to those described.

■ Reread sentences or paragraphs that you
do not understand.

■ Predict what you think will happen next.

■ Read the definitions at the bottom of the
page for words that you do not know.

■ Record words that you do not know.
Also, write questions or comments you
have about the text.

After Reading a Selection

■ Reread interesting or difficult parts of the selection.

■ Reflect on what you have learned by reading the selection.

■ Complete the After Reading the Selection review questions
and activities. The activities will help you develop your
grammar, writing, speaking, listening, viewing, technology,
media, and research skills.

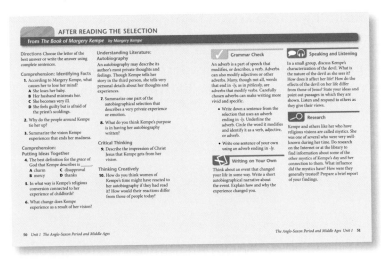

Reading Certain Types of Literature

The methods already described will help you understand all kinds of literature. You may need to use additional methods for specific types of literature.

Reading Poetry

■ Read the poem aloud.

■ Listen to the sounds of the words.

■ Picture the images the author is describing.

■ Reread poems over and over again to appreciate the author's use of language.

Reading Essays

■ Review the questions in the After Reading the Selection before you begin reading.

■ Use the questions to think about what you are reading.

■ Remember that essays usually express an author's opinions. Try to understand why the author may have formed these opinions.

Reading Plays

■ Picture the setting of the play. Since there usually is not much description given, try to relate the setting to something you have seen before.

■ Pay attention to what the characters say. How does this give clues about the character's personality? Have you ever known anyone like this? Are you like this?

Tips for Better Reading

Literary Terms

Literary Terms are words or phrases that we use to study and discuss works of literature. These terms describe the ways an author helps to make us enjoy and understand what we are reading. Some of the terms also describe a genre, or specific type of literature. In this anthology, you will see white boxes on the side of the Before Reading the Selection pages. In these boxes are Literary Terms and their definitions. These terms are important in understanding and discussing the selection being read. By understanding these Literary Terms, readers can appreciate the author's craft. You can find the definitions for all of the Literary Terms used in this book in the Handbook of Literary Terms on page 659.

setting the place and time in a story

plot the series of events in a story

theme the main idea of a literary work

Using a Graphic Organizer

A graphic organizer is visual representation of information. It can help you see how ideas are related to each other. A graphic organizer can help you study for a test, organize information before writing an essay, or organize details in a literature selection. You will use graphic organizers for different activities throughout this textbook. There are 14 different graphic organizers listed below. You can read a description and see an example of each graphic organizer in Appendix A in the back of this textbook.

■ Character Analysis Guide

■ Story Map

■ Main Idea Graphic (Umbrella)

■ Main Idea Graphic (Table)

■ Main Idea Graphic (Details)

■ Venn Diagram

■ Sequence Chain

■ Concept Map

■ Plot Mountain

■ Structured Overview

■ Semantic Table

■ Prediction Guide

■ Semantic Line

■ KWL Chart

Taking Notes

You will read many selections in this literature anthology. As you read, you may want to take notes to help remember what you have read. You can use these notes to keep track of events and characters in a story. Your notes may also be helpful for recognizing common ideas among the selections in a unit. You can review your notes as you prepare to take a test. Here are some tips for taking notes:

■ Write down only the most important information.

■ Do not try to write every detail or every word.

■ Write notes in your own words.

■ Do not be concerned about writing in complete sentences. Use short phrases.

Using the Three-Column Chart

One good way to take notes is to use a three-column chart. Make your own three-column chart by dividing a sheet of notebook paper into three equal parts. In Column 1, write the topic you are reading about or studying. In Column 2, write what you learned about this topic as you read or listened to your teacher. In Column 3, write questions, observations, or opinions about the topic, or write a detail that will help you remember the topic. Here are some examples of different ways to take notes using the three-column chart.

The topic I am studying	What I learned from reading the text or class discussion	Questions, observations, or ideas I have about the topic
Fiction	• one genre of literature • many different types of fiction—science fiction, adventure, detective stories, romance, suspense	• The book I am reading right now is fiction. It is an adventure story. • I wonder if poetry is part of the fiction genre.

Vocabulary Word	Definition	Sentence with Vocabulary Word
premises	a building or part of a building	Students are not allowed on the school **premises** during the weekend.

Literary Term	Definition	Example from Selection
Exaggeration	a use of words to make something seem more than it is; stretching the truth to a great extent	He was exactly five feet six inches in height, and six feet five inches in circumference. His head was a perfect sphere . . . . (Wouter Van Twiller)

Character	Character Traits Found in the Selection	Page Number
John Krakauer	Conflict, person against self—Krakauer wonders if he will run out of oxygen before returning to camp.	p. 355
	Determined—Krakauer is determined to make it back to camp even though his oxygen has run out and it is snowing on the mountain.	p. 358
	Thankful—After reaching camp, Krakauer is thankful that he is safe.	p. 360

Stage of Plot	Example from Text	Questions, Observations, and Ideas
Rising Action	"And how easy it would be to kill him. And he deserves it. Does he? No! What the devil!... I could cut his throat—*zip, zip!* I wouldn't give him time to resist. . . ." (p. 104)	This is a good example of rising action because it introduces the conflict of the story.

What to Do About Words You Do Not Know

- If the word is in **bold type,** look for the definition of the word at the bottom of the page.

- If the word is not in bold type, read to the end of the sentence and maybe the next sentence. Can you determine the meaning now?

- Look at the beginning sound of the unknown word. Ask yourself, "What word begins with this sound and would make sense here?"

- Sound out the syllables of the word.

- If you still cannot determine the meaning, see if you know any parts of the word: prefixes, suffixes, or roots.

- If this does not work, write the word on a note card or in a vocabulary notebook. Then look up the word in a dictionary after you have finished reading the selection. Reread the passage containing the unknown word after you have looked up its definition.

- If the word is necessary to understand the passage, look it up in a dictionary or glossary immediately.

Word Study Tips

- Start a vocabulary file with note cards to use for review.

- Write one word on the front of each card. Write the unit number, selection title, and the definition on the back.

- You can use these cards as flash cards by yourself or with a study partner to test your knowledge.

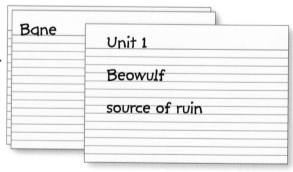

Bane

Unit 1

Beowulf

source of ruin

Before the Test Day

■ Make sure you have read all of the selections assigned.

■ Review the Literary Terms and definitions for each selection.

■ Review your answers to the After Reading the Selection questions.

■ Reread the Unit Summary and review your answers to the Unit Review.

■ Review any notes that you have taken or graphic organizers you have developed.

■ Ask your teacher what kinds of questions will be on the test.

■ Try to predict what questions will be asked. Think of and write answers to those questions.

■ Review the Test-Taking Tip at the bottom of each Unit Review page.

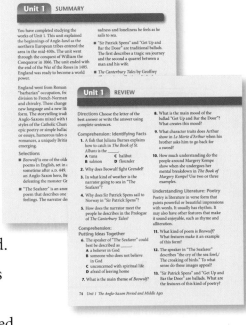

During the Test

■ Come to the test with a positive attitude.

■ Write your name on the paper.

■ Preview the test and read the directions carefully.

■ Plan your time.

■ Answer the questions that you know first.

■ Then go back and answer the more difficult questions.

■ Allow time to reread all of the questions and your answers.

How to Use This Book: A Study Guide **xix**

Les Grandes Chroniques de France,
French parchment, 15th century

S ometimes called the Dark Ages, the time of Anglo-Saxon and Norman rule in England might also be called a twilight. A uniquely English language and literature were born out of the great changes of the era. The oral storytelling traditions of the northern European tribes set the stage. The love of the written word, carried back to England by Christian monks, began the development of literature and the spread of learning and literacy. Later, Norman conquerors brought new ways of thinking and added their literary traditions to the mix.

In this unit, you will learn about these great changes and see how they are reflected in early British literature.

"So this life of man appears for a short space, but of what went before, or what is to follow, we are utterly ignorant."

—The Venerable Bede, *Ecclesiastical History of the English People,* about A.D. 731

The Anglo-Saxon Period

From the first through the fifth centuries A.D., England was part of the Roman Empire. In the early 400s, the Romans left, leaving the area unprotected. Germanic peoples from northern Europe, including the Angles, the Saxons, and the Jutes, invaded. They pushed the natives to small areas on the fringes of the land. The area became known as Angle-land, or England.

Christianity, which had flourished under Roman rule, nearly disappeared from England during the time of the Anglo-Saxons. But in 597, Augustine of Canterbury began to teach Christianity to the Anglo-Saxons. Christianity had spread throughout the island by 675. The rise of Christianity brought written texts to England. In addition to biblical texts, Anglo-Saxon poets began setting down their oral forms in writing.

In the ninth century, the Danes occupied England. A Saxon king, Alfred the Great, defeated them and united the kingdoms of southern England. However, after his death in 899, Anglo-Saxon rule weakened. The Danes then ruled until 1035. During this period, literary activity increased, with histories, grammars, and religious teachings becoming common. Still, most people could not read or write. The last great Anglo-Saxon king, Edward the Confessor, reigned from 1042 to 1066.

The Middle Ages

In 1066, William, Duke of Normandy (also known as William the Conqueror), invaded England. He defeated English forces and became king of England. Most Anglo-Saxons became serfs (people required to work the land for wealthy landowners). Gradually, the

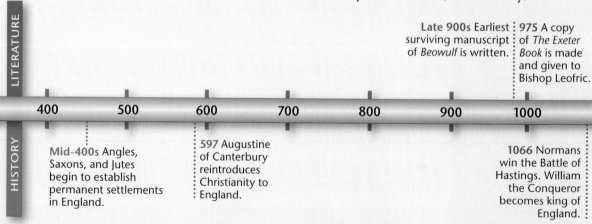

LITERATURE

Late 900s Earliest surviving manuscript of *Beowulf* is written.

975 A copy of *The Exeter Book* is made and given to Bishop Leofric.

400   500   600   700   800   900   1000

HISTORY

Mid-400s Angles, Saxons, and Jutes begin to establish permanent settlements in England.

597 Augustine of Canterbury reintroduces Christianity to England.

1066 Normans win the Battle of Hastings. William the Conqueror becomes king of England.

Norman and Anglo-Saxon cultures blended and the feudal system grew. Under feudalism, a nobleman pledged his support to the king in exchange for land and other rights.

The code of chivalry, which guided the lives of feudal nobles and knights, gave rise to the "verse romance." The King Arthur legends formed the core of this literary movement.

Between 1088 and 1154, English kings fought for power against nobles and church officials. Henry II became king in 1154. He restored the power of the king but also gave power to local courts. In the late 1100s, King John angered landowners and church leaders.

"The Four Seasons" from the Book of Hours of Jean de France, Duc de Berry

In 1215, they forced John to sign the Magna Carta. It took away some of the king's power.

The Black Death, or bubonic plague, struck Europe repeatedly during the Middle Ages. It killed up to one-third of Europe's population.

In 1337, England's King Edward III claimed the throne of France, starting the Hundred Years' War. The power struggle between the two countries continued until 1453.

At the end of this war, a conflict developed between two ruling families in England. This struggle, the War of the Roses, lasted until 1485.

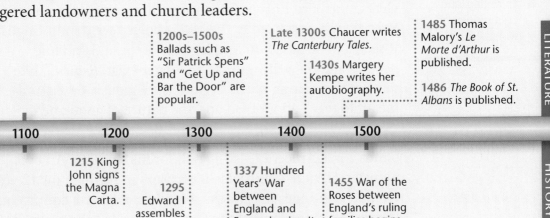

1200s–1500s Ballads such as "Sir Patrick Spens" and "Get Up and Bar the Door" are popular.

Late 1300s Chaucer writes *The Canterbury Tales.*

1430s Margery Kempe writes her autobiography.

1485 Thomas Malory's *Le Morte d'Arthur* is published.

1486 *The Book of St. Albans* is published.

LITERATURE

1100   1200   1300   1400   1500

1215 King John signs the Magna Carta.

1295 Edward I assembles the first Parliament.

1337 Hundred Years' War between England and France begins. It lasts until 1453.

1455 War of the Roses between England's ruling families begins.

HISTORY

BEFORE READING THE SELECTION

from *Beowulf* *Anonymous (translated by Seamus Heaney)*

Seamus Heaney
1939–

Objectives

- To read and understand an epic poem
- To understand the meanings of archetype, imagery, plot, character, and theme
- To understand etymologies of words

About the Author

Almost nothing is known about the original anonymous, or unknown, author of *Beowulf.* The poet was probably a Christian, because the poem reflects Christian, as well as non-Christian, beliefs.

Seamus Heaney, the translator, was born in 1939 at his family's farm near Belfast, Northern Ireland. He became a poet, publishing 14 volumes of poetry. Heaney's poetry shows respect for the land and for history. In 1995, he received the Nobel Prize for Literature. Heaney studied the Anglo-Saxon language in college. In 1999, he published a verse translation of *Beowulf.* His challenge was capturing the poem's Anglo-Saxon features while engaging modern readers.

About the Selection

The only surviving manuscript of *Beowulf* was created in the late tenth century A.D. The poem itself was written in the Old English language sometime between the early eighth century and the tenth century. Its action takes place sometime after 449, when the first Angles and Saxons arrived in England. However, its characters are Danes and Geats, northern European people who came from southern Scandinavia. It is among the oldest poems written in English. It seems to be based on oral legends of these Germanic peoples and on writings that no longer exist. *Beowulf,* like most of the writing of the period, is religiously based and meant to teach about God and the nature of good and evil.

At the beginning of the poem, Hrothgar, the Danish king, builds a magnificent feasting hall for his subjects. An evil monster, Grendel, murders 30 warriors in the hall; for 12 years Grendel continues his attacks. Finally, Beowulf, a courageous warrior from the land of the Geats, comes to kill the monster.

Literary Terms *Beowulf* is an **epic,** a long story written in verse and usually involving a heroic figure. It uses **imagery,** or pictures created by words. *Beowulf* features several **archetypes.** These are details, **plot** patterns, **character** types, or **themes** found in the literature of many different cultures. Plot is the series of events in a story. A character is a person or animal in a story, poem, or play. A theme is the main idea of a literary work.

Reading on Your Own The action and focus in this excerpt changes several times, creating four sections. Pause after reading each section (stopping at lines 34, 88, and 116) and summarize it to yourself. To summarize, state the main idea in your own words. Use your section summaries to help you understand the entire selection.

Writing on Your Own Think of a battle between two people or groups of people that you have read about or seen in a movie. Write a paragraph describing the people or groups and the reason for fighting.

Vocabulary Focus The **etymology** of a word is its history. Most dictionaries provide etymologies. Many English words can be traced back to Old English or Middle English. For example, the word *mayhem* comes from the Middle English word *mayme,* which is from the Anglo-French word *mahaim,* meaning "loss of limb." Today, *mayhem* means "damage or violence." Studying etymology helps you better understand words. Use a dictionary to find five such words in this selection. Summarize the etymology of each word.

Think Before You Read What traits do you think Beowulf will have? What traits will Grendel have?

epic a long story written in verse, usually involving a heroic figure

imagery pictures created by words that appeal to the five senses

archetype detail, plot pattern, character type, or theme found in the literature of many different cultures

plot the series of events in a story

character a person or animal in a story, poem, or play

theme the main idea of a literary work

etymology a history of a word shown by tracing its development from its first use in a language

FROM BEOWULF

As you read, think about the traits of each character in the fight.

Then out of the night
came the shadow-stalker, stealthy and swift;
the hall-guards were slack, asleep at their posts,
all except one; it was widely understood
5 that as long as God disallowed it,
the fiend could not bear them to his shadow-bourne.
One man, however, was in fighting mood,
awake and on edge, spoiling for action.

Remember that an archetype is an element that is common across time and cultures. Look for these common elements as you read. Consider how the theme and characters are like those in other stories you know.

In off the moors, down through the mist bands
10 God-cursed Grendel came greedily **loping.**
The **bane** of the race of men roamed forth,
hunting for a prey in the high hall.
Under the cloud-murk he moved towards it
until it shone above him, a sheer **keep**
15 of fortified gold. Nor was that the first time
he had scouted the grounds of Hrothgar's dwelling—
although never in his life, before or since,
did he find harder fortune or hall-defenders.

Visitors from Overseas, **Nikolai Roerich**

---

loping running   **bane** source of ruin   **keep** fort

Spurned and joyless, he journeyed on ahead
20 and arrived at the **bawn.** The iron-braced door
turned on its hinge when his hands touched it.
Then his rage boiled over, he ripped open
the mouth of the building, maddening for blood,
pacing the length of the patterned floor
25 with his loathsome tread, while a **baleful** light,
flame more than light, flared from his eyes.
He saw many men in the mansion, sleeping,
a ranked company of kinsmen and warriors
quartered together. And his glee was **demonic,**
30 picturing the mayhem: before morning
he would rip life from limb and devour them,
feed on their flesh; but his fate that night
was due to change, his days of ravening
had come to an end.
                 Mighty and **canny,**
35 Hygelac's kinsman was keenly watching
for the first move the monster would make.
Nor did the creature keep him waiting
but struck suddenly and started in;
he grabbed and mauled a man on his bench,
40 bit into his **bone-lappings,** bolted down his blood
and gorged on him in lumps, leaving the body
utterly lifeless, eaten up
hand and foot. Venturing closer,
his talon was raised to attack Beowulf
45 where he lay on the bed; he was bearing in
with open claw when the alert hero's
comeback and armlock **forestalled** him utterly.
The captain of evil discovered himself
in a handgrip harder than anything
50 he had ever encountered in any man

**Sutton Hoo helmet,
7th century** A.D.

Hygelac was the
king of the Geats
when Beowulf
was a young man.
He was Beowulf's
uncle.

spurned rejected	**demonic** possessed by a demon	**bone-lappings** joints and ligaments
bawn hall	**canny** clever; careful	**forestalled** stopped or prevented
baleful fearsome		

on the face of the earth. Every bone in his body
quailed and recoiled, but he could not escape.
He was desperate to flee to his den and hide
with the devil's litter, for in all his days
55 he had never been clamped or cornered like this.
Then Hygelac's trusty **retainer** recalled
his bedtime speech, sprang to his feet
and got a firm hold. Fingers were bursting,
the monster back-tracking, the man overpowering.
60 The dread of the land was desperate to escape,
to take a roundabout road and flee
to his lair in the **fens.** The latching power
in his fingers weakened; it was the worst trip
the terror-monger had taken to Heorot.
65 And now the timbers trembled and sang,
a hall-session that **harrowed** every Dane
inside the stockade: stumbling in fury,
the two contenders crashed through the building.
The hall clattered and hammered, but somehow
70 survived the **onslaught** and kept standing:
it was handsomely structured, a sturdy frame
braced with the best of blacksmith's work
inside and out. The story goes
that as the pair struggled, mead-benches were smashed
75 and sprung off the floor, gold fittings and all.
Before then, no Shielding elder would believe
there was any power or person upon earth
capable of wrecking their horn-rigged hall
unless the burning embrace of a fire
80 engulf it in flame. Then an extraordinary
wail arose, and bewildering fear
came over the Danes. Everyone felt it
who heard that cry as it echoed off the wall,
a God-cursed scream and strain of catastrophe,

Beowulf is the
retainer, or servant.

To what sense does
the vivid imagery
in lines 80–86
appeal? What is
the effect of the
imagery?

quailed drew back in
fear

retainer servant

fens low, wet lands

harrowed tormented

onslaught fierce
attack

85   the howl of the loser, the **lament** of the hell-serf
    keening his wound. He was overwhelmed,
    manacled tight by the man who of all men
    was foremost and strongest in the days of this life. . . .

    Then he who had harrowed the hearts of men
90   with pain and **affliction** in former times
    and had given offence also to God
    found that his bodily powers failed him.
    Hygelac's kinsman kept him helplessly
    locked in a handgrip. As long as either lived,
95   he was hateful to the other. The monster's whole
    body was in pain, a tremendous wound
    appeared on his shoulder. **Sinews** split
    and the bone-lappings burst. Beowulf was granted
    the glory of winning; Grendel was driven
100   under the fen-banks, fatally hurt,
    to his **desolate** lair. His days were numbered,
    the end of his life was coming over him,
    he knew it for certain; and one bloody clash
    had fulfilled the dearest wishes of the Danes.
105   The man who had lately landed among them,
    proud and sure, had purged the hall,
    kept it from harm; he was happy with his nightwork
    and the courage he had shown. The Geat captain
    had boldly fulfilled his boast to the Danes:
110   he had healed and relieved a huge distress,
    unremitting humiliations,
    the hard fate they'd been forced to undergo,
    no small affliction. Clear proof of this
    could be seen in the hand the hero displayed
115   high up near the roof: the whole of Grendel's
    shoulder and arm, his awesome grasp.

Hell-serf is an example of a *kenning,* a popular device in Anglo-Saxon literature. It is a compound, nonliteral noun. *Hell-serf* literally means "a servant of hell"; it refers to Grendel.

What does Beowulf's boasting show about his character?

lament wailing	**manacled** restrained from movement	**sinews** tendons
keening complaining loudly	**affliction** distress	**desolate** deserted
		unremitting constant

Then morning came and many a warrior
gathered, as I've heard, around the gift-hall,
clan-chiefs flocking from far and near
120 down wide-ranging roads, wondering greatly
at the monster's footprints. His fatal departure
was regretted by no-one who witnessed his trail,
the **ignominious** marks of his flight
where he'd **skulked** away, exhausted in spirit
125 and beaten in battle, bloodying the path,
hauling his doom to the demons' mere.
The bloodshot water wallowed and surged,
there were loathsome upthrows and overturnings
of waves and gore and wound-slurry.
130 With his death upon him, he had dived deep
into his marsh-den, drowned out his life
and his **heathen** soul: hell claimed him there.

Vikings Arriving in Britain by Sea, **English manuscript,** A.D. **1130**

| **ignominious** shameful | **skulked** moved stealthily | **heathen** uncivilized; not religious |

AFTER READING THE SELECTION

from *Beowulf*   *Anonymous (translated by Seamus Heaney)*

Directions Choose the letter of the best answer or write the answer using complete sentences.

Comprehension: Identifying Facts

1. The battle takes place _____.
   - **A** in a misty swamp
   - **B** inside Hrothgar's fortress
   - **C** near Grendel's den
   - **D** on a ship

2. How does Beowulf catch Grendel by surprise?

3. What does Beowulf hold up as proof of victory after the battle?

Comprehension: Putting Ideas Together

4. Grendel's "rage boiled over" when _____.
   - **A** the men mocked him
   - **B** Beowulf held up a sword
   - **C** he arrived at the door
   - **D** he found the men feasting

5. What traits does Beowulf show in fighting Grendel?

6. What does Grendel do when the battle is over?

Understanding Literature: Archetype

One reason some stories remain enjoyable across many centuries is because they pick up on experiences and emotions that are common to all people. These stories are not bound to a particular place or time. *Beowulf,* although written more than ten centuries ago, is still understandable and moving. It builds on ideas and themes that are still important today.

7. Define the character types represented by Beowulf and Grendel. Give two examples of these character types in other stories you know.

8. What is the theme of this selection? Explain why this is a popular theme in literature.

Critical Thinking

9. The author vividly describes the bloody, gruesome battle. Give three examples of gruesome details. What impact do they have on readers?

Thinking Creatively

10. What kinds of present-day heroes, if any, perform a service similar to the one Beowulf performed? Explain.

After Reading continued on next page

AFTER READING THE SELECTION *(continued)*

 from *Beowulf* *Anonymous (translated by Seamus Heaney)*

 Grammar Check

Many sentences in this selection from *Beowulf* contain semicolons (;). A semicolon may be used instead of a period to separate independent clauses (a group of words with a subject and verb that can stand alone as a sentence). Find examples in the poem of sentences with semicolons. Study how they are used in each case.

- Write down a sentence from the poem that uses semicolons.

- Revise the sentence by writing each independent clause as a complete sentence.

- Write a sentence about Beowulf's character. Use two independent clauses joined with a semicolon.

 Writing on Your Own

Write a description of two players in tennis, soccer, baseball, or another sport. Use strong verbs, such as *battled* or *struggled,* and vivid images to describe the traits of the players and the way they play the game.

 Speaking

Locate a section of the poem of four lines or more that includes at least one strong image. Practice reading the lines with expression to show the emotion of the section.

Listening

Listen to a partner read a section of the poem as described above. Afterward, identify the vivid images of the passage. Discuss the effect of this element on the poem's meaning.

BEFORE READING THE SELECTION

About the Author

"The Seafarer," by an unknown Anglo-Saxon author, was included in *The Exeter Book*. This was a manuscript containing a variety of poems written in Old English. The works in *The Exeter Book* include long narrative poems (poems that tell a story), brief riddles, prayers, and sermons. It even includes poems written in a woman's voice, unusual for the Anglo-Saxons. The poems were written at various times, but the manuscript was copied around A.D. 975. It was given to Exeter Cathedral by Bishop Leofric. *The Exeter Book* is the largest surviving collection of Old English poetry.

Burton Raffel
1928–

Burton Raffel translated "The Seafarer" into modern English. He has done many translations, including *Beowulf, Ten Centuries of Poetry,* and *Poems from the Old English.*

About the Selection

"The Seafarer" is similar to another poem from *The Exeter Book*, "The Wanderer." Both poems are about loss and suffering. They describe a wonderful past that is gone forever.

"The Seafarer" has two separate sections. The first describes the poet's feelings as he sets out on a long sea journey. The second describes lessons that readers should learn from the poet's experiences. The poem includes Christian, as well as non-Christian, beliefs. Like other Old English poetry, "The Seafarer" was written in unrhymed lines.

Objectives

- To read and understand a poem
- To understand and identify mood and alliteration in a literary work
- To understand first person and the role of a narrator

Before Reading **continued on next page**

The Anglo-Saxon Period and Middle Ages Unit 1   **13**

The Seafarer   Anonymous (translated by Burton Raffel)

poetry literature in verse form that usually has rhythm and paints powerful or beautiful impressions with words

mood the feeling that writing creates

first person a point of view where the narrator is also a character, using the pronouns *I* and *we*

narrator one who tells a story

alliteration repeating of sounds by using words that have beginning sounds that are the same

Literary Terms "The Seafarer" is a poem. **Poetry** is literature in verse form that usually has rhythm. It paints powerful or beautiful impressions with words. Poetry such as "The Seafarer" often uses words and images to create a specific **mood,** or feeling. This poem is written in the **first person.** The **narrator** (one who tells a story) is a character and uses the pronouns *I* and *we.* This poem also uses **alliteration.** This is the repeating of sounds by using words that have beginning sounds that are the same.

Reading on Your Own As you read the first part of the poem, picture the experience that the poet describes of sailing on the open sea. Analyze the information the poet gives to think about what this experience might have meant to him and the lessons he hopes to teach. Use your own experiences to understand the poet's meaning and define the mood.

Writing on Your Own Think of a time when you felt you were "at sea," maybe a time of uncertainty or great changes in your life. Write a paragraph describing it.

Vocabulary Focus Context clues can help you figure out the meanings of unfamiliar words as you read. Context clues are words and sentences around the word that contain information about it. For example, one line of "The Seafarer" describes the sounds of "icy-feathered terns and the eagle's screams" at sea. If you are unsure of the meaning of *terns,* use context clues to help you. The terns are described as being near the ocean and having feathers. They are associated with eagles. You could conclude that terns are seabirds. Looking up the word will give more specific details.

Think Before You Read What types of dangerous human experiences might going out to sea resemble?

The Seafarer

This tale is true, and mine. It tells
How the sea took me, swept me back
And forth in sorrow and fear and pain,
Showed me suffering in a hundred ships,
5 In a thousand ports, and in me. It tells
Of smashing surf when I sweated in the cold
Of an anxious watch, perched in the bow
As it dashed under cliffs. My feet were cast
In icy bands, bound with frost,
10 With frozen chains, and hardship groaned
Around my heart. Hunger tore
At my sea-weary soul. No man sheltered
On the quiet fairness of earth can feel
How wretched I was, drifting through winter
15 On an ice-cold sea, whirled in sorrow,
Alone in a world blown clear of love,
Hung with icicles. The hailstorms flew.
The only sound was the roaring sea,
The freezing waves. The song of the swan
20 Might serve for pleasure, the cry of the sea fowl,
The croaking of birds instead of laughter,
The mewing of gulls instead of mead.
Storms beat on the rocky cliffs and were echoed
By icy-feathered **terns** and the eagle's screams;
25 No **kinsman** could offer comfort there,
To a soul left drowning in **desolation.**

As you read, think about the nonliteral meanings the poet may be communicating, as well as the literal meaning of traveling on the sea.

Notice that the narrator uses the first person with such words as *mine, I,* and *me.*

The poet creates a vivid image in lines 8–17. What mood does the image create?

---

terns seabirds related to gulls   **kinsman** relative   **desolation** loneliness

What desire that is unreasonable to others does the poet describe in lines 27–38?

And who could believe, knowing but
The passion of cities, swelled proud with wine
And no taste of misfortune, how often, how wearily,
30 I put myself back on the paths of the sea.
Night would blacken; it would snow from the north;
Frost bound the earth and hail would fall,
The coldest seeds. And how my heart
Would begin to beat, knowing once more
35 The salt waves tossing and the towering sea!
The time for journeys would come and my soul
Called me eagerly out, sent me over
The horizon, seeking foreigners' homes.
But there isn't a man on earth so proud,
40 So born to greatness, so bold with his youth,
Grown so brave, or so graced by God,
That he feels no fear as the sails **unfurl,**
Wondering what Fate has willed and
will do.
No harps ring in his heart,
no rewards,
45 No passion for women, no worldly
pleasures,
Nothing, only the ocean's heave;
But longing wraps itself around
him.
Orchards blossom, the towns
bloom,
Fields grow lovely as the world
springs fresh,
50 And all these **admonish** that
willing mind
Leaping to journeys, always set
In thoughts traveling on a **quickening** tide.

Mariner's
compass,
about 1775

unfurl unfold   **quickening** coming to life

admonish give friendly advice to

So summer's **sentinel,** the cuckoo, sings
In his murmuring voice, and our hearts mourn
55 As he urges. Who could understand,
In ignorant ease, what we others suffer
As the paths of **exile** stretch endlessly on?

And yet my heart wanders away,
My soul roams with the sea, the whales'
60 Home, wandering to the widest corners
Of the world, returning **ravenous** with desire,
Flying solitary, screaming, exciting me
To the open ocean, breaking oaths
On the curve of a wave. Thus the joys of God
65 Are **fervent** with life, where life itself
Fades quickly into the earth. The wealth
Of the world neither reaches to Heaven nor remains.
No man has ever faced the dawn
Certain which of Fate's three threats
70 Would fall: illness, or age, or an enemy's
Sword, snatching the life from his soul.
The praise the living pour on the dead
Flowers from reputation: plant
An earthly life of profit reaped
75 Even from hatred and **rancor,** of bravery
Flung in the devil's face, and death
Can only bring you earthly praise
And a song to celebrate a place
With the angels, life eternally blessed
80 In the hosts of Heaven. The days are gone
When the kingdoms of earth **flourished** in glory;
Now there are no rulers, no emperors,
No givers of gold, as once there were,
When wonderful things were worked among them

Notice the alliteration here: *So summer's sentinel . . .*

Summarize what the poet says about death in lines 68–71.

Lines 80–102 express the common Anglo-Saxon theme that the present can never be as great as the glorious past.

sentinel guard

exile absence from one's home

ravenous having a huge appetite

fervent glowing

rancor bitter ill will

flourished thrived

**Norman ships,
1066–1086**

What images does
the poet use? How
do these images
and the vivid verbs
add to the mood?

85 And they lived in lordly magnificence.
Those powers have vanished, those pleasures are dead.
The weakest survives and the world continues,
Kept spinning by toil. All glory is **tarnished.**
The world's honor ages and shrinks,
90 Bent like the men who mold it. Their faces
Blanch as time advances, their beards
Wither and they mourn the memory of friends,
The sons of princes, **sown** in the dust.
The soul stripped of its flesh knows nothing
95 Of sweetness or sour, feels no pain,
Bends neither its hands nor its brain. A brother
Opens his palms and pours down gold
On his kinsman's grave, **strewing** his coffin

tarnished dulled; stained	**blanch** grow pale	**strewing** scattering
	sown planted	

With treasures intended for Heaven, but nothing
100   Golden shakes the wrath of God
For a soul overflowing with sin, and nothing
Hidden on earth rises to Heaven.
      We all fear God. He turns the earth,
He set it swinging firmly in space,
105   Gave life to the world and light to the sky.
Death leaps at fools who forget their God.
He who lives humbly has angels from Heaven
To carry him courage and strength and belief.
A man must conquer pride, not kill it,
110   Be firm with his fellows, **chaste** for himself,
Treat all the world as the world deserves,
With love or with hate but never with harm,
Though an enemy seek to scorch him in Hell,
Or set the flames of a funeral **pyre**
115   Under his lord. Fate is stronger
And God mightier than any man's mind.
Our thoughts should turn to where our home is,
Consider the ways of coming there,
Then strive for sure permission for us
120   To rise to that eternal joy,
That life born in the love of God
And the hope of Heaven. Praise the Holy
Grace of Him who honored us,
Eternal, unchanging Creator of earth. Amen.

> What does the poet mean by saying in line 109 that "A man must conquer pride, not kill it"?

---

chaste pure in thought and act   **pyre** pile of material set on fire

AFTER READING THE SELECTION

The Seafarer Anonymous (translated by Burton Raffel)

Directions Choose the letter of the best answer or write the answer using complete sentences.

Comprehension: Identifying Facts

1. The poet says that a person is most likely to be remembered after death for _____.
   A kindness
   B faith in God
   C family
   D bravery

2. How does the poet feel when he goes to sea in the beginning of the poem?

3. What are four sounds the poet describes hearing at sea?

Comprehension: Putting Ideas Together

4. What is the poet's attitude toward death?
   A He ignores it.
   B He is frightened by it.
   C He respects it.
   D He is angry about it.

5. According to the poet, how is present-day life different from life in the past?

6. Summarize the advice that the poet gives readers.

Understanding Literature: Mood

A writer creates a specific mood by including certain words, details, and images. The mood of a literary work may be described with words such as *scary*, *tragic*, and *cheerful*.

7. What are two words that describe the mood of the first section (lines 1–26) of the poem?

8. What are three words or phrases that help create this mood?

Critical Thinking

9. The poet describes going out to sea. What life experience does sailing out to sea seem to stand for in the poet's mind? Explain your answer.

Thinking Creatively

10. Do you think people today have feelings similar to those the poet describes? Explain.

Grammar Check

The poet of "The Seafarer" uses many gerunds (words ending in *-ing* used as nouns) and participles (words ending in *-ed* or *-ing* used as adjectives). For example, in the phrase "It tells of smashing surf," *smashing* is a participle. The word *smashing* is used as an adjective to describe the surf. In the phrase "the croaking of birds," *croaking* is a noun that names a sound the birds make.

- Write down a sentence from the poem that uses a participle and one that uses a gerund.

- Write one sentence of your own using a participle and one using a gerund.

 Writing on Your Own

Think about a place you have visited that created a specific mood, such as peace, joy, or fear. Write a paragraph describing the place. Do not state the mood of the place. Instead, use words, phrases, and images that give clues about the mood. For example, instead of *peaceful,* use *serene.*

 Speaking

Choose a small part of the poem to read aloud. Choose a part that creates a specific mood or one that gives advice to readers about how to live. Practice saying the lines with expression that fits their meaning and purpose. Then read the lines aloud to a small group. After you read your lines, lead a group discussion about the mood of the lines.

 Listening

Listen to a partner read several lines from the poem. Then explain to your partner the meaning and purpose of the lines. Some examples of a purpose are to create a mood, to describe a feeling, and to help listeners. Then read different lines and have your partner respond.

BEFORE READING THE SELECTIONS

Sir Patrick Spens and Get Up and Bar the Door   *Anonymous*

About the Author

Ballads are narrative poems that were usually sung at the time when they were written. Bishop Thomas Percy published a collection of English ballads in 1765. He had found an old manuscript of many ballads and thought they dated back to the Middle Ages. A few old ballads were originally written in Middle English. However, no one is really sure how old most of the ballads are.

Because ballads are passed down orally, most have several different versions. They continue being told and sung longest in remote areas. Many English ballads started in Scotland and in the border areas between England and Scotland. Therefore, many of the ballads are written in Scottish, the language of Scotland.

About the Selections

Many ballads, like "Sir Patrick Spens," tell about tragic events. Scholars think that this ballad tells a true story. Alexander III, king of Scotland, asked Sir Patrick Spens and other noblemen to take his daughter Margaret to Norway to be married. Many of the noblemen drowned on the way back. Twenty years later, Margaret drowned on her way to England. The version of the ballad here seems to combine the two events.

The second ballad, "Get Up and Bar the Door," does not tell of a true event. Instead, it tells a story of a married couple and the results of a disagreement they have.

Objectives

- To read and understand ballads
- To identify the climax or turning point of a literary work
- To understand the meaning of quatrain and refrain
- To know the meaning of dialect

Literary Terms "Sir Patrick Spens" and "Get Up and Bar the Door" are **ballads.** These are simple songs that have been passed from one person to another. They usually rhyme, with each **quatrain,** or group of four lines, having the rhyming pattern *abcb.* They often have a **refrain.** Ballads tell a story in a compressed way. They have a **climax,** the point of highest suspense at which a major change occurs.

Reading on Your Own As you read each ballad, think about the event that causes the rest of the events. Analyzing cause and effect helps you understand the plot of a narrative and identify its climax.

Writing on Your Own Think of an interesting, funny, or scary event that you experienced or heard about. Summarize the event and explain why it would make a good ballad.

Vocabulary Focus These two ballads are written in the Scottish **dialect.** Some words, such as *skeely,* are unfamiliar. Others are simply spelled differently. For example, words with a long *o* sound, such as *foam,* may be spelled and pronounced with a long *a* sound: *faem.* As you read the ballads, read unfamiliar words aloud. Try substituting different vowel sounds for unfamiliar words such as *mair (more).*

Think Before You Read How is a ballad likely to be different from an epic such as *Beowulf*?

---

ballad a simple song that often uses a refrain, sometimes uses rhyme, and is passed from person to person

quatrain a group of four lines

refrain repeated words or phrases that create mood or give importance to something

climax the point of highest suspense at which a major change occurs

dialect the speech of a particular part of a country or of a certain group of people

---

SIR PATRICK SPENS

As you read, notice the rhyming pattern for each quatrain.

I. The Sailing

The king sits in Dunfermline town
Drinking the blude-red wine;
"O whare will I get a **skeely** skipper
To sail this new ship o' mine?"

What does the dialect add to this ballad?

5   O up and spak an **eldern** knight,
Sat at the king's right knee;
"Sir Patrick Spens is the best sailor
That ever sail'd the sea."

Our king has written a **braid** letter,
10 And seal'd it with his hand,
And sent it to Sir Patrick Spens,
Was walking on the **strand.**

"To Noroway, to Noroway,
To Noroway o'er the faem;
15 The king's daughter o' Noroway,
'Tis thou must bring her hame."

The first word that Sir Patrick read
So loud, loud laugh'd he;
The neist word that Sir Patrick read
20 The tear blinded his e'e.

Neist means *next to.*

skeely skillful	**braid** open
eldern ancient	**strand** beach

"O wha is this has done this deed
And tauld the king o' me,
To send us out, at this time o' year,
To sail upon the sea?

What do lines 21–24 in this stanza tell you about Sir Patrick Spens's character?

25 "Be it wind, be it weet, be it hail, be it sleet,
Our ship must sail the faem;
The king's daughter o' Noroway,
'Tis we must fetch her hame."

They hoysed their sails on Monenday morn
30 Wi' a' the speed they may;
They hae landed in Noroway
Upon a Wodensday.

II. The Return

"Mak ready, mak ready, my merry men a'!
Our gude ship sails the morn."
35 "Now ever **alack,** my master dear,
I fear a deadly storm.

Lines 35–36 foreshadow, or give hints, as to the outcome of the story. What do they hint at?

"I saw the new moon late yestreen
Wi' the auld moon in her arm;
And if we gang to sea, master,
40 I fear we'll come to harm."

They hadna sail'd a **league,** a league,
A league but barely three,
When the lift grew dark, and the wind blew loud,
And **gurly** grew the sea.

---

alack interjection showing sorrow

league a measure of distance about 2.4 to 4.6 miles

gurly rough

Lines 45–60 make up the climax, or point of highest suspense, of the poem. What causes the suspense?

45 The ankers brak, and the topmast lap,
It was sic a deadly storm:
And the waves cam owre the broken ship
Till a' her sides were torn.

"Go fetch a web o' the silken claith,
50 Another o' the twine,
And wap them into our ship's side,
And let nae the sea come in."

They fetch'd a web o' the silken claith,
Another o' the twine,
55 And they wapp'd them round that gude ship's side,
But still the sea came in.

O **laith,** laith were our gude Scots lords
To wet their cork-heel'd **shoon;**
But lang or a' the play was play'd
60 They wat their hats **aboon.**

And mony was the feather bed
That flatter'd on the faem;
And mony was the gude lord's son
That never mair cam hame.

65 O lang, lang may the ladies sit,
Wi' their fans into their hand,
Before they see Sir Patrick Spens
Come sailing to the **strand!**

---

laith loath, disliking to do something **shoon** shoes **aboon** above **strand** shore

And lang, lang may the maidens sit
70 Wi' their gowd **kames** in their hair,
A-waiting for their ain dear loves!
For them they'll see nae mair.

Half-owre, half-owre to Aberdour,
'Tis fifty **fathoms** deep;
75 And there lies gude Sir Patrick Spens,
Wi' the Scots lords at his feet!

*The Ladies' Lament
from the Ballad of
Sir Patrick Spens,*
**Elizabeth
Eleanor Siddal,
1856**

kames decorative combs

fathoms units of six feet used for
measuring under water

GET UP AND BAR THE DOOR

Martinmas is the feast of Saint Martin, celebrated on November 11.

It fell about the Martinmas time,
And a gay time it was then,
When our good wife got puddings to make,
And she's boild them in the pan.

How do the rhythm and rhyme of the ballad help create a certain mood? How would you describe the mood?

5   The wind sae cauld blew south and north,
And blew into the floor;
Quoth our **goodman** to our **goodwife,**
"Gae out and bar the door."

"My hand is in my **hussyfskap,**
10   Goodman, as ye may see;
An it shoud nae be barrd this hundred year,
It's no be barrd for me."

They made a **paction** tween them twa,
They made it firm and sure,
15   That the first word whaeer shoud speak,
Shoud rise and bar the door.

Then by there came two gentlemen,
At twelve o'clock at night,
And they could neither see house nor hall,
20   Nor coal nor candle-light.

"Now whether is this a rich man's house,
Or whether is it a poor?"
But neer a word wad ane o them speak,
For barring of the door.

goodman man of a household	**hussyfskap** housework	**paction** agreement, deal
goodwife woman of a household		

25 And first they ate the white puddings,
    And then they ate the black;
    Tho **muckle** thought the goodwife to hersel,
    Yet neer a word she spake.

    Then said the one unto the other,
30 "Here, man, tak ye my knife;
    Do ye tak aff the auld man's beard,
    And I'll kiss the goodwife."

    "But there's nae water in the house,
    And what shall we do than?"
35 "What ails thee at the pudding-**broo,**
    That boils into the pan?"

> These lines are the turning point of the ballad. On what is the suspense of the poem based?

    O up then started our goodman,
    An angry man was he:
    "Will ye kiss my wife before my **een,**
40 And scad me wi pudding-bree?"

> What is the refrain of this ballad?

    Then up and started our
        goodwife,
    Gied three skips on the
        floor:
    "Goodman, you've
        spoken the foremost
        word,
    Get up and bar the door."

Cottage and Pond,
Moonlight,
Thomas Gainsborough

| **muckle** a large amount | **broo** brew: water in which something has been boiled | **een** eyes |

Directions Choose the letter of the best answer or write the answer using complete sentences.

Comprehension: Identifying Facts

1. In "Sir Patrick Spens," the king needs a good skipper to _____.
   A take his daughter to Norway
   B build some good ships
   C explore far-away lands
   D teach him how to sail

2. In "Get Up and Bar the Door," the married couple disagrees about who _____.
   A should do the housework
   B let the thieves in
   C is more friendly
   D should lock the door

3. What is Sir Patrick Spens's reaction to the king's request? Why does he have this reaction?

4. What bad signs for sailing does one sailor report to Sir Patrick Spens on the return trip?

5. What trouble does Spens's ship run into on its way home from Norway?

6. How do the men on the ship try to solve their problem?

7. For "Get Up and Bar the Door," summarize the wife's answer when her husband asks her to get up and bar the door.

8. How does the couple decide to settle their disagreement?

9. What do the men who come to the house plan to do to the couple?

10. What is the wife's response at the end of the ballad?

Comprehension: Putting Ideas Together

11. The mood of the ballad "Sir Patrick Spens" is _____.
    A funny   C sad
    B scary   D sarcastic

12. The mood of the ballad "Get Up and Bar the Door" is _____.
    A tragic   C frightening
    B scholarly   D humorous

13. Sir Patrick Spens expresses his feelings about his journey in the first section of the ballad. Why are these feelings important to the rest of the ballad?

14. What do Spens's actions show about his character?

15. Do you think the event described in "Sir Patrick Spens" was one that happened often in the Middle Ages? Explain.

16. What details at the end of "Sir Patrick Spens" emphasize the tragedy of the event?

17. Characterize the man and the woman who are married in "Get Up and Bar the Door."

18. Who are the "two gentlemen" who come to the couple's house?

19. Who finally wins the argument? Explain.

20. What lesson or theme do you find in the ballad "Get Up and Bar the Door"?

Understanding Literature: Climax

The plot of a narrative consists of a series of events arranged in an artistic way. The author creates suspense as to the final outcome of the events. The climax is the point of greatest suspense, after which the outcome will become clear.

21. What event occurs in the climax of "Sir Patrick Spens"? How many stanzas are used to describe this event?

22. What clues are given throughout the first ballad as to how the event might turn out?

23. What kinds of details are given after the climax of the first ballad?

24. Explain how the disagreement between the man and wife leads to the climax of "Get Up and Bar the Door."

25. At what point of the ballad does the climax occur? How does this differ from the arrangement of events in "Sir Patrick Spens"?

Critical Thinking

26. In what ways are the moods of these two ballads similar or different?

27. In what ways are the purposes of the two ballads similar or different?

28. Why do you think each ballad would have been popular? Explain.

Thinking Creatively

29. In what type of music today, if any, might you find songs with themes similar to these two ballads?

30. What are some ballads with which you are familiar? Why do you think ballads are still popular?

After Reading continued on next page

Sir Patrick Spens and *Get Up and Bar the Door* *Anonymous*

 Grammar Check

A contraction consists of two words that are put together. An apostrophe shows where one or more letters have been left out. For example, in "Get Up and Bar the Door," the contraction *she's* is used for *she has* in line 4, "And she's boiled them in the pan." An apostrophe can also show letters that have been left out in uncontracted forms. For example, in "Sir Patrick Spens," the apostrophe in *o'* indicates that the letter *f* has been left out of the word *of*.

- Write down each contraction in "Get Up and Bar the Door." Then write the uncontracted form of each.

- Write three words in "Sir Patrick Spens" in which an apostrophe shows that a letter has been left out. Then write the word with all its letters and without the apostrophe.

 Writing on Your Own

Refer to your previous writing about a good narrative topic for a ballad. Write three or more stanzas of a ballad on the topic. Use rhyme in your ballad. Create a plot that has a climax and an ending.

 Speaking

Choose two or more stanzas that create a specific mood from one of the ballads. With a partner, develop a choral reading from these lines. Practice your choral reading to make sure that you can communicate the intended mood. Then present your choral reading to the class.

 Listening

Locate and listen to a recording of a classic folk ballad or a modern ballad. Define the mood the ballad creates. Think about how the music, instruments, and vocals add to this effect. Write a paragraph describing these aspects of the ballad.

BEFORE READING THE SELECTION

from *The Canterbury Tales* by Geoffrey Chaucer (trans. by Nevill Coghill)

About the Author

Throughout the Middle Ages, society had three groups: nobles, church officials, and commoners. During Geoffrey Chaucer's life, the class structure was changing. Chaucer's father was a successful wine seller, and Chaucer was a member of the growing middle class. As a teenager, Chaucer worked in a prince's household. Later, he held several important positions, such as the controller of customs (taxes) and justice of the peace. Chaucer met people from all levels of society, including royalty and nobility. He learned French and read French and Italian poetry. The subject of much medieval poetry was courtly love: the idealized romances of the nobility. Around 1385, Chaucer wrote the poem *Troilus and Criseide*, about the romance of an ancient Trojan prince. It was based on a work by the Italian poet Bocaccio.

Chaucer wrote *The Canterbury Tales* between 1386 and 1400. More than 80 manuscripts of the tales still exist, showing their great popularity during the Middle Ages.

Geoffrey Chaucer
1343–1400

Objectives

- To read and understand a poem written in couplets
- To identify methods of characterization in a literary work
- To understand what an anecdote is and why it is used

About the Selection

In 1386, Chaucer lived near a road used by religious pilgrims. These people journey to an important religious place. Pilgrims were going to the shrine of the English saint Thomas à Becket. *The Canterbury Tales* has 22 linked stories. Each is told by a fictional pilgrim on the way to Canterbury. The characters come from all levels of society and include a miller, a knight, and a monk. Chaucer's characters were familiar both as real types of the age and as fictional characters. For example, knights, who fought in battles for their country, were the heroes. The Prologue introduces the characters who will tell the tales. This selection introduces the first four characters.

Before Reading continued on next page

from *The Canterbury Tales*   by *Geoffrey Chaucer*

characterization
the way a writer develops a character's traits

couplet a rhyming pair

anecdote a short account of an interesting event in someone's life

Literary Terms The Prologue to *The Canterbury Tales* contains descriptions of each character, or person who plays a part in his tales. Chaucer uses various methods of **characterization,** or the way a writer develops character traits. The poem is written in **couplets,** rhyming pairs of lines. In addition to physical descriptions, the poem includes **anecdotes,** or brief stories, about the characters.

Reading on Your Own As you read the poem, use Chaucer's descriptions to picture each character. Use your own experiences with people to make inferences, or "educated guesses," about Chaucer's characters. Reading "between the lines" in this way will make the selection easier to remember and enjoy.

Writing on Your Own Think of a person you have met who has interesting character traits. Write a brief character sketch of the person.

Vocabulary Focus A suffix is a word part added to the end of a word to change its meaning. For example, in the word *boorish, -ish* is a suffix meaning "having the characteristics of." So *boorish* means "having the characteristics of a boor." (A boor is someone who is self-centered and rude.) Knowing the meanings of suffixes can help you determine a word's meaning. Identify and find out the meaning of the suffix in each of the following words. Then explain what each word means based on its suffix: *pilgrimage, serviceable, blissful.*

Think Before You Read What types of characters might Chaucer introduce in the Prologue?

from The Canterbury Tales

When in April the sweet showers fall
And pierce the drought of March to the root, and all
The veins are bathed in liquor of such power
As brings about the **engendering** of the flower,
5　When also Zephyrus with his sweet breath
Exhales an air in every grove and heath
Upon the tender shoots, and the young sun
His half-course in the sign of the *Ram* has run,
And the small fowl are making melody
10　That sleep away the night with open eye
(So nature pricks
　　them and their
　　heart engages)
Then people long
　　to go on
　　pilgrimages
And palmers long
　　to seek the
　　stranger
　　strands
Of far-off saints,
　　hallowed in
　　sundry lands,
15　And specially, from
　　every **shire's**
　　end

A 15th-century manuscript page of *The Canterbury Tales*

As you read, notice that the poem consists of rhyming couplets, or pairs of lines that rhyme.

Zephyrus was the Greek god of the west wind. The *Ram* is Aries, a figure of the zodiac. The sun enters Aries on March 21, so a "half-course" sets the story in early April.

The trips made by pilgrims were *pilgrimages; palmers* were pilgrims wearing two crossed palm leaves to signify their journey.

engendering causing to exist

strands beaches

hallowed sacred; revered

sundry various

shire's county's

Of England, down to Canterbury they wend
To seek the holy blissful martyr, quick
To give his help to them when they were sick.
It happened in that season that one day
20 In Southwark, at *The Tabard,* as I lay
Ready to go on pilgrimage and start
For Canterbury, most devout at heart,
At night there came into that **hostelry**
Some nine and twenty in a company
25 Of sundry folk happening then to fall
In fellowship, and they were pilgrims all
That towards Canterbury meant to ride.
The rooms and stables of the inn were wide;
They made us easy, all was of the best.
30 And, briefly, when the sun had gone to rest,
I'd spoken to them all upon the trip
And was soon one with them in fellowship,
Pledged to rise early and to take the way
To Canterbury, as you heard me say.
35   But none the less, while I have time and space,
Before my story takes a further pace,
It seems a reasonable thing to say
What their condition was, the full **array**
Of each of them, as it appeared to me,
40 According to profession and **degree,**
And what apparel they were riding in;
And at a Knight I therefore will begin.
There was a *Knight,* a most distinguished man,
Who from the day on which he first began
45 To ride abroad had followed **chivalry,**
Truth, honour, generousness and courtesy.
He had done nobly in his **sovereign's** war
And ridden into battle, no man more,
As well in Christian as in heathen places,
50 And ever honoured for his noble graces.

The knight is the first character Chaucer describes. His characterization consists of direct description ("a most distinguished man") and also a description of his actions.

hostelry inn	**degree** social rank	**sovereign's** king's
array clothing and possessions	**chivalry** the customs of medieval knighthood	

When we took Alexandria, he was there.
He often sat at table in the chair
Of honour, above all nations, when in Prussia.
In Lithuania he had ridden, and Russia,
55 No Christian man so often, of his rank.
When, in Granada, Algeciras sank
Under assault, he had been there, and in
North Africa, raiding Benamarin;
In Anatolia he had been as well
60 And fought when Ayas and Attalia fell,
For all along the Mediterranean coast
He had embarked with many a noble host.
In fifteen mortal battles he had been
And **jousted** for our faith at Tramissene
65 **Thrice** in the lists, and always killed his man.
This same distinguished knight had led the **van**
Once with the Bey of Balat, doing work
For him against another **heathen** Turk;
He was of **sovereign** value in all eyes.
70 And though so much distinguished, he was wise
And in his bearing modest as a maid.
He never yet a boorish thing had said
In all his life to any, come what might;
He was a true, a perfect gentle-knight.
75   Speaking of his equipment, he possessed
Fine horses, but he was not gaily dressed.
He wore a **fustian** tunic stained and dark
With smudges where his armour had left mark;
Just home from service, he had joined our ranks
80 To do his pilgrimage and render thanks.
     He had his son with him, a fine young *Squire,*
A lover and **cadet,** a lad of fire
With locks as curly as if they had been pressed.
He was some twenty years of age, I guessed.

The names in lines 51–67 refer to locations of battles in the Near East, eastern Europe, Eurasia, and North Africa.

jousted fought on horseback with lances	**heathen** not religious or cultured	**cadet** one in training for military service
thrice three times	**sovereign** excellent	
van vanguard; troops moving before an army	**fustian** strong cotton and linen fabric	

Lydgate and the Canterbury Pilgrims Leaving Canterbury, John Lydgate, 1520

85   In **stature** he was of a moderate length,
       With wonderful agility and strength.
       He'd seen some service with the **cavalry**
       In Flanders and Artois and Picardy
       And had done valiantly in little space
90   Of time, in hope to win his lady's grace.

These are places where the English fought the French.

85   In **stature** he was of a moderate length,
With wonderful agility and strength.
He'd seen some service with the **cavalry**
In Flanders and Artois and Picardy
And had done valiantly in little space
90   Of time, in hope to win his lady's grace.
He was embroidered like a meadow bright
And full of freshest flowers, red and white.
Singing he was, or fluting all the day;
He was as fresh as is the month of May.
95   Short was his gown, the sleeves were long and wide;
He knew the way to sit a horse and ride.
He could make songs and poems and recite,
Knew how to joust and dance, to draw and write.
He loved so hotly that till dawn grew pale
100   He slept as little as a nightingale.
Courteous he was, lowly and serviceable,
And carved to serve his father at the table.

---

stature height   **cavalry** army on horseback

There was a *Yeoman* with him at his side,
No other servant; so he chose to ride.

105　This Yeoman wore a coat and hood of green,
And peacock-feathered arrows, bright and keen
And neatly sheathed, hung at his belt the while
—For he could dress his gear in yeoman style,
His arrows never drooped their feathers low—

110　And in his hand he bore a mighty bow.
His head was like a nut, his face was brown.
He knew the whole of woodcraft up and down.
A **saucy** brace was on his arm to **ward**
It from the bow-string, and a shield and sword

115　Hung at one side, and at the other slipped
A jaunty **dirk,** spear-sharp and well-equipped.
A medal of St. Christopher he wore
Of shining silver on his breast, and bore
A hunting-horn, well slung and **burnished** clean,

120　That dangled from a **baldrick** of bright green.
He was a proper forester, I guess.
　　　There also was a *Nun,* a Prioress,
Her way of smiling very simple and coy.
Her greatest oath was only "By St. Loy!"

125　And she was known as Madam Eglantyne.
And well she sang a service, with a fine
Intoning through her nose, as was most seemly,
And she spoke daintily in French, extremely,
After the school of Stratford-atte-Bowe;

130　French in the Paris style she did not know.
At meat her manners were well taught **withal;**
No morsel from her lips did she let fall,
Nor dipped her fingers in the sauce too deep;
But she could carry a morsel up and keep

135　The smallest drop from falling on her breast.

A *yeoman* was an attendant in a noble household; *him* refers to the knight.

A *prioress* was the female head of a priory, or religious house.

Stratford-atte-Bowe is a suburb of London. Chaucer makes the point that the prioress speaks French to sound stylish, but she doesn't speak it well.

saucy stylish	**burnished** polished	**intoning** reciting in musical tones
ward guard	**baldrick** ornamental belt	**withal** besides
dirk long dagger		

For **courtliness** she had a special zest,
And she would wipe her upper lip so clean
That not a trace of grease was to be seen
Upon the cup when she had drunk; to eat,
140   She reached a hand sedately for the meat.
She certainly was very entertaining,
Pleasant and friendly in her ways, and straining
To counterfeit a courtly kind of grace,
A stately bearing fitting to her place,
145   And to seem dignified in all her dealings.
As for her sympathies and tender feelings,
She was so charitably **solicitous**
She used to weep if she but saw a mouse
Caught in a trap, if it were dead or bleeding.
150   And she had little dogs she would be feeding
With roasted flesh, or milk, or fine white bread.
And bitterly she wept if one were dead
Or someone took a stick and made it smart;
She was all **sentiment** and tender heart.
155   Her veil was gathered in a seemly way,
Her nose was elegant, her eyes glass-grey;
Her mouth was very small, but soft and red,
Her forehead, certainly, was fair of spread,
Almost a **span** across the brows, I own;
160   She was indeed by no means undergrown.
Her cloak, I noticed, had a graceful charm.
She wore a coral trinket on her arm,
A set of beads, the gaudies tricked in green,
Whence hung a golden **brooch** of brightest sheen
165   On which there first was graven a crowned *A*,
And lower, *Amor vincit omnia*.

Lines 146–153 provide stories about the Prioress to illustrate her character. What can you learn about her from these details?

White bread (line 151) was the most expensive kind of bread at the time.

Amor vincit omnia is Latin for "Love conquers all."

courtliness elegance	**sentiment** emotion	**brooch** decorative pin or pendant
solicitous full of concern	**span** English unit of length equal to 9 inches	

AFTER READING THE SELECTION

from *The Canterbury Tales* by *Geoffrey Chaucer (trans. by Nevill Coghill)*

Directions Choose the letter of the best answer or write the answer using complete sentences.

Comprehension: Identifying Facts

1. The knight's appearance is _____.
- **A** flashy
- **B** modest
- **C** fashionable
- **D** sloppy

2. The pilgrim who owns dogs is the _____.
- **A** prioress
- **B** yeoman
- **C** knight
- **D** squire

3. What is the season when pilgrims set out, according to Chaucer?

4. What is the purpose of the pilgrimages that Chaucer describes?

5. According to Chaucer, how did he meet the pilgrims he describes?

6. How has the knight spent his life?

7. What talents does the squire have?

8. What does the yeoman wear on his breast?

9. Summarize the prioress's table manners.

10. How does the prioress treat other people?

Comprehension: Putting Ideas Together

11. The squire's body type could best be described as _____.
- **A** athletic
- **B** scrawny
- **C** overweight
- **D** very muscular

12. From Chaucer's description of the prioress, readers can infer that she is _____.
- **A** intelligent
- **B** unkind
- **C** unattractive
- **D** shallow

13. What mood does Chaucer create in his description of the season in the poem's beginning?

14. How do the knight's professional background and his personal manner contrast?

15. What part does the Christian faith play in the knight's professional life?

16. Describe the squire's relationships with his father and with ladies.

17. How does the squire's clothing contrast with that of the knight?

18. What weapons does the yeoman carry with him?

19. The yeoman rides at the knight's side. What do you think his job is?

After Reading **continued on next page**

20. Do you think the prioress was well educated? Explain.

Understanding Literature: Characterization

Writers use many methods to create their characters. Writers may describe their physical appearances. They may tell directly what a character is like; for example, Chaucer says about the knight that "he was wise." More often, writers *show* what a character is like. Readers must decide about their character traits from the word picture that is created.

21. Summarize the physical appearance of the prioress. Do you think her appearance is typical of that of a religious woman of the Middle Ages? Explain why or why not.

22. What does the prioress's treatment of animals show about her character?

23. According to Chaucer, did the prioress's behavior seem natural? Explain.

24. What inferences can you make about the character traits of the prioress? What details lead to your inferences?

25. How would you describe Chaucer's attitude toward the prioress?

Critical Thinking

26. Based on the details Chaucer gives about the knight, what traits did the ideal knight possess?

27. Which pilgrim does Chaucer seem to admire most? Explain.

28. Summarize a story Chaucer tells about one of the pilgrims. How does the anecdote help characterize the person?

29. Why do you think Chaucer chooses to describe each pilgrim in detail in the Prologue before telling the tale each one narrates?

Thinking Creatively

30. Suppose a writer of today created characters typical of our times as Chaucer did. Describe three character "types" that the author might create.

Grammar Check

An appositive is a phrase that renames a noun. For example, "There was a Knight, a most distinguished man." The phrase "a most distinguished man" renames the knight. It describes him. An appositive can be used to identify, define, or describe a noun.

- Find and write two other lines or sentences from the Prologue that contain appositives.

- Next to each example, tell whether the appositive phrase identifies, defines, or further describes the noun.

- Write a sentence of your own about an interesting person you know. Use an appositive in your sentence.

 ## Writing on Your Own

Write a character sketch of a person, using rhyming couplets. Write four lines or more, including details about the person's physical appearance, actions, or words that show key traits of the person's character.

 ## Speaking and Listening

Suppose that you are going on this journey and there is a character traveling with you that you do not like. What traits does the character have? How can you communicate those traits in such a way that your listeners will sympathize with you? Create a character sketch and describe your character to the class. When it is your turn to listen to others' descriptions, note how the speaker's tone and choice of details affect your feelings about the character. Share your thoughts about tone in a class discussion.

 ## Viewing

In the library or on the Internet, locate an illustration of a person whose clothing resembles one of the pilgrims described in the Prologue. Make a photocopy of the picture or make your own drawing of it. Display the picture in your classroom. Identify and discuss each illustration.

BEFORE READING THE SELECTION

from *The Book of Margery Kempe*   *by Margery Kempe*

A 14th-century noblewoman

About the Author

Margery Kempe was born in 1373 in King's Lynn, a busy trading town. Her father was the town's longtime mayor.

When Kempe was 20 years old, she married John Kempe, who worked through the years as a tax collector, brewer, and miller. After the birth of her first child, Kempe became a Christian. She could not read, so her religious knowledge came from sermons and other oral sources. Over the next 20 years, Kempe gave birth to 13 more children.

Kempe also made a pilgrimage to the Holy Land. She said she had religious visions. She responded by weeping and fasting. Many people reacted to her with scorn or disapproval. Toward the end of her life, she told her life story to two writers. Those writers wrote down her life story for her.

About the Selection

The selection comes from the first chapter of Kempe's life story. In it, Kempe tells about her first vision, which occurred soon after her first child was born. Kempe refers to herself throughout her writings as "this creature." By this, she means "a person created by God."

Literary Terms *The Book of Margery Kempe* is an **autobiography,** the story of a person's life written by the person. An autobiography may narrate important periods and events from a person's life, such as his or her childhood, friendships, and travels. However, Kempe's story is a spiritual autobiography. It mainly describes events in her religious and spiritual life. Most autobiographies are written in the first person. Kempe's, however, is written in the **third person.** This is a point of view where the narrator is not a character and refers to characters as *he* and *she*. Kempe also calls herself *this creature*.

Reading on Your Own As you read the selection, consider the difficulties of childbirth in the Middle Ages. Many women died during childbirth. Many others died of diseases that can now be cured. Use your own experiences and knowledge of religion and spirituality to understand Kempe's descriptions of her spiritual life.

Writing on Your Own The vision that Kempe describes seems to be a dreamlike experience. Write about an especially vivid dream you have had.

Vocabulary Focus In describing her spiritual journey, Kempe uses many synonyms, or words with about the same meaning, for the words *good* and *evil*. She also uses many other words associated with each. Begin two Concept Maps with the words *good* and *evil* at their centers. As you read the selection, complete the maps with synonyms and words associated with each main word. Appendix A describes this graphic organizer.

Think Before You Read How might being a woman make Kempe's spiritual journey more difficult?

from The Book of Margery Kempe

As you read, think about which experiences might be difficult for the writer to discuss.

By definition, an autobiography is a first-person account. Most autobiographies are written with the first-person pronoun *I*. However, Margery Kempe refers to herself in the third person, *she*, throughout.

When this creature was twenty years of age, or somewhat more, she was married to a worshipful **burgess** [of Lynn] and was with child within a short time, as nature would have it. And after she had conceived, she was troubled with severe attacks of sickness until the child was born. And then, what with the labour-pains she had in childbirth and the sickness that had gone before, she despaired of her life, believing she might not live. Then she sent for her **confessor,** for she had a thing on her conscience which she had never revealed before that time in all her life. For she was continually **hindered** by her enemy—the devil—always saying to her while she was in good health that she didn't need to confess but to do **penance** by herself alone, and all should be forgiven, for God is merciful enough. And therefore this creature often did great penance in fasting on bread and water, and performed other acts of **charity** with devout prayers, but she would not reveal that one thing in confession.

And when she was at any time sick or troubled, the devil said in her mind that she should be damned, for she was not **shriven** of that fault. Therefore, after her child was born, and not believing she would live, she sent for her confessor, as said before, fully wishing to be shriven of her whole lifetime, as near as she could. And when she came to the point of saying

---

burgess town leader

confessor priest who hears confessions

hindered held back

penance an act done to pay for a sin

charity goodwill or helpfulness

shriven forgiven

that thing which she had so long concealed, her confessor was a little too hasty and began sharply to **reprove** her before she had fully said what she meant, and so she would say no more in spite of anything he might do. And soon after, because of the dread she had of damnation on the one hand, and his sharp reproving of her on the other, this creature went out of her mind and was amazingly disturbed and tormented with spirits for half a year, eight weeks and odd days.

And in this time she saw, as she thought, devils opening their mouths all alight with burning flames of fire, as if they would have swallowed her in, sometimes pawing at her, sometimes threatening her, sometimes pulling her and hauling her about both night and day during the said time. And also the devils called out to her with great threats, and **bade** her that she should **forsake** her Christian faith and belief, and deny her God, his mother, and all the saints in heaven, her good works and all good virtues, her father, her mother, and all her friends. And so she did. She **slandered** her husband, her friends, and her own self. She spoke many sharp and reproving words; she recognized no virtue nor goodness; she desired all wickedness; just as the spirits tempted her to say and do, so she said and did. She would have killed herself many a time as they stirred her to, and would have been damned with

> Contrast the visions Kempe sees at the start of her madness with the one she has later in the selection.

> What is the tone of this paragraph? What traits of an autobiography do they show?

Woman Reading at the Hearth

reprove scold
bade told

forsake turn away from

slandered said false statements about

them in hell, and in witness of this she bit her own hand so violently that the mark could be seen for the rest of her life. And also she pitilessly tore the skin on her body near her heart with her nails, for she had no other **implement,** and she would have done something worse, except that she was tied up and forcibly **restrained** both day and night so that she could not do as she wanted.

And when she had long been troubled by these and many other temptations, so that people thought she should never have escaped from them alive, then one time as she lay by herself and her keepers were not with her, our merciful Lord Christ Jesus—ever to be trusted, worshipped be his name, never forsaking his servant in time of need—appeared to his creature who had forsaken him, in the likeness of a man, the most seemly, most beauteous, and most **amiable** that ever might be seen with man's eye, clad in a **mantle** of purple silk,

Dinner in a Noble Home, **15th century**

implement tool

restrained prevented from doing something

amiable pleasing; admirable

mantle cloak

sitting upon her bedside, looking upon her with so blessed a **countenance** that she was strengthened in all her spirits, and he said to her these words: "Daughter, why have you forsaken me, and I never forsook you?"

And as soon as he had said these words, she saw truly how the air opened as bright as any lightning, and he ascended up into the air, not hastily and quickly, but beautifully and gradually, so that she could clearly behold him in the air until it closed up again.

And presently the creature grew as calm in her wits and her reason as she ever was before, and asked her husband, as soon as he came to her, if she could have the keys of the **buttery** to get her food and drink as she had done before. Her maids and her keepers advised him that he should not deliver up any keys to her, for they said she would only give away such goods as there were, because she did not know what she was saying, as they believed.

Nevertheless, her husband, who always had tenderness and **compassion** for her, ordered that they should give her the keys. And she took food and drink as her bodily strength would allow her, and she once again recognized her friends and her household, and everybody else who came to her in order to see how our Lord Jesus Christ had worked his grace in her—blessed may he be, who is ever near in **tribulation**. When people think he is far away from them he is very near through his grace. Afterwards this creature performed all her responsibilities wisely and **soberly** enough, except that she did not truly know our Lord's power to draw us to him.

What is Kempe like at the end of the passage? Do you think she is completely healthy and happy? Explain.

countenance expression	**compassion** pity	**soberly** calmly
buttery pantry	**tribulation** distress; suffering	

The Anglo-Saxon Period and Middle Ages Unit 1 **49**

AFTER READING THE SELECTION

from *The Book of Margery Kempe*   *by Margery Kempe*

Directions Choose the letter of the best answer or write the answer using complete sentences.

Comprehension: Identifying Facts

1. According to Margery Kempe, what causes her to lose her mind?
   A She loses her baby.
   B Her husband mistreats her.
   C She becomes very ill.
   D She feels guilty but is afraid of the priest's scoldings.

2. Why do the people around Kempe tie her up?

3. Summarize the vision Kempe experiences that ends her madness.

Comprehension: Putting Ideas Together

4. The best definition for the *grace* of God that Kempe describes is _____.
   A charm   **C** disapproval
   B mercy   **D** thanks

5. In what way is Kempe's religious conversion connected to her experience of childbirth?

6. What change does Kempe experience as a result of her vision?

Understanding Literature: Autobiography

An autobiography may describe its author's most private thoughts and feelings. Though Kempe tells her story in the third person, she tells very personal details about her thoughts and experiences.

7. Summarize one part of the autobiographical selection that describes a very private experience or emotion.

8. What do you think Kempe's purpose is in having her autobiography written?

Critical Thinking

9. Describe the impression of Christ Jesus that Kempe gets from her vision.

Thinking Creatively

10. How do you think women of Kempe's time might have reacted to her autobiography if they had read it? How would their reactions differ from those of people today?

Grammar Check

An adverb is a part of speech that modifies, or describes, a verb. Adverbs can also modify adjectives or other adverbs. Many, though not all, words that end in -*ly*, as in *pitilessly*, are adverbs that modify verbs. Carefully chosen adverbs can make writing more vivid and specific.

- Write down a sentence from the selection that uses an adverb ending in -*ly*. Underline the adverb. Circle the word it modifies and identify it as a verb, adjective, or adverb.

- Write one sentence of your own using an adverb ending in -*ly*.

 Writing on Your Own

Think about an event that changed your life in some way. Write a short autobiographical narrative about the event. Explain how and why the experience changed you.

 Speaking and Listening

In a small group, discuss Kempe's characterization of the devil. What is the nature of the devil as she sees it? How does it affect her life? How do the effects of the devil on her life differ from those of Jesus? State your ideas and point out passages in which they are shown. Listen and respond to others as they give their views.

 Research

Kempe and others like her who have religious visions are called mystics. She was one of several who were very well-known during her time. Do research on the Internet or at the library to find information about some of the other mystics of Kempe's day and her connection to them. What influence did the mystics have? How were they generally treated? Prepare a brief report of your findings.

from *Le Morte d'Arthur*   by Thomas Malory

Objectives

- To read and understand a romance
- To understand the role of legend in literature

About the Author

Little is known about Thomas Malory. He lived during the War of the Roses, a power struggle between the Lancaster and the York families to rule England. During these years, there were many political arrests. Malory began getting into trouble with the law in 1451. He was arrested and jailed for crimes such as stealing from an abbey, escaping prison, and extortion (forcing people to give money). Malory's crimes and punishments may have been related to the political troubles of the times. Malory wrote *Le Morte d'Arthur* in prison. It was printed in 1485.

About the Selection

The stories of King Arthur are based on chivalry, the code that provided rules for a knight's behavior in battle, in his religious life, and toward women. The first knights were warriors who fought on horseback, and most came from the nobility. Being a knight was a great honor. The popularity of tales of chivalry peaked in the twelfth and thirteenth centuries. The first stories of King Arthur were told around 1150 by a Welsh storyteller, Geoffrey of Monmouth. They seem to have been based on a real king who fought against Anglo-Saxon invaders around 500. But the true story has been hidden by stories about Arthur's courage and his relationship with his knights of the Round Table. Malory translated and edited French tales about Arthur. He was the first English author to create stories that were as lively as verse.

This selection is from the beginning of *Le Morte d'Arthur*. The French title means "The Death of Arthur." His death is described in the last story of the series. The chapters that come before this selection tell of the victories and death of King Uther Pendragon, whose son Arthur had been sent away for his protection, to be raised by Sir Ector.

Literary Terms *Le Morte d'Arthur* is a **legend.** It is also considered a **romance.** It discusses the loves, as well as the battles, of heroes from a distant, idealized past. The legend contains themes involving courage, loyalty, and love.

Reading on Your Own As you read the selection, use the details to draw conclusions about facts that may seem unclear. For example, make conclusions about the rules and customs of knights and the relationships among the characters. After reading each chapter, summarize it.

Writing on Your Own Write a short summary of a legend, myth, or romance that you enjoy. Describe why you think the story is a legend, myth, or romance.

Vocabulary Focus Sometimes words and phrases in a literary work have meanings that are not literal. Instead, they are figures of speech. For example, in *Le Morte d'Arthur,* Malory says about King Uther Pendragon that "therewith he yielded up the ghost." This phrase is not literal. "Giving up the ghost" is a common phrase for dying. As you read *Le Morte d'Arthur,* list words and phrases used this way instead of literally.

Think Before You Read What parts of myths, legends, and romances do you predict you will find in the selection?

> **legend** a story from folklore featuring characters who actually lived or real events or places
>
> **romance** a story about heroes, mysterious settings, or love

from Le Morte d'Arthur

Chapter V: How Arthur Was Chosen King

Then stood the realm in great jeopardy long while, for every lord that was mighty of men made him strong, and many **weened** to have been king. Then Merlin went to the Archbishop of Canterbury, and counselled him for to send for all the lords of the realm, and all the gentlemen of arms, that they should to London come by Christmas, upon pain of **cursing;** and for this cause, that Jesus, that was born on that night, that he would of his great mercy show some miracle, as he was come to be king of mankind, for to show some miracle who should be **rightwise** king of this realm. So the Archbishop, by the advice of Merlin, sent for all the lords and gentlemen of arms that they should come by Christmas even unto London. And many of them made them clean of their life, that their prayer might be the more acceptable unto God. So in the greatest church of London, whether it were Paul's or not the French book maketh no mention, all the **estates** were long or day in the church for to pray. And when **matins** and the first mass was done, there was seen in the churchyard, against the high altar, a great stone four square, like unto a marble stone; and in midst thereof was like an anvil of steel a foot on high, and therein stuck a fair sword naked by the point, and letters there were written in gold about the sword that said thus: Whoso pulleth out this sword of this stone and anvil, is rightwise king born of all England. Then the people marvelled, and told it to the Archbishop. "I command," said the Archbishop, "that ye keep you within your church and pray unto God still, that no man touch the sword till the high mass be all done." So when all masses were done all the lords went to behold the stone and the sword. And when they saw

The *Archbishop of Canterbury* was the head of the Church of England.

Malory refers to the fact that he was translating parts of the story from the French. The original Saint Paul's Cathedral was built in London in A.D. 604. It has since been rebuilt three times.

---

weened wished

cursing calling upon divine power to send injury upon

rightwise rightful; proper

estates high social classes

matins morning prayers

the **scripture** some **assayed,** such as would have been king. But none might stir the sword nor move it. "He is not here," said the Archbishop, "that shall achieve the sword, but doubt not God will make him known. But this is my **counsel,**" said the Archbishop, "that we let **purvey** ten knights, men of good fame, and they to keep this sword." So it was **ordained,** and then there was made a cry, that every man should assay that would, for to win the sword. And upon New Year's Day the barons let make a jousts and a tournament, that all knights that would joust or tourney there might play, and all this was ordained for to keep the lord together and the **commons,** for the Archbishop trusted that God would make him known that should win the sword.

So upon New Year's Day, when the service was done, the barons rode unto the field, some to joust and some to tourney, and so it happened that Sir Ector, that had great **livelihood** about London, rode unto the jousts, and with him rode Sir Kay his son, and young Arthur that was his nourished brother; and Sir Kay was made knight at All Hallowmass afore. So as

> Knights practiced their battle skills at tournaments in which they formed two large groups and fought each other. Tournaments covered large areas of countryside and could last several days. Because tournaments could be dangerous and could cause more fighting, jousts between two knights with blunt weapons became popular.

> *All Hallowmass* is another name for All Saints' Day, November 1.

A Medieval Joust

scripture writing
assayed tried
counsel advice

purvey supply
ordained ordered

commons common people
livelihood business

What do you learn about Arthur from his willingness to go on the errand for Sir Kay? What do you learn about him from his reaction to finding the house locked?

they rode to the jousts-ward, Sir Kay lost his sword, for he had left it at his father's lodging, and so he prayed young Arthur for to ride for his sword. "I will well," said Arthur, and rode fast after the sword, and when he came home, the lady and all were out to see the jousting. Then was Arthur **wroth,** and said to himself, "I will ride to the churchyard, and take the sword with me that sticketh in the stone, for my brother Sir Kay shall not be without a sword this day." So when he came to the churchyard, Sir Arthur alighted and tied his horse to the stile, and so he went to the tent, and found no knights there, for they were at the jousting. And so he handled the sword by the handles, and lightly and fiercely pulled it out of the stone, and took his horse and rode his way until he came to his brother Sir Kay, and delivered him the sword. And as soon as Sir Kay saw the sword, he **wist** well it was the sword of the stone, and so he rode to his father Sir Ector, and said: "Sir, lo here is the sword of the stone, wherefore I must be king of this land." When Sir Ector beheld the sword, he returned again and came to the church, and there they alighted all three, and went into the church. And **anon** he made Sir Kay swear upon a book how he came to that sword. "Sir," said Sir Kay, "by my brother Arthur, for he brought it to me." "How gat ye this sword?" said Sir Ector to Arthur. "Sir, I will tell you. When I came home for my brother's sword, I found nobody at home to deliver me his sword; and so I thought my brother Sir Kay should not be swordless, and so I came hither eagerly and pulled it out of the stone without any pain." "Found ye any knights about this sword?" said Sir Ector. "Nay," said Arthur. "Now," said Sir Ector to Arthur, "I understand ye must be king of this land." "Wherefore I," said Arthur, "and for what cause?" "Sir," said Ector, "for God will have it so; for there should never man have drawn out this sword, but he that shall be rightwise king of this land. Now let me see whether ye can put the sword there as it was, and pull it out again." "That is no **mastery,**" said Arthur, and so he put it in the stone; wherewithal Sir Ector assayed to pull out the sword and failed.

How would you describe the relationship between Arthur and Sir Kay? between Arthur and Sir Ector?

wroth very angry   **anon** soon   **mastery** skill
wist knew

Chapter VI: How King Arthur Pulled Out the Sword Divers Times

Divers means many.

"Now assay," said Sir Ector unto Sir Kay. And anon he pulled at the sword with all his might; but it would not be. "Now shall ye assay," said Sir Ector to Arthur. "I will well," said Arthur, and pulled it out easily. And **therewithal** Sir Ector knelt down to the earth, and Sir Kay. "Alas," said Arthur, "my own dear father and brother, why kneel ye to me?" "Nay, nay, my lord Arthur, it is not so; I was never your father nor of your blood, but I wot well ye are of an higher blood than I weened ye were." And then Sir Ector told him all, how he was betaken him for to nourish him, and by whose commandment, and by Merlin's **deliverance.**

Then Arthur made great **dole** when he understood that Sir Ector was not his father. "Sir," said Ector unto Arthur, "will

Why do you think Sir Ector makes the requests he does of Arthur?

Prince Arthur/Excalibur,
Louis Rhead

ye be my good and gracious lord when ye are king?" "Else were I to blame," said Arthur, "for ye are the man in the world that I am most **beholden** to, and my good lady and mother your wife, that as well as her own hath **fostered** me and kept. And if ever it be God's will that I be king as ye say, ye shall desire of me what I may do, and I shall not fail you; God forbid I should fail you." "Sir," said Sir Ector, "I will ask no more of you, but that ye will make my son, your foster brother, Sir Kay, **seneschal** of all your lands."

therewithal at that	**dole** grief; sorrow	**fostered** nurtured
deliverance the act of delivering	**beholden** indebted	**seneschal** manager

"That shall be done," said Arthur, "and more, by the faith of my body, that never man shall have that office but he, while he and I live." Therewithal they went unto the Archbishop, and told him how the sword was achieved, and by whom; and on Twelfth-day all the barons came thither, and to assay to take the sword, who that would assay. But there afore them all, there might none take it out but Arthur; wherefore there were many lords wroth, and said it was great shame unto them all and the realm, to be over-governed with a boy of no high blood born. And so they fell out at that time that it was put off till Candlemas, and then all the barons should meet there again; but always the ten knights were ordained to watch the sword day and night, and so they set a **pavilion** over the stone and the sword, and five always watched. So at Candlemas many more great lords came thither for to have won the sword, but there might none **prevail.** And right as Arthur did at Christmas, he did at Candlemas, and pulled out the sword easily, whereof the barons were sore **aggrieved** and put it off in delay till the high feast of Easter. And as Arthur sped before, so did he at Easter; yet there were some of the great lords had indignation that Arthur should be king, and put it off in a delay till the feast of Pentecost.

Then the Archbishop of Canterbury by Merlin's **providence** let purvey then of the best knights that they might get, and such knights as Uther Pendragon loved best and most trusted in his days. And such knights were put about Arthur as Sir Baudwin of Britain, Sir Kay, Sir Ulfius, Sir Brastias. All these, with many other, were always about Arthur, day and night, till the feast of Pentecost.

pavilion tent

prevail win

aggrieved suffering from a denial of legal rights

providence the state of making plans for the future

AFTER READING THE SELECTION

from *Le Morte d'Arthur*   by Thomas Malory

Directions Choose the letter of the best answer or write the answer using complete sentences.

Comprehension: Identifying Facts

1. Merlin calls for the great men of the kingdom to come to London to _____.

   A have a feast
   B honor King Uther
   C discover who will be king
   D have a tournament

2. Arthur feels sad after pulling out the sword because _____.

   A everyone is jealous of him
   B he is not Sir Ector's real son
   C his brother dislikes him
   D he does not want to be king

3. What caused trouble in the kingdom after King Uther's death?

4. Who does Merlin go to speak to?

5. What appears in the churchyard after the first mass?

6. What was written about the sword in the stone?

7. Why do Sir Ector and Sir Kay go into London?

8. Why does Arthur take the sword out of the stone the first time?

9. How do the barons feel after Arthur pulls out the sword?

10. How many times does Arthur prove his ability to pull the sword out?

Comprehension: Putting Ideas Together

11. At the start of Chapter V, the kingdom is _____.

    A in a state of turmoil because there is no king
    B at peace
    C divided over whether Merlin should be king
    D ready to crown Arthur

12. What does Merlin do in the life of young Arthur?

    A threatens him
    B protects him
    C teaches him
    D ignores him

13. What are some traits of the men who attempt to pull the sword from the stone?

14. How does Sir Ector's treatment of Arthur change after Arthur pulls the sword out of the stone?

15. What is the one thing Sir Ector wants when Arthur becomes king?

After Reading **continued on next page**

from *Le Morte d'Arthur* by *Thomas Malory*

16. Describe the knights' relationship to the church. Use details from the selection to support your answer.

17. Why do the barons call for the sword to be pulled out of the stone several times?

18. Which parts of the story have traits of a legend? Which have traits of a myth?

19. Why do trusted knights stay with Arthur night and day from Easter until Pentecost?

20. Describe Arthur's treatment of Sir Ector and Sir Kay.

Understanding Literature: Theme

The theme of a literary work is usually not stated directly. The theme is implied by all the parts of the work. Examples are the characters and what they say and do, the language used, and the details and images. Readers can infer a work's theme by studying these parts.

21. Describe Arthur's character as written in the selection. How does he differ from the barons?

22. Why are the other knights upset when Arthur is the only one who can pull the sword from the stone?

23. The sword in the stone is placed in the churchyard. The attempts to pull the sword out are made on religious days. Why are these details important to the main idea?

24. Whose blessings does Arthur have in becoming king?

25. Think about Arthur's character and other details. What idea about becoming king do these details state? State the theme in a sentence.

Critical Thinking

26. What skills and character traits were knights supposed to have? Make inferences based on the details in the selection.

27. Predict what might happen later in the story. Do you think the barons will accept Arthur? Explain your answer.

28. What can you tell about the characters Sir Ector and Sir Kay?

29. Magic plays a part in most versions of the King Arthur stories. Explain why you think this is the case.

Thinking Creatively

30. Why do you think people still enjoy reading or watching movies about chivalry and knights?

Grammar Check

Commas are used to separate words, phrases, and clauses. They improve the clarity of sentences. One function of commas is to separate items in a series. For example, "King Arthur, Sir Ector, and Sir Kay went to the jousts."

- Find a sentence in *Le Morte d'Arthur* in which commas are used to separate items in a series. Write the sentence.

- Write a sentence about *Le Morte d'Arthur* that includes items in a series separated by commas.

 ## Writing on Your Own

Invent or retell a legend about a historical character. Keep in mind that a legend becomes popular because it tells of amazing events or teaches an important lesson.

 ## Speaking

With a partner, locate the dialogue between Arthur and Sir Ector. Practice reading the dialogue to show the feelings of the characters.

 ## Speaking

With a partner, identify the dialogue in the selection. Then rewrite the dialogue, using words you would use today. One partner then reads the original dialogue. The other reads the modern dialogue.

 ## Technology

The legend of King Arthur has inspired works of art in many fields. For example, the Broadway musical *Camelot* was popular in the 1960s and was later made into a film. Use the Internet to research some books and films based on the Arthurian legend. Create a short bibliography giving facts about several works.

 ## Research

Find out more about knighthood and chivalry on the Internet or at the library. Write a summary of your findings or create a poster that tells and shows interesting aspects of knights and knighthood.

from *The Book of St. Albans*   *by Juliana Barnes*

About the Author

Very little is known about Juliana Barnes. In fact, there is some doubt whether she actually existed. In different sources, her last name has different spellings—*Berners* and *Bernes*. At that time, many words and names had more than one spelling. Barnes seems to have been the daughter of a nobleman, James Berners. Being brought up as a noblewoman meant that Barnes learned many kinds of sports and had plenty of time to enjoy them. As an adult, she was the prioress of the nunnery of Sopwell, near the town of Saint Albans.

About the Selection

The Book of St. Albans was first published in 1486. However, some of the manuscript was written well before this date. It contained information about hunting, hawking (hunting birds with a trained hawk), and heraldry (coats of arms). Later, the section on angling, or sport fishing, was added. This was the first book in English on angling.

Barnes was said to be the author of the book. Much of the content was probably put together and translated from earlier works in French. At any rate, the book was very popular. In this selection, Barnes discusses in great detail some methods of fishing.

The English language has changed a lot since the time this selection was first written. To modern readers, Middle English may look like a foreign language. However, readers will notice that they are able to recognize many words if they pay close attention or if they try to read it aloud. This selection has been translated into modern English so that it can be better understood. However, also included is the first paragraph of the Middle English original. Compare the two paragraphs to identify some of the ways English has changed over time.

Objectives

■ To read and understand an essay

■ To identify imagery in a literary work

Literary Terms *The Book of St. Albans* contains vivid imagery or word pictures that appeal to the five senses. *The Book of St. Albans* contains many **essays** (also called treatises), including this one on fly fishing. An essay is a form of writing in which the writer explains facts and offers opinions on a topic.

essay a written work that shows a writer's opinions on some basic or current issue

Reading on Your Own As you read the selection, think about the author's use of language to create images. Picture or sense each image.

Writing on Your Own Think about an outdoor activity or sport that you enjoy. Write a paragraph describing the activity. Use images that appeal to the five senses.

Vocabulary Focus When you read a selection with many difficult words, use a variety of ways to figure out their meanings. Look up some words in the glossary or dictionary. In the phrase "he must avoid all quarrelsome company and all places of debate," you can probably use context clues to figure out the meaning of *quarrelsome*. In Barnes's discussion of baits, some specific names of baits may be unfamiliar. Simply identifying them as types of bait is probably enough to understand the passage.

Think Before You Read What parts of fishing might call for vivid imagery?

FROM THE BOOK OF ST. ALBANS

Compare the sample on this page to the first paragraph of the modern English translation at the top of the next page. What do you notice about word spellings?

When you read passages that are in an older style of writing or that use dialects, try reading the passage aloud. Middle English and many English dialects are often written somewhat phonetically. This means that the writer wrote words to look the way they sounded to him or her.

Original Text from Middle English

Salomon in his parables sayeth that a good spyrite maketh a flouring age that is a fayre age and a longe. And sythe it is so I aske this question, whiche be the meanes and the causes that enduce a man into a mery spyryte? Truely to my best discretion it semeth good disportes and honest games in whom a man ioyeth without any repentaunce after. Then foloweth it that good disportes and honest games: be cause of mannes fayre age and longe lyfe. And therfore nowe we wyll I chose of foure good dysportes and honest games, that is to wete of Haukyng, Huntyng, and fyshyng, and for foulyng. The best to my discrecion whiche is fyshying called anglyng with a rod, and a lyne, and an hoke, and therof to treat as my symple wyt may suffyse, both for the sayd reason of Salomon, & also for the reason that reason maketh in this wyse.

Si tibi deficiant medici, medici tibi fiant.
Heac tria, mens laeta, labor, et moderata diaeta.

The Treatise of Fishing with an Angle

Solomon in his proverbs says that a good spirit makes a flowering age, that is, a happy age and a long one. And since it is true, I ask this question, "Which are the means and the causes that lead a man into a happy spirit?" Truly, in my best judgement, it seems that they are good sports and honest games which a man enjoys without any **repentance** afterward. Thence it follows that good sports and honest games are the cause of a man's happy old age and long life. And therefore, I will now choose among four good sports and honest games: to wit, of hunting, hawking, fishing, and fowling. The best, in my simple opinion, is fishing, called angling, with a rod and a line and a hook. And of that I will talk as my simple mind will permit: not only because of the reasoning of Solomon, but also for the **assertion** that medical science makes in this manner:

> *Si tibi deficiant medici, medici tibi fiant.*
> *Heac tria, mens laeta, labor, et moderata diaeta.*

You shall understand that this means, if a man lacks **leech** or medicine, he shall make three things his leech and medicine, and he will never need any more. The first of them is a happy mind. The second is work which isn't too **onerous.** The third is a good diet. First, if a man wishes ever more to have merry thoughts and be happy, he must avoid all **quarrelsome** company and all places of debate, where he might have any causes to be upset. And if he wishes to have a job which is not too hard, he must then organise, for his relaxation and pleasure, without care, anxiety, or trouble, a cheerful **occupation** which gives him good heart and in which will raise his spirits. And if he wishes to have a moderate diet, he must avoid all places of **revelry,** which is the cause of overindulgence and sickness. And he must withdraw

Solomon was a king of ancient Israel. He was known for his wisdom and for writing a book of proverbs, or sayings.

In the sport of *hawking,* people hunt birds with a trained hawk. In *fowling,* people hunt wildfowl, such as pheasant.

This Latin sentence means "If doctors fail you, these three might succeed: a broad mind, work, and moderate diet."

repentance regret, feeling guilty	**onerous** boring, tiring	**revelry** rowdy partying
assertion claim	**quarrelsome** likely to argue	
leech doctor	**occupation** work	

himself to places of sweet and hungry air, and eat nourishing and digestible meats. . . .

The Fishes

Because the salmon is the most stately fish that anyone can angle for in fresh water, therefore I intend to begin with him. The salmon is a noble fish, but he is difficult to catch. For commonly he lies only in deep places of great rivers. And for the most part he keeps to the middle of the water: that a man cannot come at him. And he is in season from March until Michaelmas. In which season you should angle for him with these baits when you can get them. First, with a red worm in the beginning and end of the season. And also with a grub that grows in a dunghill. And especially with an excellent bait that grows on a water dock. And he doesn't bite at the bottom but at the float. Also you may take him: but it is seldom seen with a **dubbed** hook at such times as he leaps, in the same style and manner as you catch a trout or a grayling. And these baits are well proven baits for the salmon.

The trout, because he is a right dainty fish and also a right **fervent** biter, we shall speak of next. He is in season from March until Michaelmas. He is on clean gravel bottom and in a stream. You can angle for him at all times with a lying or running ground-line: except in leaping time and then with a dubbed hook; and early with a running ground-line, and later in the day with a float line. You shall angle for him in March with a minnow hung on your hook by the lower nose, without float or sinker: drawing it up and down in the stream till you feel him take. In the same time, angle for him with a ground-line with a red worm as the most sure. In April, take the same baits, and also the lamprey, otherwise named "seven eyes," also the cankerworm that grows in a great tree, and the red snail. In May, take the stone fly and the grub . . . and the silkworm, and the bait that grows on a fern leaf. In June, take a red worm and nip off the head, and put a codworm on your hook before it. In July, take the great red worm and the codworm together. In

Michaelmas is the Christian holiday for Saint Michael, celebrated on September 29.

Trout often spawn, or produce young, in lakes with gravel bottoms.

dubbed "dressed," disguised   **fervent** energetic

August, take a flesh fly and the big red worm and bacon fat, and bind them on your hook. In September, take the red worm and the minnow. In October, take the same, for they are special for the trout at all times of the year. From April to September the trout leaps; then angle for him with dubbed hook appropriate to the month. These dubbed hooks you will find at the end of this **treatise,** and the months with them. . . .

The Lines

After you have made your rod, you must learn to colour your lines of hair this way. First, you must take, from the tail of a white horse, the longest and best hairs that you can find; and the rounder it is, the better it is. Divide it into six bunches, and you shall colour every part by itself in a different colour. As yellow, green, brown, **tawny, russet,** and **dusky** colours.

Angler, **woodcut from** *The Book of St. Albans,* **1496**

And to make a good green colour on your hair, you shall do thus. Take a quart of **small ale** and put it in a little pan, and add to it half a pound of **alum.** And put your hair in it, and let it boil softly half an hour. Then take out your hair and let it dry. Then take a half-gallon of water and put it in a pan. And put in it two handfuls of a yellow dye, and press it with a tile-stone, and let it boil gently half an hour. And when it is yellow on the scum, put in your hair with half a pound **copperas,** beaten to powder, and let it boil gently half an hour. And then set it down and let it cool five or six hours. Then take out the hair and dry it. And it is then the finest green

> How is this section like a modern-day cookbook?

treatise essay	**russet** reddish brown	**alum** aluminum sulfate
tawny brownish orange to light brown	**dusky** dark brown	**copperas** green iron-sulfur compound
	small ale weak beer	

The details about colors are an example of sensory details. Which sense do they appeal to?

there is for the water. And the more copperas you add to it, the better it is. Or else instead, use **verdigris.**

Another way, you can make a brighter green, thus. **Woad** your hair in a woad vat until it is a light blue-grey colour. And then boil it in yellow vegetable dye as I have described, except that you must not add to it either copperas or verdigris.

To make your hair yellow, prepare it with alum as I have explained already. And after that with yellow vegetable dye without copperas or verdigris.

Another yellow you shall make thus. Take a half a gallon of small ale, and crush three handfuls of walnut leaves, and put them together. And put in your hair until it is as deep a yellow as you will have it.

To make russet hair, take of strong **lye** a pint and a half and half a pound of soot and a little juice of walnut leaves and a quarter of a pound of alum; and put them all together in a pan and boil them well. And when it is cold, put in your hair till it is as dark as you will have it.

To make a brown colour, take a pound of soot and a quart of ale, and boil it with as many walnut leaves as you wish. And when they turn black, take it off the fire. And put your hair in it, and let it lie still till it is as brown as you will have it.

To make another brown, take strong ale and soot and blend them together, and put therein your hair for two days and two nights, and it will be a right good colour.

To make a tawny colour, take lime and water, and put them together; and also put your hair therein four or five hours. Then take it out and put it in tanner's ooze a day, and it will be as fine a tawny colour as we need for our purpose.

The sixth part of your hair, you must keep still white for lines for the dubbed hook, to fish for the trout and grayling, and for small lines to use for the roach and the dace.

---

verdigris a poisonous green coloring

woad an herb used for blue dyes; the verb means to soak something in this dye

lye strong liquid used to make soap

from *The Book of St. Albans* by *Juliana Barnes*

Directions Choose the letter of the best answer or write the answer using complete sentences.

Comprehension: Identifying Facts

1. Barnes says the salmon is a difficult fish to catch because it _____.
   A is unusually smart
   B does not like most bait
   C lives in deep waters
   D is so large

2. The material Barnes recommends for making a fishing line is _____.
   A cotton string   C sheep's wool
   B white horsehair   D vines

3. In your own words, summarize the proverb by Solomon that the author quotes.

4. According to Barnes, what gives a person a happy spirit?

5. What four sports does the author name?

6. What three things can make a person healthy even without medicine, according to the author?

7. When is the salmon in season?

8. What baits are good for catching salmon?

9. When is the trout in season?

10. What must an angler do after making a rod?

Comprehension: Putting Ideas Together

11. In the last section, Barnes gives instructions for _____.
    A tying fishing flies
    B finding bait
    C cooking fish
    D dying horsehair for fishing lines

12. According to the author, the color of the sixth piece of horsehair should be _____.
    A russet   C brown
    B green   D white

13. What do you think the author means by sports and games that a person can enjoy without any repentance afterward? Use examples to explain.

14. How does a cheerful occupation help a person's health?

15. Summarize the reasons why the author thinks fishing is the best sport.

After Reading **continued on next page**

from *The Book of St. Albans* *by Juliana Barnes*

16. Why does the method of fishing for trout change from April to September?

17. What traits should the material used for a fishing line have?

18. About how long would it take to make a green line according to the author's first method?

19. How do the methods for making russet lines and making brown lines differ from each other?

20. What ingredient do the green, yellow, and russet dyes have in common?

Understanding Literature: Imagery

A literary image may appeal to any of the five senses: sight, sound, touch, taste, or smell. In *The Book of St. Albans,* Barnes uses vivid images to describe fishes and fishing. For example, she says that people will be happy if they spend time in places with "sweet air." This is imagery that appeals to the sense of smell.

21. In discussing trout, Barnes uses an image that appeals to the sense of taste. Find and write the image.

22. Where can trout be found? To what sense does this image appeal?

23. Give an example of a description of bait that uses vivid imagery.

24. Vivid images often use nouns as well as vivid adjectives and adverbs. Find and write an image from the essay that is vivid because of nouns.

25. Find an image in the essay that uses color words. Write the image. To what sense does the image appeal?

Critical Thinking

26. How is the first section related to the next two?

27. Do you think the author had a lot of experience fishing? Explain why or why not.

28. How important is having the properly colored fishing lines? Explain.

Thinking Creatively

29. What type or types of books published today might be like Barnes's book? Give some examples.

30. Why do you think Barnes's book was so popular in the late Middle Ages? For what different reasons might people enjoy the book today?

Grammar Check

There are four types of sentences: statements, questions, exclamations, and commands. Commands tell someone to take an action. For example, in explaining which bait to use, Barnes says: "In May take the stone fly . . ." The subject of the sentence is understood to be *you.* The verb *take* tells you what to do. Sentences that explain how to do something often use commands.

- Find two more sentences in the selection that are commands. Write the sentences and underline the verbs.

- Write a command about an action in a sport. Underline the verb in your sentence.

 ## Writing on Your Own

Write an essay explaining how to do something such as a sport or a craft. Include details about the materials needed and the steps.

 ## Speaking and Listening

Find a section of the essay that explains how to do one or more things such as catching a fish or dyeing a fishing line. Practice reading the section aloud so that a listener would be able to follow the instructions. Then read the text to a partner. Listen to your partner's reading. Discuss guidelines for making verbal instructions clear. Discuss ways each of you could make the instructions clearer.

 ## Media

Design an article for a sporting magazine that uses illustrations and parts of Barnes's essay. First decide which parts of the essay you will include. Then find illustrations in magazines to go with them, or make your own illustrations. Lay out the text and illustrations in a striking, readable way.

The mood of a literary work is the feeling it creates. For example, the selection from *Beowulf* creates a mood of suspense and excitement as Beowulf fights Grendel. All the elements of the poem add to its unique mood. First of all, the poem's setting creates a dark, melancholy mood:

"In off the moors, down through the mist bands/God-cursed Grendel came greedily loping."

The characters themselves create an air of excitement and suspense.

"God-cursed Grendel . . . the bane of the race of men" goes against Beowulf, "mighty and canny."

The author creates a suspenseful mood through this contest of good versus evil.

The action of the poem also adds to the suspenseful mood:

"The ironbraced door/turned on its hinge when his hands touched it."

What will happen when Grendel enters the room?

"His rage boiled over, he ripped open/the mouth of the building, maddening for blood."

Notice the diction, or word choice, in these lines. *Rage, boiled, ripped, maddening,* and *blood* create a mood of darkness and violence.

Answer these questions about mood in the selections of Unit 1.

Review

1. What is the setting of "The Seafarer"? What mood does the setting create? Give an example.

2. What is the mood of the ballad "Sir Patrick Spens"? How does the plot of the ballad create this mood?

3. What are some especially vivid words Margery Kempe uses to describe her breakdown and visions? What mood or moods do these words create?

4. What is the mood of *Le Morte d'Arthur*? How do the characters of Merlin and Arthur help create this mood?

5. Locate a vivid image from *The Book of St. Albans*. What mood does the imagery create?

Writing on Your Own

Write a short narrative about a conflict between two people. Use setting, character, word choice, and plot to create a mood. You may choose to create a suspenseful, funny, sad, or other mood.

You have completed studying the works of Unit 1. This unit explained the beginnings of Angle-land as the northern European tribes entered the area in the mid-400s. The unit went through the conquest of William the Conqueror in 1066. The unit ended with the end of the War of the Roses in 1485. England was ready to become a world power.

England went from Roman territory to "barbarian" occupation, from tribal division to French-Norman feudalism and chivalry. These changes helped a new language and a new literature to form. The storytelling traditions of the Anglo-Saxons mixed with the classical styles of the Catholic Church. Whether epic poetry or simple ballads, sermons or essays, humorous tales or tragic romances, a uniquely British voice was emerging.

Selections

- *Beowulf* is one of the oldest epic poems in English, set in a distant past sometime after A.D. 449. It describes an Anglo-Saxon hero, Beowulf, defeating the monster Grendel.

- "The Seafarer" is an anonymous poem that describes one person's feelings. The narrator describes the sadness and loneliness he feels as he sails to sea.

- "Sir Patrick Spens" and "Get Up and Bar the Door" are traditional ballads. The first describes a tragic sea journey and the second a quarrel between a man and his wife.

- *The Canterbury Tales* by Geoffrey Chaucer is a collection of tales by fictional pilgrims on their way to a religious shrine at Canterbury in the 1300s. The Prologue describes each character who will tell a story.

- *The Book of Margery Kempe* is the autobiography of a woman of the Middle Ages. Kempe tells of her spiritual breakdown and how a vision of Christ helped her recover.

- *Le Morte d'Arthur* by Thomas Malory tells the legend of King Arthur. The early chapters describe the death of Arthur's father and tell how Arthur became king.

- *The Book of St. Albans* by Juliana Barnes describes field sports such as hunting. This essay describes the art of fly fishing.

Unit 1 REVIEW

Directions Choose the letter of the best answer or write the answer using complete sentences.

Comprehension: Identifying Facts

1. A fish that Juliana Barnes explains how to catch in *The Book of St. Albans* is the _____.
   - **A** tuna
   - **B** salmon
   - **C** halibut
   - **D** flounder

2. Why does Beowulf fight Grendel?

3. In what kind of weather is the narrator going to sea in "The Seafarer"?

4. Why does Sir Patrick Spens sail to Norway in "Sir Patrick Spens"?

5. How does the narrator meet the people he describes in the Prologue of *The Canterbury Tales?*

Comprehension: Putting Ideas Together

6. The speaker of "The Seafarer" could best be described as _____.
   - **A** a believer in God
   - **B** someone who does not believe in God
   - **C** unconcerned with spiritual life
   - **D** afraid of leaving home

7. What is the main theme of *Beowulf?*

8. What is the main mood of the ballad "Get Up and Bar the Door"? What creates this mood?

9. What character traits does Arthur show in *Le Morte d'Arthur* when his brother asks him to go back for a sword?

10. How much understanding do the people around Margery Kempe show when she undergoes her mental breakdown in *The Book of Margery Kempe?* Use two or three examples.

Understanding Literature: Poetry

Poetry is literature in verse form that paints powerful or beautiful impressions with words. It usually has rhythm. It may also have other features that make it sound enjoyable, such as rhyme and alliteration.

11. What kind of poem is *Beowulf?* What features make it an example of this form?

12. The speaker in "The Seafarer" describes "the cry of the sea fowl,/ The croaking of birds." To what sense do these images appeal?

13. "Sir Patrick Spens" and "Get Up and Bar the Door" are ballads. What are the features of this kind of poetry?

14. In what line form is the Prologue of *The Canterbury Tales* written?

15. Which of the poems in this unit most resemble the poetry of today? Explain.

Critical Thinking

16. Do you think women had powerful positions in English society during the Anglo-Saxon period and the Middle Ages? Use examples from the Unit 1 selections to support your answer.

17. Why were knights respected and also considered romantic figures during the Middle Ages? Use examples from selections to support your answer.

18. What part did Christianity play in the literature of these periods? Use examples to support your answer.

19. For what purposes do you think people of these periods read literature? Name literary works in support of your answer.

Thinking Creatively

20. Which selection from this unit did you find most enjoyable? Use details to explain why.

Speak and Listen

Choose one of the following selections for a dramatic monologue: "The Seafarer," *The Book of Margery Kempe*, or *Beowulf*. Choose a passage that creates a mood. Practice reading the passage, then read your passage to your classmates. Listen to others read their monologues and consider insights they give into the authors and selections.

Writing on Your Own

Think about a recent event that would be a good subject for an epic. Write a poem of at least 20 lines about the event. Use some of the following elements: rhyme, rhythm, vivid imagery, alliteration.

Beyond Words

Make a drawing or painting to illustrate one of the unit selections. Display your artwork and have classmates identify the selection you have illustrated.

Test-Taking Tip

When studying for a test, review any previous tests or quizzes that cover the same information. Make sure you have the correct answers for any items you missed. Review these answers carefully before the test.

The Vanguard *Attacking the Spanish Armada,*
19th-century line engraving

Unit 2

The English Renaissance: 1485–1660

If you had lived in England 400 years ago, you would have been part of a spirited era. The English people had a new sense of what they could achieve. You could have seen a play by the exciting playwright William Shakespeare or read the latest sonnets and essays. In this unit, you will learn about the flowering of English nationality and the political and religious struggles that shaped a nation. You will read examples of the passionate literature this period inspired.

"Lords and Commons of England, consider what Nation it is whereof ye are . . . a Nation not slow and dull, but of a quick, ingenious, and piercing spirit, acute to invent, subtle and sinewy to discourse not beneath the reach of any point the highest that human capacity can soar to."

— *John Milton, Areopagitica (political pamphlet), 1644*

Renaissance means "rebirth." The Renaissance, which began in Italy, brought an awakening of creativity and philosophy in Europe. Thinkers, artists, and writers looked to the great cultures of ancient Greece and Rome for inspiration. Renaissance art, literature, and philosophy focused on the individual. By 1485, Renaissance ideas had reached England. As ideas spread, printing technology also improved. Books on many topics became more widely available.

At this time, a period of strong, stable rule began. King Henry VIII broke with the Catholic Church and founded the Church of England. England began to see itself as a strong nation.

Henry's daughter Elizabeth became queen in 1558. She was a wise leader who also encouraged literature and art. Queen Elizabeth I managed to balance growing religious tensions. She avoided war during most of her 45-year reign and made England a world power.

The reigns of King James I and his son King Charles I were times of religious and political unrest. Parliament came under the control of Puritans, who wanted religious and government reform, or change. Charles and his supporters, known as Cavaliers, fought to keep their power. From 1642 to 1649, civil war raged. The Puritans won and executed Charles. A harsh Puritan government ruled until 1660, when the monarchy was restored.

Several literary styles developed during the English Renaissance: Elizabethan, Cavalier, Metaphysical, and Puritan.

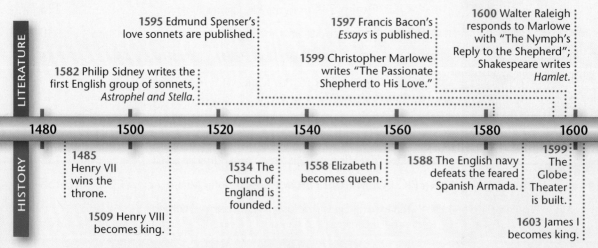

LITERATURE

1595 Edmund Spenser's love sonnets are published.

1582 Philip Sidney writes the first English group of sonnets, *Astrophel and Stella.*

1597 Francis Bacon's *Essays* is published.

1599 Christopher Marlowe writes "The Passionate Shepherd to His Love."

1600 Walter Raleigh responds to Marlowe with "The Nymph's Reply to the Shepherd"; Shakespeare writes *Hamlet.*

1480   1500   1520   1540   1560   1580   1600

HISTORY

1485 Henry VII wins the throne.

1509 Henry VIII becomes king.

1534 The Church of England is founded.

1558 Elizabeth I becomes queen.

1588 The English navy defeats the feared Spanish Armada.

1599 The Globe Theater is built.

1603 James I becomes king.

The Elizabethan literature in this unit includes formal poems, an essay, and a sample of Shakespeare's play *Hamlet*. The poems include sonnets by Philip Sidney, Edmund Spenser, and William Shakespeare, as well as a poem by Elizabeth I.

Henry VIII and His Family, 16th century

They describe the joys and pains of love, using complex rhythm and rhyme. An essay by Francis Bacon, titled "Of Studies," expresses the importance of study.

Poems by Cavaliers feature elegance and classical form. They tend to have light subjects and a light touch. They include Ben Jonson's "Still to Be Neat" and "To Celia," as well as Robert Herrick's "To the Virgins, to Make Much of Time" and Richard Lovelace's "To Lucasta, on Going to the Wars."

Metaphysical poets took on complex ideas, used complex imagery, and used less regular forms. They are represented by John Donne's "Valediction, Forbidding Mourning" and Andrew Marvell's "To His Coy Mistress."

Puritan works include *Paradise Lost,* John Milton's epic poem about Adam and Eve; and Amelia Lanier's *Eve's Apology in Defense of Women.* Both writers sought moral and political reform.

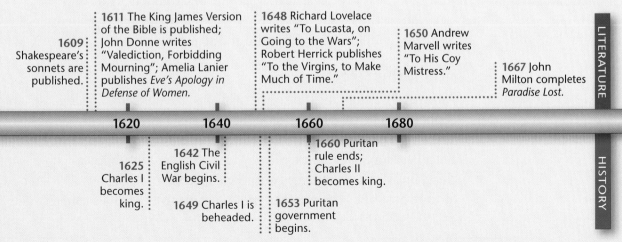

1609 Shakespeare's sonnets are published.

1611 The King James Version of the Bible is published; John Donne writes "Valediction, Forbidding Mourning"; Amelia Lanier publishes *Eve's Apology in Defense of Women.*

1648 Richard Lovelace writes "To Lucasta, on Going to the Wars"; Robert Herrick publishes "To the Virgins, to Make Much of Time."

1650 Andrew Marvell writes "To His Coy Mistress."

1667 John Milton completes *Paradise Lost.*

LITERATURE

1620   1640   1660   1680

HISTORY

1625 Charles I becomes king.

1642 The English Civil War begins.

1649 Charles I is beheaded.

1653 Puritan government begins.

1660 Puritan rule ends; Charles II becomes king.

Sonnet 31 by Philip Sidney

Philip Sidney
1554–1586

Objectives

- To read and understand a sonnet
- To analyze the use of rhyme and rhythm in a poem
- To understand iambic pentameter

About the Author

Philip Sidney was considered to be the ideal nobleman. Edmund Spenser, a great Elizabethan poet of the day, described Sidney as "the noble and virtuous gentleman most worthy of all titles both of learning and chivalry."

Sidney was born in 1554 in Kent, England. He attended Oxford University and then traveled in Europe. Sidney knew many famous writers and heads of state and was popular at the court of Queen Elizabeth I.

Sidney is famous for his essay "The Defense of Poesy," which he wrote to answer a Puritan attack against plays and poetry. In it, he explains the value of poetry and all literature that uses the imagination. Sidney contributed greatly to poetry with his group of sonnets called *Astrophel and Stella*. These 108 sonnets were modeled after similar sonnet sequences of Italian and French Renaissance poets. However, *Astrophel and Stella* was the first complete sonnet sequence in English.

During Sidney's lifetime, a conflict between Catholics and Protestants (people who left the Catholic Church to protest its teachings) raged. While traveling in Europe in 1572, Sidney had become a Protestant. In 1585, he became governor of a region in the Netherlands. He died in a battle against the Spanish in 1586. All of England mourned his death.

About the Selection

"Sonnet 31" is one of the sonnets in the *Astrophel and Stella* sequence. The title of the sequence means "Starlover and Star." The poems are based on Sidney's real-life relationship with Penelope Devereux. Sidney was engaged to her for a time, but she later married someone else. In this sonnet, Sidney describes the way the moon seems to echo his sadness.

Literary Terms Sidney's "Sonnet 31" uses both **rhyme** and **rhythm.** Rhyme occurs in words that have the same or similar sounds at the ends of lines of poetry. Rhythm is the musical beat in the pattern of stressed and unstressed syllables in each line. A **sonnet** is a 14-line poem with a strict pattern of rhyme and rhythm. The lines of this sonnet rhyme with the pattern *abba abba cdcd ee*. Each line contains five two-beat sounds, with a stress on the second syllable. This kind of pattern is called **iambic pentameter.**

Reading on Your Own Notice that the way the poet has rhymed causes the poem to fall into four sections. As you read each section, think about how he has used sound to tie the poem's ideas together. After you have read each section, stop and draw conclusions about what the poet feels and observes.

Writing on Your Own Do you find images in the sky that seem to reflect your feelings? Write a paragraph that describes something in the sky and explains your connection to it.

Vocabulary Focus Four centuries ago, the English language differed in many ways from the English we use today. In this sonnet, the poet uses *thou* and *thy* where we would say *you* and *your*. The words *climb'st* and *feel'st* (contractions for *climbest* and *feelest*) would today be replaced by the simple verb forms *climb* and *feel*.

Think Before You Read The poet addresses the moon in this poem. What do you think he will ask the moon?

---

rhyme words that end with the same or similar sounds

rhythm a pattern created by the stressed and unstressed syllables in a line of poetry

sonnet a 14-line poem divided into four sections, in iambic pentameter

iambic pentameter five two-beat sounds in a line of poetry, where the second syllable is stressed in each pair

Sonnet 31

As you read, think about the feelings the words suggest. Why does the speaker address the moon?

With how sad steps, O moon, thou climb'st the skies!
How silently, and with how **wan** a face!
What! may it be that even in heavenly place
That busy archer his sharp arrows tries?
5 Sure, if that long-with-love-acquainted eyes
Can judge of love, thou feel'st a lover's case:
I read it in thy looks; thy **languish'd** grace
To me, that feel the like, thy state **descries.**
Then, even of fellowship, O Moon, tell me,
10 Is constant love **deem'd** there but want of **wit**?
Are beauties there as proud as here they be?
Do they above love to be loved, and yet

The *busy archer* in line 4 refers to Cupid, the Roman god of love.

Look for the rhyme pattern *abba abba cdcd ee.*

Those lovers scorn
    whom that love
    doth possess?
Do they call
    "virtue" there—
    ungratefulness?

While different poets may use different rhyme patterns, all English sonnets use iambic pentameter. Read aloud a line of this sonnet. Notice that the line has five unstressed and five stressed syllables that alternate.

wan pale	**descries** reveals	**wit** intelligence
languish'd weakened	**deem'd** judged	

Directions Choose the letter of the best answer or write the answer using complete sentences.

Comprehension: Identifying Facts

1. How does the moon look to the poet?
   A scornful   **C** cold
   B beautiful   **D** sad

2. What does the poet say that shows the moon feels rejected in love?

3. In line 10, what does the poet say that women think "constant love" shows?

Comprehension: Putting Ideas Together

4. The best words to describe the poet's mood are _____.
   A sad and disappointed
   B angry and resentful
   C scornful and proud
   D meek and grateful

5. Why does the poet feel a connection to the moon?

6. What words does the poet use to describe the beauty he loves? What does this show about his experience?

Understanding Literature: Rhyme and Rhythm

Rhyme and rhythm are sound-effect tools a poet uses to create musical interest and to focus ideas. The rhyme scheme of this poem ties together lines 1–4, 5–8, 9–12, and 13–14. The poem's rhythm ties together the whole poem, because each line has five beats with two syllables each. The stress is on the second syllable in each pair. This pattern is called iambic pentameter.

7. The final two lines place rhyming words close together. How does this strong end rhyme help the poet focus his main idea?

8. How does the rhythm affect the way this poem sounds when read aloud?

Critical Thinking

9. What is the tone of this poem? Why did the poet use this tone to deliver his message?

Thinking Creatively

10. Do you think someone who is disappointed in love would react in the same way as this poet? Or does Sidney's reaction show the attitudes of his time? Explain your opinion.

After Reading **continued on next page**

AFTER READING THE SELECTION (continued)

Sonnet 31   by Philip Sidney

 ### Grammar Check

In a poem, the normal order of words in a sentence may be changed to focus on a certain point or to create sound effects. Look back at the poem to find examples. Think about how the sentence would be worded in ordinary speech.

- From the poem, write down a sentence that has unusual word order.

- Rewrite the sentence using normal word order to express the thought.

- Explain why you think the poet uses the unusual order of words.

 ### Writing on Your Own

Think about someone or something you have loved for a long time. Write a poem describing the bond you feel with the person or thing. Let your details suggest your feelings. Use rhyme and rhythm to express your ideas.

 ### Speaking

Think about the emotions this poem expresses. Practice reading the poem aloud with the expression and tone the poet would have used. Then read it aloud to the class.

 ### Listening

Listen carefully as your teacher reads the poem aloud several times. First, listen to understand its meaning. Then, notice the way rhyme and rhythm join the lines together. Take notes on any new meanings and ideas you gain from listening more than once.

 ### Media

How do movies affect our views of love? Do they make us more romantic or more gloomy than Sidney? Write an essay explaining this effect. State your main idea in an introduction. Write a paragraph for each idea you explore. Use examples from movies to illustrate your points. Sum up the main idea in your concluding paragraph.

 ### Viewing

Look at the portrait of Philip Sidney. Use it to write a description of the man. Include personal traits the painting shows. Explain why you think Sidney's society considered him the ideal gentleman.

BEFORE READING THE SELECTION

On Monsieur's Departure   by Elizabeth I

About the Author

Queen Elizabeth I was born in 1533. She was the daughter of King Henry VIII and his second wife, Anne Boleyn. When Henry died in 1547, Elizabeth's half-brother Edward became king. He was replaced after his death in 1553 first by a cousin, Lady Jane Grey, then by a half-sister, Mary. Elizabeth came to the throne five years later, when she was only 25.

Elizabeth's excellent education and keen intelligence helped her become one of England's finest rulers. She encouraged the development of literature and art in England. Elizabeth also proved herself a clever and wise ruler. During her rule, England grew rich and powerful. Elizabeth supported England's exploration of North and South America. Before this, Spain had controlled New World trade and colonies. Conflict between England and Spain grew into open war in 1588. In a great naval battle, England defeated the mighty Spanish Armada (a group of warships).

By the time of her death in 1603, Elizabeth was well loved by most of her people. It is fitting that this time period is called the Elizabethan Era.

About the Selection

This poem may have been addressed to Francis, Duke of Alencon, who tried for years to get Elizabeth to marry him. Another theory suggests that it may have been written for Robert Dudley, the Earl of Leicester. All her life, Elizabeth sought love but refused to marry. She believed marriage would weaken her as a ruler. In this poem, Elizabeth contrasts her public and private selves and reveals her inner conflict. A man she loves is leaving, and she grieves the loss. However, as queen, she must do her duty and show no emotion to others.

Elizabeth I
1533–1603

Objectives

- To read and understand a lyric poem with a distinct voice and style
- To explain a paradox in literature
- To compare and contrast a speaker's inner and outer selves
- To understand the use of stanzas in a poem
- To use antonyms to understand contrasting ideas

Before Reading **continued on next page**

On Monsieur's Departure   *by Elizabeth I*

style an author's way of writing

voice the way a writer expresses ideas and achieves purpose through style, form, and content

paradox a statement that includes opposite meanings but still makes sense

stanza a group of lines that forms a unit in a poem

Literary Terms The **style** of writing in "On Monsieur's Departure" is formal and complex. Style is the way a writer handles language, giving rise to patterns and rhythms. Style adds to an author's **voice.** An author's voice, like a fingerprint, is unique. It is the way the writer uses style, content, and form to achieve his or her purpose. This poem includes an idea called a **paradox.** A paradox is a statement that includes opposite meanings but still makes sense.

Reading on Your Own Notice that the poem is divided into three **stanzas,** or groups of lines, with the same format. As you read each stanza, pause to think about the things it compares and contrasts. List opposing emotions, ideas, and objects that are placed side by side in the poem. Then think about why the poet might combine such contrasts.

Writing on Your Own Think of a time you felt one way inside but showed another emotion to others. Write a paragraph that describes those two conflicting emotions and explains why you "covered" one emotion with another.

Vocabulary Focus To explore the meanings of words and sentences, you can compare antonyms. Antonyms are words with opposite meanings. List antonyms you see in the poem, such as *love/hate, freeze/burned,* and *cruel/kind.* Think about what these opposites show about the poet's main idea and state of mind.

Think Before You Read Whose departure do you think the title refers to?

On Monsieur's Departure

I grieve and dare not show my **discontent,**
I love and yet am forced to seem to hate,
I do, yet dare not say I ever meant,
I seem stark **mute** but inwardly do **prate.**
5   I am and not, I freeze and yet am burned,
      Since from myself another self I turned.

My care is like my shadow in the sun,
Follows me flying, flies when I pursue it,
Stands and lies by me, doth what I have done.
10 His too familiar care doth make me **rue** it.
      No means I find to rid him from my breast,
      Till by the end of things it be **suppressed.**

Some gentler passion slide into my mind,
For I am soft and made of melting snow;
15 Or be more cruel, love, and so be kind.
Let me or float or sink, be high or low.
      Or let me live with some more sweet content,
      Or die and so forget what love ere meant.

As you read, notice how formal the speaker's voice and tone are. Complex rhythms and rhymes help establish the formal voice.

Notice how the antonyms signal a paradox in the last verse. In what way might it be kind to be cruel (line 15)?

The First Thaw, 1909

discontent unhappiness; suffering

mute silent; unable to speak

prate chatter; talk a great deal

rue feel regret or sorrow

suppressed stopped; put down by force

Directions Choose the letter of the best answer or write the answer using complete sentences.

Comprehension: Identifying Facts

1. What emotions battle in the poet, according to line 2?
   A grief and love
   B love and hate
   C love and the need to hide it
   D anger and daring

2. To what does the poet compare her misery?
   A a severe storm
   B her shadow
   C floating in water
   D death

3. In line 6, what cause does the poet give for her conflicting emotions?

Comprehension: Putting Ideas Together

4. What feelings does the poet show outwardly as the man is leaving?
   A calm, silent indifference
   B angry, resentful dislike
   C sad, talkative regret
   D passionate, sweet love

5. In what ways is the poet's grief like her shadow?

6. What does the poet mean in lines 11–12?

Understanding Literature: Style, Voice, and Paradox

Style is the way an author writes, including choice of words, length of sentences, and turn of phrase. This poem's style is complex and formal. The author's voice is the way ideas are presented to achieve a purpose. Voice shows personality. A paradox seems to contradict itself, yet it contains truth.

7. How would you describe the author's voice in this poem?

8. What are two paradoxes the author expresses in this poem?

Critical Thinking

9. What do you think the poet wants to have happen? What event would make her happiest?

Thinking Creatively

10. Is the main idea in this poem one that is common today? Why or why not?

Grammar Check

In English, the subject usually comes first in a sentence. This poem reverses the normal subject-verb order in several places. For example, in line 6, the subject *I* is the next to last word. Change the word order to put the subject first: "I turned another self from myself." Study the subject-verb order in lines 11 and 12.

- Write lines 11 and 12 and circle the subject in each of these clauses.

- Reword each line so that the subject and verb come first. (Leave out the word *Till* in line 12.)

- Write a sentence telling what these lines mean.

Writing on Your Own

Imagine that you are the person to whom this poem is addressed. Write a letter to the poet explaining your feelings. Tell what you do and do not understand about the poet's actions. Be sure your sentences are complete.

Speaking and Listening

Offer advice to the speaker in this poem. How can she resolve her conflict and gain "sweet content"? With a partner, take turns presenting your advice. Be as persuasive as you can. When you listen, take notes about points you agree with or disagree with. When you have both made your presentations, discuss your reactions.

Technology

Elizabeth I thought about marrying kings from other countries. Such alliances were common to combine the power of two kingdoms. Use the Internet to find out about her relationships with rulers of other lands. (Try entering keywords *Elizabeth I* or *Elizabethan Era* into your search engine.) Summarize what you learn. Write a paragraph telling whether you believe Elizabeth's interests were romantic or political and why.

Viewing

Study the painting that illustrates this poem. Then read line 14 of the poem. How is the poet like melting snow in the painting?

Edmund Spenser
1552–1599

About the Author

Edmund Spenser was born in London in 1552. He began writing poetry while he was a student at Cambridge University. During the 1570s, he developed a close friendship with Philip Sidney. The two often met to discuss literature and read each other's poetry.

In 1579, Spenser published a series of poems called *The Shepherd's Calendar*. The 12 poems in this book were talks between shepherds. Spenser became known as a fine poet because of these poems.

In 1580, Spenser went to Ireland as a government official. He spent the rest of his life there, except for two visits to London. He spent much creative time writing a huge epic poem, *The Faerie Queene*. In the poem, characters stand for ideas such as pride and faith. This work illustrated moral ideas and told about England's history and achievements. Spenser dedicated *The Faerie Queene* to Queen Elizabeth I. The work took the rest of Spenser's life. When he died in 1599, he had completed 6 of the 12 volumes he planned.

About the Selection

"Sonnet 75" appeared in a cycle, or series, of 89 love sonnets that Spenser published in 1595. They are called *amoretti*, or "little love poems." The series is probably based on Spenser's courtship of Elizabeth Boyle, whom he married in 1594. This poem shows Spenser's very formal style and his creativity. Spenser invented his own rhyme pattern for the sonnet. Sonnets developed first in Italy but became popular throughout Europe during the Renaissance.

Literary Terms The sonnet is a 14-line poem written in iambic pentameter. Sonnets express personal feelings. They also follow a strict pattern of rhyme. Spenser used the rhyme pattern *abab bcbc cdcd ee*. This pattern joins together repeated sounds over a number of lines and ties the lines together.

A **figure of speech** is a word or phrase that has meaning different from the actual meaning of the words. Many figures of speech compare very different things to show surprising similarities between them. Figures of speech appeal to the imagination and help us see the world in new ways.

Reading on Your Own When you read this poem, watch for figures of speech. What things are being compared? Make notes about the ways these things are alike.

Writing on Your Own Think about the effect of the ocean on the shore. Write a description about the changes that occur because of tides and waves.

Vocabulary Focus Poetry written long ago may contain words that are no longer used. For example, this poem uses the word *eke* where we would say *also*. Many English words have multiple meanings. To determine the meaning that is intended, pay attention to the context, or surrounding words. The word *vain* appears twice in line 5. In the phrase *vain man*, it means "foolish"; *in vain* means "without success."

Think Before You Read This poem is set on the beach. What might the poet describe?

> **figure of speech** a word or phrase that has meaning different from the actual meaning

Sonnet

75

For *dost* in line 5, say *does*. For *quod* in line 9, say *said*.

One day I wrote her name upon the **strand,**
But came the waves and washèd it away:
Again I wrote it with a second hand,
But came the tide and made my pains his prey.
5   **Vain** man (said she) that dost **in vain assay**
A mortal thing so to **immortalise;**
For I myself shall like to this decay,
And eke my name be wipèd out likewise.
Not so (quod I); let **baser** things devise
10 To die in dust, but you shall live by fame;
My verse your virtues rare shall **eternise,**
And in the heavens write your glorious name:
    Where, when as Death shall all the world subdue,
    Our love shall live, and later life renew.

Identify the lines that are spoken by the female character in this poem. What do the actions of the waves represent to her?

Does the poet literally mean that the woman will live forever? How can you tell?

Title art: *Whitby, Yorkshire: A Deserted Beach,* **1909**

strand beach

vain foolish, silly

in vain without success

assay attempt

immortalise to cause to live forever, to give lasting fame to

baser lacking higher qualities of mind or spirit

eternise make eternal

AFTER READING THE SELECTION

Sonnet 75   by Edmund Spenser

Directions Choose the letter of the best answer or write the answer using complete sentences.

Comprehension: Identifying Facts

1. Where does the poet write a name?
   - **A** in the sand
   - **B** on a paper
   - **C** on a tree
   - **D** on his heart

2. What happens to the writing?

3. Where does the poet believe the woman he loves will become immortal?

Comprehension: Putting Ideas Together

4. The lover believes she is like the name in the sand because she _____.
   - **A** will die and be forgotten
   - **B** is frightened of the ocean
   - **C** will be washed away
   - **D** is not in control

5. Why does the woman think the poet is foolish?

6. What part of themselves does the poet believe will not die?

Understanding Literature: Sonnets and Figures of Speech

A sonnet is a rhyming, 14-line poem that expresses personal emotion or ideas. This sonnet discusses how poetry can make its subject live on, even after death. Figures of speech have an imaginative meaning beyond the actual meanings of the words. The tide is compared to a predator and the name in the sand to its prey.

7. Which words in this poem rhyme? In what two lines do rhymes occur next to each other?

8. What does the poet mean when he says his verse shall "in the heavens write your glorious name"?

Critical Thinking

9. Why do you think the poet changed the normal order of words, as in "My verse your virtues rare shall eternise"?

Thinking Creatively

10. Do you agree that literature can make a person immortal? What other ways might a person live on after death?

After Reading **continued on next page**

Sonnet 75   *by Edmund Spenser*

 Grammar Check

When a suffix or other ending is added to a base word, often the spelling does not change: *wish + ed → wished*. Words that end in vowel-consonant-*e* drop the final *e* before the ending is added: *like + ed → liked*. Words that end in consonant-*y* change the *y* to *i* before the ending is added: *heavy + ness → heaviness*.

- Find words with suffixes and other endings in the poem. Write them.

- Write the base word and the suffix or ending separately. Underline letters that change.

- List other words that follow the patterns you find.

 Writing on Your Own

Write a critique of this poem. Explain its patterns of rhyme and rhythm. Describe the language and sentences it uses. Include your opinion of the poem and your reasons for this opinion.

 Speaking and Listening

With a partner, take turns reading the poem aloud. When it is your turn to listen, notice the rhythm of the lines. Think about the meaning of each sentence. Write notes about new ideas or meanings you notice.

 Media and Technology

Find and read a famous eulogy, a speech praising someone who has died. Look on the Internet or in a library book of speeches for examples. Practice reading the eulogy with appropriate feeling. Record the speech and play your recording for the class. Pause the recording to explain difficult words or ideas that are especially important.

 Research

Spend some time researching one of these topics: Edmund Spenser, *The Faerie Queene,* or the Spenserian sonnet. Use encyclopedias, the Internet, or reference materials from the library. Take notes about your topic. Paraphrase from your notes to write an essay about your topic.

BEFORE READING THE SELECTION

Of Studies   *by Francis Bacon*

About the Author

Francis Bacon was born in London in 1561. He had a sharp
mind and attended the University of Cambridge when he
was only 13. Bacon went on to become the leading writer,
philosopher, and statesman of his time.

By 1584, he was serving in Parliament. However, he never
gained favor with Queen Elizabeth I. He did better when
James I became king. Bacon was knighted in 1603. By 1618, he
had risen to the rank of Lord Chancellor. However, in 1621, he
was accused of taking bribes and was forced to leave office in
disgrace. He spent the rest of his life studying and writing.

Bacon is famous today for introducing the idea of scientific
method and thought. He said that scientific conclusions
should be based on observation (what you can see) and
experiment (what you can test). Bacon also understood that
science could improve life and make the world better. In his
book *New Atlantis,* he predicted the invention of skyscrapers,
refrigeration, air conditioning, telephones, airplanes, and
submarines.

About the Selection

"Of Studies" appears in Bacon's *Essays,* a book that was first
published in 1597. It is a good example of his powerful, direct
style. The selection looks at the uses and effects of study on
the learner. Bacon often included aphorisms in his writings.
These short sayings about experience pack a lot of punch.
For example, in this selection he writes, "Reading maketh
a full man; conference a ready man; and writing an exact
man." Like his other writings, this one includes powerful
observations about life that are as true today as they were 400
years ago.

Francis Bacon
1561–1626

Objectives

- To read and
  understand an
  essay and its
  theme
- To paraphrase the
  main idea of an
  essay

Before Reading **continued on next page**

Of Studies   by Francis Bacon

essay a written
work that shows a
writer's opinions
on some basic or
current issue

theme the main
idea of a literary
work

main idea the
overall, general
idea that is
set forth in a
written work and
supported by
details

Literary Terms An **essay** is a short nonfiction writing about a single topic. The essay centers on a **theme,** or **main idea,** which is generally made clear in the introduction. Theme is often a deeper or hidden meaning within a writing. The essayist often shares her or his opinions on the subject.

Reading on Your Own This essay is not divided into paragraphs. However, it is organized logically, with main ideas followed by supporting examples or explanations. As you read, look for statements that express an important idea in broad terms. The first sentence ("Studies serve for delight, for ornament, and for ability") does this. Then think about the sentences following each main idea. How do they explain or clarify the idea?

Writing on Your Own What kind of books do you most enjoy reading? What kind do you find most difficult? Write a paragraph explaining how your approach to reading changes for different kinds of books. Tell why you change your approach.

Vocabulary Focus To prepare for reading this essay, you may want to look ahead at the vocabulary terms at the bottom of each page. Read the definitions given and use them to help you develop ways to remember the meaning. For example, *discourse* looks and sounds like the word *discuss,* which is a related idea. As you read, replace the vocabulary terms with the meanings you have learned.

Think Before You Read Why do you think people study?

OF STUDIES

Studies serve for delight, for ornament, and for ability. Their chief use for delight is in privateness and retiring; for ornament, is in **discourse;** and for ability, is in the judgment and disposition of business. For expert men can execute, and perhaps judge of particulars, one by one; but the general counsels, and the plots and **marshalling** of affairs, come best from those that are learned. To spend too much time in studies is **sloth;** to use them too much for ornament, is **affectation;** to make judgment wholly by their rules, is the humor of a scholar. They perfect nature, and are perfected by experience: for natural abilities are like natural plants, that need **proyning,** by study; and studies themselves do give forth directions too much at large, except they be bounded in by experience. Crafty men **contemn** studies, simple men admire them, and wise men use them; for they teach not their own use; but that is a wisdom without them, and above them, won by observation. Read not to contradict and **confute;** nor to believe and take for granted; nor to find talk and discourse; but to weigh and consider. Some books are to be tasted, others to be swallowed, and some few to be chewed and digested; that is, some books are to be read only in parts; others to be read, but not curiously; and some few to be read wholly, and with diligence and attention. Some books also may be read by

> As you read, think about what the writer is saying in this essay about the nature of studying. What is his theme? What is his main idea? Why does he say people should study?

Title art: *Still Life,*
François Bonvin,
1876

discourse talking; rational talk	**sloth** laziness	**proyning** trimming
marshalling careful ordering	**affectation** posing; pretending something one is not	**contemn** dislike
		confute overwhelm in argument

deputy, and extracts made of them by others; but that would be only in the less important arguments, and the **meaner** sort of books, else distilled books are like common distilled waters, flashy things. Reading maketh a full man; **conference** a ready man; and writing an exact man. And therefore, if a man write little, he had need have a great memory; if he confer little, he had need have a present wit; and if he read little, he had need have much cunning, to seem to know that he doth not. Histories make men wise; poets witty; the mathematics subtile; natural philosophy deep; moral grave; logic and **rhetoric** able to **contend.** *Abeunt studia in mores* [Studies pass into and influence manners]. Nay, there is no **stond** or impediment in the wit but may be wrought out by fit studies; like as diseases of the body may have appropriate exercises. Bowling is good for the stone and reins; shooting for the lungs and breast; gentle walking for the stomach; riding for the head; and the like. So if a man's wit be wandering, let him study the mathematics; for in demonstrations, if his wit be called away never so little, he must begin again. If his wit be not apt to distinguish or find differences, let him study the Schoolmen; for they are *cymini sectores* [splitters of hairs]. If he be not apt to beat over matters, and to call up one thing to prove and illustrate another, let him study the lawyers' cases. So every defect of the mind may have a special **receipt.**

What do you think the author means by *Studies pass into and influence manners*?

The *Schoolmen* were philosophers who followed a type of thought called scholasticism. They tended to focus on very precise questions, which is why Bacon calls them hair-splitters.

deputy assignment	**conference** formal discussing of views among people	**contend** debate
meaner more common		**stond** stoppage
	rhetoric the art of speaking or writing effectively	**receipt** remedy

Directions Choose the letter of the best answer or write the answer using complete sentences.

Comprehension: Identifying Facts

1. According to the author, the purpose of reading is to _____.
   A contradict and confute
   B talk and take for granted
   C believe and take for granted
   D weigh and consider

2. Why does a person who does not read much need to be cunning?

3. What is the relationship of studying to weaknesses of the mind? How is it like exercise for physical problems?

Comprehension: Putting Ideas Together

4. Which sort of books would the author agree should be "tasted"?
   A the most important books
   B mathematical books
   C histories and philosophies
   D books of minor importance

5. What role does experience play in learning? That is, how does it interact with "book learning"?

6. What sort of studies would the author recommend to learn how to argue a case?

Understanding Literature: Essay and Theme

An essay is a short nonfiction writing. It discusses the writer's thoughts and opinions about a subject. It should express the theme, or main idea, clearly and directly.

7. What is the theme of this essay?

8. Why did Bacon put these ideas into the form of an essay?

Critical Thinking

9. What would this author say about someone who was intelligent but did not study?

Thinking Creatively

10. Would you agree that every defect of the mind can be corrected by study? Give reasons for your opinion.

After Reading **continued on next page**

Of Studies   *by Francis Bacon*

 ## Grammar Check

This essay contains many examples of parallel structure. Parallel structure joins related parts of a sentence by writing them in a similar way. For example, Bacon says, "Crafty men contemn studies, simple men admire them, and wise men use them." The pattern is *adjective-noun-action verb-direct object*. Find other examples of parallel structure in the essay.

- Write another sentence from the essay that contains parallel structure.

- Underline the parallel parts.

- Write your own sentence about studying. Use parallel structure to compare, contrast, or add up similar ideas.

 ## Writing on Your Own

Think about learning from books and learning from experiences. How are they alike? How are they different? Is there any connection between these types of learning? Write an essay explaining your thoughts. State your main idea clearly. Develop it with examples and explanations.

 ## Speaking and Listening

Prepare a short talk about a book that has taught you something important. Present your talk to a small group. Give the title, author, and genre of the book. Describe its subject or subjects or summarize its plot. Then explain how it affected you. When it is your turn to listen, write down any questions you have about the book. Ask them after the talk is over.

 ## Media

In Bacon's day, students learned by reading books and listening to lectures. Today, other media are available in the classroom to help students learn. Brainstorm a list of tools and media you count on to help you understand your subjects. Number them in order of usefulness to you.

 ## Research

Choose a branch of study, such as mathematics, history, or music. Research to learn the types of skills and thinking abilities it develops. You may find the Internet most useful to locate information. Try keywords such as *educational development* and the subject name.

BEFORE READING THE SELECTIONS

About the Authors

Christopher Marlowe was born in Canterbury in 1564. In 1580, he attended Cambridge University. Marlowe went on to write exciting plays. He was England's most popular playwright in the years before Shakespeare became popular. Marlowe also did undercover work for the English government. He was stabbed to death during a fight at an inn when he was just 30. His narrative poem *Hero and Leander* was unfinished when he died, but it quickly became a classic.

Walter Raleigh was an explorer and the founder of Virginia. He was also a poet, philosopher, and historian. Raleigh was known to be reckless and free thinking. Queen Elizabeth I favored Raleigh, and he organized several expeditions to North America with her backing. He named the region he explored "Virginia," after Elizabeth, who was called the "virgin queen." When James I came to the throne in 1603, he imprisoned Raleigh until 1616. Raleigh made one more trip, this one to South America. It failed after Raleigh ordered an attack on the Spaniards in the area—something the king commanded him not to do. Raleigh's son was killed during the expedition, and Raleigh was put to death for not obeying, which was seen as an act of treason.

About the Selections

"The Passionate Shepherd to His Love" was published in 1599 and became very popular. In it, Marlowe paints an idealized picture of the shepherd's life and of love. In 1600, Raleigh published "The Nymph's Reply to the Shepherd," answering Marlowe's shepherd. His reply, which is more realistic in its views, echoes the style and form of Marlowe's poem. Like opposite sides of a coin, the poems show two opposing views of love.

Christopher Marlowe
1564–1593

Walter Raleigh
1552–1618

Objectives

- To read and understand pastoral poems
- To identify characteristics of poetry, including alliteration
- To describe traits of a pastoral poem

Before Reading **continued on next page**

Pastoral Poems   by Christopher Marlowe and Walter Raleigh

poetry literature in verse form that usually has rhythm and paints powerful or beautiful impressions with words

alliteration repeating sounds by using words whose beginning sounds are the same

pastoral dealing with shepherds or country life

Literary Terms These two works are examples of **poetry,** literature set up in verses, or stanzas, and characterized by imagery and sound effects. Rhythm, rhyme, and **alliteration** are three poetic sound effects. Alliteration involves repeated beginning sounds of words, as in "*m*elodious birds sing *m*adrigals." These are **pastoral** poems, which Elizabethan readers enjoyed a great deal. A pastoral poem focused on shepherds and showed their country life as simple and pleasant.

Reading on Your Own Notice that these poems look and sound very similar. As you read the poems, compare and contrast them. Think about ways they are alike—for example, in length, format, and rhyme pattern. Identify the important differences between them.

Writing on Your Own Imagine what a shepherd's life was like long ago. What were the shepherd's duties, surroundings, and lifestyle? Separate these into things you think you would find pleasant and unpleasant. Use your notes to write a paragraph describing what this life was like.

Vocabulary Focus A word's origin can help you learn its meaning. Word origins are word histories that trace a word's development, including ways it has changed and passed from one language to another. For example, Marlowe uses the word *swain*. It comes from the Middle English word *swein*, which meant "boy" or "servant." Originally, it came into English from the Latin word *suus*, meaning "one's own." The word's meaning changed to describe a peasant sheepherder or a suitor (lover). Knowing about the earlier meanings adds depth to the poem, in which a shepherd is the suitor.

The Passionate Shepherd to His Love

Come live with me and be my Love,
And we will all the pleasures **prove**
That hills and valleys, dale and field,
And all the craggy mountains yield.

5 There will we sit upon the rocks
And see the shepherds feed their flocks,
By shallow rivers, to whose falls
Melodious birds sing **madrigals.**

There will I make thee beds of roses
10 And a thousand fragrant posies,
A cap of flowers, and a **kirtle**
Embroider'd all with leaves of **myrtle.**

A gown made of the finest wool,
Which from our pretty lambs we pull,
15 Fair linèd slippers for the cold,
With buckles of the purest gold.

A belt of straw and ivy buds
With coral clasps and amber studs:
And if these pleasures may thee move,
20 Come live with me and be my Love.

The silver dishes for thy meat
As precious as the gods do eat,
Shall on an ivory table be
Prepared each day for thee and me.

25 The shepherd **swains** shall dance and sing
For thy delight each May-morning:
If these delights thy mind may move,
Then live with me and be my Love.

– Christopher Marlowe

As you read, notice the descriptive details. What kind of life does the shepherd promise his love?

Shepherd swains shall dance and sing is an example of alliteration.

prove experience	**kirtle** skirt	**swains** simple country peasants; male admirers
madrigals complex songs with many voice parts	**myrtle** a bush with shiny leaves and good-smelling flowers	

The Nymph's Reply to the Shepherd

As you read, notice ways this poem is like "The Passionate Shepherd to His Love." How is it different?

If all the world and love were young,
And truth in every shepherd's tongue,
These pretty pleasures might me move
To live with thee and be thy Love.

5 But Time drives flocks from field to fold;
When rivers rage and rocks grow cold;
And Philomel becometh **dumb;**
The rest complains of cares to come.

Philomel is the nightingale, a bird noted for its sweet song.

The flowers do fade, and **wanton** fields
10 To wayward Winter **reckoning** yields:
A honey tongue, a heart of **gall,**
Is fancy's spring, but sorrow's fall.

Thy gowns, thy shoes, thy beds of roses,
Thy cap, thy kirtle, and thy posies,
15 Soon break, soon wither—soon forgotten,
In **folly** ripe, in reason rotten.

What do you think *In folly ripe, in reason rotten* means?

Thy belt of straw and ivy-buds,
Thy coral clasps and amber studs,—
All these in me no means can move
20 To come to thee and be thy Love.

But could youth last, and love still breed,
Had joys no date, nor age no need,
Then these delights my mind might move
To live with thee and be thy Love.

– Walter Raleigh

dumb silent; speechless	**reckoning** summing up; settling of accounts	**folly** foolishness
wanton unchecked; lush	**gall** bitterness	

AFTER READING THE SELECTIONS

Directions Choose the letter of the best answer or write the answer using complete sentences.

Comprehension: Identifying Facts

1. What does the poet want his love to do in "The Passionate Shepherd to His Love"?

   A run away with him

   B tend sheep and grow flowers

   C live with him in the country

   D wear wool and jewels

2. In "The Nymph's Reply to the Shepherd," what does "wayward Winter reckoning" (line 10) mean?

3. In line 19 of "The Nymph's Reply," what attitude toward the shepherd's words does the nymph reveal?

Comprehension: Putting Ideas Together

4. In "The Nymph's Reply," the nymph seems most concerned with the

   _____.

   A realities of aging

   B nature of love

   C hard work of a shepherd

   D nature of truth

5. What details about their life together does the shepherd give in "The Passionate Shepherd"? How would you describe these details?

6. How are the descriptions of pastoral surroundings different in the two poems?

Understanding Literature: Poetry, Alliteration, and Pastoral

Poetry is verse that uses imagery and sound effects. For example, it may use alliteration, or repetition of the same beginning sound. A pastoral poem focuses on the simplicity and charm of the country lives of shepherds.

7. What are three examples of alliteration in these poems?

8. What makes both of these poems pastoral?

Critical Thinking

9. Compare the attitudes of the two poets toward love. Which one connects love to physical joys and beauty? Which one thinks a life of romance is a fantasy?

Thinking Creatively

10. What offer from a suitor would a young woman find romantic today? Describe the life he might offer. Then explain whether you think it is realistic.

After Reading continued on next page

AFTER READING THE SELECTIONS *(continued)*

Pastoral Poems by Christopher Marlowe and Walter Raleigh.

 ### Grammar Check

Possessive nouns show who or what owns something by adding an apostrophe (') and *s* to the singular form. In "The Nymph's Reply to the Shepherd," *Nymph's* is a singular possessive noun. (Whose reply? The reply of the nymph.) Reread this poem to find more examples.

- Locate three more examples of singular possessive nouns.

- Write the lines in which the possessives occur. Draw an arrow from each possessive to the word it modifies.

- Write three original sentences using singular possessive nouns.

 ### Writing on Your Own

Think about a person's attitudes toward love at different times of life. Write a journal entry exploring your thoughts about the meaning of love to a child, a young adult, a parent, and a grandparent.

 ### Speaking and Listening

Work with a partner. Each of you should take one of the poems and practice reading it aloud. Think about the tone of voice and attitude each speaker should have. Present the poems as a dramatic reading, as if you had become the characters in a play. When your partner is speaking, listen and react to his or her tone and gestures.

 ### Technology

Pastoral poetry has a long history. Use the Internet to find out how it began and how it changed over time. Print out examples of pastoral poems and write a summary of what you learned. Present these materials in booklet form.

BEFORE READING THE SELECTIONS

About the Author

William Shakespeare was born in 1564 in Stratford-upon-Avon, in southern England. At the age of 18, he married Anne Hathaway. By 1592, he was working as an actor and playwright in London.

Shakespeare became a member of a successful acting company, the Lord Chamberlain's Men, and soon became the company's main playwright. He produced a huge body of work. Thirty-seven of his plays have been passed down to us and are still performed. Some include *A Midsummer Night's Dream, Much Ado About Nothing, Romeo and Juliet, Hamlet,* and *Macbeth.* Shakespeare also wrote 154 sonnets. In them, he explores concerns about time, death, beauty, friendship, and love.

By 1610, Shakespeare had retired to Stratford-upon-Avon as a wealthy man. He continued to write but enjoyed the life of a well-known and respected citizen. He died in 1616. In 1623, some of his friends and fellow actors published a collection of his plays.

About the Selections

Sonnets were often written by noblemen for an inner circle of wealthy friends. However, Shakespeare broke down class barriers to make the sonnet a poem of the common people, too. The sonnets of Shakespeare are considered the most polished and perfect in the English language. Their language and expression are natural, yet beautiful. In these selections, Shakespeare considers the nature of love and beauty. In "Sonnet 130," he also pokes fun at the ideals that sonnets of his time praised so often.

William Shakespeare
1564–1616

Objectives

- To read and understand sonnets
- To analyze the sequence of a sonnet, including the final couplet
- To identify and explain examples of personification, metaphor, and hyperbole
- To understand the meaning of parody

Before Reading continued on next page

Sonnet 116 and Sonnet 130   by William Shakespeare

couplet a rhyming pair

personification giving animals or objects the characteristics or qualities of humans

hyperbole extreme exaggeration that shows something is important

metaphor a figure of speech that makes a comparison but does not use *like* or *as*

parody an exaggerated look at a situation

Literary Terms Shakespeare's sonnets are organized into three groups of four lines each and a final **couplet**. A couplet is two rhymed lines of verse. Sonnets make rich use of figurative language such as **personification, hyperbole,** and **metaphor.** Personification gives human characteristics to things, ideas, or animals. Hyperbole is an exaggeration that is meant to make a point. Metaphor is a figure of speech comparing two things without using *like* or *as*. "Sonnet 130" is a **parody** of the typical sonnet. A parody makes fun of something.

Reading on Your Own Notice the sequence of ideas set up in these poems. For example, in "Sonnet 116," the poet first states what love is not. Then he defines what love is. He then describes its nature further. As you read these poems, draw conclusions about what the poet believes about real love.

Writing on Your Own What is "true love"? People have debated this question for centuries. Write a poem or essay giving your definition and examples. Use figurative language to show what love is like.

Vocabulary Focus Often you can predict the meaning of a hard word by studying context. Context clues lie in the text around the word. Find the word *dun* in line 3 of "Sonnet 130." What does it mean? The speaker is contrasting his love's traits with those often used to praise a woman's beauty. So *dun* must contrast with the whiteness of snow. Probably, it refers to a dull color such as brown or gray. Use context to predict the meanings of *damask'd* in line 5 and *belied* in line 14.

Think Before You Read Summarize some ideas about love expressed in other poems in this unit. What themes or ideas do you think Shakespeare might touch on in these sonnets?

Sonnet 116

Let me not to the marriage of true minds
Admit **impediments.** Love is not love
Which alters when it alteration finds,
Or bends with the remover to remove:
5 O, no! it is an ever-fixèd mark,
That looks on tempests and is never shaken;
It is the star to every wand'ring **bark,**
Whose worth's unknown, although his height be taken.
Love's not Time's fool, though rosy lips and cheeks
10 Within his bending **sickle**'s compass come;
Love alters not with his brief hours and weeks,
But bears it out even to the edge of doom:—
    If this be error and upon me proved,
    I never writ, nor no man ever loved.

As you read, notice the things to which love and time are compared. What traits of love and time do these comparisons suggest?

Sonnet 130

My mistress' eyes are nothing like the sun;
Coral is far more red than her lips' red:
If snow be white, why then her breasts are **dun;**
If hairs be wires, black wires grow on her head.
5 I have seen roses **damask'd,** red and white,
But no such roses see I in her cheeks;
And in some perfumes is there more delight
Than in the breath that from my mistress **reeks.**
I love to hear her speak, yet well I know
10 That music hath a far more pleasing sound:
I grant I never saw a goddess go,—
My mistress, when she walks, treads on the ground:
    And yet, by heaven, I think my love as rare
    As any she **belied** with false compare.

As you read, note what the speaker says his lady love is *not*. Is he criticizing her or making fun of the usual hyperboles found in sonnets of that time?

In Shakespeare's day, fancy hair nets were woven from finely spun gold threads. A flattering sonnet might compare hair to "golden wire" to describe its beauty. *Black wires* (line 4) is not a flattering description.

impediments obstacles

bark boat

sickle curved blade on a wooden handle, used for cutting hay

dun dull, drab; yellowish-brown

damask'd mixed; colored grayish red like damask cloth

reeks gives off

belied gave a false impression of

Directions Choose the letter of the best answer or write the answer using complete sentences.

Comprehension: Identifying Facts

1. In the first sentence of "Sonnet 116," "true minds" means _____.
   A the souls of lovers
   B the mental part of love
   C philosophers who have studied love
   D two whose love is constant and strong

2. Who or what has a sickle in line 10 of "Sonnet 116"?

3. To what is the woman's voice compared in "Sonnet 130"?

Comprehension: Putting Ideas Together

4. In the first four lines of "Sonnet 116," love is characterized as being _____.
   A a complete mystery
   B unchanging and unshakeable
   C a prison
   D a marriage of minds

5. Why is the North Star a good object to compare with love in line 7 of "Sonnet 116"?

6. What is the poet's feeling for his love, as expressed in lines 13–14 of "Sonnet 130"?

Understanding Literature: Sonnets and Figurative Language

A sonnet expresses strong feelings about a subject. The poet may use much figurative language to create strong images and make an impression on the reader.

7. How does the final couplet in each sonnet emphasize the speaker's point?

8. Give an example of personification, metaphor, and hyperbole in these sonnets. What effect do these figures of speech have on the reader?

Critical Thinking

9. What does the poet criticize in "Sonnet 130"? Would he say that love should be based on real or ideal qualities? Explain.

Thinking Creatively

10. Do you agree that "love's not Time's fool," or does the passage of time change love? Explain your opinion.

Grammar Check

Conjunctions are words that connect words, phrases, and clauses. *And, but, or,* and *nor* are coordinating conjunctions. They join words, phrases, or clauses together. For example, in the second sentence of "Sonnet 116," *or* connects verb phrases that describe what love is not. ("Love is not love/ Which alters . . . /Or bends . . .")

- Find three more examples of coordinating conjunctions in these sonnets.

- Write the sentence parts joined by the conjunction and circle the conjunction in each one.

- Decide whether the two parts are joined to show contrast, choice, or likeness.

 ## Writing on Your Own

Think about what these poems say about the nature of real love. Write a summary of the ideas expressed, using your own words. Begin with a main idea sentence. Then write one or two sentences about each part of the poems.

 ## Speaking and Listening

Choose another of Shakespeare's sonnets. Practice reading the poem aloud. When you can read it smoothly, with expression, recite it for the class. When it is your turn to listen, note the effect of rhyme on the poem. Identify examples of figurative language.

 ## Viewing

What ideal of beauty do media advertisements show? Is it achievable for most women? Clip photographs that show this female ideal. Organize them on a poster. Add labels that explain each "desirable" trait and your opinion about its value.

 ## Research

Find sources that discuss Shakespeare's sonnets. Use the Internet and the online card catalog of libraries in your area. Prepare a bibliography for students to use when searching for discussions of the poems. See Appendix C for tips on preparing a bibliography.

from *Hamlet*   *by William Shakespeare*

William Shakespeare
1564–1616

Objectives

- To read and understand classical drama
- To know the meaning of tragedy
- To understand the parts of a drama, such as act, dialogue, and aside
- To define foil

About the Elizabethan Theater

Shakespeare's *Hamlet* would have been performed in the Globe Theater, which was just across the Thames River from London. Built in 1599, this theater could hold an audience of 2,000 to 3,000 people. All performances were held in the afternoon, for there was no lighting besides daylight. To be heard, actors shouted their lines from the open-air stage. The stage was only 43 feet by about 28 feet and raised off the ground about 5 feet. Actors used props and costumes, but there was no background scenery or curtain. Playgoers used their imaginations to picture the castles, forests, and battlegrounds where the action took place.

The Globe's stage was surrounded on three sides by the pit. Here the one-penny playgoers stood shoulder to shoulder. Set back from this was a three-story amphitheater with places where wealthier playgoers sat. The rich and the poor, the educated and the uneducated crowded into the theater.

About the Selection

This selection comes from *Hamlet*, written around 1600. Such revenge plays were popular in Elizabethan England. In these plays, a hero gets even for the murder of a relative. The story of Hamlet comes from an old Danish legend. It was already well known when Shakespeare wrote his play.

Shakespeare's *Hamlet* remains popular today. It contains some of Shakespeare's most unforgettable lines. Hamlet's "To be or not to be" speech is probably the most familiar quotation in the world. It shows that good and evil are complex issues.

Literary Terms *Hamlet* is a **drama** that tells a story with characters on a stage. It is a **classical drama,** because it tells the story of larger-than-life, noble characters. Classical drama also follows the style of ancient Greek and Latin drama. Because it has a serious theme and important characters die, it is a **tragedy.** *Hamlet* contains five **acts,** or major units that advance the plot. Most of the drama has **dialogue,** the conversations between characters. At times, however, a character may speak in an **aside** (words the other characters are not intended to hear). A character called a **foil** serves as a strong contrast to a main character to point out the main character's traits.

Reading on Your Own As you read this scene, think about each character. Compare and contrast the ideas and reactions of Claudius, Polonius, Hamlet, and Ophelia. What traits do characters' words and actions show?

Writing on Your Own Is it right or wrong to listen secretly to others speak? Write a dialogue between two characters who argue the two sides of this question. Think of a scene in which parents, for example, plan to listen in on a child.

Vocabulary Focus Elizabethan English differs from today's English. Some words used then are no longer used, such as *bodkin* ("dagger") and *fardels* ("burdens"). Some familiar words had a different meaning in Shakespeare's day. For example, Hamlet uses *doubt* where we would say *suspect* and *honest* where we would say *honorable*. Word order in sentences may seem odd. "With all my heart; and it doth much content me/To hear him so inclined" translates in today's speech as "It pleases me with all my heart to hear that Hamlet is so inclined."

Think Before You Read What do you think Hamlet is thinking and feeling as this scene opens?

drama a story told through the words and actions of characters, written to be performed, as well as read; a play

classical drama play that follows the style of ancient Greek and Latin drama

tragedy a play that ends with the suffering or death of one or more of the main characters

act a major unit of action in a play

dialogue the words that characters in a play speak

aside when a character in a play is heard by the audience but not by the other characters

foil a character who contrasts with the main character

from Hamlet

As you read, think about what each person has to hide. Who might be lying?

Act 3, Scene 1

Hamlet's father, the king of Denmark, has been murdered by Hamlet's uncle, Claudius. Claudius then married Hamlet's mother, Gertrude, and became king. Hamlet, who was away at school, suspects the murder but has no proof. He is depressed and upset. His father's ghost visits Hamlet. He asks his son to get even for his death. Hamlet fears the ghost may have been sent by the Devil, so he seeks proof. At the same time, he pretends to be insane so he will not arouse Claudius's suspicion. Hamlet arranges for a play to be performed. The play will picture his father's death. Hamlet thinks Claudius's reaction will show if he is guilty. In the scene that follows, Claudius and his chief adviser, Polonius, try to discover whether Hamlet's "madness" is really lovesickness. They get Ophelia, the woman Hamlet loves, to speak with him while they secretly listen.

[Enter King, Queen, Polonius, Ophelia, Rosencrantz, Guildenstern, and Lords.]

King And can you by no **drift of conference**
Get from him why he puts on this confusion,
Grating so harshly all his days of quiet
With **turbulent** and dangerous **lunacy?**
5 **Rosencrantz** He does confess he feels himself distracted,
But from what cause he will by no means speak.

drift of conference hint	**turbulent** violent; disorderly
grating disturbing	**lunacy** madness

Guildenstern Nor do we find him **forward** to be **sounded,**
But with a crafty madness keeps aloof
When we would bring him on to some confession
10 Of his true state.
    Queen   Did he receive you well?
Rosencrantz Most like a gentleman.
    Guildenstern But with much forcing of his disposition.
Rosencrantz Niggard of question, but of our demands
15 Most free in his reply.
    Queen Did you assay him to any pastime?
Rosencrantz Madam, it so fell out that certain players
We **o'erraught** on the way. Of these we told him,
And there did seem in him a kind of joy
20 To hear of it. They are here about the court,
And, as I think, they have already order
This night to play before him.
    Polonius   'Tis most true,
And he beseeched me to entreat your Majesties
25 To hear and see the matter.
    King With all my heart, and it doth much content me
To hear him so inclined.
Good gentlemen, give him a further **edge**
And drive his purpose into these delights.
30 **Rosencrantz** We shall, my lord.

[*Rosencrantz, Guildenstern, and Lords exit.*]

King Sweet Gertrude, leave us too,
For we have **closely** sent for Hamlet hither,
That he, as 'twere by accident, may here
Affront Ophelia.
35 Her father and myself (lawful **espials**)
Will so bestow ourselves that, seeing unseen,
We may of their encounter frankly judge

> Why do you think Hamlet is happy to have actors perform a play? Why does he especially want Claudius and Gertrude there?

> Claudius feels that he and Polonius have a right to spy on Hamlet and Ophelia.

forward eager	**edge** encouragement	**affront** meet
sounded questioned	**closely** secretly	**espials** spies
o'erraught overtook		

And gather by him, as he is behaved,
If 't be th' **affliction** of his love or no
40 That thus he suffers for.
    Queen   I shall obey you.
And for your part, Ophelia, I do wish
That your good beauties be the happy cause
Of Hamlet's wildness. So shall I hope your virtues
45 Will bring him to his **wonted** way again,
To both your honors.
    Ophelia   Madam, I wish it may.

[*Queen exits.*]

Polonius tells his daughter to read from a religious book so that she will appear virtuous to Hamlet.

Polonius Ophelia, walk you here.—Gracious, so please you,
We will bestow ourselves. [*To Ophelia.*] Read on this book,
50 That show of such an exercise may color
Your loneliness.—We are oft to blame in this
('Tis too much proved), that with devotion's **visage**
And **pious** action we do sugar o'er
The devil himself.
55 **King** [*Aside*] O, 'tis too true!
How smart a lash that speech doth give my conscience.
The **harlot's** cheek beautied with plast'ring art
Is not more ugly to the thing that helps it
Than is my deed to my most **painted** word.
60 O heavy burden!
Polonius I hear him coming. Let's withdraw, my lord.

[*They withdraw. Enter Hamlet.*]

Polonius's words awaken Claudius's guilty conscience. He is troubled by the horror of his crime and all the lies he must tell. Why does Claudius speak of his burden in an aside instead of to Polonius?

Hamlet To be or not to be—that is the question:
Whether 'tis nobler in the mind to suffer
The slings and arrows of outrageous fortune,
65 Or to take arms against a sea of troubles
And, by opposing, end them. To die, to sleep—

affliction sickness, suffering	**visage** face, mask	**harlot's** prostitute's
	pious very religious	**painted** false
wonted normal, usual		

No more—and by a sleep to say we end
The heartache and the thousand natural shocks
That flesh is heir to—'tis a **consummation**
70 Devoutly to be wished. To die, to sleep—
To sleep, perchance to dream. Ay, there's the **rub,**
For in that sleep of death what dreams may come,
When we have shuffled off this mortal coil,
Must give us pause. There's the **respect**
75 That makes calamity of so long life.
For who would bear the whips and scorns of time,
Th' oppressor's wrong, the proud man's **contumely,**
The pangs of despised love, the law's delay,
The insolence of office, and the spurns
80 That patient merit of th' unworthy takes,
When he himself might his **quietus** make
With a bare **bodkin?** Who would **fardels** bear,
To grunt and sweat under a weary life,

Hamlet talks to himself, revealing his inner conflict. He asks whether life is worth living in a world so full of evil and suffering. He thinks about and rejects suicide, since he might suffer more for this sin after death. He is sad about the way his inner conflict has left him unable to act.

Claudius and Polonius Listen to Hamlet, **John Gilbert, 1881**

consummation completion, end

rub obstacle

respect reason

contumely insulting behavior

quietus discharge, release

bodkin dagger

fardels burdens

A fear of what comes after death makes some people avoid acting like heroes.

But that the dread of something after death,
85 The undiscovered country from whose **bourn**
No traveler returns, puzzles the will
And makes us rather bear those ills we have
Than fly to others that we know not of?
Thus conscience does make cowards of us all,
90 And thus the native hue of **resolution**
Is sicklied o'er with the pale **cast** of thought,
And enterprises of great **pitch** and **moment**
With this regard their currents turn awry
And lose the name of action.—Soft you now,
95 The fair Ophelia.—Nymph, in thy **orisons**
Be all my sins remembered.
Ophelia   Good my lord,
How does your Honor for this many a day?
Hamlet I humbly thank you, well.

Ophelia tries to give Hamlet back his love letters (*remembrances*) and says he has been unkind. Hamlet thinks she has been put up to this. If so, she is being as dishonest as Claudius. He speaks bitterly because of his disappointment in her.

100 **Ophelia** My lord, I have remembrances of yours
that I have longèd long to redeliver.
I pray you now receive them.
Hamlet No, not I. I never gave you aught.
Ophelia My honored lord, you know right well you did,
105 And with them words of so sweet breath composed
As made the things more rich. Their perfume lost,
Take these again, for to the noble mind
Rich gifts **wax** poor when givers prove unkind.
There, my lord.
110 **Hamlet** Ha, ha, are you honest?
Ophelia My lord?
Hamlet Are you fair?
Ophelia What means your lordship?
Hamlet That if you be honest and fair, your honesty
115 should admit no discourse to your beauty.

Hamlet is deeply concerned with being honest in the face of all the dishonesty around him. How are Claudius and Polonius foils on this point?

bourn border, boundary	**cast** covering	**orisons** prayers
resolution determination to act	**pitch** height	**wax** become
	moment importance	

Ophelia Could beauty, my lord, have better **commerce** than with honesty?

Hamlet Ay, truly, for the power of beauty will sooner transform honesty from what it is to a **bawd** than the
120 force of honesty can translate beauty into his likeness. This was sometime a paradox, but now the time gives it proof. I did love you once.

Ophelia Indeed, my lord, you made me believe so.

Hamlet You should not have believed me, for virtue
125 cannot so inoculate our old stock but we shall **relish** of it. I loved you not.

Ophelia I was the more deceived.

Hamlet Get thee to a **nunnery.** Why wouldst thou be a breeder of sinners? I am myself **indifferent** honest, but
130 yet I could accuse me of such things that it were better my mother had not borne me: I am very proud, revengeful, ambitious, with more offenses at my beck than I have thoughts to put them in, imagination to give them shape, or time to act them in. What should such
135 fellows as I do crawling between earth and heaven? We are arrant knaves all; believe none of us. Go thy ways to a nunnery. Where's your father?

Ophelia At home, my lord.

Hamlet Let the doors be shut upon him that he may play
140 the fool nowhere but in 's own house. Farewell.

Ophelia O, help him, you sweet heavens!

Hamlet If thou dost marry, I'll give thee this plague for thy dowry: be thou as chaste as ice, as pure as snow, thou shalt not escape **calumny.** Get thee to a nunnery,
145 farewell. Or if thou wilt needs marry, marry a fool, for wise men know well enough what monsters you make of them. To a nunnery, go, and quickly too. Farewell.

Ophelia Heavenly powers, restore him!

Notice that Shakespeare changes from verse to prose during this dialogue between Hamlet and Ophelia. Why do you think he does this? How does it change the tone of the play?

Hamlet does not want Ophelia to be affected by evil, so he tells her to go to a nunnery—a place where she will not be affected.

Hamlet suddenly asks Ophelia where her father is. He knows that she is lying. Some of his angry words are aimed at those he knows are listening.

commerce interaction	**relish** have some trace	**indifferent** not very
bawd person who keeps a brothel	**nunnery** a place where one will not be tempted	**calumny** insults that call one's character into question

Hamlet I have heard of your paintings too, well enough.
150 God hath given you one face, and you make yourselves
another. You jig and **amble,** and you **lisp;** you nickname
God's creatures and make your wantonness your
ignorance. Go to, I'll no more on 't. It hath made me
mad. I say we will have no more marriage. Those that are
155 married already, all but one, shall live. The rest shall
keep as they are. To a nunnery, go.

[*He exits.*]

Ophelia O, what a noble mind is here o'erthrown!
The courtier's, soldier's, scholar's, eye, tongue, sword,
Th' expectancy and rose of the fair state,
160 The glass of fashion and the mold of form,
Th' observed of all observers, quite, quite down!
And I, of ladies most deject and wretched,
That sucked the honey of his musicked vows,
Now see that noble and most sovereign reason,
165 Like sweet bells jangled, out of time and harsh;
That unmatched form and stature of blown youth
Blasted with **ecstasy.** O, woe is me
T' have seen what I have seen, see what I see!
King [*Advancing with Polonius*]
Love? His **affections** do not that way tend;
170 Nor what he spake, though it lacked form a little,
Was not like madness. There's something in his soul
O'er which his melancholy sits on brood,
And I do doubt the hatch and the **disclose**
Will be some danger; which for to prevent,
175 I have in quick determination
Thus set it down: he shall with speed to England
For the demand of our neglected **tribute.**

amble walk in an unnatural way	**blasted** ruined	**disclose** outcome
lisp talk in a false way	**ecstasy** madness	**tribute** payments owed to a king
	affections frame of mind	

Haply the seas, and countries different,
With variable objects, shall **expel**
180 This something-settled matter in his heart,
Whereon his brains still beating puts him thus
From fashion of himself. What think you on 't?
Polonius It shall do well. But yet do I believe
The origin and commencement of his grief
185 Sprung from neglected love.—How now, Ophelia?
You need not tell us what Lord Hamlet said;
We heard it all.—My lord, do as you please,
But, if you hold it fit, after the play
Let his queen-mother all alone **entreat** him
190 To show his grief. Let her be **round** with him;
And I'll be placed, so please you, in the ear
Of all their conference. If she find him not,
To England send him, or confine him where
Your wisdom best shall think.
195 **King**   It shall be so.
Madness in great ones must not unwatched go.

[*They exit.*]

What conclusion
has the king
drawn? How
does Polonius's
conclusion differ?

*Hamlet Holding
the Skull of Yorick,*
John Gilbert, 1881.
This scene comes
later in the play,
after Hamlet returns
from England.

expel kick out	**entreat** beg	**round** direct

AFTER READING THE SELECTION

from *Hamlet*   *by William Shakespeare*

Directions Choose the letter of the best answer or write the answer using complete sentences.

Comprehension: Identifying Facts

1. What has Hamlet ordered to occur in the evening?
   A a murder   C a concert
   B spying   D a play

2. Whom does Hamlet want to attend this event?

3. What has the king arranged to happen?

4. What does the queen hope has caused Hamlet's madness?

5. What do the king and Polonius do while Hamlet speaks to Ophelia?

6. Ophelia wants to return something to Hamlet. What is it?

7. Where does Hamlet tell Ophelia to go?

8. Where does Ophelia say her father is?

9. What does Polonius believe has caused Hamlet's grief?

10. What does Polonius suggest the queen do after the play?

Comprehension: Putting Ideas Together

11. What have Rosencrantz and Guildenstern learned by talking to Hamlet?
    A that he is eager to talk
    B that he is insane
    C that he is distracted
    D what is bothering him

12. What does Polonius mean when he says we all "sugar o'er/The devil himself"? Why does the king feel guilty when he hears this?

13. How does Hamlet want to solve his problem? Why is he also afraid of solving his problem this way?

14. Why does Hamlet feel like a coward?

15. How have Hamlet's feelings for Ophelia changed? How do they seem to change in this scene?

16. Several times, Hamlet tells Ophelia to go to a nunnery. Why do you think he does this?

17. What does Ophelia think has caused Hamlet's anger? How does she feel about this?

18. What causes the king to decide to send Hamlet to England? What does he say he hopes the trip will achieve?

19. The way Polonius talks to his daughter Ophelia suggests what kind of feeling for her?

20. What does Polonius believe he will learn if the queen talks to Hamlet? Why will he be able to learn this?

Understanding Literature: Drama and Dialogue

Hamlet is one of Shakespeare's greatest tragedies. It is a drama with five acts, or major divisions. The story is developed through action and dialogue, or conversations between the characters. A character may reveal his or her thoughts to the audience in an aside, which other characters do not hear. A foil is a character who contrasts strongly with another character.

21. What subjects in this scene suggest that this drama is a tragedy?

22. What do you think has happened before this in Act 3? What do you think will happen next?

23. For what character could Claudius be a foil? How do the two characters contrast?

24. Who speaks an aside in this scene? Why must other characters not hear these words?

25. What plot actions has Shakespeare set in motion through dialogue in this scene? What ideas has he communicated?

Critical Thinking

26. Do you think Hamlet is insane or pretending to be insane? Why?

27. Whom does Hamlet want to mislead? How does it help Hamlet if they think he is insane?

28. In this scene, who is misleading whom? What could each character gain from the lie?

29. Why do you think Hamlet views death as a welcome release? What conflicts are going on within him? Why might he view people as evil and everyday life as fake?

Thinking Creatively

30. In lines 84–88, Hamlet suggests that doubt prevents him from acting. Do you think it is wise or cowardly to fail to carry out a plan because of doubt? Back up your opinion with an example.

After Reading **continued on next page**

from *Hamlet* *by William Shakespeare*

 Grammar Check

There are four kinds of sentences: declarative, interrogatory, imperative, and exclamatory. Declarative sentences make a statement. (*I never gave you aught.*) They end with a period. Interrogatory sentences ask a question. (*Are you fair?*) They end with a question mark. Imperative sentences make a command. (*Ophelia, walk you here.*) They usually end with a period. Exclamatory sentences show emotion. (*O, 'tis too true!*) They end with an exclamation point.

Find three more examples of each type of sentence in this scene. Write the sentences and label them. Write an original example of each type of sentence.

 Writing on Your Own

Choose a passage of at least 15 lines from the scene. Rewrite it in your own words, showing the meaning in today's language and grammar.

 Speaking and Listening

Practice reading aloud a part of Hamlet's speech in lines 62–96 or, with a partner, read some dialogue from the scene. Speak clearly. Use the feeling the characters express. When you are listening, listen to understand the literal meaning of the words and any other meaning that they suggest.

 Media

Watch a movie version of *Hamlet*. Make notes about what you see. Tell what you think about each character. Write a movie review for your school newspaper. Tell a little about the plot and characters of the play. Give your opinion and reasons why classmates should or should not see it.

 Research

In a classical tragedy, the hero has a flaw that leads directly to the hero's death. Does Hamlet have a flaw? Research to learn different views about this question. Use encyclopedias, the Internet, and reference materials from the library. Take notes about your findings. Summarize the opinion that makes the most sense to you.

BEFORE READING THE SELECTION

Psalm 23 *from the King James Bible*

About the King James Bible

In 1604, King James I ordered a new translation of the Bible.
Fifty-four of England's greatest scholars and churchmen set
to work. Through the Middle Ages, the Bible was written in
Latin. This meant most people could not read it. By 1600,
there were several English translations, but none of them had
been accepted by all the people. There was no "official" Bible.

James's experts studied Latin versions of the Bible and the
original Greek and Hebrew. They used these to edit current
English versions. By 1611, the King James Version was
completed. Ever since, it has been praised as a masterpiece.
The language is beautiful and full of life. Its poetic wording,
strong rhythms, and powerful imagery have left a lasting
imprint on readers. It even changed the English language. Its
phrases have made their way into our writing and everyday
speech.

About the Selection

"Psalm 23" is one of the most familiar passages from the
Bible. The word *psalm* comes from a Hebrew title meaning
"praise." The Greek form of the word means "song." The
purpose of the psalms was to sing songs praising God. In
the original Hebrew, the psalms were written as verse. Their
poetic devices mean that they are best read as poetry, not
prose.

"Psalm 23" is believed to have been written by David, the
second king of ancient Israel, who had once been a shepherd
himself. He was a great poet, musician, and ruler. Elizabethan
poets helped the scholars polish verses for the King James
Bible. Some experts believe that Shakespeare had a hand in
the final version of "Psalm 23."

King James I
1566–1625

Objectives

- To read and
  understand a
  psalm
- To identify
  examples of
  metaphor and
  parallel structure
- To explain the
  effects of imagery
  and rhythm

***Before Reading* continued on next page**

The English Renaissance Unit 2   **125**

Psalm 23   *from the King James Bible*

parallel structure the phrasing of words to balance ideas that are equally important

Literary Terms A psalm is a type of writing that praises God. Most psalms were meant to be sung or chanted. "Psalm 23" makes rich use of metaphor, a comparison that does not use *like* or *as.* Many of its sentences use **parallel structure.** Phrases and clauses are set down with the same format. This helps to unify the writing and relate the parts to each other.

Reading on Your Own As you read, notice the kind of images and metaphors used to describe God (the LORD). In reading, you can add up the details and tone to make inferences, or educated guesses, about unspoken meaning. What inferences can you make about the speaker's view of the world?

Writing on Your Own How is a poem like a song? Create a two-column table and list traits of a poem and a song in each column. Match traits that are similar. Use your notes to write a paragraph comparing the two.

Vocabulary Focus Figurative language uses words in a way that is not to be taken literally. It expresses ideas in a vivid, imaginative way. For example, "The LORD is my shepherd" compares God to a sheep herder and worshippers to sheep. This comparison helps readers understand how God cares for people. Look for other examples of figurative language in "Psalm 23." Think about how they help readers understand God's care.

Think Before You Read Why would the idea of God acting as a shepherd be comforting to people?

Psalm 23

The LORD is my shepherd; I shall not want.

He maketh me to lie down in green pastures: he leadeth me beside the still waters.

He restoreth my soul: he leadeth me in the paths of righteousness for his name's sake.

Yea, though I walk through the valley of the shadow of death, I will fear no evil: for thou art with me; thy **rod** and thy **staff** they comfort me.

Thou preparest a table before me in the presence of mine enemies: thou **anointest** my head with oil; my cup runneth over.

Surely goodness and mercy shall follow me all the days of my life: and I will dwell in the house of the LORD for ever.

Great Britain, Pembrokeshire, Colby Woodland Garden

As you read, notice the rhythms set up by the parallel structure of clauses. Picture the images and note the mood they suggest.

A shepherd's *staff* was often hooked at one end to enable the shepherd to guide sheep and pull them out of holes or tight spots. How might this image be comforting?

Anointing with oil was a mark of great honor. King David, the author of this psalm, was anointed with oil on the day he was identified as king of Israel.

rod a club used by a shepherd to protect flocks

staff a stick carried in the hand for guiding sheep

anointest to apply oil or perfume as part of a ritual

Directions Choose the letter of the best answer or write the answer using complete sentences.

Comprehension: Identifying Facts

1. What does the speaker compare the LORD to?

   A a shepherd   **C** a valley

   B a sheep   **D** a staff

2. Why does the speaker not fear death?

3. What does the speaker say the LORD anoints with oil?

Comprehension: Putting Ideas Together

4. Which detail does *not* continue the shepherd and sheep comparison?

   A leading beside waters

   B a rod and staff

   C green pastures

   D anointing with oil

5. What details suggest the goodness and mercy of the LORD?

6. What does the psalm say about the LORD's effect on life and death?

Understanding Literature: Metaphor and Parallel Structure

Poetry often uses figures of speech, especially metaphors, to make comparisons that are surprising. They help the audience see the subject in a new light. Parallel structure often helps establish the rhythm of a poem.

7. Do you think the LORD/shepherd metaphor is a fitting comparison? Why or why not?

8. What pattern does the parallel structure of the second paragraph set up? What does this structure emphasize?

Critical Thinking

9. From this psalm, what can you infer about the speaker's attitude?

Thinking Creatively

10. When the psalms were written, being a shepherd was a common and needed job. If this psalm were rewritten today, what more modern metaphor might the poet use? Why would this comparison be fitting?

Grammar Check

A number of clauses in "Psalm 23" have the same pattern: subject-action verb-direct object (S-V-DO). A subject carries out the action of the sentence. A direct object receives the action of the verb. For example, in the clause "he restoreth my soul," *he* is the subject; *restoreth* is the action verb; and *soul* is the direct object.

- Find three more clauses in the psalm with the S-V-DO pattern.

- Write the clauses. Underline the subject with one line and the verb with two lines. Circle the direct object.

 Writing on Your Own

Write a paragraph praising someone you admire. Begin with a topic sentence naming the person and telling why you admire him or her. Support your topic sentence with facts and examples. Use parallel structure in some sentences.

 Speaking and Listening

Practice reading the selection aloud until you can read it smoothly. With classmates, prepare a choral reading of the psalm and present it to the class.

As you listen to the psalm read aloud, notice the cadence, or pattern of rhythm. In what way does it remind you of poetry? How is it like prose? Take notes describing how the language and its beat affect you.

 Viewing

In the Middle Ages, monks wrote out copies of the Bible by hand. These books (called illuminated manuscripts) contained beautiful, colorful illustrations. Use the Internet or resources in your library to view samples of this religious art. Write a description of what you see.

 Research

Research to learn more about the history of the King James Version of the Bible. Use the Internet, encyclopedias, or trade books in the library. Record notes in your own words on index cards. Arrange the cards in chronological order and use them to create a time line with labels.

Valediction, Forbidding Mourning   *by John Donne*

John Donne
1572–1631

About the Author

John Donne was born in 1572 in London into a wealthy and famous Roman Catholic family. In the early 1590s, he studied law and lived a wild lifestyle. He became a favorite at the royal court and was much admired for his mind and poetic talents. Donne's early poetry (mostly love poems and satires) was witty and clever.

In 1597, he was appointed secretary to Sir Thomas Egerton, an important official. In 1601, he secretly married Egerton's 16-year-old niece, Ann More. Ann's father was furious and had Donne fired and put in prison. Out of favor, Donne struggled to support his family.

During these difficult years, Donne turned to religion. In 1615, at the urging of King James I, Donne entered the ministry of the Church of England, or Anglican Church. He quickly became famous for his powerful sermons. From 1621 until his death, Donne served as dean, or head priest, of Saint Paul's Cathedral. His later poetry includes some of the most famous religious poems in English.

About the Selection

Donne wrote "Valediction, Forbidding Mourning" in 1611. A valediction is a speech of farewell. The poem is addressed to his wife as he leaves for France. They will be apart only for a short time, but husband and wife both know that the dangers of travel could mean this goodbye is final. As you read the poem, keep in mind that, at this time, people believed the earth was the center of the universe. All stars and planets circled around it. Perfection lay beyond the circle in which the moon orbited.

Literary Terms A poet may use several tools to organize a poem. Rhyme ties lines together using repeated ending sounds of words *(away/say, go/no)*. A stanza groups a set number of lines together. A **conceit** helps connect ideas in a poem by continuing a metaphor or comparison over many lines. The **tone** of a poem also adds to the poem. Word choices of the poet reveal the tone, or attitude, of the poet.

conceit a complex or strained metaphor

tone the attitude an author takes toward a subject

Reading on Your Own Notice that the poem is organized into nine stanzas of four lines each. Each stanza presents a complete thought and ends with a natural pause. Take advantage of these pauses to think about the meaning of each stanza. On a second reading, think about how the meaning of each stanza builds on the last to express the speaker's relationship to his love.

Writing on Your Own Think about a difficult farewell you have said. Write a journal entry as though you have just said this goodbye. Describe what you said and how you felt.

Vocabulary Focus Suffixes and prefixes add to the meaning of words. A prefix is letters added at the beginning of a word, and a suffix is letters added at the end. In this poem, the word *profanation* is made by adding the suffix *–ation* to the base word *profane* (meaning "impure" or "not religious"). This suffix turns the adjective into a noun meaning "disgrace" or "dishonor." Look at the words *sublunary, inter-assured,* and *expansion* in the selection. Identify the base word and prefix or suffix used to create each word. Put together the meanings of these parts to predict the longer word's meaning.

Think Before You Read From the title, what do you think this poem is about?

Valediction, Forbidding Mourning

As you read, think about how the poet's choices of words and images set the tone, or show the poet's attitude, in the poem. How would you describe the tone?

As virtuous men pass mildly away,
    And whisper to their souls to go;
While some of their sad friends do say,
    Now his breath goes, and some say, No;

5 So let us melt, and make no noise,
    No tear-floods, nor sigh-tempests move;
'Twere **profanation** of our joys
    To tell the **laity** our love.

The poet thinks of their love as being sacred and more special than that of ordinary people (*laity*).

Moving of th' earth brings harms and fears
10   Men reckon what it did and meant;
But **trepidations** of the spheres,
    Though greater far, are innocent.

Dull **sublunary** lovers' love,
    Whose soul is sense, cannot admit
15 Absence; for that it doth remove
    Those things which elemented it.

Lines 9–12 mean movements of heavenly bodies are important but do not harm as earthquakes do.

But we, by a love so far refined,
    That ourselves know not what it is,
Inter-assurèd of the mind,
20   Careless, eyes, lips and hands to miss,

---

profanation act of disgracing or dishonoring

laity the general mass of people

trepidations tremors

sublunary of or relating to the real world (beneath the moon)

inter-assurèd jointly and equally sure or certain

—Our two souls therefore, which are one,
  Though I must go, endure not yet
A **breach,** but an expansion,
  Like gold to airy thinness beat.

25 If they be two, they are two so
     As stiff twin compasses are two;
  Thy soul, the fixt foot, makes no show
     To move, but doth if th' other do.

  And though it in the centre sit,
30   Yet when the other far doth roam,
  It leans and hearkens after it,
     And grows erect as that comes home.

  Such wilt thou be to me, who must,
     Like th' other foot, **obliquely** run;
35 Thy firmness makes my circles just,
     And makes me end where I begun.

Line 24 refers to gold beaten into a sheet of foil so light that it floats. The poet means that being apart is something that stretches their love into something beautiful and delicate.

The speaker and the woman are like the two feet of a compass. When used to draw a circle, the compass's feet are separated at one end. The fixed foot remains in the center. When the circle is complete, the feet can be straightened and closed so that they lie side by side. This extended metaphor is an example of conceit.

Celtic cross in Templebrady Cemetery

Circles in line 35 refers to the poet's journey. It also refers to a shape that symbolizes perfection because it has no beginning and no end.

breach a break, rupture, or tear   **obliquely** at an angle

AFTER READING THE SELECTION

Valediction, Forbidding Mourning   by *John Donne*

Directions Choose the letter of the best answer or write the answer using complete sentences.

Comprehension: Identifying Facts

1. In the second stanza, the poet asks his love _____.
   A to melt her cold heart
   B to remain silent
   C not to curse
   D not to cry

2. To what does "moving of th' earth" refer?

3. According to the sixth stanza, what will connect the poet and the woman while he is gone?

Comprehension: Putting Ideas Together

4. According to the poet, their love is "refined." By this, he means it is _____.
   A spiritual, as well as physical
   B passionate and physical
   C ideal and intellectual
   D shrunken and lacking in feeling

5. What images compare the love of this pair to gold? Why is this a good comparison?

6. What images tie love to movements or changes of the earth and heavens?

Understanding Literature: Tone and Conceit

A poet may use many devices to pull a poem together. Rhyme connects lines by repeated sounds (*away/say, go/no*). Stanzas group a set number of lines together. A conceit connects ideas by continuing a metaphor or comparison over many lines. Word choices reveal the poet's tone, or attitude.

7. Explain the conceit of the compasses in the final three stanzas. How are the parts and movements of the compass similar to the man and woman who must part?

8. What is the tone of the poem? Give examples of word choices that create this tone.

Critical Thinking

9. How does this poem illustrate Donne's growing concern with spiritual matters in the second half of his life?

Thinking Creatively

10. Do you believe that being apart strengthens love? Explain your opinion.

Grammar Check

An adjective describes a noun or pronoun. It answers the question *what kind? which one?* or *how many?* An adjective may be placed before the noun it describes, or it may follow a *be* verb *(is, are).* In line 1, Donne uses the adjective *virtuous* to tell what kind of men.

- Find five other adjectives in the poem. List them and the words they describe.

- Write a sentence using each adjective. Explain what it suggests about the noun it describes.

Writing on Your Own

Study the pattern of rhyme and stanza format of Donne's poem. Think about the kinds of images it contains. Choose a subject and write a poem of your own, using a similar rhyme and stanza setup. Include strong images to create a tone that suits your subject.

Speaking

In a small group, discuss your thoughts about being separated from a loved one, such as a parent, sibling, or best friend. Try to agree on a list of pros and cons in such a situation. Remember to give every member of the group a chance to speak and to avoid interrupting.

Listening

Listen to a popular song about lovers who have been parted. Make notes about the song's details and main point. How does its message compare to the message of Donne's poem?

Media

Scan the tables of contents of entertainment magazines. List titles of articles that discuss the separation of famous couples. Read one of these articles, then make a table listing ways the couple is like and unlike the couple in Donne's poem.

Technology

In a small group, discuss how the situation and ideas expressed in "Valediction, Forbidding Mourning" might be acted out in today's language. Write a short script for this scene. Include dialogue and stage directions. Have two members of the group practice and act out the script. Use a video camera to record the scene.

Still to Be Neat and *To Celia*   by Ben Jonson

Ben Jonson
1572–1637

Objectives

- To read and understand a poem and identify poetry as a genre
- To analyze repetition in a poem and explain its effect
- To explain the meaning of figurative language in a poem

About the Author

Ben Jonson was born in Westminster in 1572. His father, a minister, died when Jonson was a baby. A bricklayer adopted Jonson. Lacking wealth, he could not attend a university. However, through study and reading, he became one of the best-educated men of his time.

Jonson worked as a bricklayer and served in the army. By 1595, he had found his calling as an actor and playwright. He and his plays enjoyed great success with the public. Jonson wrote comedies, masques (dramatic poems with song, dance, and colorful costumes), and witty plays. Jonson was the first playwright to publish his plays (in 1616). This step helped make drama a serious form of literature, not just entertainment. Jonson was also the first to be named poet laureate of England. (The poet laureate is the official poet of a country. Until the 19th century, English poets laureate were paid to write poems for and about the royal family.)

Much of Jonson's poetry is set as songs within his plays. He had studied Greek and Latin poetry closely. He modeled his own poetry on its elegant, refined forms. His poems are clear and flow easily because of his mastery of rhythm and sound. Jonson had a group of loyal fans known as "Ben's Tribe." They followed Jonson's style in their own writings. This was the beginning of the neoclassical movement, which valued the characteristics of classical Greek and Latin poetry.

About the Selections

"Still to Be Neat" is a song that appears in Jonson's comedy *The Silent Woman.* This poem was first titled "Simplex Munditiis." This Latin phrase means "simple, in neat attire" or "neat, not gaudy." "To Celia" honors a lady. The poet makes a symbolic toast to Celia's perfection. The poem is a fine example of the classical style Jonson admired.

Literary Terms A **genre,** or type, of literature can be identified by its form, method, or content. These two poems belong to the genre of poetry. It is rich in sound devices and special effects. **Repetition** is a sound effect used to emphasize sounds and ideas. It involves repeating a word, phrase, or sentence. **Figurative language** gives words meanings other than their literal or usual meanings.

Reading on Your Own In "Still to Be Neat," the poet makes a broad statement about appearance. Is it a fact or an opinion? Facts can be proved true or false. They are based on evidence. Opinions involve personal beliefs. They can never be proved. We must judge for ourselves whether an opinion is convincing. In "To Celia," notice the figure of speech in the first two lines. What does it suggest about the speaker's feelings?

Writing on Your Own Think about the amount of time you spend each day on your appearance: hair, clothes, make-up. Make a graph showing what part of your day this takes up. Is this time well spent or is it wasted time? Write a paragraph explaining your opinion.

Vocabulary Focus In figures of speech, the most ordinary words may take on amazing new meanings. *Drink to me* usually means lifting a glass in my honor. It is not possible to drink to someone with your eyes. The meaning is symbolic. The gaze between lovers is as strong as wine and flushes them with pleasure, like wine. The comparison is not literally true, but it shows the feeling behind the words.

Think Before You Read Recall the meaning of the title "Simplex Munditiis." What do you predict this poem will say about clothing that is simple and not gaudy?

genre a specific type, or kind, of literature

repetition using a word, phrase, or image more than once, for emphasis

figurative language writing or speech not meant to be understood exactly as it is written; writers use figurative language to express ideas in vivid or imaginative ways

STILL TO BE NEAT

As you read, notice how smoothly the lines flow and how the sound effects such as repetition make the poem musical.

Still to be neat, still to be drest,
As you were going to a feast;
Still to be powder'd, still perfumed:
Lady, it is to be **presumed,**
5 Though art's hid causes are not found,
All is not sweet, all is not sound.

Give me a look, give me a face
That makes simplicity a grace;
Robes loosely flowing, hair as free:
10 Such sweet neglect more taketh me
Than all th' **adulteries** of art;
They strike mine eyes, but not my heart.

The poet thinks *art* (elaborate clothing and makeup) in line 11 is used to hide flaws and produce an illusion of beauty.

presumed taken for granted   **adulteries** falseness

TO CELIA

Drink to me only with thine eyes,
    And I will **pledge** with mine;
Or leave a kiss but in the cup
    And I'll not look for wine.
5 The thirst that from the soul doth rise
    Doth ask a drink divine;
But might I of Jove's nectar **sup,**
    I would not change for thine.

I sent thee late a rosy wreath,
10   Not so much honouring thee
As giving it a hope that there
    It could not wither'd be;
But thou thereon didst only breathe,
    And sent'st it back to me;
15 Since when it grows, and smells, I swear,
    Not of itself but thee!

As you read,
think about what
the speaker is
suggesting about
the woman. What
is his view of her?

Jove was another
name for Jupiter,
king of the Roman
gods. The gods
were believed to
drink *nectar,* a
perfect drink.

**A Young Woman
of the Tudor Court,
16th century**

pledge promise; toast   **sup** drink; swallow

Directions Choose the letter of the best answer or write the answer using complete sentences.

Comprehension: Identifying Facts

1. What appearance does the poet find most beautiful in "Still to Be Neat"?
   A a natural, simple look
   B a wild, tousled look
   C a neglected look
   D a woman's eyes

2. In "To Celia," what would the poet prefer to wine?

3. What did the poet give to Celia? What did she do with it?

Comprehension: Putting Ideas Together

4. In "Still to Be Neat," what words set up a contrast?
   A powder'd, perfumed/free, neglect
   B lady, presumed/give, simplicity
   C neat, feast/look, face
   D sweet, sound/flowing, free

5. In "Still to Be Neat," what does the poet mean by "adulteries of art"? What does this have to do with "art's hid causes"?

6. In "To Celia," what happens to the rosy wreath? What quality does this suggest about Celia?

Understanding Literature: Genre and Repetition

The genre of a literary work is the category of writing to which it belongs, such as poetry, fiction, or drama. A genre has its own traits. For example, poetry makes use of figurative language and sound effects. Figurative language uses words with imaginative rather than literal meanings. Repetition is a sound effect used in these poems.

7. What traits tell you these selections are poems?

8. In lines 5 and 6 of "To Celia," what does the poet compare thirst and drinking to?

Critical Thinking

9. In Jonson's time, English society valued the ability to improve on nature. Women wore fancy gowns, wigs, hats, and jewelry. Powder and paint (coloring) were applied heavily. In what sense is the speaker in this poem a rebel?

Thinking Creatively

10. Why do you think people describe being in love as heavenly? How does being in love with someone change the way you look at them?

Grammar Check

A pronoun takes the place of a noun. The noun to which a pronoun refers is its antecedent. Look at this sentence: *The English people loved Ben Jonson, because he wrote witty plays.* In this sentence, *Ben Jonson* is the antecedent of the pronoun *he.*

- Find four pronouns in "Still to Be Neat."

- Write each pronoun and its antecedent.

- Write sentences telling about the poem. Use the pronouns *she, he,* and *we.* Include the antecedent for each pronoun.

 Writing on Your Own

How would the poems be different if they were written in prose? Write a paragraph paraphrasing (putting in your own words) the ideas found in one of the poems.

 Speaking

Analyze the use of rhyme and rhythm in these poems. Prepare a lesson on these elements. Teach the lesson to classmates by explaining how Jonson used these tools. Try to involve students actively. For example, ask questions and have them read aloud or clap rhythms.

 Technology

Use the Internet to learn about current productions of Ben Jonson's plays, such as *Every Man in His Humour, The Silent Woman, Volpone,* or *The Alchemist.* (Enter *Ben Jonson's plays* or the names of the plays as keywords.) Summarize your findings and what you learn about Jonson's dramatic style. Print out pictures that show costuming or sets.

 Viewing

Search through this unit and in library books for illustrations that show how English women dressed in the early 1600s. Note how they wear their hair and whether they are made up. Then reread the poem. How does the art add to your understanding of the poem?

BEFORE READING THE SELECTION

To the Virgins, to Make Much of Time   by Robert Herrick

Robert Herrick
1591–1674

About the Author

Robert Herrick was born in 1591 in London. Soon after his birth, his father died. Herrick learned the trades of jeweler and goldsmith when he worked for an uncle. He later attended Cambridge University and in 1623 became an Anglican priest.

Herrick loved life in London. He was the most loyal of "Ben's Tribe," writers who followed Ben Jonson. Finally, in 1629, Herrick took a job as a minister in the county of Devonshire in southwest England. He was sad to leave London, but in time he came to love this beautiful countryside.

Civil war in England led to the overthrow of King Charles I and of Anglican rule. By 1647, Herrick was removed from his position. He returned to London and published his poems. He collected his secular (nonreligious) poems in one volume, *Hesperides,* and his religious poems in another, *Noble Numbers.*

Most of Herrick's poetry deals with light (rather than deep) subjects in a light-hearted way. He crafted poems that remind us of the arts he knew: jewelry and goldsmithing. Like gems set in gold, his poems are perfectly cut and balanced.

About the Selection

"To the Virgins, to Make Much of Time" was published in Herrick's 1648 book *Hesperides.* The poem is better known by its first line: "Gather ye rose-buds while ye may." Like much of his work, this poem speaks to ladies and is concerned with mortality, or death. It also expresses the Roman saying *carpe diem* (Latin for "seize the day"). This saying urges people to live in the moment.

Literary Terms Poems may use **symbols** to link an object to an idea. A symbol is a person, place, or object that stands for something beyond itself. By tying an idea, such as love, to an object, such as a rose, the poet makes it more vivid and attaches emotions to it. A poet may also set up ideas in a **sequence**, or order, that helps readers understand the theme. For example, this poem looks at cycles in terms of the time they use up. It moves from the passing of a day to the passing of a lifetime.

Reading on Your Own In this poem, Herrick uses several objects as symbols. As you read, think about what they might represent. To help you understand the poem, use your own experiences. For example, picture flowers as they bud, open, and wither. Imagine the path of the sun from sunrise to sunset. Think about how these cycles relate to our lives.

Writing on Your Own Write a description of a sunny day. Use nouns, verbs, and vivid adjectives and adverbs. Describe each part of the day as it passes. Include your feelings about the day and passing time.

Vocabulary Focus A word affects us in two ways. Usually, we are aware of its denotation, or definition. We may be less aware of its connotation, or the emotions it stirs up. For example, Herrick describes time as "a-flying." The word means "going quickly." It also suggests a bird to us. It makes time into something that darts away, something we can never catch. This word carries with it feelings of anxiety and loss about time's passing.

Think Before You Read What subject does the title of this poem suggest?

symbol something that represents something else

sequence the order of events in a literary work

To the Virgins, to Make Much of Time

As you read, picture the speaker and the young ladies to whom he speaks. Where are they? What are they doing?

Gather ye rose-buds while ye may,
    Old Time is still a-flying:
And this same flower that smiles today,
    Tomorrow will be dying.

5   The glorious Lamp of Heaven, the Sun,
        The higher he's a-getting
The sooner will his race be run,
        And nearer he's to setting.

How do flowers symbolize the passage of time in a human life?

That age is best which is the first,
10   When youth and blood are warmer:
But being spent, the worse, and worst
      Times, will **succeed** the former.

Notice the short lines and the rhyme pattern (abab). What effect do they have on the mood of the poem?

Then be not **coy,** but use your time;
    And while ye may, go marry:
15 For having lost but once your prime,
    You may for ever **tarry.**

Afternoon Tea,
Kate Greenaway, 1886

What is the sequence of this poem?

---

succeed come after   **coy** shy; timid   **tarry** delay, linger

AFTER READING THE SELECTION

To the Virgins, to Make Much of Time by Robert Herrick

Directions Choose the letter of the best answer or write the answer using complete sentences.

Comprehension: Identifying Facts

1. The virgins should gather rosebuds now because _____.

   A they need the fresh air

   B flowers add beauty to life

   C blossoms do not last long

   D a coming storm will destroy them

2. What happens to the sun when its race is run?

3. What does the poet urge the young ladies to do?

Comprehension: Putting Ideas Together

4. What tone, or attitude, do the poet's choices of words and details create?

   A serious   C sad

   B light-hearted D worried

5. Why does the poet talk about flowers and the sun?

6. What does it mean to be coy? Why should it be avoided, according to the poet?

Understanding Literature: Theme and Symbol

A writer's goal is to present and support a theme, or central idea, in writing. Poets have many tools to help convey a theme. The use of symbols, or objects that represent ideas or other things, is one of these tools.

7. What do the flowers and the sun symbolize in this poem?

8. What sequence of ideas appears in the poem? Why?

Critical Thinking

9. This poem is neoclassical. That is, it makes skillful use of balance, order, and harmony in the same way as the classical poems of ancient Rome and Greece. Point out examples of these qualities in the poem. Tell about a modern song or work of art you know that also has these qualities.

Thinking Creatively

10. What do you think makes this poem timeless? Why is it still enjoyed today?

After Reading continued on next page

To the Virgins, to Make Much of Time   *by Robert Herrick*

 ### Grammar Check

Adjectives have forms of comparison. Shorter adjectives add the endings *–er* and *–est* to show that a comparison is being made (*long, longer, longest*). Longer adjectives add *more* or *most* (*more beautiful, most beautiful*). The comparative form (*-er*) compares two things. The superlative form (*-est*) compares three or more things.

- Find five adjectives in the comparative form in the selection.

- Find two adjectives in the superlative form in the selection.

- Make a table and fill in the three forms for each adjective you listed. (For example, *high, higher, highest*.)

- Write sentences using all the forms of one of these adjectives to compare objects.

 ### Writing on Your Own

Write a paraphrase of this selection. To paraphrase means to restate what a text says, putting it your own words. Make your paraphrase prose rather than poetry.

 ### Speaking and Listening

How would a young lady today reply to the advice in this poem to marry while young? Prepare a short speech giving reasons why this may or may not be the best idea in modern society. Begin with a catchy introduction that states your main idea. Give your reasons in order of importance. When you are a listener, jot down the speaker's reasons. Star the ones you agree with.

 ### Media

How do today's media encourage people to "live for today"? Focus on one form of media: TV, movies, music, or magazines. Find examples of programs, ads, films, songs, and articles that persuade us to just do something now (buy, consume, love, and so on) rather than putting off doing what we want. Write an essay explaining the effect this form of media and its message have on society.

BEFORE READING THE SELECTION

To Lucasta, on Going to the Wars   *by Richard Lovelace*

About the Author

Richard Lovelace was born in 1618 into a wealthy family. His good looks and fine manners brought him attention when he attended Oxford University.

The 1640s were a violent, unstable period in England. Puritans and Anglicans were against each other in thought, word, and actions that led to civil war. The conflict was both religious and political. Lovelace supported King Charles I and served as a soldier in his army. The forces of Parliament (which the Puritans controlled) put him in prison twice. Lovelace lost his wealth and land because of his support for the defeated king. He died in poverty when he was just 39.

Lovelace belongs to a group known as the Cavalier poets. To be *cavalier* meant to be a gentleman of good breeding. The cavaliers paid courtly attention to women and showed heroic bravery in causes. The writing of Lovelace (and the other Cavalier poets) is witty, charming, and graceful. Most often, it deals with ideals of love, beauty, and honor. However, his poems also express a sad awareness of the passing of time.

Richard Lovelace
1618–1657

Objectives

- To read and understand a poem
- To define paradox and identify it in a poem

About the Selection

Lovelace wrote "To Lucasta, on Going to the Wars" while he was in prison in 1648. Its speaker is a gentleman soldier who addresses his lady as he leaves for war. Short lines and stanzas, strong rhythm and rhyme, and brief and snappy language mark the poem as Cavalier. It is meant to be songlike. Like many of Lovelace's poems, it may have been set to music. However, it does address a serious subject: the soldier's call to duty. This poem's ending lines give us one of the world's most famous quotes from poetry: "I could not love thee, Dear, so much,/Loved I not Honour more."

Before Reading **continued on next page**

To Lucasta, on Going to the Wars   *by Richard Lovelace*

paradox
a statement that includes opposite meanings but still makes sense

Literary Terms A **paradox** is a statement that contains parts that contradict, or oppose, each other. At the same time, the statement is true. For example, in another poem, Lovelace writes, "Stone walls do not a prison make,/Nor iron bars a cage." These are the things that do make a building a prison. But the poet is pointing out that his thoughts, love, and spirit are free, and this freedom is more important than physical freedom.

Reading on Your Own As you read this poem, pay attention to the words the speaker uses to describe his lady and war. They will allow you to make inferences, or educated guesses, about his attitudes toward love and duty. Also, think about the paradox that these words express. How is it false? How is it true?

Writing on Your Own Is being a soldier an honor? What attitude does our society have toward its military? What is a soldier called on to do? Why does the soldier do this? Answer these questions in a paragraph that explains your opinion of soldiers.

Vocabulary Focus When you come across a difficult word, break it into parts and look for parts you know. For example, in line 9 of the selection, find the word *inconstancy*. It begins with a prefix, *in-*, which means "not." It ends with a suffix, *-y*, which turns an adjective into a noun. Its middle contains the root *constans*, which is also used to form the word *constant*. *Constant* means "steady" or "faithful." Put these parts together. You can see that *inconstancy* means "the quality of being unfaithful."

Think Before You Read What do you think a soldier going to war would say to a husband, wife, or special friend? What do you expect this poem to say?

To Lucasta, on Going to the Wars

Tell me not, Sweet, I am unkind
    That from the **nunnery**
Of thy **chaste** breast and quiet mind,
    To war and arms I fly.

5   True, a new mistress now I chase,
    The first foe in the field;
And with a stronger faith embrace
    A sword, a horse, a shield.

Yet this **inconstancy** is such
10   As you too shall adore;
I could not love thee, Dear, so much,
    Loved I not Honour more.

As you read, think about the situation. To whom is the man speaking? Why? What has Lucasta probably just said to him?

What paradox is in the second stanza? How is this comparison opposite to what you expect? What is true about it?

THE
Exercise of the English, in the
Militia of the Kingdome of
ENGLAND.

A Cavalier (left) and a Roundhead, from the Time of King Charles I of England

nunnery convent; here, a metaphor for someplace pure and safe

chaste pure; virtuous

inconstancy unfaithfulness

AFTER READING THE SELECTION

To Lucasta, on Going to the Wars   by Richard Lovelace

Directions Choose the letter of the best answer or write the answer using complete sentences.

Comprehension: Identifying Facts

1. Who or what is the "new mistress" of line 5?
   A being a soldier
   B the church
   C a government position
   D another woman

2. What does the poet embrace "with a stronger faith"?

3. How does the poet believe Lucasta should feel about his leaving?

Comprehension: Putting Ideas Together

4. What words does the poet use to make us think of war in terms of love?
   A chaste, quiet
   B sword, shield
   C nunnery, faith
   D mistress, embrace

5. How does the speaker feel about Lucasta? What tells you this?

6. What do you think the final two lines of the poem mean?

Understanding Literature: Paradox

Is it possible for two opposites both to be true? Poets often use paradox to make readers think about this question. Classic examples speak of being cruel to be kind or of loving and hating the same person. Human experience teaches that these opposite emotions can still be true. This poem explores, among other paradoxes, the honor of unfaithfulness.

7. How is war unlike a mistress? In what sense is war like love?

8. Why is it a paradox for the speaker to compare the woman he loves to a nunnery?

Critical Thinking

9. What qualities of the speaker does his eagerness to go to war suggest?

Thinking Creatively

10. The speaker seems to say that love is only possible if one has honor. Do you think people feel this way today? Explain your opinion.

Grammar Check

Many verbs express physical action. Writers use vivid verbs to help readers visualize the action. The speaker in this poem *flies* to war. *Fly* is much more specific than *go*, and it suggests eagerness.

- List other action verbs in the selection.

- Beside each verb, write a phrase that suggests the feeling behind the action.

 Writing on Your Own

Write a column for a newspaper telling why fighting in a war is or is not honorable. Choose words and a style of writing that fit the audience you are trying to persuade. List your reasons and evidence in order of importance.

 Speaking and Listening

Find and prepare to present a poem or song that expresses an attitude about war. Practice saying or singing the poem clearly, with the feelings the writer intended. Write and present an introduction that gives some history about the piece. When you listen to others' presentations, note the feelings each poem or song stirs. Try to identify the words or ideas that cause these feelings. Are these feelings reasonable? Why or why not?

 Research

Use the Internet to research and learn about the reign of Charles I, the English Civil War of the 1640s, the Cavalier poets, or the Puritan influence on England. (Enter keywords such as *Charles I, Oliver Cromwell, Roundheads,* and *Cavalier poets*.) Take notes on the important ideas and facts you find about your subject. Organize them in outline form, with supporting details under main ideas.

To His Coy Mistress   by Andrew Marvell

Andrew Marvell
1621–1678

About the Author

Andrew Marvell was born in Yorkshire, in northern England, in 1621. His father was a Puritan minister. At Cambridge University, Marvell was well educated in Greek and Latin. This skill led him to become an assistant to John Milton. Milton held a high position in the Puritan government. His duty was to write important government papers in formal Latin. Both men were poets. Their closeness probably resulted in some similarities in their literary work. For example, both use similar themes in their poetry.

Marvell supported Oliver Cromwell, a Puritan, during the English Civil War of 1642–1649. In 1660, King Charles II was restored to the throne. The king threw Milton in prison and wanted to have him executed. Marvell, who had been elected to Parliament in 1659, worked behind the scenes to get Milton freed. Marvell continued to serve in Parliament until his death in 1678.

Through the early 1650s, Marvell wrote lyric poems. The tone of these poems is often witty and playful. The poems are rhythmic and graceful. However, Marvell's poems also set out important ideas and make readers look at experiences from new and surprising points of view. In later life, Marvell wrote prose against the royal court.

About the Selection

Marvell wrote "To His Coy Mistress" around 1650. Like Robert Herrick's "To the Virgins, to Make Much of Time," this poem uses the *carpe diem* theme. The poet points out that life is short and urges his mistress to make the most of life and love.

Literary Terms This selection contains several examples of **hyperbole.** Hyperbole involves a whopping exaggeration, which helps the author make a point.

Reading on Your Own In this poem, the poet is trying to persuade his mistress to enjoy their love today—not put it off. Like any good persuasive speaker, he presents facts and opinions to convince her. Facts can be proved. Opinions are personal beliefs and cannot be proved. When you read broad statements in the poem, think about whether they are facts or opinions. Make a note of which statements you found most convincing and why.

Writing on Your Own This poet compares time to a "wingèd chariot." What is time like to you? Write a creative description about the nature of time. Use images and figures of speech to make your description vivid.

Vocabulary Focus Writers sometimes use allusions in their work. An allusion refers to an event, person, or place that is important to the readers' culture. It may refer to history, religion, or even another famous work of literature. Marvell refers to the Ganges River in India (line 5). India was important to British trade but very hard to reach. The Ganges would seem colorful and glamorous to Marvell's readers. The Humber (line 7), a slow-moving river in England, would seem dull by comparison. In line 8, "the Flood" refers to the great Flood in the Bible, which destroyed all life except Noah, his family, and a boatful of animals.

Think Before You Read What does the word *coy* mean as it is used in the title? What does the title suggest will be the speaker's tone?

To His Coy Mistress

As you read, notice where the speaker uses hyperbole to make his point. What sort of reaction does he hope this brings from his mistress?

Had we but world enough, and time,
This **coyness,** Lady, were no crime
We would sit down and think which way
To walk and pass our long love's day.
5 Thou by the Indian Ganges' side
Shouldst rubies find: I by the tide
Of Humber would complain. I would
Love you ten years before the Flood,
And you should, if you please, refuse
10 Till the **conversion** of the Jews.
My **vegetable** love should grow
Vaster than empires, and more slow;
An hundred years should go to praise
Thine eyes and on thy forehead gaze;
15 Two hundred to adore each breast,
But thirty thousand to the rest;
An age at least to every part,
And the last age should show your heart.
For, Lady, you deserve this state,
20 Nor would I love at lower rate.

The poet (and his readers) knew that the event in line 10 was not likely to happen.

coyness timidity; shyness

conversion a change from one religion to another

vegetable slow-moving, not appearing to respond

But at my back I always hear
Time's wingèd chariot hurrying near;
And yonder all before us lie
Deserts of vast eternity.
25 Thy beauty shall no more be found,
Nor, in thy marble vault, shall sound
My echoing song: then worms shall try
That long preserved virginity,
And your quaint honour turn to dust,
30 And into ashes all my lust:
The grave's a fine and private place,
But none, I think, do there embrace.

     Now therefore, while the youthful hue
Sits on thy skin like morning dew,
35 And while thy willing soul **transpires**
At every pore with instant fires,
Now let us sport us while we may,
And now, like **amorous** birds of prey,
Rather at once our time devour
40 Than languish in his **slow-chapt** power
Let us roll all our strength and all
Our sweetness up into one ball,
And tear our pleasures with rough strife
Thorough the iron gates of life:
45 Thus, though we cannot make our sun
Stand still, yet we will make him run.

After death, the poet says, time will be like a desert—vast, empty, and lifeless.

The *marble vault* (line 26) refers to the tomb of an important person. Though the poet's lover's tomb may be impressive, love will no longer exist once the lover is in it.

---

transpires lives in the body   **amorous** passionate   **slow-chapt** slow jawed, slowly devouring

AFTER READING THE SELECTION

To His Coy Mistress   by Andrew Marvell

Directions Choose the letter of the best answer or write the answer using complete sentences.

Comprehension: Identifying Facts

1. The speaker says that, if time were not important, he would praise his mistress's eyes for _____.
   A eternity
   B 30,000 years
   C 100 years
   D 200 years

2. What will turn to dust and ashes?

3. Who or what is compared to "amorous birds of prey" in line 38?

Comprehension: Putting Ideas Together

4. Which image creates a feeling of slow leisure?
   A walking slowly beside rivers
   B seeing birds of prey
   C finding rubies
   D smelling dust and ashes

5. How do the images in the second half of the poem contrast with those in the first half?

6. What actions does the poet include in the final lines? How do these compare with his mistress's coyness?

Understanding Literature: Hyperbole

Writers are most likely to use hyperbole when they want to get readers' attention and make a point. Hyperbole is an overstatement. It can point out that an idea or attitude is silly.

7. What examples of hyperbole are used in the first half of this poem?

8. What effect do these exaggerations have?

Critical Thinking

9. How do you think this writing would be different it the author had written it as a letter? Would it have been more effective or less effective? Why?

Thinking Creatively

10. What makes this poem about time timeless? Why do you think people find it just as powerful today as they did 300 years ago?

Grammar Check

A prepositional phrase begins with a preposition such as *at, before, by, in, into, like, of, on, to,* or *with*. It ends with a noun or pronoun called the object of the preposition. Prepositional phrases show the relationship of the object to another word in the sentence. They act like adjectives or adverbs. For example, the prepositional phrase *by the Indian Ganges' side* acts as an adverb telling where the mistress would find rubies.

- Find five more examples of prepositional phrases in the poem.

- Write the prepositional phrases. Underline the preposition and circle its object.

- Write the word each phrase describes or tells more about. Write *adjective* if the phrase describes a noun or pronoun. Write *adverb* if it describes a verb.

 Writing on Your Own

Write a short biography about a famous person who died young. Find facts in an encyclopedia or history book. Include only the most important events and accomplishments. Point out what the person achieved in a short time.

 Speaking

Tell a brief anecdote about something that happened to you. (An anecdote is a short, funny story.) Focus on how the event shows the passing of time. Brainstorm details that made the event vivid for you. Use details that involve the five senses and show your feelings. Practice delivering your talk. Then tell your anecdote to the class.

 Media

Listen to a song about time and the changes it brings. What is the theme of the song? What details in the song support this idea? Write down your answers to these questions.

 Viewing

Look for artworks or photographs that show the effects of time's passing. For example, find ancient palaces and temples that have been worn to ruins. Write a journal entry telling how one of these images affected you.

BEFORE READING THE SELECTION

from *Paradise Lost* by John Milton

John Milton
1608–1674

About the Author

John Milton was born in 1608 in London. As a boy at Saint Paul's School, he showed a great talent for mastering ancient languages. He was an outstanding student at Cambridge University. After graduating, Milton devoted more years to reading and study. The poetry he wrote showed his mastery of language. Milton had been getting himself ready for great things.

Milton was devoted to the Puritan faith. He believed each person must be free to develop his or her own relationship to God by studying the Bible. During the English Civil War, Milton wrote pamphlets attacking the Anglican Church. Its many ceremonies and leaders, he felt, separated the individual from God. By 1652, Milton had become blind.

In 1660, Charles II was restored to the throne, and Milton was arrested and fined. Milton then retired and began to work on his masterpieces. The greatest of these is the epic poem *Paradise Lost*. In this long, heroic poem he brings together his learning and his remarkable talent for language. Milton completed the epic in 1667.

About the Selection

Paradise Lost looks at the biblical story of the Fall of Adam and Eve and what it means to people. The small section here focuses on Satan, who has been cast out of heaven for warring against God. In the opening lines of his epic, Milton says that his goal is no less than to "justify the ways of God" to people. The rich, powerful language he uses is just as grand as this goal. Many consider *Paradise Lost* the greatest long poem in English.

Literary Terms This epic poem, like a story, develops **characters** through **characterization.** Writers give a character certain looks, actions, and words to reveal personality and traits. The story's central **conflict,** or struggle, pits an **antagonist** against a protagonist. The antagonist is the enemy of the hero. Milton's epic also uses poetic sound effects such as **assonance.** Assonance is the repetition of vowel sounds.

Reading on Your Own This excerpt from *Paradise Lost* focuses on Satan. He and his troops have been cast out of heaven for rebelling against God. Details in his speech and action give clues about this character. Look for these details as you read. What can you tell about Satan's character from his actions and words?

Writing on Your Own Pretend you are making a movie of *Paradise Lost*. Write a description of hell for the director. Include details that appeal to the senses. Explain how to achieve the desired effects and appearance.

Vocabulary Focus Looking up the history of a new word can help you learn its meaning. For example, look at the word *perdition* in line 21. Find the history of *perdition* in the dictionary. It is given in brackets [ ] after the part of speech. This word came to us from the Latin word *perdere*, which means "to destroy." *Perdition* refers to hell or eternal damnation. Look up the histories of selection words such as *omnipotent, transgress, infernal, transcendent,* and *empyreal* to help you learn them.

Think Before You Read What do you think the character Satan will be like?

character
a person or animal in a story, poem, or play

characterization
the way a writer develops character qualities and personality traits

conflict the struggle of the main character against himself or herself, another person, or nature

antagonist
a person or thing in the story struggling against the main character

assonance
repeating sounds by using words with the same vowel sounds

from Paradise LOST

The *one restraint* in line 6 was the rule that Adam and Eve must not eat the fruit of a certain tree.

The Bible shows Satan as a *serpent,* or snake.

As you read, look for clues to the conflict, or struggle, in which Satan is involved. What has happened? Why? How does Satan react to this event?

Say first, for Heav'n hides nothing from thy view
Nor the deep tract of Hell, say first what cause
Moved our **grand** parents in that happy state,
Favoured of Heav'n so highly, to fall off
5   From their Creator and transgress his will
For one restraint, lords of the world besides?
Who first seduced them to that foul revolt?
Th' infernal Serpent; he it was, whose **guile**
Stirred up with envy and revenge, deceived
10   The mother of mankind, what time his pride
Had cast him out from Heav'n, with all his host
Of rebel angels, by whose aid aspiring
To set himself in glory above his peers,
He trusted to have equalled the Most High,
15   If he opposed; and with ambitious aim
Against the throne and monarchy of God
Raised **impious** war in Heav'n and battle proud
With vain attempt. Him the Almighty Power
Hurled headlong flaming from th' **ethereal** sky
20   With hideous ruin and combustion down
To bottomless **perdition,** there to dwell
In **adamantine** chains and **penal** fire,
Who durst defy th' Omnipotent to arms.

---

grand first

guile trickiness

impious unholy

ethereal heavenly

perdition eternal hell

adamantine unbreakable

penal relating to punishment

Nine times the space that measures day and night
25 To mortal men, he with his horrid crew
Lay vanquished, rolling in the fiery gulf
Confounded though immortal: but his doom
Reserved him to more wrath; for now the thought
Both of lost happiness and lasting pain
30 Torments him; round he throws his **baleful** eyes
That witnessed huge **affliction** and dismay
Mixed with **obdúrate** pride and steadfast hate:
At once as far as angels' **ken** he views
The dismal situation waste and wild,
35 A dungeon horrible, on all sides round
As one great furnace flamed, yet from those flames
No light, but rather darkness visible
Served only to discover sights of woe,
Regions of sorrow, **doleful** shades, where peace
40 And rest can never dwell, hope never comes
That comes to all; but torture without end
Still urges, and a fiery deluge, fed
With ever-burning sulphur unconsumed:
Such place Eternal Justice had prepared
45 For those rebellious, here their prison ordained
In utter darkness, and their portion set
As far removed from God and light of Heav'n
As from the centre thrice to th' utmost pole.
O how unlike the place from whence they fell!
50 There the companions of his fall, o'erwhelmed
With floods and whirlwinds of **tempestuous** fire,
He soon discerns, and welt'ring by his side
One next himself in power, and next in crime,
Long after known in Palestine, and named
55 Beëlzebub. To whom th' Arch-Enemy,
And thence in Heav'n called Satan, with bold words
Breaking the horrid silence thus began.

As bad as hell is,
Satan is even more
tormented by his
thoughts: Heaven
is lost forever to
him, and he will
suffer this way for
all time.

Satan and his rebel
army have been
cast three times
(*thrice*) farther than
the distance from
the earth to the
farthest point in
the universe. The
earth was believed
to be at the center
of the universe.

Beëlzebub (line
55) is the name
of the angel next
in command to
Satan in this poem.
Often, Beëlzebub
is used as another
name for Satan.

confounded frustrated	**affliction** suffering	**doleful** miserable
baleful evil	**obdurate** stubborn	**tempestuous** stormy
	ken sight	

Lines 58–98 are one long monologue by Satan to Beëlzebub. What do Satan's words tell you about him? Why do you think Milton chose this method of characterization?

The *potent Victor* is God, who is the great protagonist of Milton's epic. Though Satan is the main character of this selection, he is the antagonist of the story.

If thou beest he; but O how fall'n! how changed
From him, who in the happy realms of light
60 Clothed with **transcendent** brightness didst outshine
Myriads though bright: if he whom **mutual league,**
United thoughts and counsels, equal hope
And hazard in the glorious enterprise,
Joined with me once, now misery hath joined
65 In equal ruin: into what pit thou seest
From what heighth fall'n, so much the stronger proved
He with his thunder: and till then who knew
The force of those **dire** arms? yet not for those,
Nor what the **potent** Victor in his rage
70 Can else inflict, do I repent or change,
Though changed in outward lustre, that fixed mind

Paradise Lost,
wood engraving,
Gustave Doré

transcendent magnificent	**mutual league** partnership	**potent** powerful
myriads a great number	**dire** horrible	

And high disdain, from sense of injured merit,
That with the mightiest raised me to contend,
And to the fierce **contention** brought along
75   Innumerable force of Spirits armed
That **durst** dislike his reign, and me preferring,
His utmost power with adverse power opposed
In dubious battle on the plains of Heav'n,
And shook his throne. What though the field be lost?
80   All is not lost; the unconquerable will,
And study of revenge, immortal hate,
And courage never to submit or yield:
And what is else not to be overcome?
That glory never shall his wrath or might
85   Extort from me. To bow and sue for grace
With **suppliant** knee, and **deify** his power
Who from the terror of this arm so late
Doubted his empire, that were low indeed,
That were an **ignominy** and shame beneath
90   This downfall; since by Fate the strength of gods
And this empyreal substance cannot fail,
Since through experience of this great event
In arms not worse, in foresight much advanced,
We may with more successful hope resolve
95   To wage by force or guile eternal war
Irreconcilable, to our grand Foe,
Who now triúmphs, and in th' excess of joy
Sole reigning holds the tyranny of Heav'n.
     So spake th' **apostate** angel, though in pain,
100 **Vaunting** aloud, but racked with deep despair:
And him thus answered soon his bold compeer.

Read aloud portions of Satan's monologue. Listen for the various sound devices Milton uses. These include assonance (the repetition of vowel sounds within words) and alliteration (the repetition of consonant sounds at the beginning of words). How do these devices add to the effect of the poetry?

Empyreal means something comes from heaven. Heaven (called the empyrean) and those who lived there were believed to be made of a substance that could not be destroyed. Satan and his troops will never die.

contention rivalry; competition

durst dared

suppliant humbly begging

deify worship

ignominy deep disgrace

apostate abandoning a previous loyalty

vaunting bragging

AFTER READING THE SELECTION

from *Paradise Lost*   by John Milton

Directions Choose the letter of the best answer or write the answer using complete sentences.

Comprehension: Identifying Facts

1. Satan and the angels who joined him in rebelling find themselves surrounded by _____.
   A a raging battle
   B terrifying monsters
   C chains and fire
   D a dungeon

2. To whom does Satan speak?

3. Why will Satan not beg for God's forgiveness?

Comprehension: Putting Ideas Together

4. Satan and Beëlzebub have changed from what they were like in heaven. They have lost _____.
   A luster, or brightness
   B the ability to see
   C strength
   D size (have become smaller)

5. What details does Milton include that show Satan is proud?

6. What caused Satan to seek revenge by tempting Eve?

Understanding Literature: Character, Conflict, and Assonance

At the heart of every story, including epic poems, are the elements of character and conflict. A story is moved forward as the writer reveals the protagonist and antagonist and develops the conflict, or struggle, between them. Milton, like other poets, uses sound devices such as assonance to create interest and tie the poem together.

7. What characters have been introduced? Which one is the antagonist? What conflicts do you learn about?

8. Analyze lines 85–90. What words with long *a,* long *e,* and /ou/ sounds repeat there? What effect does this assonance have?

Critical Thinking

9. Why do you think Satan says, "All is not lost" (line 80)? What might he be planning to do?

Thinking Creatively

10. What do you think about the idea of good and evil? Do they exist in the world? Explain.

Grammar Check

Proper nouns name important persons, places, things, or ideas. They are capitalized. For example, capitalize religious terms such as the names of deities *(God, Satan)* and religious places or events *(the Second Coming)*.

- Find and list proper nouns in this excerpt.

- Group them into columns with these headings: *References to God, References to Satan, Places.*

- Write five sentences telling about religious places or art you have seen or read about. Capitalize all proper nouns.

 ## Writing on Your Own

Later in Book 1 of *Paradise Lost*, Satan says, "The mind is its own place, and in itself/Can make a Heaven of Hell, a Hell of Heaven." Do you think hell is a state of mind or a place? Write a paragraph giving your reasons for your opinion.

 ## Speaking and Listening

Many of Milton's sentences order words in unusual ways to focus on certain words. Practice reading aloud the sentences in lines 18–23 and 50–55. Rewrite each sentence in your own words to give its meaning in modern English. With a partner, read aloud your sentences and the original sentences from the poem. When it is your turn to listen, compare the effect of each version. Which is grander? Which is more dramatic?

 ## Technology

Gather writings, songs, and copies of artworks that deal with the themes of Adam and Eve or the battle between Satan and God. Use a computer to create a slide show and a recording of music and texts. Match spoken words to visual images. Play your multimedia presentation for classmates.

 ## Viewing

Look at the artwork used to illustrate this selection. Write a description of it. How does it add to your understanding of the characters and the conflict described in the poem?

from *Eve's Apology in Defense of Women* by Amelia Lanier

Eve, Lucien
Levy-Dhurmer

Objectives

- To read and understand a poem
- To identify the theme of a poem
- To understand and explain the point of view of a poem's speaker

About the Author

Amelia Lanier was born in 1569. She was the daughter of an Englishwoman and an Italian musician who played for Queen Elizabeth I. She grew up among the children of nobles at court and was educated with them. The little that is known of her life shows that she was quite independent for a woman of her time.

In 1592, she married Alphonso Lanier, who was also one of the queen's musicians. Although they had two children, only her son Henry lived to adulthood. After her husband died in 1613, Lanier supported herself for a time by running a school. Henry died in 1633, and Lanier helped provide for her grandchildren.

In the 1600s, society frowned on a woman writing or publishing. Nonetheless, in 1611 Lanier published *Salve Deus Rex Judaeorum* ("Hail, God, King of the Jews") under her own name. She dedicated the book to women and addressed them in it. She argued for religious and social equality for women centuries before the women's rights movement in the United States.

About the Selection

The selection that follows comes from *Salve Deus Rex Judaeorum. Eve's Apology in Defense of Women* is traditional in its form. It uses iambic pentameter and the rhyme pattern *ababab cc*. However, its theme, subject, and point of view were new for its time. Lanier argues that Adam, not Eve, was to blame for the Fall. Lanier also argues that men, not women, were responsible for killing Jesus. Her arguments lead to the idea that it is not right for men to treat women poorly. The poem explores bold ideas about the rights of women centuries before society addressed them seriously.

Literary Terms "Eve's Apology in Defense of Women" has a feminist theme and **point of view**. The theme of a literary work is its main idea. It may be stated or just suggested by the details. The point of view of a work is the position from which it is told. This work is from a female point of view on issues such as women's rights and who was to blame for the first disobedience to God.

Reading on Your Own The poem is spoken by the wife of Pontius Pilate, the Roman official who allowed Jesus to be killed. She begs her husband to spare Jesus's life. The poem makes several points about why blaming Eve (and all women) for the things humans do is wrong. As you read, think about the author's purpose carefully. What does she hope to gain by writing the poem?

Writing on Your Own The biblical book of Genesis tells the story of Adam and Eve. Review this story and summarize it in your own words. Place events in the order in which they happened. Explain the cost of Adam and Eve's actions for human beings.

Vocabulary Focus Authors may use figurative language to make a point. Used in this way, words do not make sense at the literal level. Instead, think of the comparison they make, or the idea they express. For example, in line 6, the speaker says, "Do not in innocent blood imbrue thy hands." Pilate's hands will not be bloody; he will not kill Jesus directly. However, his failure to free Jesus will stain Pilate with guilt. This comparison creates a vivid picture that helps us understand what is at stake. Find other figures of speech in the poem. Think about what meaning and feeling they add.

Think Before You Read Predict the tone and message this poem will have.

from Eve's Apology in Defense of Women

As you read, notice the speaker's point of view. Who is she? Why does she beg her husband? What are her emotions? What does she hope to gain?

Now Pontius Pilate is to judge the cause
Of faultless Jesus, who before him stands,
Who neither hath offended prince, nor laws,
Although he now be brought in woeful bands.
5   O noble governor, make thou yet a pause,
Do not in innocent blood **imbrue** thy hands;
     But hear the words of thy most worthy wife,
     Who sends to thee, to beg her Saviour's life.

Let **barb'rous** cruelty far depart from thee,
10   And in true justice take **affliction's** part;
Open thine eyes, that thou the truth may'st see.
Do not the thing that goes against thy heart,
Condemn not him that must thy Saviour be;
But view his holy life, his good desert.
15   Let not us women glory in men's fall,
     Who had power given to overrule us all.

The Bible tells that Pilate refused to have anything to do with the case brought against Jesus. By doing so, he felt he would have no guilt or blame in the torture and death of an innocent man.

Till now your **indiscretion** sets us free,
And makes our former fault much less appear;
Our mother Eve, who tasted of the tree,
20 Giving to Adam what she held most dear,
Was simply good, and had no power to see;
The after-coming harm did not appear:
     The subtle serpent that our sex betrayed
     Before our fall so sure a plot had laid.

---

imbrue soak

barb'rous (barbarous) extremely cruel, brutal

affliction's belonging to the weak or troubled

indiscretion wrongdoing

25 That **undiscerning** ignorance perceived
No guile or craft that was by him intended;
For had she known of what we were **bereaved,**
To his request she had not **condescended.**
But she, poor soul, by cunning was deceived;
30 No hurt therein her harmless heart intended:
    For she **alleged** God's word, which he denies,
    That they should die, but even as gods be wise.

But surely Adam cannot be excused;
Her fault though great, yet he was most to blame;
35 What weakness offered, strength might have refused,
Being lord of all, the greater was his shame.
Although the serpent's craft had her abused,
God's holy word ought all his actions frame,
    For he was lord and king of all the earth,
40   Before poor Eve had either life or breath,

Who being framed by God's eternal hand
The perfectest man that ever breathed on earth;
And from God's mouth received that **strait** command,
The **breach** whereof he knew was present death;
45 Yea, having power to rule both sea and land,
Yet with one apple won to lose that breath
    Which God had breathed in his beauteous face,
    Bringing us all in danger and disgrace.

And then to lay the fault on Patience' back,
50 That we (poor women) must endure it all.
We know right well he did discretion lack,
Being not persuaded thereunto at all.
If Eve did err, it was for knowledge sake;
The fruit being fair persuaded him to fall:
55   No subtle serpent's falsehood did betray him;
    If he would eat it, who had power to **stay** him?

In the 1600s, English society believed that women had less ability to think than men. Lanier uses this idea to her advantage in disproving the argument that women are to blame for the Fall.

Lanier uses sarcasm in lines 41 and 42. Does she really believe Adam was *the perfectest man that ever breathed on earth?*

undiscerning with no insight or understanding	**condescended** lowered	**strait** strict
bereaved deprived, robbed	**alleged** brought forward as an authority	**breach** violation, breaking
		stay stop

What new argument does Lanier begin at line 57?

Not Eve, whose fault was only too much love,
Which made her give this present to her dear,
That what she tasted he likewise might prove,
60 Whereby his knowledge might become more clear;
He never sought her weakness to **reprove**
With those sharp words which he of God did hear;
      Yet men will boast of knowledge, which he took
      From Eve's fair hand, as from a learned book.

Lanier points out an irony in lines 63 and 64: Men are proud of their intellect (knowledge) but blame women (Eve) for giving them the fruit that gave them this knowledge.

65 If any evil did in her remain,
Being made of him, he was the ground of all.
If one of many worlds could lay a stain
Upon our sex, and work so great a fall
To wretched man by Satan's subtle train,
70 What will so foul a fault amongst you all?
      Her weakness did the serpent's words obey,
      But you in **malice** God's dear Son betray,

Whom, if unjustly you condemn to die,
Her sin was small to what you do commit;
75 All mortal sins that do for **vengeance** cry
Are not to be compared unto it.
If many worlds would altogether try
By all their sins the wrath of God to get,
      This sin of yours **surmounts** them all as far
80   As doth the sun another little star.

Pilate shows he is corrupt by failing to save Jesus. He also will be condemned for his failing.

Then let us have our liberty again,
And challenge to yourselves no **sovereignty**.
You came not in the world without our pain,
Make that a bar against your cruelty;
85 Your fault being greater, why should you disdain
Our being your equals, free from **tyranny**?
      If one weak woman simply did offend,
      This sin of yours hath no excuse nor end,

reprove scold	**vengeance** punishment in return for a wrong; revenge	**sovereignty** supreme power; control
malice wish to hurt or cause suffering		**tyranny** oppression; cruelty
	surmounts passes	

170 *Unit 2 The English Renaissance*

To which, poor souls, we never gave consent.
90 Witness, thy wife, O Pilate, speaks for all,
Who did but dream, and yet a message sent
That thou shouldest have nothing to do at all
With that just man; which, if thy heart relent,
Why wilt thou be a **reprobate** with Saul
95   To seek the death of him that is so good,
For thy soul's health to shed his dearest blood?

Saul was the first king of Israel. David, a war hero and the best friend of Saul's son, lived in Saul's house as a court musician. In jealousy of David's accomplishments, Saul repeatedly tried to kill David.

Adam and Eve Cast Out of the Garden of Eden,
Robert Leinweber, Bible illustration

reprobate a corrupt
person

from *Eve's Apology in Defense of Women*   by Amelia Lanier

Directions Choose the letter of the best answer or write the answer using complete sentences.

Comprehension: Identifying Facts

1. The indiscretion the speaker mentions in line 17 is _____.
   A sentencing Jesus to death
   B eating the forbidden fruit
   C Pontius Pilate's lies about Jesus
   D the serpent's temptation of Eve

2. Whom does line 56 refer to? What does the line mean?

3. What does the speaker mean in lines 85–86?

Comprehension: Putting Ideas Together

4. What two things does Pilate's wife ask him to do?
   A to convert to Christianity and to study the Bible
   B to save Jesus and to recognize that women are equal to men
   C to condemn Jesus and to blame Adam for the Fall
   D to share power with her and to argue about sin

5. How does the speaker compare Eve's sin with that of Pontius Pilate? Which is the worse betrayal?

6. List three arguments Lanier makes in defense of Eve.

Understanding Literature: Theme and Point of View

The theme of a literary work is its main idea or the important truth the writer wants to express. Sometimes, the theme is stated, but most times the reader must use details in the text to figure it out.

Every piece of literature has a point of view. This has to do with who is telling the story and what attitude that person brings to the text.

7. What are two themes of this selection? Which lines in the poem best summarize these themes?

8. How would you describe the speaker's point of view? What is her attitude toward Pontius Pilate? toward men in general?

Critical Thinking

9. Do you think Lanier has achieved her purpose in this poem? Explain your opinion.

Thinking Creatively

10. How do you think readers reacted to this poem in the 1600s? How would people react differently today? Why?

Grammar Check

Verbs have different forms, or tenses, to show time. Present tense expresses present or ongoing action: *taste(s)*. Future tense expresses action in the future: *will taste*. Past tense expresses action that was completed: *tasted*.

Perfect tenses express an action completed before another past, present, or future action: *has tasted, had tasted, will have tasted*.

- Find examples of each tense in the selection.

- Write the verbs and label them with the proper tense.

- Identify stanzas that use different tenses. Explain why the verb tense changes in this selection.

 Writing on Your Own

Lanier argues that men should consider women their equals. She feels that men are morally no better—and in some ways are far worse—than women. Write a speech to persuade classmates that women and men are equals. List your arguments in order from least to most important. For each reason, provide evidence.

 Speaking and Listening

Deliver the speech you wrote for "Writing on Your Own." Practice it until you can deliver your ideas smoothly. Emphasize words that you feel will persuade listeners. When it is your turn to listen, jot down ideas that you strongly agree or disagree with. Give your reason for agreeing or disagreeing.

 Viewing

Look at a number of TV, magazine, and newspaper advertisements that picture women. What images do these ads project? What attitudes toward women do they suggest? Think about how these attitudes differ from the point of view in Lanier's poem.

 Research

Research ways the rights of women have changed over time. Trace the events that gave women the right to own property, to vote, to hold office, and to receive equal pay for equal work. Use your notes to create a time line.

A sonnet is a 14-line poem written in iambic pentameter. Every line contains 10 syllables and five beats. The beat falls on the even-numbered syllables. Here is an example line from Edmund Spenser's "Sonnet 75":

> One day I wrote her name upon the strand

A sonnet also has a set rhyme scheme, or pattern of repeated sounds at the ends of lines. English sonnets usually have the pattern *abab cdcd efef gg*. This means every other line in lines 1–12 has an end rhyme. Lines 13–14 place rhyming words side by side. In Shakespeare's "Sonnet 130" (page 109), the rhyming words are *sun/red/dun/head, white/cheeks/delight/reeks, know/sound/go/ground*, and *rare/compare*.

Sonnets are a kind of lyric poem. They usually express the love of the poet for a beautiful woman. The poet uses metaphors, or comparisons, to tell about her beauty and charms. For example, her eyes might be described as stars and her cheeks as roses.

In "Sonnet 130," Shakespeare uses metaphors to mock this tradition.

> My mistress' eyes are nothing like the sun;
> Coral is far more red than her lips' red

These lines refer to comparisons many sonnets make: eyes like the sun and lips like coral. Throughout the poem, Shakespeare mentions other unrealistic comparisons. He ends by saying that his love is "as rare/As any she belied with false compare."

Review

1. What is a sonnet?

2. What syllables and words would be accented in this line from a sonnet:

   > I grant I never saw a goddess go

3. Lines 1 and 2 from "Sonnet 130" appear at the bottom of the column at the left of this page. Which word will the final word in line 3 rhyme with?

4. What sorts of comparisons did sonnets usually make? What was their typical subject?

5. In "Sonnet 130," why do you think Shakespeare makes a point of saying his love is not like heavenly objects?

Writing on Your Own

Write the opening lines of your own sonnet, using the rhyme scheme *abab*. Include comparisons and write each line in iambic pentameter.

Unit 2 covers the period from 1485 to 1660. England's rise as a world power, the birth of new types of literature, and serious political and religious conflicts occurred during this era.

Four literary styles were popular during the English Renaissance. Elizabethan literature in this unit includes the works of Elizabeth I, Philip Sidney, Edmund Spenser, Francis Bacon, and William Shakespeare. Cavalier literature in this unit is by Ben Jonson, Robert Herrick, and Richard Lovelace. Metaphysical poets include John Donne and Andrew Marvell. John Milton and Amelia Lanier wrote works from a Puritan point of view.

Selections

- "Sonnet 31" by Philip Sidney tells of a love that is not returned.

- "On Monsieur's Departure" by Elizabeth I is a poem revealing conflicts between duty and desire.

- "Sonnet 75" by Edmund Spenser tells how words give immortality.

- "Of Studies" by Francis Bacon is an essay about the usefulness and effects of serious study.

- "The Passionate Shepherd to His Love" by Christopher Marlowe and "The Nymph's Reply to the Shepherd" by Walter Raleigh are pastoral poems with opposing views of life and love.

- "Sonnet 116" and "Sonnet 130" by William Shakespeare look at the nature of love and beauty. A scene from *Hamlet* shows a man's conflict as he tries to avenge his father's murder.

- "Psalm 23" from the King James Bible is a hymn of praise to God.

- "Valediction, Forbidding Mourning" by John Donne is a poem addressed to his wife as he leaves on a journey.

- "Still to Be Neat" and "To Celia" are poems that were set as songs in Ben Jonson's plays.

- "To the Virgins, to Make Much of Time" by Robert Herrick is a poem urging women to live in the moment.

- "To Lucasta, on Going to the Wars" by Richard Lovelace is a poem about a soldier's duty and love.

- "To His Coy Mistress" by Andrew Marvell is a love poem about making the most of life.

- *Paradise Lost* by John Milton is an epic poem about the downfall of Adam and Eve.

- *Eve's Apology in Defense of Women* by Amelia Lanier is a poem that argues against men's cruelty and injustice.

Directions Choose the letter of the best answer or write the answer using complete sentences.

Comprehension: Identifying Facts

1. Which selection is from an epic poem about Adam and Eve?
   A "Psalm 23"   C "To Celia"
   B *Paradise Lost* D "Sonnet 130"

2. How did the Elizabethan Era get its name?

3. What was England like from 1603 to 1649?

4. Who won the English Civil War?

5. Which authors in this unit represent the Metaphysical poets?

Comprehension: Putting Ideas Together

6. How is the selection "Of Studies" by Francis Bacon a contrast to other selections in the unit?
   A It imitates Latin.
   B It is a short story.
   C It is an essay.
   D It is not English.

7. List some ways the poetry of Ben Jonson, Robert Herrick, and Richard Lovelace are similar.

8. What makes Shakespeare's sonnets different from those of Sidney and Spenser?

9. What do *Paradise Lost* and *Eve's Apology in Defense of Women* have in common?

10. Name three common themes of the selections in this unit.

Understanding Literature: Sonnets, Pastorals, and Drama

Sonnets and pastorals were a popular form of poetry during the Elizabethan Era. Sonnets praised the beauty of a woman. Pastorals spoke positively about the life of shepherds. Drama became the most popular form of public entertainment. Many plays were patterned on classical drama, which told of events in the lives of powerful people, as plays of ancient Greece and Rome did.

11. Identify qualities the sonnets in this unit share.

12. Which poems in the unit are pastorals? Why are they presented together? Which poem is the more typical pastoral?

13. Give reasons *Hamlet* is a classical drama. What is one message it seems to give?

14. Which selection in the unit gives the clearest picture of life during this era? Give reasons for your choice.

15. What values does the literature of this period express?

Critical Thinking

16. Only two women, Queen Elizabeth I and Amelia Lanier, are represented in this unit. In what way are they unlike most women of that time?

17. Did you enjoy the literature of the English Renaissance in this unit? Why or why not?

18. Which author from this unit did you like most? Why?

19. Why do you think most of the selections in this unit are poetry?

Thinking Creatively

20. Today's literature and entertainment are very different from those enjoyed in 1600 in England. Do you think differences in society then and now cause these differences? Explain your thinking.

Speak and Listen

Select several poems, Bacon's essay, or part of one of the longer works in the unit. Reread the work and think about its structure and theme. Write a paragraph explaining how this work represents the English Renaissance. Practice reading the work and your paragraph aloud. Pay close attention to phrasing, expression, and rhythm. When you can read aloud smoothly, give your presentation to your class. Listen to others' presentations. Jot down what you like best about each one.

Writing on Your Own

Write an essay about the benefits of study. Name each way you think study helps a person. Give examples as evidence. Organize your writing into an introduction, body, and conclusion.

Beyond Words

Think about the selections in this unit. Make a list of symbols that would be fitting to represent the English Renaissance. Design and draw a poster that combines several of these symbols.

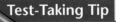

Test-Taking Tip

Before you begin a test, look at all the parts quickly. Decide how much time to give each section. Notice questions that will be easiest to answer. Answer those first.

Charles II's Return,
Based on a Dutch engraving

Unit 3

The Restoration and the 18th Century: 1660–1798

King Charles II's return to the throne in 1660 brought new hope to the English people. Despite fire and plague in London in the 1660s, the nation soon enjoyed new wealth and power. Writers used a new, simpler style. Their nonfiction and novels became popular with the public, including women and the middle class. Booksellers and publishers earned money by mass-producing what readers wanted. Literature was no longer a luxury for the upper classes. It became available to common people and reflected their thoughts and experiences, too.

In this unit, you will read and study literature from this important period.

"No entertainment is so cheap as reading, nor any pleasure as lasting."

—Mary Wortley Montagu, "A Letter to Her Daughter," 1750

In 1649, Charles I was replaced by Parliament and then by Oliver Cromwell. In 1660, Charles II came back from exile and became king. This was known as the Restoration. Shortly after the king's return, England suffered two disasters. In 1665, the plague struck, killing an estimated 100,000 in London alone. Then, in 1666, a raging fire destroyed 80 percent of London.

Great Fire of London, 1666

Two political parties formed. The Tories supported the king. They believed that only nobles could be good leaders. The Whig party was made up of the newly wealthy upper class and merchants.

Religious differences played a large part in power changes during the era. Most of the English favored Protestant leaders and limiting the powers of the king. However, Charles's brother James II, who became king in 1685, was Catholic and thought the kings should be all-powerful. English political leaders got James's son-in-law, William of Orange, to invade. William and James's daughter Mary, who were Protestants, ruled together and gave important rights to the English people.

In 1707, the Act of Union joined England, Scotland, and Wales into one country, Great Britain. In wars between

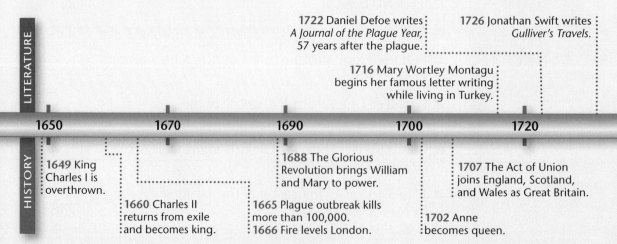

LITERATURE

1722 Daniel Defoe writes *A Journal of the Plague Year,* 57 years after the plague.

1726 Jonathan Swift writes *Gulliver's Travels.*

1716 Mary Wortley Montagu begins her famous letter writing while living in Turkey.

1650   1670   1690   1700   1720

HISTORY

1649 King Charles I is overthrown.

1660 Charles II returns from exile and becomes king.

1688 The Glorious Revolution brings William and Mary to power.

1665 Plague outbreak kills more than 100,000.
1666 Fire levels London.

1702 Anne becomes queen.

1707 The Act of Union joins England, Scotland, and Wales as Great Britain.

180 *Unit 3 The Restoration and the 18th Century*

1689 and 1763, Britain defeated France and gained lands around the world, including Canada. Queen Anne ruled Great Britain from 1702 to 1714. When she died, the crown passed to her closest Protestant relative. King George I gave much responsibility to his chief minister, Robert Walpole. He is considered the nation's first prime minister.

George III became king in 1760, as the Industrial Revolution was beginning. Technological advances helped increase Great Britain's wealth and power despite the loss of the American colonies in 1783. Still, the working classes did not share this new wealth.

Around 1660, a new literary style began to take hold. Writers turned against the complex, artificial style of some Renaissance literature. Instead, they supported a simpler, more natural style. Publishers began to earn money by selling books to the general public. Writers chose to appeal to ordinary readers instead of only to key noblemen.

Satire became a popular genre. Two of the wittiest satirists, Jonathan Swift and Alexander Pope, were Tories. They aimed their satire at the societal changes the Whigs were bringing to Britain. Many 18th-century writers became known for their prose. Samuel Johnson's literary criticism and James Boswell's biographical writing used lively prose. The century had many remarkable letter writers, including Thomas Gray and Mary Wortley Montagu. The novel also became popular. Novelists such as Daniel Defoe came from the middle class. They wrote about common people in realistic settings.

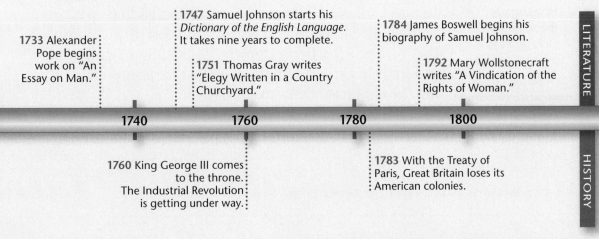

LITERATURE

1733 Alexander Pope begins work on "An Essay on Man."

1747 Samuel Johnson starts his *Dictionary of the English Language.* It takes nine years to complete.

1751 Thomas Gray writes "Elegy Written in a Country Churchyard."

1784 James Boswell begins his biography of Samuel Johnson.

1792 Mary Wollstonecraft writes "A Vindication of the Rights of Woman."

1740   1760   1780   1800

1760 King George III comes to the throne. The Industrial Revolution is getting under way.

1783 With the Treaty of Paris, Great Britain loses its American colonies.

HISTORY

BEFORE READING THE SELECTION

from *Gulliver's Travels*   by Jonathan Swift

Jonathan Swift
1667–1745

Objectives

- To read and understand a satire
- To understand the roles of irony and exaggeration in a satire
- To identify a first-person protagonist
- To recognize the roles of plot, fantasy, and description in a satire

About the Author

Jonathan Swift was born in Ireland to English parents. He studied at Trinity College in Dublin to become a minister. Swift became minister of an Anglican church in Ireland in 1700. As a young man, Swift realized he had a talent for humorous writing. He published his first writings in 1704.

Swift visited London often and made friends in powerful government positions. A strong supporter of the Tory government, he wrote many articles expressing Tory views.

In 1714, George I became king, and the Whig party gained power. Swift, head of Saint Patrick's Cathedral in Dublin, no longer had much political power. However, he served at Saint Patrick's for 30 years and continued to support political causes.

Swift never married, but he had a long friendship with a woman named Esther Johnson. Swift called her Stella and wrote her many long letters. These letters appeared in a book titled *The Journal to Stella*, published after Swift's death.

About the Selection

Gulliver's Travels, written in 1726, is about a doctor named Lemuel Gulliver. Gulliver takes four trips, ending up in an unusual place each time. This selection describes Gulliver's first voyage. After being shipwrecked, Gulliver swims ashore and finds himself in Lilliput, a land where people are a 12th the size of normal humans.

Literary Terms *Gulliver's Travels* is a **satire,** or a humorous writing that pokes fun at human behavior. It uses **irony** and **exaggeration** to call attention to certain traits of people and society. Irony is a figure of speech in which the writer says the opposite of what is meant. Exaggeration "blows up" an idea, making something seem more than it is. *Gulliver's Travels* has a **first-person protagonist.** That is, the main character is also the narrator of the story. Swift uses literary elements such as **fantasy, description,** and **plot** to tell the story. Fantasy adds imaginative details to create strange settings and characters. Description is a word picture that gives details about characters, setting, and events. Plot is the action of the story.

Reading on Your Own As you read the selection, think about the author's purpose. Is it to entertain, to inform, to persuade, or to do all of these?

Writing on Your Own What character trait or trend in society do you dislike? Describe it and tell why it bothers you.

Vocabulary Focus Some words have more than one meaning. The word *quiver* is an example. It can mean "to shake." In *Gulliver's Travels,* the narrator sees a "human Creature . . . with a Quiver at his Back." In this context, the word is used as a noun; it is something a person carries or wears to hold arrows. If you are unsure of this meaning of *quiver,* you can find it in a dictionary. Words with multiple meanings have separate entries for each different meaning. As you read the selection, make sure you know the definition in context of each of the following words: *buff, page, train,* and *dressed.* Then write a second meaning for each word.

Think Before You Read How do you think Gulliver and the people of Lilliput will react to one another?

---

satire humorous writing that makes fun of foolishness or evil

irony the use of words that seem to say one thing but mean the opposite

exaggeration the use of words to make something seem more than it is

first person a point of view where the narrator is also a character, using the pronouns *I* and *we*

protagonist the main character in a story

fantasy imaginative fiction that often has strange settings and characters

description a written picture of the characters, events, and settings in a story

plot the series of events in a story

from Gulliver's Travels

As you read, think about how the people of Lilliput are similar to and different from normal human beings.

The first-person narrator and protagonist uses the pronoun *I* as he describes the feelings, sights, and sounds he experiences.

Rules of capitalization and punctuation differed in Swift's day. Many common nouns were capitalized.

I lay down on the Grass, which was very short and soft; where I slept sounder than ever I remember to have done in my Life, and as I reckoned, above Nine Hours; for when I awaked, it was just Day-light. I attempted to rise, but was not able to stir: For as I happened to lie on my Back, I found my Arms and Legs were strongly fastened on each Side to the Ground; and my Hair, which was long and thick, tied down in the same Manner. I likewise felt several slender **Ligatures** across my Body, from my Armpits to my Thighs. I could only look upwards; the Sun began to grow hot, and the Light offended my Eyes. I heard a confused Noise about me, but in the Posture I lay, could see nothing except the Sky. In a little time I felt something alive moving on my left Leg, which advancing gently forward over my Breast, came almost up to my Chin; when bending my Eyes downwards as much as I could, I perceived it to be a human Creature not six Inches high, with a Bow and Arrow in his Hands, and a **Quiver** at his Back. In the mean time, I felt at least Forty more of the same Kind (as I **conjectured**) following the first. I was in the utmost Astonishment, and roared so loud, that they all ran back in a Fright; and some of them, as I was afterwards told, were hurt with the Falls they got by leaping from my Sides upon the Ground. However, they soon returned; and one of them, who ventured so far as to get a full Sight of my Face,

| **ligatures** bindings | **quiver** a case for holding arrows | **conjectured** supposed |

lifting up his Hands and Eyes by way of Admiration, cryed out in a shrill, but distinct Voice, *Hekinah Degul:* The others repeated the same Words several times, but I then knew not what they meant. I lay all this while, as the Reader may believe, in great Uneasiness: At length, struggling to get loose, I had the Fortune to break the Strings, and **wrench** out the Pegs that fastened my left Arm to the Ground; for, by lifting it up to my Face, I discovered the Methods they had taken to bind me; and, at the same time, with a violent Pull, which gave me excessive Pain, I a little loosened the Strings that tied down my Hair on the left Side; so that I was just able to turn my Head about two Inches. But the Creatures ran off a second time, before I could seize them; whereupon there was a great Shout in a very shrill Accent; and after it ceased, I heard one of them cry aloud, *Tolgo Phonac;* when in an Instant I felt above an Hundred Arrows **discharged** on my left Hand, which pricked me like so many Needles; and besides, they shot another Flight into the Air, as we do Bombs in *Europe;* whereof many, I suppose, fell on my Body, (though I felt them not) and some on my Face, which I immediately covered with my left Hand. When this Shower of Arrows was over, I fell a groaning with Grief and Pain; and then striving again to get loose, they discharged another **Volly** larger than the first; and some of them attempted with Spears to stick me in the Sides; but, by good Luck, I had on me a **Buff Jerkin,** which they could not pierce. I thought it the most **prudent** Method to lie still; and my Design was to continue so till Night, when my left Hand being already loose, I could easily free myself: And as for the Inhabitants, I had Reason to believe I might be a Match for the greatest Armies they could bring against me, if they were all of the same Size with him that I saw. But Fortune **disposed** otherwise of me. When the People observed I was quiet, they discharged no more Arrows: But by the Noise increasing, I knew their Numbers were greater; and

Hekinah Degul are words of the imaginary Lilliputian language. What do you think they might mean?

Find two comparisons Swift uses. How do they describe the place and situation Gulliver is in?

Plot has several parts: introduction, rising action, climax, falling action, and resolution. The selection is mostly introduction and rising action for the larger story. However, as a story in its own right, the selection includes all of these plot elements. As you continue reading, note where the shifts occur.

wrench twist violently

discharged shot

volly volley: flight of missiles

buff jerkin leather jacket

prudent wise

disposed dealt with

about four Yards from me, over-against my right Ear, I heard a Knocking for above an Hour, like People at work; when turning my Head that Way, as well as the Pegs and Strings would permit me, I saw a Stage erected about a Foot and a half from the Ground, capable of holding four of the Inhabitants, with two or three Ladders to mount it: From whence one of them, who seemed to be a Person of Quality, made me a long Speech, whereof I understood not one Syllable. But I should have mentioned, that before the principal Person began his **Oration,** he cryed out three times *Langro Dehul san:* (these Words and the former were afterwards repeated and explained to me.) Whereupon immediately about fifty of the Inhabitants came, and cut the Strings that fastened the left side of my Head, which gave me the Liberty of turning it to the right, and of observing the Person and Gesture of him who was to speak. He appeared to be of a middle Age, and taller than any of the other three who attended him; whereof one was a **Page,** who held up his **Train,** and seemed to be somewhat longer than my middle Finger; the other two stood one on each side to support him. He acted every part of an **Orator;** and I could observe many Periods of Threatnings, and others of Promises, Pity, and Kindness. I answered in a few Words, but in the most **submissive** Manner, lifting up my left Hand and both my Eyes to the Sun, as calling him for a Witness; and being almost famished with Hunger, having not eaten a Morsel for some Hours before I left the Ship, I found the Demands of Nature so strong upon me, that I could not **forbear** shewing my Impatience (perhaps against the strict Rules of Decency) by putting my Finger frequently on my Mouth, to signify that I wanted Food. The *Hurgo* (for so they call a great Lord, as I afterwards learnt) understood me very well: He descended from the Stage, and commanded that several Ladders should be applied to my Sides, on which above

How do Swift's descriptions of setting and character help accomplish his purpose in this section?

How might the leader's speech be a form of irony?

Here *shewing* means "showing."

oration formal speech

page a young attendant

train part of a robe that trails behind

orator powerful public speaker

submissive humble

forbear hold back

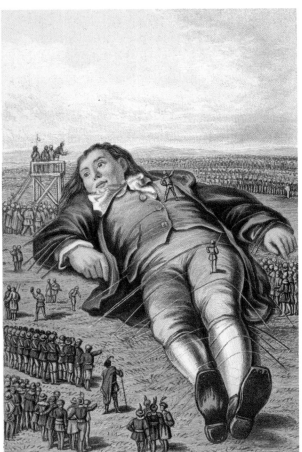

Gulliver's Travels, Illustration from a 19th-century edition of *Gulliver's Travels*

How do the details in this section show the fantasy part of the story?

What exaggerations does Swift use in this section? What effect do they have on the story?

an hundred of the Inhabitants mounted, and walked towards my Mouth, **laden** with Baskets full of Meat, which had been provided, and sent thither by the King's Orders upon the first Intelligence he received of me. I observed there was the Flesh of several Animals, but could not distinguish them by the Taste. There were Shoulders, Legs, and Loins shaped like those of **Mutton,** and very well **dressed,** but smaller than the Wings of a Lark. I eat them by two or three at a Mouthful; and took three Loaves at a time, about the bigness of Musket Bullets. They supplyed me as fast as they could, shewing a thousand Marks of Wonder and Astonishment at my Bulk and Appetite. I then made another Sign that I wanted Drink. They found by my eating that a small Quantity would not suffice me; and being a most **ingenious** People, they slung up with great **Dexterity** one of their largest **Hogsheads;** then rolled it towards my Hand, and beat out the Top; I drank it off

laden carrying a load	**dressed** prepared	**dexterity** skill
mutton sheep	**ingenious** clever	**hogsheads** barrels

at a **Draught,** which I might well do, for it hardly held half a Pint, and tasted like a small Wine of *Burgundy,* but much more delicious. They brought me a second Hogshead, which I drank in the same Manner, and made Signs for more, but they had none to give me. When I had performed these Wonders, they shouted for Joy, and danced upon my Breast, repeating several times as they did at first, *Hekinah Degul.* They made me a Sign that I should throw down the two Hogsheads, but first warned the People below to stand out of the Way, crying aloud, *Borach Mivola;* and when they saw the Vessels in the Air, there was an universal Shout of *Hekinah Degul.* I confess I was often tempted, while they were passing backwards and forwards on my Body, to seize Forty or Fifty of the first that came in my Reach, and dash them against the Ground. But the Remembrance of what I had felt, which probably might not be the worst they could do; and the Promise of Honour I made them, for so I interpreted my submissive Behaviour, soon drove out those Imaginations. Besides, I now considered my self as bound by the Laws of Hospitality to a People who had treated me with so much Expence and Magnificence. However, in my Thoughts I could not sufficiently wonder at the **Intrepidity** of these **diminutive** Mortals, who durst venture to mount and walk on my Body, while one of my Hands was at Liberty, without trembling at the very Sight of so **prodigious** a Creature as I must appear to them. After some time, when they observed that I made no more Demands for Meat, there appeared before me a Person of high Rank from his Imperial Majesty. His Excellency having mounted on the Small of my Right Leg, advanced forwards up to my Face, with about a Dozen of his **Retinue;** and producing his Credentials under the **Signet** Royal, which he applied close to my Eyes, spoke about ten Minutes, without any Signs of Anger, but with a kind of **determinate** Resolution; often

---

Whom or what is Swift satirizing in this section?

What is a simpler way to say *I could not sufficiently wonder at the Intrepidity of these diminutive Mortals?* How would you describe Swift's style here?

---

draught draft: portion drunk

intrepidity fearlessness

diminutive small

prodigious enormous

retinue group of attendants

signet seal

determinate firmly resolved

pointing forwards, which, as I afterwards found, was towards the Capital City, about half a Mile distant, whither it was agreed by his Majesty in Council that I must be conveyed. I answered in few Words, but to no Purpose, and made a Sign with my Hand that was loose, putting it to the other, (but over his Excellency's Head, for Fear of hurting him or his Train) and then to my own Head and Body, to signify that I desired my Liberty. It appeared that he understood me well enough; for he shook his Head by way of **Disapprobation,** and held his Hand in a Posture to shew that I must be carried as a Prisoner. However, he made other Signs to let me understand that I should have Meat and Drink enough, and very good Treatment.

Illustration from a 19th-century edition of *Gulliver's Travels.* This scene, which shows Gulliver with the army of Lilliput, comes from later in the story.

disapprobation disapproval

AFTER READING THE SELECTION

from *Gulliver's Travels*   by Jonathan Swift

Directions Choose the letter of the best answer or write the answer using complete sentences.

Comprehension: Identifying Facts

1. What does Gulliver feel across his body when he awakens?

   A insects   **C** sand

   B water   **D** ropes

2. The creatures Gulliver sees carry _____.

   A weapons   **C** flowers

   B food   **D** luggage

3. What plan does Gulliver make to free himself?

4. Why does Gulliver's plan not work?

5. What attitude does Gulliver have toward the speaker?

6. What is the problem with the food the Lilliputians give Gulliver?

7. What does the person of high rank indicate will happen to Gulliver next?

8. What two reasons does Gulliver think of that keep him from throwing the Lilliputians to the ground?

9. Why do the Lilliputians set up a stage?

10. How do Gulliver and the Lilliputians communicate?

Comprehension: Putting Ideas Together

11. One literary technique the author uses to make the selection interesting is _____.

   A first-person viewpoint

   B alliteration

   C rhyme

   D sound effects

12. When Gulliver first sees the creatures on his body, he feels _____.

   A relieved   **C** surprised

   B amused   **D** panic-filled

13. What advantages does Gulliver have over the Lilliputians? What advantages do the Lilliputians have over Gulliver?

14. What type of real person do you think the orator resembles?

15. Why do you think Gulliver is tempted to throw the creatures to the ground?

16. In general, how would you describe the Lilliputians' treatment of Gulliver?

17. Describe Gulliver's feelings toward the Lilliputians.

18. Is the person of high rank a funny character? Explain why or why not.

19. How do you think the Lilliputians feel about Gulliver?

20. Explain the role of exaggeration in the selection.

Understanding Literature: Fantasy

Imaginative writing that has characters or settings that cannot be real is called fantasy. In fantasy, writers can create worlds where anything can happen.

21. Describe the setting of the selection. Is it realistic or fantastic?

22. Describe a part of the selection's plot that is not realistic.

23. What is fantastic about the Lilliputians? What, if any, realistic traits do they have?

24. Is Gulliver a realistic or fantastic character? Explain how his character reinforces the fantasy elements of the selection.

25. Discuss one main idea the selection has. Explain how the fantasy elements help or hurt the telling of this idea.

Critical Thinking

26. What are the "Demands of Nature" that Gulliver mentions? How do they conflict with the "Rules of Decency"?

27. What types of real people might Swift be making fun of in the selection? Explain.

28. Describe three elements of the story that make it funny.

29. How do you think Swift pokes fun at pride in the story? How does he make fun of travel literature?

Thinking Creatively

30. Compare the selection to a fantasy you have read, such as science fiction, a fairy tale, or a tall tale.

After Reading **continued on next page**

from *Gulliver's Travels* *by Jonathan Swift*

 ### Grammar Check

The past tense of many verbs is regular, formed by adding *-ed* to the present tense verb. For example, Swift's narrator says, "I attempted to rise." The *-ed* ending is added to the regular verb *attempt* to form the past tense. Other verbs are irregular. The narrator says, "I lay down." *Lay* is the past tense of the verb *lie.* Another irregular verb used in the story is *eat.* Today, we use the irregular form *ate* to form the past tense of *eat.* In Swift's time, the irregular past tense of *eat* was *eat* or *et.*

Identify the irregular past tense verb in each of the following sentences, taken from longer sentences in the selection. Then give the present tense form of the verb.

> *But the Creatures ran off a second time.*
>
> *I fell a groaning with Grief and Pain.*
>
> *I heard a Knocking for above an Hour.*

 ### Writing on Your Own

Imagine you have been transported to a strange land under the sea, in outer space, or in another place. Write a short description of the place and the creatures you find there.

 ### Speaking

How do you think the Lilliputians speak? Choose one section in which they speak their own language. Practice saying the words using the voice and expression they might use. Share your oral interpretation with a small group.

 ### Listening

Locate and listen to a recorded version of "A Voyage to Lilliput" from *Gulliver's Travels.* Discuss how the oral version of the story affects its fantasy elements.

 ### Research

The popularity and lightheartedness of Swift's writings brought many of his made-up names and ideas into common use. Do research to find out more about Swift's influence on the English language. Make a poster to report your findings.

BEFORE READING THE SELECTION

from *A Letter to Her Daughter*   *by Mary Wortley Montagu*

About the Author

Mary Pierrepont was the daughter of a wealthy noble. While growing up, she met many important people, including writers. She also taught herself Latin. Instead of marrying the man her father had chosen for her, she married Edward Wortley Montagu, a member of Parliament. They had a son in 1713 and a daughter a few years later.

Edward was made ambassador to Turkey in 1716, and he and Mary lived in Constantinople, known today as Istanbul, for two years. Mary Montagu learned the Turkish language and customs and wrote many letters and journals. On returning to England, she wrote poems, a play, and essays. She also worked hard to make smallpox vaccinations common in England.

Montagu became friends with Alexander Pope, one of the era's greatest poets. However, they had a disagreement, and he later became very critical of her. In 1739, Montagu moved to Italy and lived there for most of the rest of her life.

Writing for publication was not proper for upper-class women at the time. Montagu's writings were often outspoken and even scandalous. Her family tried to stop their publication. However, her writings were published in 1763, after her death, and became quite popular.

Mary Wortley
Montagu
1689–1762

Objectives

- To read and understand a letter
- To recognize and understand metaphors, analogies, and metonymies in a literary work

About the Selection

As a writer, Montagu is known mainly for her letters. Many of the greatest English letter writers wrote in the 18th century, and Montagu's letters are considered among the best. When this letter was written, Montagu's daughter Mary was married to Lord Bute, who later became prime minister of Great Britain. Montagu's daughter feared that her mother's writings would hurt Lord Bute's political career.

Before Reading continued on next page

from *A Letter to Her Daughter*   by Mary Wortley Montagu

letter impressions and feelings written to a specific person

analogy a figure of speech that uses one thing to stand for another

metaphor a figure of speech that makes a comparison but does not use *like* or *as*

metonymy a figure of speech that replaces the intended word with a related word that is symbolic

Literary Terms "A Letter to Her Daughter" is a **letter** that expresses not only feelings and impressions but the beliefs of its author. The letter is written to Montagu's daughter, Mary. Montagu uses many figures of speech, including **analogy, metaphor,** and **metonymy,** to explain her views on education. Analogies and metaphors make comparisons to help readers understand the ideas better. Analogies are figures of speech in which one thing or person stands for another. Metaphors are comparisons that do not use the words *like* or *as*. A metonymy replaces a common word with a related but more symbolic word.

Reading on Your Own As you read the letter, use your own experiences to decide whether you agree or disagree with Montagu's views on education for women.

Writing on Your Own What do you think is the most important subject that you study at school? Describe it and explain why it is useful now and will be in the future.

Vocabulary Focus Several suffixes, or word endings, are used to describe a person who performs a certain action. The suffixes *-ist* and *-er* mean "one who does or performs." The suffix *-an* or *-ian* means "one skilled in or specializing in." Define the following words from the selection, based on your knowledge of these suffixes: *arithmetician, linguist, philosopher, transcriber, historian.*

Think Before You Read How do you think education for girls differed in the 18th century from today?

from A Letter to Her Daughter

As you read, think about how Montagu's advice for educating her granddaughter differs from the way Montagu educated her own daughter.

You have given me a great deal of satisfaction by your account of your eldest daughter. I am particularly pleased to hear she is a good arithmetician; it is the best proof of understanding: the knowledge of numbers is one of the chief distinctions between us and the **brutes.** If there is anything in blood, you may reasonably expect your children should be **endowed** with an uncommon share of good sense. Mr. Wortley's family and mine have both produced some of the greatest men that have been born in England: I mean Admiral Sandwich, and my grandfather, who was distinguished by the name of Wise William. I have heard Lord Bute's father mentioned as an extraordinary genius, though he had not many opportunities of showing it; and his uncle, the present Duke of Argyll, has one of the best heads I ever knew. I will therefore speak to you as supposing Lady Mary not only capable, but desirous of learning; in that case by all means let her be **indulged** in it. You will tell me I did not make it a part of your education: your **prospect** was very different from hers. As you had no defect either in mind or person to hinder, and much in your circumstances to attract, the highest offers, it seemed your business to learn how to live in the world, as it is hers to know how to be easy out of it. It is the common error of builders and parents to follow some plan they think beautiful (and perhaps is so), without

Admiral Sandwich refers to Edward Montagu (1625–1672), who was the first Earl of Sandwich, an admiral, and a friend of Cromwell. He played a part in the end of the English Civil War.

Why did Montagu present her ideas in a letter rather than in another form?

brutes animals

endowed given

indulged encouraged and supported

prospect expected future

In the first two sentences on this page, Montagu uses analogies related to building. To what two situations does she compare raising children? What point about child-rearing is she making?

considering that nothing is beautiful that is displaced. Hence we see so many **edifices** raised that the raisers can never inhabit, being too large for their fortunes. Vistas are laid open over barren heaths, and apartments **contrived** for a coolness very agreeable in Italy, but killing in the north of Britain: thus every woman endeavours to breed her daughter a fine lady, qualifying her for a station in which she will never appear, and at the same time **incapacitating** her for that retirement to which she is destined. Learning, if she has a real taste for it, will not only make her contented, but happy in it. No entertainment is so cheap as reading, nor any pleasure so lasting. She will not want new fashions, nor regret the loss of expensive **diversions,** or variety of company, if she can be amused with an author in her closet. To render this amusement extensive, she should be permitted to learn the languages. I have heard it **lamented** that boys lose so many years in mere learning of words: this is no objection to a girl, whose time is not so precious: she cannot advance herself in any profession, and has therefore more hours to spare; and as you say her memory is good, she will be very agreeably employed this way. There are two cautions to be given on this subject: first, not to think herself learned when she could read Latin, or even Greek. Languages are more properly to be called vehicles of learning than learning itself, as may be observed in many schoolmasters, who, though perhaps critics in grammar, are the most ignorant fellows upon earth. True knowledge consists in knowing things, not words. I would wish her no further a linguist than to enable her to read books in their originals, that are often **corrupted,** and always injured, by translations. Two hours' application every morning will bring this about much sooner than you can imagine, and she will have leisure enough besides to run over the English poetry, which is a more important

The study of Latin and Greek were a big part of most boys' formal education in the 18th century.

edifices buildings

contrived designed

incapacitating disabling

diversions pastimes, hobbies

lamented regretted

corrupted spoiled

part of a woman's education than it is generally supposed. Many a young damsel has been ruined by a fine copy of verses, which she would have laughed at if she had known it had been stolen from Mr. Waller. I remember, when I was a girl, I saved one of my companions from destruction, who communicated to me an **epistle** she was quite charmed with. As she had a natural good taste, she observed the lines were not so smooth as Prior's or Pope's, but had more thought and spirit than any of theirs. She was wonderfully delighted with such a demonstration of her lover's sense and passion, a little pleased with her own charms, that had force enough to inspire such elegancies. In the midst of this triumph I showed her that they were taken from Randolph's poems, and the unfortunate transcriber was dismissed with the scorn he deserved. To say truth, the poor plagiary was very unlucky to fall into my hands; that author being no longer in fashion, would have escaped any one of less universal reading than myself. You should encourage your daughter to talk over with you what she reads; and, as you are very capable of distinguishing, take care she does not mistake **pert** folly for wit and humour, or rhyme for poetry, which are the common errors of young people, and have a train of ill consequences. The second caution to be given her (and which is most absolutely necessary) is to conceal whatever learning she attains, with as much **solicitude** as she would hide crookedness or lameness; the parade of it can only serve to draw on her the envy, and consequently the most **inveterate** hatred, of all he and she fools, which will certainly be at least three parts in four of all her acquaintance. The use of knowledge in our sex, besides the amusement of **solitude,** is to moderate the passions, and learn to be contented with a small expense, which are the certain effects of a studious life; and it may be preferable even to that fame which men have

Mr. Waller refers to Edmund Waller, a popular and witty 17th-century English poet.

Here Montagu tells an anecdote from her youth. What idea does it teach?

Randolph's refers to Thomas Randolph, another 17th-century poet and a follower of Ben Jonson. *Plagiary* refers to copying another person's work and accepting or claiming credit for it. Montagu is saying the young man tried to pass off a poem by Randolph as his own writing.

epistle letter	**solicitude** care	**solitude** being alone
pert lively, light	**inveterate** firmly established	

Lady Reading a Letter,
Gerard Ter Borch

engrossed to themselves, and will not suffer us to share. You will tell me I have not observed this rule myself; but you are mistaken: it is only **inevitable** accident that has given me any reputation that way. I have always carefully avoided it, and ever thought it a misfortune. The explanation of this paragraph would occasion a long **digression,** which I will not trouble you with, it being my present design only to say what I think useful for the instruction of my granddaughter, which I have much at heart. If she has the same **inclination**

inevitable unavoidable	**digression** comments that are off the main point	**inclination** preference

(I should say passion) for learning that I was born with, history, geography, and philosophy will furnish her with materials to pass away cheerfully a longer life than is allotted to mortals. I believe there are few heads capable of making Sir I. Newton's calculations, but the result of them is not difficult to be understood by a moderate capacity. Do not fear this should make her affect the character of Lady ----, or Lady ----, or Mrs. ----: those women are ridiculous, not because they have learning but because they have it not. One thinks herself a complete historian, after reading Echard's *Roman History;* another a **profound** philosopher, having got by heart some of Pope's **unintelligible** essays; and a third an able **divine,** on the strength of Whitefield's sermons: thus you hear them screaming politics and controversy.

It is a saying of Thucydides, ignorance is bold, and knowledge reserved. Indeed, it is impossible to be far advanced in it without being more humbled by a conviction of human ignorance, than **elated** by learning. At the same time I recommend books, I neither exclude work nor drawing. I think it as scandalous for a woman not to know how to use a needle, as for a man not to know how to use a sword. I was once extremely fond of my pencil, and it was a great **mortification** to me when my father turned off my master, having made a considerable progress for a short time I learnt. My over-eagerness in the pursuit of it had brought a weakness on my eyes, that made it necessary to leave it off; and all the advantage I got was the improvement of my hand. I see, by hers, that practice will make her a ready writer: she may attain it by serving you for a secretary, when your health or affairs make it troublesome to you to write yourself; and custom will make it an agreeable amusement to her. She cannot have too many for that station of life which will probably be her fate.

Sir I. Newton is Isaac Newton (1642–1727), an English scientist, astronomer, and mathematician. He developed the theory of gravity and invented calculus. *Pope's* refers to Alexander Pope (1688–1744), one of the leading poets of the time. *Whitefield's* refers to George Whitefield (1714–1770), an Anglican preacher who played a part in founding the Methodist Church.

I was once extremely fond of my pencil is a metonymy. What activity does *pencil* stand for?

The word *hers* here refers to Montagu's granddaughter. The girl's writing shows that she could be a good writer.

profound having intellectual insight

unintelligible not capable of being understood

divine clergyman

elated filled with pride

mortification denial of a passion

The ultimate end of your education was to make you a good wife (and I have the comfort to hear that you are one): hers ought to be, to make her happy in a **virgin** state. I will not say it is happier; but it is undoubtedly safer than any marriage. In a lottery, which there are (at the lowest computation) ten thousand blanks to a prize, it is the most prudent choice not to **venture.** I have always been so thoroughly persuaded of this truth, that, notwithstanding the flattering views I had for you (as I never intended you a sacrifice to my vanity), I thought I owed you the justice to lay before you all the hazards attending **matrimony:** you may recollect I did so in the strongest manner. Perhaps you may have more success in the instructing of your daughter: she has so much company at home, she will not need seeking it abroad, and will more readily take the notions you think fit to give her. As you were alone in my family, it would have been thought a great cruelty to suffer you no companions of your own age, especially having so many near relations, and I do not wonder their opinions influenced yours. I was not sorry to see you not determined on a single life, knowing it was not your father's intention, and contented myself with endeavouring to make your home so easy that you might not be in haste to leave it.

Montagu uses a metaphor when she writes *I never intended you a sacrifice to my vanity.* What is she comparing?

virgin unmarried   **venture** take risks   **matrimony** marriage

AFTER READING THE SELECTION

from *A Letter to Her Daughter* by Mary Wortley Montagu

Directions Choose the letter of the best answer or write the answer using complete sentences.

Comprehension: Identifying Facts

1. Montagu thinks that the study of math for girls is ____.
   A important
   B a waste of time
   C too difficult
   D natural

2. What subject does Montagu *not* recommend for her granddaughter to study?
   A mathematics
   B languages
   C fencing
   D history

3. For what purpose should young women learn foreign languages?

4. What activities does Montagu recommend for girls in addition to reading?

5. What type of learning separates humans from animals?

6. What reason does Montagu give for why her grandchildren can be expected to be unusually bright?

7. Why does Montagu think it is better to read a book in its original language?

8. What are two errors of young people that parents can correct?

9. Why was Montagu forced to give up drawing as a pastime?

10. Does Montagu expect her granddaughter to get married? Explain.

Comprehension: Putting Ideas Together

11. Montagu says that a girl's time "is not so precious" as a boy's because ____.
   A boys are more important than girls
   B girls don't train for work
   C girls are not as smart as boys
   D boys must serve in the military

12. Learning should have the result of making the learner more ____.
   A humble
   B foolish
   C prideful
   D ignorant

13. What is Montagu's explanation for giving different advice about educating her granddaughter than she followed for her own daughter?

14. Does knowing another language mean a person is smart? What example does Montagu give?

15. How can copied poetry "ruin" a girl who hasn't read widely?

After Reading continued on next page

from *A Letter to Her Daughter*   *by Mary Wortley Montagu*

16. What is the difference between "pert folly" and wit?

17. How is learning likely to make a person less likeable?

18. Montagu calls the three women she uses as examples "ridiculous." Why?

19. What is Montagu's opinion of marriage?

20. What does Montagu think of how her daughter "turned out"?

Understanding Literature: Metaphor

A metaphor is a figure of speech that compares two unlike things in a nonliteral way. A metaphor does not use the words *like* or *as* to compare things.

21. Montagu says a young woman will not want new fashions "if she can be amused with an author in her closet." It is clear that she is not really describing having an author in the closet. What two things are being compared in this metaphor?

22. In what way is language a "vehicle of learning" (page 196)?

23. Montagu compares marriage to a lottery. What does this metaphor reveal about Montagu's opinion about marriage?

24. Locate and quote another nonliteral phrase or sentence in the letter. Explain why it is a metaphor or not.

25. What effect does the use of metaphors have on a piece of writing?

Critical Thinking

26. Montagu says, "True knowledge consists in knowing things, not words." Explain this statement in your own words. Then tell why you agree or disagree.

27. Give an example from your own experience to support the idea from the letter that "nothing is beautiful that is displaced."

28. Give examples of activities or traits that are considered "masculine." How do such stereotypes affect young people?

29. Montagu's most famous line comes from this letter: "No entertainment is so cheap as reading, nor any pleasure so lasting." Do you agree with her? Why or why not?

Thinking Creatively

30. What advice about learning would you give a young woman today? How would it differ from Montagu's advice about her granddaughter?

Grammar Check

A colon (:) is a punctuation mark that signals that an explanation or a list of items will follow. For example, Montagu writes, "Mr. Wortley's family and mine have both produced some of the greatest men that have been born in England: I mean Admiral Sandwich, and my grandfather . . ." The colon shows that the words that follow will name some of these great men.

- Write down another sentence from the letter that uses a colon to show that an explanation or list will follow.

- Write one sentence of your own about Montagu's beliefs about education, using a colon.

Writing on Your Own

How important is learning a second language to young people today? Write a letter to someone younger than yourself. Express your views and give advice on this question.

Speaking

Find a piece of good advice or a wise saying in the letter. Write a short speech telling more about the statement. Give the speech to a small group of classmates.

Listening

Choose four related sentences from the letter. Read them aloud to a partner. Use vocal intonation (the controlled rise and fall of your voice) and expression to make the meaning clear. Listen to your partner's reading and suggest ways to make the meaning clearer.

Media

One of the key activities Montagu recommends is reading. In your school or local library, look for some ways people try to get others to read more often. Think about the different ways this is done (posters, book drives, celebrity support, media coverage, and so on). Evaluate the efforts in a brief report.

BEFORE READING THE SELECTION

from *A Journal of the Plague Year* by Daniel Defoe

Daniel Defoe
1660–1731

About the Author

Daniel Defoe was born to a middle-class family. He became a successful merchant but later had financial problems. He then became a political journalist to earn a living.

When he was nearly 60 years old, Defoe wrote his first novel, *Robinson Crusoe.* This tale of the adventures of a shipwrecked man was published in 1719. It was one of the first English novels. Many critics believe that Defoe's finest novel was *Moll Flanders,* published in 1722. Defoe is known for creating realistic dialogue and vividly detailed settings.

About the Selection

The Romans built the city of London around A.D. 43 and built a wall around it in the early 200s. By the mid-1660s, London had a population of about a half million people. Most people lived outside the walls in neighborhoods that included many crowded slums. The area inside the walls was known as the City. In 1665, the bubonic plague struck London. This disease, carried by fleas that infested the rats in London's slums, spread quickly. Within a year, 100,000 Londoners had died of the disease.

Then, in the early morning of September 3, 1666, a baker's house caught on fire. The fire spread throughout London and burned for days. By the time it was put out, about four-fifths of the city had been destroyed. Only 16 people died in the fire. However, most of the city's rats were apparently killed. After the fire, the deadly plague disappeared.

Daniel Defoe was 5 years old when the plague struck. He wrote this fictional journal in 1722 based on the events surrounding the disease.

Literary Terms *A Journal of the Plague Year* is **historical fiction.** This is fiction that draws on factual events of history. This selection is set in London during the plague. It is written in the form of a **journal,** a first-person account of an event.

Reading on Your Own As you read the selection, think about cause and effect. What causes the public and city officials to behave as they do? What are the effects of the plague and people's reactions to it?

Writing on Your Own Describe a historical event from any time period that you would have liked to witness.

Vocabulary Focus The dictionary definition of a word is its denotation. In addition to this meaning, many words also have connotations: positive or negative emotions attached to them over and above their dictionary definitions. For example, the denotation of *home* is "dwelling place." But the word *home* has positive connotations of comfort, warmth, and love. The word *plague* has negative connotations of fear, disease, disaster, and death. Find other words in the selection whose negative connotations help create a mood.

Think Before You Read How do you think the people living in London in 1665 reacted to news of the plague?

historical fiction fictional writing that draws on factual events of history

journal writing that expresses an author's feelings or first impressions about a subject

from A Journal of the Plague Year

As you read, think about how you would feel about the plague if you were a poor person, a wealthy person, a doctor, and a government official.

Plague, also called bubonic plague or the black death, first appeared in England in 1348. Within a five-year period, as much as half of the population was dead. Outbreaks occurred repeatedly in the centuries that followed. People learned to live under the shadow of this dreaded illness.

The return of the plague in the 1660s led to great panic. The rich fled into the countryside, and the gates of London were barred to keep the infected from carrying the disease abroad. At the peak of the outbreak, in August 1665, about 6,000 victims fell to the plague each week.

The bubonic plague was often carried from seaport to seaport by rats that traveled on ships. The *Levant* is made up of the countries bordering the eastern Mediterranean Sea. *Candia* is a name for Crete, a Greek island. *Cyprus* is an island of the eastern Mediterranean.

It was about the beginning of September, 1664, that I, among the rest of my neighbours, heard in ordinary **discourse** that the plague was returned again in Holland; for it had been very violent there, and particularly at Amsterdam and Rotterdam, in the year 1663, **whither,** they say, it was brought, some said from Italy, others from the Levant, among some goods which were brought home by their Turkey **fleet;** others said it was brought from Candia; others from Cyprus. It mattered not from whence it came; but all agreed it was come into Holland again.

We had no such thing as printed newspapers in those days to spread rumours and reports of things, and to improve them by the **invention** of men, as I have lived to see practised

discourse talk

whither where

fleet group of ships

invention products of imagination

since. But such things as these were gathered from the letters of merchants and others who corresponded abroad, and from them was handed about by word of mouth only; so that things did not spread instantly over the whole nation, as they do now. But it seems that the Government had a true account of it, and several councils were held about ways to prevent its coming over; but all was kept very private. Hence it was that this rumour died off again, and people began to forget it as a thing we were very little concerned in, and that we hoped was not true; till the latter end of November or the beginning of December 1664 when two men, said to be Frenchmen, died of the plague in Long Acre. . . . it was printed in the weekly bill of **mortality** in the usual manner, thus — Plague, 2. **Parishes** infected, 1.

The people showed a great concern at this, and began to be alarmed all over the town, and the more, because in the last week in December 1664 another man died in the same house, and of the same **distemper.** And then we were easy again for about six weeks, when none having died with any marks of infection, it was said the distemper was gone; but after that, I think it was about the 12th of February, another died in another house, but in the same parish and in the same manner.

This turned the people's eyes pretty much towards that end of the town, and the weekly bills showing an increase of burials in St. Giles's parish more than usual, it began to be suspected that the plague was among the people at that end of the town, and that many had died of it, though they had taken care to keep it as much from the knowledge of the public as possible. This **possessed** the heads of the people very much, and few cared to go through Drury Lane, or the other streets suspected, unless they had extraordinary business that obliged them to it. . . .

The *bill of mortality* is an account of how many people have died, where, and of what cause. This report shows that two people in the same area died of plague that week.

---

mortality death

parishes smaller parts of a city or county

distemper illness

possessed took control of

[T]he richer sort of people, especially the nobility and **gentry** from the west part of the city, **thronged** out of town with their families and servants in an unusual manner; and this was more particularly seen in Whitechappel; that is to say, the Broad Street where I lived; indeed, nothing was to be seen but waggons and carts, with goods, women, servants, children, etc.; coaches filled with people of the better sort and horsemen attending them, and all hurrying away; then empty waggons and carts appeared, and spare horses with servants, who, it was apparent, were returning or sent from the countries to fetch more people; besides **innumerable** numbers of men on horseback, some alone, others with servants, and, generally speaking, all loaded with baggage and fitted out for travelling, as anyone might perceive by their appearance.

This was a very terrible and **melancholy** thing to see, and as it was a sight which I could not but look on from morning to night (for indeed there was nothing else of **moment** to be seen), it filled me with very serious thoughts of the misery that was coming upon the city, and the unhappy condition of those that would be left in it. . . .

ow
napel,
of east
orth of
the ⅓⅓ mes River.

What traits of a journal do you find in this paragraph?

Londoners flee into the countryside

gentry wealthy owners of property	**innumerable** countless	**moment** importance
thronged crowded together	**melancholy** depressing	

ORDERS CONCERNING INFECTED HOUSES AND PERSONS SICK OF THE PLAGUE.

Notice to be given of the Sickness.

The master of every house, as soon as any one in his house complaineth, either of blotch or purple, or swelling in any part of his body, or falleth otherwise dangerously sick, without apparent cause of some other disease, shall give knowledge thereof to the examiner of health within two hours after the said sign shall appear.

Sequestration of the Sick.

As soon as any man shall be found by this examiner, **chirurgeon,** or searcher to be sick of the plague, he shall the same night be **sequestered** in the same house; and in case he be so sequestered, then though he afterwards die not, the house wherein he sickened should be shut up for a month, after the use of the due **preservatives** taken by the rest...

Burial of the Dead.

That the burial of the dead by this **visitation** be at most convenient hours, always either before sun-rising or after sun-setting, with the **privity** of the churchwardens or constable, and not otherwise; and that no neighbours nor friends be **suffered** to accompany the corpse to church, or to enter the house visited, upon pain of having his house shut up or be imprisoned.

And that no corpse dying of infection shall be buried, or remain in any church in time of common prayer, sermon, or lecture. And that no children be suffered at time of burial of any corpse in any church, churchyard, or burying-place to come near the corpse, coffin, or grave. And that all the graves shall be at least six feet deep.

And further, all public assemblies at other burials are to be **foreborne** during the continuance of this visitation.

---

chirurgeon surgeon

sequestered set apart

preservatives things used to protect against decay or spoilage

visitation outbreak

privity knowledge of a private matter

suffered allowed

foreborne done without

This s— laws abo— the sick and dead. Such law— would have been posted publicly and published in newspapers. How does the voice of this section differ from the first section of the selection?

The symptoms of bubonic plague are swellings of lymph glands, called buboes. Some forms of the disease create spots of blood that become black under the skin. This is how the disease earned the name Black Death.

People in the 1600s treated the plague with herbs. They also used vinegar to clean up the area where the disease was present. These were among the *preservatives* recommended.

If I may be allowed to give my opinion, by what I saw with my eyes and heard from other people that were eye-witnesses, I do **verily** believe the same, **viz.,** that there died at least 100,000 of the plague only, besides other distempers and besides those which died in the fields and highways and secret Places out of the **compass** of the communication, as it was called, and who were not put down in the bills though they really belonged to the body of the inhabitants. It was known to us all that abundance of poor despairing creatures who had the distemper upon them, and were grown stupid or melancholy by their misery, as many were, wandered away into the fields and Woods, and into secret **uncouth** places almost anywhere, to creep into a bush or hedge and die.

Aspects of the Great Plague of London, 1665

verily truly	**compass** boundary
viz. that is	**uncouth** rugged

AFTER READING THE SELECTION

from *A Journal of the Plague Year*   by Daniel Defoe

Directions Choose the letter of the best answer or write the answer using complete sentences.

Comprehension: Identifying Facts

1. The first information Londoners receive about the plague concerns cases of it in ____.
   A Italy
   B Turkey
   C Holland
   D Cyprus

2. The members of the public who receive the first information about the plague overseas are ____.
   A health officials
   B journalists
   C poor people
   D tradesmen

3. Why do people stop worrying about the plague for six weeks after news that a man died in December?

4. What action do the people who have business in London take after hearing about a plague death in February?

5. What do wealthy people do after news of the plague becomes public?

6. What feelings does the narrator experience when he witnesses the actions of the wealthy people?

7. How long do people whose families were infected have to notify the examiner?

8. What is done to the house of the victim of the plague?

9. At what time of day are victims of the plague buried?

10. According to the narrator, how many people died in this plague?

Comprehension: Putting Ideas Together

11. The narrator of the journal is ____.
    A an ordinary citizen
    B a plague victim
    C a government official
    D a newspaper reporter

12. The weekly "bill of mortality" is probably ____.
    A a letter to debtors
    B an ad for doctors
    C a notice of recent deaths
    D a political pamphlet

13. How much information does the public receive about the plague? How does this affect their mood?

14. Why do you think the government kept information about the plague secret?

After Reading **continued on next page**

from *A Journal of the Plague Year*   by Daniel Defoe

15. Many people stay away from infected areas or leave the city. What do these actions show about people's understanding of the disease?

16. Do you think the measures described in the second section are wise or overreaction?

17. How does one's social class affect his or her ability to avoid the plague?

18. What attitudes toward the plague does the selection show?

19. Characterize the narrator of the journal. Support your answer with evidence from the selection.

20. How does Defoe build suspense in the selection?

Understanding Literature: Historical Fiction

Historical fiction is based on historical events. Good historical fiction creates a setting and characters that bring the events vividly to life.

21. What event is the starting point for Defoe's journal? About when does the journal end?

22. What main event does the journal describe? What mood does the description of the event create?

23. What is the setting of the journal? Describe two details that make the setting seem realistic.

24. From what viewpoint does the journal's narrator observe the events? How does this viewpoint make the story suspenseful?

25. Do you think the event Defoe chose was a good one for vivid historical fiction? Explain why or why not.

Critical Thinking

26. Why do you think Defoe includes the "Orders Concerning Infected Houses and Persons Sick of the Plague"?

27. Why do you think Defoe chooses to describe the plague in a work of historical fiction instead of a work of nonfiction?

28. Describe Defoe's style in the selection. Explain why this is fitting for his subject matter.

29. What is the author's purpose in the selection?

Thinking Creatively

30. If you had not known this selection was fiction before reading, would you have believed it was factual? Explain why or why not.

Grammar Check

Prepositional phrases include a preposition (words such as *in, to, from,* and *at*). They also have a noun that is the object of the preposition. For example, in "the plague was returned again in Holland," *in Holland* is a prepositional phrase. Prepositional phrases may tell where something or someone is located or goes.

- In the selection, find three more prepositional phrases that answer the question *where*. Underline each prepositional phrase. Circle each preposition.

- Write a sentence of your own about the setting of the selection, using a prepositional phrase that tells *where*.

 ## Writing on Your Own

Choose a recent historical event that you have heard much about. Write a fictional journal entry that describes some aspect of the event as if you had witnessed it or participated in it.

 ## Speaking and Listening

Suppose you are a town crier, assigned to announce the orders described in the second section of the selection. With a partner, take turns saying one paragraph of the orders as you would announce them to a public gathering. Then discuss how you would feel if you were a member of the public hearing the announcement.

 ## Research

Use the Internet and library resources to find out more about the London plague of 1665–1666 and about another serious disease. For example, you might choose the flu outbreak of 1918–1919 or AIDS in the 20th century. Compare facts about the two diseases on a graphic organizer such as a Venn diagram.

 ## Viewing

Locate illustrations that were drawn to accompany reports of the plague. How does the artwork represent the disease? Compare two or more pieces of art from different eras. Discuss the differences.

from *An Essay on Man*   *by Alexander Pope*

Alexander Pope
1688–1744

About the Author

Alexander Pope was born to a wealthy Roman Catholic merchant in London. He was sickly as a child, and his family moved to the country. Because of his religion, Pope could not attend a university. (He also could not vote or hold public office.) But in the country, Pope educated himself through wide reading. He also learned to love the beauty of nature.

Pope showed a talent for poetry quite early. His first successful work, *An Essay on Criticism,* was published in 1711. It discussed the qualities that make literature excellent. In 1712, he published *The Rape of the Lock.* It displayed his skill as a satirist.

Pope became friends with some of the greatest writers of his time, including Jonathan Swift. In addition to writing original poetry, Pope translated Homer and edited Shakespeare. In his satires and his more philosophical works, Pope criticized popular literature that used scandal to appeal to the public. He fought for art that showed good taste and virtue.

About the Selection

Pope wrote "An Essay on Man" in 1733. In the poem, he discusses philosophical and moral issues. It has four epistles, or parts. This selection is from the first epistle, which discusses the way the universe is organized and people's place in it. The second epistle discusses how people can live with both passion and reason to be mentally healthy. The third epistle discusses how people can get along in society. The last deals with finding happiness through loving God and other people.

Literary Terms "An Essay on Man" is written in heroic **couplets,** pairs of rhyming lines written in **iambic pentameter.** Iambic pentameter is a poetic rhythm that has five two-beat sounds per line. The second syllable is stressed in each set of sounds.

Reading on Your Own As you read the poem, think about the author's purpose. Did Pope write the poem to entertain, to inform, to share his opinions, or to persuade? You might also make inferences about Pope's philosophy as you read. When you make inferences, you use your own knowledge and experiences to find connections between details in a text and ideas from other sources.

Writing on Your Own People have always asked questions about the meaning of life and people's place in the universe. What questions of this type do you wonder about? Write a journal entry about them.

Vocabulary Focus In *An Essay on Man,* Pope discusses God. As you read the poem, write synonyms for the word *God,* such as *Providence,* or related to it, such as *heaven.* Create a Concept Map or other type of graphic organizer to organize the words. A description of a Concept Map can be found in Appendix A.

Think Before You Read What questions about man and the universe do you think Pope will ask in the poem?

couplet a rhyming pair

iambic pentameter five two-beat sounds in a line of poetry where the second syllable is stressed in each pair of sounds

from An Essay on Man

As you read, think about the position in which Pope places people in the context of the entire universe.

Epistle 1. Of the Nature and State of Man, with Respect to the Universe

    1. Say first, of God above, or man below,
What can we reason, but from what we know?
Of man, what see we but his **station** here,
From which to reason, or to which refer?
5   Through worlds unnumbered though the God be known,
'Tis ours to trace him only in our own.
He, who through vast immensity can pierce,
See worlds on worlds compose one universe,
Observe how system into system runs,
10   What other planets circle other suns,
What varied being peoples every star,
May tell why Heaven has made us as we are.
But of this frame the bearings, and the ties,
The strong connections, nice dependencies,
15   **Gradations** just, has thy **pervading** soul
Looked through? or can a part contain the whole?
    Is the great chain, that draws all to agree,
And drawn supports, upheld by God, or thee?

In lines 17 and 18, Pope refers to a concept of a chain of being. This chain includes a linking of living things from the smallest parasites to four-legged animals to humans to God. What question does Pope ask about this chain?

station position

gradations shadings; gradual variations

pervading spread throughout every part

2. Presumptuous man! the reason wouldst thou find,
20 Why formed so weak, so little, and so blind?
First, if thou canst, the harder reason guess,
Why formed no weaker, blinder, and no less!
Ask of thy mother earth, why oaks are made
Taller or stronger than the weeds they shade?
25 Or ask of yonder **argent** fields above,
Why Jove's **satellites** are less than Jove?
    Of systems possible, if 'tis confessed
That Wisdom Infinite must form the best,
Where all must full or not **coherent** be,
30 And all that rises, rise in due degree;
Then, in the scale of reasoning life, 'tis plain,
There must be, somewhere, such a rank as man:
And all the question (wrangle e'er so long)
Is only this, if God has placed him wrong?
35   Respecting man, whatever wrong we call,
May, must be right, as relative to all.
In human works, though labored on with pain,
A thousand movements scarce one purpose gain;
In God's, one single can its end produce;
40 Yet serves to second too some other use.
So man, who here seems **principal** alone,
Perhaps acts second to some sphere unknown,
Touches some wheel, or **verges** to some goal;
'Tis but a part we see, and not a whole.
45   When the proud **steed** shall know why man restrains
His fiery course, or drives him o'er the plains;
When the dull ox, why now he breaks the clod,
Is now a victim, and now Egypt's god:
Then shall man's pride and dullness comprehend
50 His actions', passions', being's use and end;

Jove in line 26 is the planet Jupiter; its satellites are its moons. In this analogy, to what is Pope comparing Jupiter and its moons?

Summarize lines 27–30. What question does Pope hear people asking? What question does he think they should ask instead?

In lines 37–40, what comparison between God and humans does Pope make?

In what way are people like animals, according to lines 45–52?

---

presumptuous overstepping proper bounds

argent silver or white

satellites moons

coherent consistent; understandable

principal person in a leading position

verges moves toward

steed horse

Why doing, suffering, checked, impelled; and why
This hour a slave, the next a **deity.**
　　Then say not man's imperfect, Heaven in fault;
Say rather, man's as perfect as he ought;
55　His knowledge measured to his state and place,
His time a moment, and a point his space.
If to be perfect in a certain **sphere,**
What matter, soon or late, or here or there?
The blest today is as completely so,
60　As who began a thousand years ago. . . .

What does the poet mean when he says *man's as perfect as he ought* (line 54)? Do you agree?

Orrery, **model of the solar system made by Edward Troughton, about 1800**

deity god　　　　　　　　**sphere** area or range

4. Go, wiser thou! and, in thy scale of sense,
Weigh thy opinion against Providence;
Call imperfection what thou fancy'st such,
Say, here he gives too little, there too much;
65 Destroy all creatures for thy sport or **gust,**
Yet cry, if man's unhappy, God's unjust;
If man alone **engross** not Heaven's high care,
Alone made perfect here, immortal there:
Snatch from his hand the balance and the rod,
70 Rejudge his justice, be the God of God!
    In pride, in reasoning pride, our error lies;
All quit their sphere, and rush into the skies.
Pride still is aiming at the blest abodes,
Men would be angels, angels would be gods.
75 **Aspiring** to be gods, if angels fell,
Aspiring to be angels, men rebel:
And who but wishes to **invert** the laws
Of order, sins against the Eternal Cause.

Fancy'st in line 63 means "imagines."

The *balance* is an instrument for weighing; the *rod* is an instrument both for measurement and for punishment.

The *blest abodes* of line 73 are the heavens.

gust delight

engross engage the whole attention of

aspiring seeking to reach a goal

invert reverse

from *An Essay on Man*   by Alexander Pope

Directions Choose the letter of the best answer or write the answer using complete sentences.

Comprehension: Identifying Facts

1. According to Pope, who can understand why people were made as they were?

A everyone   **C** God

B no one   **D** religious people

2. According to Pope, when will humans understand the meaning of life?

3. In what character flaw does people's main error lie, according to Pope?

Comprehension: Putting Ideas Together

4. In the introduction, Pope compares "vindicating the ways of God to man" to ____.

A traveling to a distant land

B exploring nature

C reading a book

D stargazing

5. How do you think Pope would answer the question he asks at the end of the first stanza? Explain.

6. What makes human beings "presumptuous"?

Understanding Literature: Heroic Couplets

A couplet is a poetic form consisting of a set of two rhyming lines. A heroic couplet is written in iambic pentameter. This refers to the number of stressed and unstressed syllables in the line when it is read aloud.

7. Write a couplet from the poem. Explain how you know it is a couplet.

8. Suppose the poem were written in prose or in a poetic form with a different rhyme scheme, such as four-line stanzas with the rhyme scheme *abab*. Explain why it would be more effective or less so.

Critical Thinking

9. What is Pope's answer to the question of whether people should have been created more knowledgeable, powerful, or godlike?

Thinking Creatively

10. Do you think people today ask the same kinds of questions Pope discusses in the poem? Explain.

Grammar Check

An apostrophe is used to show a possessive noun. For example, Pope says the ox "Is now a victim, and now Egypt's god." An apostrophe and *s* indicate that *Egypt's* is a singular possessive noun. In the sentence "Weeds are in the oaks' shade," an apostrophe comes after the *s* in the plural noun *oaks*. This indicates that *oaks* is a plural possessive noun.

- Find the three possessive nouns in line 50 of the poem.

- Write each possessive noun. Then tell whether it is a singular possessive or a plural possessive.

 Writing on Your Own

Suppose you have a friend who asks many questions about people and the universe. Write a letter to the friend. Give advice about seeking answers to these questions, based on the ideas Pope provides in "An Essay on Man."

 Speaking and Listening

Find a meaningful passage in "An Essay on Man" of at least eight lines. With a partner, practice reading the lines in a sing-song rhythm, emphasizing the stressed and unstressed syllables. Then practice reading the lines as if you were talking normally. How does each way affect the reading?

 Research

Writers and critics in Pope's day seemed to go out of their way to create controversy. Pope, though widely recognized as a great writer, had many enemies. Find out more about some of Pope's bitter literary feuds. What effect did they have on Pope's style and choice of subjects? Write a brief paper outlining your thoughts.

Thomas Gray
1716–1771

- To read and understand a poem
- To understand and identify personification in a literary work
- To analyze sequence in a literary work
- To recognize imagery and rhythm in a poem

About the Author

Thomas Gray lived a very quiet life. He was educated at Eton, one of England's most famous private schools. He became a history professor at Cambridge University. He also studied pre-Renaissance poetry and old Welsh and Norse literature. As a young man, Gray traveled in France and Italy. Later, he rarely left Cambridge except to enjoy nature in England's Lake District or in Scotland.

Unlike later poets such as Wordsworth, Gray believed that "the language of the age is never the language of poetry." So his poems often contain unnatural word order and word choice. Critics such as Samuel Johnson criticized some of Gray's poems for this reason. (You will read more about Johnson in the next selection.)

About the Selection

"Elegy Written in a Country Churchyard," written in 1751, is Thomas Gray's masterpiece. An *elegy* is a sad poem, sometimes written to mourn someone's death. The churchyard Gray writes about was in the village of Stoke Poges, where his mother lived. Samuel Johnson once said, "The Churchyard abounds with images which find a mirror in every mind, and with sentiments to which every bosom returns an echo."

Literary Terms "Elegy Written in a Country Churchyard" is a poem that uses **imagery,** rhyme, and **rhythm.** Imagery is words that appeal to the five senses to create word pictures. Rhyme is the repetition of ending sounds. Rhythm is a musical quality created through changes in stressed syllables. The selection also uses figurative language to express ideas and feelings. It includes **personification,** a form of figurative language in which an animal or nonliving object is described as if it were a person. References to the past, present, and future create a **sequence** of events in the poem.

Reading on Your Own In this poem, the poet describes some details that are facts. From these facts, he reaches certain conclusions that are his own opinion. As you read the poem, distinguish between the facts and the poet's opinions. Summarize the meaning of each stanza as you read.

Writing on Your Own Imagine walking through a cemetery or graveyard. Write a journal entry describing your thoughts and feelings.

Vocabulary Focus Prefixes can help you figure out the meanings of unfamiliar words as you read. For example, Gray describes "some mute inglorious Milton." If you know that the prefix *in-* means "not," you can determine that *inglorious* means "not having glory or fame." Figure out the meanings of *ignoble* and *uncouth* by looking up the meanings of each prefix and root word and combining them.

Think Before You Read What thoughts and ideas might a walk in a graveyard cause?

imagery
pictures created by words that appeal to the five senses

rhythm a pattern created by the stressed and unstressed syllables in a line of poetry

personification giving animals or objects the characteristics or qualities of humans

sequence the order of events in a literary work

Elegy Written in a Country Churchyard

As you read, think about the ideas about life and death that being in the churchyard inspires in the poet.

The **Curfew** tolls the knell of parting day,
    The lowing herd wind slowly o'er the lea,
The plowman homeward plods his weary way,
    And leaves the world to darkness and to me.

5 Now fades the glimmering landscape on the sight,
    And all the air a solemn stillness holds,
Save where the beetle wheels his droning flight,
    And drowsy tinklings lull the distant folds;

The *tinklings* are the sounds of the sheep's bells in their *folds,* or pens. What other examples of sound imagery do you find in the first three stanzas?

Save that from yonder ivy-mantled tow'r
10   The moping owl does to the moon complain
Of such as, wand'ring near her secret bow'r,
    Molest her ancient solitary reign.

Beneath those rugged elms, that yew-tree's shade,
    Where heaves the turf in many a **mould'ring** heap,
15 Each in his narrow cell for ever laid,
    The **rude** Forefathers of the **hamlet** sleep.

Line 10 is an example of personification. What other examples of personification can you find in the poem?

The breezy call of incense-breathing Morn,
    The swallow twitt'ring from the straw-built shed,
The cock's shrill **clarion,** or the echoing horn,
20   No more shall rouse them from their lowly bed.

curfew sounding of a bell at evening	**mould'ring** decomposing	**hamlet** small village
molest disturb	**rude** simple	**clarion** a loud, clear trumpet

For them no more the blazing hearth shall burn,
    Or busy housewife ply her evening care:
No children run to lisp their sire's return,
    Or climb his knees the envied kiss to share.

25 Oft did the harvest to their sickle yield,
    Their furrow oft the stubborn **glebe** has broke:
How **jocund** did they drive their team afield!
    How bow'd the woods beneath their sturdy stroke!

Let not Ambition mock their useful toil,
30   Their homely joys, and destiny obscure;
Nor Grandeur hear with a disdainful smile
    The short and simple **annals** of the poor.

The boast of **heraldry,** the pomp of pow'r,
    And all that beauty, all that wealth e'er gave,
35 Awaits alike th' **inevitable** hour:
    The paths of glory lead but to the grave.

Nor you, ye Proud, **impute** to These the fault,
    If Memory o'er their Tomb no Trophies raise,
Where through the long-drawn aisle and fretted vault
40   The pealing anthem swells the note of praise.

Can storied urn or animated bust
    Back to its mansion call the fleeting breath?
Can Honour's voice provoke the silent dust,
    Or Flatt'ry soothe the dull cold ear of death?

45 Perhaps in this neglected spot is laid
    Some heart once pregnant with celestial fire;
Hands, that the rod of empire might have sway'd,
    Or waked to ecstasy the living **lyre.**

Beginning in line 15, Gray is describing the dead people buried in the churchyard.

A *fretted vault* is a decorated ceiling. This and the *long-drawn aisle* in line 39 describe the inside of a cathedral. How does this image contrast with the setting of the poem?

A *storied urn* (line 41) is a funeral urn, or container, decorated with words or designs describing the dead person.

glebe field	**heraldry** family history	**impute** blame
jocund merrily		**lyre** stringed instrument
annals chronicles	**inevitable** unavoidable	

To figure out the meaning of lines 49–50, rearrange the word order: "Knowledge never unrolled her ample page to their eyes."

But Knowledge to their eyes her ample page
50   Rich with the spoils of time did ne'er unroll;
Chill **Penury** repress'd their noble rage,
       And froze the **genial** current of the soul.

Full many a gem of purest ray serene
       The dark unfathom'd caves of ocean bear:
55   Full many a flower is born to blush unseen,
       And waste its sweetness on the desert air.

Hampden refers to John Hampden (1594–1643), a statesman who defended the rights of the people. *Milton* refers to John Milton (1608–1674), a great English poet. *Cromwell* refers to Oliver Cromwell (1599–1658), a general who led Parliament to victory over King Charles I in the English Civil War.

Some village Hampden that with **dauntless** breast
       The little tyrant of his fields withstood,
Some mute inglorious Milton here may rest,
60   Some Cromwell guiltless of his country's blood.

Th' applause of list'ning senates to command,
       The threats of pain and ruin to despise,
To scatter plenty o'er a smiling land,
       And read their history in a nation's eyes,

65   Their lot forbade: nor **circumscribed** alone
       Their glowing virtues, but their crimes confined;
Forbade to wade through slaughter to a throne,
       And shut the gates of mercy on mankind,

The struggling pangs of conscious truth to hide,
70   To quench the blushes of **ingenuous** shame,
Or heap the shrine of Luxury and Pride
       With incense kindled at the Muse's flame.

A *muse* is a poet's source of inspiration. In lines 71–72, Gray criticizes poets who write to please wealthy people.

Far from the **madding** crowd's ignoble strife,
       Their sober wishes never learn'd to stray;
75   Along the cool **sequester'd** vale of life
       They kept the noiseless tenor of their way.

penury severe poverty	**circumscribed** limited	**sequester'd** isolated
genial friendly, warm	**ingenuous** innocent	
dauntless fearless	**madding** frenzied	

Yet ev'n these bones from insult to protect
    Some frail memorial still erected nigh,
With uncouth rhymes and shapeless sculpture deck'd,
80   Implores the passing tribute of a sigh.

Their name, their years, spelt by th' unletter'd muse,
    The place of fame and elegy supply:
And many a holy text around she strews,
    That teach the **rustic moralist** to die.

85 For who, to dumb Forgetfulness a prey,
    This pleasing anxious being e'er resign'd,
Left the warm precincts of the cheerful day,
    Nor cast one longing ling'ring look behind?

On some fond breast the parting soul relies,
90   Some pious drops the closing eye requires;
Ev'n from the tomb the voice of Nature cries,
    Ev'n in our Ashes live their **wonted** Fires.

For thee, who, mindful of th' unhonour'd dead,
    Dost in these lines their artless tale relate;
95 If chance, by lonely contemplation led,
    Some kindred spirit shall inquire thy fate,

Haply some **hoary-headed Swain** may say,
    "Oft have we seen him at the peep of dawn
Brushing with hasty steps the dews away
100   To meet the sun upon the upland lawn.

"There at the foot of yonder nodding beech
    That wreathes its old fantastic roots so high,
His listless length at noontide would he stretch,
    And pore upon the brook that babbles by.

An *unletter'd muse* is an uneducated poet.

To whom do you think *thee* ("you") refers in line 93?

Beginning in line 97, the poet imagines a man recalling the young man about whom the epitaph (lines 117–128 on page 229) is written. Note the sequence, or order of events, in his recollection.

rustic rural; in the country	**wonted** usual	**hoary-headed** gray- or white-haired
moralist philosopher	**haply** perhaps	**swain** peasant; shepherd

105 "Hard by yon wood, now smiling as in scorn,
    Mutt'ring his wayward fancies he would rove,
Now drooping, woeful wan, like one forlorn,
    Or crazed with care, or cross'd in hopeless love.

"One morn I miss'd him on the custom'd hill,
110   Along the heath and near his fav'rite tree;
Another came; nor yet beside the **rill,**
    Nor up the lawn, nor at the wood was he;

"The next with **dirges** due in sad array
    Slow through the church-way path we saw him borne.
115 Approach and read (for thou canst read) the **lay**
    Graved on the stone beneath yon aged thorn:"

> Do you think the swain knew the young man personally? How do the details support your answer?

Stoke Poges Church, the subject of Gray's *Elegy*

rill small brook	**dirges** mournful hymns	**lay** ballad

THE EPITAPH.

Here rests his head upon the lap of Earth
  A Youth to Fortune and to Fame unknown.
Fair Science frown'd not on his humble birth,
120   And Melancholy mark'd him for her own.

Large was his **bounty,** and his soul sincere,
  Heav'n did a **recompense** as largely send:
He gave to Mis'ry all he had, a tear,
  He gain'd from Heav'n ('twas all he wish'd) a friend.

125 No farther seek his merits to disclose,
  Or draw his frailties from their dread abode,
(There they alike in trembling hope repose,)
  The bosom of his Father and his God.

An *epitaph* is writing on a gravestone. What is the main idea of this epitaph?

Read the epitaph aloud and listen for the rhythm of the poetry. How does the regular rhythm suit this poem?

bounty generosity   **recompense** payment

Directions Choose the letter of the best answer or write the answer using complete sentences.

Comprehension: Identifying Facts

1. The people buried in the country churchyard are ____.
   A former village leaders
   B soldiers
   C common villagers
   D priests

2. According to the epitaph, the dead young man is ____.
   A sadder than ever before
   B with God in heaven
   C reunited with his dead parents
   D a great war hero

3. How does poverty affect the lives of the villagers?

4. Where is the "moping owl"?

5. What household or family activities will no longer take place for the people in the churchyard?

6. What crimes or sins has death stopped (lines 65–72)?

7. Where does the poet see "uncouth rhymes and shapeless sculpture" (line 79)?

8. Whom is the "hoary-headed swain" talking about beginning in line 98?

9. According to lines 105–108, what emotions did the young man show when he was alive?

10. Where is the epitaph written?

Comprehension: Putting Ideas Together

11. The mood of the setting created in the first three stanzas is ____.
    A humorous   C peaceful
    B scary   D sad

12. The purpose of an epitaph is to ____.
    A reveal a secret
    B tell about a dead person
    C keep evil spirits away
    D record family histories

13. What does the poet contrast in the fourth and fifth stanzas?

14. Why are the rich and powerful warned not to mock the people in the churchyard?

15. According to the poet, what is one advantage the villagers had due to being poor?

16. In line 55, for what is the flower a metaphor?

17. How do the gravestones teach people about death (lines 81–84)?

18. According to the epitaph, what did the young man lose by dying? What did he gain?

19. For what does the "voice of Nature" (line 91) cry? Do you think this is true? Tell why you think as you do.

20. Why does the poet bring in the swain as a character in this poem? What role does he play?

Understanding Literature: Personification

Personification is a figure of speech in which a writer compares an animal or a nonliving object to a person. For example, in line 10 Gray says that an owl is moping and complaining. These are actions that only people do in real life. Sometimes, the animal or thing being personified is shown by capitalizing the word used for it.

21. Identify and explain the personification in this line: "Let not Ambition mock their useful toil."

22. Find and quote three other examples of personification in the poem.

23. What human traits does the poet give to the nonhuman things in these examples?

24. How does personification affect the mood of the poem?

25. Why do you think writers use personification? How is it an effective tool?

Critical Thinking

26. One of the poem's most famous lines is "The paths of glory lead but to the grave." Explain how this line expresses the poem's theme.

27. According to lines 49–52, poverty (*penury*) and a lack of knowledge are what kept these people from becoming great. Do you think this still happens? Explain.

28. What did the swain see about the young man's life? How do his observations and the epitaph fit together?

29. Why do you think this is one of the most popular and well-known poems in the English language?

Thinking Creatively

30. What qualities or details from your life do you hope people will remember after you are gone? Why are those important to you? What could they teach others?

After Reading continued on next page

Grammar Check

Exclamations are sentences that express strong feeling such as surprise, fear, or joy. An exclamation ends with an exclamation point (!).

- Write down two exclamations from the poem.

- Identify the emotion expressed in each sentence.

 Writing on Your Own

Think about a place you went that created a mood, such as peace, joy, or fear. Write a paragraph describing the place. Don't state the mood of the place. Instead, use words, phrases, and images that help suggest the mood.

 Speaking

Choose a small part of the poem to read aloud. Choose a part that creates a specific mood or one that gives readers ideas about how to live. Practice saying the lines with expression that fits their meaning and purpose. Then read the lines aloud to a small group.

 Listening

Listen to a partner read several lines from the poem. Then explain to your partner the meaning and purpose of the lines. Some examples of a purpose are to create a mood, to describe a feeling, and to help listeners. Then read different lines and have your partner respond.

 Viewing

In the library or online, find a painting or photograph that could illustrate the setting of "Elegy Written in a Country Churchyard." Make a photocopy of the picture and display it on a bulletin board along with those your classmates have chosen.

BEFORE READING THE SELECTION

from *Dictionary of the English Language*   by Samuel Johnson

About the Author

Samuel Johnson was the son of a bookseller. He attended Oxford University but could afford to go for only two years. He became a writer in London to support himself. His poetry soon got the public's attention. He also wrote a biography and journalistic pieces.

As a young man, Johnson married a widow much older than himself. Known for his brilliant conversation, he became friends with many talented people. James Boswell became close friends with Johnson and later wrote Johnson's biography, based on shared journeys and talks.

In 1750–1752, Johnson wrote a popular group of essays in *The Rambler,* a twice-weekly newsletter. These made him famous for his wisdom and keen moral sense. Toward the end of his life, Johnson wrote *The Lives of the English Poets.* This book helped him become known as an honest and insightful critic. Despite his success, Johnson also suffered hardships: poverty, depression, and the death of his wife.

Samuel Johnson
1709–1784

Objectives

■ To read and understand nonfiction

■ To analyze an author's style and voice

About the Selection

Johnson's *Dictionary of the English Language* was the first English dictionary. Many scholars had feared that the English they spoke would die out if its words were not recorded. Johnson started work on the project in 1747 with the help of six assistants. Johnson did much of the work on this nine-year project himself. He gathered and defined words and located quotations containing examples of their use. Many entries contain humor or personal references. However, most entries are clear, thorough definitions. This selection includes only a few entries. The meanings of some words have changed, but others are still used in dictionaries through the present day.

Before Reading continued on next page

The Restoration and the 18th Century Unit 3   **233**

BEFORE READING THE SELECTION *(continued)*

from *Dictionary of the English Language*   by Samuel Johnson

nonfiction
writing containing
information that
is factual; may
be presented
through detailed
descriptions or
examples

voice the way an
author expresses
ideas through style,
form, content, and
purpose

style an author's
way of writing

Literary Terms Johnson's *Dictionary of the English Language* is **nonfiction,** or writing about factual information. Johnson was known for his unique **voice.** His wit and desire to inform his readers caused them to trust in his judgments. His **style,** or choice of words and way of constructing sentences, also made his writing a success.

Reading on Your Own As you read the selection, keep in mind the author's purpose. Also consider the cause of Johnson's writing the dictionary and how this adds to its effect.

Writing on Your Own Choose one of the following words: *sports, peace, politics, popularity.* Write a paragraph in which you define the word in your own way.

Vocabulary Focus Many English words are based on Greek and Latin roots. For example, the word *lexis* is Greek for "speech" or "word." The Greek root *graph* comes from the verb "to write." The word *lexicographer* means "a writer who focuses on words." Find the meanings of *innovation, censure,* and *immutably* by finding their Greek or Latin roots and their meanings.

Think Before You Read How do you think Johnson might have felt about the challenge of creating a dictionary from scratch?

from *Dictionary*
of the English Language

Preface.

It is the fate of those who toil at the lower employments of life, to be rather driven by the fear of evil, than attracted by the prospect of good; to be exposed to censure, without hope of praise; to be disgraced by **miscarriage,** or punished for neglect, where success would have been without applause, and diligence without reward.

Among these unhappy mortals is the writer of dictionaries; whom mankind have considered, not as the pupil, but the slave of science, the pionier of literature, doomed only to remove rubbish and clear obstructions from the paths of Learning and Genius, who press forward to conquest and glory, without bestowing a smile on the humble drudge that **facilitates** their progress. Every other authour may aspire to praise; the lexicographer can only hope to escape reproach, and even this negative **recompence** has been yet granted to very few.

I have, notwithstanding this discouragement, attempted a dictionary of the *English* language, which, while it was employed in the cultivation of every species of literature, has itself been hitherto neglected, suffered to spread, under the direction of chance, into wild exuberance, resigned to the tyranny of time and fashion, and exposed to the corruptions of ignorance, and **caprices** of innovation. . . .

> As you read, think about the kinds of facts and details that add to a person's understanding of a word.

> What figure of speech does Johnson use here?

> Voice is the writer's personality coming out in the writing. What can you tell about Johnson from his word choices and style of writing?

miscarriage failure	**recompence** payment, reward	**caprices** sudden whims
facilitates brings about		

In this work, when it shall be found that much is omitted, let it not be forgotten that much likewise is performed; and though no book was ever spared out of tenderness to the authour, and the world is little **solicitous** to know whence proceeded the faults of that which it condemns; yet it may gratify curiosity to inform it, that the *English Dictionary* was written with little assistance of the learned, and without any patronage of the great; not in the soft **obscurities** of retirement, or under the shelter of academick bowers, but amidst inconvenience and distraction, in sickness and in sorrow: and it may repress the triumph of **malignant** criticism to observe, that if our language is not here fully displayed, I have only failed in an attempt which no human powers have hitherto completed. If the lexicons of ancient tongues, now immutably fixed, and comprised in a few volumes, be yet, after the toil of successive ages, inadequate and **delusive;** if the **aggregated** knowledge, and co-operating diligence of the *Italian* academicians, did not secure them from the censure of *Beni;* if the embodied criticks of *France,* when fifty years had been spent upon their work, were obliged to change its oeconomy, and give their second edition another form, I may surely be contented without the praise of perfection, which, if I could obtain, in this gloom of solitude, what would it **avail** me? I have **protracted** my work till most of those whom I wished to please, have sunk into the grave, and success and miscarriage are empty sounds: I therefore dismiss it with frigid tranquillity, having little to fear or hope from censure or from praise.

Beni refers to Paolo Beni, who, in 1612, wrote a violent attack on the first edition of the Italian dictionary. The French lexicographers changed their dictionary's *oeconomy,* or organization, due to criticism.

❦ ❦ ❦ ❦ ❦ ❦ ❦ ❦ ❦

B

B, the second letter of the English alphabet, is pronounced as in most other European languages, by pressing the whole length of the lips together, and forcing them open with a

solicitous eager	**malignant** mean; meaning to do harm	**aggregated** collected
obscurities states of being secluded	**delusive** false	**avail** help
		protracted delayed

strong breath. It has a near **affinity** with the other labial letters, and is **confounded** by the Germans with *P*, and by the Gascons with *V*; from which an epigrammatist remarks, that *bibere* and *vivere* are in Gascony the same. The Spaniards, in most words, use *B* or *V* **indifferently.**

buffleheaded adj. [from *buffle* and *head*.] A man with a large head, like a buffalo; dull; stupid; foolish.

electricity n.s. [from *electrick*. See *electre*.] A property in some bodies, whereby, when rubbed so as to grow warm, they draw little bits of paper, or such like substances, to them. Quincy.

Such was the account given a few years ago of electricity; but the industry of the present age, first excited by the experiments of Gray, has discovered in electricity a multitude of philosophical wonders. Bodies electrified by a sphere of glass, turned nimbly round, not only emit flame, but may be fitted with such a quantity of the electrical vapour, as, if discharged at once upon a human body, would endanger life. The force of this vapour has hitherto appeared instantaneous, persons at both ends of a long chain seeming to be struck at once. The philosophers are now endeavouring to intercept the strokes of lightning.

enthusiasm n.s. A vain belief of private **revelation;** a vain confidence of divine favour or communication.

hatchet-face n.s. An ugly face; such, I suppose, as might be **hewn** out of a block by a hatchet.

lexicographer n.s. [*lexicographe*, French] A writer of dictionaries; a harmless drudge, that busies himself in tracing the original, and detailing the **signification** of words.

Labial sounds such as *b* and *v* are made by using the lips. *Gascons* are from *Gascony*, a region in southwest France. The word *bibere* means "to drink"; *vivere* means "to live."

The abbreviation *n.s.* means the word is a singular noun.

Johnson uses irony to describe himself. What is the effect of the irony?

affinity kinship	**revelation** sudden understanding of truth or reality	**signification** meaning
confounded confused		
indifferently not differentiated	**hewn** cut with blows of a heavy tool	

Dr. Johnson in the Ante-Room of Lord Chesterfield Waiting for an Audience, Edward Matthew Ward

In Johnson's time some literary figures got money and support from wealthy *patrons.* The Earl of Chesterfield had offered patronage to Johnson. He then ignored Johnson until the dictionary was finished, but expected Johnson to dedicate the *Dictionary* to him.

Cleaveland is John Cleveland (1613–1658), a poet and political satirist. His poetry was popular with the public but not with critics. What point does Johnson make about Cleveland in the entry for *skilt*?

newfangled adj. [*new* and *fangle.*] Formed with vain or foolish love of novelty.

oats n.s. [*aten*, Saxon.] A grain, which in England is generally given to horses, but in Scotland supports the people.

patron n.s. [*patron*, Fr. *patronus*, Latin.] One who **countenances,** supports or protects. Commonly a wretch who supports with **insolence,** and is paid with flattery.

skilt n.s. [A word used by Cleaveland, of which I know not either the **etymology** or meaning.]
> Smectymnus! ha! what art?
> Syriack? Or Arabick? Or Welsh? What skilt?
> Ape all the bricklayers that Babel built.   Cleaveland.

tory n.s. [A **cant** term, derived, I suppose, from an Irish word signifying a savage.] One who adheres to the ancient constitution of the state, and the **apostolical hierarchy** of the church of England, opposed to a whig.

countenances approves	**etymology** history of a word	**apostolical** related to religious authority
insolence insulting treatment	**cant** word used by a particular group	**hierarchy** ranking; proper order

AFTER READING THE SELECTION

from *Dictionary of the English Language*   *by Samuel Johnson*

Directions Choose the letter of the best answer or write the answer using complete sentences.

Comprehension: Identifying Facts

1. According to Johnson, the most likely response to a dictionary is _____.

   A criticism   **C** gratitude

   B praise   **D** scorn

2. Summarize three problems Johnson had in writing the dictionary.

3. From what language does the word *oats* come from?

Comprehension: Putting Ideas Together

4. The reason Johnson gives for writing the dictionary is to _____.
   A become famous
   B compete with the French
   C save English from corruption
   D help English writers

5. How important are the quotations in helping readers understand the words' definitions? Give an example that helps or hurts understanding.

6. Describe Johnson's style in the dictionary. Use examples from the selection to support your answer.

Understanding Literature: Voice

A writer's voice is communicated through what the writer says and how he or she says it. For example, a writer with a scholarly voice might use difficult words and complex sentences.

7. Think of two adjectives that describe Johnson's voice. Give examples from the selection to support your descriptions.

8. Give an example of a word entry in which Johnson has a humorous voice. Give an example of one in which his voice is more serious.

Critical Thinking

9. Some of Johnson's definitions discuss *connotation,* or the emotions surrounding a word. Most dictionaries today list the *denotation,* the actual definition. Explain why this makes Johnson's dictionary more valuable or less so.

Thinking Creatively

10. Suppose there was no dictionary containing standard spellings and definitions of words. How would the language change over time?

After Reading **continued on next page**

The Restoration and the 18th Century Unit 3 **239**

from *Dictionary of the English Language*   *by Samuel Johnson*

 ### Grammar Check

One use of commas is to separate a less important statement from the rest of a sentence. For example, Johnson defines *tory* as "A cant term, derived, I suppose, from an Irish word signifying a savage." In this sentence, "I suppose" is not important to the meaning of the sentence and is set off by commas. Here is another example of a less important statement set off by commas: *Johnson was, it seems, weary of work on the dictionary.*

- Find another example of this use of commas by Johnson and write it down.

- Write one sentence of your own about Johnson or his dictionary using commas to set off a less important statement.

 ### Writing on Your Own

Suppose you were adding three new words or slang terms to a dictionary. Tell what you would add and how you would define each.

 ### Speaking and Listening

Look up one of the words from Johnson's dictionary in a current dictionary. Read aloud Johnson's entry and the current entry to a partner. Listen to your partner's entries. Then discuss how the style and voice of the current entries are similar to or different from those of Johnson's entries.

 ### Media

Create a magazine or newspaper ad for Johnson's dictionary that might have appeared when it was published. "Sell" the dictionary in the ad by telling about its usefulness, its unique qualities, and so on. You may use pictures, as well as words, in your ad.

BEFORE READING THE SELECTION

from *The Life of Samuel Johnson*   by James Boswell

About the Author

James Boswell was born in Edinburgh, Scotland. His father was a respected judge. Boswell studied law and became a lawyer in 1766, but he wanted to become a writer and be around people in the literary world.

Boswell traveled through Europe, where he met Voltaire and Rousseau, great French writers. He also met Pasquale Paoli, a patriot of the Italian province of Corsica. Paoli was leading Corsica in a fight for independence from the Republic of Genoa, which is now part of Italy. Boswell supported Paoli's efforts. He then wrote a book about the event, *Account of Corsica,* which became popular.

Boswell much admired Samuel Johnson, who was the most famous writer of the period. After meeting through a mutual friend, the two men became friends. In 1773, Boswell invited Johnson on a trip through the Hebrides, which are Scottish islands. He wrote a book about the journey, *Journal of a Tour to the Hebrides.* Boswell is best known for his writings about Samuel Johnson.

About the Selection

During his years of friendship with Johnson, Boswell took many notes. He even wrote exact accounts of Johnson's conversations. He began writing about Johnson after Johnson died in 1784. He was assisted by Edmond Malone, a literary scholar. The writing presented vivid dramatic scenes of its subject. It also showed the faults, as well as the admirable traits, of its subject.

James Boswell
1740–1795

Objectives

- To read and understand biography
- To analyze prose style
- To recognize a character who serves as a foil

Before Reading continued on next page

from *The Life of Samuel Johnson*   *by James Boswell*

biography
a person's life story told by someone else

prose writing that is not poetry

foil a minor character who shows the traits of a major character through contrast

Literary Terms *The Life of Samuel Johnson* is a **biography,** the story of a person's life. A biography often describes the life and achievements of someone who has excelled in some field. Biographies are written in **prose,** or nonpoetical form. Well-written prose can make the person and events described come alive for readers. One method that is often used in biography to highlight the traits of the subject is using **foils.** Foils are minor characters who are contrasted with the main character—the subject of the biography.

Reading on Your Own As you read the selection, think about which parts are fact and which are the author's opinion. How do you know which is which?

Writing on Your Own Write a description of a biography you have read. Explain why the biography was memorable.

Vocabulary Focus You can often use context clues to figure out the meaning of an unfamiliar word. For example, in *The Life of Samuel Johnson,* Boswell says that Johnson "was totally absorbed in the business of the moment; his looks seemed rivetted to his plate." If you are unsure of the meaning of *rivetted,* the first part of the sentence gives helpful clues. It says Johnson was "totally absorbed." This can help you infer that *rivetted* means "firmly attached." Use context clues to figure out the meanings of *arduous, noble,* and *undaunted* in the first paragraph of the selection. Write the meaning of each in your own words and describe the context clues that provide hints.

Think Before You Read What character traits do you think Samuel Johnson might have?

FROM *The Life of* SAMUEL JOHNSON

As you read, think about the traits that made Samuel Johnson a special person.

That he was fully aware of the **arduous** nature of the undertaking, he acknowledges; and shews himself perfectly sensible of it in the conclusion of his "Plan"; but he had a **noble** consciousness of his own abilities, which enabled him to go on with **undaunted** spirit.

Dr. Adams found him one day busy at his Dictionary, when the following dialogue ensued. "*Adams.* This is a great work, Sir. How are you to get all the **etymologies?** *Johnson.* Why, Sir, here is a shelf with Junius, and Skinner, and others; and there is a Welch gentleman who has published a collection of Welch proverbs, who will help me with the Welch. *Adams.* But, Sir, how can you do this in three years? *Johnson.* Sir, I have no doubt that I can do it in three years. *Adams.* But the French Academy, which consists of forty members, took forty years to compile their Dictionary. *Johnson.* Sir, thus it is. This is the proportion. Let me see; forty times forty is sixteen hundred. As three to sixteen hundred, so is the proportion of an Englishman to a Frenchman." With so much ease and pleasantry could he talk of that **prodigious** labour which he had undertaken to execute.

Dr. Adams is William Adams, who became master of Pembroke College at Oxford University in 1775. He had been a fellow (professor) at the college while Johnson was a student there. How does Adams serve as a foil to Johnson in this conversation?

Junias (in the second paragraph) refers to Franciscus Junius (1589–1677), a scholar of English language and literature. *Skinner* refers to Stephen Skinner (1623–1667), who researched the origins of many English words and wrote an important book of etymology.

arduous difficult; tiring

noble superior in mind and character

undaunted not discouraged

etymologies histories of words

prodigious enormous

Holborn, Gough-square, and *Fleet-street* are areas of London.

While the Dictionary was going forward, Johnson lived part of the time in Holborn, part in Gough-square, Fleet-street; and he had an upper room fitted up like a **counting-house** for the purpose, in which he gave to the **copyists** their several tasks. The words, partly taken from other dictionaries, and partly supplied by himself, having been first written down with spaces left between them, he delivered in writing their etymologies, definitions, and various **significations.** The authorities were copied from the books themselves, in which he had marked the passages with a black-lead pencil, the traces of which could easily be **effaced.** It is remarkable, that he was so attentive in the choice of the passages in which words were authorised, that one may read page after page of his Dictionary with improvement and pleasure; and it should not pass unobserved, that he has quoted no authour whose writings had a tendency to hurt sound religion and morality. . . .

Why do you think Boswell points out that Johnson made no references that had *a tendency to hurt sound religion and morality?*

At supper this night he talked of good eating with uncommon satisfaction. "Some people (said he,) have a foolish way of not minding, or pretending not to mind, what they eat. For my part, I mind my belly very studiously, and very carefully; for I look upon it, that he who does not mind his belly will hardly mind any thing else." I never knew any man who **relished** good eating more than he did. When at table, he was totally absorbed in the business of the moment; his looks seemed **rivetted** to his plate; nor would he, unless when in very high company, say one word, or even pay the least attention to what was said by others, till he had satisfied his appetite, which was so fierce, and indulged with such intenseness, that while in the act of eating, the veins of his forehead swelled, and generally a strong perspiration was visible. But it must be owned, that Johnson, though he could

counting-house office

copyists ones who make copies; assistants

significations subtle meanings or usages

effaced erased

relished enjoyed

rivetted riveted: fastened firmly

be rigidly **abstemious**, was not a **temperate** man either in eating or drinking. He could refrain, but he could not use moderately. He told me, that he had fasted two days without inconvenience, and that he had never been hungry but once. They who beheld with wonder how much he eat upon all occasions when his dinner was to his taste, could not easily conceive what he must have meant by hunger; and not only was he remarkable for the extraordinary quantity which he eat, but he was, or affected to be, a man of very nice **discernment** in the science of cookery. He used to **descant** critically on the dishes which had been at table where he had dined or **supped**, and to recollect very minutely what he had liked. When invited to dine, even with an intimate friend, he was not pleased if something better than a plain dinner was not prepared for him. I have heard him say on such an occasion, "This was a good dinner enough, to be sure; but it was not a dinner to *ask* a man to."

Part of Boswell's prose style in this section is the use of contrast. What two sets of contrasting words does he use?

Samuel Johnson, James Boswell, and Author Oliver Goldsmith at the Mitre Tavern in London

abstemious not taking much food or drink

temperate enjoying in small amounts

discernment power to see what is not evident

descant comment

supped ate supper

AFTER READING THE SELECTION

from *The Life of Samuel Johnson*   by James Boswell

Directions Choose the letter of the best answer or write the answer using complete sentences.

Comprehension: Identifying Facts

1. Johnson planned to write the dictionary in ____.

  A one year   **C** six years

  B three years   **D** ten years

2. According to Boswell, what do the quoted passages in the dictionary have in common?

3. What did Johnson mainly focus on at the dinner table?

Comprehension: Putting Ideas Together

4. Johnson thought Frenchmen were ____.

  A unintelligent

  B good hosts

  C not as efficient as Englishmen

  D the best dictionary writers

5. What character traits are shown by Johnson's behavior about food?

6. Judging by the biography, what was the relationship of Johnson and Boswell?

Understanding Literature: Biography

In telling the story of a person's life, a biographer chooses certain events and stories that best characterize the person. A biographer's goal is to reflect the subject's life accurately. Biographers can create an interesting story with the same literary techniques used in fiction, such as dialogue and a lively prose style.

7. Which direct quotation by Johnson best reflects his character and personality? Explain what it shows about him.

8. Contrast the two main anecdotes, or short stories about certain events, in this selection.

Critical Thinking

9. Why do you think Boswell admired Johnson so much? Support your answer with examples from the selection.

Thinking Creatively

10. Would you have enjoyed having Samuel Johnson for a friend? Explain why or why not.

Grammar Check

Italics are used to set off the titles of books, movies, and other long works. They may also be used to emphasize certain words. For example, Boswell quotes Johnson: ". . . but it was not a dinner to *ask* a man to." The italics show the word that Johnson stressed when speaking. Italics should be used only rarely for this purpose. When writing by hand, use an underline.

- Write down another sentence from the selection that uses italics for emphasis. Explain why the words in italics were emphasized.

 ## Writing on Your Own

Write a short biographical article about a person you know who has done something unusual or who has a strong or interesting character. Use one or more of the techniques Boswell uses in his biography of Samuel Johnson.

 ## Speaking and Listening

With a partner, practice reading the dialogue in the selection between Dr. Adams and Samuel Johnson. Discuss how Dr. Adams, as the foil, would best be portrayed to highlight Johnson's character.

 ## Research

After Shakespeare, Samuel Johnson might be the most quoted writer in the English language. Use reference materials and the Internet to locate some of Johnson's famous quotes. Compile them in a booklet.

 ## Media

Samuel Johnson was the leading critic of his day, and—as Boswell points out—he did not limit his criticism to literature. Review the media sources you use regularly to see how criticism is presented today. What effect does it have on your views and choices? Write a brief reflection paper on criticism in the media.

BEFORE READING THE SELECTION

from *A Vindication of the Rights of Woman* by Mary Wollstonecraft

Mary Wollstonecraft
1759–1797

Objectives

■ To read and
understand an
essay

■ To recognize the
theme of a literary
work

About the Author

Mary Wollstonecraft's father was a wealthy farmer, but
he drank and wasted the wealth he had inherited. At 19,
Wollstonecraft went to work as the companion to a wealthy
widow.

Later, Wollstonecraft, two sisters, and a friend started a school
for girls. The school began successfully, but Wollstonecraft's
friend soon became ill. When she died and the school had
financial problems, Wollstonecraft became deeply depressed.

Wollstonecraft wrote her first book, *Thoughts on the
Education of Daughters,* to try to earn a living. After working
as a governess (a woman who lives with a family to care for
their children) in Ireland, Wollstonecraft returned to London
and wrote a novel and a children's book. She sympathized
with supporters of the French Revolution and wrote a book
defending its principles, *A Vindication of the Rights of Man.*

In 1792, Wollstonecraft turned her attention to injustices
against women, writing *A Vindication of the Rights of
Woman.* She also went to France to observe the French
Revolution firsthand. In 1796, she married William Godwin,
a philosopher. Shortly after that, she gave birth to a baby girl
but died of childbirth complications. Her daughter, Mary,
wrote the novel *Frankenstein.*

About the Selection

In the 18th century, women had very few rights. They could
not vote and had to give up their property to their husbands
when they married. They had few ways to make a living; they
could be nurses, servants, governesses, or shopkeepers. In *A
Vindication of the Rights of Woman,* Wollstonecraft describes
these injustices. She discusses the effects of unfair treatment
not only on women, but also on men.

Literary Terms *A Vindication of the Rights of Woman* is an **essay.** It is a written work that shows an author's opinions on an issue. The **theme** of this essay is women's position in society.

Reading on Your Own As you read the essay, think about the author's purpose for writing it. Is she writing to inform, offer opinions, or persuade, or is it a combination of these?

Writing on Your Own Think of an injustice you have observed in your community or in the society as a whole. Think of the theme of this injustice or event. How did it make you feel? Write a description of it.

Vocabulary Focus Some English words have roots from other languages, such as Greek and Latin. Other words come directly into English from other languages. For instance, Wollstonecraft uses the word *harem.* It comes from Arabic words meaning "something forbidden" or "sanctuary." It was a place where women lived in a Muslim household. She also uses the word *seraglio.* This was the Italian word for a harem.

Think Before You Read What kinds of evidence might Wollstonecraft use to support her opinions?

essay a written work that shows the author's opinions on some basic or current issue

theme the main idea of a literary work

from A Vindication of the Rights of Woman

As you read, consider what the theme, or underlying message, is. Think about how the author says both men and women should change to improve the condition of women.

After considering the historic page, and viewing the living world with anxious **solicitude,** the most melancholy emotions of sorrowful **indignation** have depressed my spirits, and I have sighed when obliged to confess that either Nature has made a great difference between man and man, or that the civilization which has hitherto taken place in the world has been very partial. I have turned over various books written on the subject of education, and patiently observed the conduct of parents and the management of schools; but what has been the result?—a profound conviction that the neglected education of my fellow-creatures is the grand source of the misery I **deplore,** and that women, in particular, are rendered weak and wretched by a variety of concurring causes, originating from one hasty conclusion. The conduct and manners of women, in fact, evidently prove that their minds are not in a healthy state; for, like the flowers which are planted in too rich a soil, strength and usefulness are sacrificed to beauty; and the flaunting leaves, after having pleased a **fastidious** eye, fade, disregarded on the stalk, long before the season when they ought to have arrived at maturity. One cause of this barren blooming I attribute to a false system of education, gathered from the books written on this subject by men who, considering females rather as women

Wollstonecraft compares women to flowers. What kind of flowers does she say women are like? How are they alike?

solicitude care, concern

indignation anger caused by injustice

deplore feel or express sorrow for

fastidious having a demanding attitude

than human creatures, have been more anxious to make them alluring mistresses than affectionate wives and rational mothers; and the understanding of the sex has been so **bubbled** by this **specious homage,** that the civilized women of the present century, with a few exceptions, are only anxious to inspire love, when they ought to cherish a nobler ambition, and by their abilities and virtues exact respect.

In a treatise, therefore, on female rights and manners, the works which have been particularly written for their improvement must not be overlooked, especially when it is asserted, in direct terms, that the minds of women are enfeebled by false refinement; that the books of instruction, written by men of genius, have had the same tendency as more frivolous productions; and that, in the true style of Mahometanism, they are treated as a kind of subordinate beings, and not as a part of the human species, when improvable reason is allowed to be the dignified distinction which raises men above the brute creation, and puts a natural sceptre in a feeble hand.

Yet, because I am a woman, I would not lead my readers to suppose that I mean violently to **agitate** the contested question respecting the quality or inferiority of the sex; but as the subject lies in my way, and I cannot pass it over without subjecting the main tendency of my reasoning to **misconstruction,** I shall stop a moment to deliver, in a few words, my opinion. In the government of the physical world it is observable that the female in point of strength is, in general, inferior to the male. This is the law of Nature; and it does not appear to be suspended or **abrogated** in favor of woman. A degree of physical superiority cannot, therefore, be denied, and it is a noble **prerogative!** But not content with this natural preeminence, men endeavor to sink us still lower, merely

Mahometanism is the practice of Islam. Many Europeans of the time mistakenly believed that the Koran, the sacred text of Islam, taught that women do not have souls.

Wollstonecraft uses a *sceptre* (scepter), a symbol of royal power, in a figurative way. According to her, what puts "a natural sceptre" in the hands of men?

bubbled made into something that lacks firmness or reality	**homage** expression of high regard	**abrogated** made invalid
specious having a false look of truth	**agitate** stir up	**prerogative** exclusive right, power, or privilege
	misconstruction misunderstanding	

to render us alluring objects for a moment; and women, intoxicated by the adoration which men, under the influence of their senses, pay them, do not see, to obtain a durable interest in their hearts, or to become the friends of the fellow-creatures who find amusement in their society.

What inference is Wollstonecraft referring to?

I am aware of an obvious inference. From every quarter have I heard exclamations against masculine women, but where are they to be found? If by this **appellation** men mean to **inveigh** against their ardor in hunting, shooting, and gaming, I shall most cordially join in the cry; but if it be against the imitation of manly virtues, or, more properly speaking, the attainment of those talents and virtues, the exercise of which ennobles the human character, and which raises females in the scale of animal being, when they are comprehensively termed mankind, all those who view them with a philosophic eye must, I should think, wish with me, that they may every day grow more and more masculine. . . .

What contrast does Wollstonecraft use? Why do you think such a contrast would require women to excuse the writer?

My own sex, I hope, will excuse me, if I treat them like rational creatures, instead of flattering their *fascinating graces,* and viewing them as if they were in a state of **perpetual** childhood, unable to stand alone. I earnestly wish to point out in what true dignity and human happiness consists, I wish to persuade women to endeavor to acquire strength, both of mind and body, and to convince them that the soft phrases, **susceptibility** of heart, delicacy of sentiment, and refinement of taste, are almost synonymous with **epithets** of weakness, and that those beings who are only the objects of pity, and that kind of love which has been termed its sister, will soon become objects of **contempt**. . . .

The education of women has of late been more attended to than formerly; yet they are still reckoned a **frivolous** sex, and ridiculed or pitied by the writers who endeavor by satire

---

appellation name or title

inveigh protest

perpetual going on forever

susceptibility openness; responsiveness

epithets abusive words or phrases

contempt lack of respect

frivolous silly, useless

The Letter,
Ludwig Guttenbrunn,
18th century

or instruction to improve them. It is acknowledged that they spend many of the first years of their lives in acquiring a smattering of accomplishments; meanwhile strength of body and mind are sacrificed to **libertine** notions of beauty, to the desire of establishing themselves—the only way women can rise in the world—by marriage. And this desire making mere animals of them, when they marry they act as such children may be expected to act,—they dress, they paint, and nickname God's creatures. Surely these weak beings are only fit for a **seraglio!** Can they be expected to govern a family with judgment, or take care of the poor babes whom they bring into the world?

If, then, it can be fairly deduced from the present conduct of the sex, from the **prevalent** fondness for pleasure which takes place of ambition and those nobler passions that open and enlarge the soul, that the instruction which women have hitherto received has only tended, with the **constitution** of civil society, to render them insignificant objects of desire—mere **propagators** of fools!—if it can be proved that

In Shakespeare's *Hamlet,* Hamlet criticizes Ophelia of having faults common to women by saying, "You jig and amble, you lisp, you nickname God's creatures." Wollstonecraft's point is that some women act weak or silly because people expect them to.

---

libertine not held back by morals

seraglio harem

prevalent widespread

constitution law or custom

propagators those who create offspring

According to Wollstonecraft, what happens to women when they get older?

in aiming to accomplish them, without cultivating their understandings, they are taken out of their sphere of duties, and made ridiculous and useless when the short-lived bloom of beauty is over, I presume that *rational* men will excuse me for endeavoring to persuade them to become more masculine and respectable. . . .

Youth is the season for love in both sexes; but in those days of thoughtless enjoyment provision should be made for the more important years of life, when reflection takes place of sensation. But Rousseau, and most of the male writers who have followed his steps, have warmly **inculcated** that the whole tendency of female education ought to be directed to one point—to render them pleasing.

Rousseau is Jean-Jacques Rousseau (1712–1778), a French philosopher.

Let me reason with the supporters of this opinion who have any knowledge of human nature. Do they imagine that marriage can **eradicate** the habitude of life? The woman who has only been taught to please will soon find that her charms are **oblique** sunbeams, and that they cannot have much effect on her husband's heart when they are seen every day, when the summer is passed and gone. Will she then have sufficient native energy to look into herself for comfort, and cultivate her dormant faculties? or is it not more rational to expect that she will try to please other men, and, in the emotions raised by the expectation of new conquests, endeavor to forget the mortification her love or pride has received? When the husband ceases to be a lover, and the time will inevitably come, her desire of pleasing will then grow languid, or become a spring of bitterness; and love, perhaps, the most **evanescent** of all passions, gives place to jealousy or vanity.

The phrase *her charms are oblique sunbeams* is a metaphor. What two things are being compared? What does the author mean by the comparison?

I now speak of women who are restrained by principle or prejudice. Such women, though they would shrink from an **intrigue** with real **abhorrence,** yet, nevertheless, wish to be convinced by the homage of **gallantry** that they are cruelly

In what ways might a person be *restrained by principle?* by prejudice?

inculcated taught by repeated teaching

eradicate get rid of completely

oblique not direct

evanescent vanishing quickly

intrigue secret love affair

abhorrence hate

gallantry romantic attention or pursuit

neglected by their husbands; or, days and weeks are spent in dreaming of the happiness enjoyed by congenial souls, till their health is undermined and their spirits broken by discontent. How then can the great art of pleasing be such a necessary study? It is only useful to a mistress. The chaste wife and serious mother should only consider her power to please as the polish of her virtues, and the affection of her husband as one of the comforts that render her task less difficult, and her life happier. But, whether she be loved or neglected, her first wish should be to make herself respectable, and not to rely for all her happiness on a being subject to like infirmities with herself. . . .

Women ought to endeavor to purify their heart; but can they do so when their **uncultivated** understandings make them entirely dependent on their senses for employment and amusement, when no noble pursuits set them above the little **vanities** of the day, or enable them to curb the wild emotions that agitate a reed, over which every passing breeze has power? To gain the affections of a virtuous man, is **affectation** necessary? Nature has given woman a weaker frame than man; but, to ensure her husband's affections, must a wife, who by the exercise of her mind and body whilst she was discharging the duties of a daughter, wife, and mother, has allowed her constitution to retain its natural strength, and her nerves a healthy tone,—is she, I say, to **condescend** to use art, and **feign** a sickly delicacy, in order to secure her husband's affection? Weakness may excite tenderness, and gratify the arrogant pride of man; but the lordly caresses of a protector will not gratify a noble mind that pants for and deserves to be respected. Fondness is a poor substitute for friendship!

In a seraglio, I grant, that all these arts are necessary; the epicure must have his palate tickled, or he will sink into **apathy;** but have women so little ambition as to be satisfied

An *epicure* is a person devoted to sensual pleasure. Wollstonecraft is comparing a woman's relationship with her husband to that of a harem member with her master.

uncultivated unrefined; unencouraged

vanities things that are empty or valueless

affectation artificial behavior

condescend stoop to an undignified level

feign pretend

apathy lack of interest or concern

with such a condition? Can they **supinely** dream life away in the lap of pleasure, or the **languor** of weariness, rather than assert their claim to pursue reasonable pleasures, and render themselves **conspicuous** by practicing the virtues which dignify mankind? Surely she has not an immortal soul who can loiter life away merely employed to adorn her person, that she may amuse the languid hours, and soften the cares of a fellow-creature who is willing to be enlivened by her smiles and tricks, when the serious business of life is over.

Besides, the woman who strengthens her body and exercises her mind will, by managing her family and practicing various virtues, become the friend, and not the humble dependent of her husband; and if she, by possessing such substantial qualities, merit his regard, she will not find it necessary to conceal her affection, nor to pretend to an unnatural coldness of **constitution** to excite her husband's passions. In fact, if we revert to history, we shall find that the women who have distinguished themselves have neither been the most beautiful nor the most gentle of their sex.

What kind of relationship does the writer see as most natural? What are the benefits of such a relationship?

supinely lazily

languor lack of energy

conspicuous obvious

constitution nature

AFTER READING THE SELECTION

from *A Vindication of the Rights of Woman* by Mary Wollstonecraft

Directions Choose the letter of the best answer or write the answer using complete sentences.

Comprehension: Identifying Facts

1. According to Wollstonecraft, the miserable condition of women has been caused by their ____.
   A lack of intelligence
   B poor education
   C beauty
   D weak physical condition

2. Wollstonecraft says the ambition of most women is to be ____.
   A respected   C loved
   B famous   D wealthy

3. In what way is the female generally inferior to the male, according to Wollstonecraft?

4. What "masculine" activities does Wollstonecraft think are inappropriate for women?

5. What ambition do women have instead of becoming well educated?

6. What has women's instruction taught them to become?

7. What have male writers said that women should be taught?

8. What activities does Wollstonecraft think women should focus on?

9. According to the author, what do women pretend in order to attract their husbands?

10. What main thing does Wollstonecraft think should connect a husband and wife?

Comprehension: Putting Ideas Together

11. According to the author, the attitude of most women of her time toward their poor education was ____.
    A anger   C gratitude
    B unconcern   D rebellion

12. What makes people different from animals?
    A kindness
    B refinement
    C ability to use tools
    D capacity to learn

13. Summarize Wollstonecraft's view of the issue of physical strength.

14. Should women copy "manly virtues"? Explain.

15. According to the author, will women of her time make good mothers? Why or why not?

After Reading **continued on next page**

16. According to the author, how do men and women differ in regard to romantic love as they grow older?

17. Is romantic love between two people often permanent, according to Wollstonecraft? Explain.

18. Explain why teaching women only to please others has bad effects for both men and women.

19. According to Wollstonecraft, why might a woman's weakness be attractive to a man?

20. According to the author, are women involved in "the serious business of life"? If not, who is?

Understanding Literature: Essay

In an essay, an author must offer facts, examples, and other details to support his or her opinion. If readers decide these supporting details are true, readers will accept the author's opinion.

21. Summarize two figures of speech Wollstonecraft uses to make her point. Explain why these help make her opinion more or less valid.

22. Summarize one scientific observation Wollstonecraft makes. How does it support her argument?

23. In your own words, state the main idea of Wollstonecraft's essay.

24. Summarize one reference to another culture that Wollstonecraft makes. How does it support her argument?

25. Do you agree or disagree with Wollstonecraft's opinion? Explain why or why not.

Critical Thinking

26. Which descriptions of women's lives are still true? Which are not? Explain your answers.

27. Wollstonecraft says that women have a "fondness for pleasure which takes place of ambition and those nobler passions that open and enlarge the soul." What do you think she means by "nobler passions"?

28. Do you agree with Wollstonecraft that women cannot be both strong and soft-hearted (page 252)? Explain your answer.

29. What do you think Wollstonecraft's purpose in writing the essay is?

Thinking Creatively

30. Suppose you are a newspaper advice columnist. What advice for women today might you find in Wollstonecraft's essay?

Grammar Check

Pronouns are words like *I, you, he,* and *they* that take the place of nouns. A pronoun must agree with the noun it refers to in person and in number. This means that the third-person pronouns *he* and *him* agree with the noun *man;* the third-person pronouns *she* and *her* agree with the noun *woman.* The third-person pronouns *they* and *them* agree with the noun *men* and the noun *women.* Identify each pronoun and the noun it replaces in the following sentences from *A Vindication of the Rights of Woman.*

- The education of women has of late been more attended to than formerly; yet they are still reckoned a frivolous sex.

- I presume that rational men will excuse me for endeavouring to persuade them to become more masculine and respectable.

- The woman who has only been taught to please will soon find that her charms are oblique sunbeams.

 Writing on Your Own

Create a Main Idea graphic organizer for this essay. See Appendix A for a model of this graphic organizer. Use the graphic organizer to write a summary of the selection.

 Speaking

Has the condition of women changed greatly since Wollstonecraft wrote her essay? Write a short speech answering this question. Then present your speech to a small group of classmates.

 Listening

With a partner, take turns reading aloud one paragraph of Wollstonecraft's essay. Listen carefully to your partner's reading and summarize the ideas expressed in it.

Irony is the use of words that seem to say one thing but mean the opposite. If you look at a rainy, gloomy sky and say, "It looks like another beautiful day," you are using irony. Your real meaning is different from your stated meaning.

Writers sometimes use irony for effect. For example, in *Dictionary of the English Language,* Samuel Johnson defines *lexicographer* as "a harmless drudge." In his introduction, Johnson discusses the difficult job of writing a dictionary. In contrast, a "harmless drudge" is a worker who labors dully over an unimportant task. So Johnson's ironic description calls attention to his brilliance and the difficult goal he has achieved. It also has a humorous effect.

Writers of satire, novels, and essays also use irony. It can call attention to social problems and to people's flaws. When you read, watch for statements that contradict the author's viewpoint. Recognizing irony can ensure that you understand an author's meaning.

Review

1. After receiving food and drink from the Lilliputians, Gulliver says he has been treated with "Expence and Magnificence." Why is this statement ironic? What is its effect?

2. In "A Letter to Her Daughter," Montagu says her granddaughter should "conceal whatever learning she attains, with as much solicitude as she would hide crookedness or lameness." Is Montagu being ironic? What does her advice say about women's place in society?

3. Defoe says that, during the plague, there were no newspapers "to spread rumours and reports of things, and to improve them by the invention of men." Explain the irony in this statement.

4. In *An Essay on Man,* Pope tells people to criticize Providence and to "Destroy all creatures for thy sport or gust." Is Pope's advice ironic? Tell why you think as you do.

5. Why do you think irony was popular with 18th-century writers?

Writing on Your Own

Write an essay about getting along with your parents. Use irony at least twice to help make a point.

In the late 1600s, London experienced two disasters: a plague and a destructive fire. In the next 100 years, however, the nation became wealthier and more powerful. England, Wales, and Scotland came together as Great Britain. After defeating France in a series of wars, Britain controlled lands all over the world. The Industrial Revolution began, making the country wealthier. Unfortunately, the working classes did not always share the wealth.

During the Restoration and the century that followed, literature became more available to the middle class. Literary style became simpler. Many kinds of nonfiction, such as letters, biography, and essays, were published. Samuel Johnson published the first dictionary of the English language. Writers like Jonathan Swift and Alexander Pope used satire to criticize poor taste in art and in life. The novel's popularity increased due to novelists like Daniel Defoe. Mary Wollstonecraft proposed better education for women.

Selections

- "A Voyage to Lilliput" is part of the satire *Gulliver's Travels* by Jonathan Swift. In it, Swift's narrator, Lemuel Gulliver, discovers a land of tiny human-like creatures.

- In "A Letter to Her Daughter," Mary Wortley Montagu explains how and why girls should be educated.

- *A Journal of the Plague Year* by Daniel Defoe is a work of fiction set during the plague that killed many thousands in London in 1665.

- In the poem "An Essay on Man," Alexander Pope seeks to explain humans' place in the universe.

- "Elegy Written in a Country Churchyard" is a poem by Thomas Gray that expresses thoughts about death. It describes the natural nobility of common people buried in a village cemetery.

- Samuel Johnson's *Dictionary of the English Language*, the first comprehensive English dictionary, reflects Johnson's brilliance and wit.

- In *The Life of Samuel Johnson*, James Boswell creates a biography that brings its subject vividly to life and describes his failings, as well as his achievements.

- In *A Vindication of the Rights of Woman,* Mary Wollstonecraft explains why women should receive an education equal to that of men.

Directions Choose the letter of the best answer or write the answer using complete sentences.

Comprehension: Identifying Facts

1. "A Voyage to Lilliput" is narrated by _____.

   A Jonathan Swift
   B a Lilliputian
   C Lemuel Gulliver
   D an orator

2. In *A Journal of the Plague Year,* what do officials say should be done with people who get the plague?

3. According to Pope in "An Essay on Man," what error does pride lead people to make?

4. In "Elegy Written in a Country Churchyard," what does the poet describe?

5. What subjects does Montagu think her granddaughter should study?

Comprehension: Putting Ideas Together

6. Which detail about a word does *not* appear in Johnson's dictionary listings?

   A part of speech **C** etymology
   B definition   **D** pronunciation

7. Why was writing the *Dictionary of the English Language* difficult for Johnson?

8. Summarize two details in *The Life of Samuel Johnson* that show character traits of Johnson that are negative or unappealing.

9. Name three character traits of the "rude Forefathers of the hamlet" described in "Elegy Written in a Country Churchyard."

10. According to Wollstonecraft, what traits and habits in a woman lead to a happy marriage?

Understanding Literature: Nonfiction

Nonfiction is writing, usually prose, about real people and events. Essays, letters, biography, and dictionaries are all forms of nonfiction.

11. How does Montagu's "A Letter to Her Daughter" differ from a typical friendly letter of today? What other forms of nonfiction is it like?

12. Defoe's *A Journal of the Plague Year* is historical fiction. In what ways is historical fiction similar to nonfiction? In what ways does it differ?

13. What supporting details does Boswell use in his biography to describe Samuel Johnson?

14. What is Wollstonecraft's purpose for writing *A Vindication of the Rights of Woman*? How does she accomplish it?

15. How do the quotations in *Dictionary of the English Language* help support the word entries?

Critical Thinking

16. How are Montagu's and Wollstonecraft's opinions about women's education similar and different?

17. What differing views of death are found in *A Journal of the Plague Year* and "Elegy Written in a Country Churchyard"?

18. Do you think it is a good idea for a biographer to know his subject personally, as Boswell did? Explain why or why not. Use examples from the selections to support your answer.

19. Which writer in this unit has the most optimistic view of people and life? Use examples to support your answer.

Thinking Creatively

20. Which author in this unit would you most like to meet? Explain why and tell what you would discuss with the person.

Speak and Listen

With a partner, choose two authors from this unit who have themes or issues in common, such as Wollstonecraft and Montagu. Create a dialogue between the two that shows similarities and differences between their points of view.

Writing on Your Own

Research an event in British history from 1660 to 1798 that interests you. Write either a work of nonfiction or of historical fiction about the event.

Beyond Words

In the library or on the Internet, locate a drawing or map of London in the 1600s, before or after the fire of 1666. Make a sketch of the drawing or map. Use labels to show important buildings and other locations.

Test-Taking Tip

Studying together in small groups and asking questions of one another is one way to review for tests.

Winter Sunset,
Joseph Farquharson

As the 19th century began, the British people had witnessed two revolutions—one in America and one in France. The British views of a quiet and ordered social world no longer seemed important. A new wave of energetic writers felt strongly about the value of the individual, freedom, and the imagination. They turned to the beauty of the natural world and their private experience to create poems with new forms and messages. This was the start of Romantic literature.

In this unit, you will learn about the restless state of English society and read some of the excellent Romantic literature its writers produced.

"These sublime and magnificent scenes [in nature] . . . elevated me from all littleness of feeling, and . . . diverted my mind from the thoughts over which it had brooded. . . ."

—*Mary Shelley*, Frankenstein, *1818*

By 1800, there was no going back to the calm, orderly ways of earlier times in England. The American and French revolutions had filled the air with ideas of freedom and equal rights. When the French Revolution spiraled into chaos and murder, a strong leader, Napoleon Bonaparte, emerged. He took control of France, ending democracy there. However, the ideas of democracy remained.

Napoleon on Board **Bellerophon, William Orchardson**

In addition, the Industrial Revolution had changed cities and patterns of work forever. People came to the cities to work. Cities had become dirty and overcrowded. Workers slaved for very little pay. A wealthy middle class had emerged to join the upper class. But most people were poor and unhappy.

Social unrest marked the first decades of the 1800s in England and led to the Reform Bill passed by Parliament in 1832. More people could vote, and the upper class lost some privileges.

A new generation of writers supported the struggle for freedom. They spoke out against the society that held people down. In their work, these writers turned away from cold reason and used

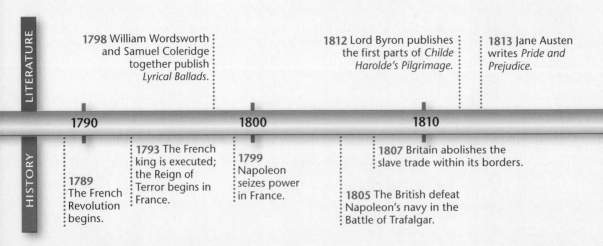

LITERATURE

1798 William Wordsworth and Samuel Coleridge together publish *Lyrical Ballads.*

1812 Lord Byron publishes the first parts of *Childe Harolde's Pilgrimage.*

1813 Jane Austen writes *Pride and Prejudice.*

1790   1800   1810

HISTORY

1789 The French Revolution begins.

1793 The French king is executed; the Reign of Terror begins in France.

1799 Napoleon seizes power in France.

1807 Britain abolishes the slave trade within its borders.

1805 The British defeat Napoleon's navy in the Battle of Trafalgar.

imagination and emotion instead. They valued the human and the individual, not society as a whole. They stood up for freedom. They loved nature and the rural setting, not machinery. And they wrote in more natural, conversational language, not the formal language of the 18th century.

At the same time, England had expanded its empire into many colonies. A new sense of the world brought the magic of far-off lands and ancient myths and mysteries into the new literature.

This period falls into two parts, the first and second generations of Romantic writers. The first generation defined the new spirit of renewal that they were witnessing in the world. The second generation poured its heart into political beliefs. They saw themselves as outcasts and would not live by society's unjust rules.

Many writings in this unit represent the first generation of Romantic writers. These include the poems of William Wordsworth and Samuel Taylor Coleridge, which focus on the beauty and power of nature and the mystery of far-off lands; the journals of Dorothy Wordsworth; and a novel by Jane Austen, which looks humorously at society and marriage. The second generation of Romantic writers includes four excellent authors who died young. Poems by Lord Byron, Percy Shelley, and John Keats explore the nature of beauty, change, and the power of art and imagination. A part of Mary Shelley's novel *Frankenstein* is also included. It finds the negative possibilities in science and shows the need for responsibility and caring for others.

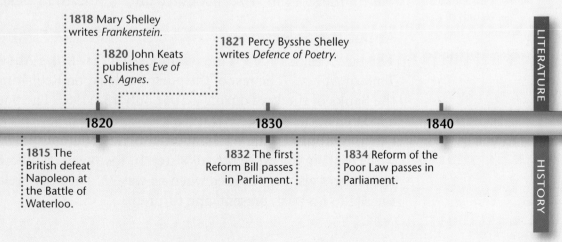

1818 Mary Shelley writes *Frankenstein*.

1820 John Keats publishes *Eve of St. Agnes*.

1821 Percy Bysshe Shelley writes *Defence of Poetry*.

1820   **1830**   **1840**

1815 The British defeat Napoleon at the Battle of Waterloo.

1832 The first Reform Bill passes in Parliament.

1834 Reform of the Poor Law passes in Parliament.

LITERATURE

HISTORY

Lines Composed a Few Miles Above Tintern Abbey   *by William Wordsworth*

William Wordsworth
1770–1850

About the Author

William Wordsworth was born in Cockermouth near the Lake District of northwest England. His mother died when he was 8. His father died when Wordsworth was 13. Wordsworth spent many of his early years going to school near Esthwaite Lake. There he spent much time being with and admiring nature.

Wordsworth attended St. John's College, Cambridge, and graduated in 1791. Later, he met Samuel Taylor Coleridge. The two poets built a close friendship. In 1798, they published a collection of poems called *Lyrical Ballads*, which was very popular. The works used a new style of poetry that included regular language in poetic form. The poems helped start the Romantic movement.

Wordsworth was very close to his sister Dorothy. They lived together for many years. She helped him with his writing. In 1802, Wordsworth married Mary Hutchinson, a woman whom he had known since childhood. The two cared for Dorothy for the last 20 years of her life.

In addition to *Lyrical Ballads,* Wordsworth is known for his *Poems, in Two Volumes.* Perhaps his greatest work, *The Prelude,* was his life story in verse, published after his death in 1850.

About the Selection

This selection is called "Lines Composed a Few Miles Above Tintern Abbey." The rest of the poem's title is "on Revisiting the Banks of the Wye during a Tour, July 13, 1798." The poem appeared at the end of *Lyrical Ballads.* Tintern Abbey was a very old monastery in Wales. Wordsworth wrote this poem while touring the area with his sister. In the poem, Wordsworth remembers visiting the area when he was 23. The poem relates the site to his past, present, and future.

Literary Terms This poem is written in **blank verse.** This verse is unrhymed **iambic pentameter.** Each line has five two-beat sounds, and the second syllable is stressed in each pattern. The ends of the lines do not rhyme with each other. This poem includes an idea called a **paradox.** This is a statement that includes opposite meanings but still makes sense.

Reading on Your Own Notice that this poem has four breaks: in line 22, in line 49, after line 57, and in line 111. When you reach each break, stop to think about what you have read. Summarize that part—state the meaning in your own words. When you are finished with the poem, use your summary to help you understand what you have read.

Writing on Your Own Think of a time when you visited a place that made you feel a certain way. Write a paragraph that describes the place and how it made you feel.

Vocabulary Focus One way to learn about the meanings of new words is to make a list of synonyms and antonyms. A synonym is a word that has nearly the same meaning as another word. An antonym is a word that has the opposite meaning of a word. Look at the terms for this poem at the bottom of each page. *Tranquil* has the synonym *calm.* An antonym for *calm* is *nervous.* Create a list of synonyms and antonyms for difficult words in this poem.

Think Before You Read Predict how this poem will describe nature.

LINES COMPOSED A FEW MILES ABOVE TINTERN ABBEY

As you read, think about what the poet is trying to say about the place he is visiting. What does it mean to him?

Five years have past; five summers, with the length
Of five long winters! and again I hear
These waters, rolling from their mountain-springs
With a soft inland murmur.—Once again
5   Do I behold these steep and lofty cliffs,
That on a wild **secluded** scene impress
Thoughts of more deep seclusion; and connect
The landscape with the quiet of the sky.
The day is come when I again repose
10 Here, under this dark sycamore, and view
These plots of cottage-ground, these orchard-tufts,
Which at this season, with their unripe fruits,
Are clad in one green hue, and lose themselves
'Mid groves and copses. Once again I see
15 These hedge-rows, hardly hedge-rows, little lines
Of **sportive** wood run wild: these **pastoral** farms,
Green to the very door; and wreaths of smoke
Sent up, in silence, from among the trees!
With some uncertain notice, as might seem
20 Of **vagrant** dwellers in the houseless woods,
Or of some **Hermit's** cave, where by his fire
The Hermit sits alone.

Read aloud several lines of the poem and listen for the stress pattern in each line. Ten-syllable lines with a pattern of alternating unstressed and stressed syllables is called iambic pentameter. For example: Do I behold these steep and lofty cliffs . . . (line 5).

secluded screened or hidden from view; by itself

sportive playful or reckless

pastoral out in the country

vagrant wandering without a home

Hermit's belonging to one who lives alone away from others

These beauteous forms,
Through a long absence, have not been to me
As is a landscape to a blind man's eye:
25 But oft, in lonely rooms, and 'mid the din
Of towns and cities, I have owed to them,
In hours of weariness, sensations sweet,
Felt in the blood, and felt along the heart;
And passing even into my purer mind,
30 With **tranquil restoration:**—feelings too
Of unremembered pleasure: such, perhaps,
As have no slight or **trivial** influence
On that best portion of a good man's life,
His little, nameless, unremembered, acts
35 Of kindness and of love. Nor less, I trust,
To them I may have owed another gift,
Of aspect more **sublime;** that blessed mood,
In which the burthen of the mystery,
In which the heavy and the weary weight
40 Of all this **unintelligible** world,
Is lightened:—that serene and blessed mood,
In which the affections gently lead us on,—
Until, the breath of this **corporeal** frame
And even the motion of our human blood
45 Almost suspended, we are laid asleep
In body, and become a living soul:
While with an eye made quiet by the power
Of **harmony,** and the deep power of joy,
We see into the life of things.

> How does blank verse suit the subject and theme of this poem?

> What do you think the poet means by *We see into the life of things* (line 49)?

tranquil calm	**sublime** important or lofty	**harmony** melody; pleasing arrangement of parts; calmness
restoration the act of returning something to what it once was	**unintelligible** unable to be understood	
trivial common, ordinary	**corporeal** of the physical body	

Notice the language used in lines 50–57: *oft* (often), *thee* (you), *thou* (you), *thro'* (through).

The River *Wye* forms part of the border between England and Wales. The river valley is well known even today for its great natural beauty and scenic views.

Starting in line 65, the poem begins to discuss how the poet has changed from when he was last at this place.

If this
50   Be but a vain belief, yet, oh! how oft—
       In darkness and amid the many shapes
       Of joyless daylight; when the fretful stir
       Unprofitable, and the fever of the world,
       Have hung upon the beatings of my heart—
55   How oft, in spirit, have I turned to thee,
          O **sylvan** Wye! thou wanderer thro' the woods,
       How often has my spirit turned to thee!
             And now, with gleams of half-extinguished thought,
       With many **recognitions** dim and faint,
60   And somewhat of a sad **perplexity,**
       The picture of the mind revives again:
       While here I stand, not only with the sense
       Of present pleasure, but with pleasing thoughts
       That in this moment there is life and food
65   For future years. And so I dare to hope,
       Though changed, no doubt, from what I was when first
       I came among these hills; when like a **roe**
       I bounded o'er the mountains, by the sides
       Of the deep rivers, and the lonely streams,
70   Wherever nature led: more like a man
       Flying from something that he dreads than one
       Who sought the thing he loved. For nature then
       (The coarser pleasures of my boyish days,
       And their glad animal movements all gone by)
75   To me was all in all.—I cannot paint
       What then I was. The sounding **cataract**
       Haunted me like a passion: the tall rock,
       The mountain, and the deep and gloomy wood,
       Their colours and their forms, were then to me
80   An appetite; a feeling and a love,
       That had no need of a remoter charm,
       By thought supplied, nor any interest
       Unborrowed from the eye.—That time is past,

sylvan related to or found in wooded areas	**perplexity** confusion	**cataract** waterfall
recognitions figuring something out	**roe** a type of deer native to the British Isles	

And all its aching joys are now no more,
85 And all its dizzy **raptures.** Not for this
Faint I, nor mourn nor murmur; other gifts
Have followed; for such loss, I would believe,
Abundant **recompense.** For I have learned
To look on nature, not as in the hour
90 Of thoughtless youth; but hearing oftentimes
The still, sad music of humanity,
Nor harsh nor grating, though of ample power
To **chasten** and **subdue.** And I have felt
A presence that disturbs me with the joy
95 Of elevated thoughts; a sense sublime
Of something far more deeply **interfused,**
Whose dwelling is the light of setting suns,
And the round ocean and the living air,
And the blue sky, and in the mind of man:
100 A motion and a spirit, that **impels**
All thinking things, all objects of all thought,
And rolls through all things. Therefore am I still
A lover of the meadows and the woods,

> How has the poet changed since coming to this spot at a younger age?

> *Disturbs me with joy* (line 94) is an example of a paradox. This is a connection of two ideas that seem to contradict each other but are, in fact, both true. In what ways might joy be disturbing?

Tintern Abbey

raptures delight and pleasure

recompense repayment

chasten punish

subdue bring under control

interfused blended together

impels urges forward

And mountains; and of all that we behold
105 From this green earth; of all the mighty world
Of eye, and ear,—both what they half create,
And what **perceive;** well pleased to recognise
In nature and the language of the sense
The anchor of my purest thoughts, the nurse,
110 The guide, the guardian of my heart, and soul
Of all my moral being.

                                    Nor perchance,
If I were not thus taught, should I the more
Suffer my **genial** spirits to decay:
For thou art with me here upon the banks
115 Of this fair river; thou my dearest Friend,
My dear, dear Friend; and in thy voice I catch
The language of my former heart, and read
My former pleasures in the shooting lights
Of thy wild eyes. Oh! yet a little while
120 May I behold in thee what I was once,
My dear, dear Sister! and this prayer I make,
Knowing that Nature never did betray
The heart that loved her; 'tis her privilege,
Through all the years of this our life, to lead
125 From joy to joy: for she can so inform
The mind that is within us, so impress
With quietness and beauty, and so feed
With lofty thoughts, that neither evil tongues,
Rash judgments, nor the sneers of selfish men,
130 Nor greetings where no kindness is, nor all
The dreary **intercourse** of daily life,
Shall e'er prevail against us, or disturb
Our cheerful faith, that all which we behold
Is full of blessings. Therefore let the moon
135 Shine on thee in thy **solitary** walk;

The poet is referring to his sister, Dorothy, when he says *friend* in these lines.

perceive to become aware through the senses	**intercourse** dealings between persons or groups
genial cheerful	**solitary** lonely

And let the misty mountain-winds be free
To blow against thee: and, in after years,
When these wild **ecstasies** shall be matured
Into a sober pleasure; when thy mind
140 Shall be a mansion for all lovely forms,
Thy memory be as a dwelling-place
For all sweet sounds and harmonies; oh! then,
If solitude, or fear, or pain, or grief,
Should be thy portion, with what healing thoughts
145 Of tender joy wilt thou remember me,
And these my **exhortations!** Nor, perchance—
If I should be where I no more can hear
Thy voice, nor catch from thy wild eyes these gleams
Of past existence—wilt thou then forget
150 That on the banks of this delightful stream
We stood together; and that I, so long
A worshipper of Nature, hither came
Unwearied in that service: rather say
With warmer love—oh! with far deeper **zeal**
155 Of holier love. Nor wilt thou then forget
That after many wanderings, many years
Of absence, these steep woods and lofty cliffs,
And this green pastoral landscape, were to me
More dear, both for themselves and for thy sake!

The poet's sister reminds him of himself and what he was like when last visiting this place. *Of past existence* means the author's past existence as a younger man.

---

ecstasies wild emotions

exhortations acts of advice, warning, or encouragement

zeal eagerness

Directions Choose the letter of the best answer or write the answer using complete sentences.

Comprehension: Identifying Facts

1. The poet describes the farms as _____.

   A sportive   **C** trivial

   B pastoral   **D** genial

2. Line 147 refers to the poet's _____.

   A death   **C** wife

   B writing   **D** view of nature

3. How long has it been since the poet has visited this place?

4. What does the poet hear at the beginning of the story?

5. Where does the poem take place?

6. What does the poet mean by *unintelligible* in line 40?

7. What are some of the objects the poet describes in this poem?

8. How does the waterfall make the poet feel?

9. Who is the friend the poet mentions in line 115?

10. What does the poet hope for this friend in the future?

Comprehension: Putting Ideas Together

11. Since returning to this place, the poet believes he has _____.

    A become angry

    B stayed the same

    C learned to dislike his sister

    D changed in the way he views nature

12. The poet thinks nature is _____.

    A an important part of his life

    B something he liked only when he was younger

    C something only his sister likes

    D boring

13. What descriptions does the poet use to tell about this place? How does this add to the poem?

14. How did the poet's memory of this place help him in his life?

15. What does the poet seem to be saying about human life away from nature?

16. How has the poet changed since his last visit?

17. The poet mentions "spirit" throughout the poem. What does he mean by a spirit?

18. Lines 139–140 read: "when thy mind/Shall be a mansion for all lovely forms." What does this mean?

19. What does the poet think of nature?

20. How are the past, present, and future represented in this poem?

Understanding Literature: Blank Verse and Iambic Pentameter

Blank verse is one way a poem can sound like normal speech but still be poetic. The blank verse of this poem (unrhymed iambic pentameter) has five two-beat sounds per line. The second syllable is stressed in each pattern. The ends of the lines do not rhyme.

21. How do you know this poem is written in iambic pentameter?

22. How is this poem different from others you have read?

23. Describe how this poem sounds as you read it aloud.

24. What effects do blank verse and iambic pentameter have on this poem?

25. What makes this selection a poem rather than an essay or short story?

Critical Thinking

26. How do you think the poet's choice of words is different from the way people talk today?

27. What feelings does this poem create? Do you think the poet was happy to write this poem? Explain.

28. What does this poem tell you about the author?

29. How might this writing be different if the author chose not to write it as a poem?

Thinking Creatively

30. Do you think people today still have the same feelings toward nature that the poet does? Explain your opinion.

After Reading **continued on next page**

✓ Grammar Check

The poem you have just read uses exclamation points (!). These are used to show strong feelings in writing. Look back at the poem to find examples. Study how they are used.

- Write down three sentences from the poem that use exclamation points.

- Next to each sentence, describe what the exclamation point does to show strong feelings. Are the feelings good? bad? neither?

- Write three original sentences of your own, using an exclamation point in each.

Writing on Your Own

Go to a place that you enjoy. Spend some time observing the place and thinking about what it means to you. Then write a short blank verse poem describing the place and how it makes you feel. Provide many details about the place in your poem. Pay close attention to your choice of words to get the most meaning out of your writing.

Speaking and Listening

With a partner, take turns reading the poem aloud to each other. Make sure each of you spends the same amount of time reading and listening. When not reading, listen for meanings in the poem that you did not notice when reading it the first time. Take notes about your observations as you listen.

Media

Write and design a magazine article to describe this poem. First think about what the main idea of your article will be. Then include facts and details from the poem to support the main idea. Include pictures (such as photographs of the setting) to support the topic. Write captions for any artwork or photos.

Technology

Tourists can visit Tintern Abbey and the Wye Valley today. Use the Internet to find out about the things visitors can do at these places. (Enter the words *Tintern Abbey* or *Wye Valley* into a search engine as keywords.) Plan a trip as if you are actually going to visit. Find out places to stay and things to do. Write a summary of what you find.

BEFORE READING THE SELECTION

from *Grasmere Journals*   by Dorothy Wordsworth

About the Author

Dorothy Wordsworth was born in 1771 in Cockermouth, Cumberland, England. Her mother's death in 1778 caused the Wordsworth children to be separated. Various relatives helped raise Dorothy. However, she was close to her brother William. They made a home together for most of their adult lives.

William, Dorothy, and poet Samuel Taylor Coleridge traveled together in Europe from 1796 to 1798. Dorothy's thoughts and writings inspired the poets. Although she did not think of herself as a writer, her writings are imaginative and her style natural. Urged to publish her work, she insisted she was only writing to entertain family and friends.

Dorothy Wordsworth
1771–1855

In 1799, Dorothy, William, and William's wife, Mary, settled in the Lake District, an out-of-the-way area in England with beautiful lakes and mountains. Wordsworth's writings record her observations of the natural world she loved and of the quiet cottage life in the village of Grasmere. In 1829, she became seriously ill. Her illness left her in need of care by others. For the last 20 years of her life, she had mental health challenges. Her brother's family, whom she had looked after for many years, cared for her lovingly until her death in 1855.

About the Selection

This entry was written on April 15, 1802. It appeared in Wordsworth's *Grasmere Journals*. It shows her delight in nature and her ability to observe and describe it exactly. It describes a scene in nature that her brother William later described in his poem "Daffodils." This excerpt shows the strong influence Dorothy had on her brother's work. It also shows the way her record of shared experiences provides clues to how and when William wrote his poems.

Objectives

- To read and understand a journal entry
- To identify characteristics of journal writing
- To describe the types of information likely to be included in a journal
- To define prose

Before Reading continued on next page

diary a daily record of personal events, thoughts, or private feelings

journal writing that expresses an author's feelings or first impressions about a subject

prose all writing that is not poetry

Literary Terms A **diary** or **journal** is written in **prose.** This writing includes all written language that is not verse. In a diary, a writer records events and feelings of each day, usually with the idea of keeping them private. This selection from Dorothy Wordsworth's *Grasmere Journals* records her impressions and feelings about the events of a day. However, unlike a diary entry, it is intended to be shared.

Reading on Your Own The journal entry you are about to read describes nature and the actions of people. It suggests the interests and personality of the writer. It includes both facts and opinions about what the writer observes. As you read, decide what inferences you can make about Wordsworth's feelings for nature.

Writing on Your Own Write a journal entry about the events of a memorable day. Place events in the order in which they happened. Describe the surroundings that were important to the events. Be sure to state or suggest your feelings and reactions to what happened.

Vocabulary Focus This selection mentions various plants seen on a spring walk. To get a complete picture of the scene, you need to know a little about the plants Wordsworth describes. For example, a furze bush is a shrub with yellow flowers. Hawthorns are spiny shrubs with glossy leaves and white or pink flowers. Look up *birches, primroses, woodsorrel, anemone,* and *daffodils* in a dictionary. Picture the scene these plants would create in springtime. Daffodils are pictured on page 282.

Think Before You Read Use what you know about spring weather and colors to predict what this description will report.

from
Grasmere Journals

Thursday 15th. It was a threatening misty morning—but mild. We set off after dinner from Eusemere. Mrs. Clarkson went a short way with us but turned back. The wind was furious and we thought we must have returned. We first rested in the large Boat-house, then under a furze Bush opposite Mr. Clarkson's. Saw the plough going in the field. The wind seized our breath the Lake was rough. There was a Boat by itself floating in the middle of the Bay below Water Millock. We rested again in the Water Millock Lane. The hawthorns are black and green, the birches here and there greenish but there is yet more of purple to be seen on the Twigs. We got over into a field to avoid some cows—people working, a few primroses by the roadside, woodsorrel flower, the **anemone,** scentless violets, strawberries, and that starry yellow flower which Mrs. C. calls pile wort.

When we were in the woods beyond Gowbarrow park we saw a few **daffodils** close to the water side. We fancied that the lake had floated the seeds ashore and that the little colony had so sprung up. But as we went along there were more and yet more and at last under the boughs of the trees, we saw that there was a long belt of them along the shore, about the breadth of a country turnpike road. I never saw daffodils so beautiful they grew among the mossy stones about and about them, some rested their heads upon these stones as on a

As you read, picture the scenes the writer is experiencing. What is the weather like? What does the countryside look like?

The bushes and flowers Wordsworth mentions would be in bloom. The *furze,* or gorse, bush has yellow blooms. Most of the other plants mentioned have yellow, white, or pink blossoms. What is the importance of color to this selection?

A *turnpike* is a toll road.

anemone flowering plant in the buttercup family

daffodils jonquils; plant with trumpet-shaped yellow flowers

What mood does Wordsworth associate with the daffodils?

pillow for weariness and the rest tossed and reeled and danced and seemed as if they **verily** laughed with the wind that blew upon them over the lake, they looked so gay ever glancing ever changing. This wind blew directly over the lake to them. There was here and there a little knot and a few **stragglers** a few yards higher up but they were so few as not to disturb the simplicity and unity and life of that one busy highway. We rested again and again.

The Bays were stormy, and we heard the waves at different distances and in the middle of the water like the sea. Rain came on—we were wet when we reached Luffs but we called in. Luckily all was cheerless and gloomy so we faced the storm—we *must* have been wet if we had waited—put on

Dobson's is an inn where the travelers can change and eat dinner.

dry clothes at Dobson's. I was very kindly treated by a young woman, the Landlady looked sour but it is her way. She gave us a goodish supper. Excellent ham and potatoes. We paid 7 when we came away. William was sitting by a bright fire when I came downstairs. He soon made his way to the Library piled up in a corner of the window. He brought out a volume of Enfield's *Speaker,* another **miscellany,** and an odd volume of Congreve's plays. We had a glass of warm rum and water.

Mary is William Wordsworth's wife.

We enjoyed ourselves and wished for Mary. It rained and blew when we went to bed. N.B. Deer in Gowbarrow park like skeletons.

Daffodils, Cumbria, England

---

verily truly, really

stragglers things trailing off from others

miscellany separate writings collected in one volume

Directions Choose the letter of the best answer or write the answer using complete sentences.

Comprehension: Identifying Facts

1. This journal entry covers a time period of _____.
   - **A** days
   - **B** hours
   - **C** weeks
   - **D** years

2. Where do the walkers see daffodils?

3. What do they do at Dobson's?

Comprehension: Putting Ideas Together

4. The day this entry describes can best be called _____.
   - **A** cold and snowy
   - **B** mild and warm
   - **C** windy and stormy
   - **D** dry and uncomfortable

5. Would the writer say this walk was frightening or rousing? What details show how she felt about it?

6. Based on the details in this entry, what were some ways people entertained themselves around 1800?

Understanding Literature: Prose and Diary/Journal Entries

This journal entry is written in prose, not verse. A journal is like a diary because it maintains a record of personal events and thoughts. It is less private and more likely to be shared with other people.

7. What characteristics show that this selection is prose rather than verse?

8. What details suggest that the author wants to share this memory with others, not record it just for herself?

Critical Thinking

9. Which experience does the author find most delightful on that day? How do you know?

Thinking Creatively

10. This experience took place in 1802. Later, William Wordsworth wrote a poem called "Daffodils." In what way do you think this prose helped him write his poem?

After Reading **continued on next page**

from *Grasmere Journals* by Dorothy Wordsworth

 Grammar Check

Description often uses vivid adjectives to create word pictures. Adjectives tell more about nouns or pronouns by telling what kind, which one, or how many. In the first sentence of the selection, three adjectives describe the morning of April 15, 1802: *threatening, misty,* and *mild.* These adjectives modify *morning* by telling what kind.

- List 10 more adjectives from the selection.

- Beside each adjective, write the word it modifies, or describes.

- Write several sentences explaining what adjectives add to this journal entry. How would it be different if they were left out?

 Writing on Your Own

Write a paragraph describing something in nature you have observed closely. Begin with a topic sentence introducing the object or place. Use spatial order (left to right, top to bottom, or near to far) to organize your details. Include vivid adjectives, strong verbs, and specific nouns to create clear pictures in your reader's mind.

 Speaking and Listening

Find and read William Wordsworth's poem "Daffodils." Practice reading it and the second paragraph of this selection. Note differences between the prose and verse descriptions of the daffodils. When you can read both writings smoothly, present them to a partner. Take a turn as the audience. As you listen, write down ways you find the prose and poetry versions alike and different.

 Viewing

Find and look at a picture of spring flowers other than daffodils. Write your own description of the flowers. Use precise language that involves the five senses. Compare your description to Wordsworth's. What similarities do you see? What differences?

BEFORE READING THE SELECTION

Kubla Khan   by Samuel Taylor Coleridge

About the Author

Samuel Taylor Coleridge was born in 1772 in Devonshire, the youngest of 14 children. His father died when Coleridge was 10, and Coleridge was sent to live in London. A brilliant student, he attended Cambridge University. However, his studies did not interest him.

In 1795, Coleridge met William Wordsworth. Their friendship was important, for each helped the other with poems and ideas. Together they produced *Lyrical Ballads* in 1798. The volume included poems by both men. It opened with Coleridge's great poem "The Rime of the Ancient Mariner." This book drew attention, for it introduced a new poetic language. This new style used ordinary language, praised common subjects, and valued freedom of imagination.

For much of his life, Coleridge had ill health. He became addicted to opium, a common pain reliever of the day. In spite of this, he produced fine poems and prose explaining his theory of poetry. His ideas about the nature of poetry are still read and valued today. Coleridge died in 1834.

About the Selection

"Kubla Khan" was written in 1797 or 1798 but not published until 1816. It is about Kublai Khan, who founded the great Mongol kingdom in China in the 13th century. Coleridge had been reading *The Travels of Marco Polo*, which describes the might of this ruler. He fell asleep and claimed to have composed "two or three hundred lines" while asleep. When he awoke, he began writing down the words, but he was interrupted. He could never remember the rest of the poem he had dreamed.

Samuel Taylor
Coleridge
1772–1834

Objectives

- To read and understand a poem
- To define and identify examples of onomatopoeia and alliteration
- To explain reasons for the author's word choices

Before Reading continued on next page

Kubla Khan by Samuel Taylor Coleridge

onomatopoeia
using words that
sound like their
meaning

alliteration
repeating sounds
by using words
whose beginning
sounds are the
same

Literary Terms Poems use many sound devices to make words sound musical. **Onomatopoeia** is the use of words that imitate the sound they name; for example, *bang* and *burst*. **Alliteration** occurs when beginning consonant sounds are repeated, as in "a *w*aning moon was haunted/By *w*oman *w*ailing." The repeated sounds add to the emotional effect and call attention to the ideas expressed.

Reading on Your Own The poem you are about to read weaves sound and meaning together skillfully. The poet has chosen words whose sounds add to their meanings. As you read, first think about what each sentence is saying. Then reread the poem aloud to notice repeated sounds and rhythms. Finally, think about why the poet chose specific words. For example, why did he use *sunless* instead of *dark* to describe the sea?

Writing on Your Own Dreams often include events and places that are not possible in real life. Recall a dream you have had. Describe what you can remember of the dream. Tell how you felt when you woke up from dreaming.

Vocabulary Focus This poem becomes richer if you understand the poet's references to faraway, ancient places and people. What Coleridge calls *Xanadu* was part of Tartary, a huge region including much of Asia and Eastern Europe. In line 3, *Alph* probably refers to Alpheus, a river god in mythology. The *Abyssinian maid* of line 39 calls up images of the East African empire Abyssinia. *Mount Abora* (line 41) might refer to Amara, a real mountain in Abyssinia where an earthly paradise was supposed to exist.

Think Before You Read Predict what this poem will say about an ancient Chinese kingdom.

Kubla Khan

In Xanadu did Kubla Khan
A stately pleasure-dome decree:
Where Alph, the sacred river, ran
Through caverns measureless to man
5   Down to a sunless sea.
So twice five miles of fertile ground
With walls and towers were girdled round:
And there were gardens bright with **sinuous** rills
Where blossomed many an incense-bearing tree;
10   And here were forests ancient as the hills,
Enfolding sunny spots of greenery.

But oh! that deep romantic **chasm** which slanted
Down the green hill **athwart** a cedarn cover!
A savage place! as holy and enchanted
15   As e'er beneath a waning moon was haunted
By woman wailing for her demon-lover!
And from this chasm, with ceaseless **turmoil** seething,
As if this earth in fast thick pants were breathing,
A mighty fountain momently was forced:
20   Amid whose swift half-intermitted burst
Huge fragments **vaulted** like rebounding hail,
Or chaffy grain beneath the thresher's flail:

> As you read, think about the nature of Kubla Khan's kingdom. How has the poet used the words and their sounds to suggest this nature? Where does he use onomatopoeia and alliteration?

> Beginning with line 12, the poet describes the deep gorge through which the river runs. It runs downhill through a thick stand of cedar trees.

> The river's water explodes from the chasm with great force, throwing up rocks.

sinuous winding; twisting	**athwart** from side to side; crosswise	**vaulted** leaped
chasm deep gorge	**turmoil** uproar	

And mid these dancing rocks at once and ever
It flung up momently the sacred river.
25 Five miles meandering with a **mazy** motion
Through wood and dale the sacred river ran,
Then reached the caverns measureless to man,
And sank in **tumult** to a lifeless ocean:
And 'mid this tumult Kubla heard from far
30 Ancestral voices **prophesying** war!
    The shadow of the dome of pleasure
    Floated midway on the waves;
    Where was heard the mingled measure
    From the fountain and the caves.
35 It was a miracle of rare device,
A sunny pleasure-dome with caves of ice!

    A damsel with a **dulcimer**
    In a vision once I saw:
40   It was an Abyssinian maid,
    And on her dulcimer she played,
    Singing of Mount Abora.
    Could I revive within me
    Her symphony and song,
    To such a deep delight 'twould win me,
45 That with music loud and long,
I would build that dome in air,
That sunny dome! those caves of ice!
And all who heard should see them there,
And all should cry, Beware! Beware!
50 His flashing eyes, his floating hair!
Weave a circle round him **thrice,**
And close your eyes with holy dread,
For he on **honey-dew** hath fed,
And drunk the milk of **Paradise.**

The river's final destination is an underground sea beneath a network of caves.

Kublai Khan, 1216–1294

The poet dreams of creating the pleasure dome *in air* from a vision he once saw. What kind of power is he contrasting with the power of nature and kings, described earlier?

mazy like a maze	**dulcimer** musical instrument with metal strings and a sweet sound	**honey-dew** a sweet deposit on the leaves of plants
tumult violent uproar		
prophesying predicting, foretelling	**thrice** three times	**Paradise** may refer to Eden, heaven, or a state of bliss

AFTER READING THE SELECTION

Kubla Khan   by Samuel Taylor Coleridge

Directions Choose the letter of the best answer or write the answer using complete sentences.

Comprehension: Identifying Facts

1. In the poem, what does Kubla Khan build and where does he build it?
   A a pleasure dome on a sacred river
   B a network of caves in Xanadu
   C a kingdom in China
   D a deep chasm by a river

2. What does the poem's speaker see in a vision?

3. What would the speaker do if he could "revive" his vision of the damsel?

Comprehension: Putting Ideas Together

4. Compared to the sunny pleasure dome, the sacred river seems
   A sad and lifeless
   B happier and sunnier
   C violent and more powerful
   D calmer and holier

5. Compare the pleasure dome to the "dome in air."

6. What is the nature of the river? What details tell you this?

Understanding Literature: Alliteration and Onomatopoeia

"Kubla Khan" is rich in musical sound effects. In addition to rhyme and rhythm, it uses alliteration, or repeated beginning consonant sounds. It also contains onomatopoeia, or the use of words that sound like their meaning.

7. Give three examples of alliteration used in the poem. What overall effect does alliteration have on the poem?

8. List examples of onomatopoeia from the poem. Explain how their sound adds to meaning.

Critical Thinking

9. How does the attitude of Khan compare to the attitude of the poet?

Thinking Creatively

10. This poem presents three kinds of power: a king's, nature's, and the imagination's. Which of these three do you think is most powerful? Why?

After Reading **continued on next page**

Grammar Check

Irregular verbs do not form the past tense and past participle forms in regular ways. For example, the past tense of *run* is *ran*, not *runned*. The past participle of *run* is *have run*. The verb *are* has the past tense *was* (or *were*) and the past participle *has been* (or *have been*).

- Find the past tense or past participle forms of these verbs in the poem: *fling, sink, hear, see, feed.*

- Write the verb forms in a chart with these headings: *Present, Past, Past Participle.* Use a dictionary to find missing forms and complete the chart.

 Writing on Your Own

Write about "Kubla Khan." Begin with a paragraph that summarizes what the poem is about. Then explain how the poet used sound effects and word choices to bring the subject into focus. Finally, give your opinion of the poem and your reasons for thinking as you do.

 Speaking

Practice reading "Kubla Khan" aloud. Use expression and tone that fit the mood and theme of the poem. When you can read the poem well, record your reading. Listen to your recording. What effect do rhyme, alliteration, onomatopoeia, and rhythm have on the impression the poem makes? Make notes about changes you want to make. Record the poem over until you are satisfied with your recording.

 Listening

In a small group, discuss the theme, or main idea, of "Kubla Khan." In writing, theme is often a greater meaning than just simple concepts. Note ideas that you think are most interesting. Write your reasons for disagreeing with other ideas you hear.

 Research

Spend some time researching the life of Kublai Khan. Use encyclopedias, the Internet, or library books on the history of China. Take notes about achievements of this ruler. Use your notes to write a short biographical sketch about the man.

BEFORE READING THE SELECTION

from *Pride and Prejudice*   by *Jane Austen*

About the Author

Jane Austen was born in 1775 in Steventon, a small town in southwest England. She spent much of her life in this rural area. As the daughter of a minister, she lived a quiet life and grew up happily. She went to school briefly at a boarding school. This was more education than most girls received at that time.

Austen was engaged once but broke it off. She never married. She seemed content to live with other family members. While in her 20s, she began writing. She wrote *Pride and Prejudice* in 1796. Like all her works, it was not published until later in her life. Austen was respected as an author during her lifetime, and her reputation has grown steadily ever since.

Austen's writings use irony skillfully to show the effects of social customs. She wrote about human weakness truthfully, but with kindness and humor. She also showed real affection for the everyday life she knew. Her elegant, clever writing style is still greatly admired. Each of her books involves a man and woman overcoming problems—often humorous—to marry. As the characters struggle, they learn about themselves and grow, giving readers confidence that they will be happy together.

About the Selection

The chapters you are about to read are from *Pride and Prejudice*. It begins with a statement of the theme: "It is a truth universally acknowledged that a single man in possession of a good fortune, must be in want of a wife." So she begins her satire about marriage in middle-class, 18th-century England. She pokes gentle fun at her society's customs and concerns for money in making a match.

Jane Austen
1775–1817

Objectives

- To read and understand an excerpt from a novel
- To identify theme in a work of fiction
- To describe characters and identify conflict in a work of fiction

Before Reading continued on next page

BEFORE READING THE SELECTION *(continued)*

from *Pride and Prejudice*   by Jane Austen

novel a long work of fiction

fiction writing that is imaginative and designed to entertain; the author creates the events and characters

character a person or animal in a story, poem, or play

conflict the struggle of the main character against himself or herself, another person, or nature

Literary Terms This selection consists of the opening chapters of a **novel.** A novel is a long work of **fiction** meant to entertain. Fiction is writing with a made-up plot and characters. The plot involves **characters** (the people in the story) in a **conflict** they must resolve. Conflict can be a mental struggle, a challenge in nature or society, or problems created by other characters. In Austen's novels, the actions of the characters in solving the problem create entertaining situations.

Reading on Your Own A work of fiction has a theme, or main idea. The author may state the theme or suggest it through what characters do and say. In this selection, the theme is stated in the opening paragraph. As you read, think about how the characters show their opinion of this theme.

Writing on Your Own How should a man or woman choose a marriage partner? What role should parents play? Give your opinions and the reasons for them as you answer these questions.

Vocabulary Focus The context around a new word can help you predict its meaning. Context is the words and sentences surrounding a word. It offers clues to meaning. For example, Mrs. Bennet says to her husband, "You take delight in vexing me. You have no compassion for my nerves." These words and the conversation in which they are set suggest that the word *vexing* means "annoying" or "upsetting."

Think Before You Read Read the opening sentence of the selection. Read to find out what the characters and their actions say about marriage.

FROM *Pride and* PREJUDICE

As you read, list each character that is introduced. Notice what the character's words and actions show about his or her personality.

Chapter I

It is a truth **universally acknowledged,** that a single man in possession of a good fortune, must be in want of a wife.

However little known the feelings or views of such a man may be on his first entering a neighbourhood, this truth is so well fixed in the minds of the surrounding families, that he is considered as the rightful property of some one or other of their daughters.

"My dear Mr. Bennet," said his lady to him one day, "have you heard that Netherfield Park is **let** at last?"

Mr. Bennet replied that he had not.

"But it is," returned she; "for Mrs. Long has just been here, and she told me all about it."

Mr. Bennet made no answer.

"Do not you want to know who has taken it?" cried his wife impatiently.

"*You* want to tell me, and I have no objection to hearing it."

This was invitation enough.

"Why, my dear, you must know, Mrs. Long says that Netherfield is taken by a young man of large fortune from the north of England; that he came down on Monday in a **chaise and four** to see the place, and was so much delighted with it

What tone does the narrator use to tell this story? Keep in mind the author is making gentle fun of her society as she tells about it.

universally everywhere	**acknowledged** agreed upon as true	**chaise and four** light carriage pulled by four horses
	let rented	

The Romantic Period Unit 4   **293**

that he agreed with Mr. Morris immediately; that he is to take possession before Michaelmas, and some of his servants are to be in the house by the end of next week."

"What is his name?"

"Bingley."

"Is he married or single?"

"Oh! single, my dear, to be sure! A single man of large fortune; four or five thousand a year. What a fine thing for our girls!"

"How so? how can it affect them?"

"My dear Mr. Bennet," replied his wife, "how can you be so **tiresome**! You must know that I am thinking of his marrying one of them."

"Is that his **design** in settling here?"

"Design! nonsense, how can you talk so! But it is very likely that he *may* fall in love with one of them, and therefore you must visit him as soon as he comes."

"I see no occasion for that. You and the girls may go, or you may send them by themselves, which perhaps will be still better, for as you are as handsome as any of them, Mr. Bingley might like you the best of the party."

"My dear, you flatter me. I certainly *have* had my share of beauty, but I do not pretend to be any thing extraordinary now. When a woman has five grown up daughters, she ought to give over thinking of her own beauty."

"In such cases, a woman has not often much beauty to think of."

"But, my dear, you must indeed go and see Mr. Bingley when he comes into the neighbourhood."

"It is more than I **engage** for, I assure you."

"But consider your daughters. Only think what an **establishment** it would be for one of them. Sir William and Lady Lucas are determined to go, merely on that account, for

---

Mr. Bennet quickly asks whether the newcomer is married or single. What does this say about his interest?

In Austen's day, the women of a family could not visit an unmarried gentleman without first being introduced to him through a third person.

---

tiresome annoying

design plan

engage promise

establishment act of setting up on a solid basis

in general you know they visit no new comers. Indeed you must go, for it will be impossible for *us* to visit him, if you do not."

"You are over **scrupulous** surely. I dare say Mr. Bingley will be very glad to see you; and I will send a few lines by you to assure him of my hearty consent to his marrying which ever he chuses of the girls; though I must throw in a good word for my little Lizzy."

Notice the old spelling of *chooses* as *chuses*.

"I desire you will do no such thing. Lizzy is not a bit better than the others; and I am sure she is not half so handsome as Jane, nor half so good humoured as Lydia. But you are always giving *her* the preference."

"They have none of them much to recommend them," replied he; "they are all silly and ignorant like other girls; but Lizzy has something more of quickness than her sisters."

"Mr. Bennet, how can you abuse your own children in such a way? You take delight in **vexing** me. You have no compassion on my poor nerves."

How would you describe Mr. Bennet's way of interacting with his wife? Does he speak in a serious or teasing way?

"You mistake me, my dear. I have a high respect for your nerves. They are my old friends. I have heard you mention them with consideration these twenty years at least."

"Ah! you do not know what I suffer."

"But I hope you will get over it, and live to see many young men of four thousand a year come into the neighbourhood."

"It will be no use to us, if twenty such should come since you will not visit them."

"Depend upon it, my dear, that when there are twenty, I will visit them all."

Mr. Bennet was so odd a mixture of quick parts, **sarcastic** humour, **reserve,** and **caprice,** that the experience of three and twenty years had been insufficient to make his wife understand his character. *Her* mind was less difficult to develop. She was a woman of **mean** understanding, little information, and uncertain temper. When she was

Here the author gives a direct description of Mr. and Mrs. Bennet. How would you compare them?

---

scrupulous proper

vexing annoying; irritating

sarcastic meant to ridicule

reserve caution in words and actions

caprice impulsiveness

mean low in quality or value

discontented she fancied herself **nervous.** The business of her life was to get her daughters married; its **solace** was visiting and news.

Chapter II

Mr. Bennet was among the earliest of those who waited on Mr. Bingley. He had always intended to visit him, though to the last always assuring his wife that he should not go; and till the evening after the visit was paid, she had no knowledge of it. It was then **disclosed** in the following manner. Observing his second daughter employed in trimming a hat, he suddenly addressed her with,

"I hope Mr. Bingley will like it, Lizzy."

"We are not in a way to know *what* Mr. Bingley likes," said her mother resentfully, "since we are not to visit."

"But you forget, mama," said Elizabeth, "that we shall meet him at the **assemblies,** and that Mrs. Long has promised to introduce him."

"I do not believe Mrs. Long will do any such thing. She has two nieces of her own. She is a selfish, **hypocritical** woman, and I have no opinion of her."

"No more have I," said Mr. Bennet; "and I am glad to find that you do not depend on her serving you."

Mrs. Bennet **deigned** not to make any reply; but unable to contain herself, began scolding one of her daughters.

"Don't keep coughing so, Kitty, for heaven's sake! Have a little compassion on my nerves. You tear them to pieces."

"Kitty has no **discretion** in her coughs," said her father; "she times them ill."

"I do not cough for my own amusement," replied Kitty fretfully.

"When is your next ball to be, Lizzy?"

What are some sources of conflict within the Bennet family? What is a possible source of conflict outside the family?

Lizzy (Elizabeth) is decorating a hat.

Mrs. Bennet is a caricature, or a character with features and behaviors that the author exaggerates for humorous effect. How do you imagine the character of Mrs. Bennet being played in a stage or movie production of this novel?

---

nervous having a condition affecting the nerves

solace way of comforting or calming

disclosed revealed

assemblies gatherings of people

hypocritical phony; acting against one's beliefs

deigned stooped; lowered oneself

discretion good judgment

"To-morrow fortnight."

"Aye, so it is," cried her mother, "and Mrs. Long does not come back till the day before; so, it will be impossible for her to introduce him, for she will not know him herself."

"Then, my dear, you may have the advantage of your friend, and introduce Mr. Bingley to *her*."

"Impossible, Mr. Bennet, impossible, when I am not acquainted with him myself; how can you be so teazing?"

"I honour your **circumspection.** A fortnight's acquaintance is certainly very little. One cannot know what a man really is by the end of a fortnight. But if *we* do not venture, somebody else will; and after all, Mrs. Long and her nieces must stand their chance; and therefore, as she will think it an act of kindness, if you decline the office, I will take it on myself."

The girls stared at their father. Mrs. Bennet said only, "Nonsense, nonsense!"

"What can be the meaning of that **emphatic** exclamation?" cried he. "Do you consider the forms of introduction, and the stress that is laid on them, as nonsense? I cannot quite agree with you *there*. What say you, Mary? for you are a young lady of deep reflection I know, and read great books, and make **extracts.**"

Mary wished to say something very sensible, but knew not how.

"While Mary is adjusting her ideas," he continued, "let us return to Mr. Bingley."

"I am sick of Mr. Bingley," cried his wife.

"I am sorry to hear *that*; but why did not you tell me so before? If I had known as much this morning, I certainly would not have called on him. It is very unlucky; but as I have actually paid the visit, we cannot escape the acquaintance now."

A *fortnight* is two weeks. The term is uniquely British.

Notice how Mr. Bennet mistakes on purpose the meaning with which his wife uses the word *acquaintance*. She has not met Mr. Bingley at all; Mr. Bennet pretends she is saying they do not know him well enough.

Why has Mr. Bennet waited to tell his family he paid a visit to Mr. Bingley?

---

circumspection caution   **emphatic** strong   **extracts** summaries or parts of larger works

The astonishment of the ladies was just what he wished; that of Mrs. Bennet perhaps **surpassing** the rest; though when the first **tumult** of joy was over, she began to declare that it was what she had expected all the while.

"How good it was in you, my dear Mr. Bennet! But I knew I should persuade you at last. I was sure you loved your girls too well to neglect such an acquaintance. Well, how pleased I am! and it is such a good joke, too, that you should have gone this morning, and never said a word about it till now."

"Now, Kitty, you may cough as much as you chuse," said Mr. Bennet; and, as he spoke, he left the room, **fatigued** with the **raptures** of his wife.

"What an excellent father you have, girls," said she, when the door was shut. "I do not know how you will ever make

Elizabeth Bennet Meets Mr. Bingley and His Daughters

him **amends** for his kindness; or me either, for that matter. At our time of life, it is not so pleasant I can tell you, to be making new acquaintance every day; but for your sakes, we would do any thing. Lydia, my love, though you *are* the youngest, I dare say Mr. Bingley will dance with you at the next ball."

"Oh!" said Lydia stoutly, "I am not afraid; for though I *am* the youngest, I'm the tallest."

The rest of the evening was spent in **conjecturing** how soon he would return Mr. Bennet's visit, and determining when they should ask him to dinner.

> **How is Mrs. Bennet's reaction typical of her personality?**

surpassing going beyond	**fatigued** tired	**amends** repayment
tumult great excitement	**raptures** expressions of joyful emotion	**conjecturing** wondering; guessing

Directions Choose the letter of the best answer or write the answer using complete sentences.

Comprehension: Identifying Facts

1. Which character is rich and single?
   A Mr. Bennet   **C** Mrs. Long
   B Mr. Bingley   **D** Mrs. Bennet

2. When they learn of Mr. Bennet's visit, the family is _____.
   A upset   **C** overjoyed
   B resentful   **D** puzzled

3. What does Mrs. Bennet want Mr. Bennet to do?

4. Why doesn't she do this herself?

5. When will Mr. Bingley move into the neighborhood?

6. Which daughter is Mr. Bennet's favorite?

7. How long have the Bennets been married?

8. What has Mrs. Long promised to do?

9. When does Mr. Bennet tell his family he has visited Mr. Bingley?

10. What does the family do after learning of the visit?

Comprehension: Putting Ideas Together

11. Mrs. Bennet feels that it is natural and likely that _____.
    A Mr. Bingley will want to marry one of her daughters
    B she should visit a strange, single man
    C husbands torment their wives
    D others will find her more beautiful than her daughters

12. Judging from their conversations in these chapters, which daughter seems brightest?
    A Kitty   **C** Mary
    B Lydia   **D** Lizzy

13. How would you describe Mr. Bennet's personality?

14. How would you describe Mrs. Bennet's personality?

15. What is ironic, or opposite of what you expect, about the Bennets' marriage?

16. How does the conversation between the Bennets highlight the contrast between them?

After Reading continued on next page

from *Pride and Prejudice*   *by Jane Austen*

17. What clues in the reading suggest Mrs. Bennet has often been unhappy?

18. Why does she accuse Mrs. Long of being selfish and hypocritical?

19. What does Mr. Bennet's surprise show about his relationship to his family?

20. Do you think it likely that many people in the neighborhood have visited Mr. Bingley? Why?

Understanding Literature: Fiction

Fiction is imaginative writing of stories with a plot and characters. This selection is from the novel *Pride and Prejudice*. It focuses on the theme of marriage. Its plot involves finding suitable husbands for the Bennets' daughters. The characters' actions lead to humorous situations.

21. What shows that this work is fiction?

22. How does the author reveal the personality of characters in the story?

23. What problem has been introduced in these chapters?

24. How do you think the problem will be resolved?

25. What feeling or mood does the dialogue give to these chapters?

Critical Thinking

26. How do you think Austen feels about these characters? about marriage? Explain.

27. In what ways would the Bennet girls' situation be different today?

28. Irony is the use of words to express something other than, or opposite to, the literal meaning. How is the novel's opening sentence ironic?

29. What is one way social customs of Austen's day differ from ours today?

Thinking Creatively

30. Do you think it is likely that one of the Bennet girls will marry Mr. Bingley? Which one? Why do you think so?

Grammar Check

Adverbs modify, or tell more about, verbs, adjectives, or other adverbs. They answer the questions *when, where, how,* and *to what degree.* For example, the first sentence contains the adverb *universally,* which modifies the verb *acknowledged.* It tells to what degree a truth is acknowledged. Mr. Bennet says "a woman has not often much beauty." The adverbs *not often* modify the verb *has.* They tell when a woman has beauty.

- Find five other adverbs in the selection.

- List each adverb. Then write the word it modifies and tell what question it answers.

- Explain how the author has used adverbs to make actions more clear and specific.

 ## Writing on Your Own

Imagine what happens when Mr. Bennet meets Mr. Bingley. Write a narrative including your description of Mr. Bingley and the dialogue between the two men. Include conversation and details to show what the two are like. Suggest the motives of both speakers.

 ## Speaking and Listening

In a small group, discuss what Mr. and Mrs. Bennet are like. Point out clues that suggest the traits of each person. Explain whether you think they are well matched or mismatched, and why you think so. As you listen to others, jot down ideas that interest you and questions that occur to you.

 ## Viewing

Look at the art used in this selection and the picture of Jane Austen on page 291. Describe the way women and men dressed in the early 1800s. How do these pictures help you understand the customs of this time and the way men and women interacted?

 ## Technology

Use the Internet to learn about the social customs and the rights of women in the 1800s in England. Use a computer to gather and organize a report that includes both words and pictures.

George Gordon,
Lord Byron
1788–1823

Objectives

■ To read and understand a poem

■ To define and find examples of similes

About the Author

George Gordon grew up at first in Scotland. He was handsome but had been born with a club foot. (His foot was twisted and out of position.) That made him self-conscious all his life, but it also drove him to become a great athlete. At the age of 10, he inherited a fortune and the title Lord Byron from a great-uncle. He also moved to London. While attending Cambridge University, he entertained richly and began writing poetry. He lived a colorful, shocking lifestyle for which he became famous. For example, he had a pet bear.

As an adult, Byron traveled widely in Europe and the Near East. His adventurous, daring travels gave him material for the poems that made him famous. Two of his long poems, *Childe Harolde's Pilgrimage* and *Don Juan*, follow the adventures of heroes in the countries Byron had visited. These works established the "Byronic hero"—a sad but proud adventurer who goes against the expected and pursues his goals. There is little doubt that Byron saw himself as a hero in this mold.

Byron left England for good in 1816. He lived in Italy mostly and became committed to the cause of freedom in Italy and Greece. He joined the Greeks in their war for independence from the Ottoman (Turkish) Empire, became ill, and died there in 1823.

About the Selection

Byron wrote "She Walks in Beauty" in 1814. It is a poem of praise for his cousin by marriage, Lady Anne Wilmot Horton. He describes her as she appeared at the evening party where they met, wearing a black mourning dress. The poem was published in *Melodies* in 1815.

Literary Terms Many poems use figurative language such as **similes** to suggest what a subject is like. A simile compares a subject to another thing. On the surface, the things appear very different, but an underlying similarity becomes clear in the poem. A simile uses the word *like* or *as* to make a comparison.

Reading on Your Own Scan the poem and notice its strong rhyme scheme, or pattern, and stanza organization. Every other line rhymes *(ababab)*. Each stanza has six lines with four metrical beats. After you read each stanza, pause and paraphrase what it says about the woman the speaker has just seen.

Writing on Your Own Write a description of night. What contrasts does it contain? Use comparisons and vivid, specific language to create a word picture.

Vocabulary Focus Suffixes are letters added to the end of a word that change its meaning. Every suffix has a meaning of its own. Here are some common suffixes and their meanings:

Suffix	Meaning	Example	Part of Speech Formed
-less	"without"	loveless	adjective
-y	"characterized by, full of"	sunny	adjective
-ly	"in the manner or way mentioned"	slowly	adverb
-ness	"condition, quality"	happiness	noun

Find words with these suffixes in the poem. Write the meaning and part of speech of each word.

Think Before You Read What makes a woman beautiful or a man handsome? List these traits. Then read to compare your ideas with those of the poet.

She Walks in Beauty

As you read, notice how the poet uses contrasts to express the woman's beauty.

The word *like* in line 1 signals a simile. What is the poet comparing?

I

She walks in Beauty, like the night
    Of cloudless **climes** and starry skies;
And all that's best of dark and bright
    Meet in her **aspect** and her eyes:
5 Thus mellowed to that tender light
    Which Heaven to gaudy day denies.

II

One shade the more, one ray the less,
    Had half **impaired** the nameless grace
Which waves in every **raven tress,**
10   Or softly lightens o'er her face;
Where thoughts **serenely** sweet express,
    How pure, how dear their dwelling-place.

III

And on that cheek, and o'er that brow,
    So soft, so calm, yet **eloquent,**
15 The smiles that win, the tints that glow,
    But tell of days in goodness spent,
A mind at peace with all below,
    A heart whose love is innocent!

Mrs. Downey, About 1790, Henry Raeburn

climes climates	**impaired** damaged, lessened	**serenely** calmly
aspect face		**eloquent** expressive
	raven tress black curl of hair	

AFTER READING THE SELECTION

She Walks in Beauty   *by George Gordon, Lord Byron*

Directions Choose the letter of the best answer or write the answer using complete sentences.

Comprehension: Identifying Facts

1. The poet in this poem is describing _____.

   A a beautiful woman
   B the moonlight
   C a beautiful evening
   D moonlight on the waves

2. What does the poet mean by saying "all that's best of dark and bright/ Meet in her aspect and her eyes"?

3. According to the poet, what does the outward beauty tell of?

Comprehension: Putting Ideas Together

4. Day is less desirable than night in this poem because _____.

   A it is too bright and lacks contrasts of dark and light
   B it is too hot and powerful for this delicate beauty
   C only night has stars
   D it is the time when people are busiest

5. What creates the contrasts of dark and bright that the poet finds so beautiful?

6. What is the character of the lady in this poem?

Understanding Literature: Simile

A simile is a figure of speech that compares one thing to another using *like* or *as*. It points out a surprising similarity between the two things.

7. To what is the woman in this poem compared? Why?

8. The poet points out physical contrasts. What are they? How are they like the contrasts of night?

Critical Thinking

9. The poet finds goodness, peace, and innocence reflected in this woman's beauty. How does the tone of the poem express these characteristics?

Thinking Creatively

10. The poet suggests that outer beauty indicates inner beauty. Do you think this is true? Explain.

After Reading **continued on next page**

She Walks in Beauty *by George Gordon, Lord Byron*

 Grammar Check

An apostrophe (') is used to show where letters are left out in a contraction. For example, in the contraction *can't*, the apostrophe has replaced the letters *no* in *cannot*.

- Find three contractions in this poem.

- Write the contractions, then write the longer word or the words used to form them.

- List 10 other contractions and their long forms. Write sentences using the contractions you have written.

 Writing on Your Own

How would you define *beauty*? Write an essay in which you define and explain the term. Begin with a general definition that explains your view. Develop each part of your definition with examples, comparisons, and contrasts.

 Speaking and Listening

Prepare an oral reading of "She Walks in Beauty." As you practice, remember to use punctuation, not the ends of lines, as a guide to pauses. Decide on a tone for your reading. After you practice, read your poem for a partner or a small group. When it is your turn to listen, notice any new meanings that become clear.

 Research

Research the life of George Gordon, Lord Byron. You may find information in encyclopedias, online biographies, or print biographies. Take notes on the facts of his life that you find especially adventurous or interesting. Organize your notes and use them to write an imaginary interview with the poet. Have him answer your questions in the way you think he would speak.

BEFORE READING THE SELECTION

from *Frankenstein*   by *Mary Shelley*

About the Author

Mary Wollstonecraft Shelley was born in 1797 in London. Her parents were well-known writers. Her father wrote about the rights of the common people. Her mother wrote about the rights of women. (Shelley's mother, Mary Wollstonecraft, wrote *A Vindication of the Rights of Woman,* part of which is included in Unit 3.) Writers and thinkers constantly visited the house. Mary enjoyed writing and read many books.

At age 16, Mary met poet Percy Bysshe Shelley. They fell in love and, although he was married, ran away together. They married only after Shelley's wife died in 1816. In 1818, the couple was visiting Lord Byron in Switzerland. Byron suggested that they write ghost stories to pass the time. Mary Shelley's was the most terrifying of the stories. She developed it into the novel *Frankenstein,* which was published that year. It became her most famous work.

After her husband drowned in 1822, Shelley wrote to support herself and her son. She also edited her husband's poetry. Of her other works, *The Last Man* is best known. Shelley spent the final years of her life living with her son and his wife.

About the Selection

Frankenstein is a novel that looks at issues important to readers of the time. Its themes include fears about the rapid advance of technology and anger at the mistreatment of the poor. Its famous monster, created by Victor Frankenstein, raises questions about science and the effects of rejection. In this excerpt, Frankenstein is troubled after the monster kills Frankenstein's brother. He clashes with the monster on a mountain slope.

Mary Shelley
1797–1851

Objectives

- To read and understand an excerpt from a novel

- To explain plot elements in a work of fiction

- To identify character traits and conflict in fiction

- To recognize and understand allusions in a work of literature

Before Reading **continued on next page**

from *Frankenstein*   *by Mary Shelley*

genre a specific type, or kind, of literature

plot the series of events in a story

character trait a character's way of thinking, behaving, or speaking

allusion a reference to a historical event, person, place, or work of literature

Literary Terms The **genre** of this selection is fiction. It involves characters in conflict that is explained, increased, and resolved within the **plot,** or story action. Characters struggle against each other, nature, or themselves. We learn about **character traits** by observing the characters' actions, words, thoughts, and other details the author provides about them. To help readers understand more about the characters, Shelley also makes **allusions,** or references, to other works of literature with which her readers might be familiar.

Reading on Your Own The excerpt you will read makes clear the conflict between a scientist and his living creation. It also suggests conflicts within each of these characters. As you read, stop from time to time to predict what will happen. For example, when they meet, what will they have to say to each other?

Writing on Your Own What do you know about the *Frankenstein* story? Make an outline telling what you have learned from movies or the media about the plot, characters, and main idea of the story.

Vocabulary Focus This selection contains many difficult words. Remember, when you come across a new word, use the context clues around it. They can help you predict what the unfamiliar word might mean. However, you will have to look up some words or read the short definitions provided for some words in the margin. After reading the meaning, reread the sentence, substituting the definition for the word. Check to be sure it makes sense and helps you understand what you are reading.

Think Before You Read Read the summary before the excerpt from *Frankenstein.* List several questions you want to answer as you read. Then read to find out what both characters are thinking and feeling.

from Frankenstein

Victor Frankenstein is a bright young man who is interested in science. At the university, he becomes very involved in his studies. He succeeds at bringing a dead body to life using chemistry and electricity. However, Frankenstein feels fear, disgust, and guilt for the monstrous thing he has created, so he runs away. The monster wanders the countryside. Frankenstein learns that his younger brother has been murdered and realizes that the monster is the murderer.

As you read, list each character that is introduced. Notice what the character's words and actions show about his or her personality.

Chapter 10

I spent the following day roaming through the valley. I stood beside the sources of the Arveiron, which take their rise in a glacier, that with slow pace is advancing down from the summit of the hills to **barricade** the valley. The abrupt sides of vast mountains were before me; the icy wall of the glacier overhung me; a few shattered pines were scattered around; and the solemn silence of this glorious presence-chamber of **imperial** nature was broken only by the **brawling** waves or the fall of some vast fragment, the thunder sound of the avalanche or the cracking, **reverberated** along the mountains, of the **accumulated** ice, which, through the silent working of **immutable** laws, was ever and **anon** rent and torn, as if it

Arveiron is a stream near Mont Blanc. Its source is at Montanvert.

barricade block

imperial grand

brawling fighting

reverberated echoed

accumulated piled up

immutable absolute, unchanging

anon again

had been but a plaything in their hands. These **sublime** and magnificent scenes afforded me the greatest **consolation** that I was capable of receiving. They elevated me from all littleness of feeling, and although they did not remove my grief, they subdued and **tranquillized** it. In some degree, also, they diverted my mind from the thoughts over which it had brooded for the last month. I retired to rest at night; my slumbers, as it were, waited on and ministered to by the assemblance of grand shapes which I had contemplated during the day. They congregated round me; the unstained snowy mountaintop, the glittering **pinnacle,** the pine woods, and ragged bare ravine, the eagle, soaring amidst the clouds— they all gathered round me and bade me be at peace.

Where had they fled when the next morning I awoke? All of soul-inspiring fled with sleep, and dark melancholy clouded every thought. The rain was pouring in torrents, and thick mists hid the summits of the mountains, so that I even saw not the faces of those mighty friends. Still I would penetrate their misty veil and seek them in their cloudy retreats. What were rain and storm to me? My mule was brought to the door, and I resolved to ascend to the summit of Montanvert. I remembered the effect that the view of the tremendous and ever-moving glacier had produced upon my mind when I first saw it. It had then filled me with a sublime ecstasy that gave wings to the soul and allowed it to soar from the obscure world to light and joy. The sight of the **awful** and majestic in nature had indeed always the effect of solemnizing my mind and causing me to forget the passing cares of life. I determined to go without a guide, for I was well acquainted with the path, and the presence of another would destroy the solitary grandeur of the scene.

The ascent is **precipitous,** but the path is cut into continual and short windings, which enable you to surmount the **perpendicularity** of the mountain. It is a

Montanvert means "green mountain." It is one of three large glaciers on *Mont Blanc* (which means "white mountain"). Mont Blanc (referred to on page 312) is the highest of the Alps. It is a peak that borders France, Italy, and Switzerland.

sublime having unearthly beauty	**pinnacle** peak	**perpendicularity** condition of rising at right angles to another surface
consolation comfort	**awful** creating a sense of awe or wonder	
tranquillized calmed	**precipitous** steep	

scene terrifically desolate. In a thousand spots the traces of the winter avalanche may be perceived, where trees lie broken and strewed on the ground, some entirely destroyed, others bent, leaning upon the jutting rocks of the mountain or **transversely** upon other trees. The path, as you ascend higher, is intersected by ravines of snow, down which stones continually roll from above; one of them is particularly dangerous, as the slightest sound, such as even speaking in a loud voice, produces a **concussion** of air sufficient to draw destruction upon the head of the speaker. The pines are not tall or **luxuriant,** but they are sombre and add an air of **severity** to the scene. I looked on the valley beneath; vast mists were rising from the rivers which ran through it and curling in thick wreaths around the opposite mountains, whose summits were hid in the uniform clouds, while rain poured from the dark sky and added to the melancholy impression I received from the objects around me. Alas! Why does man boast of **sensibilities** superior to those apparent in the brute; it only renders them more necessary beings. If our impulses were confined to hunger, thirst, and desire, we might be nearly free; but now we are moved by every wind that blows and a chance word or scene that that word may convey to us.

> We rest; a dream has power to poison sleep. We rise; one wand'ring thought pollutes the day. We feel, conceive, or reason; laugh or weep, embrace fond woe, or cast our cares away; it is the same: for, be it joy or sorrow, the path of its departure still is free. Man's yesterday may ne'er be like his morrow; nought may endure but **mutability!**

It was nearly noon when I arrived at the top of the ascent. For some time I sat upon the rock that overlooks the sea of ice. A mist covered both that and the surrounding mountains. Presently a breeze **dissipated** the cloud, and I descended upon

How does Frankenstein feel about nature? How does it ease his pain?

These lines are the final two stanzas of a poem, "Mutability," by Percy Shelley, the author's husband. What do they add to Frankenstein's thoughts about how our thoughts and emotions enslave us?

transversely in a crosswise way	**severity** harshness	**dissipated** scattered
concussion hard blow	**sensibilities** abilities to receive sensations	
luxuriant lush, thriving	**mutability** changeableness	

Glacier of Rosenlaui,
John Brett, 1856

Notice the differences in this selection between natural (mountains, glaciers, climate) and unnatural (Frankenstein's creation). What does this tell you about the author's views on nature?

the glacier. The surface is very uneven, rising like the waves of a troubled sea, descending low, and interspersed by rifts that sink deep. The field of ice is almost a **league** in width, but I spent nearly two hours in crossing it. The opposite mountain is a bare perpendicular rock. From the side where I now stood Montanvert was exactly opposite, at the distance of a league; and above it rose Mont Blanc, in awful majesty. I remained in a recess of the rock, gazing on this wonderful and stupendous scene. The sea, or rather the vast river of ice, wound among its dependent mountains, whose aerial summits hung over its recesses. Their icy and glittering peaks shone in the sunlight over the clouds. My heart, which was before sorrowful, now swelled with something like joy; I exclaimed, "Wandering spirits, if indeed ye wander, and do not rest in your narrow beds, allow me this faint happiness, or take me, as your companion, away from the joys of life."

league a unit of distance, from 2.4 to 4.6 miles

As I said this I suddenly beheld the figure of a man, at some distance, advancing towards me with superhuman speed. He bounded over the crevices in the ice, among which I had walked with caution; his **stature,** also, as he approached, seemed to exceed that of man. I was troubled; a mist came over my eyes, and I felt a faintness seize me, but I was quickly restored by the cold gale of the mountains. I perceived, as the shape came nearer (sight tremendous and abhorred!) that it was the wretch whom I had created. I trembled with rage and horror, resolving to wait his approach and then close with him in mortal combat. He approached; his **countenance** bespoke bitter anguish, combined with disdain and **malignity,** while its unearthly ugliness rendered it almost too horrible for human eyes. But I scarcely observed this; rage and hatred had at first deprived me of **utterance,** and I recovered only to overwhelm him with words expressive of furious **detestation** and contempt.

"Devil," I exclaimed, "do you dare approach me? And do not you fear the fierce vengeance of my arm wreaked on your miserable head? Begone, vile insect! Or rather, stay, that I may trample you to dust! And, oh! That I could, with the extinction of your miserable existence, restore those victims whom you have so **diabolically** murdered!"

"I expected this reception," said the daemon. "All men hate the wretched; how, then, must I be hated, who am miserable beyond all living things! Yet you, my creator, detest and spurn me, thy creature, to whom thou art bound by ties only **dissoluble** by the annihilation of one of us. You purpose to kill me. How dare you sport thus with life? Do your duty towards me, and I will do mine towards you and the rest of mankind. If you will comply with my conditions, I will leave

What effect does the arrival of the monster have on the pace of the plot and the tension in the story?

Frankenstein resolves to fight the monster to the death. What is unexpected about the creature's response to him? Does this change how you feel toward him?

stature size; height	**utterance** speech	**dissoluble** able to be ended
countenance face	**detestation** hatred	
malignity meanness	**diabolically** devilishly	

them and you at peace; but if you refuse, I will **glut** the **maw** of death, until it be **satiated** with the blood of your remaining friends."

"Abhorred monster! Fiend that thou art! The tortures of hell are too mild a vengeance for thy crimes. Wretched devil! You reproach me with your creation, come on, then, that I may extinguish the spark which I so **negligently** bestowed."

My rage was without bounds; I sprang on him, impelled by all the feelings which can arm one being against the existence of another.

He easily eluded me and said—

"Be calm! I entreat you to hear me before you give vent to your hatred on my devoted head. Have I not suffered enough, that you seek to increase my misery? Life, although it may only be an accumulation of anguish, is dear to me, and I will defend it. Remember, thou hast made me more powerful than thyself; my height is superior to thine, my joints more supple. But I will not be tempted to set myself in opposition to thee. I am thy creature, and I will be even mild and docile to my natural lord and king if thou wilt also perform thy part, the which thou owest me. Oh, Frankenstein, be not **equitable** to every other and trample upon me alone, to whom thy justice, and even thy **clemency** and affection, is most due. Remember that I am thy creature; I ought to be thy Adam, but I am rather the fallen angel, whom thou drivest from joy for no misdeed. Everywhere I see bliss, from which I alone am **irrevocably** excluded. I was benevolent and good; misery made me a fiend. Make me happy, and I shall again be virtuous."

"Begone! I will not hear you. There can be no community between you and me; we are enemies. Begone, or let us try our strength in a fight, in which one must fall."

How does the monster's state of mind compare to Frankenstein's? What does the monster ask? What does it warn?

The monster compares himself to Adam and to Satan, "the fallen angel." This is an allusion to Milton's *Paradise Lost.* In what way is the monster like Adam? like Satan? In what way is Frankenstein like God?

glut fill	**negligently** without attention or care	**clemency** mercy
maw mouth		**irrevocably** permanently
satiated satisfied	**equitable** fair	

"How can I move thee? Will no entreaties cause thee to turn a favourable eye upon thy creature, who implores thy goodness and compassion? Believe me, Frankenstein, I was **benevolent;** my soul glowed with love and humanity; but am I not alone, miserably alone? You, my creator, abhor me; what hope can I gather from your fellow creatures, who owe me nothing? They spurn and hate me. The desert mountains and dreary glaciers are my refuge. I have wandered here many days; the caves of ice, which I only do not fear, are a dwelling to me, and the only one which man does not **grudge.** These bleak skies I hail, for they are kinder to me than your fellow beings. If the **multitude** of mankind knew of my existence, they would do as you do, and arm themselves for my destruction. Shall I not then hate them who **abhor** me? I will keep no terms with my enemies. I am miserable, and they shall share my wretchedness. Yet it is in your power to **recompense** me, and deliver them from an evil which it only remains for you to make so great, that not only you and your family, but thousands of others, shall be swallowed up in the whirlwinds of its rage. Let your compassion be moved, and do not **disdain** me. Listen to my tale; when you have heard that, abandon or **commiserate** me, as you shall judge that I deserve. But hear me. The guilty are allowed, by human laws, bloody as they are, to speak in their own defence before they are condemned. Listen to me, Frankenstein. You accuse me of murder, and yet you would, with a satisfied conscience, destroy your own creature. Oh, praise the eternal justice of man! Yet I ask you not to spare me; listen to me, and then, if you can, and if you will, destroy the work of your hands."

"Why do you call to my remembrance," I rejoined, "circumstances of which I shudder to reflect, that I have been the miserable origin and author? Cursed be the day, abhorred devil, in which you first saw light! Cursed (although I curse myself) be the hands that formed you! You have made me

What kind of repayment do you think the monster is looking for from Frankenstein? Why does he feel he is owed something?

The monster points out that Frankenstein wants to kill him because the monster has committed murder. However, this act would make Frankenstein a murderer, too. Would these crimes be equal? Is Frankenstein no better than his creation?

benevolent kind

grudge be unwilling to give

multitude large number

abhor hate

recompense repay

disdain scorn

commiserate pity; feel compassion for

wretched beyond expression. You have left me no power to consider whether I am just to you or not. Begone! Relieve me from the sight of your detested form."

"Thus I relieve thee, my creator," he said, and placed his hated hands before my eyes, which I flung from me with violence; "thus I take from thee a sight which you abhor. Still thou canst listen to me and grant me thy compassion. By the **virtues** that I once possessed, I demand this from you. Hear my tale; it is long and strange, and the temperature of this place is not fitting to your fine sensations; come to the hut upon the mountain. The sun is yet high in the heavens; before it descends to hide itself behind your snowy **precipices** and illuminate another world, you will have heard my story and can decide. On you it rests, whether I quit forever the neighbourhood of man and lead a harmless life, or become the **scourge** of your fellow creatures and the author of your own speedy ruin."

As he said this he led the way across the ice; I followed. My heart was full, and I did not answer him, but as I proceeded, I weighed the various arguments that he had used and determined at least to listen to his tale. I was partly urged by curiosity, and compassion confirmed my resolution. I had hitherto supposed him to be the murderer of my brother, and I eagerly sought a **confirmation** or denial of this opinion. For the first time, also, I felt what the duties of a creator towards his creature were, and that I ought to render him happy before I complained of his wickedness. These motives urged me to **comply** with his demand. We crossed the ice, therefore, and ascended the opposite rock. The air was cold, and the rain again began to descend; we entered the hut, the fiend with an air of **exultation,** I with a heavy heart and depressed spirits. But I consented to listen, and seating myself by the fire which my **odious** companion had lighted, he thus began his tale.

Frankenstein experiences both internal and external conflict. What is he struggling with mentally? What kind of struggle does he have with the monster?

Why is Frankenstein persuaded to listen to the monster's story?

virtues good traits	**scourge** curse; plague	**comply** to do as asked
precipices steep slopes	**confirmation** something that proves truth	**exultation** great joy
		odious disgusting

Chapter 11

"It is with considerable difficulty that I remember the original **era** of my being; all the events of that period appear confused and indistinct. A strange **multiplicity** of sensations seized me, and I saw, felt, heard, and smelt at the same time; and it was, indeed, a long time before I learned to distinguish between the operations of my various senses. By degrees, I remember, a stronger light pressed upon my nerves, so that I was obliged to shut my eyes. Darkness then came over me and troubled me, but hardly had I felt this when, by opening my eyes, as I now suppose, the light poured in upon me again. I walked and, I believe, descended, but I presently found a great alteration in my sensations. Before, dark and **opaque** bodies had surrounded me, **impervious** to my touch or sight; but I now found that I could wander on at liberty, with no obstacles which I could not either surmount or avoid. The light became more and more oppressive to me, and the heat wearying me as I walked, I sought a place where I could receive shade. This was the forest near Ingolstadt; and here I lay by the side of a brook resting from my fatigue, until I felt tormented by hunger and thirst. This roused me from my nearly **dormant** state, and I ate some berries which I found hanging on the trees or lying on the ground. I **slaked** my thirst at the brook, and then lying down, was overcome by sleep.

"It was dark when I awoke; I felt cold also, and half frightened, as it were, instinctively, finding myself so desolate. Before I had quitted your apartment, on a sensation of cold, I had covered myself with some clothes, but these were insufficient to secure me from the dews of night. I was a poor, helpless, miserable wretch; I knew, and could distinguish, nothing; but feeling pain invade me on all sides, I sat down and wept.

"Soon a gentle light stole over the heavens and gave me a sensation of pleasure. I started up and beheld a **radiant** form

> How is the newly awakened monster like a newborn?

> *Ingolstadt* is a city in Bavaria, a region of southern Germany.

era time period	**opaque** not see-through	**dormant** sleeping
multiplicity large number	**impervious** resisting, obstructing	**slaked** satisfied
		radiant glowing

In what ways
is the monster
like his creator,
Frankenstein in
his misery and his
reaction to nature?

rise from among the trees. I gazed with a kind of wonder. It moved slowly, but it enlightened my path, and I again went out in search of berries. I was still cold when under one of the trees I found a huge cloak, with which I covered myself, and sat down upon the ground. No distinct ideas occupied my mind; all was confused. I felt light, and hunger, and thirst, and darkness; innumerable sounds rang in my ears, and on all sides various scents saluted me; the only object that I could distinguish was the bright moon, and I fixed my eyes on that with pleasure.

The *orb of night* is the moon. (An orb is a round object.) The moon has waned, or become smaller, as time has passed.

"Several changes of day and night passed, and the orb of night had greatly lessened, when I began to distinguish my sensations from each other. I gradually saw plainly the clear stream that supplied me with drink and the trees that shaded me with their **foliage.** I was delighted when I first discovered that a pleasant sound, which often saluted my ears, proceeded from the throats of the little winged animals who had often intercepted the light from my eyes. I began also to observe, with greater accuracy, the forms that surrounded me and to perceive the boundaries of the **radiant** roof of light which canopied me. Sometimes I tried to imitate the pleasant songs of the birds but was unable. Sometimes I wished to express my sensations in my own mode, but the **uncouth** and **inarticulate** sounds which broke from me frightened me into silence again."

foliage leaves
radiant glowing

uncouth untrained, wild

inarticulate making no sense

AFTER READING THE SELECTION

from *Frankenstein* by Mary Shelley

Directions Choose the letter of the best answer or write the answer using complete sentences.

Comprehension: Identifying Facts

1. When Victor Frankenstein dreams at night, he is soothed by dreams of _____.

   A the creature he has created
   B family and friends
   C natural beauty he has seen
   D revenge for his brother's death

2. When Frankenstein describes the scene as desolate, he means it is _____.

   A beautiful in a severe way
   B ugly and unappealing
   C steep and dangerous
   D dreary and barren

3. Why does Frankenstein want to reach Montanvert?

4. What feeling do the mountains and glaciers stir in Frankenstein?

5. Who approaches Frankenstein?

6. Why does Frankenstein hate the monster he created?

7. Why does the monster say people hate him?

8. Where has the monster been living?

9. What does Frankenstein agree to do?

10. Where does the monster first take shelter when he leaves Frankenstein's apartment?

Comprehension: Putting Ideas Together

11. The mountains help Frankenstein by _____.
    A granting his wishes
    B presenting a challenge
    C sending boulders down on the monster
    D helping him forget his misery

12. When he says, "I ought to be thy Adam," the monster means that _____.

    A Frankenstein should consider him before others
    B Frankenstein should love him as God loved Adam
    C the monster knows he has sinned
    D Frankenstein should have given his creation a human name

13. Describe Frankenstein's climb to Montanvert.

14. What is the monster like physically and mentally?

After Reading **continued on next page**

from *Frankenstein* *by Mary Shelley*

15. What ties bind Frankenstein and the monster to each other?

16. What do you think the monster means when he asks Frankenstein to "do your duty towards me"?

17. What does the monster have in common with Adam? with Satan?

18. What actions and reactions have made the monster a fiend?

19. Describe the monster's first reactions to the world around him.

20. How is the monster's description of his feelings as he lives in the forest like Frankenstein's description of his feelings as he climbs to Montanvert?

Understanding Literature:
Conflict, Plot, and Character Traits

The genre of fiction entertains by inventing a plot, or series of events, that happens to characters. A conflict or conflicts cause them to struggle against each other, against nature, or against themselves. The plot builds to create ever more difficult struggles. Character traits are revealed by the way characters talk, think, and behave.

21. List at least three conflicts that are acted out in this selection.

22. Is the main conflict between characters, within a character, or between a character and nature? Explain your thinking.

23. What plot events occur in this selection?

24. What do you learn about Frankenstein from his thoughts, words, and actions?

25. What does the monster's explanation in Chapter 11 add to his character?

Critical Thinking

26. What role does nature play in this selection?

27. Why has the monster murdered? Do you think he has had good reason to do this?

28. What is the relationship between Frankenstein and the monster? How does each of them feel about this relationship?

29. Why does the monster have little ability to describe his surroundings at first?

Thinking Creatively

30. Do you have more sympathy for Frankenstein or the monster? Why?

Grammar Check

Parts of a sentence may be compound. For example, this sentence has a compound verb: *Still I <u>would penetrate</u> their misty veil and <u>seek</u> them in their cloudy retreats.* This clause has a compound direct object: *I will leave <u>them</u> and <u>you</u> at peace.*

- Write these sentences from the selection:

  These sublime and magnificent scenes afforded me the greatest consolation.
  Rage and hatred had at first deprived me of utterance.
  I saw, heard, felt, and smelt at the same time.
  I felt tormented by hunger and thirst.

- Underline the compound parts and circle the conjunction *(and* or *or)* that joins them.

- Identify each compound part as a subject, adjective, verb, or object.

 Writing on Your Own

You have begun to read the monster's autobiography—his own story of his life. Pretend you are the monster and continue his story. Tell what happened to you next and how you felt about it. Use language like the kind the monster uses in the selection.

 Speaking and Listening

Do you agree or disagree with the monster that he is right to hate "them who abhor me"? Write the reasons for your opinion. Then form two debate teams with classmates and argue your case. When you listen to opposing arguments, make notes on how you can answer the opposing team.

 Media

The monster from *Frankenstein* has always fascinated people. Locate images from paintings and movies that show different ideas of what the monster looks like. Describe differences in the way he has been viewed and shown.

 Research

Shelley subtitled her novel *The Modern Prometheus.* Prometheus is a character in Greek mythology. Do research to find out more about Prometheus and why Shelley compares her character Frankenstein to him.

BEFORE READING THE SELECTION

Ozymandias   by Percy Bysshe Shelley

Percy Bysshe Shelley
1792–1822

About the Author

Percy Bysshe Shelley was born in 1792 into a wealthy, powerful family. As a young man, Shelley developed new ideas about politics and spirituality. He was expelled from Oxford University in 1811 for writing the pamphlet *The Necessity of Atheism*. That same year, he married 16-year-old Harriet Westbrook.

Shelley often visited William Godwin, whose liberal ideas he admired. He met Godwin's daughter, Mary, then 16 years old, and they fell in love. The two ran away together. They married after Harriet's death in 1816. The couple became good friends with Lord Byron. The exchange of ideas among them led to some of the best work of all three writers.

Shelley felt that the imagination held the key to truth and spirituality. He wanted people to live free lives. He lived in Italy from 1818 until his death. The poet wrote some of his best work there, including the long poem *Prometheus Unbound,* the play *The Cenci,* and the funeral poem *Adonais* for John Keats.

His essay *A Defence of Poetry* gives valuable insights into poetry and Shelley's views of the imagination. He realized his ideals would not gain a hold in his lifetime but hoped others would like his work in the future. Shelley had great influence on the next generation of poets. Tragically, he drowned while sailing off the coast of Italy in 1822.

About the Selection

Shelley wrote the poem "Ozymandias" for a writing contest in 1817. The title comes from the Greek name for the ancient Egyptian king Ramses II (1304–1237 B.C.). Shelley's poem contrasts the pride and impermanence of a ruler's power with the more lasting power of art and truth.

Literary Terms "Ozymandias" uses a **figure of speech** called **irony.** Figures of speech give words meanings different from their actual meaning. In irony, words seem to say one thing but mean the opposite. The poem is rich in **imagery;** its words create vivid pictures in the mind. It is a poem of **romance** because it has a mysterious, far-off setting and its subject is larger than life.

Reading on Your Own The poem first describes a desert scene and ruins. Then it gives the words that a king put on his monument. As you read, picture the place and the person depicted in stone. Think about the words used to describe these things. Contrast this with the king's words.

Writing on Your Own Do you think world leaders are the most powerful people on earth? Who holds real power? Write your thoughts about these questions. Tell your reasons for thinking this way.

Vocabulary Focus Reading about the history of a new word can help you understand its meaning. For example, the word *visage* in line 4 came into English through the French language. *Vis* meant "face" in medieval times. It came into French from the Latin *visus*, meaning "sight." *Visage* refers to the face or the expression on a face. Use a dictionary to learn the histories of *pedestal* and *colossal*.

Think Before You Read The poem uses words of an ancient king and striking images. What effect do you imagine this poem had on its first readers?

figure of speech a word or phrase that has meaning different from the actual meaning, such as idioms, metaphors, and similes

irony the use of words that seem to say one thing but mean the opposite

imagery pictures created by words; the use of words that appeal to the five senses

romance a story about heroes, mysterious settings, or love

OZYMANDIAS

As you read, pay attention to the kinds of words used to describe the statue and its surroundings. What is ironic about them?

I met a traveller from an antique land,
Who said—"Two vast and trunkless legs of stone
Stand in the desert. . . . Near them, on the sand,
Half sunk a shattered **visage** lies, whose frown,
5   And wrinkled lip, and sneer of cold command,
Tell that its sculptor well those passions read
Which yet survive, stamped on these lifeless things,
The hand that mocked them, and the heart that fed;
And on the **pedestal,** these words appear:
10   My name is Ozymandias, King of Kings,
Look on my Works, ye Mighty, and despair!
Nothing beside remains. Round the decay
Of that **colossal** Wreck, boundless and bare
The lone and level sands stretch far away."—

Notice the older spelling *(desart)* for *desert* in line 3.

In line 8, *the hand* refers to the sculptor's hand; *the heart* refers to the king's heart.

The Temple of Ramses II at Abu Simbel, Egypt, about 1880

visage face   **pedestal** base   **collosal** huge

Directions Choose the letter of the best answer or write the answer using complete sentences.

Comprehension: Identifying Facts

1. Who is the speaker for most of this poem?

A Shelley

B a king

C Ozymandias

D one who traveled in Egypt

2. Whose statue lies broken in the desert? What expression is on its face?

3. What exists around the statue?

Comprehension: Putting Ideas Together

4. What passions did the sculptor record?

A power and cruelty

B decay and ugliness

C love and ambition

D revenge and hate

5. In what sense did the sculptor "mock" those passions?

6. What contrast does the poem show?

Understanding Literature: Figures of Speech, Irony, Imagery, and Romance

Figures of speech give words a meaning different from their actual meaning. Irony uses words to say one thing but mean the opposite. Imagery creates word pictures by appealing to the five senses. A romance in literature refers to the heroic quality of the subject and the mysterious setting, not just to love stories.

7. What two examples of irony appear in the poem?

8. Which images help you picture Ozymandias and the desert? What is romantic about these images?

Critical Thinking

9. In what sense is this poem about a sculptor as well as a king? What does it suggest about artists?

Thinking Creatively

10. One theme of this poem is that everything changes and nothing lasts. Do you agree? List examples of events or things that support this theme.

After Reading **continued on next page**

Ozymandias   *by Percy Bysshe Shelley*

 Grammar Check

Quotation marks (" ") are used to set off the words someone speaks: *"Did you read the poem?" asked Ms. Talley.* If one speaker quotes someone else, the inside quotation is set off with single quotation marks (' '): *James reported, "Then she said, 'Don't get smart with me, young man.'"* Quotation marks are also used to enclose titles of short works of literature.

- Find the part of "Ozymandias" that is enclosed in quotation marks.

- Tell whose words these are. Then find the lines which give another person's words. How could these be set off?

- Write a paragraph explaining the use of quotation marks in the poem. Use quotation marks as needed in your writing.

 Writing on Your Own

Write a summary of this poem, using your own words to describe what happens in it. Also explain why this poem is important or explain the main idea it shows.

 Speaking and Listening

Find and practice saying aloud a joke or anecdote whose humor is based on figures of speech. For example, it may be ironic, or have words that appear to say one thing but really mean the opposite. Or it may be based on puns, words that sound the same but have different meanings. In a small group, deliver your joke or tell your anecdote. As a listener, jot down the figure of speech that makes the presentation humorous.

 Media and Technology

Pull together news stories, copies of paintings, poems, speeches, and other media items whose subject is power. They may show how power is gained and lost or suggest that it is an illusion. Organize the materials you find, add explanations, and create a magazine article or audiovisual presentation with them.

BEFORE READING THE SELECTION

Ode on a Grecian Urn   by John Keats

About the Author

John Keats was born in 1795, the son of a stable keeper. Keats's troubles began when his father died in 1803. His mother took the family to live with Keats's grandmother. At first, he attended a school that taught him to love literature. However, after his mother died of tuberculosis, a lung disease, in 1810, his guardians made him leave school to get medical training. He spent much of his time studying literature. When he left his medical studies to become a poet, his disapproving guardians did not give him his inheritance. For the rest of his life, Keats lived in poverty.

John Keats
1795–1821

From 1816, when Keats published his first volume of poetry, until 1818, when his brother died of tuberculosis, he worked hard, and his poems improved steadily. Critics attacked and made fun of his work. In 1818, Keats met Fanny Brawne and fell in love. In the following year, he wrote constantly. In less than 12 months, he produced some of the finest poems in the English language, including six great odes ("Ode on a Grecian Urn" among them).

However, by 1820, it was clear that Keats also had tuberculosis. His engagement and the great promise of his talent were ended. Although he went to Italy in the hope of improving his health, he died there in 1821.

About the Selection

An ode is a formal lyric poem on a serious subject. "Ode on a Grecian Urn" describes Keats's reaction to the artwork painted on an ancient Greek urn, a piece of pottery. He enjoys the beauty of the artwork. However, this is contrasted with what he feels when he sees that the figures on the urn will never know the joys and pains of life.

Objectives

■ To read and understand a poem

■ To identify and explain metaphors

■ To explain important ideas expressed in a poem

Before Reading continued on next page

Ode on a Grecian Urn by John Keats

metaphor
a figure of speech
that makes a
comparison but
does not use *like*
or *as*

Literary Terms A **metaphor** is a figure of speech that compares two unlike things without using the words *like* or *as*. The comparison may be direct. The metaphor *Life is a dream* compares life to a dream. Some metaphors are implied, for example, *the words stabbed sharply into my heart*. Words are compared to a knife, although a knife is not mentioned directly.

Reading on Your Own In this poem, the poet describes figures painted on a marble vase. They are so artfully created that he can imagine their lives in ancient Greece. Keats uses language just as skillfully to give his impressions of the figures. Each stanza looks at the scene on the urn from a new point of view. Pause after each stanza and note in your own words what it says.

Writing on Your Own Think of a painting, statue, or other artwork you have seen. Describe the artwork, using vivid words. Explain what thoughts it brought to mind. In what sense was it "living"?

Vocabulary Focus In this poem, Keats uses several proper nouns to refer to ancient Greece. Knowing their meanings helps you better understand the poem's meaning. *Tempe* is a lovely valley in Thessaly, Greece. *Arcady* is a pastoral, or rural, region in that country. The carving on the urn reminds the poet of these beautiful places. *Attic* is a synonym for *Athenian*. The art of ancient Athens was known for its grace and simplicity. *Attic* implies the type of beauty of the urn.

Think Before You Read Explain ways your imagination is involved in understanding a work of art, a poem, or a musical composition.

ODE ON A GRECIAN URN

1

Thou still **unravish'd** bride of quietness,
　　Thou foster-child of silence and slow time,
Sylvan historian, who canst thus express
　　A flowery tale more sweetly than our rhyme:
5　What leaf-fring'd legend haunts about thy shape
　　Of deities or mortals, or of both,
　　　　In Tempe or the dales of Arcady?
　　What men or gods are these? What maidens **loth?**
What mad pursuit? What struggle to escape?
10　　　　What pipes and **timbrels?** What wild ecstasy?

2

Heard melodies are sweet, but those unheard
　　Are sweeter; therefore, ye soft pipes, play on;
Not to the **sensual ear,** but, more endear'd,
　　Pipe to the spirit ditties of no tone:
15　Fair youth, beneath the trees, thou canst not leave
　　Thy song, nor ever can those trees be bare;
　　　　Bold Lover, never, never canst thou kiss,

As you read, think about the opposites this poem contains. For example, the images on the urn are frozen in time, but they show passion and are full of life.

In lines 1–4, the poet uses the metaphors of a bride, a foster child, and a historian to describe the urn. How is it like each of these people?

The poet contrasts the ideal world frozen on the vase with the real world. Which does he prefer?

---

unravish'd pure

sylvan related to or found in a wooded area

loth unwilling

timbrels hand drums or tambourines

sensual ear appealing to the sense of hearing

Though winning near the goal—yet, do not grieve;
    She cannot fade, though thou hast not thy bliss,
20   For ever wilt thou love, and she be fair!

3

Ah, happy, happy boughs! that cannot shed
    Your leaves, nor ever bid the Spring **adieu;**
And, happy melodist, unwearied,
    For ever piping songs for ever new;
25 More happy love! more happy, happy love!
    For ever warm and still to be enjoy'd,
        For ever panting, and for ever young;
All breathing human passion far above,
    That leaves a heart high-sorrowful and **cloy'd,**
30   A burning forehead, and a **parching** tongue.

4

Who are these coming to the sacrifice?
    To what green altar, O mysterious priest,
Lead'st thou that **heifer** lowing at the skies,
    And all her silken **flanks** with garlands drest?
35 What little town by river or sea shore,
    Or mountain-built with peaceful **citadel,**
        Is emptied of this folk, this **pious** morn?
And, little town, thy streets for evermore
    Will silent be; and not a soul to tell
40   Why thou art desolate, can e'er return.

> What does the poet point out as an advantage of the unchanging world on the urn?

> The poet describes another scene on the vase. How does it contrast with the first scene?

> The art stirs the imagination, and the poet sees more than is shown on the vase. What does he imagine?

---

adieu goodbye (in French)

cloy'd overfull

parching becoming dry

heifer young cow

flanks part of the side of a cow, toward the back

citadel walled city

pious devoted to worship

5

O Attic shape! Fair attitude! with **brede**
　　Of marble men and maidens **overwrought,**
With forest branches and the **trodden** weed;
　　Thou, silent form, dost tease us out of thought
45　As doth eternity: Cold Pastoral!
　　When old age shall this generation waste,
　　　Thou shalt remain, in midst of other woe
Than ours, a friend to man, to whom thou say'st,
　　"Beauty is truth, truth beauty,"—that is all
50　　　Ye know on earth, and all ye need to know.

> The poet compares the urn to eternity. In what sense does it *tease us out of thought?*

Black-figured storage jar from Greece:
Olive Harvesting, **about 520 B.C.**

brede embroidery	**overwrought** made all over a surface	**trodden** stepped on

Directions Choose the letter of the best answer or write the answer using complete sentences.

Comprehension: Identifying Facts

1. The fair youth and bold lover addressed in stanza 2 are _____.
   A the bride and foster child of stanza 1
   B the poet's companions
   C figures painted on the urn
   D symbols imagined by the poet

2. In stanza 3, what leaves the poet's heart "high-sorrowful and cloy'd"?

3. In the final stanza, what is the "Cold Pastoral"?

Comprehension: Putting Ideas Together

4. The speaker is jealous of the figures on the urn mostly because _____.
   A they look happy
   B they cannot achieve their goals
   C time will not age them
   D he imagines their lives

5. Why are the figures on the urn above "all breathing human passion" (line 28)?

6. What two scenes are painted on the urn? What two aspects of life do they represent?

Understanding Literature: Metaphor

A metaphor is a figure of speech that compares two things without using the words *like* or *as*. Metaphors allow this poet to suggest surprising ways two seemingly very different things are alike.

7. To what three things is the urn compared in stanza 1?

8. In what sense is the urn an "unravish'd bride"? How is it like a "foster-child"? Why is it like a "sylvan historian"?

Critical Thinking

9. What do you think "Beauty is truth, truth beauty" means? How does the urn communicate this?

Thinking Creatively

10. The beauty and passion shown on the vase will remain forever. However, the figures will never really get to live through these experiences either. Do you think that is better than real life, where the young couple would kiss, enjoy their love, and grow old? Explain your thinking.

Grammar Check

Words can change their spelling and part of speech when a suffix or ending is added. Words that end in a consonant plus *y* change spelling before adding a suffix or ending. Change the *y* to *i* before adding the suffix, unless the suffix begins with *i*. For example, *spy* becomes *spied* when *ed* is added. But when *–ing* is added, the word is *spying*.

- List words in the poem that are made from the following words plus a suffix: *history, melody, ditty, unweary, mystery, empty.*

- Make a chart listing each word and showing the parts from which it is made.

- Put a * next to a new word if it changes part of speech. (For example, *happy* is an adjective; *happiness* is a noun.)

 Writing on Your Own

Write a response to this poem. Explain what you think each stanza means and suggest a main idea you think Keats is expressing. Refer specifically to the wording in the poem. End by telling whether you agree or disagree with Keats in his view of art versus life.

 Listening

Interview someone who knows a great deal about a piece of art. For example, ask a relative questions about a family antique or painting. Find out what meaning the work has for this person, and how the person's experiences add personal meaning to it. Listen carefully to the answers. Record the interview if possible. Write a summary of what you learned.

 Viewing

Find pictures of ancient Greek art on the Internet or in a printed book. Write a description of each artwork you observe. What characteristics apply to all the Greek artworks? Which artwork seems most beautiful to you? Think about how Keats's descriptions of the urn apply to the art you have viewed.

 Research

Read about the life of John Keats. Use encyclopedias, Internet biographies, and reference books in the library. Take notes about important events in his life and how they affected him. Use what you have learned to write a one-page magazine article about Keats.

Fiction stories develop around a series of events called the plot. Plot has five parts: exposition, rising action, climax, falling action, and resolution.

An author begins by presenting the situation and characters. This beginning part is known as exposition. For example, in the selection from *Pride and Prejudice,* Jane Austen introduces several characters and tells what problem they will try to solve:

Mr. and Mrs. Bennet are eager to find husbands for their five daughters. They are excited because of the arrival in the neighborhood of Mr. Bingley, a rich, single man. We know that the plot development will involve the pursuit of Mr. Bingley and other men the daughters may marry.

The way a plot develops is called the rising action. Conflict increases or becomes more urgent until the climax, or high point, of the action. We see part of the rising action of the novel *Frankenstein* in the selection you read:

Frankenstein feels grief, guilt, and hate, because the monster he created has killed Frankenstein's brother. When the monster confronts Frankenstein, the conflict becomes more complex and exciting. We feel the tension build as we await the climax.

After the climax, the action falls, leading to the resolution, where the outcome of the story is clear. (This is also called the denouement.) If the story is tragic, then the hero or heroes will suffer a disaster. If the story is comic, then there will be a happy ending.

Review

1. What is plot?

2. What should happen in the exposition of a story?

3. What part of the plot does the selection from *Frankenstein* illustrate? What part does the selection from *Pride and Prejudice* illustrate?

4. What event could be the climax of *Pride and Prejudice?* of *Frankenstein?*

5. Why will the resolution of *Frankenstein* likely be unhappy, but that of *Pride and Prejudice* happy?

Writing on Your Own

Think of a story you would like to write. Write a summary of the plot. Explain what happens in each part: exposition, rising action, climax, falling action, resolution.

Unit 4 covers the period from 1798 to 1832. During this time, the American and French revolutions, the rise of Napoleon in France, and the Industrial Revolution affected English society and thinking.

The Romantic Period includes two distinct sets of writers. William and Dorothy Wordsworth, Samuel Taylor Coleridge, and Jane Austen helped start the early Romantic Period. Lord Byron, Percy and Mary Shelley, and John Keats wrote during the later Romantic Period.

Selections

- "Lines Composed a Few Miles Above Tintern Abbey" is a poem by William Wordsworth exploring a person's different feelings toward nature over time.

- A selection from *Grasmere Journals* by Dorothy Wordsworth creates a record of a day spent in nature with her brother and reveals her powers of observation.

- "Kubla Khan" by Samuel Taylor Coleridge is a poem that records a dream fantasy about a real Mongolian ruler.

- A selection from the novel *Pride and Prejudice* by Jane Austen celebrates and satirizes British society's customs.

- "She Walks in Beauty" by George Gordon, Lord Byron, is a poem describing the outer and inner beauty of a woman.

- A selection from the novel *Frankenstein* by Mary Shelley focuses on the Romantic fascination with nature, the strange, the danger of scientific progress, and the rights of the individual.

- "Ozymandias" by Percy Bysshe Shelley is an ironic poem about the illusion of worldly power.

- "Ode on a Grecian Urn" by John Keats is a formal poem about the interaction between a work of art and the imagination of a viewer.

Unit 4   REVIEW

Directions Choose the letter of the best answer or write the answer using complete sentences.

Comprehension: Identifying Facts

1. Which selection tells a tale of terror?
   A "Kubla Khan"
   B *Frankenstein*
   C *Grasmere Journals*
   D *Pride and Prejudice*

2. What were three events that affected England and English attitudes in the 1800s?

3. What happened in British cities during the 1800s?

4. Identify some examples from the Unit 4 selections of the Romantic writers' preference for nature over technology.

5. Which writers in this unit represent the first generation of Romantic writers?

Comprehension: Putting Ideas Together

6. Which selection shows that pride in power is ironic?
   A "Ode on a Grecian Urn"
   B "She Walks in Beauty"
   C "Kubla Khan"
   D "Ozymandias"

7. What common thread runs through the selections by Dorothy and William Wordsworth?

8. Tell how "Ozymandias" and "Kubla Khan" are alike and how they differ.

9. Name three ways Jane Austen's work differs from that of other Romantic writers.

10. What are three common Romantic themes you observed in the works in this unit?

Understanding Literature: Diary/Journal Entries

A diary is a personal and private daily record of events, experiences, and one's feelings about them. A journal also records events and one's impressions of them, but it is more likely to be shared.

11. Is a journal fiction or nonfiction? Why?

12. How were the journals of Dorothy Wordsworth useful?

13. Contrast the selection from *Grasmere Journals* with the opening paragraphs of the selection from *Frankenstein*. How do they differ in language, subject matter, and style?

14. Which selection best reflects English society at this time? Why?

15. Dorothy Wordsworth did not consider herself a writer. How do her journals disprove this belief?

Critical Thinking

16. During the Romantic era, society still did not think writing was fit for women. Why might male Romantic writers have welcomed women writers?

17. What changes from 18th-century writing do you see in Romantic writing?

18. Which author in this unit do you find most interesting? Why?

19. What aspects of the Romantic Era do you think have carried over into today's thinking?

Thinking Creatively

20. If Romantic writers could have written for movies, what kinds of scripts do you think they would have written? Why?

Speak and Listen

Think about the high value Romantic authors placed on the natural world, the emotions, the individual, and the imagination. What joys and challenges do each of these bring you? Make notes about your answer to this question and organize the notes to contribute to a group discussion. When it is your turn to talk, speak clearly. When it is your turn to listen, think about whether you agree or disagree with the speaker's points.

Writing on Your Own

Write an original poem that reflects Romantic ideas and language. First, decide on a subject and format for your poem. Then brainstorm vivid words and figures of speech that capture the subject and your view of it. Write your poem and share it with a classmate.

Beyond Words

Think about the selections in Unit 4. What kind of music would best fit the ideas and language in these poems, stories, and journal? List pieces of music you could use to play along with the selections. Record them and prepare to play them for the class while you explain your choices.

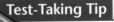

Test-Taking Tip

When reviewing for a test, first survey the headings, graphics, and captions to get the main ideas in mind. Then look for important supporting details in the paragraphs under each heading.

Queen Victoria of England,
George Hayter, 1838

The Victorian Age: 1832–1901

During Queen Victoria's rule (1837–1901), Britain seemed to be strongest and best at everything. The nation grew to be the world's greatest military and economic power. Middle-class values and ideas took center stage. Energy, duty, and seriousness well describe the attitude of Victorian society. At the same time, its writers expressed many styles and ideas with great energy. They believed in the values of their time, but they also questioned them. In this unit, you will learn how Victorian society changed Britain. You also will listen to the voices its literature produced.

"We live, as I hope you know, Mr. Worthing, in an age of ideals. The fact is constantly mentioned in the more expensive monthly magazines, and has reached the provincial pulpits, I am told."

—Gwendolen Fairfax, speaking to the man she hopes to marry in Oscar Wilde's The Importance of Being Earnest, 1894

The years from the 1830s to 1901 were a time of promise and problems in England and the rest of Britain. As the nation built an empire around the world, the middle class became the

Workers in a London Gas Factory, **Gustave Doré**

most powerful group. However, most British workers lived with hardship. Some reforms helped the poor during this period. For example, the lower middle classes gained the right to vote. However, reform happened slowly. The middle class did not want to upset the system that had built its wealth.

The world changed rapidly, thanks to advances in technology. These advances

made the British feel that their way of life was the best. They believed their mission was to spread their way of life to the rest of the world.

Toward the end of this period, Britain was sure of itself and proud. Queen Victoria had ruled for 60 years. The British Empire stretched around the world, and Britain had much success in the world market. Victorian society believed that its values of hard work and moral seriousness had made Britain successful. However, lower classes were fed up with slow change. A political idea called socialism became popular.

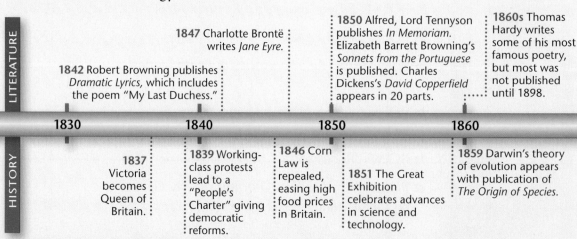

LITERATURE

1842 Robert Browning publishes *Dramatic Lyrics,* which includes the poem "My Last Duchess."

1847 Charlotte Brontë writes *Jane Eyre.*

1850 Alfred, Lord Tennyson publishes *In Memoriam.* Elizabeth Barrett Browning's *Sonnets from the Portuguese* is published. Charles Dickens's *David Copperfield* appears in 20 parts.

1860s Thomas Hardy writes some of his most famous poetry, but most was not published until 1898.

| 1830 | 1840 | 1850 | 1860 |

HISTORY

1837 Victoria becomes Queen of Britain.

1839 Working-class protests lead to a "People's Charter" giving democratic reforms.

1846 Corn Law is repealed, easing high food prices in Britain.

1851 The Great Exhibition celebrates advances in science and technology.

1859 Darwin's theory of evolution appears with publication of *The Origin of Species.*

Victorians began to wonder if the future might not be so rosy after all.

Victorian writers cannot be put into neat groups. Many of them hold up some Victorian ideas as good. However, they rebelled against other Victorian ideas. They pointed out the narrow-minded and prideful attitude behind these values. They expressed the growing doubts of British society.

Victorian poets used many styles and voices. The public eagerly read novels that were published in parts. They were published chapter by chapter in popular magazines. These novels reflected Victorian society and issues.

Three poets represent the early Victorian period. Alfred, Lord Tennyson's *In Memoriam* searches for meaning in life when a loved one dies. Robert Browning's "My Last Duchess" reveals the flaws of a Renaissance nobleman as he speaks about his first wife. Elizabeth Barrett Browning's "Sonnet 43" describes a wife's love.

Charlotte Brontë's *Jane Eyre* and Charles Dickens's *David Copperfield* are dramatic novels about orphans who learn life lessons and prove their inner worth. Matthew Arnold's poem "Dover Beach" speaks to the worry of losing religious faith, which was a common theme of the era. Gerard Manley Hopkins's "Pied Beauty" praises the unique beauty of creation.

Late in the period, *The Importance of Being Earnest*, by playwright Oscar Wilde, pokes fun at the self-importance of British society. Poets A. E. Housman, Thomas Hardy, and Rudyard Kipling use plain language to explain some of the false beliefs the British clung to.

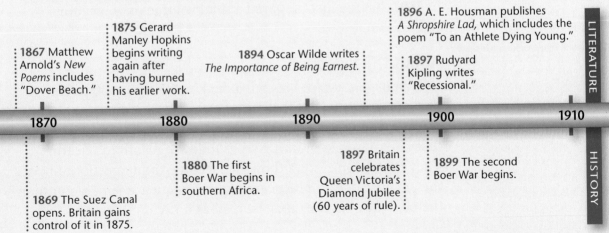

LITERATURE

1867 Matthew Arnold's *New Poems* includes "Dover Beach."

1875 Gerard Manley Hopkins begins writing again after having burned his earlier work.

1894 Oscar Wilde writes *The Importance of Being Earnest.*

1896 A. E. Housman publishes *A Shropshire Lad,* which includes the poem "To an Athlete Dying Young."

1897 Rudyard Kipling writes "Recessional."

1870   1880   1890   1900   1910

HISTORY

1869 The Suez Canal opens. Britain gains control of it in 1875.

1880 The first Boer War begins in southern Africa.

1897 Britain celebrates Queen Victoria's Diamond Jubilee (60 years of rule).

1899 The second Boer War begins.

BEFORE READING THE SELECTIONS

from *In Memoriam*　by Alfred, Lord Tennyson

Alfred,
Lord Tennyson
1809–1892

Objectives

- To read and understand a poem
- To identify the mood of a poem and explain how mood is created
- To understand how rhythm and figurative language add to a poem

About the Author

At Cambridge University, Tennyson became close friends with a gifted young man named Arthur Hallam. Hallam's sudden death in 1833 threw Tennyson into a period of grief and shock for several years. During this time, he wrote a long elegy (a poem mourning someone's death) called *In Memoriam* in honor of his friend. Its greatness was recognized immediately. It made Tennyson a famous poet. In 1850, Queen Victoria appointed him poet laureate, the chief poet of Great Britain. That same year, Tennyson married Emily Sellwood, whom he had loved since 1836. A shy man, Tennyson preferred to avoid public notice. He and his wife built a home on the Isle of Wight, where Tennyson remained for the rest of his life.

In 1859, Tennyson published *Idylls of the King.* These poems about the legendary King Arthur praise Arthur's hopeful vision of the perfect state and suggest that it failed because the king's followers betrayed him.

Tennyson wrote many books of poetry and was praised as a master poet. His poems dealt with political, scientific, and spiritual issues important to British citizens. The queen awarded him the title of baron in 1883. He died peacefully in 1892, having just prepared a final volume of poetry for publication.

About the Selection

In Memoriam, which was published in 1850, has 130 poems that mourn his friend Hallam's death. Many of the poems consider the meaning of life and art. They grew out of a poetic diary Tennyson kept in the years following Hallam's death. They reveal Tennyson's thoughts, feelings, and questions about the purpose of life. The poems form a sequence with a common theme. However, they may be read as individual poems.

Literary Terms An author creates a **mood,** or feeling, in writings. The words, images, **rhythms,** and sound effects the writer chooses combine to suggest the emotion the writer wants to get across.

Reading on Your Own You will read three numbered poems from a longer work with many sections. Each section contains the poet's thoughts and questions about life and death. After you read each section, state its main idea. Has the poet stated it directly or just suggested it? If the main idea is not stated, you will have to make an inference by thinking about the details.

Writing on Your Own Is it "better to have loved and lost/ Than never to have loved at all"? How would you respond to this statement? Write a letter to someone close to you giving your thoughts on the idea.

Vocabulary Focus Writers use **figurative language** to show how their ideas are related to other things. For example, in lines 10 and 11 of poem 27, a heart is described as turning bad "in the weeds of sloth." You may know all the words used here but still not understand the meaning of the sentence. Think about the comparison the author is making: the heart that is not given to someone loved is compared to a weedy patch of still water. Since it has no energy or movement, its power is wasted. What special meaning do the words in lines 7 and 8 of poem 82 have?

Think Before You Read Imagine your best friend has died. What emotions would you have? What do you think would help Tennyson accept his friend's death?

mood the feeling that writing creates

rhythm a pattern created by the stressed and unstressed syllables in a line of poetry

figurative language writing or speech not meant to be understood exactly as it is written

from In Memoriam

As you read, think about the images each poem contains. What mood is suggested? What does each mood say about the author's state of mind?

27

I envy not in any moods
    The captive **void** of noble rage,
    The **linnet** born within the cage,
That never knew the summer woods:

5   I envy not the beast that takes
    His **license** in the field of time,
    Unfetter'd by the sense of crime,
To whom a conscience never wakes;

Nor, what may count itself as blest,
10   The heart that never plighted troth
    But **stagnates** in the weeds of **sloth:**
Nor any **want-begotten** rest.

I hold it true, whate'er befall;
    I feel it, when I sorrow most;
15   'T is better to have loved and lost
Than never to have loved at all.

In line 10, *plighted* means "pledged" and *troth* is "faithfulness." When two people plighted troth, they became engaged. (Hallam was engaged to Tennyson's sister.)

void empty

linnet a small brown bird

license permission to act

unfetter'd not held back

stagnates lies still and idle

sloth laziness

want-begotten undeserved

82

I wage not any feud with Death
    For changes **wrought** on form and face;
    No lower life that earth's embrace
May breed with him can fright my faith.

5 Eternal process moving on,
    From state to state the spirit walks;
    And these are but the shatter'd stalks,
Or ruin'd **chrysalis** of one.

Nor blame I Death, because he bare
10   The use of virtue out of earth:
    I know transplanted human worth
Will bloom to profit, **otherwhere.**

For this alone on Death I **wreak**
    The wrath that **garners** in my heart;
15   He put our lives so far apart
We cannot hear each other speak.

What is the poet's attitude toward death?

In line 7, *these* refers to the changes mentioned in line 2.

What aspect of death has the poet not accepted?

Lake District/Ullswater

wrought worked
chrysalis cocoon of a butterfly

otherwhere elsewhere
wreak avenge

garners gathers

130

How has the poet's love for the person who has died changed? In what sense has the poet not lost this person?

Thy voice is on the rolling air;
    I hear thee where the waters run;
    Thou standest in the rising sun,
And in the setting thou art fair.

5   What art thou then? I cannot guess;
    But tho' I seem in star and flower
    To feel thee some **diffusive** power,
I do not therefore love thee less.

My love involves the love before;
10   My love is vaster passion now;
    Tho' mix'd with God and Nature thou,
I seem to love thee more and more.

Far off thou art, but ever **nigh;**
    I have thee still, and rejoice;
15   I **prosper,** circled with thy voice;
I shall not lose thee tho' I die.

In line 6, *tho'* is a poetic contraction, or shortened form, of *though.*

diffusive scattered   **nigh** near   **prosper** do very well

Directions Choose the letter of the best answer or write the answer using complete sentences.

Comprehension: Identifying Facts

1. The beast mentioned in line 5 of poem 27 is _____.
   A death
   B Tennyson
   C Hallam
   D a wild animal that kills without guilt

2. In poem 82, for what does the speaker hate death?

3. In poem 130, how can the dead person be "far off . . . but ever nigh"?

Comprehension: Putting Ideas Together

4. Poem 27 states, "'T is better to have loved and lost/Than never to have loved at all." This means that the great value of love lies in _____.
   A having experienced it
   B not getting hurt by it
   C having avoided it
   D knowing it brings joy

5. How are the images of death different in poems 82 and 130?

6. What change in attitude occurs over the course of these three poems?

Understanding Literature: Mood

The mood, or feeling, of a piece of writing comes out of the words and images a writer chooses.

7. How does the speaker's mood change in each of the parts of *In Memoriam* presented here?

8. What images in poem 130 create its mood?

Critical Thinking

9. In what ways has the speaker's love become a "vaster passion"? How is this related to the "diffusive power" (poem 130, line 7) of the dead person?

Thinking Creatively

10. Do you agree with Tennyson that we do not lose a person who has died? Explain your opinion.

After Reading continued on next page

from *In Memoriam*   by Alfred, Lord Tennyson

 ### Grammar Check

Adjectives and adverbs have forms that are used to show that a comparison is being made. The comparative form compares two things by adding *-er* or the word *more*. The superlative form compares three or more things by adding *-est* or the word *most*.

- List adjectives in the poem that are forms of comparison.

- Make a chart with columns for the positive (regular) form, the comparative form, and the superlative form. Place the adjectives you found in the chart. Complete each row by filling in the two missing forms. These can be found in the dictionary entry for the word.

 ### Writing on Your Own

Choose one of the numbered poems of *In Memoriam* you have just read. Write a paraphrase—a rewording of it in your own words. Then add a paragraph explaining whether you agree or disagree with the main idea of the poem.

 ### Speaking and Listening

Select a poem you like that expresses a strong mood. Think about the expression needed to convey this feeling when reading the poem aloud. Practice reading the poem aloud, then read it for a partner. When you are the audience, listen to decide what mood the poem expresses. Tell whether you think this mood is appropriate for the subject of the poem.

 ### Media and Technology

Death is a subject common in art and writings of all time periods. Find poems, stories, articles, artworks, songs, and films that express different views about death. Gather words, music, and images and organize them to create a multimedia presentation about the subject. For example, you might create a slide show of artworks that runs while a recording of songs and readings plays.

BEFORE READING THE SELECTION

My Last Duchess   by Robert Browning

About the Author

Robert Browning was raised in a London suburb. He received little formal education, but his father taught him Latin and Greek. Reviewers criticized his early poems so harshly that he decided he would never again express his own emotions in poetry. Instead, he wrote long poems in which a historical or imaginary character speaks. The character reveals a great deal about his or her personal situation and ways of thinking— usually without meaning to.

In 1846, Browning met Elizabeth Barrett, who was already a respected poet. Their secret courtship and marriage is one of the world's most famous romances. They lived happily in Italy until her death in 1861. He then returned to London with their son. Not until Browning was about 60 years old did the public recognize him as a great poet. His poems are dramatic and use words that imitate the irregular rhythms of speech. The poems are often startling because of the speaker's unexpected point of view.

About the Selection

"My Last Duchess" was published in 1842. It is set in the castle of the Duke of Ferrara, a powerful Italian nobleman who lived during the Renaissance. The duke is speaking to a man who has been sent to arrange the details of the duke's second marriage. The duke is showing a painting of his first wife to the man. Although the duke seems unaware of it, he reveals his own flaws through the way he describes his first wife.

Robert Browning
1812–1889

Objectives

- To read and understand a dramatic monologue
- To understand iambic pentameter
- To describe character traits and point out details that reveal them

Before Reading continued on next page

My Last Duchess by Robert Browning

dramatic monologue
a poem in which a character talks to the reader or to a silent second character

iambic pentameter
five two-beat sounds in a line of poetry where the second syllable is stressed in each pattern

character traits characters' ways of thinking, behaving, or speaking

Literary Terms "My Last Duchess" is a **dramatic monologue.** It is a poem made up of the words a character speaks to someone who listens but does not reply. It is written in **iambic pentameter.** Each line of iambic pentameter has five strong beats and 10 syllables. This poem's rhythm is rough, not perfectly smooth, to imitate natural speech. The monologue also reveals **character traits.** The way the speaker in this poem talks and acts shows his personality.

Reading on Your Own The details the speaker chooses to tell his listener suggest his personality, as well as what happened to his first wife. As you read, think about what happened in his marriage and what might have made the duke act as he did.

Writing on Your Own Think of a historical person you have learned about. Write a dramatic monologue from that person's point of view. Remember to reveal some important character traits through your character's words.

Vocabulary Focus "My Last Duchess" is set in 13th-century Italy. Some of the words it contains are no longer familiar to us. For example, in line 16, the word *mantle* refers to a kind of cloak worn over other clothes. The word *dowry* in line 51 refers to money, property, and other valuables a man receives from his bride's family as the couple is married. The sentence in lines 53–54 may puzzle you, too. The count calls his companion to walk at his side. Because the man was of lower rank than the count, he would have walked behind the count to show respect.

Think Before You Read What do you imagine the setting in the duke's palace is like in this poem?

My Last DUCHESS

That's my last Duchess painted on the wall,
Looking as if she were alive. I call
That piece a wonder, now: Frà Pandolf's hands
Worked busily a day, and there she stands.
5 Will't please you sit and look at her? I said
"Frà Pandolf" by design, for never read
Strangers like you that pictured **countenance,**
The depth and passion of its earnest glance,
But to myself they turned (since none puts by
10 The curtain I have drawn for you, but I)
And seemed as they would ask me, if they **durst,**
How such a glance came there; so, not the first
Are you to turn and ask thus. Sir, 'twas not
Her husband's presence only, called that spot
15 Of joy into the Duchess' cheek: perhaps
Frà Pandolf chanced to say "Her **mantle** laps
Over my lady's wrist too much," or "Paint
Must never hope to reproduce the faint
Half-flush that dies along her throat": such stuff
20 Was **courtesy,** she thought, and cause enough
For calling up that spot of joy. She had
A heart—how shall I say?—too soon made glad,
Too easily impressed; she liked whate'er
She looked on, and her looks went everywhere.

As you read, picture the palace scene, the duke, and the portrait he is describing. Think about what he says and the tone in which you think he says it.

Frà Pandolf (line 3) is an imaginary monk and painter of the Renaissance period. Frà means "brother."

Note the rhythm of this poem. Each line is written in iambic pentameter: 10 syllables with alternating unstressed and stressed syllables.

countenance face and its expression   **durst** dared   **courtesy** thoughtfulness
mantle loose cloak

25 Sir, 'twas all one! My **favour** at her breast,
The dropping of the daylight in the West,
The **bough** of cherries some **officious** fool
Broke in the orchard for her, the white mule
She rode with round the terrace—all and each
30 Would draw from her alike the approving speech,
Or blush, at least. She thanked men,—good! but thanked
Somehow—I know not how—as if she ranked
My gift of a nine-hundred-years-old name
With anybody's gift. Who'd stoop to blame
35 This sort of **trifling?** Even had you skill
In speech—(which I have not)—to make your will
Quite clear to such an one, and say, "Just this
Or that in you disgusts me; here you miss,
Or there exceed the mark"—and if she let
40 Herself be **lessoned** so, nor plainly set
Her wits to yours, **forsooth,** and made excuse,
—E'en then would be some stooping; and I choose
Never to stoop. Oh sir, she smiled, no doubt,
Whene'er I passed her; but who passed without
45 Much the same smile? This grew; I gave commands;
Then all smiles stopped together. There she stands
As if alive. Will't please you rise? We'll meet

The duke's noble heritage is 900 years old. He thinks his heritage is a great gift to his wife.

What character trait does the duke show in lines 42–43?

favour token of love or respect	**officious** bossy, overbearing	**lessoned** taught
bough branch	**trifling** silly activity	**forsooth** indeed

The company below, then. I repeat,
The Count your master's known **munificence**
50 Is ample **warrant** that no just **pretence**
Of mine for **dowry** will be **disallowed;**
Though his fair daughter's self, as I **avowed**
At starting, is my object. Nay, we'll go
Together down, sir. Notice Neptune, though,
55 Taming a sea-horse, thought a rarity,
Which Claus of Innsbruck cast in bronze for me!

Who is the duke addressing in his monologue? What effect might this speech have on the listener?

Lady in Red,
William Turner Dannatt, 1889

munificence generosity

warrant certification, proof

pretence claim, expectation

dowry money and property given by a woman's family to the man she marries

disallowed denied

avowed swore

My Last Duchess   by Robert Browning

Directions Choose the letter of the best answer or write the answer using complete sentences.

Comprehension: Identifying Facts

1. In line 1, "my last Duchess" refers to _____.

    A the speaker's mother
    B the speaker's first wife
    C the speaker's bride-to-be
    D a noble ancestor of the duke

2. What does the speaker mean when he says in line 22 that the duchess had a "heart . . . too soon made glad"?

3. What does it mean that "all smiles stopped together" (line 46)?

Comprehension: Putting Ideas Together

4. As you read this poem, you gradually become aware that the duke _____.

    A is arrogant, proud, and possessive
    B did not love his first wife
    C loves people and entertaining
    D will never marry again

5. What details in the poem suggest that the duke is intelligent and cultured?

6. What did the duke seem to expect and need from his wife?

Understanding Literature: Dramatic Monologue, Character Traits, and Iambic Pentameter

In a dramatic monologue, one speaker talks to another speaker who remains silent. The poem is usually long enough to reveal some character traits of the speaker through the things said and the way in which they are said. This poem is written in iambic pentameter; each line has 10 syllables and five beats.

7. Which words or phrases give clues about the duke's opinion of his first wife? Is his opinion a fair one? Tell why you think as you do.

8. This poem uses meter and rhyme in irregular ways. How does Browning play with these elements to make the poem sound like natural speech?

Critical Thinking

9. At the end of the poem, the duke points out another work of art. What does this sculpture suggest about the duke? about the poem's main idea?

Thinking Creatively

10. What does the duke report in lines 45–46? What do you think happened to the last duchess? Why do you think so?

Grammar Check

A dash (—) is a punctuation mark used to set off a thought or a less important comment that interrupts a sentence. In line 22, *how shall I say?* is set off from the sentence *She had a heart too soon made glad.* No other punctuation mark is needed before or after a dash.

- Write two more examples from this poem of sentences that use dashes.

- Read the sentences aloud. Use pauses and expression to show the change in the speaker's thoughts.

- Write a sentence of your own that uses dashes. Read your sentence to a partner and have him or her write the sentence, adding dashes. Check to see if your partner placed dashes in the correct places.

 ## Writing on Your Own

Write a character analysis of the duke. In your introduction, summarize his character traits. Then write a paragraph explaining each trait. In your conclusion, sum up how you feel about this character. A Character Analysis Guide can help you organize your thoughts. See Appendix A for a description of this graphic organizer.

 ## Speaking and Listening

The duke wants to marry another woman. In a small group, discuss whether you would advise her to marry him. Give your reasons in clear, simple sentences and support them with evidence from the poem. When others are speaking, be polite and give them your full attention. If you disagree, offer your reasons and point out other evidence in the poem.

 ## Research

The artists mentioned in this poem are imaginary. Read more about the art of the Renaissance. Choose one real Renaissance artist and take notes about the work and accomplishments of that artist. Prepare a short talk about the artist. Show pictures of some of his or her paintings or sculptures.

Elizabeth Barrett
Browning
1806–1861

Objectives

- To read and understand a sonnet
- To identify words that rhyme and explain the pattern of rhyme in a sonnet

About the Author

Elizabeth Barrett Browning had a happy childhood in the English countryside. However, at age 15, she injured her spine. It seemed likely that she would be physically weak for the rest of her life. The family moved to London, and she spent much time in a dark room, where she wrote poetry and letters. Her verse was widely admired. One admirer was Robert Browning, who wrote to her about her poetry.

The two writers met and fell in love but kept their love a secret. Elizabeth's father did not approve of the match. Doctors advised her to go to Italy for her health, but her father refused. Robert and she then married secretly. The couple moved to Italy and had a son. The Brownings supported the cause of Italian unification (creating one nation out of many smaller states) and independence from Austria. Elizabeth wrote *Casa Guidi Windows,* in which she tried to win sympathy for the cause of freedom in the city of Florence.

Browning was more famous than her husband during her lifetime. Although she was very popular with the public, critics were less impressed with her talent.

About the Selection

This poem is a sonnet, a 14-line poem invented in Italy during the 1200s. English writers changed the form and began writing sonnets in the 1400s. For this sonnet, Browning used a rhyme scheme that was common to Italian sonnets. This is appropriate, because Italy had become her home. Sonnets express emotion about one subject. In this case, the subject is Browning's love for her husband. This sonnet is one of 44 that are in *Sonnets from the Portuguese,* a popular book of love poetry published in 1850.

Literary Terms The poem you are about to read is a **sonnet,** a 14-line poem written in iambic pentameter. Each line has five beats and 10 syllables. It follows a strict pattern of **rhyme.** Words rhyme when they repeat the same or similar ending sound, as in *height* and *sight.*

Reading on Your Own In this poem, Browning describes the different ways in which she loves her husband. Pause after reading each sentence that begins *I love thee* and think about the kind of love it describes.

Writing on Your Own Name and describe several different kinds of love. Write several sentences about each, giving examples you have observed.

Vocabulary Focus Some words have more than one meaning or mean slightly different things in different contexts. Understanding what you read requires that you know which meaning the writer is using. For example, *grace* can refer to smoothness of movement (as with a graceful dancer). It can also be a religious term for undeserved goodness done for another. However, in this poem, "Ideal Grace" is more likely the goodness of the poet being the very best that she can be. As you read, consider the different shades of meaning connected to *freely, right,* and *faith.*

Think Before You Read What do you think was the nature of Elizabeth Barrett Browning's love for Robert Browning, the man she felt rescued her?

> **sonnet** a 14-line poem written in iambic pentameter
>
> **rhyme** words that end with the same or similar sounds

Sonnet 43

As you read, notice the pattern of rhymes Browning uses. How does she use rhyme to emphasize her meaning? Why do you think the poet chose the strict form of a sonnet instead of free verse?

What adverbs describe the way the poet loves in lines 7–10? What do these words suggest about the nature of the poet's love?

What has the poet regained that was lost in childhood?

How do I love thee? Let me count the ways!—
I love thee to the depth and breadth and height
My soul can reach, when feeling out of sight
For the ends of Being and Ideal **Grace.**
5   I love thee to the level of everyday's
Most quiet need, by sun and candlelight—
I love thee freely, as men **strive** for Right,—
I love thee purely, as they turn from **Praise;**
I love thee with the passion, put to use
10   In my old griefs, . . . and with my childhood's faith:
I love thee with the
        love I seemed
        to lose
With my lost
        Saints,—I love
        thee with the
        breath,
Smiles, tears, of all
        my life!—and, if
        God choose,
I shall but love thee
        better after death.

Young Girl with a Candle,
Godfried Schalcken

Grace beauty of form, movement, or manner	**strive** work hard, strain	**praise** worship

Directions Choose the letter of the best answer or write the answer using complete sentences.

Comprehension: Identifying Facts

1. The phrase "by sun and candlelight" in line 6 shows that the poet's love for her husband ____.
   A lights up her life
   B is a force of nature
   C is a part of her soul
   D is present day and night

2. What does the poet mean when she says, "I love thee freely, as men strive for Right" (line 7)?

3. What does the phrase "the love I seemed to lose/With my lost Saints" (lines 11–12) mean?

Comprehension: Putting Ideas Together

4. The nature of the poet's love for her husband is ____.
   A simple
   B intense
   C like that of a servant for a master
   D sad

5. What images appear in the sonnet? What do they suggest about the poet's love?

6. What does this poem tell about the nature of the person to whom she speaks?

Understanding Literature: Sonnet and Rhyme

A sonnet is a 14-line poem written in iambic pentameter. Each line has 10 syllables with five strong beats. A sonnet uses rhyme, or repeated ending sounds of words at the ends of lines. Rhyme emphasizes some ideas in this sonnet.

7. Which words in this sonnet rhyme with *ways*? Which words rhyme with *height*?

8. What ideas are emphasized by the *breath/death* rhyme?

Critical Thinking

9. Is the speaker's love for her husband more spiritual or earthly? Explain your opinion.

Thinking Creatively

10. Is it good or bad to love one person with all your being? Explain your thinking.

After Reading continued on next page

Sonnet 43   by Elizabeth Barrett Browning

Grammar Check

A noun names a person, place, thing, or idea. Many nouns are concrete nouns; they name things you can see and touch (*face, hat, sky*). Others are abstract; they name ideas you cannot see or touch (*love, sorrow, pity*).

- List nouns you can find in the selection.

- Write *concrete* beside each concrete noun. Write *abstract* beside each abstract noun.

- Write a paragraph explaining which kind of noun is used most often in the poem. Explain what effect these nouns have.

Writing on Your Own

Write a biographical sketch about another real couple famous for their love. Jot down the facts you know. Find more information in encyclopedias and library books, if necessary. Write your sketch, putting events in the order in which they happened.

Speaking and Listening

Practice reading this poem or another love poem aloud until you can recite it smoothly. Record your reading and play it back. Listen to hear whether the sentences sound natural or artificial. Note whether your tone and expression are suitable to the poem's viewpoint. Record the poem again until you are satisfied with your reading.

Media and Technology

Which form of media today would portray a love like that described in this poem: TV, radio, movies, magazines, or newspapers? Look for examples. Copy examples; for instance, you might record a portion of a soap opera or photocopy a story in a magazine. Prepare a presentation using one or more kinds of media.

BEFORE READING THE SELECTION

from *Jane Eyre*   *by Charlotte Brontë*

About the Author

Charlotte Brontë was the oldest of three talented sisters. With Emily and Anne and their brother Bram, Brontë was raised in the lonely countryside of Yorkshire in northern England. The girls attended boarding schools and worked at times as governesses, who looked after children in wealthy people's homes, and as schoolteachers. They were shy, poor, and lonely, but they entertained themselves with music, drawing, reading, and—most of all—writing stories. All three sisters wrote novels. Charlotte Brontë's *Jane Eyre* became successful right after it was published in 1847.

Brontë used her experiences in boarding schools and as a governess in writing *Jane Eyre*. However, the novel's romantic hero, Mr. Rochester, is invented. In *Jane Eyre,* Brontë creates a strong, independent-minded heroine. She also develops themes of love, independence, and forgiveness. Brontë wrote three other books, also based on her experiences as a single working woman.

Brontë refused several offers of marriage during her life. Not until 1854 did she marry. While she was pregnant in 1855, she became sick and died.

About the Selection

Jane Eyre tells the story of an orphan who (like Brontë) attends a harsh, unpleasant boarding school, then becomes a governess. She falls in love with Edward Rochester, the guardian of the child she is hired to teach. *Jane Eyre* startled readers of its day because its heroine, though poor, is an independent woman of strong passions and moral ideals. She longs for love but refuses to accept it at the cost of her self-respect.

Charlotte Brontë
1816–1855

Objectives

- To read and understand an excerpt from a novel
- To identify point of view in a work of fiction
- To explain the author's purpose for writing

Before Reading **continued on next page**

The Victorian Age Unit 5   **361**

novel fiction that is book-length and has more plot and character details than a short story

point of view the position from which the author or storyteller tells the story

Literary Terms This selection presents a chapter from a **novel,** a long work of fiction. The novel *Jane Eyre* is told from the heroine's **point of view.** Every story has a point of view—a vantage point from which it is told. Readers see the plot and all the other characters through this person's eyes.

Reading on Your Own The chapter you are about to read tells how Mr. Rochester at last confesses his love for Jane and asks her to marry him. Their words and reactions tell us a great deal about their characters. Pay close attention to what each person says, how he or she says it, and how nature reflects the actions and emotions of the scene.

Writing on Your Own This novel is written as an autobiography of the character Jane. An autobiography is one's own life story. Jot down five important facts you would include in your autobiography. Then describe what is most important about your beliefs, dreams, and plans.

Vocabulary Focus Writers sometimes define a new word where it appears. For example, on page 364, Jane says, "Do you think I am an automaton?" The next phrase gives the meaning of *automaton:* "a machine without feelings." Authors may also suggest a word's meaning by providing an antonym, or a word that means the opposite. On page 368, the "paradise of union" follows the "nightmare of parting." *Paradise* and *nightmare* are antonyms. *Paradise* suggests delight. Read the sentences on page 368 in which *solace* and *sanctions* occur. Find an antonym for each word and use it to predict the word's meaning.

Think Before You Read In the 1800s, women were expected to marry. Without a husband, money, or family, a single woman had no way to provide for her future. What is at stake as Jane insists she will leave Rochester's home forever?

from Jane Eyre

Jane teaches a little girl who is in the care of Mr. Rochester, a mysterious and gloomy gentleman who holds himself apart. Like Jane, he is independent, proud, and out of the ordinary. Her fascination with him soon turns to love. Her hopes are crushed when he seems to court a noblewoman. Jane decides she must leave his estate. She does not realize that, secretly, Rochester loves her. She also does not know he has a dark secret.

As you read, notice ways in which Jane and Mr. Rochester are alike and different.

"I have known you, Mr. Rochester; and it strikes me with terror and **anguish** to feel I absolutely must be torn from you for ever. I see the necessity of departure; and it is like looking on the necessity of death."

"Where do you see the necessity?" he asked, suddenly.

"Where? You, sir, have placed it before me."

"In what shape?"

"In the shape of Miss Ingram; a noble and beautiful woman,—your bride."

"My bride! What bride? I have no bride!"

"But you will have."

"Yes;—I will—I will!" He set his teeth.

"Then I must go—you have said it yourself."

"No: you must stay! I swear it—and the oath shall be kept."

Rochester's response that he will have a bride means one thing to him and something very different to Jane.

anguish suffering

"I tell you I must go!" I retorted, roused to something like passion. "Do you think I can stay to become nothing to you? Do you think I am an **automaton?**—a machine without feelings? and can bear to have my **morsel** of bread snatched from my lips, and my drop of living water dashed from my cup? Do you think, because I am poor, **obscure,** plain, and little, I am soulless and heartless? You think wrong!—I have as much soul as you,—and full as much heart! And if God had gifted me with some beauty and much wealth, I should have made it as hard for you to leave me, as it is now for me to leave you. I am not talking to you now through the medium of custom, **conventionalities,** nor even of mortal flesh—it is my spirit that addresses your spirit; just as if both had passed through the grave, and we stood at God's feet, equal,—as we are!"

"As we are!" repeated Mr. Rochester—"so," he added, enclosing me in his arms, gathering me to his breast, pressing his lips on my lips: "so, Jane!"

"Yes, so, sir," I **rejoined:** "and yet not so; for you are a married man—or as good as a married man, and wed to one inferior to you—to one with whom you have no sympathy—whom I do not believe you truly love; for I have seen and heard you sneer at her. I would scorn such a union: therefore I am better than you—let me go!"

"Where, Jane? To Ireland?"

"Yes—to Ireland. I have spoken my mind, and can go anywhere now."

"Jane, be still; don't struggle so, like a wild, frantic bird that is **rending** its own **plumage** in its desperation."

"I am no bird; and no net ensnares me: I am a free human being with an independent will; which I now exert to leave you."

Jane sees herself as Rochester's equal. This would have been a shocking point of view in the 1800s.

What causes Jane to say she is better than Rochester? Is this true?

How does Rochester's view of Jane differ from her idea of who she is?

automaton robot	**conventionalities** behaviors accepted by society	**rending** tearing
morsel small piece		**plumage** feathers
obscure unknown	**rejoined** answered	

Another effort set me at liberty, and I stood erect before him.

"And your will shall decide your **destiny**," he said: "I offer you my hand, my heart, and a share of all my possessions."

"You play a **farce,** which I merely laugh at."

"I ask you to pass through life at my side—to be my second self, and best earthly companion."

"For that fate you have already made your choice, and must abide by it."

"Jane, be still a few moments; you are over-excited: I will be still too."

A **waft** of wind came sweeping down the **laurel** walk, and trembled through the boughs of the chestnut: it wandered away—away—to an indefinite distance—it died. The nightingale's song was then the only voice of the hour: in listening to it, I again wept. Mr. Rochester sat quiet, looking at me gently and seriously. Some time passed before he spoke; he at last said:—"Come to my side, Jane, and let us explain and understand one another."

"I will never again come to your side: I am torn away now, and cannot return."

"But, Jane, I summon you as my wife: it is you only I intend to marry."

I was silent: I thought he mocked me.

"Come, Jane—come **hither.**"

"Your bride stands between us."

He rose, and with a stride reached me.

"My bride is here," he said, again drawing me to him, "because my equal is here, and my likeness. Jane, will you marry me?"

Still I did not answer, and still I **writhed** myself from his grasp: for I was still **incredulous.**

"Do you doubt me, Jane?"

"Entirely."

How does Rochester show that he knows Jane must make her own decision?

Notice that nature reflects the characters' emotions.

Why does Rochester say he wants to marry Jane? What does he recognize?

destiny fate	**laurel** a type of evergreen tree	**writhed** twisted, wriggled
farce mockery	**hither** here	**incredulous** not believing
waft breeze		

"You have no faith in me?"

"Not a whit."

"Am I a liar in your eyes?" he asked passionately. "Little **sceptic,** you *shall* be convinced. What love have I for Miss Ingram? None: and that you know. What love has she for me? None: as I have taken pains to prove; I caused a rumour to reach her that my fortune was not a third of what was supposed, and after that I presented myself to see the result; it was coldness both from her and her mother. I would not—I could not—marry Miss Ingram. You—you strange—you almost unearthly thing!—I love as my own flesh. You—poor and obscure, and small and plain as you are—I **entreat** to accept me as a husband."

"What, me!" I **ejaculated:** beginning in his earnestness— and especially in his **incivility**—to credit his **sincerity:** "me who have not a friend in the world but you—if you are my friend: not a shilling but what you have given me?"

"You, Jane. I must have you for my own—entirely my own. Will you be mine? Say yes, quickly."

"Mr. Rochester, let me look at your face: turn to the moonlight."

"Why?"

"Because I want to read your **countenance;** turn!"

"There: you will find it scarcely more legible than a crumpled, scratched page. Read on: only make haste, for I suffer."

His face was very much **agitated** and very much flushed, and there were strong workings in the features, and strange gleams in the eyes.

"Oh, Jane, you torture me!" he exclaimed. "With that searching and yet faithful and generous look, you torture me!"

"How can I do that? If you are true, and your offer real, my only feelings to you must be gratitude and devotion—they cannot torture."

> What does his test of Miss Ingram show about Rochester's character?

> What finally begins to convince Jane that Rochester is not lying?

sceptic doubter	**incivility** rudeness	**agitated** upset; not calm
entreat beg	**sincerity** honesty	
ejaculated cried out	**countenance** face	

"Gratitude!" he ejaculated; and added wildly—"Jane, accept me quickly. Say, Edward—give me my name—Edward—I will marry you."

"Are you in earnest?—Do you truly love me? Do you sincerely wish me to be your wife?"

"I do; and if an oath is necessary to satisfy you, I swear it."

"Then, sir, I will marry you."

"Edward—my little wife!"

"Dear Edward!"

"Come to me—come to me entirely now," said he: and added, in his deepest tone, speaking in my ear as his cheek was laid on mine, "Make my happiness—I will make yours."

"God pardon me!" he **subjoined ere** long; "and man meddle not with me: I have her, and will hold her."

"There is no one to meddle, sir. I have no **kindred** to interfere."

"No—that is the best of it," he said.

What does Rochester's cry suggest about his situation? What does it suggest about his morals?

Rochester, Jane Eyre, and Adèle, Frederick Walter, 1847

subjoined added   **ere** before   **kindred** relatives

Rochester's words here show he is suffering an inner conflict. What might cause him to argue with himself even after Jane has agreed to marry him?

And if I loved him less I should have thought his accent and look of **exultation** savage; but, sitting by him, roused from the nightmare of parting—called to the paradise of union—I thought only of the bliss given me to drink in so abundant a flow. Again and again he said, "Are you happy, Jane?" and again and again I answered, "Yes." After which he murmured, "It will **atone**—it will atone. Have I not found her friendless, and cold, and comfortless? Will I not guard, and cherish, and **solace** her? Is there not love in my heart, and constancy in my resolves? It will **expiate** at God's tribunal. I know my Maker **sanctions** what I do. For the world's judgment—I wash my hands thereof. For man's opinion—I defy it."

What does the change in the weather suggest about the step Rochester and Jane have taken?

But what had **befallen** the night? The moon was not yet set, and we were all in shadow: I could scarcely see my master's face, near as I was. And what ailed the chestnut tree? it writhed and groaned; while wind roared in the laurel walk, and came sweeping over us.

"We must go in," said Mr. Rochester: "the weather changes. I could have sat with thee till morning, Jane."

"And so," thought I, "could I with you." I should have said so, perhaps, but a **livid,** vivid spark leapt out of a cloud at which I was looking, and there was a crack, a crash, and a close rattling peal; and I thought only of hiding my dazzled eyes against Mr. Rochester's shoulder.

The rain rushed down. He hurried me up the walk, through the grounds, and into the house; but we were quite wet before we could pass the threshold. He was taking off my shawl in the hall, and shaking the water out of my loosened hair, when Mrs. Fairfax emerged from her room. I did not observe her at first, nor did Mr. Rochester. The lamp was lit. The clock was on the stroke of twelve.

Mrs. Fairfax is Rochester's housekeeper.

exultation triumph	**solace** comfort	**befallen** happened to
atone make up for something	**expiate** pay a penalty	**livid** furious
	sanctions blesses	

"**Hasten** to take off your wet things," said he; "and before you go, good-night—good-night, my darling!"

He kissed me repeatedly. When I looked up, on leaving his arms, there stood the widow, pale, grave, and amazed. I only smiled at her, and ran upstairs. "Explanation will do for another time," thought I. Still, when I reached my chamber, I felt a pang at the idea that she should even temporarily **misconstrue** what she had seen. But joy soon **effaced** every other feeling; and loud as the wind blew, near and deep as the thunder crashed, fierce and frequent as the lightning gleamed, **cataract-like** as the rain fell during a storm of two hours' duration, I experienced no fear, and little awe. Mr. Rochester came thrice to my door in the course of it, to ask if I was safe and **tranquil**: and that was comfort, that was strength for anything.

Before I left my bed in the morning, little Adèle came running in to tell me that the great horse-chestnut at the bottom of the orchard had been struck by lightning in the night, and half of it split away.

Why do you think Mrs. Fairfax is shocked by what she sees? What does it tell about Jane's character that she doesn't want Mrs. Fairfax to get the wrong idea?

Adèle is the child Jane takes care of for Rochester.

hasten hurry	**effaced** wiped away	**tranquil** peaceful
misconstrue misunderstand	**cataract-like** like a waterfall	

AFTER READING THE SELECTION

Directions Choose the letter of the best answer or write the answer using complete sentences.

Comprehension: Identifying Facts

1. Jane is convinced that she must leave Rochester's estate because _____.
   - **A** he is supposed to marry someone else
   - **B** he and Jane are engaged
   - **C** she cannot earn money there
   - **D** he does not trust her

2. What happens that forces the lovers to go indoors?
   - **A** It grows too late.
   - **B** Mrs. Fairfax finds them.
   - **C** A violent storm begins.
   - **D** They fear what people will say.

3. In what ways does Jane say she is Rochester's equal?

4. In what way does she consider herself better than Rochester?

5. Why does Jane not answer Rochester's first proposal?

6. What did Rochester do that convinced him that Miss Ingram did not love him?

7. What does Jane do to be sure Rochester is telling the truth?

8. Whom does Rochester address after Jane accepts his proposal? What does he say?

9. What keeps Jane from being afraid during the storm?

10 What happens to the chestnut tree during the night?

Comprehension: Putting Ideas Together

11. Within this chapter, Jane's mood changes from anguish to _____.
    - **A** acceptance
    - **C** joy
    - **B** dislike
    - **D** questioning

12. Jane and Rochester agree that _____.
    - **A** he loves Miss Ingram
    - **B** they are equals
    - **C** they have every right to marry
    - **D** a man must care for a woman

13. In what way would society say Jane and Rochester are unequal? In what ways does Jane say they are equals?

14. What convinces Jane that Rochester is being truthful?

15. In this chapter, how is nature made to seem like a character?

16. In what ways are Jane and Rochester alike?

17. How do the reactions of Jane and Rochester differ after she says yes?

18. What values does Jane reveal by her behavior?

19. What values does Rochester reveal?

20. Why does Rochester love Jane?

Understanding Literature: Novel and Point of View

A novel is a book-length work of fiction. In a novel, characters and plot are fleshed out in great detail. Like all stories, novels are told by someone. This person's point of view controls and limits the readers' understanding of characters and their actions.

21. What plot events occurred in *Jane Eyre* before this excerpt?

22. What plot events occur in this excerpt?

23. From whose point of view is the story told?

24. Why do you think Brontë chose to tell this story from this point of view?

25. Why do you think Brontë spent an entire chapter on Rochester's proposal?

Critical Thinking

26. Why does Rochester speak to Jane using her first name, while she calls him "Mr. Rochester"? When is she able to call him by his first name?

27. Why do you think Brontë makes both characters different from what society expects?

28. Both Rochester and Jane insist on marrying for love. Why was this unique in the 1800s?

29. How did you react to this chapter? How might the reaction of Victorian readers have been different?

Thinking Creatively

30. Why do you think Rochester asks for God's pardon at such a happy time? What things could prevent two adults from marrying each other today?

After Reading **continued on next page**

from *Jane Eyre*   *by Charlotte Brontë*

 Grammar Check

A comma is used to set off a noun of direct address: "I have known you, Mr. Rochester." If the noun of direct address comes in the middle of a sentence, it is set off by two commas: "You, sir, have placed it before me."

- In the selection, find more examples of nouns of direct address, two with one comma and two with two commas.

- Write the sentences in which these nouns occur. Use punctuation correctly.

- Write two or three lines of dialogue that use nouns of direct address.

 Writing on Your Own

Rochester does not care whether other people will dislike that he marries Jane. Do you agree with this attitude? Write a letter to Rochester explaining your reasons for agreeing or disagreeing with him.

 Speaking and Listening

Select a longer speech by Jane or Rochester from this chapter and practice reading it aloud. Think about how the character feels. Use a tone and expression that fit the emotions the words express. Present your reading to a partner. Ask him or her for suggestions to make your reading better.

 Viewing

Find a copy of a movie version of *Jane Eyre*. Watch the part that includes the proposal scene. Listen to the characters speak. Does their acting add to your understanding of the passage? How do the surroundings and costumes add to the emotions you experience?

Research

Research one of these topics: Charlotte Brontë's *Villette* or Emily Brontë's *Wuthering Heights*. Locate a plot summary on the Internet. Read what critics have to say about the book. Watch a movie version of the story if possible. Then compare the work to *Jane Eyre*.

BEFORE READING THE SELECTION

from *David Copperfield*   *by Charles Dickens*

About the Author

Charles Dickens was born in 1812. He was the son of a poor clerk. Because of money problems, Dickens's father went to debtor's prison. At age 12, Dickens had to work in a London factory for a time. He attended school off and on until about age 15 but received a poor education. Dickens sharpened his writing skills and began writing short stories after he went to work as a reporter.

Dickens observed life and people closely. By the 1830s, he had become a famous novelist. His understanding of human nature and his sympathy for the poor come to life in his books. Among his famous works are *A Christmas Carol, Oliver Twist, David Copperfield, A Tale of Two Cities,* and *Great Expectations.*

Dickens's personal life was not happy. His marriage ended in 1858. However, his great energy went into creating some of the most famous characters ever invented. His sense of drama brought life into his plots. His warmth and humor shine through in his works. Dickens worked tirelessly until his death in 1870.

About the Selection

In *David Copperfield,* Dickens combines social criticism with autobiography. Its hero is a novelist who first works as a reporter. Like Dickens, David also is forced to work in a factory as a youngster. The book describes a young man's journey to understanding the world and what life is about. *David Copperfield* has the many subplots and huge cast of characters typical of Dickens's work. It was written in 20 monthly parts that appeared in a popular magazine in 1849 and 1850.

Charles Dickens
1812–1870

Objectives

- To read and understand an excerpt from a novel
- To describe dialect and appreciate dramatic dialogue
- To identify plot elements and describe a protagonist

Before Reading **continued on next page**

from *David Copperfield* by Charles Dickens

dialogue
the conversation among characters in a story

dialect the speech of a particular part of a country or of a certain group of people

plot the series of events in a story

protagonist
the main character; also called the hero

Literary Terms This novel uses **dialogue,** or the conversations among characters, skillfully. The **dialect,** or regional speech, of some characters identifies their social background. Its **plot,** or sequence of events, follows the **protagonist,** or hero, as he learns about life and makes his way in the world.

Reading on Your Own The selection you are about to read describes a meeting between the hero, David, and an evil character, Uriah Heep. In this excerpt, Heep tries to worm his way into power and a marriage to David's dear friend Agnes. Pay close attention to the contrasts in the way each character speaks and the way Dickens describes Heep.

Writing on Your Own Think about the unique ways people in a region talk. Write a dialogue between people speaking in a dialect with which you are familiar. Take care to use words and expressions common to that dialect. You may want to invent word spellings that will help a reader "hear" the dialect the way it is spoken.

Vocabulary Focus The history of a word can help you understand its current meaning. Word histories appear in brackets [ ] before definitions in a dictionary entry. For example, Dickens uses the word *propitiatory* to describe a movement of a character. This word is built from the Latin *pro*, meaning "for" and *petere*, meaning "to seek." An action is propitiatory when it is carried out to get someone's favor or good will. Look up the word histories of *stratagem*, *malevolent*, and *temperate*. Predict each word's meaning.

Think Before You Read What do you think David Copperfield and Uriah Heep might talk about?

from David Copperfield

As a boy, David lives with his Aunt Betsey. Her lawyer, Mr. Wickfield, and Wickfield's sweet daughter Agnes become dear friends to David. Uriah Heep is a law clerk who works for Mr. Wickfield. He wants to take over his employer's business and marry Agnes. Just before this passage, David has returned from a long absence. He observes that Uriah Heep and his mother hover around the Wickfields. It is as if David's friends have become the Heeps' prisoners. Uriah follows David on his evening walk.

I had not walked out far enough to be quite clear of the town, upon the Ramsgate road, where there was a good path, when I was hailed, through the dust, by somebody behind me. The **shambling** figure, and the scanty **great-coat,** were not to be mistaken. I stopped, and Uriah Heep came up.

"Well?" said I.

"How fast you walk!" said he. "My legs are pretty long, but you've given 'em quite a job."

"Where are you going?" said I.

"I am going with you, Master Copperfield, if you'll allow me the pleasure of a walk with an old acquaintance." Saying this, with a jerk of his body, which might have been either **propitiatory** or **derisive,** he fell into step beside me.

> David Copperfield is both the protagonist and narrator of this story. Pay attention to what David's words and actions reveal about him. Also notice how the character Uriah Heep clashes and contrasts with him.

> Contrast the two characters' speech. Heep expresses himself as a member of a lower class and chooses his words to make himself seem less "worthy." David's speech is more cultured and proud.

---

shambling awkward

great-coat heavy overcoat

propitiatory meaning to win favor

derisive mocking

What can you tell about the plot actions that have happened before this scene?

"Uriah!" said I, as **civilly** as I could, after a silence.

"Master Copperfield!" said Uriah.

"To tell you the truth (at which you will not be offended), I came out to walk alone, because I have had so much company."

He looked at me sideways, and said with his hardest grin, "You mean mother."

"Why yes, I do," said I.

What does Heep mean when he describes himself as *umble*?

"Ah! But you know we're so very umble," he returned. "And having such a knowledge of our own umbleness, we must really take care that we're not pushed to the wall by them as isn't umble. All **stratagems** are fair in love, sir."

Raising his great hands until they touched his chin, he rubbed them softly, and softly chuckled; looking as like a **malevolent** baboon, I thought, as anything human could look.

Heep's dialect (dropping the *h* from *humble* and *harsh,* for example) contrasts with David's proper speech.

"You see," he said, still hugging himself in that unpleasant way, and shaking his head at me, "you're quite a dangerous rival, Master Copperfield. You always was, you know."

"Do you set a watch upon Miss Wickfield, and make her home no home, because of me?" said I.

"Oh! Master Copperfield! Those are very arsh words," he replied.

"Put my meaning into any words you like," said I. "You know what it is, Uriah, as well as I do."

"Oh no! You must put it into words," he said. "Oh, really! I couldn't myself."

"Do you suppose," said I, **constraining** myself to be very **temperate** and quiet with him, on account of Agnes, "that I regard Miss Wickfield otherwise than as a very dear sister?"

"Well, Master Copperfield," he replied, "you perceive I am not bound to answer that question. You may not, you know. But then, you see, you may!"

---

civilly politely	**malevolent** wicked; mean	**temperate** calm and controlled
stratagems tricks; plans	**constraining** holding back	

Anything to equal the low cunning of his **visage,** and of his shadowless eyes without the ghost of an eyelash, I never saw.

"Come then!" said I. "For the sake of Miss Wickfield—"

"My Agnes!" he exclaimed, with a sickly, **angular contortion** of himself. "Would you be so good as call her Agnes, Master Copperfield!"

"For the sake of Agnes Wickfield—Heaven bless her!"

"Thank you for that blessing, Master Copperfield!" he **interposed.**

"I will tell you what I should, under any other circumstances, as soon have thought of telling to—Jack Ketch."

"To who, sir?" said Uriah, stretching out his neck, and shading his ear with his hand.

"To the hangman," I returned. "The most unlikely person I could think of,"—though his own face had suggested the **allusion** quite as a natural sequence. "I am engaged to another young lady. I hope that contents you."

"Upon your soul?" said Uriah.

I was about indignantly to give my **assertion** the confirmation he required, when he caught hold of my hand, and gave it a squeeze.

"Oh, Master Copperfield!" he said. "If you had only had the **condescension** to return my confidence when I poured out the fulness of my art, the night I put you so much out of the way by sleeping before your sitting-room fire, I never should have doubted you. As it is, I'm sure I'll take off mother directly, and only too appy. I know you'll excuse the precautions of affection, won't you? What a pity, Master Copperfield, that you didn't condescend to return my confidence! I'm sure I gave you every opportunity. But

What are Heep's physical traits? How do they serve as outward signs of his bad character?

Jack Ketch was a public executioner of the 1600s—awkward, wild, and clumsy.

How does Heep's manner toward David change here? Who is in control of the situation?

Notice Heep's dialect: *art* for *heart* and *appy* for *happy.*

visage facial features

angular sharp; not smooth

contortion twisting of the body

interposed interrupted

allusion reference

assertion claim

condescension stooping to a lower level

you never have condescended to me, as much as I could have wished. I know you have never liked me, as I have liked you!"

All this time he was squeezing my hand with his damp fishy fingers, while I made every effort I decently could to get it away. But I was quite unsuccessful. He drew it under the sleeve of his mulberry-coloured great-coat, and I walked on, almost upon **compulsion,** arm-in-arm with him.

"Shall we turn?" said Uriah, by and by wheeling me face about towards the town, on which the early moon was now shining, silvering the distant windows.

"Before we leave the subject, you ought to understand," said I, breaking a pretty long silence, "that I believe Agnes Wickfield to be as far above *you,* and as far removed from all *your* **aspirations,** as that moon herself!"

"Peaceful! Ain't she!" said Uriah. "Very! Now confess, Master Copperfield, that you haven't liked me quite as I have liked you. All along you've thought me too umble now, I shouldn't wonder?"

David openly states his low opinion of Heep. How does Heep respond?

compulsion force   **aspirations** goals

"I am not fond of **professions** of humility," I returned, "or professions of anything else."

"There now!" said Uriah, looking flabby and lead-coloured in the moonlight. "Didn't I know it! But how little you think of the rightful umbleness of a person in my station, Master Copperfield! Father and me was both brought up at a foundation school for boys; and mother, she was likewise brought up at a public, sort of charitable, establishment. They taught us all a deal of umbleness—not much else that I know of, from morning to night. We was to be umble to this person, and umble to that; and to pull off our caps here, and to make bows there; and always to know our place, and **abase** ourselves before our betters. And we had such a lot of betters! Father got the monitor-medal by being umble. So did I. Father got made a **sexton** by being umble. He had the character, among the gentlefolks, of being such a well-behaved man, that they were determined to bring him in. 'Be umble, Uriah,' says father to me, 'and you'll get on. It was what was always being dinned into you and me at school; it's what goes down best. Be umble,' says father, 'and you'll do!' And really it ain't done bad!"

It was the first time it had ever occurred to me, that this **detestable cant** of false humility might have originated out of the Heep family. I had seen the harvest, but had never thought of the seed.

"When I was quite a young boy," said Uriah, "I got to know what umbleness did, and I took to it. I ate umble pie with an appetite. I stopped at the umble point of my learning, and says I, 'Hold hard!' When you offered to teach me Latin, I knew better. 'People like to be above you,' says father, 'keep yourself down.' I am very umble to the present moment, Master Copperfield, but I've got a little power!"

> Monitors are students who are selected to watch the behavior of other students. A *monitor-medal* is a badge showing this rank.

> How have the Heeps found success in exaggerating the importance of their "betters"? What does Uriah Heep's upbringing have to do with his way of behaving?

> What does Heep's father mean by *keep yourself down*? What does Heep's "umbleness" cover up?

---

professions claims

abase make lower; put down

sexton person who takes care of church property

detestable hateful

cant insincere speech

Why does David think Heep has told him about his upbringing and his power? For what do you think Heep feels he is entitled to reward himself?

What effect do you think this conversation will have on David's future actions? How might it help to move the plot along?

And he said all this—I knew, as I saw his face in the moonlight—that I might understand he was resolved to **recompense** himself by using his power. I had never doubted his meanness, his **craft** and **malice;** but I fully comprehended now, for the first time, what a **base, unrelenting,** and revengeful spirit, must have been **engendered** by this early, and this long, **suppression.**

His account of himself was so far attended with an agreeable result, that it led to his withdrawing his hand in order that he might have another hug of himself under the chin. Once apart from him, I was determined to keep apart; and we walked back, side by side, saying very little more by the way.

recompense reward	**base** low	**engendered** caused
craft trickiness	**unrelenting** never becoming less harsh	**suppression** holding down
malice wicked feelings		

AFTER READING THE SELECTION

from *David Copperfield* *by Charles Dickens*

Directions Choose the letter of the best answer or write the answer using complete sentences.

Comprehension: Identifying Facts

1. Whom does David see on his walk?
  A Agnes Wickfield
  B Mr. Wickfield
  C Uriah Heep
  D Jack Ketch

2. David continues to walk with Heep because _____.
  A Heep will not let go of him
  B David is frightened of Heep
  C Heep is David's friend
  D David needs more information

3. What does Heep mean when he says, "All stratagems are fair in love"?

4. In what way does Heep consider David dangerous?

5. What does David tell Heep to prove that he is not Heep's rival?

6. Who is Jack Ketch?

7. What does David tell Heep about Agnes?

8. Why does Heep believe David does not like him?

9. Where were Heep and his parents raised and educated?

10. What advice did Uriah Heep's father give his son?

Comprehension: Putting Ideas Together

11. What does David feel toward Uriah Heep?
  A curiosity and liking
  B affection and sympathy
  C a scientific interest
  D dislike

12. Heep makes himself "umble" to _____.
  A show respect for others
  B make a joke
  C show he feels inferior
  D trick others into feeling they are better

13. What traits does Heep reveal through his words?

14. What is the nature of Heep's humility?

15. What impression do David's descriptions of Heep create?

16. Who controls whom in this scene? How do you know?

17. Why have Heep and his mother been spending all their time with Mr. Wickfield and Agnes?

After Reading **continued on next page**

18. What has Heep "suppressed" all his life?

19. Why does David try to be polite at first, then speak rudely?

20. Throughout the passage, David describes Heep in animal terms. How is this appropriate to David's view of Heep?

Understanding Literature: Dialect, Dialogue, Plot, and Protagonist

This novel uses dialect, or regional speech, in its dialogue. Dialogue is the conversation of characters in a story. The plot involves the protagonist, or hero, in a series of events that may bring him trouble but finally help him learn about himself and life.

21. List several examples of Heep's dialect.

22. How does the dialogue in this passage increase your understanding of the two characters?

23. What may happen next in the plot of this story? What details in this passage suggest this?

24. Who is the protagonist of *David Copperfield*? How do you know?

25. Do you think this passage is more important to understanding character or to moving the plot forward? Explain.

Critical Thinking

26. What is the difference between the way Heep and David use the words *humble* and *humility*?

27. How does Heep use his body to establish control? How do you think this makes David feel?

28. How does David's view of Heep change during the selection? Do you think he is wise to change the way he views Heep?

29. Heep talks on and on about his "betters." Do people in American society today believe some people are better than others? If so, what makes them better?

Thinking Creatively

30. How do you think people of a lower class feel about those who have power over them? Explain your thinking.

Grammar Check

A participial phrase begins with a form of a verb and is used as an adjective to tell about a noun or a pronoun: *Stretching its neck upward, the giraffe tore leaves from a high branch.* The participial phrase *Stretching its neck upward* describes the giraffe.

- Find three examples of participial phrases in this passage.

- Write the sentences in which the phrases occur. Underline each participial phrase and draw an arrow to the word it modifies.

- Write an original sentence using a participial phrase.

Writing on Your Own

Uriah Heep has gotten where he is by acting humble and keeping himself down. This is a paradox. It contains ideas that seem to contradict each other, and yet both ideas are true. Write a paragraph explaining why the statement is true.

Speaking and Listening

Prepare a one-minute talk about the character Uriah Heep. Make notes telling what he is like and what you think causes him to act this way. In a small group, take turns presenting your thoughts. When you listen to others' presentations, make notes on the main ideas. Star ideas you find especially interesting and give the speaker feedback about those ideas.

Research

Find information about child labor in Victorian England. Use the Internet to find history sites, using keywords such as *child labor in England* or *Victorian society and child labor.* Encyclopedias are another useful reference source. Print out or make copies of artworks and photos that illustrate child labor. Summarize and paraphrase the information you find. Prepare a short talk or illustrated report about the history of child labor in England.

Dover Beach   by Matthew Arnold

Matthew Arnold
1822–1888

Objectives

■ To read and understand a poem

■ To identify figurative language and explain its effect

■ To explain how imagery supports a theme

About the Author

Matthew Arnold was born in 1822, the son of an important religious and educational thinker. Arnold attended Rugby School, where his father was headmaster. He then attended Oxford University. At first, Arnold seemed to rebel against his father's ideas. As a student, he was not serious about studying. He focused on being stylish and popular. However, beneath all this, Arnold had a great mind and imagination. His thoughtful poetry amazed his friends and family.

In 1851, he became an inspector of schools. He held this job until two years before his death. Although his work gave him little free time, Arnold wrote fine poetry and criticism. He wrote important works about religion and education and was the major literary critic of his time.

Arnold wrote most of his poetry before 1855. His prose came later. Arnold's work expresses ideas and concerns that arose during Victorian times. New scientific discoveries had shaken traditional religious belief. His poems raise questions without giving easy answers. They often have a haunting quality because of the loneliness and isolation they express.

About the Selection

"Dover Beach," written in 1867, is Arnold's most famous poem. It expresses the fear and loneliness of a person who faces a stormy period in history and the loss of faith. One reason for the poem's success is the power with which it uses descriptions of the sea and tides to represent the withdrawal of faith.

Literary Terms "Dover Beach" is rich in **imagery**—pictures created by vivid, specific words that appeal to the senses. Details such as "the long line of spray" and "the grating roar of pebbles" flung and dragged by waves help readers experience the ocean as though they were there. The poem also uses figurative language to make imaginative comparisons.

imagery pictures created by words; the use of words that appeal to the five senses

Reading on Your Own In this poem, the poet finds larger meanings for the ebb and flow of the ocean. As you read, think about how the setting matches the poet's thoughts and concerns. How does he relate his thoughts to history and religion?

Writing on Your Own Read an explanation of tides and their effects. Write a paragraph summarizing what you learned. Be sure to paraphrase the ideas, or write them in your own words.

Vocabulary Focus Context clues can add to your understanding of unfamiliar words. For example, *tremulous cadence* (line 13) can be better understood by reading the next line about the "eternal note of sadness." Even without knowing the exact definition of the words, you can learn from context that this is a sad-sounding musical quality in the waves. Use context, in addition to other aids, to get a fuller picture of what new words mean.

Think Before You Read Look at the poem you are about to read. What are some ways it differs from other poems you have read in this book?

Dover Beach

As you read, picture the scene the poet looks at. What imagery helps you form a picture in your mind?

The *Straits* of Dover is the crossing place between England and France.

The sea is calm to-night,
The tide is full, the moon lies fair
Upon the **straits**;—on the French coast the light
Gleams and is gone; the cliffs of England stand,
5 Glimmering and vast, out in the **tranquil** bay.
Come to the window, sweet is the night air!
Only, from the long line of spray
Where the sea meets the **moon-blanch'd** land,
Listen! you hear the grating roar
10 Of pebbles which the waves draw back, and fling,
At their return, up the high **strand.**
Begin, and cease, and then again begin,
With **tremulous cadence** slow, and bring
The eternal note of sadness in.

Sophocles was a writer in ancient Greece. The *Aegean* Sea is an arm of the Mediterranean Sea between Greece and Turkey.

15 Sophocles long ago
Heard it on the Aegean, and it brought
Into his mind the **turbid** ebb and flow
Of human misery; we
Find also in the sound a thought,
20 Hearing it by this distant northern sea.

---

straits narrow passageway connecting two bodies of water

tranquil peaceful

moon-blanch'd made pale by the moonlight

strand shore

tremulous trembling

cadence rhythm; beat

turbid murky; cloudy

The Sea of Faith
Was once, too, at the full, and round earth's shore
Lay like the folds of a bright **girdle furl'd.**
But now I only hear
25 Its **melancholy,** long, withdrawing roar,
Retreating, to the breath
Of the night-wind, down the vast edges drear
And naked **shingles** of the world.
Ah, love, let us be true
30 To one another! for the world, which seems
To lie before us like a land of dreams,
So various, so beautiful, so new,
Hath really neither joy, nor love, nor light,
Nor **certitude,** nor peace, nor help for pain;
35 And we are here as on a **darkling** plain
Swept with confused alarms of struggle
and flight,
Where ignorant armies clash by night.

The poet is not speaking about an actual sea. What does he think has happened to the *Sea of Faith*?

How has the poet's mood changed?

Dover cliffs at night

girdle something that wraps around

furl'd folded up

melancholy sad

shingles coarse stones and material deposited on the shore by the sea

certitude certainty; sureness

darkling in the dark

AFTER READING THE SELECTION

Dover Beach   by Matthew Arnold

Directions Choose the letter of the best answer or write the answer using complete sentences.

Comprehension: Identifying Facts

1. The setting of this poem is _____.
   A in ancient Greece by the sea
   B in an art gallery with sea paintings
   C at sea on a dark night
   D a seashore on a moonlit night

2. What emotion does the poet connect to the sound of the waves hitting the shore?

3. What does the poet think is happening to the Sea of Faith?

Comprehension: Putting Ideas Together

4. While the poem begins with a view of the beauty of the world, it ends with the understanding that the world is _____.
   A bright and reassuring
   B growing smaller all the time
   C a dark, confused place
   D full of joy and love

5. How does the poet's attitude toward his readers change?

6. With the Sea of Faith at low tide, what does the poet see that the Earth has to offer humans?

Understanding Literature: Figurative Language and Imagery

Figurative language uses the reader's imagination as it makes unusual comparisons. It is not meant to be taken word for word. Imagery creates pictures through words that appeal to the senses. It draws the reader into the poem.

7. What comparison does the poet make in lines 17–18 and 21–23? Why is it fitting for this poem?

8. How do the images in the opening of the poem contrast with those at the end? Which images support the main idea of the poem?

Critical Thinking

9. What does the poet see has happened to faith? What mood does this understanding cause?

Thinking Creatively

10. Do you agree with the poet that the world is a dark, confused place where humans struggle and "ignorant armies clash by night"? Explain your thinking.

Grammar Check

Verb tenses show the time when action occurs or a state of being exists. The simple verb tenses are present, past, and future (*meet/meets, met, will meet; is/are, was/were, will be*). Arnold's poem begins, "The sea is calm to-night." *Is* expresses present time. When he says "Sophocles long ago/Heard it" (lines 15–16), the poet changes to past-tense verbs. (*Heard* is the past-tense form of *hear.*)

- Read the poem and divide it into sections based on changes in verb tense.

- Write the numbers of lines that make up each section and label them with *present* or *past.*

- Write several verbs from each section that illustrate the tense of the section.

 ## Writing on Your Own

Study the way this poem uses rhyme, rhythm, and meter (number of beats per line). Write an essay describing these elements in the poem. Write at least one paragraph for each of these elements. Explain how they are suitable to the theme of the poem (loss of religious faith in the modern world). Be sure you begin with a general introduction and end with a strong conclusion.

 ## Speaking and Listening

Interview an older friend or family member about his or her beliefs. Ask questions that encourage the person to describe his or her attitudes about life. Listen carefully to the person's responses. They may suggest more questions you want to ask.

Research

Read about Matthew Arnold's ideas on Victorian society and writing, which he expressed in his prose. You may find information in encyclopedias, in books, or on the Internet. Take notes on ideas you find most interesting. Write a summary of what you learn.

Pied Beauty   *by Gerard Manley Hopkins*

Gerard Manley
Hopkins
1844–1889

Objectives

- To read and understand a poem
- To describe the effects of alliteration
- To analyze the rhythms in a poem

About the Author

Gerard Manley Hopkins had a brilliant mind that blossomed while he studied at Oxford University. He also thought deeply about religion. In 1866, he joined the Roman Catholic Church. By 1868, he had decided to become a Catholic priest. He did not think his poetry suitable for his new calling, so he burned it all. Hopkins began writing again in 1875 when one of his superiors encouraged him. His work was very original in its sound and expression. Hopkins often wrote about God's mystery and greatness as expressed in nature.

As a priest, Hopkins served various churches and institutions. He also taught at University College in Dublin in Ireland. He died of typhoid fever in 1889.

Hopkins's poetry was not published in his lifetime. His friend and fellow poet Robert Bridges published Hopkins's work in 1918. Readers and poets recognized Hopkins's way of writing as very original.

About the Selection

In "Pied Beauty," Hopkins praises God for the beauty in the world. This beauty is not smooth, same, or easy but "dappled," or varying. (The word *pied* in the title means "many-colored.") The poem contains sound effects and powerful, unusual structures for which Hopkins is famous. We could think of it as a rich soundscape that matches his theme perfectly.

Literary Terms "Pied Beauty" makes rich use of the sound device called **alliteration.** Alliteration involves the repetition of beginning sounds in a group of words. It emphasizes the words in which it occurs and gives them a pleasing sound. Rhythm is the pattern of stressed and unstressed syllables in a poem. Most Victorian poetry used a predictable rhythm. Hopkins used what he called sprung rhythm. He thought traditional rhythm forced poems to sound too "same and tame." Sprung rhythm includes one stressed syllable and a varying number of unstressed syllables in a section.

alliteration
repeating sounds by using words whose beginning sounds are the same

Reading on Your Own The poem lists a number of things that Hopkins finds beautiful for the contrasts and mixtures they contain. Think about each thing he lists. In what ways are all these things alike?

Writing on Your Own Is something beautiful because it is regular or because it is strange? Is it pleasing because of its evenness or its unexpected combinations? Observe something you find beautiful in nature. Write an explanation for why you find it beautiful.

Vocabulary Focus Sometimes, authors create words to show just the right meaning for their ideas. In "Pied Beauty," Hopkins has joined some words to create new meanings. *Couple-color*, for example, describes a sky in which various colors are joined. *Rose-moles* describes reddish spots on trout. *Fresh-firecoal chestnut-falls* makes us picture the colors in chestnut leaves in autumn. *Fathers-forth* is used instead of *creates* to suggest the power and care with which God creates. Notice how all these invented words use repeated consonant or vowel sounds to add to the poem's musical quality.

Think Before You Read Hopkins lists different objects that have something in common that makes them beautiful. What common trait do you think the poet finds beautiful?

PIED BEAUTY

As you read, think about the kind of beauty Hopkins is celebrating. What is unusual about it?

Glory be to God for **dappled** things—
    For skies of couple-colour as a **brinded** cow;
For rose-moles all in **stipple** upon trout that swim;
    Fresh-firecoal chestnut-falls; finches' wings;
5 Landscape **plotted** and pieced—fold, **fallow,** and plough;
    And all trades, their gear and tackle and trim.

All things **counter,** original, spare, strange;
    Whatever is **fickle,** freckled (who knows how?)
With swift, slow; sweet, sour; adazzle, dim;
10   He fathers-forth whose beauty is past change:
    Praise him.

Pay attention to where the beats are. The changes in stress create the sprung rhythm that Hopkins liked to use in his poetry.

Look for examples of alliteration in the poem and read those lines aloud. How does alliteration add to the musical quality of a poem?

Trout Breaking, Winslow Homer, 1889

dappled spotted with different colors	**stipple** dots or spots	**counter** opposite; different
brinded streaked with dark hairs	**plotted** laid out according to a plan	**fickle** likely to change
	fallow unplowed land	

Directions Choose the letter of the best answer or write the answer using complete sentences.

Comprehension: Identifying Facts

1. The poet praises God for things whose beauty is dappled, or _____.
   A ordinary
   B calming
   C rarely seen
   D created through a mixture

2. What part of God's creation does Hopkins praise in line 6?

3. What is the nature of God's beauty in line 10?

Comprehension: Putting Ideas Together

4. All the things listed in lines 2–6 are made of _____.
   A simple objects with few parts
   B many colors and forms
   C organic, or living, parts
   D parts made by humans

5. How does line 9 fit in with the format and theme of the poem?

6. How does the beauty of God compare to the beauty of creation?

Understanding Literature: Alliteration and Rhythm

When poets repeat beginning sounds of words, they are using alliteration. With rhythm, they set up a pattern of stressed and unstressed beats in each line. Both tools help make a poem musical.

7. Point out five examples of alliteration in lines 1–6. Write the words with the same beginning sounds.

8. How many syllables are found in lines 1 and 2? How many are stressed, or have strong beats? How is this pattern different from iambic pentameter?

Critical Thinking

9. Why do you think the poet included only two words in the last line? Do you think this is fitting? Explain.

Thinking Creatively

10. Do you agree with Hopkins that God's beauty is "past change" (line 10)? Explain your thinking.

After Reading **continued on next page**

Pied Beauty   *by Gerard Manley Hopkins*

 ### Grammar Check

Semicolons (;) are used to separate items in a list when each listed item already contains a comma. For example: *Ancient Egyptians worshipped Ra, the sun god; Isis, the mother goddess; and Osiris, the god of the underworld.*

- Find the list in "Pied Beauty" that uses commas and semicolons.

- Write the pairs of words that are most closely related. Tell how they are related.

- Write a sentence of your own that contains a list using semicolons and commas.

 ### Writing on Your Own

How are Hopkins's words "pied"? In other words, how do the words he chooses imitate the kind of beauty he is praising? Write a paragraph explaining how the sounds and looks of words in "Pied Beauty" add to its meaning. Cite specific words and phrases and tell about their sound effects or appearance.

 ### Speaking and Listening

Take turns reading "Pied Beauty" aloud to a partner. As the listener, close your eyes and listen for the sound effects that come through repeating sounds and rhythm. Each partner should read the poem aloud several times. Discuss how your understanding of the poem changed after you had heard it several times.

 ### Viewing

Collect pictures and small natural objects you think illustrate the idea of "pied beauty." Make a collage of the items. Add your artwork to your classmates' to create a classroom gallery. Be ready to explain your choices by referring to the poem.

 ### Research

Use several sources to gather facts about Gerard Manley Hopkins's life and poetry. Make a separate note card for each important event. Write facts of publication for each source. Organize your notes and write a report. Attach a bibliography of the sources you used. (See Appendix C for tips on preparing a bibliography.)

BEFORE READING THE SELECTION

from *The Importance of Being Earnest*   *by Oscar Wilde*

About the Author

Oscar Wilde was born in Dublin, Ireland. His father was a surgeon and writer. His mother was a poet and expert on ancient Irish writings. Wilde left Ireland to study at Oxford University in London. His intelligence, wit, and colorful style soon made him a public figure. He believed strongly that life was a work of art. He lived in a dramatic way to prove it.

Not until the last decade of his life did Wilde create his major works. He wrote a novel, *The Picture of Dorian Gray*, which critics called immoral. His greatest successes were four plays written in the 1890s. They breathed new life into English theater. In them, Wilde made fun of English high society, pointing out its shallowness and fakeness. His dialogue had short, witty sayings that often contain apparent opposites.

His plays made Wilde very popular, but his fame turned to disgrace. He was tried on a morals charge in 1895 and sent to prison. Released from prison in 1897, he went to France. He lived there in poverty for the last years of his life.

About the Selection

The Importance of Being Earnest, written in 1894, has a wildly unbelievable plot. It pokes fun at the foolishness of British society. On the surface, it seems very light and funny. Beneath the surface, it takes a hard look at the two-faced attitudes of Victorian upper classes. The play's hero, Jack Worthing, leads a double life. At his country estate, he is known as Jack. In London, he is known as Ernest. The *Ernest/Earnest* play on words gives the play one of its double meanings: Victorians considered being earnest (serious and sincere) a virtue.

Oscar Wilde
1854–1900

Objectives

- To understand drama
- To read and understand an excerpt from a comedy
- To define and point out traits of satire and farce
- To describe character and explain elements of characterization

Before Reading **continued on next page**

from *The Importance of Being Earnest*   *by Oscar Wilde*

drama a story told through the words and actions of characters, written to be performed, as well as read; a play

comedy a play with a happy ending, intended to amuse its audience

farce writing that uses satire and comedy, with an unlikely plot

satire humorous writing that makes fun of foolishness or evil

characterization the way a writer develops character qualities and personality traits

Literary Terms *The Importance of Being Earnest* is a **drama,** or play. It is also a **comedy,** because it ends happily and is meant to amuse. More specifically, it is a **farce**—a play with a silly plot and clever dialogue that includes **satire.** In a satire, a writer makes fun of things he or she considers foolish or evil. **Characterization,** or developing the traits of characters, must take place through dialogue and costumes in a play.

Reading on Your Own This play tells about the double lives that two friends have created. Algernon has made up Bunbury, a sickly friend whom Algernon uses as an excuse to get himself out of unpleasant social duties. Jack has made up Ernest, a younger brother, whose name he uses when he is in London. In this selection, notice how Algernon and Jack use these "imaginary friends" and how Jack's lie creates a problem. Keep these main ideas in mind as you read.

Writing on Your Own Write an anecdote, or a brief, interesting story, about a time when you made up a story to avoid having to do something you did not want to do. Did your plot work? Why or why not?

Vocabulary Focus The prefixes *ir-*, *in-*, and *un-* all add a negative meaning to a word. For example, *rational* and *irrational* are opposite in meaning. So are *capable* and *incapable* and *usual* and *unusual*. Find the words *irresistible*, *indecorous*, and *unsound* in the selection. Write them with and without the prefixes and give the meaning of each word.

Think Before You Read How do you think Algernon's and Jack's lies will get them in trouble?

from *The Importance of* Being Earnest

> **Characters**
>
> **Jack Worthing** A young man who leads a double life. He calls himself Ernest when he is in London. He is in love with his friend Algernon's cousin, Gwendolen Fairfax.
>
> **Algernon Moncrieff** A charming, idle bachelor; nephew of Lady Bracknell, cousin of Gwendolen Fairfax, and best friend of Jack Worthing, whom he knows as Ernest.
>
> **Lady Bracknell** Algernon's snobbish, bossy aunt, Augusta; Gwendolen's mother.
>
> **Gwendolen Fairfax** Algernon's cousin and Lady Bracknell's daughter. She is in love with Jack, whom she knows as Ernest.

Jack has dropped by to visit his friend Algernon. Lady Bracknell and her daughter Gwendolen Fairfax enter. Gwendolen and Jack sit down together in the corner.

Algernon I am afraid, Aunt Augusta, I shall have to give up the pleasure of dining with you to-night after all.

Lady Bracknell [*Frowning.*] I hope not, Algernon. It would put my table completely out. Your uncle would have to dine upstairs. Fortunately he is accustomed to that.

Algernon It is a great bore, and, I need hardly say, a terrible disappointment to me, but the fact is I have just had a telegram to say that my poor friend Bunbury is very ill again. [*Exchanges glances with Jack.*] They seem to think I should be with him.

Algernon is using his invented friend, *Bunbury*, to get out of going to his aunt's dinner party.

Lady Bracknell It is very strange. This Mr. Bunbury seems to suffer from curiously bad health.

Algernon Yes; poor Bunbury is a dreadful **invalid.**

Lady Bracknell Well, I must say, Algernon, that I think it is high time that Mr. Bunbury made up his mind whether he was going to live or to die. This **shilly-shallying** with the question is absurd. Nor do I in any way approve of the modern sympathy with invalids. I consider it **morbid.** Illness of any kind is hardly a thing to be encouraged in others. Health is the primary duty of life. I am always telling that to your poor uncle, but he never seems to take much notice . . . as far as any improvement in his **ailment** goes. I should be much obliged if you would ask Mr. Bunbury, from me, to be kind enough not to have a **relapse** on Saturday, for I rely on you to arrange my music for me. It is my last reception, and one wants something that will encourage conversation, particularly at the end of the season when every one has practically said whatever they had to say, which, in most cases, was probably not much.

Algernon I'll speak to Bunbury, Aunt Augusta, if he is still conscious, and I think I can promise you he'll be all right by Saturday. Of course the music is a great difficulty. You see, if one plays good music, people don't listen, and if one plays bad music people don't talk. But I'll run over the programme I've drawn out, if you will kindly come into the next room for a moment.

Lady Bracknell Thank you, Algernon. It is very thoughtful of you. [*Rising and following Algernon.*] I'm sure the programme will be delightful, after a few **expurgations.** French songs I cannot possibly allow. People always seem to think that they are improper, and either look shocked, which is **vulgar,** or laugh, which is worse. But German sounds a thoroughly respectable language, and indeed, I believe is so. Gwendolen, you will accompany me.

> Lady Bracknell has no sympathy for the sick. What is her main concern?

> What do Algernon's and Lady Bracknell's comments suggest about her guests?

invalid someone who is often sick	**morbid** gloomy	**expurgations** deletions
shilly-shallying showing a lack of decisiveness	**ailment** illness	**vulgar** not polite
	relapse return to previous illness	

Gwendolen Certainly, mamma.

[*Lady Bracknell and Algernon go into the music-room, Gwendolen remains behind.*]

Jack Charming day it has been, Miss Fairfax.

Gwendolen Pray don't talk to me about the weather, Mr. Worthing. Whenever people talk to me about the weather, I always feel quite certain that they mean something else. And that makes me so nervous.

Jack I do mean something else.

Gwendolen I thought so. In fact, I am never wrong.

Jack And I would like to be allowed to take advantage of Lady Bracknell's temporary absence . . .

Gwendolen I would certainly advise you to do so. Mamma has a way of coming back suddenly into a room that I have often had to speak to her about.

Jack [*Nervously.*] Miss Fairfax, ever since I met you I have admired you more than any girl . . . I have ever met since . . . I met you.

Gwendolen Yes, I am quite well aware of the fact. And I often wish that in public, at any rate, you had been more **demonstrative.** For me you have always had an **irresistible** fascination. Even before I met you I was far from **indifferent** to you. [*Jack looks at her in amazement.*] We live, as I hope you know, Mr. Worthing, in an age of ideals. The fact is constantly mentioned in the more expensive monthly magazines, and has reached the **provincial pulpits,** I am told; and my ideal has always been to love some one of the name of Ernest. There is something in that name that inspires absolute confidence. The moment Algernon first mentioned to me that he had a friend called Ernest, I knew I was destined to love you.

Jack You really love me, Gwendolen?

Gwendolen Passionately!

> Notice that Gwendolen gets Jack to declare his love quickly. Who seems more assured and mature: Jack or Gwendolen?

> Remember that Algernon, Gwendolen, and Lady Bracknell all know Jack only as Ernest. What is Gwendolen's motive for marrying Jack?

demonstrative obvious	**indifferent** not caring	**pulpits** preaching positions; here, it refers to what ministers say in church
irresistible too strong to fight against	**provincial** in the countryside	

Jack Darling! You don't know how happy you've made me.

Gwendolen My own Ernest!

Jack But you don't really mean to say that you couldn't love me if my name wasn't Ernest?

Gwendolen But your name is Ernest.

Jack Yes, I know it is. But supposing it was something else? Do you mean to say you couldn't love me then?

Gwendolen [*Glibly.*] Ah! that is clearly a **metaphysical speculation,** and like most metaphysical speculation has very little reference at all to the actual facts of real life, as we know them.

Jack Personally, darling, to speak quite **candidly,** I don't much care about the name of Ernest. . . . I don't think the name suits me at all.

Gwendolen It suits you perfectly. It is a divine name. It has a music of its own. It produces vibrations.

Jack Well, really, Gwendolen, I must say that I think there are lots of other much nicer names. I think Jack, for instance, a charming name.

Gwendolen Jack? . . . No, there is very little music in the name Jack, if any at all, indeed. It does not thrill. It produces absolutely no vibrations. . . . I have known several Jacks, and they all, without exception, were more than usually plain. Besides, Jack is a **notorious domesticity** for John! And I pity any woman who is married to a man called John. She would probably never be allowed to know the **entrancing** pleasure of a single moment's **solitude.** The only really safe name is Ernest.

> What is humorous about Gwendolen's extreme fondness of the name Ernest? Victorians thought it a great virtue to be earnest. What does *earnest* mean?

metaphysical abstract	**notorious** known to be bad	**entrancing** delightful
speculation thought	**domesticity** nickname	**solitude** being alone
candidly truthfully		

Jack Gwendolen, I must get **christened** at once—I mean we must get married at once. There is no time to be lost.

Gwendolen Married, Mr. Worthing?

Jack [*Astounded.*] Well . . . surely. You know that I love you, and you led me to believe, Miss Fairfax, that you were not absolutely indifferent to me.

Gwendolen I adore you. But you haven't proposed to me yet. Nothing has been said at all about marriage. The subject has not even been touched on.

Jack Well . . . may I propose to you now?

Gwendolen I think it would be an admirable opportunity. And to spare you any possible disappointment, Mr. Worthing, I think it only fair to tell you quite frankly beforehand that I am fully determined to accept you.

Jack Gwendolen!

Gwendolen Yes, Mr. Worthing, what have you got to say to me?

Jack You know what I have got to say to you.

Gwendolen Yes, but you don't say it.

Jack Gwendolen, will you marry me?   [*Goes on his knees.*]

Gwendolen Of course I will, darling. How long you have been about it! I am afraid you have had very little experience in how to propose.

Jack My own one, I have never loved any one in the world but you.

Gwendolen Yes, but men often propose for practice. I know my brother Gerald does. All my girl friends tell me so. What wonderfully blue eyes you have, Ernest! They are quite, quite, blue. I hope you will always look at me just like that, especially when there are other people present.

[*Enter Lady Bracknell.*]

> Gwendolen wants a formal proposal but tells Jack she will accept him before he proposes. How would you describe Gwendolen's character?

> What does Gwendolen's comment suggest about the nature of her love?

---

christened named (or renamed)

Lady Bracknell Mr. Worthing! Rise, sir, from this **semi-recumbent posture**. It is most **indecorous**.

Gwendolen Mamma! [*He tries to rise; she restrains him.*] I must beg you to **retire**. This is no place for you. Besides, Mr. Worthing has not quite finished yet.

Lady Bracknell Finished what, may I ask?

Gwendolen I am engaged to Mr. Worthing, mamma.

[*They rise together.*]

Lady Bracknell Pardon me, you are not engaged to any one. When you do become engaged to some one, I, or your father, should his health permit him, will inform you of the fact. An engagement should come on a young girl as a surprise, pleasant or unpleasant, as the case may be. It is hardly a matter that she could be allowed to arrange for herself. . . . And now I have a few questions to put to you, Mr. Worthing. While I am making these inquiries, you, Gwendolen, will wait for me below in the carriage.

Gwendolen [*Reproachfully.*] Mamma!

Lady Bracknell In the carriage, Gwendolen! [*Gwendolen goes to the door. She and Jack blow kisses to each other behind Lady Bracknell's back. Lady Bracknell looks vaguely about as if she could not understand what the noise was. Finally turns around.*] Gwendolen, the carriage!

Gwendolen Yes, mamma. [*Goes out, looking back at Jack.*]

Lady Bracknell [*Sitting down.*] You can take a seat, Mr. Worthing. [*Looks in her pocket for note-book and pencil.*]

Jack Thank you, Lady Bracknell, I prefer standing.

Lady Bracknell [*Pencil and note-book in hand.*] I feel bound to tell you that you are not down on my list of **eligible** young men, although I have the same list as the dear Duchess of Bolton has. We work together, in fact. However, I am quite ready to enter your name, should your answers be what a really affectionate mother requires. Do you smoke?

Jack Well, yes, I must admit I smoke.

> What is Lady Bracknell's view of love and marriage?

> Lady Bracknell prepares to question Jack. What sort of questions do you predict she will ask him?

---

semi-recumbent almost lying down

posture body position

indecorous improper

retire go away

eligible suitable and single

Lady Bracknell I am glad to hear it. A man should always have an occupation of some kind. There are far too many idle men in London as it is. How old are you?

Jack Twenty-nine.

Lady Bracknell A very good age to be married at. I have always been of opinion that a man who desires to get married should know either everything or nothing. Which do you know?

Jack [*After some hesitation.*] I know nothing, Lady Bracknell.

Lady Bracknell I am pleased to hear it. I do not approve of anything that **tampers** with natural ignorance. Ignorance is like a delicate exotic fruit; touch it and the bloom is gone. The whole theory of modern education is **radically unsound.** Fortunately in England, at any rate, education produces no effect whatsoever. If it did, it would prove a serious danger to the upper classes, and probably lead to acts of violence in Grosvenor Square.

Lady Bracknell

What is Lady Bracknell's view about ignorance? Why do you think she believes effective education would be dangerous to the upper classes?

---

tampers makes changes (usually bad)   **radically** totally   **unsound** wrong; unsafe

AFTER READING THE SELECTION

from *The Importance of Being Earnest*   by Oscar Wilde

Directions Choose the letter of the best answer or write the answer using complete sentences.

Comprehension: Identifying Facts

1. Lady Bracknell says that having sympathy for invalids is _____.
  A noble   **C** admirable
  B morbid   **D** encouraging

2. What kind of age does Gwendolyn say they live in?
  A an age of ideals
  B an age of changes
  C a cynical age
  D an innocent age

3. Why does Algernon say he cannot come to dinner that evening?

4. Why do Algernon and Lady Bracknell go into the next room?

5. What does Gwendolen not want Jack to talk to her about? Why?

6. What does the name Ernest mean to Gwendolen?

7. Why does Lady Bracknell send Gwendolen to the carriage?

8. How does Lady Bracknell react when Jack tells her he smokes?

9. What does Jack confess about his knowledge?

10. To what does Lady Bracknell compare ignorance?

Comprehension: Putting Ideas Together

11. What does Lady Bracknell care about most?
  A other people
  B her husband
  C marrying her daughter well
  D making others comfortable

12. The best word to describe Lady Bracknell's relationship to Gwendolen is _____.
  A affectionate   **C** caring
  B stressful   **D** controlling

13. How are Bunbury and Ernest alike?

14. How is the proposal scene the reverse of what you would expect in Victorian society?

15. Why does Jack need to "get christened at once"?

16. Contrast Gwendolen's love of the name Ernest with the idea from the title of being earnest, or serious and sincere.

17. How are Lady Bracknell and Gwendolen alike in their views on engagement? How are they different?

18. What kind of relationship do Lady Bracknell and her husband seem to have?

19. Where does Gwendolen hope Jack will give her the most attention and affection?

20. Based on what she says about health and education, how would you describe Lady Bracknell?

Understanding Literature: Comedy, Satire, Farce, and Characterization

A comedy is a humorous play. Satire and farce are often used in comedies to make fun of society or people and to set up ridiculous plot situations. What characters say and how they dress and move are part of their characterization.

21. What does Wilde satirize in Lady Bracknell?

22. What is satirical about Gwendolen's love of the name Ernest?

23. What parts of this scene suggest that it is a farce?

24. What parts of the scene do you find humorous?

25. Lady Bracknell makes many strong statements of opinion. What character traits do these statements show?

Critical Thinking

26. What do Lady Bracknell's questions to Jack show about her values?

27. Why does Gwendolen love Jack? Do you think this kind of love will lead to a happy marriage?

28. Gwendolen loves the sound of the name Ernest. Why do you think it is important that she does not seem to care whether her husband is actually earnest?

29. Lady Bracknell approves of "natural ignorance." What do you think she means by this?

Thinking Creatively

30. Lady Bracknell suggests that educating the lower classes would be "a serious danger to the upper classes." What do you think about this? Explain.

After Reading continued on next page

from *The Importance of Being Earnest*   *by Oscar Wilde*

 Grammar Check

Commas are used to set off expressions such as *I am afraid* and *in fact* and mild interjections such as *Oh* and *Well.* Set off a conjunctive adverb (such as *however*) with a comma, too.

- Find example sentences from the selection that use commas in the ways described above.

- Write each sentence and underline the words and comma or commas that set them off.

- Write original sentences using *in fact, well,* and *however.* Be sure to use commas correctly.

 Writing on Your Own

Write an essay explaining what is humorous about *The Importance of Being Earnest.* In your introduction, list the kinds of humor it contains. In the body, give examples of each kind of humor. Write a conclusion telling one way in which the play is serious.

 Speaking and Listening

In a small group, discuss this statement: *Wilde suggests that Victorian society cares only about the way things and people look or sound, not their actual character.* Point out lines in the play that prove or disprove this statement. Tell what they mean to you. Be sure you take part in the discussion both by speaking clearly and listening courteously to others.

 Viewing

Search in printed books or on the Internet for paintings, drawings, and photographs that show Victorian society. Notice the clothes people wore, the buildings and homes they created, and other details about Victorian life. Write a caption for each picture, summarizing what it tells you about life in Victorian England.

About the Author

Alfred Edward Housman was born in 1859. He was close to his mother, who died when he was 12 years old. Her early death may be one reason for the gloomy outlook of Housman's poetry. Although he was a brilliant student, Housman did not pass his final exam at Oxford University.

Housman became a clerk in London's Patent Office and studied Latin at night. He mastered that language, and his articles in journals brought him attention. He became a professor of Latin at University College in London. From 1911 until near the time of his death in 1936, he taught at Cambridge University.

Housman lived a lonely life. He turned to his notebooks, where he wrote short, sad poems in a simple style. He modeled his poems after the poems of ancient Greece, the sonnets of Shakespeare, and Scottish ballads. His poems express intense emotion with few words. The speaker in his poems is usually a simple farm laborer. Housman published *A Shropshire Lad* in 1896. Its popularity grew slowly but surely. When *Last Poems* came out in 1922, it became successful right away.

A. E. Housman
1859–1936

Objectives

- To read and understand lyric poetry
- To analyze rhythm in a poem
- To identify and explain figures of speech

About the Selection

"To an Athlete Dying Young" appeared in *A Shropshire Lad*. The poem speaks to an athlete who enjoyed success and fame very early but also died young. Housman's training as a scholar of Greek and Latin can be seen in the poem's style and the situation it presents. Its language is simple and direct but emotional.

Before Reading continued on next page

To an Athlete Dying Young   by A. E. Housman

lyric poetry
a short poem that expresses a person's emotions or feelings

figure of speech
a word or phrase that has meaning different from the actual meaning, such as idioms, metaphors, and similes

Literary Terms "To an Athlete Dying Young" is an example of **lyric poetry,** which expresses the poet's emotions in brief verse. A strict rhythm balances the emotion. Each line contains four beats; most lines contain eight syllables. The poet uses **figures of speech** to bring ideas to life. These comparisons are not meant to be taken literally.

Reading on Your Own This poem contrasts two processions, or parades. Read the poem to learn what happens in each procession. What do these different images help emphasize?

Writing on Your Own Think about a famous athlete. What do you imagine being so famous is like? Is it something to be jealous about? Write a paragraph answering these questions and explaining your answers.

Vocabulary Focus At times, writers use familiar words in new ways. For example, writers may make comparisons that cannot be taken literally. Such a comparison is puzzling if you think of the words with their usual meanings. For example, in line 8 of Housman's poem, the dead athlete is called "Townsman of a stiller town." The stiller town is not really a town at all, but death, whose "townsmen" the athlete has gone to join. As you read the poem, think about the figurative meaning of phrases such as "shady night" (line 13), "Runners whom renown outran" (line 19), and "The fleet foot on the sill of shade" (line 22).

Think Before You Read This poem is addressed to a young athlete who has died. What do you predict Housman will have to say to the athlete?

To an Athlete Dying Young

The time you won your town the race
We **chaired** you through the market-place;
Man and boy stood cheering by,
And home we brought you shoulder-high.

5   To-day, the road all runners come,
Shoulder-high we bring you home,
And set you at your **threshold** down,
Townsman of a stiller town.

Smart lad, to slip **betimes** away
10 From fields where glory does not stay,
And early though the laurel grows
It withers quicker than the rose.

Eyes the shady night has shut
Cannot see the record cut,
15 And silence sounds no worse than cheers
After earth has stopped the ears:

Now you will not swell the **rout**
Of lads that wore their honours out,
Runners whom **renown** outran
20 And the name died before the man.

So set, before its echoes fade,
The fleet foot on the sill of shade,
And hold to the low **lintel** up
The still-defended challenge-cup.

25 And round that early-laurelled head
Will flock to gaze the strengthless dead,
And find unwithered on its curls
The **garland** briefer than a girl's.

As you read, notice the kinds of words Housman uses. What effect do these simple, one- and two-syllable words have on the tone of the poem?

Laurel was used in ancient Greece to crown athletes who won.

Lyric poetry expresses the poet's emotions in brief verse. In what ways is this poem a good example of lyric poetry?

The *challenge-cup* (line 24) is a trophy given to winning athletes. The *garland* (line 28) refers to the laurel wreath used to crown the victor.

chaired carried	**rout** crowd	**lintel** beam in a building that holds up a wall or roof
threshold doorway	**renown** fame	
betimes early		**garland** strand of leaves or flowers

Directions Choose the letter of the best answer or write the answer using complete sentences.

Comprehension: Identifying Facts

1. In the first stanza, "Man and boy" cheer to _____.

   A celebrate the athlete's victory

   B celebrate the town's victory

   C begin the competition

   D honor the dead

2. Why does the poet think the athlete is smart?

3. In the final stanza, who gathers to admire the athlete's triumph?

Comprehension: Putting Ideas Together

4. The poet says that one benefit of dying young is _____.

   A avoiding old age and sickness

   B leaving as a hero, not a has-been

   C having a large funeral

   D the peacefulness of death

5. What are the contrasts between the first and second processions the poem describes?

6. How does the admiring crowd differ in stanza 1 and stanza 7?

Understanding Literature: Lyric Poetry, Figures of Speech, and Rhythm

This lyric poem focuses on emotions with simple, direct language. It makes use of figures of speech in the form of imaginative comparisons called metaphors. In these comparisons, words cannot be understood with their usual, or literal, meanings. The poem also has a strict rhythm of four strong beats per line.

7. What do *fleet foot, sill of shade,* and *low lintel* represent in stanza 6?

8. How do the short words and lines of the poem and its strict rhythm prevent the poem's emotion from being weepy and sentimental?

Critical Thinking

9. The poet says that the athlete was lucky to have died before his fame did. Yet the tone with which he speaks is sad and ironic. How do you think the poet really feels about death? Why do you think so?

Thinking Creatively

10. Do you agree that it is better to die young and famous than to live into old age and have no one remember you? Give reasons for your opinion.

✔️ Grammar Check

Hyphens (-) are used to create compound adjectives that come before nouns. A compound adjective contains two words combined to describe a noun, for example: *well-known actor*. Hyphens are also used in some compound nouns: *great-grandparents*.

- Find three compound adjectives in "To an Athlete Dying Young." Find two compound nouns.

- Write each compound adjective and the noun it describes. Then write the compound nouns.

- Make up your own compound adjective and compound noun. Write each compound word in an original sentence.

Writing on Your Own

Write a biography of a great athlete or other famous person you admire. Find important facts and events in the person's life in reference books or on the Internet. Focus on highlights in the person's life, placing events in order. Did the person's fame die before he or she did? Comment on the person's place in history.

Speaking and Listening

Is it glorious to be famous, or is there a "down side" to fame? Form two teams based on answers to this question. In your team, discuss reasons why your opinion is convincing. Have the two teams present their arguments. Listen to the other team's arguments. Make notes about points that would counter, or disprove, their arguments.

Media

Look through newspapers and magazines to find articles that celebrate the victories of great athletes. What do they have in common? Notice the photographs or other visuals included with the articles. What attitude toward the athletes do the words and pictures suggest? Make a drawing, collage, or sculpture that conveys the American attitude toward its sports heroes.

BEFORE READING THE SELECTION

Rudyard Kipling
1865–1936

Objectives

- To read and understand a poem with hymn-like qualities
- To identify mood and recognize how it is created
- To draw conclusions about a writer's views

About the Author

Rudyard Kipling was born in India, which was a British colony at the time. Kipling's father taught at an art school in Bombay. Kipling loved India and learned Hindi, one of the languages spoken in India.

From age 5 to 17, Kipling lived in England and attended boarding schools and a military school. This was a difficult time for him, for the schools were harsh, and he missed India.

Kipling returned to India to work as a journalist. His articles, stories, and poems gained him many readers. He published books in India, and his fame quickly spread. By the time he returned to England in 1889, he was famous. In 1907, he became the first English person to receive the Nobel Prize for literature. To this day, he is still the youngest person to receive that honor.

Many of Kipling's stories and books are set in India and show his love of that land and its people. Ballads, music-hall songs, and popular hymns influenced his poetry. Much of Kipling's poetry is focused on the duty of England as a world power and the progress that might result. Today, Kipling's work is enjoyed for its colorful, vivid pictures of life in India.

About the Selection

"Recessional" was written for Queen Victoria's Diamond Jubilee (60th anniversary celebration) in 1897. This event celebrated the power of the British Empire. However, Kipling does not applaud England for being a world power. Instead, he warns against becoming arrogant, proud, and smug. The poem is written as a prayer that God would keep them from the pride that might ruin them.

Literary Terms "Recessional" gets its **mood**, or feeling, from its hymn-like rhythm and language. (A hymn is a song of praise to God.) Other elements that can have an emotional effect include figurative language and imagery.

mood the feeling that writing creates

Reading on Your Own In this poem, Kipling repeats the phrase *Lest we forget* many times. The poem echoes these words from Deuteronomy in the Bible: "Then beware lest thou forget the Lord." After each stanza, pause and ask yourself what Kipling is warning his audience about. What conclusions can you draw about his belief in England?

Writing on Your Own Review what you know about great world powers of the past, such as Rome, Spain, and the Soviet Union. None of these empires still exists today. Write a paragraph explaining why you think powerful empires crumble and fall.

Vocabulary Focus In "Recessional," Kipling refers to places and people that have a historical importance to his theme. In line 8, "Captains" and "Kings" represent the military and political leaders who seek power over others. In line 16, "Nineveh and Tyre" name ancient cities that were once great. Nineveh was an ancient Assyrian city located in what is now Iraq. Tyre was the main city of Phoenicia (now Lebanon). They were the seats of great power, now vanished. Think about how these words represent larger ideas in the poem.

Think Before You Read How do you think most British people felt about their country and its empire in 1897?

RECESSIONAL

As you read,
think about how
powerful the
British Empire had
become by 1897.
What is Kipling
saying about
its power and
attitude? What is
the mood of this
poem?

God of our fathers, known of old,
    Lord of our far-flung battle-line,
Beneath whose awful Hand we hold
    Dominion over palm and pine—
5 Lord God of **Hosts,** be with us yet,
    Lest we forget—lest we forget!

The **tumult** and the shouting dies;
    The Captains and the Kings depart:
Still stands Thine ancient sacrifice,
10   An humble and a **contrite** heart.
Lord God of Hosts, be with us yet,
Lest we forget—lest we forget!

Far-called, our navies melt away;
    On dune and **headland** sinks the fire:
15 Lo, all our **pomp** of yesterday
    Is one with Nineveh and Tyre!
Judge of the Nations, spare us yet,
Lest we forget—lest we forget!

Colonies of
England stretched
around the world,
from tropics (*palm*)
to the far north
(*pine*). At one time,
the saying that
"the sun never
set on the British
Empire" was true.
It was always
daylight in some
part of the empire.

dominion control	**lest** in case	**headland** point of high land jutting out into a body of water
hosts huge armies (here, referring to the angels that God commands)	**tumult** uproar	
	contrite sorry; regretful	**pomp** display of greatness

If, drunk with sight of power, we loose
20 Wild tongues that have not Thee in awe,
Such boastings as the Gentiles use,
  Or lesser breeds without the Law—
Lord God of Hosts, be with us yet,
Lest we forget—lest we forget!

25 For **heathen** heart that puts her trust
  In **reeking** tube and iron **shard,**
All **valiant** dust that builds on dust,
  And guarding, calls not Thee to guard.
For **frantic** boast and foolish word—
30 Thy mercy on Thy People, Lord!

In the Bible, *Gentiles* (line 21) were any people who were not Israelites (and therefore did not live by God's laws). Here, *Gentiles* and *heathen* (line 25) refer to other power-hungry countries of Kipling's time, such as Germany and Italy.

Notice the images of war in the last stanza—the stink of gunpowder and the cutting sharpness of metal bits after an explosion.

Queen Victoria's Diamond Jubilee procession, 1897

heathen uncivilized; not religious

reeking stinking

shard fragment

valiant brave, heroic

frantic wild with rage or fear

Directions Choose the letter of the best answer or write the answer using complete sentences.

Comprehension: Identifying Facts

1. The refrain (repeated lines) of this poem warns the British people not to forget _____.
   A the past
   B God and his laws
   C the need for watchfulness
   D captains and kings

2. In lines 15–16, why does Kipling compare "all our pomp" to "Nineveh and Tyre"?

3. In lines 25–26, what does the "heathen heart" put its trust in? Why is this unwise?

Comprehension: Putting Ideas Together

4. The poem recognizes Britain's great power in the world and points out that _____.
   A it will not last
   B the navy is not strong
   C other nations are threatening England
   D God helps the mighty

5. What does this poem say is more important than power?

6. What descriptions suggest that Kipling sees an ugly, dangerous side to English attitudes?

Understanding Literature: Mood

A writer produces a mood, or emotional feeling, in a work by choosing details and words and setting up rhythms that create that feeling.

7. What is the mood of "Recessional"?

8. Point out specific words and details that create this feeling. Tell how the rhythm underscores, or accents, this feeling.

Critical Thinking

9. Write the meaning of lines 25–28 in your own words. Do you agree with what they say? Explain why.

Thinking Creatively

10. Kipling warns his people not to forget the Lord. Sacrifice and a humble heart are values Kipling holds up as having real, lasting power. Tell how you think Kipling believed British rulers should behave toward the peoples they controlled. Do you think governments today behave like this?

✔ Grammar Check

A preposition is the first word in a prepositional phrase. The noun that ends the phrase is the object of the preposition. A prepositional phrase acts as an adjective or adverb; it modifies or describes a noun, pronoun, or verb. Study the following prepositional phrase and noun:

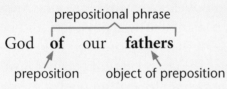

prepositional phrase

God **of** our **fathers**

preposition   object of preposition

Of our fathers is a prepositional phrase modifying the noun *God*. It tells which God, so it acts as an adjective. Some common prepositions are: *above, for, in, on, to, beneath, from, of, over, with*.

- Find as many prepositional phrases as you can in "Recessional."

- Write each phrase. Circle the preposition and underline the object of the preposition.

- In a second column, write the word that the phrase modifies.

- In a third column, tell whether the phrase acts as an adjective or an adverb.

✎ Writing on Your Own

The United States is considered the greatest world power today, as Britain was in 1897. Do you think America will lose its power? Write an essay explaining your opinion. Include a paragraph explaining why you believe as you do.

💬🎧 Speaking and Listening

"Recessional" suggests that war helped England get and hold power. Is military might the most important power for a nation to have today? Jot down your thoughts on this question. Share your ideas with a small group of classmates. Listen carefully to others' ideas.

🔍 Research

Read about the British Empire in Victorian times. How did the British govern their colonies? When did the empire begin to crumble and why? Use encyclopedias and other reference books, such as historical atlases. On the Internet, enter the keywords *British Empire, British imperialism,* and *Victorian England* to find information. Organize your notes and use them to write a summary of what you learned. Include a world map showing British colonies.

BEFORE READING THE SELECTION

Thomas Hardy
1840–1928

Objectives

- To read and understand a poem written in dialogue form
- To appreciate the effect of a surprise ending
- To explain the meaning of irony in a poem

About the Author

Thomas Hardy was born and grew up in rural southwestern England. He did not receive much formal education. Instead, he went to work as an architect's assistant. He studied hard on his own time and began writing. He loved writing poetry, but he first had success with fiction. In the early 1870s, Hardy gave up architecture to write full time.

Most of Hardy's stories and novels are set in a countryside like the one where he grew up—lonely, marshy heaths (level, open land). His stories show his view of life's unfairness. Their characters fight a losing battle against fate and come to a tragic end. Because of their frankness and questioning of some Victorian social values, several of Hardy's novels outraged the public. He turned to writing poetry for the last 30 years of his life.

Hardy wrote poems in plain language, to sound like the speech of rural people. He wrote this way by choice. He did not like the fancy language many Victorian poets used. Many of his poems are touched with sadness and point out human misunderstandings. Hardy died in 1928, a widely admired poet and novelist.

About the Selection

"Ah, Are You Digging on My Grave?" is written in the form of a dialogue. It illustrates Hardy's grim sense of humor. It also exposes romantic ideas about love, life, and death as misunderstandings. One speaker (a woman who has died) asks questions of a second speaker (someone who is digging on her grave).

Literary Terms In this poem, Hardy takes an ironic look at romantic ideas about love and death. **Irony** contrasts what we expect to happen with what actually happens. "Ah, Are You Digging on My Grave?" slowly reveals the story of what happens after a loved one dies. The poem has a **surprise ending.** Because it is not what we expect, the ending wakes us up to reality.

Reading on Your Own The dead person speaking in the poem asks who is visiting her grave. She goes through several possibilities. As you read each stanza, think about why the dead person might assume that person is her visitor.

Writing on Your Own Think about a romantic poem, story, or movie you have read or seen in which one of the lovers dies. Summarize what happens in the plot. Then give your reaction to this outcome. Is it satisfying? Is it realistic? Why or why not?

Vocabulary Focus You can often use the context, or surrounding words, to figure out the meaning of a new word. The sentence in which the word is used gives clues because it describes a situation. Your past experiences also help you to predict what the word must be. For example, in line 2 of this selection, the word *rue* appears. You know from the sentence that the scene is a grave and someone is digging on a grave. Rue is something that is planted. Therefore, it is probably a low-growing plant that lives a long time. Read lines 11–12 and 27–30. Use the context to predict the meanings of *tendance*, *gin*, and *fidelity*.

Think Before You Read Who do you think is digging on the dead person's grave?

irony
the difference between what is expected to happen in a story and what does happen

surprise ending
an ending in a narrative that has an unusual, unexpected twist and usually makes a strong point

"Ah, Are You Digging on My Grave?"

As you read, imagine the tone of voice of the first speaker (the dead woman). How do you think her tone changes with each answer she receives?

"Ah, are you digging on my grave,
    My loved one?—planting **rue?**"
—"No: yesterday he went to wed
One of the brightest wealth has bred.
5 'It cannot hurt her now,' he said,
    'That I should not be true.'"

"Then who is digging on my grave?
    My nearest dearest **kin?**"
—"Ah, no: they sit and think, 'What use!
10 What good will planting flowers produce?
No **tendance** of her mound can loose
    Her spirit from Death's **gin.**'"

"But some one digs upon my grave?
    My enemy?—**prodding sly?**"
15 —"Nay: when she heard you had passed the Gate
That shuts on all flesh soon or late,
She thought you no more worth her hate,
    And cares not where you lie."

Death's gin is a grim metaphor. It is both a trap from which one does not escape and a machine that grinds up the body into its basic parts and returns it to earth.

rue a small, bushy herb	**tendance** tending; action of caring for	**prodding** poking
kin relative	**gin** machine for separating parts; trap	**sly** sneaky

"Then, who is digging on my grave?
20   Say—since I have not guessed!"
—"O it is I, my mistress dear,
Your little dog, who still lives near,
And much I hope my movements here
        Have not disturbed your rest?"

25 "Ah, yes! *You* dig upon my grave . . .
        Why flashed it not on me
That one true heart was left behind!
What feeling do we ever find
To equal among human kind
30   A dog's **fidelity!**"

"Mistress, I dug upon your grave
        To bury a bone, in case
I should be hungry near this spot
When passing on my daily trot.
35 I am sorry, but I quite forgot
        It was your resting-place."

Why has the dead woman not guessed who is digging on her grave?

What is ironic about the dog's explanation for his visit? How is this surprise ending a "wake-up call" to readers?

fidelity faithfulness

"Ah, Are You Digging on My Grave?" by Thomas Hardy

Directions Choose the letter of the best answer or write the answer using complete sentences.

Comprehension: Identifying Facts

1. The questions in this poem are asked by _____.
   A a faithful lover
   B an outside observer
   C a faithful pet
   D a woman who has died

2. Why do the speaker's family members not visit her grave?

3. Who is the visitor at the grave? What is the visitor doing?

Comprehension: Putting Ideas Together

4. The speaker from the grave learns that the emotion the living feel toward her is _____.
   A pity   C indifference
   B hate   D love

5. What did the dead woman hope for? What does the second speaker do to this hope?

6. List the people the first speaker guesses, in order. Why does she mention them in this order?

Understanding Literature: Irony and Surprise Ending

The irony of this poem comes from our expecting one thing to happen, when another is what actually happens. By not telling who the visitor is until the end, Hardy creates an ironic surprise ending.

7. Who did you expect the visitor to be? Did your idea change as you read the poem? Why?

8. The word *rue* in line 2 can refer to a plant with bitter leaves, sometimes used as medicine, and to an attitude of regret. What is ironic about both meanings of this word, after you know what is really happening?

Critical Thinking

9. Many people feel the bond of humans and their dogs is very strong and loving. What does the ending of the poem suggest about that belief? Do you agree or disagree with Hardy about this?

Thinking Creatively

10. Do you think Hardy is being cruel, realistic, or practical in this poem? Explain why you think this.

Grammar Check

Quotation marks (" ") are placed around spoken words in a story, poem, or play: *"Ah, are you digging on my grave?"* If a speaker reports another person's words, those words are set off by single quotation marks ('): *"No: yesterday he went to wed . . ./'It cannot hurt her now,' he said,/'That I should not be true.'"*

- Keep track of how many times each of the following characters in the poem speaks: the dead woman, her lover, her kin, her dog.

- Study several of the quotations in this poem to see where end punctuation marks go.

- Write a short question-and-answer dialogue between two people. Use quotation marks correctly.

Writing on Your Own

What do you think causes the close bond between dogs and their masters? Write an essay on the subject. Begin with a main idea statement. Develop your ideas in several paragraphs. End with a strong conclusion. You may wish to use a Main Idea Graphic Organizer to organize your ideas. See Appendix A for a description of this graphic organizer.

Speaking and Listening

With a partner, prepare a dramatic reading of "Ah, Are You Digging on My Grave?" Discuss the tones of voice the speakers should use. Practice reading your lines aloud. When your partner reads, listen and offer helpful feedback about his or her expression. After you have practiced reading your parts together, present your reading to a group of classmates.

Media

With a partner, brainstorm a list of movies and TV shows that focus on how people react after a loved one has died. Beside each title, write a sentence summarizing the story or program's view of love and death. For example, you might say a movie shows that after death a loved one can still communicate with us. Separate the titles you have into "Realistic" and "Unrealistic" categories. Which category is larger?

The narrator, or storyteller, determines the story's point of view. Point of view is the position from which a story or novel is told. The writer's choice of a narrator limits the type and amount of information readers get.

A *first-person narrator* is a character telling the story in his or her own words. *David Copperfield* is a novel told by a first-person narrator, David. The reader learns about events and characters through the experiences of the narrator:

"All this time he was squeezing my hand with his damp fishy fingers, while I made every effort I decently could to get away."

A first-person storyteller can tell us only what he or she sees, hears, and thinks. For example, David Copperfield thinks Uriah Heep looks

"like a malevolent baboon."

We do not know how Uriah feels about David. Because we see the world only through David's eyes, he colors the way we think about all other characters.

Is the narrator a reliable reporter? This is a question to ask about any first-person narrator. If not, we must read between the lines to decide. For example, in the poem "My Last Duchess," we hear only the duke's view.

However, we get clues that he is arrogant, proud, and cruel. Perhaps we cannot rely on his account of his wife.

If a voice from outside the story narrates, then the story has a *third-person narrator*. In many works of fiction, a third-person narrator can look into any character's head and heart. Then we learn what each character thinks and feels.

Review

1. What is point of view?

2. What is the difference between a first-person and third-person narrator?

3. What is the point of view in *Jane Eyre*? Through whose eyes do we see the story?

4. Do you think David Copperfield is a reliable first-person narrator? Explain.

5. How do you think *David Copperfield* would have been different if a third-person narrator had told the story?

Writing on Your Own

Write a paragraph for *David Copperfield* as it would be if told from Uriah Heep's point of view.

Unit 5 covers the years from 1832 to 1901. This period saw Britain become the world's most powerful nation, with an empire that spanned the globe. The confident British people believed they should spread their views and technology around the world.

Literature of the Victorian Era changed over time. Earlier poems by Alfred, Lord Tennyson, Robert Browning, and Elizabeth Barrett Browning expressed a more positive view. Novels by Charlotte Brontë and Charles Dickens entertained while they pointed out problems. Later works, like those by Matthew Arnold, A. E. Housman, and Thomas Hardy, expressed a gloomier outlook. Oscar Wilde used humor to point out the flaws in British society. Rudyard Kipling expressed doubts about the British Empire.

Selections

- Poems from *In Memoriam* by Alfred, Lord Tennyson explore grief and find what makes life worth living.

- "My Last Duchess" by Robert Browning reveals the flaws of a proud duke and how his wife died.

- "Sonnet 43" from *Sonnets from the Portuguese* by Elizabeth Barrett Browning explores the depth of love between a man and woman.

- A selection from the novel *Jane Eyre* by Charlotte Brontë shows the difficulties a poor woman faces and tells the love story of two social opposites.

- A selection from the novel *David Copperfield* by Charles Dickens observes the way a young man learns about the motives of a bad man.

- "Dover Beach" is a poem by Matthew Arnold that comments on the disappearance of faith in the world.

- "Pied Beauty" by Gerard Manley Hopkins is a poem that celebrates the varieties of beauty that God created.

- The play *The Importance of Being Earnest* by Oscar Wilde pokes fun at British society and points out some of its uglier aspects.

- "To an Athlete Dying Young" by A. E. Housman is a poem that finds the ironic good in a young man's death.

- "Recessional" is Rudyard Kipling's hymn-like poem that warns Britain against pride and suggests that its power will not last.

- "Ah, Are You Digging on My Grave?" is a poem by Thomas Hardy that shows how the living forget the dead.

Directions Choose the letter of the best answer or write the answer using complete sentences.

Comprehension: Identifying Facts

1. Queen Victoria was queen for _____.
   A 40 years
   B 45 years
   C 50 years
   D more than 60 years

2. Who held the most power in England during this period?

3. What happened because of scientific advances and new theories?

4. Which selection is a satiric play?

5. Which selection warns that Britain is fated to lose its power?

Comprehension: Putting Ideas Together

6. Which selection suggests that British society twists the minds of the poor?
   A "Ah, Are You Digging on My Grave?"
   B "To an Athlete Dying Young"
   C *Jane Eyre*
   D *David Copperfield*

7. How do "Dover Beach" and "Pied Beauty" differ in their themes?

8. Explain how Gerard Manley Hopkins's poem differs from traditional Victorian poetry.

9. Tell how the poems *In Memoriam* and "Ah, Are You Digging on My Grave?" are alike and different.

10. List some ways the speakers in "Sonnet 43" and "Ah, Are You Digging on My Grave?" differ.

Understanding Literature: Fiction

Fiction is prose (nonpoetical) writing that is imaginative and designed to entertain. An author makes up events and characters to tell a story. Fiction includes short stories and novels. A novel is longer and can develop more characters and a more complicated plot.

11. What are some ways in which fiction differs from poetry?

12. Which selections in this unit are fiction?

13. Why is *The Importance of Being Earnest* not fiction? How is it like fiction?

14. Which selection in this unit do you think best shows the nature of Victorian society?

15. Which poem in this unit is most like a play? Explain your choice.

Critical Thinking

16. Which selection in this unit do you think expresses the strongest religious faith? Explain your choice.

17. Which selection from the unit do you think seems most modern in its wording and attitudes? Why?

18. Which author's works are you most likely to see today in movies or on television? Why do you think this is so?

19 Which author in this unit do you like best? Tell why.

Thinking Creatively

20. Do you find any areas in which American society today is similar to Victorian society? Explain your answer.

Speak and Listen

Work with a partner to write a dialogue between two of the authors in this unit. Think about each author's outlook and ideas. How did each one feel about his or her society? Let their conversation show their agreement or disagreement about issues such as the future of England. Read the dialogue, with each partner taking one author's role. Try to speak in a way you think suits the author. Listen to your partner and give each other suggestions for improving the dialogue. When you have practiced the dialogue several times, present it for a group of classmates.

Writing on Your Own

Choose a poem from Unit 5 that you think expresses an important ideal or attitude of Victorian England. Write an essay explaining how the poem illustrates this point of view. Use examples from the poem for supporting details. End with a conclusion that sums up the poem's importance.

Beyond Words

Think about the selections in Unit 5. Choose one you liked and note its theme, images, and language. Decide on a symbol or set of symbols that suits the selection. Create an artwork using the symbols you chose.

Test-Taking Tip

Skim through a test before you begin answering its questions. If there are essay questions, allow more time for answering them than you do for short-answer or multiple-choice questions.

Bursting Shell,
Christopher R. W. Nevinson, 1915

Unit 6

Contemporary British Literature: 1901–Present

During the contemporary period, the world endured two bloody, costly world wars, the threat of nuclear war, and the violence of terrorism. At the same time, advances in technology, agriculture, and medical science promised a better world. While the British nation lost much power and economic influence, its people made gains in health, housing, and education.

In this unit, you will learn how British authors responded to the destruction of war and the promise of human potential they saw everywhere.

"We are sharply cut off from our predecessors. A shift in the scale—the war, the sudden slip of masses held in position for ages—has shaken the fabric from top to bottom, alienated us from the past and made us perhaps too vividly conscious of the present. Every day we find ourselves doing, saying, or thinking things that would have been impossible for our fathers."

—*Virginia Woolf, 1924*

During the 20th century, Britain lost international power as a result of world events. The trench warfare and poison gas of World War I convinced many that war was horrible, not heroic. A deadly influenza outbreak in 1918 and 1919 killed 30 million people worldwide.

A nurse reads to wounded British sailors, 1940.

However, the new century also brought reforms in Britain. Women gained the right to vote. The Irish Free State was formed in 1921. The working class gained a better standard of living.

The Great Depression began in the United States in 1929. Its effects spread throughout the world. Dictators, or unelected leaders, came to power in Germany, Italy, and Russia. In Germany, the rise of Adolf Hitler and Nazism was a threat. Germany's military power grew, and it invaded other nations. This led to World War II (1939–1945).

New weapons and techniques created new horrors. The militaries bombed entire cities, causing widespread damage. Millions died in death camps. More than 50 million people died during the war.

After World War II, Britain formed the Commonwealth. Former colonies became independent nations. This era also brought a different kind of war: a

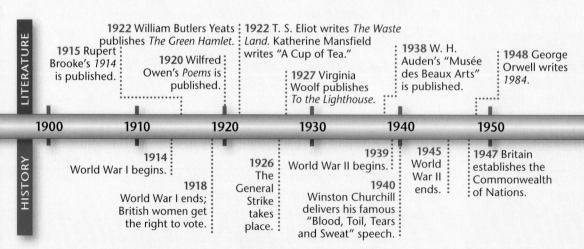

LITERATURE

1915 Rupert Brooke's *1914* is published.

1922 William Butlers Yeats publishes *The Green Hamlet.*

1920 Wilfred Owen's *Poems* is published.

1922 T. S. Eliot writes *The Waste Land.* Katherine Mansfield writes "A Cup of Tea."

1927 Virginia Woolf publishes *To the Lighthouse.*

1938 W. H. Auden's "Musée des Beaux Arts" is published.

1948 George Orwell writes *1984.*

1900   1910   1920   1930   1940   1950

HISTORY

1914 World War I begins.

1918 World War I ends; British women get the right to vote.

1926 The General Strike takes place.

1939 World War II begins.

1940 Winston Churchill delivers his famous "Blood, Toil, Tears and Sweat" speech.

1945 World War II ends.

1947 Britain establishes the Commonwealth of Nations.

"cold war" between the United States and the Soviet Union. The threat of nuclear war terrified the world, and the threat of terrorism grew.

The writers in this unit vary widely. Generally, the poets use shorter forms than earlier poets did. The focus shifts from teaching a lesson to letting readers draw their own lessons. Prose writers deal more with social problems and mental health issues.

The poems "The Soldier" by Rupert Brooke and "Dulce et decorum est" by Wilfred Owen are responses to World War I. The essay "Shooting an Elephant" by George Orwell points out the folly of British control in India. William Butler Yeats's "The Second Coming," T. S. Eliot's "The Hollow Men," Virginia Woolf's story "The Duchess and the Jeweller," and Katherine Mansfield's story "A Cup of Tea" use new techniques for writing. Woolf and Mansfield focus on small moments that reveal characters' motives. W. H. Auden's poem "Musée des Beaux Arts" and Stephen Spender's "What I Expected" explore questions about human suffering. A wartime speech by Winston Churchill, "Blood, Toil, Tears and Sweat," reveals the British will to win despite hardship. Dylan Thomas's "Do Not Go Gentle into That Good Night" urges a man to fight death. "The Horses" by Ted Hughes tells about an experience of the natural world. Graham Greene's story "A Shocking Accident" and Stevie Smith's poem "Not Waving But Drowning" use a light touch to discuss responses to the lack of kindness in the world. Jane Shilling's column "Beat the Blues with Brian" explores mental health issues with honesty and humor.

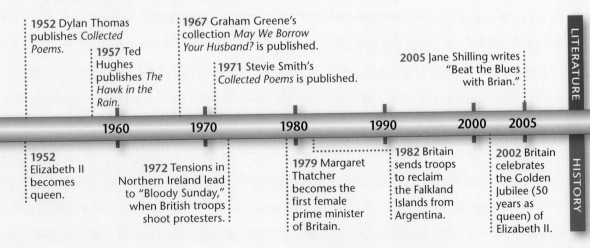

LITERATURE

1952 Dylan Thomas publishes *Collected Poems.*

1957 Ted Hughes publishes *The Hawk in the Rain.*

1967 Graham Greene's collection *May We Borrow Your Husband?* is published.

1971 Stevie Smith's *Collected Poems* is published.

2005 Jane Shilling writes "Beat the Blues with Brian."

1960   1970   1980   1990   2000   2005

HISTORY

1952 Elizabeth II becomes queen.

1972 Tensions in Northern Ireland lead to "Bloody Sunday," when British troops shoot protesters.

1979 Margaret Thatcher becomes the first female prime minister of Britain.

1982 Britain sends troops to reclaim the Falkland Islands from Argentina.

2002 Britain celebrates the Golden Jubilee (50 years as queen) of Elizabeth II.

The Soldier **by Rupert Brooke**

Rupert Brooke
1887–1915

- To read and understand a sonnet
- To identify the tone of a poem and identify language that establishes tone
- To compare a poem to the Victorian style
- To identify rhyme scheme, rhythm, and iambic pentameter

About the Author

Rupert Brooke was born in 1887 in the town of Rugby in central England. His first poetry caused him to be called a Georgian poet. Georgian poets wrote traditional, hopeful poems about nature and country living. After going through an unhappy love affair, Brooke turned back to a Victorian outlook.

In 1913 and 1914, Brooke traveled in the United States, Canada, and the Pacific islands. Some of his most famous poems are set in Tahiti. Shortly after World War I began, he joined the British navy. He served briefly in Belgium. He died of blood poisoning in 1915, while traveling with his unit to the Dardanelles in Turkey. Brooke's death became a symbol of the end of Georgian poetry.

Brooke never experienced the horrors of trench warfare, which may be one reason his poetry is more positive toward war. In trench warfare, soldiers spent days or weeks in trenches (deep ditches) where they were safe from enemy bullets but in constant danger from bombs, poisonous gas, and bad weather. The terrible experiences of the trenches, along with new forms of media that helped broadcast news and images of the war, changed how people viewed war.

About the Selection

"The Soldier" is one of Brooke's war poems, written while he was in Belgium. It was included in *1914*, a book of poetry published in 1915 after the poet's death. Brooke's poem creates a heroic and patriotic picture of the life and death of a soldier.

Literary Terms "The Soldier" is a **sonnet.** Like all sonnets, it has 14 lines and uses **iambic pentameter.** This is a kind of **rhythm,** or sound pattern, in which each line contains five strong beats and each "foot" generally contains two beats. Its **rhyme scheme,** or pattern of end rhymes, is *ababcdcd efgefg.* This makes it different from a Shakespearean sonnet, which has the pattern *abab cdcd efef gg.* Brooke's pattern ties together the final six lines with rhyme. Shakespeare's pattern more heavily emphasizes the final two lines.

Tone is found in every piece of writing. It is the attitude of the writer, revealed through the choice of words and details. It may be happy or sad, formal or informal, serious or playful.

Reading on Your Own In this poem, a soldier speaks about his view of England and the possibility of his death. As you read, think about the details he uses to describe his homeland. What conclusions can you draw about the tone of his writing? What is his attitude toward England?

Writing on Your Own Imagine you are a soldier, serving your country in a foreign land. Write a letter to a friend or family member explaining how you feel about doing this.

Vocabulary Focus Regular English verbs form the past tense by adding *-ed*: *wash* becomes *washed*, *shape* becomes *shaped*. Notice, though, that in "The Soldier," Brooke uses the ending *-t* to form the past tense of two verbs: *bless* and *learn*. In line 8, *blest* appears where we would usually use *blessed*. In line 13, *learnt* appears where we would usually use *learned*. The form the poet has used was used more in the past.

Think Before You Read What was the Victorian attitude toward war and England? What attitude do you expect from Brooke?

sonnet a 14-line poem written in iambic pentameter

iambic pentameter five two-beat sounds in a line of poetry where the second syllable is stressed in each pair

rhythm a pattern created by the stressed and unstressed syllables in a line of poetry

rhyme scheme the pattern created by the ending sounds of the lines of a poem

tone the attitude an author takes toward a subject

The Soldier

As you read, notice the rhythms of the lines and the effect of the rhyme scheme. In what ways does this poem remind you of the work of Victorian poets?

If I should die, think only this of me:
That there's some corner of a foreign field
That is for ever England. There shall be
In that rich earth a richer dust concealed;
5   A dust whom England bore, shaped, made aware,
Gave, once, her flowers to love, her ways to roam,
A body of England's, breathing English air,
Washed by the rivers, blest by suns of home.

The poet speaks of himself as a spirit; he will no longer have a physical body or pulse, but he will exist in a spiritual form (*the eternal mind,* line 10).

And think, this heart, all
    evil shed away,
10   A pulse in the eternal
    mind, no less
Gives somewhere back
    the thoughts by
    England given;
Her sights and sounds;
    dreams happy as her
    day;
And laughter, learnt of
    friends; and
    gentleness,
In hearts at peace, under
    an English heaven.

What words help set the tone of the poem?

RALLY ROUND THE FLAG

"WE MUST HAVE MORE MEN"

British Recruitment Poster in World War I

AFTER READING THE SELECTION

The Soldier *by Rupert Brooke*

Directions Choose the letter of the best answer or write the answer using complete sentences.

Comprehension: Identifying Facts

1. The "richer dust concealed" in line 4 refers to _____.
   A the wealth given by England
   B the soldier's belongings
   C the soldier's mind
   D the soldier's body

2. Where does the soldier expect to be buried if he is killed?

3. What things does the soldier think he will give back after death?

Comprehension: Putting Ideas Together

4. The soldier gives credit to England for _____.
   A all that he has become
   B supporting its soldiers
   C its rich earth
   D peacefulness

5. What traditional English qualities does the poet stress?

6. What feelings does the poet express for England and the cause for which he is fighting?

Understanding Literature: Tone

Tone is the attitude of the writer toward his or her subject. Readers sense this attitude through the details and kinds of words the writer has chosen.

7. What is the tone of "The Soldier"?

8. What details and words create this tone?

Critical Thinking

9. Do you think the poet is expressing what his life has really been like or an ideal of happiness? How does line 9 suggest an answer to this question?

Thinking Creatively

10. The poems in Brooke's poetry book *1914* were traditional and hopeful. They were the last to express this sort of patriotism about the war. Do you think such poems would be written today? Why or why not?

After Reading **continued on next page**

The Soldier　　by Rupert Brooke

 ## Grammar Check

The apostrophe (') is used to replace missing letters in a contraction (as in *can't, might've, she's*) or to show possession (as in *a nation's army* or *a soldier's uniform*).

- List the two words in "The Soldier" that contain an apostrophe. Write *contraction* or *possessive* beside each word to show how the apostrophe is used.

- If there is a contraction, write the words used to form it. If there is a possessive, write the noun that it tells about.

- Write a sentence of your own using the contraction or the possessive phrase.

 ## Writing on Your Own

Write a short scene for a play in which a soldier talks to a person protesting war. First jot down ideas each might want to express and questions they might ask each other. Then imagine the situation that led to their meeting. Write the conversation, using language each person would be likely to use.

 ## Speaking and Listening

With a partner, prepare a dramatic reading of this poem. Focus on how you can use vocal expression and tone of voice to show the mood of the poem. Present your reading to the class. When it is your turn to listen, make note of techniques others use to get across the same ideas.

 ## Research

Work with a small group to find out about World War I. Which countries fought on each side? How long did the war last? How many people were killed or wounded? What was the fighting like? Make notes and visuals, such as a world map. Decide how to organize your material. As a group, present your information to the class.

Media

Find a recording of a documentary about World War I or a movie that is set during that war. As you watch and listen, make notes about what the war was like. How was it unlike the wars that had come before it? How did people of the world react to it?

BEFORE READING THE SELECTION

About the Author

Wilfred Owen was born in Shropshire County in 1893. Like Rupert Brooke, he joined the military and fought in World War I. Unlike Brooke, he experienced the horrors of trench warfare. In poor health, Owen collapsed while in France and was hospitalized in England. When he recovered, he returned to the fighting. He was killed in action just seven days before the war ended.

Owen's collection *Poems* was published in 1920. Unlike Brooke's poems, these are painfully clear about the suffering, bloodshed, and waste of war. They also experiment with more modern sound effects and rhythms. Owen's work influenced many 20th-century poets who followed him.

Wilfred Owen
1893–1918

About the Selection

"Dulce et decorum est" is one of the poems Owen wrote in 1917 and 1918 to suggest "the pity of war." Owen uses words and sound effects to create ideas of the harshness and confusion of war. He uses poetic forms and language that were not as polished as in earlier poetry.

Dulce et decorum est pro patria mori is a Latin saying taken from the writings of the ancient Roman poet Horace. It means "It is sweet and proper to die for your fatherland (country)." These words were widely understood by the British, who often quoted them in a positive way at the beginning of the war. Owen did not believe the words were true. His poem tells how horrible war is. Owen wrote this poem to challenge an author who wrote war poems for children.

Objectives

- To read and understand a poem
- To identify figures of speech and explain their meaning
- To infer the poet's view of war

Before Reading continued on next page

Dulce et decorem est   by Wilfred Owen

figure of speech a word or phrase that has meaning different from the actual meaning

Literary Terms **Figures of speech** are phrases that cannot be understood just by thinking of the literal, or exact, meanings of the words. When we say "You are the apple of my eye," we do not mean that eyes contain apples. This figure of speech describes someone who is much loved. Figures of speech are often used in poetry for imaginative, emotional effect.

Reading on Your Own The soldier who is speaking in this poem sees his fellow soldiers as beggars and old women. They are so exhausted that they are blind and deaf to the chaos around them. Think about the images Owen has chosen. What inferences can you make about his state of mind?

Writing on Your Own Mustard gas was used as a weapon in World War I. Read about it and write a summary of what you learn. For example, what is it made of? How does it kill?

Vocabulary Focus Poets sometimes invent words or new uses for words to make their images more effective. For example, the word *hoots* appears in line 7 of Owen's poem. This word usually refers either to the sound of an owl or to scornful laughter. Owen uses it to describe the sound that falling bombs make. *Hoots* captures the sound and the feeling that the soldiers are victims of a scornful enemy. Find the word *guttering* in line 16. How do you think Owen invented this word? What do you think he intends it to mean?

Think Before You Read What do you know about the kind of weapons and techniques used in World War I combat? How do you think this poet will describe them?

Dulce et decorum est

As you read, picture the scene suggested by the details and images. What atmosphere is suggested?

Bent double, like old beggars under sacks,
Knock-kneed, coughing like hags, we cursed
    through **sludge,**
Till on the haunting flares we turned our backs,
And towards our distant rest began to trudge.

5   Men marched asleep. Many had lost their boots,
But limped on, blood-shod. All went lame, all blind;
Drunk with **fatigue;** deaf even to the hoots
Of tired, **outstripped** Five-Nines that dropped behind.

    Flares were rockets shot up to light up targets.

   Gas! GAS! Quick, boys!—An **ecstasy** of fumbling
10 Fitting the clumsy helmets just in time
But someone still was yelling out and stumbling
And **flound'ring** like a man in fire or **lime.**—
Dim through the misty panes and thick green light,
As under a green sea, I saw him drowning.

    Five-Nines are a type of explosive shell. The soldiers struggled beyond their reach.

15 In all my dreams before my helpless sight
He plunges at me, **guttering,** choking, drowning.

    The *misty panes* in line 13 are the glass fronts of the gas masks.

sludge mud

fatigue state of being very tired

outstripped passed, as in a race

ecstasy frenzied state

flound'ring struggling to move, but without making progress

lime chemical that reacts with air, heating quickly and creating dangerous fumes

guttering perhaps a combination of *gurgling* and *stuttering;* the word can also refer to a candle flickering out or the sound of water draining down a gutter

Which figure of speech in this poem is most striking to you? What does it add to the poem?

If in some **smothering** dreams, you too could pace
Behind the wagon that we flung him in,
And watch the white eyes **writhing** in his face,
20   His hanging face, like a devil's sick of sin,
If you could hear, at every jolt, the blood
Come gargling from the **froth-corrupted** lungs
Obscene as cancer, bitter as the cud
Of **vile**, incurable sores on innocent tongues,—
25   My friend, you would not tell with such high **zest**
To children **ardent** for some desperate glory,
The old Lie: *Dulce et decorum est*
Pro patria mori.

Gas masks protected British soldiers from poison gas in the trenches of World War I.

smothering choking	**froth-corrupted** filled with fluid	**zest** enthusiasm
writhing twisting in pain	**vile** terrible	**ardent** eager

Directions Choose the letter of the best answer or write the answer using complete sentences.

Comprehension: Identifying Facts

1. In the first sentence of the poem, the soldiers are _____.
   A trudging through mud away from the battle
   B involved in a fierce battle
   C trying to disguise themselves as beggars
   D badly outnumbered but determined

2. What happens to the soldier who cannot get his gas mask on?

3. Where do the soldiers put this man?

Comprehension: Putting Ideas Together

4. Overall, this poem depicts the soldiers as _____.
   A inspiring patriots
   B helpless, exhausted victims
   C cruel, efficient warriors
   D cowardly and unprepared men

5. What contrast does Owen use in the poem?

6. How does the poet show the sudden, unexpected terror of war?

Understanding Literature: Figures of Speech

Figures of speech are words or phrases with a meaning other than the usual meaning the words have. Often, they involve a surprising comparison or create a vivid word picture.

7. What does the poet compare in line 6 when the soldiers are described as being "blood-shod"?

8. A soldier is described as drowning. How is his death like drowning?

Critical Thinking

9. The person to whom the poem is addressed described war as a glorious, patriotic duty. Why does the poet call this the "old Lie"? Who usually encourages young men to serve in war? Why?

Thinking Creatively

10. What is your opinion of war? Give examples from wars you have read about to support your opinion.

After Reading **continued on next page**

AFTER READING THE SELECTION *(continued)*

 ## Grammar Check

When two or more adjectives are used to tell about the same noun, separate them with commas: *a crisp, clear, sunny day*. If one of the adjectives in the series modifies another adjective, then no comma comes between them: *a dark brown package*. If the word next to the noun is very closely associated with it, no comma is needed: *a bubbly, talkative young lady*. (*Young lady* can be thought of as a single unit.)

- Find at least two examples of adjectives in a series in the selection. Write them correctly on your paper. Draw arrows from the adjectives to the nouns they tell about.

- Find one place where two adjectives appear before a noun without any comma. Write this phrase and explain why it does not need a comma.

 ## Writing on Your Own

Study this poem's use of harsh consonant sounds and pauses within lines. Write an essay explaining the techniques Owen uses to create a tone and mood that suit his theme.

 ## Speaking and Listening

Practice reading "Dulce et decorum est" aloud. Use punctuation as a guide for when to pause. Use a tone you think is fitting and change it when the mood of the poem changes. You may want to record your reading and listen to it to decide on any changes you want to make. When you feel ready, recite the poem for classmates.

 ## Media

Locate recordings or sheet music for war songs from World War I. Find out about their history. Try grouping them into categories, or types. For example, which ones are patriotic and intended to inspire men to enlist? Which ones inspire patriotism and loyalty among the people left at home? Which ones express sorrow over the losses of war? Which ones might have been meant to entertain and cheer up the soldiers?

BEFORE READING THE SELECTION

The Second Coming   *by William Butler Yeats*

About the Author

William Butler Yeats was considered by many to be the greatest poet of his time. He was born in Dublin, Ireland. His family moved from there to London several times, but to Yeats, Ireland was home. Yeats spent much of his life working to help the Irish learn their heritage and be proud of it. With others, he established the Irish Literary Theater and wrote many plays for it. It was later called the Abbey Theater and became world famous. He published many poems and tales based on his understanding of Irish myth.

William Butler Yeats
1865–1939

His poetry, which began as beautiful song-like poems, grew tougher and more "modern" as he grew older. His style became closer to natural speech. Yeats saw in history a cycle of events that repeats about every 2,000 years. As one age winds down, another age—opposite to the first—begins. Yeats used the gyre (whirlwind) to represent a historic cycle. Each era begins with an important event.

Yeats loved Irish actress Maude Gonne, a leader in the Irish fight for independence from Britain. She married someone else, and Yeats threw himself into his work. His poetry improved throughout his life. He received the Nobel Prize for Literature in 1923.

About the Selection

In "The Second Coming," Yeats draws on his ideas about cycles of history. Its opening lines describe a falcon leaving the hand of the falconer and rising in ever-widening circles. This expresses the unwinding (ending) of an era. This poem was written in 1919. The world was trying to recover after World War I, revolution in Russia, and a bloody Irish rebellion.

Objectives

- To identify and explain metaphors, symbols, and allusions in a poem
- To explain the theme of a poem
- To identify and explain the effects of consonance

Before Reading **continued on next page**

The Second Coming by William Butler Yeats

metaphor
a figure of speech that makes a comparison but does not use *like* or *as*

symbol something that represents something else

consonance the repetition of consonant sounds, usually within the context of several words

allusion something referring to a historical event, a person, a place, or a work of literature

theme the main idea of a literary work

Literary Terms **Metaphor** and **symbol** are two forms of figurative language. Metaphors compare two things that seem different without using the words *like* or *as*. Symbols are people, places, or things that stand for something else. **Consonance** is the repetition of the same consonant sound in nearby words. Writers also make **allusions,** or references, to historical events or other literature. Poets use these tools to emphasize their **theme,** or main idea.

Reading on Your Own "The Second Coming" uses animals as symbols of an ending era and a beginning era in world history. As you read, think about the world events Yeats had witnessed. Why might Yeats have chosen these symbols?

Writing on Your Own What do *anarchy* and *revelation* mean? Write the dictionary meanings of these words. Then write about the actions and emotions you connect with them.

Vocabulary Focus Readers need to understand the poet's allusions to get at a poem's meaning. In "The Second Coming," Yeats uses several allusions. The phrase *Second Coming* refers to a future event told about in the Bible when Jesus Christ will bring a new era of peace and success. *Spiritus Mundi* is the spirit or soul of the universe. Yeats thought it connected all souls through the "Great Memory"—a collection of all the memories of the human race. It was therefore a source of symbolic images for the poet. *Twenty centuries* is the 2,000-year Christian era, according to Yeats's system.

Think Before You Read What sort of Second Coming do you think Yeats will describe?

THE SECOND COMING

As you read, think about how the theme of the poem is presented differently in each stanza.

Turning and turning in the widening gyre
The falcon cannot hear the falconer;
Things fall apart; the centre cannot hold;
Mere **anarchy** is loosed upon the world,
5   The blood-dimmed tide is loosed, and everywhere
The ceremony of innocence is drowned;
The best lack all **conviction,** while the worst
Are full of passionate **intensity.**

Surely some **revelation** is at hand;
10   Surely the Second Coming is at hand.
The Second Coming! Hardly are those words out
When a vast image out of *Spiritus Mundi*
Troubles my sight: somewhere in sands of the desert
A shape with lion body and the head of a man,
15   A gaze blank and pitiless as the sun,
Is moving its slow thighs, while all about it
Reel shadows of the **indignant** desert birds.
The darkness drops again; but now I know
That twenty centuries of stony sleep
20   Were **vexed** to nightmare by a rocking cradle,
And what rough beast, its hour come round at last,
Slouches towards Bethlehem to be born?

The ceremony of innocence refers to the customs on which a society is based.

Which metaphors and symbols tell about the age that is ending? Which tell about the coming age?

The image of the *rocking cradle* and the reference to *Bethlehem* are allusions to the birth of Jesus.

anarchy lawless disorder

conviction strong belief

intensity focused strength

revelation time in which truth or reality becomes known

indignant angry

vexed troubled

slouches creeps, sneaks

Directions Choose the letter of the best answer or write the answer using complete sentences.

Comprehension: Identifying Facts

1. In the first two lines, the thing that is circling is _____.

   A a hunter   C war

   B a bird   D a bomber

2. What does the poet believe is about to happen?

3. What does the poet see in his imagination?

Comprehension: Putting Ideas Together

4. The symbol in the first two lines of this poem represents _____.

   A the ending of a cycle of history

   B mankind and nature

   C war and its suffering

   D the coming of Christ

5. The poem begins by recognizing the chaos and confusion in the world. How have people reacted to this?

6. How does the poet feel about this new age? How can you tell?

Understanding Literature: Metaphor, Symbol, Consonance, Allusion, and Theme

Metaphors show how one thing is like another (without using *like* or *as*). Symbols are things, places, or people that stand for something else. Consonance is the repetition of consonant sounds. Allusions remind readers of ideas from history and literature. These tools help a poet tell the theme, or main idea.

7. What consonant sounds are repeated in lines 7–8 and 19–20? How do these sounds affect the meaning of these lines?

8. Find an example of a metaphor, a symbol, and an allusion in the poem. How does each help support the theme?

Critical Thinking

9. In the second stanza, Yeats symbolizes a new era by a "rough beast." What do his details suggest this age will be like?

Thinking Creatively

10. Yeats uses Christian imagery, but the new age he sees does not seem Christian. What do you think is the "character" of our time? What symbols would you use to show this?

Grammar Check

A clause contains a subject and a verb and is used as part of a sentence. A clause that can stand alone as a sentence is called an independent clause. A clause that cannot stand alone is called a dependent clause. Clauses may be joined by conjunctions such as *and, but,* or *because* or by a semicolon (;). "Things fall apart; the center cannot hold" contains two independent clauses.

- Find another example of clauses joined by a semicolon in the poem.

- Analyze the clauses that appear in lines 7–8. Which one is an independent clause? Which one is dependent?

- Write a sentence of your own that contains two or more clauses.

Writing on Your Own

According to the Bible, the Second Coming of Christ will bring an era of peace. Write a paragraph explaining how Yeats's use of this phrase is ironic. That is, tell how he uses it with a meaning opposite to its usual meaning. Begin with a topic sentence. Then present your explanation. Put your supporting details in a logical order.

Speaking and Listening

In a small group, discuss what you think these things stand for in Yeats's poem: (1) the falcon and falconer and (2) the figure with a lion's body and man's head. Speak clearly when you present your ideas. Refer to the context of the poem and your own knowledge of history to support your ideas. Listen carefully to others' ideas. As a group, make a chart showing possible meanings for these symbols. Study the chart and decide which meanings the poet most likely intended.

Media and Technology

Look through headline stories in a newspaper and major news stories on TV or the Internet. Summarize the content of five stories you think are most important. Do these reports seem to prove or disprove Yeats's thinking that "anarchy is loosed upon the world"? Explain your thinking.

BEFORE READING THE SELECTION

Shooting an Elephant   by George Orwell

George Orwell
1903–1949

Objectives

- To read and understand an essay
- To define irony and point out examples in the selection
- To recognize the effect of figurative language in a work of literature

About the Author

George Orwell was the pen name (a name used by writers who did not want their real names to be public) of Eric Blair. He was born in 1903 in Bengal, India, where his father was a government employee. Orwell was sent to boarding schools in England, including a very competitive school called Eton. From 1922 to 1927, he served with the Indian Imperial Police in Burma (now called Myanmar).

Orwell wrote novels and essays that warned against holding power unjustly and ruling cruelly. His most famous books were *Animal Farm* (1945) and *1984* (1948). *Animal Farm* is a story that warns of the outcome of Communism. *1984* presents a frightening picture of a society mistreated by its government.

Orwell was middle class and well educated. However, he chose to live among the working class. Because he sought to change what he disliked about society, he sought out experiences among the poor. Most of his writings are drawn from his experiences. For example, "Shooting an Elephant" reports one of his experiences as a police officer in Burma.

Near the end of his life, Orwell married. However, he had a lung disease that caused his death at the age of 46.

About the Selection

"Shooting an Elephant" appeared in Orwell's 1950 book of the same name. All the book's writings reported on the behavior of colonial officers in India. This selection shows Orwell's precise, clear style. Orwell wanted his writing to be free of falseness and pretending. He believed that being precise in writing and thinking helped protect individuals against the misuse of political power.

Literary Terms An **essay** is a kind of nonfiction writing in which the writer expresses personal beliefs or opinions. "Shooting an Elephant" is an informal essay. In this kind of writing, the writer speaks to the reader in a personal, conversational way. Much of this essay's impact comes from **irony.** This is **figurative language** or situations in which the thing that is said or that happens is the opposite of what is expected.

Reading on Your Own In this essay, Orwell shows how natives of Burma and British government officials interact. As you read about the behavior of people in each of these groups, think about what causes them to act this way. How do they affect each other?

Writing on Your Own In Orwell's time, the British controlled the countries in their empire through imperialism. British officials managed the government and economy of these nations. Write a paragraph describing how the people in those nations probably felt about the British.

Vocabulary Focus When writing about other cultures, authors often use words from those cultures. For example, in this essay, Orwell uses the words *Raj, mahout, Dravidian,* and *sahib. Raj* means "government or rule." *Mahout* is the word for a person who keeps and controls an elephant. *Dravidian* names a group of people in southern India. They make up most of the population. *Sahib* is a title Indians used during the colonial period to address a man from the West.

Think Before You Read What feelings about the Burmese people and the British officers do you think Orwell will express?

essay a written work that shows a writer's opinion on some basic or current issue

irony difference between what is expected to happen in a story and what does happen; the use of words that seem to say one thing but mean the opposite

figurative language writing or speech not meant to be understood exactly as it is written

Shooting an Elephant

As you read, notice that Orwell feels inner conflict. How do his feelings about the Burmese and about his role conflict?

Betel juice is a liquid produced by chewing the leaves and nuts of the betel plant, a type of pepper.

In Moulmein, in lower Burma, I was hated by large numbers of people—the only time in my life that I have been important enough for this to happen to me. I was sub-divisional police officer of the town, and in an **aimless, petty** kind of way anti-European feeling was very bitter. No one had the guts to raise a riot, but if a European woman went through the **bazaars** alone somebody would probably spit betel juice over her dress. As a police officer I was an obvious target and was **baited** whenever it seemed safe to do so. When a **nimble** Burman tripped me up on the football field and the referee (another Burman) looked the other way, the crowd yelled with hideous laughter. This happened more than once. In the end the **sneering** yellow faces of young men that met me everywhere, the insults hooted after me when I was at a safe distance, got badly on my nerves. The young Buddhist priests were the worst of all. There were several thousands of them in the town and none of them seemed to have anything to do except stand on street corners and jeer at Europeans.

All this was **perplexing** and upsetting. For at that time I had already made up my mind that imperialism was an evil thing and the sooner I chucked up my job and got out of it

aimless without a goal

petty small and mean

bazaars outdoor markets

baited did something to get someone else to react

nimble quick

sneering showing dislike and scorn

perplexing puzzling

the better. Theoretically—and secretly, of course—I was all for the Burmese and all against their **oppressors,** the British. As for the job I was doing, I hated it more bitterly than I can perhaps make clear. In a job like that you see the dirty work of Empire at close quarters. The wretched prisoners huddling in the stinking cages of the lock-ups, the gray, **cowed** faces of the long-term convicts, the scarred buttocks of the men who had been flogged with bamboos—all these oppressed me with an **intolerable** sense of guilt. But I could get nothing into **perspective.** I was young and ill educated and I had had to think out my problems in the utter silence that is imposed on every Englishman in the East. I did not even know that the British Empire is dying, still less did I know that it is a great deal better than the younger empires that are going to **supplant** it. All I knew was that I was stuck between my hatred of the empire I served and my rage against the evil-spirited little beasts who tried to make my job impossible. With one part of my mind I thought of the British Raj as an unbreakable tyranny, as something clamped down, IN SAECULA SAECULORUM, upon the will of **prostrate** peoples; with another part I thought that the greatest joy in the world would be to drive a bayonet into a Buddhist priest's guts. Feelings like these are the normal by-products of imperialism; ask any Anglo-Indian official, if you can catch him off duty.

One day something happened which in a roundabout way was enlightening. It was a tiny incident in itself, but it gave me a better glimpse than I had had before of the real nature of imperialism—the real motives for which **despotic** governments act. Early one morning the sub-inspector at a police station the other end of the town rang me up

What is ironic about Orwell's hatred for British oppressors?

At the time of this story, British world power was decreasing while Communism was spreading.

The Latin phrase *in saecula saeculorum* means "forever and ever."

oppressors those who abuse their power over others	**intolerable** not bearable	**prostrate** flat and face down; bowing low
cowed frightened; beaten down	**perspective** reasonable mental view	**despotic** ruling unfairly or cruelly
	supplant replace	

What problems might Orwell encounter as he reaches the place where the elephant has caused damage?

Must is an annual period of aggressiveness in male elephants, related to mating, during which the animals can become violent.

on the phone and said that an elephant was **ravaging** the bazaar. Would I please come and do something about it? I did not know what I could do, but I wanted to see what was happening and I got on to a pony and started out. I took my rifle, an old .44 Winchester and much too small to kill an elephant, but I thought the noise might be useful IN TERROREM. Various Burmans stopped me on the way and told me about the elephant's doings. It was not, of course, a wild elephant, but a tame one which had gone "must." It had been chained up, as tame elephants always are when their attack of "must" is due, but on the previous night it had broken its chain and escaped. Its **mahout,** the only person who could manage it when it was in that state, had set out in pursuit, but had taken the wrong direction and was now twelve hours' journey away, and in the morning the elephant had suddenly reappeared in the town. The Burmese population had no weapons and were quite helpless against it. It had already destroyed somebody's bamboo hut, killed a cow and raided some fruit-stalls and devoured the stock; also it had met the **municipal** rubbish van and, when the driver jumped out and took to his heels, had turned the van over and **inflicted** violences upon it.

The Burmese sub-inspector and some Indian constables were waiting for me in the quarter where the elephant had been seen. It was a very poor quarter, a **labyrinth** of squalid bamboo huts, **thatched** with palmleaf, winding all over a steep hillside. I remember that it was a cloudy, stuffy morning at the beginning of the rains. We began questioning the people as to where the elephant had gone and, as usual, failed to get any definite information. That is **invariably** the case in the East; a story always sounds clear enough at a distance, but the nearer you get to the scene of events the vaguer it

---

ravaging causing damage to

mahout elephant keeper

municipal belonging to a town or city

inflicted caused

labyrinth maze

thatched roofed

invariably always

becomes. Some of the people said that the elephant had gone in one direction, some said that he had gone in another, some **professed** not even to have heard of any elephant. I had almost made up my mind that the whole story was a pack of lies, when we heard yells a little distance away. There was a loud, **scandalized** cry of "Go away, child! Go away this instant!" and an old woman with a switch in her hand came round the corner of a hut, violently shooing away a crowd of naked children. Some more women followed, clicking their tongues and exclaiming; evidently there was something that the children ought not to have seen. I rounded the hut and saw a man's dead body sprawling in the mud. He was an Indian, a black Dravidian coolie, almost naked, and he could not have been dead many minutes. The people said that the elephant had come suddenly upon him round the corner of the hut, caught him with its trunk, put its foot on his back and ground him into the earth. This was the rainy season and the ground was soft, and his face had scored a trench a foot deep and a couple of yards long. He was lying on his belly with arms **crucified** and head sharply twisted to one side. His face was coated with mud, the eyes wide open, the teeth bared and grinning with an expression of **unendurable** agony. (Never tell me, by the way, that the dead look peaceful. Most of the corpses I have seen looked devilish.) The friction of the great beast's foot had stripped the skin from his back as neatly as one skins a rabbit. As soon as I saw the dead man I sent an **orderly** to a friend's house nearby to borrow an elephant rifle. I had already sent back the pony, not wanting it to go mad with fright and throw me if it smelt the elephant.

The orderly came back in a few minutes with a rifle and five **cartridges,** and meanwhile some Burmans had arrived and told us that the elephant was in the **paddy fields**

Dravidian refers to a dark-skinned people from southern India. The term *coolie* comes from a Hindi (Indian) word that means "laborer." It usually referred to an unskilled worker. The word is now considered offensive.

How does the man's death make Orwell's situation more difficult?

professed claimed

scandalized outraged

crucified stretched out and pinned down

unendurable unbearable

orderly assistant

cartridges small containers that hold bullets and gunpowder

paddy fields flooded areas of land used for growing rice

below, only a few hundred yards away. As I started forward practically the whole population of the quarter flocked out of the houses and followed me. They had seen the rifle and were all shouting excitedly that I was going to shoot the elephant. They had not shown much interest in the elephant when he was merely ravaging their homes, but it was different now that he was going to be shot. It was a bit of fun to them, as it would be to an English crowd; besides they wanted the meat. It made me vaguely uneasy. I had no intention of shooting the elephant—I had merely sent for the rifle to defend myself if necessary—and it is always **unnerving** to have a crowd following you. I marched down the hill, looking and feeling a fool, with the rifle over my shoulder and an ever-growing army of people **jostling** at my heels. At the bottom, when you got away from the huts, there was a **metalled** road and beyond that a **miry** waste of paddy fields a thousand yards across, not yet ploughed but soggy from the first rains and dotted with coarse grass. The elephant was standing eight yards from the road, his left side toward us. He took not the slightest notice of the crowd's approach. He was tearing up bunches of grass, beating them against his knees to clean them, and stuffing them into his mouth.

I had halted on the road. As soon as I saw the elephant I knew with perfect certainty that I ought not to shoot him. It is a serious matter to shoot a working elephant—it is comparable to destroying a huge and costly piece of machinery—and obviously one ought not to do it if it can possibly be avoided. And at that distance, peacefully eating, the elephant looked no more dangerous than a cow. I thought then and I think now that his attack of "must" was already passing off; in which case he would merely wander harmlessly about until the mahout came back and caught him. Moreover, I did not in the least want to shoot him. I decided that I would watch him for a little while to make sure that he did not turn savage again, and then go home.

Notice how the crowd of natives and their expectations affect Orwell. Why do you think this is so?

---

unnerving upsetting   **jostling** crowding and pushing   **metalled** paved

miry muddy

But at that moment I glanced round at the crowd that had followed me. It was an immense crowd, two thousand at the least and growing every minute. It blocked the road for a long distance on either side. I looked at the sea of yellow faces above the **garish** clothes—faces all happy and excited over this bit of fun, all certain that the elephant was going to be shot. They were watching me as they would watch a **conjurer** about to perform a trick. They did not like me, but with the magical rifle in my hands I was momentarily worth watching. And suddenly I realized that I should have to shoot the elephant after all. The people expected it of me and I had got to do it; I could feel their two thousand wills pressing me forward, irresistibly. And it was at this moment, as I stood there with the rifle in my hands, that I first grasped the hollowness, the **futility** of the white man's **dominion** in the East. Here was I, the white man with his gun, standing in front of the unarmed native crowd—seemingly the leading actor of the piece; but in reality I was only an absurd puppet pushed to and fro by the will of those yellow faces behind. I perceived in this moment that when the white man turns **tyrant** it is his own freedom that he destroys. He becomes a sort of hollow, posing dummy, the **conventionalized** figure of a sahib. For it is the condition of his rule that he shall spend his life in trying to impress the "natives," and so in every crisis he has go to do what the "natives" expect of him. He wears a mask, and his face grows to fit it. I had got to shoot the elephant. I had committed myself to doing it when I sent for the rifle. A sahib has got to act like a sahib; he has got to appear **resolute,** to know his own mind and do definite things. To come all that way, rifle in hand, with two thousand people marching at my heels, and then to trail feebly away, having done nothing—no, that was impossible. The crowd would laugh at me. And my whole life, every white man's life in the East, was one long struggle not to be laughed at.

> What is ironic about Orwell's position of power in this situation?

> According to Orwell, what makes the *white man* a helpless victim of his own attempt to be all-powerful?

> *Sahib* was a title used to address European men in colonial India.

garish bright	**dominion** control and authority	**conventionalized** expected
conjurer magician		
futility uselessness	**tyrant** cruel ruler	**resolute** set in one's mind

But I did not want to shoot the elephant. I watched him beating his bunch of grass against his knees with that **preoccupied** grandmotherly air that elephants have. It seemed to me that it would be murder to shoot him. At that age I was not **squeamish** about killing animals, but I had never shot an elephant and never wanted to. (Somehow it always seems worse to kill a *large* animal.) Besides, there was the beast's owner to be considered. Alive, the elephant was worth at least a hundred pounds; dead, he would only be worth the value of his tusks, five pounds, possibly. But I had got to act quickly. I turned to some experienced-looking Burmans who had been there when we arrived, and asked them how the elephant had been behaving. They all said the same thing: he took no notice of you if you left him alone, but he might **charge** if you went too close to him.

It was perfectly clear to me what I ought to do. I ought to walk up to within, say, twenty-five yards of the elephant and test his behavior. If he charged, I could shoot; if he took no notice of me, it would be safe to leave him until the mahout came back. But also I knew that I was going to do no such thing. I was a poor shot with a rifle and the ground was soft mud into which one would sink at every step. If the elephant charged and I missed him, I should have about as much chance as a toad under a steam-roller. But even then I was not thinking particularly of my own skin, only of the watchful yellow faces behind. For at that moment, with the crowd watching me, I was not afraid in the ordinary sense, as I would have been if I had been alone. A white man mustn't be frightened in front of "natives"; and so, in general, he isn't frightened. The **sole** thought in my mind was that if anything went wrong those two thousand Burmans would see me pursued, caught, trampled on, and reduced to a grinning corpse like that Indian up the hill. And if that happened it

Why does Orwell not move closer to the elephant? How would it help if he could?

preoccupied lost in thought

squeamish nervous; afraid

charge run toward something with force

sole only

was quite probable that some of them would laugh. That would never do. There was only one **alternative.** I shoved the cartridges into the **magazine** and lay down on the road to get a better aim.

The crowd grew very still, and a deep, low, happy sigh, as of people who see the theater curtain go up at last, breathed from **innumerable** throats. They were going to have their bit of fun after all. The rifle was a beautiful German thing with cross-hair sights. I did not then know that in shooting an elephant one would shoot to cut an imaginary bar running from ear-hole to ear-hole. I ought, therefore, as the elephant was sideways on, to have aimed straight at his ear-hole; actually I aimed several inches in front of this, thinking the brain would be further forward.

When I pulled the trigger I did not hear the bang or feel the kick—one never does when a shot goes home—but I heard the devilish roar of glee that went up from the crowd. In that instant, in too short a time, one would have thought, even for the bullet to get there, a mysterious, terrible change had come over the elephant. He neither stirred nor fell, but every line of his body had **altered.** He looked suddenly **stricken,** shrunken, immensely old, as though the frightful impact of the bullet had paralyzed him without knocking him down. At last, after what seemed a long time—it might have been five seconds, I dare say—he sagged **flabbily** to his knees. His mouth slobbered. An enormous **senility** seemed to have settled upon him. One could have imagined him thousands of years old. I fired again into the same spot. At the second shot he did not collapse but climbed with desperate slowness to his feet and stood weakly upright, with legs sagging and head drooping. I fired a third time. That was the shot that did for him. You could see the agony of it jolt his whole body and knock the last

Orwell does not know how to kill the elephant without causing it great pain. How is this situation ironic?

How does Orwell make the crowd seem inhuman? How does he make the elephant seem human?

---

alternative choice

magazine part of a weapon that holds the bullets

innumerable countless

altered changed

stricken suffering

flabbily weakly

senility frailty due to old age

remnant of strength from his legs. But in falling he seemed for a moment to rise, for as his hind legs collapsed beneath him he seemed to tower upward like a huge rock toppling, his trunk reaching skyward like a tree. He trumpeted, for the first and only time. And then down he came, his belly toward me, with a crash that seemed to shake the ground even where I lay.

Notice the exact description of the elephant's death. What effect does Orwell want to achieve with it?

I got up. The Burmans were already racing past me across the mud. It was obvious that the elephant would never rise again, but he was not dead. He was breathing very **rhythmically** with long rattling gasps, his great mound of a side painfully rising and falling. His mouth was wide open—I could see far down into **caverns** of pale pink throat. I waited a long time for him to die, but his breathing did not weaken. Finally I fired my two remaining shots into the spot where I thought his heart must be. The thick blood welled out of him like red velvet, but still he did not die. His body did not even jerk when the shots hit him, the tortured breathing continued without a pause. He was dying, very slowly and in great agony, but in some world **remote** from me where not even a bullet could damage him further. I felt that I had got to put an end to that dreadful noise. It seemed dreadful to see the great beast lying there, powerless to move and yet powerless to die, and not even to be able to finish him. I sent back for my small rifle and poured shot after shot into his heart and down his throat. They seemed to make no **impression.** The tortured gasps continued as steadily as the ticking of a clock.

In the end I could not stand it any longer and went away. I heard later that it took him half an hour to die. Burmans were bringing **dahs** and baskets even before I left, and I was told they had stripped his body almost to the bones by the afternoon.

remnant leftover part	**caverns** caves	**impression** effect
rhythmically steadily	**remote** far away	**dahs** large knives

Afterward, of course, there were endless discussions about the shooting of the elephant. The owner was furious, but he was only an Indian and could do nothing. Besides, legally I had done the right thing, for a mad elephant has to be killed, like a mad dog, if its owner fails to control it. Among the Europeans opinion was divided. The older men said I was right, the younger men said it was a damn shame to shoot an elephant for killing a coolie, because an elephant was worth more than any damn Coringhee coolie. And afterward I was very glad that the coolie had been killed; it put me legally in the right and it gave me a sufficient **pretext** for shooting the elephant. I often wondered whether any of the others grasped that I had done it solely to avoid looking a fool.

What is ironic about the Europeans' reaction to Orwell's killing the elephant? What might the elephant symbolize?

Coringhee may refer to someone from the seaport of Coringa in British-controlled India.

Elephant Stacking Timber in Burma, 1928

pretext excuse

AFTER READING THE SELECTION

Shooting an Elephant   by George Orwell

Directions Choose the letter of the best answer or write the answer using complete sentences.

Comprehension: Identifying Facts

1. Where does this incident take place?
   A southern India   **C** Africa
   B lower Burma   **D** Coringa

2. Orwell is about to decide the story is not true when he finds _____.
   A the body of a coolie the elephant has trampled
   B a man who tells him where the elephant is now
   C a large crowd surrounding the elephant
   D the elephant rampaging through the neighborhood

3. What is Orwell's job? In what city does he work?

4. Why does Orwell feel guilty?

5. What makes him hate the Burmese?

6. Why does Orwell take a rifle with him when he goes to see about the elephant?

7. Why does Orwell send for the elephant gun?

8. Why does the crowd become excited when the elephant gun arrives?

9. How does Orwell know he will have to shoot the elephant?

10. What two opinions do the Europeans have about the shooting of the elephant?

Comprehension: Putting Ideas Together

11. The actions of the Burmese toward the Europeans show _____.
    A admiration   **C** puzzlement
    B fear   **D** resentment

12. The main thing Orwell hates about the Burmese is _____.
    A their culture
    B their silence
    C their laughing at him
    D their fear of him

13. What does Orwell hate about imperialism?

14. From the facts you learned, do you think the elephant should have been shot? Why or why not?

15. Who has more control in this situation, Orwell or the native Burmese? Why?

16. How do Orwell's intentions change during the incident?

17. What emotions do the Burmese feel toward the British? What tells you this?

18. What does this statement mean: "A sahib has got to act like a sahib."

19. How would you describe the elephant's death?

20. How do European reactions to the shooting illustrate Orwell's thinking that imperialism is "an evil thing"?

Understanding Literature: Symbol and Irony

This essay uses irony effectively. Events take a turn that is the opposite of what is expected. It also uses symbols. The elephant and the gun that kill it represent something more than themselves.

21. What is ironic about Orwell being a police officer in Burma?

22. What is ironic about the peacefulness of the elephant?

23. What is ironic about Orwell deciding he must shoot the elephant?

24. What do the elephant and the gun symbolize?

25. What tone does Orwell take in the first and last paragraphs of the essay?

Critical Thinking

26. List at least two ways in which this essay shows problems of imperial rule.

27. What does Orwell mean when he says the incident was "enlightening"?

28. Orwell says that he was like "an absurd puppet" of the crowd. Do you agree?

29. Orwell wrote this essay years after he had shot the elephant. Do you think his attitudes and ideas had changed? How does he seem to view his younger self?

Thinking Creatively

30. Do you think it was wrong to shoot the elephant? Why or why not?

After Reading **continued on next page**

Shooting an Elephant   *by George Orwell*

✓ Grammar Check

An interesting writing style uses a variety of sentence lengths and styles. "Shooting an Elephant" contains a mixture of short and long sentences. The contrast creates drama and holds interest. For example, Orwell places these sentences side by side: "I had halted on the road. As soon as I saw the elephant I knew with perfect certainty that I ought not to shoot him." The short sentence focuses on action. It has only a subject, verb, and prepositional phrase. The long sentence explains Orwell's thinking. It is complex and has one independent clause and two dependent clauses.

- Find at least one more example of paired short and long sentences in the essay.

- Write the sentences and compare their length and contents.

- Explain the effect of this combination of different types of sentences.

Writing on Your Own

Pick a sentence from the essay that you think expresses Orwell's theme. Write an essay telling why you chose this statement. Include supporting details from the essay to support your choice.

Speaking

Locate photographs, articles, and TV programs or films that inform about elephants. Use the visuals and information to gain a good idea of what an elephant is like. Prepare a short talk to inform your classmates.

Listening

Write down three questions you have after reading this essay. In a small group, ask your questions. Listen carefully to what classmates say. If the group cannot answer them, discuss where the answers might be found.

Research

Orwell fought in the Spanish Civil War in the 1930s. Research the causes and results of this war. Write a paragraph summarizing what the war was about. Tell why you think Orwell fought.

BEFORE READING THE SELECTION

The Hollow Men   by T. S. Eliot

About the Author

Thomas Stearns Eliot was born in Saint Louis, Missouri, in 1888 into a socially important family. He was educated at Harvard University and studied in Paris and London. He settled in England in 1914. In 1927, he became a British citizen.

Eliot burst on the poetry scene with a style, techniques, and subject matter no one had used before. He was the most influential poet writing in the first half of the 20th century. His originality at first shocked readers. However, his work seemed to express perfectly the doubt that followed the Victorian Era. Important works, such as *The Waste Land* (1922), spoke about the lack of values many felt after World War I. A late poem, *Four Quartets* (1936–1942), has a more hopeful tone.

Eliot also wrote verse dramas. His light verse *Old Possum's Book of Practical Cats* (1939) was adapted to create the musical comedy *Cats* (1981). Eliot received the Nobel Prize for Literature in 1948. He died of a lung disease in 1965.

About the Selection

In "The Hollow Men," Eliot expresses what it feels like not to believe in anything and yet to want to believe in something. Much hard thinking went into making the poem, and the reader must think hard to understand it. Some statements seem unconnected. This is because Eliot has not explained the connections between his ideas. It is the reader's job to piece together the logic of the ideas.

T. S. Eliot
1888–1965

Objectives

■ To read and understand a free verse poem

■ To explain the effects of repetition in a poem

Before Reading continued on next page

The Hollow Men by T. S. Eliot

free verse poetry that does not have a strict rhyming pattern or regular line length and uses actual speech patterns for the rhythms of sound

repetition using a word, phrase, or image more than once, for emphasis

Literary Terms This poem does not use traditional rhythms. It is **free verse** and has no regular rhythm or rhyme. Instead, it takes its rhythms from the way people actually speak. Eliot uses **repetition,** or repeated words and phrases, to emphasize ideas.

Reading on Your Own "The Hollow Men" is divided into five sections. Pause after reading each section and think about its allusions and images. What idea about "the hollow men" does it express?

Writing on Your Own Think of an idea, image, or comparison that represents sadness to you. Write a brief poem in free verse that uses this idea to tell about experiencing sadness.

Vocabulary Focus Poetry uses words in unusual ways. Readers therefore need to pay attention to how and why the writer chooses certain words. For example, compound words such as *headpiece* and *crowskin* call to mind pictures that are more vivid than *top* or *bumpy.* Eliot chooses words very carefully to create a powerful effect. As you read, think about new or unusual words in the poem. What images do they create in your mind? How are they related to other words in the poem?

Think Before You Read What characteristics do you expect Eliot's "hollow men" to have?

The Hollow Men

I

We are the hollow men
We are the stuffed men
Leaning together
Headpiece filled with straw. Alas!
5 Our dried voices, when
We whisper together
Are quiet and meaningless
As wind in dry grass
Or rats' feet over broken glass
10 In our dry cellar

Shape without form, shade without colour,
Paralysed force, gesture without motion;

Those who have crossed
With direct eyes, to death's other Kingdom
15 Remember us—if at all—not as lost
Violent souls, but only
As the hollow men
The stuffed men.

As you read, notice the kinds of adjectives used to describe the men. What seems to be lacking in their character and lives?

Lines 11–14 refer to Dante's *Divine Comedy.* In this long poem written in the 1300s, Dante makes an imaginary journey through purgatory (a place of temporary punishment), hell (a place of eternal punishment), and paradise (heaven). Those with *direct eyes* (line 14) are the blessed souls in paradise.

paralysed without the ability to move

II

Eyes I dare not meet in dreams
20 In death's dream kingdom
These do not appear:
There, the eyes are
Sunlight on a broken column
There, is a tree swinging
25 And voices are
In the wind's singing
More distant and more solemn
Than a fading star.

Let me be no nearer
30 In death's dream kingdom
Let me also wear
Such deliberate disguises
Rat's coat, crowskin, crossed **staves**
In a field
35 Behaving as the wind behaves
No nearer—

Not that final meeting
In the twilight kingdom

III

This is the dead land
40 This is cactus land
Here the stone images
Are raised, here they receive
The **supplication** of a dead man's hand
Under the twinkle of a fading star.

Death's dream kingdom appears to refer to death by illusion. The hollow men are cut off from life's reality.

Crossed staves/In a field refers to scarecrows. How is a scarecrow a fitting symbol for the people Eliot is describing?

The *dead land* where the hollow men dwell has no spiritual presence. It is a place where people feel no connection with nature, either.

staves rods or staffs   **supplication** prayer, plea

45 Is it like this
In death's other kingdom
Waking alone
At the hour when we are
Trembling with tenderness
50 Lips that would kiss
Form prayers to broken stone.

IV
The eyes are not here
There are no eyes here
In this valley of dying stars
55 In this hollow valley
This broken jaw of our lost kingdoms

In this last of meeting places
We **grope** together
And avoid speech
60 Gathered on this beach of the **tumid** river

Sightless, unless
The eyes reappear
As the **perpetual** star
Multifoliate rose
65 Of death's twilight kingdom
The hope only
Of empty men.

V
Here we go round the prickly pear
Prickly pear prickly pear
70 *Here we go round the prickly pear*
At five o'clock in the morning.

The *tumid river* (line 60) is the River Acheron in Dante's *Divine Comedy.* Dead souls on their way to hell must cross this river to enter the land of the dead.

Dante describes paradise as a rose with many petals (*multifoliate*).

Lines 68–71 mimic a popular nursery rhyme, "Here We Go Round the Mulberry Bush." The *prickly pear* (cactus) contrasts with the rose of paradise.

grope fumble and feel about for

tumid swollen

perpetual everlasting

multifoliate having many leaves, petals, or layers

Lines 72–76 refer to Shakespeare's *Julius Caesar:* "Between the acting of a dreadful thing/And the first motion, all the interim is/Like a phantasma or a hideous dream."

Between the idea
And the reality
Between the motion
75 And the act
Falls the Shadow

For Thine is the Kingdom

Between the **conception**
And the creation
80 Between the emotion
And the response
Falls the Shadow

Life is very long

Between the desire
85 And the **spasm**
Between the **potency**
And the existence
Between the **essence**
And the **descent**
90 Falls the Shadow

For Thine is the Kingdom

For Thine is
Life is
For Thine is the

95 *This is the way the world ends*
This is the way the world ends
This is the way the world ends
Not with a bang but a whimper.

For Thine is the Kingdom is part of a prayer in the Bible. The Lord's Prayer, as it is known, ends with "For thine is the kingdom, and the power, and the glory, forever and ever."

What words, phrases, and ideas are repeated in Part V? How does this repetition add to or change the meaning of the poem?

conception beginning of an idea	**spasm** shudder; sudden motion	**essence** core; most basic parts
	potency strength	**descent** fall; decline

Directions Choose the letter of the best answer or write the answer using complete sentences.

Comprehension: Identifying Facts

1. In Part I, the poet compares the "hollow men" to _____.

A rats

B scarecrows

C those who died from violence

D those who see clearly

2. What do the lips "trembling with tenderness" (line 49) do?

3. In Part IV, what gives some hope of a renewed vision (as "eyes reappear")?

Comprehension: Putting Ideas Together

4. In this poem, eyes seem to be connected to _____.

A strength, faith, and vision

B the beauty of Earth

C weakness, tears, and blindness

D the failure of modern society

5. What hope, if any, do the hollow men have of becoming better or more solid?

6. What references to nursery rhymes do you find in this poem? Why do you think Eliot included them?

Understanding Literature: Free Verse, Allusion, and Repetition

This poem is written in free verse, which is meant to sound like human speech. It lacks a regular pattern of rhythm and rhyme. The poem also contains allusions (references to past or fictional acts and people) and repetition (repeating a word, phrase, or image) that add meaning and emphasis.

7. Why is it appropriate for Eliot's hollow men to use simple, unsteady words and repetitions?

8. Why does Eliot refer several times to places and things in Dante's *Divine Comedy?*

Critical Thinking

9. In Part V, again and again "the Shadow" falls between what might be (the idea) and what is (the reality). What do you think this shadow is? What seems to be its final effect?

Thinking Creatively

10. The hollow men seem like walking dead men, unable to feel, see, or communicate. What do you think makes them hollow?

After Reading **continued on next page**

The Hollow Men　by T. S. Eliot

✔ Grammar Check

The adverb *only* can be placed in different places in the same sentence and lead to very different meanings:

The *only* dog belonged to Joan. (There was just one dog.)

The dog belonged *only* to Joan. (The dog belonged to Joan and no one else.)

- Read lines 65–67 again. Does Eliot mean that Dante's rose (salvation, or paradise) is their only hope (their last chance) or only a hope (something to be wished for but not possible)?

- Write what these lines mean in your own words. Why do you think Eliot put the word *only* in a place where its meaning would be uncertain?

Writing on Your Own

Eliot is not concerned with presenting a beautiful world. Do you prefer Eliot's style or that of a traditional Victorian poet such as Tennyson? Write an essay to persuade your classmates that one of these types of poetry is better. Give your reasons in order of importance. Develop them with details from poems.

Speaking and Listening

In a small group, prepare a dramatic reading of "The Hollow Men." Pick sound effects your group can use as background for the reading. Decide if you want to use props or costumes. Discuss the appropriate expression, posture, and gestures for this poem. Listen to ideas from all members of your group and try to find a way to combine them. Assign lines and decide which parts should be read by one person, two people, and so on. After you have practiced, present your reading.

Research

Use library books and encyclopedias to learn about the art of the 1920s, when Eliot wrote "The Hollow Men." What details about this art seem to match Eliot's ideas and tone? What new methods did artists use that could be compared to Eliot's inventive use of language?

BEFORE READING THE SELECTION

The Duchess and the Jeweller   by Virginia Woolf

About the Author

Virginia Woolf was born in 1882 in London into a family of scholars and writers. Her life seemed charmed, for she spent much time with the brightest and best writers and artists. In 1912, she married Leonard Woolf, also a writer and editor. The Woolfs' home became a center where many talented writers, artists, and thinkers met.

Woolf had many losses in her life and developed mental illness. First her mother, and then a close aunt, died when Woolf was a teenager. Her father died of cancer in 1904. When her brother died in 1906, she had a mental breakdown. It was the first of several serious breakdowns that led her to kill herself in 1941 at the age of 59.

Woolf was a gifted novelist, essayist, and critic. She was also a leader in a literary movement called Modernism. Woolf used a technique in which she followed the thought processes of the people in her stories. This allowed her to represent life in the same way people experience it. Through their thoughts, characters revealed themselves. Woolf captured each moment in time from the inside out. Among her most famous novels are *Mrs. Dalloway* (1925), *To the Lighthouse* (1927), and *The Waves* (1931). Her new technique allowed her to reveal women's experience and criticize the social system using powerful, poetic language.

About the Selection

"The Duchess and the Jeweller" tells a story through the thoughts and experiences of one man. The story does not have much of a plot. However, it is still rich in detail and personality as the narrator presents the flow of the man's thoughts and his reactions to others.

Virginia Woolf
1882–1941

Objectives

- To read and understand a short story
- To recognize a writer's use of stream of consciousness
- To identify similes and metaphors and explain their effect
- To understand characterization and draw conclusions about a character

Before Reading continued on next page

short story
a brief work of prose fiction that includes plot, setting, characters, point of view, and theme

stream of consciousness
a writing technique that develops the plot by allowing the reader to see how and what the characters are thinking

character
a person or animal in a story, poem, or play

characterization
the way a writer develops character qualities and personality traits

simile a figure of speech in which two things are compared using a phrase that includes the word *like* or *as*

Literary Terms "The Duchess and the Jeweller" is a **short story,** or a brief work of fiction. In it, Woolf uses a technique called **stream of consciousness.** This is a method that develops the plot, or action of the story, by letting readers see what a **character** (person in the story) is thinking. The details about the main character are part of his **characterization.**

Woolf uses **simile** and metaphor to give an idea of what characters are like. A simile compares two unlike things using *like* or *as (his nose was like an elephant's trunk).* A metaphor compares two unlike things directly *(his nose was an elephant's trunk).*

Reading on Your Own The story follows Oliver Bacon as he goes to his store and has a meeting with a duchess. As you read, pay attention to the way he thinks and interacts with people. List several words you think describe his character.

Writing on Your Own Think of a time when you made a promise to another person. Write about the event. Tell how and why you made the promise. Then explain the outcome and how you felt about it.

Vocabulary Focus Woolf names a number of places in London to help set the scene. They are places where the rich and powerful live and work. For example, from his house, Bacon can see Piccadilly, a busy London street filled with entertainment. Bacon gets his clothing made in Savile Row, famous for tailors who make expensive suits. Hatton Garden is the famous jewelry district of London. Mayfair is an upper-class district in western London. Agincourt is a French village where, in 1415, the English defeated the French.

Think Before You Read Oliver Bacon was a poor boy who became rich. What attitude do you think he will have toward wealth and the wealthy?

The Duchess and the JEWELLER

Oliver Bacon lived at the top of a house overlooking the Green Park. He had a flat; chairs jutted out at the right angles—chairs covered in **hide.** Sofas filled the **bays** of the windows—sofas covered in tapestry. The windows, the three long windows, had the proper allowance of **discreet** net and **figured** satin. The mahogany **sideboard** bulged discreetly with the right brandies, whiskeys and liqueurs. And from the middle window he looked down upon the glossy roofs of fashionable cars packed in the narrow **straits** of Piccadilly. A more central position could not be imagined. And at eight in the morning he would have his breakfast brought in on a tray by a manservant; the manservant would unfold his crimson dressing-gown; he would rip his letters open with his long pointed nails and would **extract** thick white cards of invitation upon which the engraving stood up roughly from duchesses, countesses, viscountesses and Honourable Ladies. Then he would wash; then he would eat his toast; then he would read his paper by the bright burning fire of electric coals.

"Behold Oliver," he would say, addressing himself. "You who began life in a filthy little alley, you who . . ." and he would look down at his legs, so shapely in their perfect

As you read, notice the colors and animals that are linked with the jeweler and the duchess. What do these comparisons tell about each character?

Notice how carefully Bacon has put together his home and life. What image does he project?

Much of the story comes through Bacon's thoughts and memories. This is a feature of stream of consciousness writing.

hide the skin of an animal; leather

bays outward curved portions of a window

discreet not calling attention to itself

figured richly decorated or trimmed

sideboard piece of furniture used for storage, especially of glassware or dishes

straits narrow passageways

extract remove

Why might a wealthy man *dismantle himself*, or mentally take apart the image he has built up, to think about his past poverty?

What does Bacon do to show his mother he has some sense?

trousers; at his boots; at his **spats.** They were all shapely, shining; cut from the best cloth by the best scissors in Savile Row. But he **dismantled** himself often and became again a little boy in a dark alley. He had once thought that the height of his ambition—selling stolen dogs to fashionable women in Whitechapel. And once he had been done. "Oh, Oliver," his mother had wailed. "Oh, Oliver! When will you have sense, my son?" . . . Then he had gone behind a counter; had sold cheap watches; then he had taken a **wallet** to Amsterdam. . . . At that memory he would chuckle—the old Oliver remembering the young. Yes, he had done well with the three diamonds; also there was the **commission** on the emerald. After that he went into the private room behind the shop in Hatton Garden; the room with the scales, the safe, the thick magnifying glasses. And then . . . and then . . . He chuckled. When he passed through the knots of jewellers in the hot evening who were discussing prices, gold mines, diamonds, reports from South Africa, one of them would lay a finger to the side of his nose and murmur, "Hum-m-m," as he passed. It was no more than a murmur; no more than a nudge on the shoulder, a finger on the nose, a buzz that ran through the cluster of jewellers in Hatton Garden on a hot afternoon—oh, many years ago now! But still Oliver felt it purring down his spine, the nudge, the murmur that meant, "Look at him— young Oliver, the young jeweller—there he goes." Young he was then. And he dressed better and better; and had, first a **hansom cab;** then a car; and first he went up to the dress circle, then down into the stalls. And he had a **villa** at Richmond, overlooking the river, with **trellises** of red roses; and Mademoiselle used to pick one every morning and stick it in his buttonhole.

spats cloth or leather pieces for covering the top of the foot and the ankle

dismantled took apart; uncovered

wallet folding case

commission fee paid for a service

hansom cab light, two-wheeled, covered carriage

villa large country home and grounds

trellises frame used as a support for climbing plants

"So," said Oliver Bacon, rising and stretching his legs. "So . . ."

And he stood beneath the picture of an old lady on the **mantelpiece** and raised his hands. "I have kept my word," he said, laying his hands together, palm to palm, as if he were doing **homage** to her. "I have won my bet." That was so; he was the richest jeweller in England; but his nose, which was long and flexible, like an elephant's trunk, seemed to say by its curious quiver at the nostrils (but it seemed as if the whole nose quivered, not only the nostrils) that he was not satisfied yet; still smelt something under the ground a little further off. Imagine a giant hog in a pasture rich with **truffles;** after unearthing this truffle and that, still it smells a bigger, a blacker truffle under the ground further off. So Oliver snuffed always in the rich earth of Mayfair another truffle, a blacker, a bigger further off.

Now then he straightened the pearl in his tie, cased himself in his smart blue overcoat; took his yellow gloves and his cane; and swayed as he descended the stairs and half snuffed, half sighed through his long sharp nose as he passed out into Piccadilly. For was he not still a sad man, a dissatisfied man, a man who seeks something that is hidden, though he had won his bet?

He swayed slightly as he walked, as the camel at the zoo sways from side to side when it walks along the asphalt paths **laden** with grocers and their wives eating from paper bags and throwing little bits of silver paper crumpled up on to the path. The camel **despises** the grocers; the camel is dissatisfied with its **lot;** the camel sees the blue lake and the fringe of palm trees in front of it. So the great jeweller, the greatest jeweller in the whole world, swung down Piccadilly, perfectly dressed, with his gloves, with his cane; but dissatisfied still, till he reached the dark little shop, that was famous in France,

> How does Bacon feel about his mother?

> To what two animals is Bacon compared here? What do these comparisons show about him?

> Why do you think Bacon is still not satisfied?

---

mantelpiece beam above a fireplace

homage worship; honor

truffles rare, expensive mushrooms prized for their flavor

laden full

despises hates

lot place in life; destiny

in Germany, in Austria, in Italy, and all over America—the dark little shop in the street off Bond Street.

As usual he strode through the shop without speaking, though the four men, the two old men, Marshall and Spencer, and the two young men, Hammond and Wicks, stood straight behind the counter as he passed and looked at him, envying him. It was only with one finger of the amber-coloured glove, waggling, that he **acknowledged** their presence. And he went in and shut the door of his private room behind him.

Then he unlocked the **grating** that barred the window. The cries of Bond Street came in; the purr of the distant traffic. The light from reflectors at the back of the shop struck upwards. One tree waved six green leaves, for it was June. But Mademoiselle had married Mr. Pedder of the local brewery—no one stuck roses in his buttonhole now.

"So," he half sighed, half snorted, "so . . ."

Then he touched a spring in the wall and slowly the panelling slid open, and behind it were the steel safes, five,

no six of them, all of **burnished** steel. He twisted a key; unlocked one; then another. Each was lined with a pad of deep crimson velvet; in each lay jewels—bracelets, necklaces, rings, **tiaras, ducal coronets;** loose stones in glass shells; rubies, emeralds, pearls, diamonds. All safe, shining, cool, yet burning, eternally, with their own **compressed** light.

What is Bacon's shop like? How does this fit his character?

Mademoiselle, the woman with whom Bacon had a relationship, chose to marry someone else. Why do you think this happened?

acknowledged recognized

grating a metal screen used to close an opening

burnished polished

tiaras women's jeweled headbands

ducal coronets dukes' crowns, smaller than a king's

compressed pressed together tightly

"Tears!" said Oliver, looking at the pearls.

"Heart's blood!" he said, looking at the rubies.

"Gunpowder!" he continued, rattling the diamonds so that they flashed and blazed.

"Gunpowder enough to blow up Mayfair—sky high, high, high!" He threw his head back and made a sound like a horse neighing as he said it.

The telephone buzzed **obsequiously** in a low muted voice on his table. He shut the safe.

"In ten minutes," he said. "Not before." And he sat down at his desk and looked at the heads of the Roman emperors that were graved on his sleeve links. And again he dismantled himself and became once more the little boy playing marbles in the alley where they sell stolen dogs on Sunday. He became that wily **astute** little boy, with lips like wet cherries. He dabbled his fingers in ropes of tripe; he dipped them in pans of frying fish; he dodged in and out among the crowds. He was slim, **lissome,** with eyes like licked stones. And now—now—the hands of the clock ticked on. One, two, three, four. . . The Duchess of Lambourne waited his pleasure; the Duchess of Lambourne, daughter of a hundred Earls. She would wait for ten minutes on a chair at the counter. She would wait his pleasure. She would wait till he was ready to see her. He watched the clock in its **shagreen** case. The hand moved on. With each tick the clock handed him—so it seemed—**pâté de foie gras;** a glass of champagne; another of fine brandy; a cigar costing one **guinea.** The clock laid them on the table beside him, as the ten minutes passed. Then he heard soft slow footsteps approaching; a rustle in the corridor. The door opened. Mr. Hammond flattened himself against the wall.

"Her Grace!" he announced.

And he waited there, flattened against the wall.

To what does Bacon compare the jewels in his safes? What does this suggest about how he got them?

Bacon enjoys making the duchess wait. Why do you think this is so?

obsequiously respectfully	**shagreen** rough, untanned leather	**guinea** British unit of money
astute shrewd	**pâté de foie gras** a spread of chopped goose livers	
lissome quick		

And Oliver, rising, could hear the rustle of the dress of the Duchess as she came down the passage. Then she loomed up, filling the door, filling the room with the aroma, the **prestige,** the arrogance, the pomp, the pride of all the Dukes and Duchesses swollen in one wave. And as a wave breaks, she broke, as she sat down, spreading and splashing and falling over Oliver Bacon the great jeweller, covering him with sparkling bright colours, green, rose, violet; and odours; and **iridescences;** and rays shooting from fingers, nodding from plumes, flashing from silk; for she was very large, very fat, tightly girt in pink **taffeta,** and past her prime. As a **parasol** with many flounces, as a peacock with many feathers, shuts its **flounces,** folds its feathers, so she **subsided** and shut herself as she sank down in the leather armchair.

"Good morning, Mr. Bacon," said the Duchess. And she held out her hand which came through the slit of her white glove. And Oliver bent low as he shook it. And as their hands touched the link was forged between them once more. They were friends, yet enemies; he was master, she was mistress; each cheated the other, each needed the other, each feared the other, each felt this and knew this every time they touched hands thus in the little back room with the white light outside, and the tree with its six leaves, and the sound of the street in the distance and behind them the safes.

"And today, Duchess—what can I do for you today?" said Oliver, very softly.

The Duchess opened; her heart, her private heart, gaped wide. And with a sigh, but no words, she took from her bag a long wash-leather pouch—it looked like a lean yellow **ferret.** And from a slit in the ferret's belly she dropped pearls—ten pearls. They rolled from the slit in the ferret's belly—one, two, three, four—like the eggs of some heavenly bird.

What colors and animals are compared to the duchess? What impression does she make?

The relationship between the jeweler and the duchess is complex. Read to find out why.

Note the word *like* in *it looked like a lean yellow ferret.* This signals that the comparison is a simile.

---

prestige status

iridescences shining, rainbow-like plays of color

taffeta a crisp, shiny fabric

parasol dainty umbrella for keeping off the sun

flounces gathered ruffles used as trim

subsided settled; sunk

ferret small animal related to the weasel

"All that's left me, dear Mr. Bacon," she moaned. Five, six, seven—down they rolled, down the slopes of the vast mountain sides that fell between her knees into one narrow valley—the eighth, the ninth, and the tenth. There they lay in the glow of the peach-blossom taffeta. Ten pearls.

"From the Appleby **cincture**," she mourned. "The last . . . the last of them all."

Oliver stretched out and took one of the pearls between finger and thumb. It was round, it was **lustrous.** But real was it, or false? Was she lying again? Did she dare?

She laid her plump padded finger across her lips. "If the Duke knew . . ." she whispered. "Dear Mr. Bacon, a bit of bad luck . . ."

Been gambling again, had she?

"That villain! That sharper!" she hissed.

The man with the chipped cheek bone? A bad'un. And the Duke was straight as a poker; with side whiskers; would cut her off, shut her up down there if he knew—what I know, thought Oliver, and glanced at the safe.

"Araminta, Daphne, Diana," she moaned. "It's for *them*."

The Ladies Araminta, Daphne, Diana—her daughters. He knew them; adored them. But it was Diana he loved.

"You have all my secrets," she **leered.** Tears slid; tears fell; tears, like diamonds, collecting powder in the ruts of her cherry-blossom cheeks.

"Old friend," she murmured, "old friend."

"Old friend," he repeated, "old friend," as if he licked the words.

"How much?" he **queried.**

She covered the pearls with her hand.

"Twenty thousand," she whispered.

But was it real or false, the one he held in his hand? The Appleby cincture—hadn't she sold it already? He would ring for Spencer or Hammond. "Take it and test it," he would say. He stretched to the bell.

> Why is the duchess dependent on Bacon? How is Bacon dependent on the duchess?

---

cincture sash **leered** looked slyly **queried** asked

lustrous shining

"You will come down tomorrow?" she urged, she interrupted. "The Prime Minister—His Royal Highness . . ." She stopped. "And Diana," she added.

Oliver took his hand off the bell.

He looked past her, at the backs of the houses in Bond Street. But he saw, not the houses in Bond Street, but a **dimpling** river; and trout rising and salmon; and the Prime Minister; and himself too; in white **waistcoats;** and then, Diana. He looked down at the pearl in his hand. But how could he test it, in the light of the river, in the light of the eyes of Diana? But the eyes of the Duchess were on him.

"Twenty thousand," she moaned. "My honour!"

The honour of the mother of Diana! He drew his cheque book towards him; he took out his pen.

"Twenty," he wrote. Then he stopped writing. The eyes of the old woman in the picture were on him—of the old woman, his mother.

"Oliver!" she warned him. "Have sense? Don't be a fool!"

"Oliver!" the Duchess entreated—it was "Oliver" now, not "Mr. Bacon." "You'll come for a long week-end?"

Alone in the woods with Diana! Riding alone in the woods with Diana!

"Thousand," he wrote, and signed it.

"Here you are," he said.

And there opened all the flounces of the parasol, all the plumes of the peacock, the radiance of the wave, the swords and spears of Agincourt, as she rose from her chair. And the two old men and the two young men, Spencer and Marshall, Wicks and Hammond, flattened themselves behind the counter envying him as he led her through the shop to the door. And he **waggled** his yellow glove in their faces, and she held her honour—a cheque for twenty thousand pounds with his signature—quite firmly in her hands.

How does the duchess pay Bacon? How does she cheat him?

Notice the British spelling of *cheque* (*check*).

The *Agincourt* reference hints that the duchess left after winning a major battle.

A *pound* is a basic unit of British money, similar to the American dollar.

---

dimpling marked on the surface with dimples or notches   **waistcoats** fancy vests   **waggled** waved back and forth

"Are they false or are they real?" asked Oliver, shutting his private door. There they were, ten pearls on the blotting paper on the table. He took them to the window. He held them under his lens to the light. . . . This, then, was the truffle he had routed out of the earth! Rotten at the centre—rotten at the core!

"Forgive me, oh my mother!" he sighed, raising his hands as if he asked pardon of the old woman in the picture. And again he was a little boy in the alley where they sold dogs on Sunday.

"For," he murmured, laying the palms of his hands together, "it is to be a long week-end."

Why do you think Bacon feels at the end like the little boy he once was? Why does he need to ask his mother's pardon?

Directions Choose the letter of the best answer or write the answer using complete sentences.

Comprehension: Identifying Facts

1. As a boy Oliver Bacon sold _____.
   A cheap watches
   B wallets and purses
   C goods at Whitecastle
   D stolen dogs

2. Who used to put a rose in Bacon's buttonhole each morning?
   A his mother
   B Mademoiselle
   C the duchess
   D his manservant

3. How does Bacon show homage, or respect, to his dead mother?

4. Why is Bacon sad and dissatisfied?

5. Where is his place of business?

6. Where does Bacon keep his jewels?

7. Who is waiting to see him? How long does she wait?

8. What does she want him to do?

9. Who is Diana and what does she mean to Bacon?

10. Why doesn't Bacon test the pearls to see if they are fake?

Comprehension: Putting Ideas Together

11. Bacon's boyhood is to his present life as _____.
    A poor is to rich
    B spring is to winter
    C happy is to sad
    D cold is to warm

12. Most ordinary people think of Bacon as a _____.
    A criminal
    B nobleman
    C person to be avoided
    D highly successful businessman

13. What does Bacon's promise to his mother (or his bet with her) mean to him?

14. From the way he lives and dresses, what can you tell is most important to Bacon?

15. Does Bacon like or dislike the wealthy people and nobles who are his clients? What details show this?

16. What is Bacon's relationship with his employees?

17. What makes the duchess a friend to Bacon? What makes her an enemy?

18. What makes Bacon a friend to the duchess? What makes him an enemy?

19. Why does Bacon give the duchess 20,000 pounds for her pearls?

20. Why does he ask his mother's forgiveness after he buys the pearls?

Understanding Literature: Character, Characterization, Simile, and Metaphor

Writers use many methods to develop the characters, or people, in their writing. Figures of speech are one method. Some figures of speech compare two unlike things to show some way they are alike. A simile compares them in a phrase introduced by *like* or *as*. A metaphor says one thing *is* another. It does not use *like* or *as*.

21. To what three animals is Bacon compared? Write *simile* or *metaphor* beside each animal to identify the figure of speech used to make the comparison.

22. What do the comparisons to these animals tell about Bacon's character?

23. To Bacon, the jewels are tears, blood, and gunpowder. Explain why these metaphors are fitting.

24. In what ways is the duchess like a wave, a parasol, and a peacock?

25. The duke is "straight as a poker." What does this tell you about his character?

Critical Thinking

26. Do you think Bacon is a different person from the little boy in the dark alley or is he the same? Explain why you think so.

27. Why might crimson (red) be an important color for Bacon? What do you think it symbolizes?

28. Did Bacon and the Duchess of Lambourne both get what they wanted? Explain your thinking.

29. Bacon socializes with wealthy people and nobles, but his background is poor and criminal. How do you think he feels about his closeness to nobility?

Thinking Creatively

30. What do you think is more important to most people: their wealth or their feeling that they are important and respectable? Explain.

After Reading continued on next page

Contemporary British Literature **Unit 6 483**

The Duchess and the Jeweller by Virginia Woolf

 Grammar Check

A dash (—) is used in writing to signal change. It can show a break or change in thought within a sentence. It can set off extra information added to a sentence for emphasis or explanation. (*"Look at him—young Oliver, the young jeweller—there he goes."*)

- Find three more examples in the story of sentences that use dashes.

- Write an original sentence that uses dashes. Read it to a partner and see if he or she can predict where the dashes go.

 Writing on Your Own

Write a description of a person whom you know well. Choose details that you think show something important about the person. Use vivid adjectives, such as colors, to help create a clear picture of the person. Include at least one simile or metaphor that tells something about the person's character.

 Speaking and Listening

Interview a parent, grandparent, or other adult about his or her childhood. Prepare questions that are not easily answered with "yes" or "no." Find out how the person feels he or she has changed since childhood. Does the person look back on that time happily or with regret? Listen carefully to the person's responses. Record them or make notes.

Research

What training is needed to become a gem buyer or a jeweler? Find a copy of the *Occupational Outlook Handbook* in your school counselor's office, or use a computer to find the online version. (Enter the keywords *U.S. Department of Labor, Bureau of Labor Statistics,* and *Occupational Outlook Handbook* in a search engine.) Summarize the traits and training needed for this job. Explain whether it would be a good profession for you.

BEFORE READING THE SELECTION

A Cup of Tea   by Katherine Mansfield

About the Author

Katherine Mansfield's real name was Kathleen Beauchamp. She was born in New Zealand in 1888, the daughter of a wealthy family. As a young girl, she studied cello (a stringed musical instrument) in London. She later returned there to become a writer.

Her first book, *In a German Pension* (1911) received little notice, but the stories in *Bliss* (1920) and *The Garden Party* (1922) established her as a major writer. She modeled her stories after those of Anton Chekhov, a brilliant Russian writer. They are simple, yet they suggest a great deal. Her language is delicate, but plain. The stories present brief moments of decision, defeat, or victory for her characters.

In 1918, Mansfield married John Middleton Murry, an editor and critic. That same year, she got a lung disease called tuberculosis. For the next five years, she spent much time in hospitals and special clinics. Work became difficult for her. She died in 1923 at the age of 35.

About the Selection

"A Cup of Tea" is a short story that focuses on the thoughts and actions of Rosemary Fell, a wealthy young lady. Rather than focus on exciting action, it allows us to enter the mind and world of Rosemary. She encounters a new situation when she comes face to face with a poor, hungry woman about her age. Through her thoughts and reactions, Rosemary tells a lot about her character.

Katherine Mansfield
1888–1923

Objectives

- To read and understand a short story
- To identify point of view and recognize the use of third-person narration
- To explain a character's motive

Before Reading continued on next page

A Cup of Tea   by Katherine Mansfield

point of view
the position from
which the author
or storyteller tells
the story

third person
a point of view
where the narrator
is not a character
and refers to
characters as *he*
or *she*

motive a reason
a character does
something

Literary Terms A story's **point of view** is the position from which it is told. This story uses **third-person** point of view. The narrator is not a character in the story but observes and reports what happens. The narrator has limited understanding of what characters are thinking but seems able to understand the main character's **motives** well. Motives are the reasons a character does something.

Reading on Your Own This story follows the main character, Rosemary Fell, as she shops and finds a poor girl begging for money for food and drink. As you read, carefully analyze the information you learn about Rosemary. What are the motives behind her actions?

Writing on Your Own Make a list of synonyms for *beautiful*. Not all of them mean exactly the same thing. Rank the synonyms according to degree. For example, a *beautiful* thing is more pleasing than a *pretty* one. Write a paragraph explaining the slight differences in meaning among these words.

Vocabulary Focus When you come across a new word in reading, use the context to get clues to its meaning. Read the sentence in which it occurs. The writer may provide a synonym or an antonym as a clue. Look at other sentences in the paragraph. The situation itself may help you predict a word's meaning. For example, in paragraph 3, the word *gratified* describes the shopkeeper. Other phrases in the paragraph (*ridiculously fond, beamed, clasped his hands*) suggest that the man is happy to see Rosemary. These clues suggest that *gratified* means "very pleased."

Think Before You Read Rosemary Fell is bright, wealthy, well read, and socially skilled. However, she is not beautiful. What do you think will be most important to her?

A Cup of Tea

Rosemary Fell was not exactly beautiful. No, you couldn't have called her beautiful. Pretty? Well, if you took her to pieces . . . But why be so cruel as to take anyone to pieces? She was young, brilliant, extremely modern, **exquisitely** well dressed, amazingly well read in the newest of the new books, and her parties were the most delicious mixture of the really important people and . . . artists—**quaint** creatures, discoveries of hers, some of them too terrifying for words, but others quite **presentable** and amusing.

Rosemary had been married two years. She had a **duck** of a boy. No, not Peter—Michael. And her husband absolutely adored her. They were rich, really rich, not just comfortably well off, which is **odious** and stuffy and sounds like one's grandparents. But if Rosemary wanted to shop she would go to Paris as you and I would go to Bond Street. If she wanted to buy flowers, the car pulled up at that perfect shop in Regent Street, and Rosemary inside the shop just gazed in her dazzled, rather exotic way, and said: "I want those and those and those. Give me four bunches of those. And that jar of roses. Yes, I'll have all the roses in the jar. No, no lilac. I hate lilac. It's got no shape." The attendant bowed and put the lilac out of sight, as though this was only too true; lilac

As you read, think about what motivates, or causes the actions of, each character.

Notice Rosemary's view of the artists she "discovers" and introduces to her friends.

---

exquisitely perfectly

quaint unusual; not refined

presentable fit to be seen

duck British slang for darling

odious hateful

was dreadfully shapeless. "Give me those stumpy little tulips. Those red and white ones." And she was followed to the car by a thin shopgirl staggering under an **immense** white paper armful that looked like a baby in long clothes . . .

One winter afternoon she had been buying something in a little antique shop in Curzon Street. It was a shop she liked. For one thing, one usually had it to oneself. And then the man who kept it was ridiculously fond of serving her. He beamed whenever she came in. He clasped his hands; he was so **gratified** he could scarcely speak. Flattery, of course. All the same, there was something . . .

"You see, madam," he would explain in his low respectful tones, "I love my things. I would rather not part with them than sell them to someone who does not appreciate them, who has not that fine feeling which is so rare. . . ." And, breathing deeply, he unrolled a tiny square of blue velvet and pressed it on the glass counter with his pale fingertips.

Today it was a little box. He had been keeping it for her. He had shown it to nobody as yet. An exquisite little enamel box with a glaze so fine it looked as though it had been baked in cream. On the lid a **minute** creature stood under a flowery tree, and a more minute creature still had her arms around his neck. Her hat, really no bigger than a **geranium** petal, hung from a branch; it had green ribbons. And there was a pink cloud like a watchful **cherub** floating above their heads. Rosemary took her hands out of her long gloves. She always took off her gloves to examine such things. Yes, she liked it very much. She loved it; it was a great duck. She must have it. And, turning the creamy box, opening and shutting it, she couldn't help noticing how charming her hands were against the blue velvet. The shopman, in some dim cavern of his mind, may have dared to think so too. For he took a pencil, leaned over the counter, and his pale bloodless fingers crept

What does Rosemary think of the shopgirl at the flower shop and the man at the antique shop who serve her?

What can you tell so far about how Rosemary views herself?

immense huge	**minute** tiny	**cherub** angel
gratified very pleased	**geranium** a type of flowering plant	

timidly towards those, rosy, flashing ones, as he murmured gently: "If I may **venture** to point out to madam, the flowers on the little lady's **bodice.**"

"Charming!" Rosemary admired the flowers. But what was the price? For a moment the shopman did not seem to hear. Then a murmur reached her. "Twenty-eight **guineas,** madam."

"Twenty-eight guineas." Rosemary gave no sign. She laid the little box down; she buttoned her gloves again. Twenty-eight guineas. Even if one is rich . . . She looked vague. She stared at a plump teakettle like a plump hen above the shopman's head, and her voice was dreamy as she answered: "Well, keep it for me—will you? I'll . . ."

But the shopman had already bowed as though keeping it for her was all any human being could ask. He would be willing, of course, to keep it for her forever.

The **discreet** door shut with a click. She was outside on the step, gazing at the winter afternoon. Rain was falling, and with the rain it seemed the dark came too, spinning down like ashes. There was a cold bitter taste in the air, and the new-lighted lamps looked sad. Sad were the lights in the houses opposite. Dimly they burned as if regretting something. And people hurried by, hidden under their hateful umbrellas. Rosemary felt a strange pang. She pressed her muff to her breast; she wished she had the little box, too, to cling to. Of course, the car was there. She'd only to cross the pavement. But still she waited. There are moments, horrible moments in life, when one emerges from shelter and looks out, and it's awful. One oughtn't to give way to them. One ought to go home and have an extra-special tea. But at the very instant of thinking that, a young girl, thin, dark, shadowy—where had she come from?—was standing at Rosemary's elbow and a voice like a sigh, almost like a sob, breathed: "Madam, may I speak to you a moment?"

Rosemary is taken over by a *horrible moment.* What do you think has caused her to feel despair and darkness?

venture dare	**guinea** British unit of money
bodice top portion of a dress, covering the torso	**discreet** not calling attention to itself

"Speak to me?" Rosemary turned. She saw a little battered creature with enormous eyes, someone quite young, no older than herself, who clutched at her coat-collar with reddened hands, and shivered as though she had just come out of the water.

"M-madam," stammered the voice. "Would you let me have the price of a cup of tea?"

"A cup of tea?" There was something simple, sincere in that voice; it wasn't in the least the voice of a beggar. "Then have you no money at all?" asked Rosemary.

"None, madam," came the answer.

"How **extraordinary!**" Rosemary peered through the dusk, and the girl gazed back at her. How more than extraordinary! And suddenly it seemed to Rosemary such an adventure. It was like something out of a novel by Dostoyevsky, this meeting in the dusk. Supposing she took the girl home? Supposing she did do one of those things she was always reading about or seeing on the stage, what would happen? It would be thrilling. And she heard herself saying afterwards to the amazement of her friends: "I simply took her home with me," as she stepped forward and said to that dim person beside her: "Come home to tea with me."

The girl drew back **startled.** She even stopped shivering for a moment. Rosemary put out a hand and touched her arm. "I mean it," she said, smiling. And she felt how simple and kind her smile was. "Why won't you? Do. Come home with me now in my car and have tea."

"You—you don't mean it, madam," said the girl, and there was pain in her voice.

"But I do," cried Rosemary. "I want you to. To please me. Come along."

The girl put her fingers to her lips and her eyes **devoured** Rosemary. "You're—you're not taking me to the police station?" she stammered.

extraordinary strange and amazing

startled surprised; scared

devoured ate greedily; in this case, looked over carefully

"The police station!" Rosemary laughed out. "Why should I be so cruel? No, I only want to make you warm and to hear—anything you care to tell me."

Hungry people are easily led. The footman held the door of the car open, and a moment later they were **skimming** through the dusk.

"There!" said Rosemary. She had a feeling of triumph as she slipped her hand through the velvet strap. She could have said, "Now I've got you," as she gazed at the little captive she had netted. But of course she meant it kindly. Oh, more than kindly. She was going to prove to this girl that—wonderful things did happen in life, that—fairy godmothers were real, that—rich people had hearts, and that women were sisters. She turned **impulsively,** saying: "Don't be frightened. After all, why shouldn't you come back with me? We're both women. If I'm the more **fortunate,** you ought to expect . . ."

But happily at that moment, for she didn't know how the sentence was going to end, the car stopped. The bell was rung, the door opened, and with a charming, protecting, almost embracing movement, Rosemary drew the other into the hall. Warmth, softness, light, a sweet scent, all those things so familiar to her she never even thought about them, she watched that other receive. It was fascinating. She was like the little rich girl in her nursery with all the cupboards to open, all the boxes to unpack.

"Come, come upstairs," said Rosemary, longing to begin to be generous. "Come up to my room." And, besides, she wanted to spare this poor little thing from being stared at by the servants; she decided as they mounted the stairs she would not even ring for Jeanne, but take off her things by herself. The great thing was to be natural!

> What does Rosemary want to prove? To whom does she want to prove this?

> Rosemary had not really thought through what she was doing. What does this say about Rosemary? What outcome do you predict from this?

> What does it mean to Rosemary to *be natural?* Do you think the hungry girl shares Rosemary's definition?

skimming going quickly

impulsively on a whim; done without thought

fortunate lucky; wealthy

And "There!" cried Rosemary again, as they reached her beautiful big bedroom with the curtains drawn, the fire leaping on her wonderful **lacquer** furniture, her gold cushions and the primrose and blue rugs.

The girl stood just inside the door; she seemed dazed. But Rosemary didn't mind that.

"Come and sit down," she cried, dragging her big chair up to the fire, "in this **comfy** chair. Come and get warm. You look so dreadfully cold."

"I daren't, madam," said the girl, and she edged backwards.

"Oh, please,"—Rosemary ran forward—"you mustn't be frightened, you mustn't, really. Sit down, and when I've taken off my things we shall go into the next room and have tea and be cozy. Why are you afraid?" And gently she half pushed the thin figure into its deep cradle.

But there was no answer. The girl stayed just as she had been put, with her hands by her sides and her mouth slightly open. To be quite sincere, she looked rather stupid. But Rosemary wouldn't **acknowledge** it. She leaned over her, saying: "Won't you take off your hat? Your pretty hair is all wet. And one is so much more comfortable without a hat, isn't one?"

There was a whisper that sounded like "Very good, madam," and the crushed hat was taken off.

"Let me help you off with your coat, too," said Rosemary.

The girl stood up. But she held on to the chair with one hand and let Rosemary pull. It was quite an effort. The other scarcely helped her at all. She seemed to stagger like a child, and the thought came and went through Rosemary's mind, that if people wanted helping they must respond a little, just a little, otherwise it became very difficult indeed. And what was she to do with the coat now? She left it on the floor, and the hat too. She was just going to take a cigarette off the

We see the girl from Rosemary's point of view. How does Rosemary seem to regard her?

How is Rosemary's attitude toward the girl changing? How does Rosemary view the girl's helplessness?

lacquer a varnish or glaze that gives a glossy finish

comfy comfortable

acknowledge accept as true

mantelpiece when the girl said quickly, but so lightly and strangely: "I'm very sorry, madam, but I'm going to faint. I shall go off, madam, if I don't have something."

"Good heavens, how thoughtless I am!" Rosemary rushed to the bell.

"Tea! Tea at once! And some brandy immediately!"

The maid was gone again, but the girl almost cried out. "No, I don't want no brandy. I never drink brandy. It's a cup of tea I want, madam." And she burst into tears.

It was a terrible and fascinating moment. Rosemary knelt beside her chair.

"Don't cry, poor little thing," she said. "Don't cry." And she gave the other her lace handkerchief. She really was touched beyond words. She put her arm round those thin, birdlike shoulders.

Now at last the other forgot to be shy, forgot everything except that they were both women, and gasped out: "I can't go on no longer like this. I can't bear it. I shall do away with myself. I can't bear no more."

"You shan't have to. I'll look after you. Don't cry anymore. Don't you see what a good thing it was that you met me? We'll have tea and you'll tell me everything. And I shall arrange something. I promise. Do stop crying. It's so exhausting. Please!"

The other did stop just in time for Rosemary to get up before the tea came. She had the table placed between them. She **plied** the poor little creature with everything, all the sandwiches, all the bread and butter, and every time her cup was empty she filled it with tea, cream and sugar. People always said sugar was so **nourishing.** As for herself she didn't eat; she smoked and looked away **tactfully** so that the other should not be shy.

The girl confesses she is about to faint. How does this change Rosemary's view?

It is Rosemary's turn to be startled. Why does the girl's crying catch Rosemary off guard? What does Rosemary promise? Do you think she means it?

Does Rosemary mean crying is exhausting for the girl or exhausting for herself? How might both be true in Rosemary's mind?

mantelpiece cross beam above a fireplace	**nourishing** healthful; giving strength
plied tried to tempt	**tactfully** politely

Coffee and Teaset, 1760

And really the effect of that slight meal was marvelous. When the tea table was carried away a new being, a light, frail creature with tangled hair, dark lips, deep, lighted eyes, lay back in the big chair in a kind of sweet **languor,** looking at the blaze. Rosemary lit a fresh cigarette; it was time to begin.

What does it mean that *it was time to begin?*

"And when did you have your last meal?" she asked softly. But at that moment the door-handle turned.

"Rosemary, may I come in?" It was Philip.

"Of course."

He came in. "Oh, I'm so sorry," he said, and stopped and stared.

"It's quite all right," said Rosemary smiling. "This is my friend, Miss—"

"Smith, madam," said the **languid** figure, who was strangely still and unafraid.

Rosemary does not learn the girl's name until Philip comes in. What does this tell about Rosemary's motives?

"Smith," said Rosemary. "We are going to have a little talk."

"Oh, yes," said Philip. "Quite," and his eye caught sight of the coat and hat on the floor. He came over to the fire and turned his back to it. "It's a beastly afternoon," he said

---

languor relaxation   **languid** limp

curiously, still looking at that **listless** figure, looking at its hands and boots, and then at Rosemary again.

"Yes, isn't it?" said Rosemary enthusiastically. "**Vile**."

Philip smiled his charming smile. "As a matter of fact," said he, "I wanted you to come into the library for a moment. Would you? Will Miss Smith excuse us?"

The big eyes were raised to him, but Rosemary answered for her. "Of course she will." And they went out of the room together.

"I say," said Philip, when they were alone. "Explain. Who is she? What does it all mean?"

Rosemary, laughing, leaned against the door and said: "I picked her up in Curzon Street. Really. She's a real pick-up. She asked me for the price of a cup of tea, and I brought her home with me."

"But what on earth are you going to do with her?" cried Philip.

"Be nice to her," said Rosemary quickly. "Be **frightfully** nice to her. Look after her. I don't know how. We haven't talked yet. But show her—treat her—make her feel—"

"My darling girl," said Philip, "you're quite mad, you know. It simply can't be done."

"I knew you'd say that," retorted Rosemary. "Why not? I want to. Isn't that a reason? And besides, one's always reading about these things. I decided—"

"But," said Philip slowly, and he cut the end of a cigar, "she's so astonishingly pretty."

"Pretty?" Rosemary was so surprised that she blushed. "Do you think so? I—I hadn't thought about it."

"Good Lord!" Philip struck a match. "She's absolutely lovely. Look again, my child. I was bowled over when I came into your room just now. However . . . I think you're making a ghastly mistake. Sorry, darling, if I'm crude and all that. But let me know if Miss Smith is going to dine with us in time for me to look up *The **Milliner**'s Gazette*."

On what is Rosemary's idea about helping Miss Smith based?

The Milliner's Gazette was a fashion magazine. Philip may be suggesting that Miss Smith should be a fashion model.

---

listless lacking energy

vile awful

frightfully very

milliner person who makes hats

What reason does Philip give to explain why Rosemary cannot help Miss Smith? Why do you think he gives this reason? How does Rosemary react to Philip's reason? Why?

"You absurd creature!" said Rosemary, and she went out of the library, but not back to her bedroom. She went to her writing-room and sat down at her desk. Pretty! Absolutely lovely! Bowled over! Her heart beat like a heavy bell. Pretty! Lovely! She drew her checkbook towards her. But no, checks would be no use, of course. She opened a drawer and took out five **pound** notes, looked at them, put two back, and holding the three squeezed in her hand, she went back to her bedroom.

Half an hour later Philip was still in the library, when Rosemary came in.

"I only wanted to tell you," said she, and she leaned against the door again and looked at him with her dazzled **exotic** gaze, "Miss Smith won't dine with us tonight."

Philip put down the paper. "Oh, what's happened? Previous engagement?"

What is ironic about Rosemary's explanation to Philip?

Rosemary came over and sat down on his knee. "She insisted on going," said she, "so I gave the poor little thing a present of money. I couldn't keep her against her will, could I?" she added softly.

Rosemary had just done her hair, darkened her eyes a little, and put on her pearls. She put up her hands and touched Philip's cheeks.

"Do you like me?" said she, and her tone, sweet, husky, troubled him.

What are Rosemary's motives for picking up Miss Smith? for sending her away? Which do you think are a truer reflection of Rosemary's character?

"I like you awfully," he said, and he held her tighter. "Kiss me."

There was a pause.

Then Rosemary said dreamily, "I saw a fascinating little box today. It cost twenty-eight guineas. May I have it?"

Philip jumped her on his knee. "You may, little wasteful one," said he.

But that was not really what Rosemary wanted to say.

What three things does Rosemary ask of Philip? Why?

"Philip," she whispered, and she pressed his head against her bosom, "am I pretty?"

---

pound British unit of money   **exotic** strange; uncommon

AFTER READING THE SELECTION

Directions Choose the letter of the best answer or write the answer using complete sentences.

Comprehension: Identifying Facts

1. Rosemary Fell is well known in her circle for her _____.
   A beauty
   B kindness
   C clever parties
   D love of flowers

2. What does Rosemary want to buy on Curzon Street?
   A roses
   B an enamel box
   C books
   D a tailor-made dress

3. Who approaches Rosemary on the street?

4. What does this person ask?

5. Why does the girl not want to go with Rosemary at first?

6. Why does Rosemary remove the girl's coat?

7. What does the girl tell Rosemary when she breaks down crying?

8. How is the girl changed by the tea?

9. What happens before Rosemary and Miss Smith can have their talk?

10. Why does Philip say Rosemary cannot help Miss Smith?

Comprehension: Putting Ideas Together

11. Rosemary's typical attitude toward people who serve her is _____.
   A thoughtless   **C** cruel
   B kind   **D** humble

12. During the course of the story, the girl's attitude changes from _____.
   A pleasant to demanding
   B angry to pleasant
   C self-centered to kind
   D frightened to relaxed

13. How would Rosemary probably describe herself, compared to other people in her wealthy social circle?

14. How does the girl contrast with Rosemary?

15. How does Rosemary's thinking about Miss Smith change after she brings her home?

16. What is Miss Smith's situation?

17. What probably happens to Miss Smith?

After Reading **continued on next page**

18. How does the cost of the enamel box compare to the money Rosemary gives Miss Smith? Why is this important?

19. What does the little enamel box seem to mean to Rosemary in the story's beginning? at the end?

20. What happens to Rosemary's intention to prove "the rich people had hearts, and that women *were* sisters"?

Understanding Literature: Third-Person Point of View and Motive

A story's point of view is the position from which it is told. It determines how much we know about each character's thoughts and motives (reasons for acting). In third person, the narrator is not a character but knows the thoughts and actions of one or more of the characters.

21. Who tells this story? What type of point of view is this?

22. How much does the narrator understand about each character's thoughts and ideas?

23. How might the story have been different if Rosemary had told it?

24. What motives caused Rosemary to take Miss Smith home with her?

25. What motives seem most important in Rosemary's life?

Critical Thinking

26. What clues do you get early in the story that Rosemary may not follow through on her decision to help Miss Smith?

27. How is the scene painted on the enamel box symbolic of Rosemary's life?

28. What do you think causes the "horrible moment" Rosemary experiences when she emerges from the antique shop?

29. Do you think Rosemary ever really sees Miss Smith as a human being? Explain why or why not.

Thinking Creatively

30. Do you agree or disagree with Rosemary's words that rich people have hearts and want to help the poor? Explain why you think as you do.

Grammar Check

Writers may use three periods, called ellipsis points (. . .), to show that speech stops or trails off. Ellipses may suggest a speaker's uncertainty, distress, or confusion. They may also invite the reader to think about what a description or statement says. For example, the narrator says of Rosemary, "Well, if you took her to pieces . . ." This trailing off suggests that Rosemary is not pretty.

- Find three more examples in the story of sentences that use ellipsis points.

- Write the sentences. Explain how the ellipsis points add to your understanding of each sentence.

- Write an original sentence that uses ellipsis points.

 ## Writing on Your Own

Write an essay persuading classmates to volunteer to help feed the hungry. Include a surprising or shocking fact in your introduction. Then focus on the action you want readers to take. Provide convincing reasons.

 ## Speaking and Listening

Choose a side for debating this statement: *The wealthy should pay a special tax to provide food for the poor.* Meet with your debate team and brainstorm reasons supporting your position. Then think of reasons the other team is likely to present, and brainstorm answers to those reasons. Present your team's position using clear, logical language. Respond to the other team's presentation. Have the class vote on which side was most convincing.

 ## Media

Advertising and movies influence our views about material things, value, beauty, and style. Make a list of items that you think show a person is rich and important. Look through mass media advertising, stories, and articles to find images and words that influence your views. Do you think the media reflect what is most important? Make a collage to illustrate your view.

Musée des Beaux Arts by W. H. Auden

W. H. Auden
1907–1973

Objectives

■ To read and
understand
a poem with
allusions to
fine art

■ To define diction
and explain its
effect in a poem

About the Author

Wystan Hugh Auden was born, raised, and educated in England. As a young man, he formed friendships with a number of other great poets (T. S. Eliot, Stephen Spender, Louis MacNeice). They shared an interest in politics and the creation of new techniques and attitudes in poetry. In 1939, Auden left England for the United States. He became a U.S. citizen in 1946 but returned to England in 1956 to teach.

Auden wrote poems in a number of forms, from ballads to sonnets and free verse. He combined great technical skill with an informal style to create poems that speak clearly to many readers. Auden's work showed his concern and commitment to revealing the social problems of his time. Later in his life, Auden wrote more about spiritual themes. He died in 1973.

About the Selection

"Musée des Beaux Arts" is set in the Museum of Fine Arts in Brussels, Belgium. The poet thinks aloud as he looks at three paintings by Pieter Brueghel the Elder. The poem's first part refers to the paintings *The Massacre of the Innocents* and *The Numbering at Bethlehem*. These paintings show scenes of cruelty by King Herod in the Roman-controlled area of Judea. The stories took place at the time of Jesus's birth as told by the Bible. Herod ordered the killing of all boys aged two years and younger in an attempt to kill the newborn "king of the Jews," Jesus. The second part of the poem refers to *The Fall of Icarus*. In all these paintings, people carry out their busy lives without appearing to notice the amazing events going on around them.

Literary Terms **Diction** in a literary work refers to the words the author chooses. Especially in poems, where each word has great value, just the right word is needed to express the exact meaning and feeling intended. Irony increases the importance of a work, too, by highlighting the difference between what we expect to happen and what actually happens.

diction proper choice of words; saying words correctly

Reading on Your Own What kinds of words would you expect an author to use in a poem about human suffering? Predict what Auden will have to say and how he will say it. As you read, think about how Auden's word choices affect your understanding of and feelings about the subject.

Writing on Your Own Think about a painting you have observed that impressed you. Write a description of the objects, people, or events it shows. What was the painter's attitude toward the subject? Explain how you know.

Vocabulary Focus In "Musée des Beaux Arts," Auden uses words with very different meanings and connotations (associations) to set up contrasts. For example, after he introduces the subject, *suffering*, he lists very ordinary things (*eating*, *opening*, *walking*) that happen at the same time. In line 6, *miraculous birth* sets up one set of emotions and expectations. In line 10, *dreadful martyrdom* reverses them. Find other examples of opposite words and phrases that help create tension in the poem.

Think Before You Read How might history and art play a role in this poem?

Musée des Beaux Arts

As you read, keep in mind the setting—an art museum filled with the works of *Old Masters.*

About suffering they were never wrong,
The Old Masters: how well they understood
Its human position; how it takes place
While someone else is eating or opening a window or
　　　　　　　　　just walking dully along;
5　How, when the aged are **reverently,** passionately waiting
For the miraculous birth, there always must be
Children who did not specially want it to happen, skating
On a pond at the edge of the wood:
They never forgot
10　That even the dreadful **martyrdom** must run its course
Anyhow in a corner, some untidy spot
Where the dogs go on with their doggy life and the
　　　　　　　　　torturer's horse
Scratches its innocent behind on a tree.

In Brueghel's *Icarus,* for instance: how everything
　　　　　　　　　turns away

Brueghel refers to Pieter Brueghel the Elder (1522–1569), a Flemish artist who painted *The Fall of Icarus.* In Greek mythology, *Icarus* is a boy who received wings made of wax as a gift. Though warned not to, he flew too near the sun. The wings melted, and he fell to his death.

reverently respectfully

martyrdom suffering or death for one's beliefs

15 Quite **leisurely** from the disaster; the **ploughman** may
    Have heard the splash, the forsaken cry,
    But for him it was not an important failure; the sun shone
    As it had to on the white legs disappearing into the green
    Water; and the expensive delicate ship that must have seen
20 Something amazing, a boy falling out of the sky,
    Had somewhere to get to and sailed calmly on.

Forsaken (line 16) is a word that means "rejected and forgotten." Why do you think Auden chose this word to describe Icarus's cry instead of *sad* or *frightened*?

Landscape with the Fall of Icarus, Pieter Brueghel the Elder, about 1558

leisurely without concern

ploughman one who uses a plow (plough) to break up soil for planting; farm worker

AFTER READING THE SELECTION

Musée des Beaux Arts   by W. H. Auden

Directions Choose the letter of the best answer or write the answer using complete sentences.

Comprehension: Identifying Facts

1. In line 2, "Old Masters" refers to _____.

A artists   **C** rulers
B the aged   **D** philosophers

2. The "white legs disappearing" in line 18 belong to whom?

3. A ship sails by just as Icarus falls into the sea. What do the people on the ship do?

Comprehension: Putting Ideas Together

4. The poet and the painters suggest that humans suffer _____.
A very little
B alone
C more than animals
D mentally rather than physically

5. What is true about the "public"—regular people—in each of the paintings the poet sees?

6. What is the ordinary world like, judging from the details described in the poem?

Understanding Literature: Diction and Irony

Diction refers to the choice of words in a writing, including the meanings and emotions they express. Irony can refer to words used to mean the opposite of their usual meaning. Irony can also describe events that turn out the opposite of what is expected.

7. What is the effect of phrases like "doggy life" and "scratches its innocent behind" in lines 12–13?

8. Explain the irony of what the man plowing and the ship do when Icarus falls into the sea.

Critical Thinking

9. What does this poem suggest is the nature of suffering?

Thinking Creatively

10. Do you think Auden was writing about the world long ago or today? Explain why you think so. Use details in the poem for support.

Grammar Check

Pronouns must agree with their antecedents in number, gender, and person. An antecedent is the word or group of words a pronoun replaces. For example, in line 1 of "Musée des Beaux Arts," *they* replaces the phrase *The Old Masters.* (In this sentence, the pronoun appears before the antecedent. Normally, the opposite is true.)

- Write the antecedent for each of these pronouns from the poem: *it* (line 3); *they* (line 9); *its* (line 13); *him* (line 17); *it* (line 18).

- Write a sentence about W. H. Auden and another one about "Musée des Beaux Arts." Include these proper nouns as antecedents and a pronoun that refers to them.

Writing on Your Own

Think of an event from the 20th or 21st century that caused people to suffer. Write a paragraph explaining whether this event and the world reaction to it proves or disproves the theme of "Musée des Beaux Arts." Summarize the poem's main idea and state how your event is related to it. Provide facts and details that explain this relationship.

Speaking and Listening

Make a copy of a painting you like and prepare a short talk about it. Tell about the artist and the era in which it was painted. Describe the techniques the artist used and the scene the painting shows. Explain the theme, or main idea, of the painting and what you like about it. Share your talk in a small group. When you listen to others, take notes on the most important facts and ideas. Ask questions based on your viewing of the painting.

Research

Learn more about the life and art of Pieter Brueghel the Elder. You may find information in encyclopedias or art reference books in the library and on the Internet. Take notes about Brueghel's style and the kinds of subjects he preferred. Write a summary of the most interesting facts you learn.

What I Expected   *by Stephen Spender*

Stephen Spender
1909–1995

Objectives

- To read and understand a poem
- To describe imagery in a poem
- To understand how images contribute to meaning

About the Author

Stephen Spender was born in London in 1909. While attending Oxford University, he became part of a group of poets led by W. H. Auden. This group looked for order and beauty in modern technological society. For example, in one poem, Spender celebrates the beauty of a freight train. However, the group did not always have an optimistic tone about the future.

Spender published criticism, drama, fiction, and translations, as well as his poems, journals, and an autobiography. He helped found, and served as editor of, two literary journals: *Horizon* and *Encounter.* Queen Elizabeth II made him a knight in 1983. Spender died in 1995.

About the Selection

"What I Expected" contrasts what one expects from life with what one actually experiences. It begins with the cheerfulness and idealism of youth and moves on to the disappointment and failure that come with "the wearing of Time." Although it does not use a regular pattern of rhythm, it uses rhyme informally. Even-numbered lines rhyme or have similar ending sounds (*fighting/climbing, strong/long).*

Literary Terms Poems rely on **imagery**, language that creates pictures, or images, in the reader's mind. Images use specific, concrete language and appeal directly to the five senses. Therefore, they make a poem seem alive and help give it meaning.

imagery pictures created by words; the use of words that appeal to the five senses

Reading on Your Own What images do you see in your mind when you think about your future? As you read, notice how what the poet finds differs from what he expects.

Writing on Your Own Think of an experience you looked forward to with great expectation. Describe what you thought it would be like. Then describe what it was actually like. Use details that appeal to the five senses to create vivid images.

Vocabulary Focus Poets often use figurative language to make comparisons. In these figures of speech, words do not keep their literal, or everyday, meanings. For example, Spender speaks of "The fading of body and soul," comparing it to "Smoke before wind." This comparison shows how the poet came to feel physically and spiritually empty ("Corrupt, unsubstantial"). What meaning do you get from the comparison of crippled limbs to question marks in lines 18–21? from the comparison of the poem to a faceted crystal in lines 31–32?

Think Before You Read How does our life experience change what we expect from life?

WHAT I EXPECTED

As you read, allow the images of the scenes to fill your mind.

What I expected, was
Thunder, fighting,
Long struggles with men
And climbing.

5 After **continual** straining
I should grow strong;
Then the rocks would shake
And I rest long.

As a young man, the poet expects that struggle will only strengthen him and he will prevail.

What I had not foreseen
10 Was the gradual day
Weakening the will
Leaking the brightness away,
The lack of good to touch,
The fading of body and soul

What actions does the poet experience instead?

15 Smoke before wind,
Corrupt, unsubstantial.

---

continual constant　　**corrupt** spoiled, harmed　　**unsubstantial** not lasting or real

The wearing of Time,
And the watching of cripples pass
With limbs shaped like questions
20 In their odd twist,
The **pulverous** grief
Melting the bones with pity,
The sick falling from earth—
These, I could not foresee.

25 Expecting always
Some brightness to hold in trust
Some final innocence
Exempt from dust,
That, hanging solid,
30 Would dangle through all
Like the created poem,
Or the **faceted** crystal.

What does the poet suggest about the nature of life by his focus in stanza 3 on the disabled and the sick?

Twilight: Short Arbiter 'Twixt Day and Night, **Frederic Edwin Church, 1850**

pulverous created by grinding

exempt excused

faceted having many surfaces, as on the face of a cut gem

Directions Choose the letter of the best answer or write the answer using complete sentences.

Comprehension: Identifying Facts

1. When young, the poet expects that his life will involve _____.
   A a struggle
   B much sickness
   C plenty of rest
   D goodness

2. What does he discover about his will? about his body and soul?

3. What does the poet still hope for?

Comprehension: Putting Ideas Together

4. This poet would agree most strongly that life is _____.
   A difficult but inspiring
   B innocent and good
   C full of gradual losses and sorrows
   D full of the unexpected

5. Compare the images in the first stanza to those in the third stanza. What is the effect of life's struggles?

6. What is the difference between the "brightness" of line 12 and the "brightness" mentioned in line 26?

Understanding Literature: Imagery

Imagery creates mental pictures using vivid language that appeals to the senses. In this poem, images suggest the poet's changing perceptions and feelings about life.

7. What do you picture the poet doing in the first stanza? What do you picture in the third stanza?

8. What do the words *leaking, fading, corrupt,* and *unsubstantial* add to your picture of the change in the poet from the first stanza to the second stanza?

Critical Thinking

9. Does the poet believe he will discover a "brightness" that is "exempt from dust," or does he only hope this? What might this brightness represent in the world? Explain.

Thinking Creatively

10. Do you think people can create goodness in life by careful crafting, as a poet creates a poem? Explain your thinking.

Grammar Check

Nouns name people, places, things, or ideas. We can classify nouns as concrete or abstract. Concrete nouns name things that can be identified by the five senses: *thunder, rocks, men.* Abstract nouns name ideas that the senses cannot identify: *will, goodness.*

- Identify the nouns in stanzas 2–4 of "What I Expected." List each one under the heading *Concrete Nouns* or *Abstract Nouns.*

- If you have difficulty classifying a noun (such as *smoke*), try making a picture of it or imagining its smell, taste, and so on.

- Write original sentences using five of the nouns. Use both concrete and abstract nouns.

Writing on Your Own

Write a poem about your own expectations—in school, in love, in work, or in some other aspect of life. Compare these expectations to the reality you have experienced. Use images to make your poem vivid.

Speaking and Listening

"What I Expected" has a pattern of rhyme and approximate rhyme. (Approximate rhymes are words that end with similar, but not exactly the same, sounds, as in *soul/unsubstantial.*) Take turns reading the poem aloud with a partner. When you listen, notice the effect of the rhyme scheme. Why is it not obvious at first reading?

Viewing

Search in magazines, newspapers, and books for images that represent youth and age or inexperience and experience. Use them to create a collage to illustrate the theme of "What I Expected."

Blood, Toil, Tears and Sweat   *by Winston Churchill*

Winston Churchill
1874–1963

Objectives

- To read and understand a speech
- To analyze the style of a speech
- To describe the voice of a speaker

About the Author

Winston Leonard Spencer Churchill was born in 1874, the son of Lord Randolph Churchill and his American wife. After training at Sandhurst Military Academy, Churchill served in the army and as a war reporter. By 1900, Churchill was serving in Parliament, the British group of lawmakers. Over the next three decades, he held many high government offices.

In 1940, Churchill became prime minister and minister of defense for Britain. World War II was raging, and it was going badly for the Allies (which included Britain and the United States). Churchill emerged from this war as a widely admired world leader. He was an intelligent planner, an inspiring leader, and a brilliant speaker. Churchill was also known for his fine writing. Among his works are biographies of his father and another relative, a history of World War I, memoirs of World War II, and a history of English-speaking peoples. His speeches fill many volumes. Queen Elizabeth II knighted him in 1953. That same year, he received the Nobel Prize for Literature.

About the Selection

Churchill gave this famous speech to the House of Commons, part of the British Parliament, in May 1940. He had just become prime minister and knew he must quickly achieve three goals. First, he must introduce the new government and its policies and goals. Second, he must show the country that a forceful, confident, and decisive leader had taken control. Finally, he must begin to speak honestly to his country about the real danger and extent of the war and try to rally his people to a long struggle.

Literary Terms An author's **style** comes from his or her use of language. For example, a style may be serious or humorous. Most writers adopt a style that fits their theme and goals. Style is just one element that helps create the author's unique **voice.** Word choices, rhythms of sentences, and liveliness are all aspects that reveal the writer's personality. Because it is a **speech,** this work depends on clear expression and forceful language.

Reading on Your Own Imagine the air of suspense and expectation as this speech was given. In reading the speech, notice the way Churchill chooses words and constructs sentences. How does Churchill achieve the three goals explained in "About the Selection"?

Writing on Your Own Recall what you know about World War II, including the years before the United States entered it. Summarize what you think was at stake and how this situation spurred governments to action.

Vocabulary Focus When you come across difficult longer words, try to find a familiar root within the word. Think of other words that can be formed using this root. Then predict the meaning of the new word. For example, *inflexible* contains *flex*. When you flex your bicep, you bend your arm. *Flexible* and *flexibility* also contain *flex*. *Inflexible* probably means "not bending." Use this method to predict the meanings of *urgency, adjournment, complexity, reconstruction, lamentable,* and *buoyancy.*

Think Before You Read In 1940, German air raids battered Britain. Germany seemed unbeatable. How do you think Churchill inspired the British people in this speech?

style an author's way of writing

voice the way a writer expresses ideas through style, form, content, and purpose

speech a written work meant to be read aloud

Blood, Toil, Tears and Sweat

As you read, think about the sentence structures and language Churchill has used. What feeling do they add to the speech?

The *War Cabinet* was the highest level of the British government during World War II. It included the prime minister, foreign secretary, and others. The *Fighting Services,* or British Armed Forces, are made up of the Naval Services, the British Army, and the Royal Air Force.

I beg to move,

That this House welcomes the formation of a Government representing the united and **inflexible resolve** of the nation to **prosecute** the war with Germany to a victorious conclusion.

On Friday evening last I received His Majesty's **commission** to form a new Administration. It was the evident wish and will of Parliament and the nation that this should be conceived on the broadest possible basis and that it should include all parties, both those who supported the late Government and also the parties of the Opposition. I have completed the most important part of this task. A War Cabinet has been formed of five Members, representing, with the Opposition Liberals, the unity of the nation. The three party Leaders have agreed to serve, either in the War Cabinet or in high executive office. The three Fighting Services have been filled. It was necessary that this should be done in one single day, on account of the extreme urgency and **rigour** of events. A number of other positions, key positions, were filled yesterday, and I am submitting a further list to His Majesty to-night. I hope to complete the appointment of the principal Ministers during to-morrow. The appointment of the other Ministers usually takes a little longer, but I trust

inflexible stubborn; fixed

resolve firmness of mind

prosecute follow to the end

commission charge; assignment

rigour harshness

that, when Parliament meets again, this part of my task will be completed, and that the administration will be complete in all respects.

I considered it in the public interest to suggest that the House should be summoned to meet today. Mr. Speaker agreed, and took the necessary steps, in accordance with the powers **conferred upon** him by the Resolution of the House. At the end of the proceedings today, the **Adjournment** of the House will be proposed until Tuesday, 21st May, with, of course, provision for earlier meeting, if need be. The business to be considered during that week will be notified to Members at the earliest opportunity. I now invite the House, by the Motion which stands in my name, to record its approval of the steps taken and to declare its confidence in the new Government.

To form an Administration of this scale and complexity is a serious **undertaking** in itself, but it must be remembered that we are in the **preliminary** stage of one of the greatest battles in history, that we are in action at many other points in Norway and in Holland, that we have to be prepared in the Mediterranean, that the air battle is continuous and that many preparations, such as have been indicated by my honorable Friend below the Gangway, have to be made here at home. In this crisis I hope I may be pardoned if I do not address the House at any length today. I hope that any of my friends and colleagues, or former colleagues, who are affected by the political **reconstruction,** will make **allowance,** all allowance, for any lack of ceremony with which it has been necessary to act. I would say to the House, as I said to those who have joined this government: "I have nothing to offer but blood, toil, tears and sweat."

Below the Gangway refers to seats next to the center aisle of the Commons chamber. Former prime ministers usually occupy the first seat below the gangway. Churchill refers to Neville Chamberlain, whom he has just replaced.

conferred upon given to	**undertaking** task	**reconstruction** rebuilding
adjournment ending until a later time	**preliminary** beginning	**allowance** excuse

We have before us an ordeal of the most **grievous** kind. We have before us many, many long months of struggle and of suffering. You ask, what is our policy? I can say: It is to wage war, by sea, land and air, with all our might and with all the strength that God can give us; to wage war against a monstrous tyranny, never **surpassed** in the dark, **lamentable catalogue** of human crime. That is our policy. You ask, what is our aim? I can answer in one word: It is victory, victory at all costs, victory in spite of all terror, victory, however long and hard the road may be; for without victory, there is no survival. Let that be realised; no survival for the British Empire, no survival for all that the British Empire has stood for, no survival for the urge and impulse of the ages, that mankind will move forward towards its goal. But I take up my task with **buoyancy** and hope. I feel sure that our cause will not be suffered to fail among men. At this time I feel entitled to claim the aid of all, and I say, "Come then, let us go forward together with our united strength."

Winston Churchill surveys damage from a bombing in London in 1940.

grievous terrible	**lamentable** making one sorry or sad	**buoyancy** optimism; good spirits
surpassed passed, exceeded	**catalogue** list	

Directions Choose the letter of the best answer or write the answer using complete sentences.

Comprehension: Identifying Facts

1. In his introduction, Churchill makes clear that his goal is _____.
   A being a good Prime Minister
   B introducing a new government
   C introducing himself to legislators
   D defeating Germany

2. What steps did Churchill take to form a new government before giving this speech?

3. What does Churchill mean when he says, "I have nothing to offer but blood, toil, tears and sweat"?

Comprehension: Putting Ideas Together

4. Churchill's most urgent theme in this speech is _____.
   A war's difficulty
   B soothing enemies
   C preparing a united, determined people
   D the evil of tyranny

5. What details show that Churchill has proceeded quickly?

6. How is Churchill preparing the British realistically for this war?

Understanding Literature: Style, Voice, and Speech

In this speech, Churchill's style (use of language) and voice project urgency and determination. From the words he chooses to the length and organization of sentences, he has set up a rhythm and emotional appeal that will unite people for a struggle.

7. How does the first sentence in the paragraph that begins "On Friday evening last . . ." help listeners follow ideas presented in the paragraph?

8. Why are the sentences in the final paragraph short? What words have a strong emotional appeal?

Critical Thinking

9. Summarize what Churchill accomplishes in each paragraph of this speech. What shows he is speaking to the entire British population, as well as to Parliament?

Thinking Creatively

10. Why do you think the sentence "I have nothing to offer but blood, toil, tears and sweat" is remembered today throughout the world?

After Reading continued on next page

Grammar Check

In parallel structure, equal and closely related ideas are expressed in similar ways. For example, Churchill says "I have nothing to offer but *blood, toil, tears* and *sweat*." This wording is more effective than saying, for example, "I have nothing to offer but *bleeding, a lot of hard work, weeping,* and *sweat*."

- Study the first sentence of the paragraph that begins "To form an Administration . . ." Write the sentence from "but it must be remembered" to the end. Highlight each parallel clause. For each clause, underline the subject and circle the verb.

- Find another example of parallel structure in this speech. Copy it onto your paper and highlight the parallel parts. Explain how this structure strengthens the speech.

 Writing on Your Own

Think of an issue that needs action. Write a speech explaining its importance and calling for action. Use direct, short sentences or sentence parts (set off by commas) and precise words to make your ideas and suggestions easy to follow. Organize your ideas logically.

 Speaking and Listening

If possible, listen to an audio recording of Churchill's delivery of this speech. Then practice delivering this speech or the one you wrote for "Writing on Your Own." As you practice your delivery, pause for commas and periods. Vary your pitch, rate, and emotional level to suit the content of each part. Record your speech and listen to it to decide where you need to make changes. Then present the speech to the class.

 Research

Research one of the following topics: Winston Churchill, World War II, Battle of Britain. Find information on the Internet, in encyclopedias, in biographies, or in printed reference books. Paraphrase your sources, or enclose quotations in quotation marks (" "). Then prepare a brief report or biography based on your notes.

BEFORE READING THE SELECTION

Do Not Go Gentle into That Good Night   *by Dylan Thomas*

About the Author

Dylan Thomas was born in Wales in 1914, the son of an English teacher from whom he learned his love of language. Before age 20, Thomas had published his first volume of poetry, *Eighteen Poems* (1934). It dazzled readers and critics with its remarkable verbal energy. In the books that followed, Thomas continued to prove his genius.

Unlike Auden and Eliot, Thomas wrote poems with a personal focus. His poems feature intensity, driving emotions, and grand language. Many 20th-century poets showed both distrust of and longing for the modern world. Thomas simply took it by storm.

The many emotions and personal images Thomas packed into his poems make some of them difficult to understand. However, they are not wild and rash, but carefully crafted. As he grew older, Thomas wrote fewer poems but expressed himself with simpler, more direct language.

Thomas gave many public readings in Britain and the United States. His colorful character and the feeling with which he read his work made these readings very popular. Thomas died at age 39 from pneumonia and alcoholism.

Dylan Thomas
1914–1952

Objectives

- To read and understand a formal lyric poem
- To identify and explain the effects of rhythm and rhyme in a poem
- To describe the style of a poem

About the Selection

Thomas wrote "Do Not Go Gentle into That Good Night" late in his life. It is a *villanelle*—an old French form of poetry with a strictly controlled form. It contains just two rhymes and alternately repeats the two most important lines. Thomas uses this tight, formal structure to control his poem and focus on his passionate, urgent message about grief and death. He pleads with his dying father to fight against death and hold onto life as long as possible.

Before Reading continued on next page

Do Not Go Gentle into That Good Night   *by Dylan Thomas*

rhythm a pattern created by the stressed and unstressed syllables in a line of poetry

Literary Terms A poem's **rhythm** comes from the pattern of stressed and unstressed syllables in each line. In this poem, unlike many poems of the 20th century, the rhythm is regular. So is its pattern of rhyme. In this poem, the poet's voice, or unique personality, issues from his style, or use of language, as well his attitude.

Reading on Your Own What drives a person to fight against death? In each stanza of this poem, look for what causes different people to "rage against the dying of the light."

Writing on Your Own Think about a lesson you have learned by observing death in nature or society. Write a paragraph or a poem about this lesson. Include vivid details, as well as the conclusions you have drawn.

Vocabulary Focus Poets often use figurative language to make us look at familiar ideas in new ways. For example, in "Do Not Go Gentle into That Good Night," Thomas explains that wise men realize at life's end "their words had forked no lightning." What does this mean? Wise men should be able to make others understand what is important in life. Like lightning, their words should strike us suddenly and light up our understanding. Because the wise men, nearing death, realize they have not done this, they fight against death. Think about other figurative language in the poem and how it adds to the main idea.

Think Before You Read What is the symbolic meaning of night and dying light in a poem about death?

Do Not Go Gentle into That Good Night

Do not go gentle into that good night,
Old age should burn and **rave** at close of day;
Rage, rage against the dying of the light.

Though wise men at their end know dark is right,
5   Because their words had **forked** no lightning they
Do not go gentle into that good night.

Good men, the last wave by, crying how bright
Their frail deeds might have danced in a green bay,
Rage, rage against the dying of the light.

10   Wild men who caught and sang the sun in flight,
And learn, too late, they grieved it on its way,
Do not go gentle into that good night.

Grave men, near death, who see with blinding sight
Blind eyes could blaze like meteors and be gay,
15   Rage, rage against the dying of the light.

And you, my father, there on the sad height,
Curse, bless, me now with your fierce tears, I pray.
Do not go gentle into that good night.
Rage, rage against the dying of the light.

As you read, be aware of the arrangement of lines and their rhyme pattern. Which lines repeat?

Good night is a way of saying goodbye and also a metaphor for death. If night, or death, is "good," why does the speaker say the dying man should not accept it easily?

---

rave speak wildly   **forked** struck with two or more parts   **grave** serious; thoughtful

Do Not Go Gentle into That Good Night by Dylan Thomas

Directions Choose the letter of the best answer or write the answer using complete sentences.

Comprehension: Identifying Facts

1. Whom does the poet address in this poem?
   A wise men
   B wild men
   C good men
   D his father

2. What is the poet asking the listener to do?

3. Who are the "wild men" of line 10? What does it mean that they "sang the sun in flight"?

Comprehension: Putting Ideas Together

4. Examples of other men's deaths in this poem suggest that most people _____.
   A are afraid to die
   B feel death is unfair
   C want to live longer to accomplish their goals
   D accept death calmly because it is "right"

5. What images of light does the poem contain? What do they symbolize?

6. What knowledge have wise men gained at the end of their lives? good men? wild men? grave men?

Understanding Literature: Rhythm, Style, and Voice

This poem has a strict rhythm. Each line contains 10 syllables and five strong beats. Its regularity helps contain the passionate, urgent voice of the speaker. The poem's style mixes great control with violent emotion; the result is a powerful appeal to fight death.

7. What do you think the strict rhythm of the poem adds that a free verse format would lack?

8. Explain why words such as *burn and rave at close of day* and *blaze like meteors* are good choices to express this poet's theme.

Critical Thinking

9. Does this poet think a human can defeat death by fighting it? What tells you this?

Thinking Creatively

10. At life's end, what do you think most people would like to do over or do differently? Explain your choice.

Grammar Check

Verbs have tenses that show when different actions occur. Present tense expresses current, constant, or repeated action (They *rage* against death). Past tense expresses past action (They *raged* until the end). One kind of tense expresses continuing action by combining a form of the verb *be* with the *-ing* form of the verb (Someone *is raging*). Some verbs change spelling when different tenses are formed. For example, the present participle form of *die* is spelled *dying*. The *ie* is replaced by a *-y* before *-ing* is added.

- Write the present, past, and present participle forms of *cry*. Underline any changes in spelling. Use each verb form in a sentence.

- Write the same three forms for these verbs: *try, belie*. Underline the changes in spelling you see.

 Writing on Your Own

How would you reply to this poem's commands? Write a response telling your view of the proper way to meet death. Choose words and construct sentences that are appropriate to your subject and mood.

 Speaking

The obituary column of a newspaper contains articles about people who have recently died. Read an obituary column and choose one article that interests you. Use the information in it to prepare a brief eulogy, or speech praising someone who has died. Practice your presentation until you can say it smoothly and with expression. Give the eulogy to classmates.

Listening

Find a recording of Dylan Thomas reading his poems. (You can find Internet audio files by entering the keywords *Dylan Thomas readings audio* in a search engine.) If possible, listen to Thomas's reading of "Do Not Go Gentle into That Good Night." Discuss what his reading adds to your understanding of the poem.

BEFORE READING THE SELECTION

The Horses *by Ted Hughes*

Ted Hughes
1930–1998

Objectives

- To read and understand a poem
- To describe the style of a poem
- To identify elements that help create style in a poem

About the Author

Edward James (Ted) Hughes was born in 1930 in Yorkshire. The rugged wilderness and mountains of this region of northern England greatly affected Hughes's imagination. The starkness of the land and the nature he observed there have an important place in his work. Hughes's poetry contains powerful descriptions of the beauty and harshness he saw in nature and animals. However, it also shows tenderness.

Hughes studied at Cambridge University. In 1957, he published his first book of poetry, *The Hawk in the Rain*. It was the beginning of a writing career of great energy and variety. In all, Hughes wrote more than 90 books, including poetry, children's books, short stories, plays, and translations. He became poet laureate of England in 1984 and held the position until his death 14 years later.

From 1956 to 1962, Hughes was married to American poet Sylvia Plath. She committed suicide in 1963 after they separated. Hughes died of liver cancer in 1998.

About the Selection

"The Horses" appeared in Hughes's first volume, *The Hawk in the Rain*. Its theme is one he returned to again and again: human relationships with nature. Its landscape is that of his youth, filled with wild, barren bogs and bounded by mountains and sea. The poem's powerful metaphors and realistic view of nature are typical of his work.

Literary Terms This poem's **style**, or use of language, is simple and powerful. Hughes's technique focuses the readers' attention on the stark and violent nature of the world and the loneliness of living things in that world. Hughes uses sentence structure, word choice, and figurative language to create his voice. His personality in print is matter-of-fact but at the same time filled with awe for the power of nature.

style an author's way of writing

Reading on Your Own Before you read the selection, think about your views of dawn. Then read to see how the poet's perceptions of the world change as light gradually enters the darkened world.

Writing on Your Own Write a description of a horse or a herd of horses. You may work from a photograph, an artwork, a film you have seen, or a real experience. Choose words to give your writing a style that is appropriate to your feeling about horses.

Vocabulary Focus Poets may invent words or combinations of words to describe places or events with a precise meaning and mood. In "The Horses," Hughes describes the darkness just before sunrise as "hour-before-dawn." This informs readers that it is still quite dark out but will soon begin to lighten. Stillness is described as "frost-making." What quality does this suggest? Find more of Hughes's invented words (*moorline* in line 7, *megalith-still* in line 10, *moor-ridge* in line 16). Read the sentence in which each word is used and predict what the word means.

Think Before You Read What sort of mood is suggested by a moor—an open, rolling bogland on which only grasses grow?

THE HORSES

As you read, think about the adjectives Hughes uses to describe the nonliving parts of nature. What images of Earth and the universe are created?

I climbed through woods in the hour-before-dawn dark.
Evil air, a frost-making stillness,

Not a leaf, not a bird—
A world cast in frost. I came out above the wood

5   Where my breath left **tortuous** statues in the iron light.
But the valleys were draining the darkness

Till the **moorline**—blackening **dregs** of the brightening
        grey—
Halved the sky ahead. And I saw the horses:

Huge in the dense grey—ten together—
10 **Megalith**-still. They breathed, making no move,

With **draped** manes and tilted hind-hooves,
Making no sound.

The poet describes his first impression of the horses. Do they seem living or nonliving?

I passed: not one snorted or jerked its head.
Grey silent fragments

15 Of a grey silent world.

I listened in emptiness on the **moor-ridge.**
The curlew's tear turned its edge on the silence.

Slowly detail leafed from the darkness. Then the sun
Orange, red, red erupted

The *curlew* is a wading bird of coastal marshes and moors. Its ringing cry cuts through the silence dramatically here.

tortuous twisted; complex	**dregs** remains	**draped** arranged in flowing folds
moorline edge where the forest ends and the moor begins; horizon	**megalith** large stone used as building block by prehistoric peoples	**moor-ridge** highest part of the moor

20 Silently, and splitting to its core tore and flung cloud,
Shook the gulf open, showed blue,

And the big planets hanging—.
I turned

Stumbling in the fever of a dream, down towards
25 The dark woods, from the **kindling** tops,

And came to the horses.
                              There, still they stood,
But now steaming and glistening under the flow of light,

Their draped stone manes, their tilted hind-hooves
30 **Stirring** under a thaw while all around them

The frost showed its fires. But still they made no sound.
Not one snorted or stamped,

Their hung heads patient as the horizons,
High over valleys, in the red levelling rays—

35 In **din** of the crowded streets, going among the years,
       the faces,
May I still meet my memory in so lonely a place

Between the streams and
       the red clouds,
            hearing curlews,
Hearing the horizons **endure.**

What kind of change does the sunrise bring? What is its effect on the world and the poet?

How does the light change the poet's view of the horses?

| **kindling** catching fire | **din** loud, continual noise | **endure** continue without change |
| **stirring** beginning to move; waking | | |

Directions Choose the letter of the best answer or write the answer using complete sentences.

Comprehension: Identifying Facts

1. Before dawn, the horses seem to the speaker to be most like _____.

   A stone   **C** the moon
   B frost   **D** humans

2. To what is the sun's rising compared?

3. In what way are the horses like the horizons revealed at dawn?

Comprehension: Putting Ideas Together

4. Which statement best summarizes what happens in this poem?

   A A walk before dawn reveals nature's power through the sunrise.
   B Horses that have run away are found by a stranger at dawn.
   C The dark frightens a walker who finds the way with dawn.
   D A dreamer awakes from a nightmare about stone horses.

5. What is the effect of the sun on the world in this poem?

6. What is the same about the horses before and after the sunrise? What is different?

Understanding Literature: Style and Voice

A writer's style is expressed through the words chosen and the kinds of sentences they form. The writer's voice, or personality, is reflected in the style, pace, sounds, and feelings of the language.

7. As Hughes describes the world, his voice is both blunt and awed. Point out some of the language that reveals these attitudes.

8. Hughes uses many commas, colons, and dashes in his sentences. What effect does punctuation have on his style and voice?

Critical Thinking

9. Why do you think the poet admires the horses so much by the end of the poem?

Thinking Creatively

10. Hughes finds a violence in nature that shakes him. What have you seen in the natural world? How has it affected you?

Grammar Check

Participle forms of verbs may be used as part of a verb phrase (as in line 1, "I *climbed*," and line 6, "valleys *were draining* the darkness"). They may also be adjectives (as in line 7, "*blackening* dregs of the *brightening* grey"). Present participles are -*ing* forms of a verb. Past participles are -*ed* forms.

- Find the participles in lines 11, 21, 25, 28, 30, 34, and 35. Write each participle and the noun it modifies.

- Choose three of the participles from your list. Write your own sentences using them as adjectives.

 Writing on Your Own

Write a journal entry describing an act of nature you have experienced. Use vivid adjectives and strong verbs to create clear images of the event. Use time order to give a sense of the event's beginning, middle, and end. Tell how the event affected you.

 Speaking

Find out more about a breed, or type, of horse and prepare a brief oral report about it. Organize your ideas around key topics, such as physical descriptions, human use, and where the breed orginated. Use photographs and other visual aids to enhance your presentation. Then present your report to the class.

 Listening

Listen as your teacher or a volunteer reads "The Horses" aloud. What do you notice that was not clear when you read it silently? Make notes about any new insights you gain into the poem.

 Technology

The relationship between people and horses is thousands of years old. Use the Internet to locate images of the horse in art through time. Use a computer to download and print copies of some of these images. Use them to create a poster about what horses mean to humans.

BEFORE READING THE SELECTION

Graham Greene
1904–1991

Objectives

- To read and understand a short story
- To define setting and understand its importance in a story
- To recognize humor and analyze what creates it
- To identify the point of view in a short story and explain its effects

About the Author

Graham Greene was born in 1904 in Hertfordshire, a county in southeast England, just north of London. As a boy, he attended the school where his father was headmaster. Being teased by classmates made his time there very unhappy. His parents sent him to a therapist in London, who advised Greene to write. When he attended Balliol College, Greene became interested in politics and sharpened his writing skills.

After college, Greene worked as an editor and kept writing. By 1929, he had published a successful novel. He left his job to write full time. His next novels did not sell well. Desperate for money, he wrote the novel *Stamboul Train* "to please the public." It was very successful and was adapted as a film— *Orient Express*—in 1934. Many of Greene's 26 novels enjoyed great success with the public. He also wrote plays for stage and screenplays for movies. Among his best-known works are *The Power and the Glory* (1940), *The End of the Affair* (1951), *A Burnt-Out Case* (1960), and *The Honorary Consul* (1973).

Greene led a colorful life. He traveled far and wide—often to "hot spots" of the world—to get material for writing. However, he also apparently was useful to the British secret service, for whom he spied. Greene lived his final years in Switzerland and died there in 1991.

About the Selection

"A Shocking Accident" was published in 1967 in Greene's short-story collection *May We Borrow Your Husband?* It looks humorously at things Greene actually lived. The story's protagonist attends a private school and is teased by classmates. Jerome's father is an author and a world traveler. However, unlike Greene, he writes dull travel books. Greene has Jerome imagine his father as a spy for the British secret service, a role Greene really did fill.

Literary Terms A short story is a brief piece of fiction. It has a plot, **setting** (a time and place), characters, point of view, and theme, or main idea. The point of view, or the storyteller's view, controls how we see the story's events and characters. In this story, the narrator's point of view creates **humor** with its light look at a boy's difficulties with his father's death.

Reading on Your Own Greene gives details and dialogue to show readers the traits of his main character. As you read the story, evaluate Jerome's words, actions, and way of thinking to help you decide what sort of person he is.

Writing on Your Own Think of something that happened to you that would make a good story. Write about how you could approach the incident to make it dramatic. Then write about how you could change your approach to make it funny.

Vocabulary Focus Several suffixes may be added to verbs or adjectives to create nouns. For example, adding -*sion* turns the verb *apprehend* into the noun *apprehension*. Adding -*ity* turns the verb *perplex* into the noun *perplexity*. Find the nouns *convulsion, callousness, commiseration,* and *obscurity* in the story. Write each word and identify the verb or adjective from which it is formed. Underline the suffix in the word. Use context and your analysis of the word's parts to predict its meaning.

Think Before You Read How would you feel if listeners laughed at a sad story you told? Predict how the main character of this story will react when this happens to him.

A Shocking Accident

As you read, notice how much the narrator shares about Jerome. Also note details that inform you of the story's setting and characters.

Marlborough and *Rugby* are private schools that these students hope to attend.

1

Jerome was called into his housemaster's room in the break between the second and the third class on a Thursday morning. He had no fear of trouble, for he was a warden—the name that the **proprietor** and headmaster of a rather expensive preparatory school had chosen to give to approved, reliable boys in the lower **forms** (from a warden one became a guardian and finally before leaving, it was hoped for Marlborough or Rugby, a crusader). The housemaster, Mr. Wordsworth, sat behind his desk with an appearance of **perplexity** and **apprehension.** Jerome had the odd impression when he entered that he was a cause of fear.

"Sit down, Jerome," Mr. Wordsworth said. "All going well with the **trigonometry?**"

"Yes, sir."

"I've had a telephone call, Jerome. From your aunt. I'm afraid I have bad news for you."

"Yes, sir?"

"Your father has had an accident."

"Oh."

Mr. Wordsworth looked at him with some surprise. "A serious accident."

"Yes, sir?"

---

proprietor owner	**perplexity** confusion	**trigonometry** mathematical study of properties of triangles
forms grade levels in school	**apprehension** nervousness; fear	

Jerome worshipped his father: the verb is exact. As man re-creates God, so Jerome re-created his father—from a restless **widowed** author into a mysterious adventurer who travelled in far places—Nice, Beirut, Majorca, even the Canaries. The time had arrived about his eighth birthday when Jerome believed that his father either "ran guns" or was a member of the British Secret Service. Now it occurred to him that his father might have been wounded in "a hail of machine-gun bullets."

Mr. Wordsworth played with the ruler on his desk. He seemed at a loss how to continue. He said, "You know your father was in Naples?"

"Yes, sir."

"Your aunt heard from the hospital today."

"Oh."

Mr. Wordsworth said with desperation, "It was a street accident."

"Yes, sir?" It seemed quite likely to Jerome that they would call it a street accident. The police of course had fired first; his father would not take human life except as a last **resort.**

"I'm afraid your father was very seriously hurt indeed."

"Oh."

"In fact, Jerome, he died yesterday. Quite without pain."

"Did they shoot him through the heart?"

"I beg your pardon. What did you say, Jerome?"

"Did they shoot him through the heart?"

"Nobody shot him, Jerome. A pig fell on him." An **inexplicable convulsion** took place in the nerves of Mr. Wordsworth's face; it really looked for a moment as though he were going to laugh. He closed his eyes, **composed** his features and said rapidly as though it were necessary to **expel** the story as rapidly as possible. "Your father was walking along a street in Naples when a pig fell on him. A shocking accident. Apparently in the poorer quarters of Naples they keep pigs on

Jerome has invented a fantasy about his father's life. *Nice,* France, and *Beirut,* Lebanon, are port cities on the Mediterranean Sea. *Majorca* is an island in the Mediterranean, off the southeast coast of Spain. *The Canaries* are a group of islands off the west coast of North Africa. *Naples* is a city in Italy. These were, and continue to be, popular vacation spots.

How does Jerome react when he learns his father is dead? Why does he assume his father was shot?

widowed had a spouse die	**inexplicable** not explainable	**composed** calmed
resort option; way out	**convulsion** fit of shaking or twitching	**expel** force out

What makes Mr. Wordsworth shake *with emotion?* What emotion is he trying to hide?

their balconies. This one was on the fifth floor. It had grown too fat. The balcony broke. The pig fell on your father."

Mr. Wordsworth left his desk rapidly and went to the window, turning his back on Jerome. He shook a little with emotion.

Jerome said, "What happened to the pig?"

2

What do you learn about Jerome's character in this paragraph?

This was not **callousness** on the part of Jerome, as it was interpreted by Mr. Wordsworth to his colleagues (he even discussed with them whether, perhaps, Jerome was yet fitted to be a warden). Jerome was only attempting to **visualize** the strange scene to get the details right. Nor was Jerome a boy who cried; he was a boy who **brooded,** and it never occurred to him at his preparatory school that the circumstances of his father's death were comic—they were still part of the mystery of life. It was later, in his first term at his public school, when he told the story to his best friend, that he began to realize how it affected others. Naturally after that **disclosure** he was known, rather unreasonably, as Pig.

Capri is an island near Naples and a popular area for tourists. *Fariglione* is a famous rock formation in that area.

Unfortunately his aunt had no sense of humour. There was an enlarged snapshot of his father on the piano; a large sad man in an unsuitable dark suit posed in Capri with an umbrella (to guard him against sunstroke), the Faraglione rocks forming the background. By the age of sixteen Jerome was well aware that the portrait looked more like the author of *Sunshine and Shade* and *Rambles in the Balearics* than an agent of the Secret Service. All the same he loved the memory of his father: he still possessed an album fitted with picture-postcards (the stamps had been soaked off long ago for his other collection), and it pained him when his aunt **embarked** with strangers on the story of his father's death.

callousness coldness
visualize imagine

brooded worried; thought dark thoughts

disclosure confession

embarked started

"A shocking accident," she would begin, and the stranger would compose his or her features into the correct shape for interest and **commiseration.** Both reactions, of course, were false, but it was terrible for Jerome to see how suddenly, midway in her rambling **discourse,** the interest would become genuine. "I can't think how such things can be allowed in a civilized country," his aunt would say. "I suppose one has to regard Italy as civilized. One is prepared for all kinds of things abroad, of course, and my brother was a great traveller. He always carried a water-filter with him. It was far less expensive, you know, than buying all those bottles of mineral water. My brother always said that his filter paid for his dinner wine. You can see from that what a careful man he was, but who could possibly have expected when he was walking along the Via Dottore Manuele Panucci on his way to the Hydrographic Museum that a pig would fall on him?" That was the moment when the interest became genuine.

Jerome's father had not been a very **distinguished** writer, but the time always seems to come, after an author's death, when somebody thinks it worth his while to write a letter to the *Times Literary Supplement* announcing the preparation of a biography and asking to see any letters or documents or receive any anecdotes from friends of the dead man. Most of the biographies, of course, never appear—one wonders

What is humorous about the way Jerome's aunt tells about her brother's death? about the way listeners react?

commiseration sympathy

discourse talk

distinguished honored; famous

Jerome is afraid that biographers will contact him. Why is this fear needless?

Jerome's career as a *chartered* (licensed) accountant makes him more "official" and serious. As you read, think about how this choice of career affects his relationships, his communication style, and his own emotional state.

A *Neapolitan* is a person from Naples, Italy.

Jerome rehearses and plots ways of telling about his father's death that people will not laugh at. Why?

whether the whole thing may not be an **obscure** form of blackmail and whether many a potential writer of a biography or **thesis** finds the means in this way to finish his education at Kansas or Nottingham. Jerome, however, as a chartered accountant, lived far from the literary world. He did not realize how small the **menace** really was, or that the danger period for someone of his father's obscurity had long passed. Sometimes he rehearsed the method of **recounting** his father's death so as to reduce the comic element to its smallest dimensions—it would be of no use to refuse information, for in that case the biographer would undoubtedly visit his aunt who was living to a great old age with no sign of **flagging.**

It seemed to Jerome that there were two possible methods—the first led gently up to the accident, so that by the time it was described the listener was so well prepared that the death came really as an **anti-climax.** The chief danger of laughter in such a story was always surprise. When he rehearsed this method Jerome began boringly enough.

"You know Naples and those high **tenement** buildings? Somebody once told me that the Neapolitan always feels at home in New York just as the man from Turin feels at home in London because the river runs in much the same way in both cities. Where was I? Oh, yes. Naples, of course. You'd be surprised in the poorer quarters what things they keep on the balconies of those sky-scraping tenements—not washing, you know, or bedding, but things like livestock, chickens or even pigs. Of course the pigs get no exercise whatever and fatten all the quicker." He could imagine how his hearer's eyes would have glazed by this time. "I've no idea, have you, how heavy a pig can be, but these old buildings are all badly in need of repair. A balcony on the fifth floor gave way under one of those pigs. It struck the third floor balcony on its way down

obscure not well known	**menace** threat	**anti-climax** letdown
thesis scholarly paper	**recounting** telling	**tenement** slum
	flagging slowing down	

and sort of **ricochetted** into the street. My father was on the way to the Hydrographic Museum when the pig hit him. Coming from that height and that angle it broke his neck." This was really a masterly attempt to make an **intrinsically** interesting subject boring.

The other method Jerome rehearsed had the virtue of **brevity.**

"My father was killed by a pig."

"Really? In India?"

"No, in Italy."

"How interesting. I never realized there was pig-sticking in Italy. Was your father keen on polo?"

In course of time, neither too early nor too late, rather as though, in his **capacity** as a chartered accountant, Jerome had studied the **statistics** and taken the average, he became engaged to be married: to a pleasant fresh-faced girl of twenty-five whose father was a doctor in Pinner. Her name was Sally, her favourite author was still Hugh Walpole, and she had adored babies ever since she had been given a doll at the age of five which moved its eyes and made water. Their relationship was contented rather than exciting, as became the love-affair of a chartered accountant; it would never have done if it had interfered with the figures.

One thought worried Jerome, however. Now that within a year he might himself become a father, his love for the dead man increased; he realized what affection had gone into the picture-postcards. He felt a longing to protect his memory, and uncertain whether this quiet love of his would survive if Sally were so **insensitive** as to laugh when she heard the story of his father's death. **Inevitably** she would hear it when Jerome brought her to dinner with his aunt. Several times he tried to tell her himself, as she was naturally anxious to know all she could that concerned him.

> What kind of relationship do Sally and Jerome have? How do you think he will tell her about his father?

ricochetted bounced	**capacity** position; job	**insensitive** unfeeling, rude
intrinsically basically	**statistics** branch of math dealing with numerical data	**inevitably** unavoidably
brevity shortness		

"You were very small when your father died?"

"Just nine."

"Poor little boy," she said.

"I was at school. They broke the news to me."

"Did you take it very hard?"

"I can't remember."

"You never told me how it happened."

"It was very sudden. A street accident."

"You'll never drive fast, will you, Jemmy?" (She had begun to call him "Jemmy.") It was too late then to try the second method—the one he thought of as the pig-sticking one.

They were going to marry quietly in a **registry-office** and have their honeymoon at Torquay. He avoided taking her to see his aunt until a week before the wedding, but then the night came, and he could not have told himself whether his **apprehension** was more for his father's memory or the security of his own love.

The moment came all too soon. "Is that Jemmy's father?" Sally asked, picking up the portrait of the man with the umbrella.

"Yes, dear. How did you guess?"

"He has Jemmy's eyes and brow, hasn't he?"

"Has Jerome lent you his books?"

"No."

"I will give you a set for your wedding. He wrote so tenderly about his travels. My own favourite is *Nooks and Crannies*. He would have had a great future. It made that shocking accident all the worse."

"Yes?"

Jerome longed to leave the room and not see that loved face crinkle with irresistible amusement.

"I had so many letters from his readers after the pig fell on him." She had never been so abrupt before.

And then the miracle happened. Sally did not laugh. Sally sat with open eyes of horror while his aunt told her the story,

Torquay is a city in the area of southwest England known as the English Riviera. People like to take vacations there.

Why is Sally's reaction a *miracle?*

registry-office government office where marriages are recorded

and at the end, "How horrible," Sally said. "It makes you think, doesn't it? Happening like that. Out of a clear sky."

Jerome's heart sang with joy. It was as though she had **appeased** his fear for ever. In the taxi going home he kissed her with more passion than he had ever shown and she returned it. There were babies in her pale blue pupils, babies that rolled their eyes and made water.

"A week today," Jerome said, and she squeezed his hand. "Penny for your thoughts, my darling."

"I was wondering," Sally said, "what happened to the poor pig?"

"They almost certainly had it for dinner," Jerome said happily and kissed the dear child again.

Why is Jerome so happy?

What theme or underlying message does the writer intend to give in this story?

appeased calmed; soothed

AFTER READING THE SELECTION

A Shocking Accident   by Graham Greene

Directions Choose the letter of the best answer or write the answer using complete sentences.

Comprehension: Identifying Facts

1. What killed Jerome's father?
   - **A** a hail of bullets
   - **B** an automobile accident
   - **C** a rare disease
   - **D** a falling pig

2. Why does Mr. Wordsworth have to calm himself and speak quickly?
   - **A** He is overcome with emotion.
   - **B** He is fighting not to laugh aloud.
   - **C** He feels sorry for Jerome.
   - **D** He is not well.

3. Why does Jerome want to know what happened to the pig?

4. What do Mr. Wordsworth and others at the school assume from Jerome's response to the news?

5. What did Jerome's father do for a living?

6. How does Jerome's aunt cause him pain?

7. What profession does Jerome go into?

8. Who is Sally?

9. Why doesn't Jerome tell Sally about the way his father died?

10. How does Sally react when she hears the story?

Comprehension: Putting Ideas Together

11. As a boy, Jerome is _____.
    - **A** brooding and imaginative
    - **B** very unhappy at school
    - **C** angry with his father
    - **D** closer to his mother than to his father

12. Most people who hear about how Jerome's father died react with _____.
    - **A** horror
    - **C** sympathy
    - **B** amusement
    - **D** real concern

13. How does Jerome's attitude toward his father change throughout his life?

14. How did Jerome's father differ from Jerome's childhood idea of him?

15. Why is it unlikely that anyone will write a biography about Jerome's father?

16. What shows you that the adult Jerome is still hurt by people laughing at the way his father died?

17. Describe the love that Sally and Jerome share.

18. How is this love changed when Sally hears the story about Jerome's father?

19. What is ironic about this change?

20. How is Sally's response like Jerome's when he first learns of his father's death? How is it different?

Understanding Literature: Short Story, Point of View, Theme, and Humor

A short story is a brief work of fiction with a plot, setting, characters, and theme, or main idea. Its point of view, or the storyteller's position, determines the way readers see these elements. In this selection, the storyteller uses humor to shape readers' attitudes toward characters.

21. Describe the setting of this story and name its characters.

22. Which seems more important in this story: plot or character development? Why?

23. Which character does the storyteller know the most about? How is this helpful?

24. What makes the aunt's and Jerome's different methods for telling about the accident funny?

25. What is humorous about the death of Jerome's father?

Critical Thinking

26. How did Greene draw on his own life experience to write this story?

27. Why do you think Jerome believed his father was a spy or a gun runner?

28. How was Jerome's father the opposite of his son's idea of him?

29. Do you think Jerome grew up to become much like his father—a careful man? Explain your thinking.

Thinking Creatively

30. Do you think people usually remember a loved one who has died as that person actually was, or do they make the dead person better than he or she actually was? Explain.

After Reading **continued on next page**

A Shocking Accident *by Graham Greene*

 ### Grammar Check

Proper nouns name persons, places, or things and are capitalized. Names of streets, buildings, countries, cities, books, and newspapers are some examples of proper nouns. Some proper nouns, such as titles, contain more than one word. In these proper nouns, capitalize the first word and every important word, as in *Sunshine and Shade.*

- Find and list as many proper nouns in this selection as you can.

- Beside each noun, write the class in which it belongs, for example, *Thursday, day of the week.*

- Compare your lists with a classmate's list. Add any proper nouns you missed.

 ### Writing on Your Own

Write an autobiography telling about your life at school. Select events that are important to you. Arrange events in time order. See Appendix C for tips on how to make your writing specific and lively.

 ### Speaking

Find or make up your own joke or humorous anecdote (brief, amusing story). It should be long enough to take at least 30 seconds to tell. Make notes to remind you of key ideas or phrases. Practice delivering your joke or anecdote. Decide where you need to pause and change your tone of voice or pace. Present your anecdote before a small group or the class.

 ### Listening

Talk with a travel agent or watch a television program about touring Italy. Listen and observe to decide what cities or areas of Italy you would like to visit and why. Make notes about the places that interest you.

 ### Research

Research Graham Greene's role in the British secret service. Search the Internet, biographies, and magazine articles for facts and theories about where and how Greene spied for his country. Take notes on your findings, but separate documented facts from opinions and unproven ideas.

BEFORE READING THE SELECTION

Not Waving but Drowning   by Stevie Smith

About the Author

Margaret Florence Smith was born in 1902 in Yorkshire in northern England. At the age of 3, she moved with her mother and sister to London. When her mother became ill, Smith's aunt came to live with them. Smith lived with her aunt until her own death in 1971.

After graduating from college, Smith went to work in a publisher's office as a private secretary. She remained in this job for 30 years but soon decided to try writing her own works. Her first book, *Novel on Yellow Paper*, was published in 1936. Her first volume of poetry, *A Good Time Was Had by All*, appeared in 1937 and established her as a poet. In all, Smith wrote three novels and nine books of poetry under the pen name Stevie Smith. Gradually, her reputation grew. In 1969, she received the Queen's Gold Medal for Poetry. *Stevie*, a play based on her life, was filmed in 1978.

Smith wrote in a wide variety of styles, but her style was usually dark and strange. Her witty voice masks meanings that are deeper and darker than readers expect. Closer reading reveals themes such as death, loss of innocence, love, and religion.

Stevie Smith
1902–1971

Objectives

- To read and understand a free verse poem
- To identify and explain symbolism in a poem

About the Selection

"Not Waving but Drowning" is a poem in Smith's 1957 book by the same name. It is her most famous poem and is largely autobiographical. It tells the very brief story of a drowning man whose thrashing in the sea is mistaken for waving by people on the shore. It is also a metaphor for any situation in which cries for help are unheard or ignored.

Before Reading continued on next page

Not Waving but Drowning   by Stevie Smith

symbolism
the larger meaning
of a person, place,
or object

Literary Terms This selection is an example of free verse. Notice that its lines do not have a regular length or strict rhyming pattern (although even-numbered lines in each stanza feature rhyme or approximate rhyme). This poem's rhythms come from patterns of actual speech. It also relies on **symbolism** to communicate its meaning. The entire story of the drowning man represents a larger meaning.

Reading on Your Own This poem does not explain the situation. Instead, it relies on details that suggest the situation. Read the poem to infer what has happened and why.

Writing on Your Own Think about the different meanings *drowning* and *cold* can have. List each definition and write a sentence using the word with this meaning. Include idioms and figures of speech such as *the cold shoulder*.

Vocabulary Focus There are differences in the vocabulary of British and American English. Where Americans might say "poor fellow," Smith says "poor chap." The word *chap* is a shortened form of *chapman*. This word comes from Old English *ceapman,* which meant "peddler." Over time, the word's meaning became more general. Smith says, "He always loved larking." Americans would be more likely to say, "He always was a joker." To *lark* is to amuse oneself through harmless fun or mischief.

Think Before You Read What do you think the drowned man in this poem will have to say?

Not *Waving* but Drowning

Nobody heard him, the dead man,
But still he lay moaning:
I was much further out than you thought
And not waving but drowning.

As you read,
think about what,
or whom, the
dead man might
symbolize.

5 Poor chap, he always loved **larking**
And now he's dead
It must have been too cold for him his heart gave way,
They said.

How is this poem
like natural speech?

Oh, no no no, it was too cold always
10 (Still the dead one lay moaning)
I was much too far out all my life
And not waving but drowning.

larking fooling around; joking

Directions Choose the letter of the best answer or write the answer using complete sentences.

Comprehension: Identifying Facts

1. This poem seems at first to be about _____.

    A someone who drowned
    B dangers of the sea
    C a day at the beach
    D practical jokes

2. Who is speaking in lines 3–4? Who is speaking in lines 5–8?

3. What do people think the swimmer was doing, according to line 5?

Comprehension: Putting Ideas Together

4. What is this poem about, mostly?
    A dangers of swimming
    B practical joking
    C unheard cries for help
    D how people are remembered after they die

5. On a deeper level, the "dead man" represents the poet. What does it mean that she was "much further out than you thought"?

6. Is the tone of this poem humorous or serious? Is its subject humorous or serious?

Understanding Literature: Free Verse and Symbolism

This poem is written in free verse. It has no strict rhyming pattern or regular line length. Its rhythm proceeds from the language of speech. It does not state its main idea but relies on symbolism to establish a larger meaning for the incident.

7. Why is free verse appropriate for this poem?

8. What do drowning and cold symbolize in this poem?

Critical Thinking

9. What do you think is the main idea of this poem? Why might the poet have hidden it?

Thinking Creatively

10. Do you think most people have trouble asking for help? Explain why you think this.

Grammar Check

This poem contains quotations, the spoken words of people. Usually, a person's exact words are placed in quotation marks (" "). A comma sets them off from words of saying (such as *he said* or *she groaned*). If the quotation ends with a question mark or exclamation mark, that mark goes inside the final quotation mark. If it would normally end with a period and is followed by words of saying, a comma goes inside the final quotation mark: *"What are you doing?" she cried. "I'm going home," he explained.*

- Rewrite the parts of this poem that represent spoken words. Include words of saying, or add them, if necessary. Use quotation marks, end marks, and commas correctly.

- Compare your quotations with a partner's. Correct any errors.

- Discuss why you think Smith did not include quotation marks in her poem.

 Writing on Your Own

Do you think some people cover their hurt and loneliness by joking around? Write a journal entry about an incident you observed that illustrates this defense. Use Appendix C for tips on using specific, concrete language and imagery to capture action and feeling vividly.

 Speaking and Listening

Talk with a guidance counselor (or listen to a presentation by a guidance counselor in class) to find out about actions that represent "cries for help" by troubled people. Ask questions about any explanations you do not understand.

Research

Find data about the main causes of death among young people and the general population. Search government databases online to locate information. Try entering keywords such as *U.S. teen deaths, statistics on causes of death*. Compile your data into a table comparing these statistics. Write a paragraph summarizing what the data show. Are you surprised by what you found?

Beat the Blues with Brian *by Jane Shilling*

Jane Shilling

Objectives

- To read and understand a newspaper column
- To explain why news writing is nonfiction
- To analyze a journalist's writing style

About the Author

Jane Shilling has been a columnist and critic with *The Times* newspaper in London for many years. She also is a book reviewer for the newspapers *Sunday Telegraph* and *Evening Standard*. Shilling is a graduate of Oxford University. She lives in Greenwich, England, with her son.

Shilling's first book, *The Fox in the Cupboard*, is about her experiences with learning to ride a horse and taking up fox hunting. It was published in 2005.

About the Selection

While a newspaper column is nonfiction, it is not like a typical news story, which reports facts objectively. Columnists give their own opinions and understanding of people and events. They become recognized for their unique styles and opinions.

This selection shows Shilling's witty, sharp delivery of both fact and opinion about current events. She draws on personal experience for examples to support her ideas and opinions. Using a comic presentation, she makes us smile about serious topics.

"Beat the Blues with Brian" takes aim at current social issues such as depression. However, Shilling's style is so entertaining and conversational that the reader hardly realizes something serious has been shared until after reading.

Literary Terms This selection is a newspaper **column** and therefore a type of **nonfiction.** It reports about real people and events. A column is a special kind of article that appears regularly in a newspaper or magazine. Generally, a columnist focuses on one subject area, such as sports, entertainment, or current events. In each column, he or she discusses issues and expresses views about them based on experience.

Reading on Your Own As you read Shilling's column, consider which statements tell facts and which tell opinions. Look for Shilling's biases, or "slant." Weighing fact and opinion will help you judge the issues Shilling covers.

Writing on Your Own Make a word web showing the different kinds of exercise you get. Rank them in order according to your preference. Write a paragraph explaining why your top form of exercise is best.

Vocabulary Focus If context does not provide enough clues to a word's meaning, look up the word's definition in a dictionary or glossary. For example, in paragraph 7, Shilling uses the word *gambit*. From the sentence we can tell that a gambit is something she is waiting for a therapist to say or do to begin a session. However, a clear meaning cannot be predicted. The dictionary offers several definitions for *gambit*. One definition fits well: "a remark intended to start a conversation or make a telling point." It is logical that a therapist would begin with words that set the direction for therapy. Other selection words that may require you to use a dictionary include *mid-ablative, psychotic, exhortation, mortification,* and *affront.*

Think Before You Read What are the blues? What do you predict Shilling will suggest as a good way to "beat the blues"?

> **column** an article that appears regularly in a newspaper or magazine
>
> **nonfiction** writing about real people and events

Beat the Blues with Brian

As you read, pay attention to the offbeat details and images that create humor. What tone do they help create?

One of the reasons I love the radio so much is the extraordinary parallel universe contained within the dull box of greyish plastic that squats like a toad on the corner of my kitchen table. Flick the switch and you never know what **surreal** oddity is going to come squirting out of the holey bit on the front.

On Saturday night, while giving the cat the late-night snack that is supposed to discourage him from roaming the house in the small hours, making a noise like the Questing Beast in search of something to eat, I turned idly to Radio 3 and came upon some **bloke** spouting in Latin about the **raucous** elephant and **sibilant** serpent. It seemed rude to turn him off in mid-**ablative absolute,** so I felt obliged to perch on the kitchen steps in my nightie, listening attentively until he'd got it all off his chest.

Then a couple of days later, there was Brian Perkins, reading the headlines in that voice of his that assures you all's right with the world because he's in charge (whatever the Prime Minister and Cabinet may think to the contrary), announcing that a charity called the Mental Health Foundation says that the cure for depression is **vigorous** exercise.

Brian Perkins, a news broadcaster, is the Brian named in the title. Note the "role" he plays in Shilling's column.

surreal dreamlike, strange	**raucous** wild	**ablative absolute** a Latin grammatical term
bloke man	**sibilant** hissing	**vigorous** energetic

The thing about depression is that it bears the same relationship to sadness as **migraine** does to ordinary headaches. I should know, having grappled on and off throughout my life with this **grisly quartet** of **maladies.** And the reason that I'm astonished by the Voice of Brian assuring me that getting out more will cheer me up no end, is that my very first episode of depression was brought on by physical exercise.

It happened when I was in my teens, a reluctant pupil at a school where a good many things made me sad—maths, German, wearing glasses and not having any friends, for a start. I can taste the sadness now—a dull sense of unease, quite distinct from the wintry depression whose unique cause was physical exercise. Hockey, netball, even girly tennis—all **conjured** the same unmistakable feeling, of a large stone dropped from a height into my chest cavity, squashing the air out of my lungs and the spirit out of my heart.

Fast forward a decade and a half, and you find me in the grip of a proper depression. Not a stone on the heart, this time, but a full-blown, life-threatening, career-wrecking nervous breakdown. Oddly enough, none of my friends noticed that it was happening, until the moment at which I was carried off in great **disarray** to a clinic and found myself giving a history to a blissfully kind male nurse, who cheered me up so much with his Julian Claryesque squeaks of "No! He never! I can't believe I'm hearing this!" that by the time I'd finished I felt all better and said sorry for wasting your time, I'm off home now.

Julian was having none of it. You come back here in the morning and see the doctor, he said. He'll sort you out, girl. Which he did, with the aid of human kindness and a brief course of drugs. The trouble began when he passed me on, if not quite cheerful, at least no longer **psychotic,** to a series

Here Shilling gives examples from her life to illustrate the difference between sadness and depression.

Shilling speaks lightly about what were very bad times in her life. How does this affect the tone of the column?

Julian Clary is a popular comedian and TV entertainer in Britain, known especially for his outrageous costumes.

migraine severe headache with nausea	**quartet** set of four	**disarray** confusion
grisly awful	**maladies** illnesses	**psychotic** out of contact with reality
	conjured called up	

How is the *badger* metaphor funny? What trait or traits does it suggest?

of therapists, each (it struck me) madder than the last. There was the one who insisted that I take my shoes off and then remained in total silence, **snuffling** like a badger while I waited for his opening **gambit**. Then there was the woman who complained that I was depressing her with my negative mental attitude.

After half a dozen such encounters, it struck me that I had two options: one was to keep searching for a therapist who didn't sound like a badger. The other was to get on with life and see what happened.

Of the two options, the second was a lot cheaper, so I took it. Shortly afterwards I bought a horse, largely by accident and, having bought it, found that I had to ride it several times a week. Which meant that, like it or not, I was taking exercise, under the supervision of the terrifying Mrs. Rogers, BHSI, MFH.

The initials after her name show Mrs. Rogers's official qualifications to teach horseback riding and jumping (as training for fox hunting).

Mrs. Rogers wasn't interested in my personal problems. She didn't care if I had writer's block, boyfriend problems or indeed psychotic episodes. What she cared about was my ability to kick on. Eventually I came to share her view.

The significance of my emotional life shrank to a pea. If I survived one of her lessons—an ordeal by fire of **exasperated exhortation**—my psychological problems vanished in a **welter** of exhaustion and triumph. If I didn't, they were entirely eclipsed by the terrible **mortification** of failing to jump a **titchy** spread of 2 ft 3 in.

These days I notice (and so does my son): that the graph of my sanity can be plotted by my encounters with the horse. When I can't ride it, I'm a monster. When I can, I can pass for what Mary Norton's Borrowers used to call a human bean.

snuffling sniffing noisily	**exasperated** fed up, annoyed	**mortification** embarrassment
gambit opening remark intended to make a telling point	**exhortation** urging or encouraging	**titchy** very small
	welter mix	

From someone with my background of disdain for physical activity, it seems almost an **affront** to admit that the fragile balance between normality and despair can be maintained by a few hours' exercise. But there it is. If you're not happy, don't talk about it: get moving.

Brian Perkins says so. And you know, Brian Knows Best.

How does Shilling summarize her views of and experiences with depression? What lesson does she want readers to learn?

affront insult

Directions Choose the letter of the best answer or write the answer using complete sentences.

Comprehension: Identifying Facts

1. Shilling says that depression is related to sadness as _____.
   A migraine is related to headaches
   B sports is related to winning
   C comedy is related to science fiction
   D writing is related to reading

2. What does the Mental Health Foundation identify as the cure for depression?

3. What activity helps Shilling get rid of her depression?

Comprehension: Putting Ideas Together

4. Shilling concludes that exercise _____.
   A can bring on depression
   B is a form of therapy
   C can help one overcome depression
   D can cause migraines

5. How do Shilling's therapists compare to her riding instructor?

6. Of the "characters" Shilling introduces, which seems most helpful to her? Explain your answer.

Understanding Literature: Columns and Nonfiction

Nonfiction is any writing that deals with real people and events. A newspaper column is one special type of nonfiction. The columnist writes a regular article for the paper. Columns focus on current issues or a special topic on which the columnist is an expert.

7. What makes Shilling's column nonfiction? What makes it entertaining?

8. How would you describe the contents and style of Shilling's column?

Critical Thinking

9. How can you explain that school sports caused depression in Shilling but riding a horse helped her overcome it?

Thinking Creatively

10. Shilling writes humorously about her teenage sadness and depression. Do you think she could have done this as a teenager? Explain why you think as you do.

✔️ Grammar Check

A colon (:) can be used to introduce a list. For example, *For your project you may choose from these options: a painting, a report, or a poem.* A colon can also introduce an illustration or explanation of the preceding statement. *My riding experience taught me a lot about myself: I have a great love for horses and good instincts in the saddle.*

- Find three example sentences in the selection that use colons. Write them and circle the colon in each.

- Write *list* beside a sentence using a colon to introduce a list. Write *explain* or *illustrate* beside a sentence using a colon to introduce an illustration or explanation.

Writing on Your Own

Think of a topic on which you could write a column. Brainstorm a list of issues related to that topic. Choose one and make a Concept Map of facts, opinions, and examples that could go into your column. (See Appendix A for a description of a Concept Map.) Organize your ideas logically and write the column. Think about how to bring out your voice in the writing.

Speaking and Listening

Scan several newspapers for columns by regular columnists. Clip one that you find interesting and highlight or summarize its focus and main idea. In a small group, share your columns by reading them aloud. Discuss whether you agree or disagree with the columnists' opinions. Listen without interrupting others. Before you respond, think about whether your reaction to a column is based on logic or emotion.

Media

Brainstorm a list of TV programs that address mental health issues. Consider different genres, such as talk shows, reality programs, dramas, and comedies. Watch one or more of these programs and summarize its story line or topic. Explain what makes it interesting, helpful, or amusing. Give your conclusion about whether it presents an accurate or reliable impression about mental health issues.

A simile is a figure of speech that makes a comparison. It compares two things using the words *like* or *as*. The things compared are very different, but in some surprising way they are alike. Consider the following sentences:

Her fingers are like her mother's.
Her fingers moved like pale spiders on the piano keys.

The first comparison is not a simile because the things compared are so similar. The second is a simile because the things compared are different, but alike in one startling way. This simile compares fingers playing the piano to spiders moving on the keys.

Similes add interest and meaning to writing by forcing readers to see certain qualities in one of the things compared. The simile above makes us picture slender, white fingers moving across piano keys. It suggests gracefulness and at the same time a forbidding, anxious mood—perhaps due to a haunting quality of the music.

The following similes appear in Wilfred Owen's "Dulce et decorum est":

"Bent double, like old beggars under sacks,"

"Knock-kneed, coughing like hags, we cursed through sludge . . ."

The first simile compares exhausted soldiers to beggars carrying heavy loads. The second simile compares them to demon-like witches. These comparisons focus our attention on the pitiful condition of the soldiers and the terrible scene around them.

Review

1. What is a simile?

2. Why is "Hal is like his mother" not a simile?

3. In "The Hollow Men," T. S. Eliot says, "Our dried voices . . . / Are quiet and meaningless/ As wind in dry grass." How are voices and wind in grass alike?

4. How do similes make writing more effective?

5. What are some reasons you think authors use similes?

Writing on Your Own

Write two similes of your own that show a surprising, but true, comparison between two things or places.

Unit 6 covers literature written between 1901 and the present. During this period, two world wars, a cold war, and worry over terrorism affected the world.

In the face of such violence and evil, old values and ideas no longer worked. Writers broke with traditional forms and attitudes. Fiction turned to stream of consciousness. Poetry used freer forms. Literature expressed the searching for values that society faced.

Selections

■ "The Soldier" by Rupert Brooke expresses a soldier's love of country.

■ "Dulce et decorum est" by Wilfred Owen unmasks the horror of war.

■ "The Second Coming" by William Butler Yeats envisions the coming of a pitiless new era.

■ The essay "Shooting an Elephant" by George Orwell shows the ugliness of colonial rule.

■ "The Hollow Men" by T. S. Eliot reveals and grieves for the spiritual emptiness of the century.

■ Virginia Woolf's story "The Duchess and the Jeweller" explores the character of a self-made man who hates, yet depends upon, the nobility.

■ "A Cup of Tea" is a short story by Katherine Mansfield that reveals the shallowness and insecurity of a wealthy young woman.

■ "Musée des Beaux Arts" is a poem by W. H. Auden about the indifference of the world to individual suffering.

■ Stephen Spender's poem "What I Expected" shows the difference between his expectations and reality.

■ "Blood, Toil, Tears and Sweat" is Winston Churchill's speech to rally the British people in May 1940.

■ In the poem "Do Not Go Gentle into That Good Night," Dylan Thomas urges his father to fight death.

■ In his poem "The Horses," Ted Hughes tells about a moving memory of natural beauty.

■ "A Shocking Accident" is a short story by Graham Greene that follows a man's attempt to come to terms with his father's humorous death.

■ In the poem "Not Waving but Drowning" Stevie Smith uses humor to mask the pain of loneliness.

■ "Beat the Blues with Brian" is a column by Jane Shilling that looks at depression from a viewpoint of personal experience.

Unit 6   REVIEW

Directions Choose the letter of the best answer or write the answer using complete sentences.

Comprehension: Identifying Facts

1. What disease killed 30 million people right after World War I?

  A measles   **C** polio
  B depression   **D** influenza

2. What was the Commonwealth of Nations?

3. List at least three reasons World War II caused so much destruction.

4. Which selection shows human problems of British imperialism?

5. Which selection is a rallying cry for Britain during World War II?

Comprehension: Putting Ideas Together

6. Which selection sees modern civilization as a grim wasteland?

  A "The Soldier"
  B "The Duchess and the Jeweller"
  C "The Hollow Men"
  D "A Shocking Accident"

7. How are "The Soldier" and "Dulce et decorum est" alike and different?

8. Describe differences between "Musée des Beaux Arts" and "Do Not Go Gentle into That Good Night."

9. What do "A Cup of Tea" and "Musée des Beaux Arts" both suggest about human suffering?

10. Which selections use humor to deliver a serious message? Why is this an effective tool?

Understanding Literature: Media

The word *media* refers to various means by which the public receives information and entertainment. Newspapers, radio, TV, movies, and magazines are traditional media. The Internet is a newer form. Media allow information to reach many people. Readers and listeners need to distinguish between fact and opinion in print and broadcasts.

11. What was Churchill's purpose in his "Blood, Toil, Tears and Sweat" speech?

12. How does his language help him achieve this purpose?

13. Is Jane Shilling's column mostly fact or opinion? Why is it entertaining?

14. "A Shocking Accident" was made into a movie. Describe what sort of person you would cast as Jerome.

15. Write down the genre of each selection in this unit. Place a * beside those that are mass media.

Critical Thinking

16. Which selection in this unit do you think shows the most positive outlook on people and the future?

17. Which poem in this unit seems least "modern"? Explain your choice.

18. How would you describe the general tone of the writing in this unit?

19. Which author in this unit do you like best? Why?

Thinking Creatively

20. How do you think the focus of writing will change in the 21st century? Why do you think this?

Speak and Listen

Choose a selection or part of a selection from the unit to present as an oral reading for the class. Decide whether your presentation should be serious or humorous. Write a brief introduction about the selection, explaining what it shows about contemporary Britain. Practice delivering your selection. Vary your loudness and expression to fit the meaning. As you listen to other presentations, write one thing you liked best about each one.

Writing on Your Own

Write your own newspaper column about an issue that has been important to contemporary writers. Fear about nuclear war and excitement about the growing uses of the computer are two possibilities. You may use a combination of facts and opinions. Use words that express your feelings and create a consistent tone and voice.

Beyond Words

Choose the selection from Unit 6 that affected you the most. Think about what it describes or the story it tells. How did it make you feel? Why do you think it had that effect on you? Create an original song, dance, or artwork that represents the selection and expresses these feelings.

Test-Taking Tip

When taking a multiple-choice test, read every choice before choosing an answer. Cross out answers you know are wrong. Choose the best answer from the remaining choices.

Peasant Girls,
Shiavax Dhajibhoj Chavda, 1965

Unit 7

From the British Dominions

British colonies lived under the rule of Great Britain. They gained their independence slowly, most of them in the 20th century. At first, Britain gave colonies limited independence, and with it came a new name: dominion. Dominions gained control over their own national concerns, but not over international matters. By stages, many of these nations became republics—fully self-governing nations.

Though they became independent, these countries were still deeply affected by British attitudes, culture, and language. Those ties are reflected in the literature of writers from the British dominions. These writers were often educated in British schools or in schools modeled after those in Britain.

In this unit, you will learn how authors from the British dominions gave original voices to their new nations. You will also see how their common history with Britain influenced those voices.

"Break a vase, and the love that reassembles the fragments is stronger than that love which took its symmetry for granted when it was whole. . . . It is such a love that reassembles our African and Asiatic fragments. . . ."

Derek Walcott,
Nobel lecture, 1992

When the 20th century began, Britain controlled lands around the world. However, throughout the century, wars and social problems weakened Britain. In addition, world attitudes changed. People in the colonies wanted freedom and wealth of their own.

A world map showing the British Empire in red, late 19th century

Those lands that had lived under British rule wanted independence. Gradually, they received it.

Many were first made dominions, or self-governing states. A dominion controlled its own internal affairs, or issues inside the borders of the country. However, Britain still managed that country's foreign affairs, defense, and trade. In addition, sometimes the governor of a dominion was British.

In 1931, the British government gave greater freedom to the dominions. Ireland had gained independence in 1922 after a bitter civil war. The Irish Free State (later the Republic of Ireland) was the first dominion to appoint a non-British governor. Its leaders pulled farther away from Britain politically and ended all government links in 1949.

During World War II, the dominions fought on the side of the British. After the war, they felt they had earned the right to be independent. India gained independence in 1947. Countries in Africa followed in the 1950s. Most of these newly independent nations

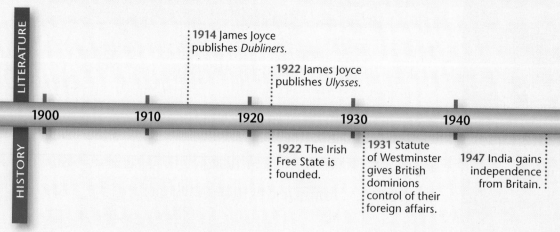

LITERATURE

1914 James Joyce publishes *Dubliners.*

1922 James Joyce publishes *Ulysses.*

1900   1910   1920   1930   1940

HISTORY

1922 The Irish Free State is founded.

1931 Statute of Westminster gives British dominions control of their foreign affairs.

1947 India gains independence from Britain.

became republics. A republic is a government with a president rather than a king or queen. Citizens of a republic elect their government officials.

The group of nations that still recognize the British ruler is called the Commonwealth of Nations. Members include Australia, Canada, New Zealand, and Jamaica. Britain ended control of its last colony, Hong Kong, in 1997. The city returned to Chinese rule.

The authors in this unit bring together diverse cultures and backgrounds. However, they have in common the influence of Britain, which affected the language, literature, and customs of colonies. Their writing has helped to establish a national identity for newly independent nations. At the same time, it reflects the history, literature, and language they share with Britain.

The story "Araby" by James Joyce reveals a boy's love-hate relationship with his country, Ireland. Penelope Lively's story "Next Term We'll Mash You" shows the fear of a youngster preparing to go to a boarding school. Many young people from the dominions were sent away to England for school. Doris Lessing, who grew up on a farm in Rhodesia (now called Zimbabwe), writes in "A Mild Attack of Locusts" about the overwhelming power of nature to crush human wants and purposes. In "Games at Twilight," Anita Desai explores the challenges of young children in a city in India, where blazing heat affects daily activities and movements. An excerpt from the epic poem *Omeros* by Derek Walcott gives a taste of the dignity, culture, and language of natives in a West Indies island nation.

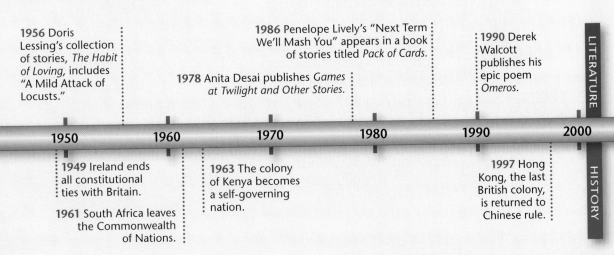

LITERATURE

1956 Doris Lessing's collection of stories, *The Habit of Loving,* includes "A Mild Attack of Locusts."

1978 Anita Desai publishes *Games at Twilight and Other Stories.*

1986 Penelope Lively's "Next Term We'll Mash You" appears in a book of stories titled *Pack of Cards.*

1990 Derek Walcott publishes his epic poem *Omeros.*

1950 — 1960 — 1970 — 1980 — 1990 — 2000

HISTORY

1949 Ireland ends all constitutional ties with Britain.

1961 South Africa leaves the Commonwealth of Nations.

1963 The colony of Kenya becomes a self-governing nation.

1997 Hong Kong, the last British colony, is returned to Chinese rule.

BEFORE READING THE SELECTION

James Joyce
1882–1941

Objectives

- To read and understand a short story written in stream of consciousness
- To describe setting and plot
- To identify characters, first-person narration, and the protagonist in a work of literature
- To define epiphany and identify an example

About the Author

James Joyce was born in Dublin, Ireland, in 1882. His father's business failures meant the large Joyce family often had money troubles. Joyce graduated from University College in Dublin in 1902. He moved to France, but the action in his books takes place in Dublin. Though he tried to escape the hardships he had known in that city, Joyce never left it in his imagination.

Joyce worked in a language school, but he focused on his writing. Money was always in short supply. Joyce's first book was *Dubliners*, a collection of stories published in 1914 in London. He wrote *A Portrait of the Artist as a Young Man*, a mostly autobiographical novel, soon after. Joyce's masterwork, *Ulysses*, appeared in 1922. In this novel, Joyce tells about one day in the life of Leopold Bloom. The entire book is made up of the thoughts of its characters. It brings the world of Dublin to life through a flood of inventive language. Joyce's last novel, *Finnegan's Wake*, is the story of the life and death of a Dublin bricklayer, told through the events of a single night.

Joyce lived most of his adult life in Paris and Switzerland. He died in Switzerland in 1941.

About the Selection

"Araby" was one of the stories in *Dubliners*, published in 1914. The story reflects both the sadness of Irish life and the promise of youth. *Araby* was the ancient name for Arabia. In the main character's mind, it represents romance and adventure. However, it refers literally to a bazaar (a kind of marketplace) in Dublin.

Literary Terms "Araby" is a **short story**, or a shorter work of fiction that has a complete **plot** (story action) and developed **characters** (the people doing the action). The story **setting** is its time and place. This story is told in the **first person.** That means the **narrator,** or storyteller, is a character in the story. In this case, the narrator is also the **protagonist,** or hero. He is a boy whose head is full of romantic ideas and idealism. By the story's end, he has an **epiphany**, or an experience which reveals to him an important truth. Joyce uses a technique called **stream of consciousness** in this story. In this method, the reader follows the story through the thoughts of the characters.

Reading on Your Own In "Araby," the main character's view of the world is as important as the story action. To help yourself focus, stop after every few paragraphs and summarize what you have read. That is, tell what has happened and what you think it means in your own words.

Writing on Your Own Imagine what a bazaar would be like. Write a description that includes details that appeal to all five senses.

Vocabulary Focus When you come across a long, difficult word in reading, try to analyze its parts. It may contain the base of a word that is familiar to you. For example, Joyce uses the word *intolerable* in "Araby." What word that you know contains the base *toler*? Perhaps you know *tolerance* or *tolerate*. The prefix *in-* means "not"; the suffix *-able* means "able to be." Putting these meanings together, you can predict that *intolerable* refers to something one cannot bear. Find the words *charitable*, *resignedly*, *odorous*, and *amiability* in the story. Analyze their parts and predict their meanings.

Think Before You Read What kind of epiphany do you think the hero of this story will have?

short story
a brief work of prose fiction that includes plot, setting, point of view, characters, and theme

plot the series of events in a story

character
a person or animal in a story, poem, or play

setting the time and place in a story

first person
a point of view where the narrator is also a character, using the pronouns *I* and *we*

narrator one who tells a story

protagonist
the main character; also called the hero

epiphany the moment in a story when a character recognizes an important truth

stream of consciousness
a writing technique that develops the plot by allowing the reader to see how and what the characters are thinking

Araby

As you read, notice the things that attract the protagonist and how he reacts to them.

North Richmond Street, being blind, was a quiet street except at the hour when the Christian Brothers' School set the boys free. An uninhabited house of two storeys stood at the blind end, detached from its neighbours in a square ground. The other houses of the street, conscious of decent lives within them, gazed at one another with brown **imperturbable** faces.

The Abbot is a romantic novel. *The Devout Communicant* is a religious manual. *The Memoirs of Vidocq* is a memoir by a French adventurer. They reflect the boy's romantic view of life.

The former **tenant** of our house, a priest, had died in the back drawing-room. Air, musty from having been long enclosed, hung in all the rooms, and the waste room behind the kitchen was littered with old useless papers. Among these I found a few paper-covered books, the pages of which were curled and damp: *The Abbot*, by Walter Scott, *The Devout Communicant* and *The Memoirs of Vidocq*. I liked the last best because its leaves were yellow. The wild garden behind the house contained a central apple-tree and a few straggling bushes under one of which I found the late tenant's rusty bicycle-pump. He had been a very **charitable** priest; in his will he had left all his money to institutions and the furniture of his house to his sister.

This story is told in first person by the main character. How does this add interest to the story? How does this limit the story?

When the short days of winter came dusk fell before we had well eaten our dinners. When we met in the street the houses had grown **sombre.** The space of sky above us was the

---

imperturbable not having strong emotions

tenant renter

charitable generous

sombre (somber) solemn; sad

colour of ever-changing violet and towards it the lamps of the street lifted their **feeble** lanterns. The cold air stung us and we played till our bodies glowed. Our shouts echoed in the silent street. The career of our play brought us through the dark muddy lanes behind the houses where we ran the **gantlet** of the rough tribes from the cottages, to the back doors of the dark dripping gardens where odours arose from the ashpits, to the dark **odorous** stables where a coachman smoothed and combed the horse or shook music from the buckled harness. When we returned to the street light from the kitchen windows had filled the areas. If my uncle was seen turning the corner we hid in the shadow until we had seen him safely housed. Or if Mangan's sister came out on the doorstep to call her brother in to his tea we watched her from our shadow peer up and down the street. We waited to see whether she would remain or go in and, if she remained, we left our shadow and walked up to Mangan's steps **resignedly.** She was waiting for us, her figure defined by the light from the half-opened door. Her brother always teased her before he obeyed and I stood by the railings looking at her. Her dress swung as she moved her body and the soft rope of her hair tossed from side to side.

Every morning I lay on the floor in the front parlour watching her door. The blind was pulled down to within an inch of the **sash** so that I could not be seen. When she came out on the doorstep my heart leaped. I ran to the hall, seized my books and followed her. I kept her brown figure always in my eye and, when we came near the point at which our ways **diverged,** I quickened my pace and passed her. This happened morning after morning. I had never spoken to her, except for a few casual words, and yet her name was like a **summons** to all my foolish blood.

feeble weak

gantlet a series of tests or challenges

odorous smelly

resignedly in a way showing one is giving in

sash bottom of a window frame

diverged parted

summons call; command

Her image accompanied me even in places the most **hostile** to romance. On Saturday evenings when my aunt went marketing I had to go to carry some of the parcels. We walked through the **flaring** streets, jostled by drunken men and bargaining women, amid the curses of labourers, the shrill **litanies** of shop-boys who stood on guard by the barrels of pigs' cheeks, the nasal chanting of street-singers, who sang a *come-all-you* about O'Donovan Rossa, or a ballad about the troubles in our native land. These noises **converged** in a single sensation of life for me: I imagined that I bore my chalice safely through a throng of foes. Her name sprang to my lips at moments in strange prayers and praises which I myself did not understand. My eyes were often full of tears (I could not tell why) and at times a flood from my heart seemed to pour itself out into my bosom. I thought little of the future. I did not know whether I would ever speak to her or not or, if I spoke to her, how I could tell her of my confused adoration. But my body was like a harp and her words and gestures were like fingers running upon the wires.

One evening I went into the back drawing-room in which the priest had died. It was a dark rainy evening and there was no sound in the house. Through one of the broken panes I heard the rain **impinge** upon the earth, the fine **incessant** needles of water playing in the **sodden** beds. Some distant lamp or lighted window gleamed below me. I was thankful that I could see so little. All my senses seemed to desire to veil themselves and, feeling that I was about to slip from them, I pressed the palms of my hands together until they trembled, murmuring: *O love! O love!* many times.

At last she spoke to me. When she addressed the first words to me I was so confused that I did not know what to answer. She asked me was I going to *Araby*. I forget whether I answered yes or no. It would be a splendid bazaar, she said; she would love to go.

O'Donovan Rossa was an Irish patriot.

In Catholic tradition, a *chalice* is a cup that hold's the blood of Jesus. Allowing any of the liquid inside the cup to spill dishonors him.

When the narrator actually talks to Mangan's sister, he does not know what to say. How does this compare to the way he reacts to her in his imagination?

hostile unfriendly	**converged** came together	**incessant** endless; constant
flaring lively		
litanies chants; repeated calls	**impinge** intrude	**sodden** soaked

—And why can't you? I asked.

While she spoke she turned a silver bracelet round and round her wrist. She could not go, she said, because there would be a retreat that week in her convent. Her brother and two other boys were fighting for their caps and I was alone at the railings. She held one of the spikes, bowing her head towards me. The light from the lamp opposite our door caught the white curve of her neck, lit up her hair that rested there and, falling, lit up the hand upon the railing. It fell over one side of her dress and caught the white border of a petticoat, just visible as she stood at ease.

—It's well for you, she said.

—If I go, I said, I will bring you something.

What innumerable follies laid waste my waking and sleeping thoughts after that evening! I wished to **annihilate** the **tedious** intervening days. I **chafed** against the work of school. At night in my bedroom and by day in the classroom her image came between me and the page I **strove** to read. The syllables of the word *Araby* were called to me through the silence in which my soul **luxuriated** and cast an Eastern enchantment over me. I asked for leave to go to the bazaar on Saturday night. My aunt was surprised and hoped it was not some Freemason affair. I answered few questions in class. I watched my master's face pass from **amiability** to sternness; he hoped I was not beginning to idle. I could not call my wandering thoughts together. I had hardly any patience with the serious work of life which, now that it stood between me and my desire, seemed to me child's play, ugly **monotonous** child's play.

On Saturday morning I reminded my uncle that I wished to go to the bazaar in the evening. He was fussing at the hallstand, looking for the hat-brush, and answered me curtly:

—Yes, boy, I know.

> Do you think the girl is trying to get the narrator to do something? Or is the narrator just focusing on how much he likes her?

> *Freemasons* were part of a secret society.

> The narrator thinks only of the bazaar. What does he now consider *the serious work of life?*

annihilate wipe out

tedious boring

chafed rubbed raw; became irritated

strove tried hard

luxuriated delighted in

amiability friendliness

monotonous dull

As he was in the hall I could not go into the front parlour and lie at the window. I left the house in bad humour and walked slowly towards the school. The air was pitilessly raw and already my heart **misgave** me.

When I came home to dinner my uncle had not yet been home. Still it was early. I sat staring at the clock for some time and, when its ticking began to irritate me, I left the room. I mounted the staircase and gained the upper part of the house. The high cold empty gloomy rooms **liberated** me and I went from room to room singing. From the front window I saw my companions playing below in the street. Their cries reached me weakened and **indistinct** and, leaning my forehead against the cool glass, I looked over at the dark house where she lived. I may have stood there for an hour, seeing nothing but the brown-clad figure cast by my imagination, touched discreetly by the lamplight at the curved neck, at the hand upon the railings and at the border below the dress.

When I came downstairs again I found Mrs. Mercer sitting at the fire. She was an old **garrulous** woman, a pawnbroker's widow, who collected used stamps for some **pious** purpose. I had to endure the gossip of the tea-table. The meal was prolonged beyond an hour and still my uncle did not come. Mrs. Mercer stood up to go: she was sorry she couldn't wait any longer, but it was after eight o'clock and she did not like to be out late, as the night air was bad for her. When she had gone I began to walk up and down the room, clenching my fists. My aunt said:

—I'm afraid you may put off your bazaar for this night of Our Lord.

At nine o'clock I heard my uncle's latchkey in the halldoor. I heard him talking to himself and heard the hallstand rocking when it had received the weight of his overcoat. I could interpret these signs. When he was midway through his dinner I asked him to give me the money to go to the bazaar. He had forgotten.

How does the change of setting affect the narrator? Why?

How is the hero's view of other characters affected by how he feels?

misgave began to doubt or fear	**liberated** freed	**garrulous** talkative
	indistinct not clear	**pious** religious

—The people are in bed and after their first sleep now, he said.

I did not smile. My aunt said to him energetically:

—Can't you give him the money and let him go? You've kept him late enough as it is.

My uncle said he was very sorry he had forgotten. He said he believed in the old saying: *All work and no play makes Jack a dull boy*. He asked me where I was going and, when I had told him a second time he asked me did I know *The Arab's Farewell to his Steed*. When I left the kitchen he was about to recite the opening lines of the piece to my aunt.

I held a **florin** tightly in my hand as I strode down Buckingham Street towards the station. The sight of the streets thronged with buyers and glaring with gas recalled to me the purpose of my journey. I took my seat in a third-class carriage of a deserted train. After an **intolerable** delay the train moved out of the station slowly. It crept onward among **ruinous** houses and over the twinkling river. At Westland Row Station a crowd of people pressed to the carriage doors; but the porters moved them back, saying that it was a special train for the bazaar. I remained alone in the bare carriage. In a few minutes the train drew up beside an **improvised** wooden platform. I passed out on to the road and saw by the lighted dial of a clock that it was ten minutes to ten. In front of me was a large building which displayed the magical name.

I could not find any sixpenny entrance and, fearing that the bazaar would be closed, I passed in quickly through a turnstile, handing a shilling to a weary-looking man. I found myself in a big hall **girdled** at half its height by a gallery. Nearly all the stalls were closed and the greater part of the hall was in darkness. I recognised a silence like that which **pervades** a church after a service. I walked into the centre of the bazaar timidly. A few people were gathered about the

> Contrast the way Dublin feels and looks to the narrator now to the way it appeared to him when he went to market with his aunt.

> The narrator compares the silence of the bazaar with the silence of an empty church. What does this help you understand about the setting? about the character's state of mind?

florin silver coin	**ruinous** in bad shape	**girdled** surrounded
intolerable unbearable	**improvised** set up for temporary use	**pervades** fills

Is the bazaar as the narrator imagined it would be? Why not?

stalls which were still open. Before a curtain, over which the words *Café Chantant* were written in coloured lamps, two men were counting money on a **salver.** I listened to the fall of the coins.

Remembering with difficulty why I had come I went over to one of the stalls and examined **porcelain** vases and flowered tea-sets. At the door of the stall a young lady was talking and laughing with two young gentlemen. I remarked their English accents and listened vaguely to their conversation.

—O, I never said such a thing!

—O, but you did!

—O, but I didn't!

—Didn't she say that?

—Yes. I heard her.

—O, there's a . . . fib!

Compare this young lady to Mangan's sister. How does she treat the narrator?

Observing me the young lady came over and asked me did I wish to buy anything. The tone of her voice was not encouraging; she seemed to have spoken to me out of a sense of duty. I looked humbly at the great jars that stood like eastern guards at either side of the dark entrance to the stall and **murmured:**

—No, thank you.

The young lady changed the position of one of the vases and went back to the two young men. They began to talk of the same subject. Once or twice the young lady glanced at me over her shoulder.

What truth does the narrator learn? What do you think leads to this epiphany?

I lingered before her stall, though I knew my stay was useless, to make my interest in her wares seem the more real. Then I turned away slowly and walked down the middle of the bazaar. I allowed the two pennies to fall against the sixpence in my pocket. I heard a voice call from one end of the gallery that the light was out. The upper part of the hall was now completely dark.

---

salver serving dish   **porcelain** china   **murmured** spoke in low tones

Gazing up into the darkness I saw myself as a creature driven and **derided** by **vanity;** and my eyes burned with **anguish** and anger.

---

derided mocked   **vanity** foolish pride   **anguish** great pain

AFTER READING THE SELECTION

Directions Choose the letter of the best answer or write the answer using complete sentences.

Comprehension: Identifying Facts

1. The narrator, or storyteller, in this story is _____.

A a talkative widow

B an outside observer

C a kind priest

D a romantic boy

2. After school, the narrator and his friends usually _____.

A read books

B watch people

C play outside

D fight with a gang

3. What does the narrator do every morning before leaving home?

4. Why does the narrator go out with his aunt on Saturday evenings?

5. What does Mangan's sister ask the narrator?

6. What does he tell her he will do?

7. Why does the narrator's schoolmaster become irritated with him?

8. Why does it seem likely that the narrator will not be able to go to Araby?

9. When does he reach the bazaar?

10. What does he buy?

Comprehension: Putting Ideas Together

11. The best word to describe the narrator's view of the world at the beginning of the selection is _____.

A bitter   **C** romantic

B accepting   **D** practical

12. Which character is intended to contrast with Mangan's sister?

A the narrator's aunt

B Mrs. Mercer

C the narrator's uncle

D the shopgirl at the bazaar

13. What is suggested about the narrator's character by the books he likes to read?

14. Why does the narrator become impatient with "child's play"?

15. What events suggest that the narrator will not get what he wants from Araby?

16. What facts do you learn about Mangan's sister?

17. What actions suggest that the narrator's love for Mangan's sister is based on things the narrator has made up in his head?

18. When does the story refer to religion and piety? What is suggested about the religious people?

19. Why does the narrator go to Araby?

20. How does the reality of Araby compare with what the narrator expected of it?

Understanding Literature: Setting, Protagonist, and Epiphany

The setting of a story is the time and place it takes place. Its protagonist is the hero, or main character. In this story, the protagonist experiences an epiphany. He reaches an important understanding about life.

21. What is the setting of this story?

22. Why is the setting important?

23. Who is the protagonist? What makes him the hero of the story?

24. What epiphany does the narrator have?

25. Do you think the narrator's new view of himself is correct? Why or why not?

Critical Thinking

26. Compare the adult characters to the child characters in this story.

27. How does the decision to go to Araby change the narrator's world?

28. Do you think the narrator's experience of the bazaar and his epiphany about himself would have been different if he had arrived earlier? Explain your opinion.

29. Do you think this story tells something about childhood in general or just about one boy's childhood? Explain.

Thinking Creatively

30. What do you consider to be "the serious work of life"? Why?

After Reading continued on next page

Grammar Check

Dialogue, the spoken words of characters in a story or play, is set off by quotation marks (" "). Joyce does not use these marks (he uses dashes: —), so you have to insert them mentally:

> *"It's well for you," she said.*

> *"If I go," I said, "I will bring you something."*

Notice the placement of punctuation inside the quotation marks. When the words of saying (*he said, she said*) follow a quotation, add a comma inside the ending quotation mark. If the quotation ends the sentence, put the appropriate end mark inside the ending quotation mark. If the words of saying interrupt the quotation, use commas before the first closing quotation mark and after the words of saying.

Find and rewrite three more quotations from later in the story. Add quotation marks and appropriate punctuation. Also add words of saying to make the speaker clear.

Writing on Your Own

Think about a place or event to which you longed to go. Did it live up to your expectations? Write a short narrative about your expectations and your actual experience. Use a comparison and contrast plan of organization.

Speaking and Listening

In a small group, discuss the point of view of the story's narrator. Be prepared to describe his personality and the way he views the world around him. Point out details in the story that support this analysis. Listen carefully as others in the group speak. As a group, prepare a summary about the narrator.

Media

A hundred years ago, "Araby" was an unusual, romantic place to an Irish boy. How is your perception of Arab countries different? What role does the media play in your perception? Gather newspaper and magazine articles or take notes on TV news stories that focus on countries of the Middle East. Discuss with a friend or family member how you think attitudes toward this region might change in the future.

BEFORE READING THE SELECTION

Next Term We'll Mash You   by Penelope Lively

About the Author

Penelope Lively was born in 1933 in Cairo, Egypt. She was educated at home, using books that were ordered from England. At the age of 12, she was sent to a boarding school in England. After attending St. Anne's College at Oxford, Lively settled in England.

Lively began writing children's fiction in 1970 and soon won awards for her work. She turned to writing novels for adults in 1977. Her children's books and her adult novels have won a number of awards, including the Carnegie Medal, the Whitbread Award, the Booker Prize, and the Arts Council National Book Award.

About the Selection

"Next Term We'll Mash You" appeared in the short story collection *Pack of Cards*, published in 1986. This story describes an ordinary experience: parents take their child to look at a boarding school. There is little obvious action or conflict. However, the details reveal a boy's terrified loneliness in a threatening world.

Penelope Lively
1933–

Objectives

- To read and understand a short story
- To analyze how dialogue and other methods of characterization reveal character
- To identify mood and elements that create it
- To understand idioms and similes in a work of literature

Before Reading **continued on next page**

Next Term We'll Mash You   *by Penelope Lively*

characterization
the way a writer
develops character
qualities and
personality traits

dialogue
the conversation
among characters
in a story

idiom a phrase
that has a different
meaning than its
words really mean

mood the feeling
that writing creates

simile a figure of
speech in which
two things are
compared, using
a phrase that
includes *like* or *as*

Literary Terms Writers use many methods to show the traits of a character. This is called **characterization.** Writers often let **dialogue,** or the words spoken by characters to each other in a story, reveal important information. In spoken language, characters often use **idioms,** or expressions that have a different meaning from the actual words. Idioms are usually particular to one culture. Dialogue also helps create a **mood.** A story's mood is the feeling or state of mind it generates. Another tool writers use to describe characters is comparison, such as **similes.** These comparisons show how two things are alike in a surprising way, using *like* or *as.*

Reading on Your Own What would you expect a family to talk about as they drove to a school where the child might soon be living? What might be the family's mood? As you read this story, think what is probably going on in the boy's mind and how he feels. Pretend you are listening to the conversation. What does it show you about the parents?

Writing on Your Own Think of a time when you were introduced to a group and were the only new person in the room. How did you feel? How did the people react to you? Write a brief summary of this encounter and what you learned from it.

Vocabulary Focus To help you learn about new words, you can make a list of synonyms and antonyms. A synonym for a word has nearly the same meaning. An antonym means the opposite. The word *subdued* has the synonym *quiet.* An antonym for *subdued* is *loud.* Make a list of synonyms and antonyms for six difficult words in this story. Use a thesaurus if you need help.

Think Before You Read How do you think the boy and his parents will react to the school?

Next Term We'll Mash You

Inside the car it was quiet, the noise of the engine even and **subdued,** the air just the right temperature, the windows tight-fitting. The boy sat on the back seat, a box of chocolates, unopened, beside him, and a comic, folded. The trim Sussex landscape flowed past the windows: cows, white-fenced fields, highly priced period houses. The sunlight was glassy, remote as a colored photograph. The backs of the two heads in front of him swayed with the motion of the car.

His mother half-turned to speak to him. "Nearly there now, darling."

The father glanced downwards at his wife's wrist. "Are we all right for time?"

"Just right. Nearly twelve."

"I could do with a drink. Hope they lay something on."

"I'm sure they will. The Wilcoxes say they're awfully nice people. Not really the schoolmaster-type at all, Sally says."

The man said, "He's an Oxford chap."

"Is he? You didn't say."

"Mmn."

"Of course, the fees are that much higher than the Seaford place."

"Fifty **quid** or so. We'll have to see."

The car turned right, between white gates and high, dark, tight-clipped hedges. The whisper of the road under

As you read, pay attention to the dialogue of the parents. What do you learn about these characters through their words?

Lay something on is an idiom that means "provide some refreshments."

---

subdued quiet

quid slang for pound, a British unit of money

the tires changed to the crunch of gravel. The child, staring sideways, read black lettering on a white board: "St. Edward's **Preparatory** School. Please Drive Slowly." He shifted on the seat, and the leather sucked at the bare skin under his knees, stinging.

The mother said, "It's a lovely place. Those must be the playing fields. Look, darling, there are some of the boys." She clicked open her handbag, and the sun caught her mirror and flashed in the child's eyes; the comb went through her hair and he saw the grooves it left, neat as distant ploughing.

"Come on, then, Charles, out you get."

The building was red brick, early nineteenth century, spreading out long arms in which windows glittered blackly. Flowers, trapped in neat beds, were alternate red and white. They went up the steps, the man, the woman, and the child two paces behind.

What do the parents' thoughts reveal about their choice of a school?

The woman, the mother, smoothing down a skirt that would be ridged from sitting, thought: I like the way they've got the maid all done up properly. The little white apron and all that. She's foreign, I suppose. **Au pair.** Very nice. If he comes here, there'll be Speech Days and that kind of thing. Sally Wilcox says it's quite dressy—she got that cream linen coat for coming down here. You can see why it costs a bomb. Great big grounds and only an hour and a half from London.

The phrase *costs a bomb* is another British idiom. Use context to figure out what it means. As you continue reading, look for other idioms.

They went into a room looking out into a terrace. Beyond, **dappled** lawns, gently shifting trees, black and white cows grazing behind iron railings. Books, leather chairs, a table with magazines—*Country Life, The Field, The Economist.* "Please, if you would wait here. The Headmaster won't be long."

Alone, they sat, inspected. "I like the atmosphere, don't you, John?"

preparatory having to do with getting ready for something	**au pair** foreign person who cares for children in exchange for room and board and a chance to learn the language of employers	**dappled** marked with small spots of contrasting color; in this case, a mix of shade and sunlight

"Very pleasant, yes." Four hundred a term, near enough. You can tell it's a cut above the Seaford place, though, or the one at St. Albans. Bob Wilcox says quite a few City people send their boys here. One or two of the merchant bankers, those kind of people. It's the sort of contact that would do no harm at all. You meet someone, get talking at a **cricket** match or what have you . . . Not at all a bad thing.

"All right, Charles? You didn't get sick in the car, did you?"

The child had black hair, slicked down smooth to his head. His ears, too large, jutted out, transparent in the light from the window, laced with tiny, delicate veins. His clothes had the shine and crease of newness. He looked at the books, the dark brown pictures, his parents, said nothing.

Why do you think Charles does not speak?

"Come here, let me tidy your hair."

The door opened. The child hesitated, stood up, sat, then rose again with his father.

"Mr. and Mrs. Manders? How very nice to meet you—I'm Margaret Spokes, and will you please forgive my husband who is tied up with some wretch who broke the cricket **pavilion** window and will be just a few more minutes. We try to be organized but a schoolmaster's day is always just that bit unpredictable. Do please sit down and what will you have to revive you after that beastly drive? You live in Finchley, is that right?"

"Hampstead, really," said the mother. "Sherry would be lovely." She worked over the headmaster's wife from shoes to hairstyle, pricing and assessing. Shoes old but expensive— Russell and Bromley. Good skirt. Blouse could be Marks and Sparks—not sure. Real pearls. Super Victorian ring. She's not gone to any particular trouble—that's just what she'd wear anyway. You can be confident, with a voice like that, of course. Sally Wilcox says she knows all sorts of people.

The headmaster's wife said, "I don't know how much you know about us. **Prospectuses** don't tell you a thing, do they? We'll look round everything in a minute, when you've

Finchley and *Hampstead* are parts of London. Hampstead is a more fashionable location.

The adults are all concerned with appearances. What do you think the boy is concerned about?

cricket team sport played with balls and flat wooden bats

pavilion a large, covered outdoor area

prospectuses advertisements

From the British Dominions Unit 7 **581**

had a chat with my husband. I gather you're friends of the Wilcoxes, by the way. I'm awfully fond of Simon—he's down for Winchester, of course, but I expect you know that."

The mother smiled over her sherry. Oh, I know that all right. Sally Wilcox doesn't let you forget that.

"And this is Charles? My dear, we've been forgetting all about you! In a minute I'm going to borrow Charles and take him off to meet some of the boys because after all you're choosing a school for him, aren't you, and not for you, so he ought to know what he might be letting himself in for and it shows we've got nothing to hide."

The parents laughed. The father, sherry warming his guts, thought that this was an amusing woman. Not attractive, of course, a bit **homespun,** but impressive all the same. Partly the voice, of course; it takes a bloody expensive education to produce a voice like that. And other things, of course. Background and all that stuff.

"I think I can hear the thud of the Fourth **Form** coming in from games, which means my husband is on the way, and then I shall leave you with him while I take Charles off to the common-room."

For a moment the three adults centered on the child, looking, judging. The mother said, "He looks so hideously pale, compared to those boys we saw outside."

"My dear, that's London, isn't it? You just have to get them out, to get some color into them. Ah, here's James. James— Mr. and Mrs. Manders. You remember, Bob Wilcox was mentioning at Sports Day . . ."

The headmaster reflected his wife's style, like paired cards in Happy Families. His clothes were mature rather than old, his skin well-scrubbed, his shoes clean, his **geniality untainted** by the least **condescension.** He was genuinely sorry to have kept them waiting, but in this business one lurches

---

Which character is most sympathetic toward Charles?

The adults judge Charles as they have been judging each other and the school silently. What does the mother's comment suggest about her attitude toward Charles?

---

homespun plain	**geniality** friendliness	**condescension** the attitude that one is better than others
form grade level	**untainted** not spoiled	

from one minor crisis to the next . . . And this is Charles? Hello, there, Charles. His large hand rested for a moment on the child's head, quite **extinguishing** the thin, dark hair. It was as though he had but to clench his fingers to crush the skull. But he took his hand away and moved the parents to the window, to observe the **mutilated** cricket pavilion, with **indulgent** laughter.

And the child is borne away by the headmaster's wife. She never touches him or tells him to come, but simply bears him away like some relentless tide, down corridors and through swinging glass doors, towing him like a frail craft, not bothering to look back to see if he is following, confident in the strength of magnetism, or obedience.

And delivers him to a room where boys are scattered among inky tables and rungless chairs and sprawled on a **mangy** carpet. There is a scampering, and a rising, and a silence falling, as she opens the door.

"Now this is the Lower Third, Charles, who you'd be with if you come to us in September. Boys, this is Charles Manders, and I want you to tell him all about things and answer any questions he wants to ask. You can believe about half of what they say, Charles, and they will tell you the most fearful lies about the food, which is excellent."

The boys laugh and groan; **amiable,** exaggerated groans. They must like the headmaster's wife: There is **licensed repartee.** They look at her with bright eyes in open, eager faces. Someone leaps to hold the door for her, and close it behind her. She is gone.

> The simile compares Charles to a small boat and the schoolmaster's wife to the tide. This comparison emphasizes the boy's helplessness and increases the mood of anxiety.

> What do you think will happen now that the schoolmaster's wife has left?

extinguishing causing to disappear

mutilated damaged

indulgent allowing something to happen

mangy shabby

amiable friendly

licensed allowed

repartee teasing talk

How does the sense of movement and changing colors and noise add to the mood?

The child stands in the center of the room, and it draws in around him. The circle of children **contracts,** faces are only a yard or so from him; strange faces, looking, assessing.

Asking questions. They help themselves to his name, his age, his school. Over their heads he sees beyond the window an **inaccessible** world of shivering trees and high racing clouds and his voice which has floated like a feather in the dusty schoolroom air dies altogether and he becomes mute, and he stands in the middle of them with shoulders humped, staring down at feet: grubby **plimsolls** and kicked brown sandals. There is a noise in his ears like rushing water, a **torrential din** out of which voices boom, blotting each other out so that he cannot always hear the words. Do you? they say, and Have you? and What's your? and the faces, if he looks up, swing into one another in **kaleidoscopic** patterns and the floor under his feet is unsteady, lifting and falling.

And out of the noises comes one voice that is complete, that he can hear. "Next term, we'll mash you," it says. "We always mash new boys."

The one clear detail Charles picks up in the confusion is the claim that the boys will mash him, or beat him up, when he arrives at the school. Why is this important to the story?

English schoolboy cricket team, 1964

contracts grows smaller

inaccessible unreachable

plimsolls sneakers

torrential hammering

din noise

kaleidoscopic having a constantly shifting shape or pattern

And a bell goes, somewhere beyond doors and down corridors, and suddenly the children are all gone, clattering away and leaving him there with the heaving floor and the walls that shift and swing, and the headmaster's wife comes back and tows him away, and he is with his parents again, and they are getting into the car, and the high hedges skim past the car windows once more, in the other direction, and the gravel under the tires changes to black **tarmac.**

"Well?"

"I liked it, didn't you?" The mother adjusted the car around her, closing windows, shrugging into her seat.

"Very pleasant, really. Nice chap."

"I liked him. Not quite so sure about her."

"It's pricey, of course."

"All the same . . ."

"Money well spent, though. One way and another."

"Shall we settle it, then?"

"I think so. I'll drop him a line."

The mother pitched her voice a notch higher to speak to the child in the back of the car. "Would you like to go there, Charles? Like Simon Wilcox. Did you see that lovely gym, and the swimming pool? And did the other boys tell you all about it?"

The child does not answer. He looks straight ahead of him, at the road coiling beneath the bonnet of the car. His face is **haggard** with **anticipation.**

> Charles is not part of the decision. He does not answer his mother. Does this outcome seem true to life?

---

tarmac pavement   **haggard** tired   **anticipation** looking ahead

AFTER READING THE SELECTION

Next Term We'll Mash You   by Penelope Lively

Directions Choose the letter of the best answer or write the answer using complete sentences.

Comprehension: Identifying Facts

1. The Manderses and their son Charles travel to a _____.
   A London public school
   B hospital for children
   C country fair
   D private school outside London

2. The family first talks to _____.
   A the headmaster
   B a maid
   C the headmaster's wife
   D several students

3. What about the headmaster's wife do Mr. and Mrs. Manders find admirable and reassuring?

4. What keeps the headmaster from greeting the family right away?

5. What does the headmaster's wife offer Mr. and Mrs. Manders?

6. Where does Charles go with the headmaster's wife?

7. What shows that the boys like the headmaster's wife?

8. What do the boys do when she leaves the room?

9. What is the one clear statement Charles hears in all the noise?

10. What does Charles say to his parents as they leave?

Comprehension: Putting Ideas Together

11. Mr. and Mrs. Manders seem most concerned with _____.
    A their son's future
    B having a good time
    C money and social class
    D finding a quiet, peaceful place

12. The best phrase to describe Charles is _____.
    A small, quiet, and withdrawn
    B proud and tough
    C tall, thin, and thoughtful
    D curious and outgoing

13. What impression of the school do you get from the words and images used to describe it?

14. How does the room in which the Manders meet the headmaster differ from the room where Charles meets the other boys?

15. What do the parents associate with the high price of attending St. Edwards?

16. Why is the Wilcox family important to Mr. and Mrs. Manders?

17. What does the broken cricket pavilion window suggest about the school and its students?

18. What do all the descriptions of Charles tell about him?

19. What shows that his parents do not consider what Charles wants?

20. How does the author use clothing to establish and contrast characters?

Understanding Literature: Dialogue, Characterization, and Mood

Dialogue is the spoken words between characters in a story. In this story, dialogue is used for characterization to reveal a great deal about various characters. Mood is the feeling created by the writing in a story. The state of mind may be suggested by word choices, images, and actions.

21. Who does most of the talking in this story?

22. What do you learn from the dialogue among the adults?

23. Why is it meaningful that Charles does not take part in the dialogue?

24. What mood is established by the opening paragraph of the story?

25. How does the mood change when Charles meets with the students?

Critical Thinking

26. The characters in this story judge each other. On what do they base their judgments?

27. What do you think will happen to Charles at this school? Why?

28. What is the theme, or main idea, of this story?

29. How will life at St. Edwards be different than it has been so far for Charles?

Thinking Creatively

30. Should children be able to choose the school they attend? Explain your thinking.

After Reading continued on next page

Next Term We'll Mash You by *Penelope Lively*

 ### Grammar Check

When you add the suffix *-y* to a word, you may need to change the word's spelling. If the word ends in silent *e*, usually the *e* is dropped, as in *tasty*. There are exceptions, however, as in *dicey*. One-syllable words that end in a vowel and a consonant usually require that the final consonant be doubled before *-y* is added, as in *tinny*. Find the following words in the story: *glassy, grubby, mangy, pricey*. Write the word, then write the base word without the suffix.

 ### Writing on Your Own

Is a private school or a public school better? Write a persuasive essay expressing your opinion and convincing others that it is right. Include your arguments in order of importance. Provide supporting evidence for each argument.

 ### Speaking and Listening

Interview a parent, grandparent, or other adult about his or her elementary school days. Prepare questions that encourage descriptions and explanations rather than one-word answers. Remember to ask questions politely and listen closely to answers. They may suggest other questions to ask.

 ### Media

Locate and watch a TV show or movie about a child or family entering a new neighborhood or school. As you watch, make notes about how the situation is shown. What challenges does the "new kid on the block" face? What solution or outcome is presented?

 ### Technology

Find out the names of several preparatory schools or universities near where you live. Locate the Web site for each school and gather information about it: number of students, student/teacher ratio, cost to attend, types of programs and sports offered, and so on. Combine the data in a table and compare the schools. Write a paragraph telling which school you would prefer to attend and why.

BEFORE READING THE SELECTION

A Mild Attack of Locusts   by Doris Lessing

About the Author

Doris Lessing was born Doris May Tayler in Persia (now Iran) in 1919 to British parents. In 1925, the family moved to Southern Rhodesia (now Zimbabwe) in Africa to farm. The 1,000-acre farm failed. Lessing attended a religious school but dropped out at age 14. She married at age 19, but her marriage ended a few years later. Her second marriage, to German political activist Gottfried Lessing, also failed. Lessing moved to England in 1949 with her youngest child and a manuscript of her first novel, *The Grass Is Singing.*

Most of Lessing's work is based on her experiences in Africa. She draws on her childhood memories and her political and social concerns. For example, she writes about the mistreatment of black Africans by white colonial settlers. *The Golden Notebook,* published in 1962, deals with subjects important to the women's rights movement.

Lessing was so outspoken about social and political matters that she was banned from Southern Rhodesia and South Africa in 1956. She went on to write dozens of books and received many awards and honors. She is now welcomed in Africa for the very topics for which she was once banished.

About the Selection

"A Mild Attack of Locusts" appeared in Lessing's 1957 story collection, *The Habit of Loving.* This story draws upon her childhood experience in Africa. The characters in the story struggle to keep the farm from failing. They must fight a swarm of locusts that threaten their crops.

Doris Lessing
1919–

Objectives

- To read and understand a short story
- To recognize description and metaphor
- To identify person-against-nature conflict
- To explain rising action, climax, falling action, and resolution in a story's plot

Before Reading continued on next page

BEFORE READING THE SELECTION (continued)

A Mild Attack of Locusts   by Doris Lessing

description
a written picture of the characters, events, and settings in a story

metaphor
a figure of speech that makes a comparison but does not use *like* or *as*

conflict
the struggle of the main character against himself or herself, another person, or nature

rising action
the buildup of excitement in a story

climax the high point of interest or suspense in a story

falling action
the action that occurs after the climax to wind up the story

resolution
the act of solving the conflict in a story

Literary Terms "A Mild Attack of Locusts" is filled with **description**—word pictures—of African farm life. **Metaphors,** or direct comparisons, add to the picture that is painted for readers. Writers also add **conflict** in a story to make it interesting. With whom or what does the protagonist struggle? A character may struggle with his or her own inner thoughts, with other people, or with nature. The conflict becomes more intense or complex as the plot of the story unfolds. This is known as the **rising action.** After the **climax,** when the conflict is resolved, the story winds down. This is known as the **falling action.** The **resolution,** where the conflict is resolved, comes last.

Reading on Your Own "A Mild Attack of Locusts" describes the battle of farmers with a swarm of locusts. It is seen through the eyes of a young woman from the city. Predict how her lack of experience with nature will affect her view of the conflict. As you read, stop every page or so and think about how the conflict has increased or decreased.

Writing on Your Own Think about an experience in which you had to struggle with nature. Write a journal entry describing the conflict and how it ended.

Vocabulary Focus Some words in this story help you understand the African farmer's life. An *escarpment* is a steep slope or cliff that separates two level surfaces. It may occur at a split in the Earth's crust or result from erosion (wearing away of soil). The farm in this story is near an escarpment, which hints at the disturbance of nature the farmers face. The *veldt* is the grassland of southern Africa, dotted with shrubs and trees. *Mealies* are the young sprouts of maize, or corn, growing on the vast farm. *Hoppers* are the immature form of the locusts.

A Mild Attack of Locusts

The rains that year were good; they were coming nicely just as the crops needed them—or so Margaret gathered when the men said they were not too bad. She never had an opinion of her own on matters like the weather, because even to know about what seems a simple thing like the weather needs experience. Which Margaret had not got. The men were Richard her husband, and old Stephen, Richard's father, a farmer from way back; and these two might argue for hours whether the rains were **ruinous** or just **ordinarily exasperating.** Margaret had been on the farm three years. She still did not understand how they did not go bankrupt altogether, when the men never had a good word for the weather, or the soil, or the government. But she was getting to learn the language. Farmers' language. And they neither went bankrupt nor got very rich. They jogged along doing comfortably.

Their crop was maize. Their farm was three thousand acres on the ridges that rise up toward the Zambesi **escarpment**—high, dry windswept country, cold and dusty in winter, but now, in the wet season, steamy with the heat rising in wet soft waves off miles of green **foliage**. Beautiful it was, with the sky blue and brilliant halls of air, and the bright green folds and hollows of country beneath, and the mountains lying sharp and bare twenty miles off across the

As you read, contrast Margaret's views about life on the farm with those of her husband and father-in-law.

The *Zambesi* is a river in southeast Africa.

---

ruinous disastrous

ordinarily in the same way as usual

exasperating annoying

escarpment steep slope separating two level surfaces

foliage leaves of a plant or tree

How does the response of Richard and Stephen differ from Margaret's response to the news about the locusts?

rivers. The sky made her eyes ache; she was not used to it. One does not look so much at the sky in the city she came from. So that evening when Richard said: "The government is sending out warnings that locusts are expected, coming down from the breeding grounds up North," her instinct was to look about her at the trees. Insects—swarms of them—horrible! But Richard and the old man had raised their eyes and were looking up over the mountain. "We haven't had locusts in seven years," they said. "They go in cycles, locusts do." And then: "There goes our crop for this season!"

But they went on with the work of the farm just as usual until one day they were coming up the road to the **homestead** for the midday break, when old Stephen stopped, raised his finger and pointed: "Look, look, there they are!"

A streak of rust-colored air is a metaphor that helps readers picture the coming swarm.

Out ran Margaret to join them, looking at the hills. Out came the servants from the kitchen. They all stood and gazed. Over the rocky levels of the mountain was a streak of rust-colored air. Locusts. There they came.

At once Richard shouted at the cookboy. Old Stephen yelled at the houseboy. The cookboy ran to beat the old ploughshare hanging from a tree branch, which was used to summon the laborers at moments of crisis. The houseboy ran off to the store to collect tin cans, any old bit of metal. The farm was ringing with the **clamor** of the gong; and they could see the laborers come pouring out of the **compound,** pointing at the hills and shouting excitedly. Soon they had all come up to the house, and Richard and old Stephen were giving them orders—Hurry, hurry, hurry.

How has the scene changed all of a sudden? What does this suggest about the coming battle with the locusts?

And off they ran again, the two white men with them, and in a few minutes Margaret could see the smoke of fires rising from all around the farmlands. Piles of wood and grass had been prepared there. There were seven patches of bared soil, yellow and oxblood color and pink, where the new mealies

| **homestead** home and accompanying land | **clamor** loud, continuous noise | **compound** group of buildings, usually within a wall or fence |

were just showing, making a film of bright green; and around each drifted up thick clouds of smoke. They were throwing wet leaves on to the fires now, to make it **acrid** and black. Margaret was watching the hills. Now there was a long, low cloud advancing, rust-color still, swelling forward and out as she looked. The telephone was ringing. Neighbors—quick, quick, there come the locusts. Old Smith had had his crop eaten to the ground. Quick, get your fires started. For of course, while every farmer hoped the locusts would overlook his farm and go on to the next, it was only fair to warn each other; one must play fair. Everywhere, fifty miles over the countryside, the smoke was rising from **myriads** of fires. Margaret answered the telephone calls, and between calls she stood watching the locusts. The air was darkening. A strange darkness, for the sun was blazing—it was like the darkness of a **veldt** fire, when the air gets thick with smoke. The sunlight comes down **distorted,** a thick, hot orange. **Oppressive** it was, too, with the heaviness of a storm. The locusts were coming fast. Now half the sky was darkened. Behind the reddish veils in front, which were the advance guards of the swarm, the main swarm showed in dense black cloud, reaching almost to the sun itself.

What feeling do the locusts give before they reach the farm?

Margaret was wondering what she could do to help. She did not know. Then up came old Stephen from the lands. "We're finished, Margaret, finished! Those beggars can eat every leaf and blade off the farm in half an hour! And it is only early afternoon—if we can make enough smoke, make enough noise till the sun goes down, they'll settle somewhere else perhaps. . . ." And then: "Get the kettle going. It's thirsty work, this."

Notice the description of noises made by the locusts and the people, as well as the sights and colors. What does the description add to your understanding of the scene?

So Margaret went to the kitchen, and **stoked** up the fire, and boiled the water. Now, on the tin roof of the kitchen she could hear the thuds and bangs of falling locusts, or a scratching slither as one skidded down. Here were the first

| **acrid** bitter | **veldt** dry grassland | **oppressive** stifling |
| **myriads** uncountable numbers | **distorted** twisted out of its true condition | **stoked** added fuel to make hotter |

of them. From down on the lands came the beating and banging and clanging of a hundred gasoline cans and bits of metal. Stephen impatiently waited while one gasoline can was filled with tea, hot, sweet and orange-colored, and the other with water. In the meantime, he told Margaret about how twenty years back he was eaten out, made bankrupt, by the locust armies. And then, still talking, he **hoisted** up the gasoline cans, one in each hand, by the wood pieces set cornerwise across each, and jogged off down to the road to the thirsty laborers. By now the locusts were falling like hail on to the roof of the kitchen. It sounded like a heavy storm. Margaret looked out and saw the air dark with a crisscross of the insects, and she set her teeth and ran out into it—what the men could do, she could. Overhead the air was thick, locusts everywhere. The locusts here flopping against her, and she brushed them off, heavy red-brown creatures, looking at her with their beady old-men's eyes while they clung with hard, **serrated** legs. She held her breath with disgust and ran through into the house. There it was even more like being in a heavy storm. The iron roof was **reverberating,** and the clamor of iron from the lands was like thunder. Looking out, all the trees were queer and still, clotted with insects, their boughs weighed to the ground. The earth seemed to be moving, locusts crawling everywhere, she could not see the lands at all, so thick was the swarm. Toward the mountains it was like looking into driving rain—even as she watched, the sun was blotted out with a fresh onrush of them. It was a half-night, a **perverted** blackness. Then came a sharp crack from the bush—a branch had snapped off. Then another. A tree down the slope leaned over and settled heavily to the ground. Through the hail of insects a man came running. More tea, more water was needed. She supplied them. She kept the fires stoked and filled cans with liquid, and then it was four in the afternoon, and the locusts had been pouring across overhead

Margaret attempts to join the fight against the locusts. What are the locusts like up close? How does her conflict increase here?

hoisted lifted	**reverberating** echoing	**perverted** not natural; distorted
serrated notched or toothed on the edge		

for a couple of hours. Up came old Stephen again, crunching locusts underfoot with every step, locusts clinging all over him; he was cursing and swearing, banging with his old hat at the air. At the doorway he stopped briefly, hastily pulling at the clinging insects and throwing them off, then he plunged into the locust-free living room.

"All the crops finished. Nothing left," he said.

But the gongs were still beating, the men still shouting, and Margaret asked: "Why do you go on with it, then?"

"The main swarm isn't settling. They are heavy with eggs. They are looking for a place to settle and lay. If we can stop the main body settling on our farm, that's everything. If they get a chance to lay their eggs, we are going to have everything eaten flat with hoppers later on." He picked a stray locust off his shirt and split it down with his thumbnail—it was clotted inside with eggs. "Imagine that multiplied by millions. You ever seen a hopper swarm on the march? Well, you're lucky."

Margaret thought an adult swarm was bad enough. Outside now the light on the earth was a pale, thin yellow, clotted with moving shadows; the clouds of moving insects thickened and lightened like driving rain. Old Stephen said, "They've got the wind behind them, that's something."

"Is it very bad?" asked Margaret fearfully, and the old man said **emphatically:** "We're finished. This swarm may pass over, but once they've started, they'll be coming down from the North now one after another. And then there are the hoppers—it might go on for two or three years."

Margaret sat down helplessly, and thought: Well, if it's the end, it's the end. What now? We'll all three have to go back to town. . . . But at this, she took a quick look at Stephen, the old man who had farmed forty years in this country, been bankrupt twice, and she knew nothing would make him go and become a clerk in the city. Yet her heart ached for him, he looked so tired, the worry lines deep from nose to mouth.

> The end of the crop is not the end of the battle. How does the conflict become more complicated in the rising action here?

emphatically forcefully

Despite the ruin brought by the locusts, Stephen can still admire them. What effect does this reaction have on Margaret?

Poor old man. . . . He had lifted up a locust that had got itself somehow into his pocket, holding it in the air by one leg. "You've got the strength of a steel-spring in those legs of yours," he was telling the locust, good-humoredly. Then, although he had been fighting locusts, squashing locusts, yelling at locusts, sweeping them in great mounds into the fires to burn for the last three hours, nevertheless he took this one to the door and carefully threw it out to join its fellows, as if he would rather not harm a hair of its head. This comforted Margaret; all at once she felt irrationally cheered. She remembered it was not the first time in the last three years the man had announced their final and **irremediable** ruin.

"Get me a drink, lass," he then said, and she set the bottle of whisky by him.

In the meantime, out in the **pelting** storm of insects, her husband was banging the gong, feeding the fires with leaves,

African farmers fighting locusts, 1951

irremediable permanent; not able to be fixed   **pelting** striking hard

the insects clinging to him all over—she shuddered. "How can you bear to let them touch you?" she asked. He looked at her, **disapproving.** She felt suitably humble—just as she had when he had first taken a good look at her city self, hair waved and golden, nails red and pointed. Now she was a proper farmer's wife, in sensible shoes and a solid skirt. She might even get to letting locusts settle on her—in time.

Having tossed back a whisky or two, old Stephen went back into the battle, wading now through glistening brown waves of locusts.

Five o'clock. The sun would set in an hour. Then the swarm would settle. It was as thick overhead as ever. The trees were ragged mounds of glistening brown.

Margaret began to cry. It was all so hopeless—if it wasn't a bad season, it was locusts; if it wasn't locusts, it was army-worm or veldt fires. Always something. The rustling of the locust armies was like a big forest in the storm; their settling on the roof was like the beating of the rain; the ground was invisible in a sleek, brown, **surging** tide—it was like being drowned in locusts, **submerged** by the **loathsome** brown flood. It seemed as if the roof might sink in under the weight of them, as if the door might give in under their pressure and these rooms fill with them—and it was getting so dark . . . she looked up. The air was thinner; gaps of blue showed in the dark, moving clouds. The blue spaces were cold and thin—the sun must be setting. Through the fog of insects she saw figures approaching. First old Stephen, marching bravely along, then her husband, drawn and **haggard** with weariness. Behind them the servants. All were crawling all over with insects. The sound of the gongs had stopped. She could hear nothing but the **ceaseless** rustle of a myriad of wings.

The two men slapped off the insects and came in.

How has Margaret changed since coming to the farm from the city? How is this experience with the locusts likely to change her even more?

Why does Margaret feel hopeless?

The climax, or high point of interest and emotion, occurs as the locusts seem to win and Margaret begins to feel hopeless. What happens to the conflict at this point?

disapproving not agreeing; stern

surging moving; bulging forward

submerged sunk beneath the surface

loathsome disgusting

haggard tired

ceaseless never-ending

"Well," said Richard, kissing her on the cheek, "the main swarm has gone over."

"For the Lord's sake," said Margaret angrily, still half-crying, "what's here is bad enough, isn't it?" For although the evening air was no longer black and thick, but a clear blue, with a pattern of insects whizzing this way and that across it, everything else—trees, buildings, bushes, earth, was gone under the moving brown masses.

"If it doesn't rain in the night and keep them here—if it doesn't rain and weight them down with water, they'll be off in the morning at sunrise."

"We're bound to have some hoppers. But not the main swarm—that's something."

Margaret **roused** herself, wiped her eyes, pretended she had not been crying, and fetched them some supper, for the servants were too exhausted to move. She sent them down to the compound to rest.

She served the supper and sat listening. There is not one maize plant left, she heard. Not one. The men would get the planters out the moment the locusts had gone. They must start all over again.

But what's the use of that, Margaret wondered, if the whole farm was going to be crawling with hoppers? But she listened while they discussed the new government pamphlet that said how to defeat the hoppers. You must have men out all the time, moving over the farm to watch for movement in the grass. When you find a patch of hoppers, small lively black things, like crickets, then you dig trenches around the patch or spray them with poison from pumps supplied by the government. The government wanted them to cooperate in a world plan for **eliminating** this **plague** forever. You should attack locusts at the source. Hoppers, in short. The men were talking as if they were planning a war, and Margaret listened, amazed.

The rest of the story is falling action, or winding down to the resolution of the story. Read to find out how Margaret continues to learn and change through the action.

Contrast Margaret's reaction to losing the battle with the reaction of Stephen and Richard.

roused stirred to action	**eliminating** getting rid of	**plague** destructive invasion or disease

In the night it was quiet; no sign of the settled armies outside, except sometimes a branch snapped, or a tree could be heard crashing down.

Margaret slept badly in the bed beside Richard, who was sleeping like the dead, exhausted with the afternoon's fight. In the morning she woke to yellow sunshine lying across the bed—clear sunshine, with an occasional blotch of shadow moving over it. She went to the window. Old Stephen was ahead of her. There he stood outside, gazing down over the bush. And she gazed, astounded—and entranced, much against her will. For it looked as if every tree, every bush, all the earth, were lit with pale flames. The locusts were fanning their wings to free them of the night dews. There was a shimmer of red-tinged gold light everywhere.

How does the description of the morning mark an important change from the day before?

She went out to join the old man, stepping carefully among the insects. They stood and watched. Overhead the sky was blue, blue and clear.

"Pretty," said old Stephen, with satisfaction.

Well, thought Margaret, we may be ruined, we may be bankrupt, but not everyone has seen an army of locusts fanning their wings at dawn.

What does the beauty of the locusts taking off add to your view of the swarm?

Over the slopes, in the distance, a faint red smear showed in the sky, thickened and spread. "There they go," said old Stephen. "There goes the main army, off south."

And now from the trees, from the earth all round them, the locusts were taking wing. They were like small aircraft, **maneuvering** for the take-off, trying their wings to see if they were dry enough. Off they went. A reddish brown steam was rising off the miles of bush, off the lands, the earth. Again the sunlight darkened.

And as the **clotted** branches lifted, the weight on them lightening, there was nothing but the black spines of branches, trees. No green left, nothing. All morning they watched,

---

maneuvering making changes in direction and position for a purpose

clotted made thick

the three of them, as the brown crust thinned and broke and dissolved, flying up to mass with the main army, now a brownish-red smear in the southern sky. The lands which had been filmed with green, the new tender mealie plants, were stark and bare. All the trees stripped. A **devastated** landscape. No green, no green anywhere.

By midday the reddish cloud had gone. Only an occasional locust flopped down. On the ground were the corpses and the wounded. The African laborers were sweeping these up with branches and collecting them in tins.

"Ever eaten sun-dried locust?" asked old Stephen. "That time twenty years ago, when I went broke, I lived on mealie meal and dried locusts for three months. They aren't bad at all—rather like smoked fish, if you come to think of it."

But Margaret preferred not even to think of it.

After the midday meal the men went off to the lands. Everything was to be replanted. With a bit of luck another swarm would not come traveling down just this way. But they hoped it would rain very soon, to spring some new grass, because the cattle would die otherwise—there was not a blade of grass left on the farm. As for Margaret, she was trying to get used to the idea of three or four years of locusts. Locusts were going to be like bad weather, from now on, always **imminent.** She felt like a survivor after war—if this devastated and **mangled** countryside was not ruin, well, what then was ruin?

But the men ate their supper with good appetites.

"It could have been worse," was what they said. "It could be much worse."

---

devastated completely destroyed   **imminent** about to happen   **mangled** torn up

A Mild Attack of Locusts   by Doris Lessing

Directions Choose the letter of the best answer or write the answer using complete sentences.

Comprehension: Identifying Facts

1. Margaret does not know what to expect on the farm because _____.
   A she is a newcomer
   B it keeps changing
   C her husband does not talk to her
   D she does not pay attention

2. Margaret is there because she _____.
   A is married to Richard
   B wants adventure
   C is the housekeeper
   D is Stephen's daughter

3. Describe the farm.

4. What threatens the farm in this story? Why are they a threat?

5. What actions do the farmers and workers take against the locusts?

6. How effective are their actions?

7. What does Margaret do to help?

8. Why does the sky become dark early that day?

9. Why do the men keep fighting after all the crops and plants have been eaten?

10. What do Margaret and Stephen watch at dawn the next morning?

Comprehension: Putting Ideas Together

11. The way the men talk about the weather and other things that affect the farm can best be described as _____.
    A positive   C dishonest
    B negative   D honest

12. The locust swarm described in this story seems most like _____.
    A a terrible storm   C a monster
    B an earthquake   D ants

13. How does the power of humans compare to the power of nature in this story?

14. In what ways is Margaret different from Richard and Stephen?

15. What qualities do the farmers of this region need to have?

After Reading **continued on next page**

16. How do Margaret's feelings about the locusts change through the story?

17. How does the night contrast with the battle of the daylight hours?

18. Contrast the way the farm looks before the locust attack and after.

19. What must the farmers do after the battle is over?

20. How is Margaret's view of herself different after the locust swarm?

Understanding Literature: Conflict and Rising Action

A story's conflict is the struggle of the main character against self, others, or nature. Conflict becomes more intense as the plot progresses. This buildup of excitement in a story is known as rising action. It is solved during the resolution.

21. What is the main conflict in this story?

22. What other conflict does Margaret feel?

23. How does the author show that conflict is increasing?

24. How is the main conflict resolved? Is there a winner? Explain.

25. When does the rising action of the story end and the resolution occur?

Critical Thinking

26. What is the theme, or main idea, of this story?

27. Why do you think the author follows Margaret most closely to tell this story?

28. Do you think the government plan to rid the world of locust plagues will work? Explain.

Thinking Creatively

29. Do you think of nature as beautiful and inviting or destructive and cruel? Provide support for your opinion.

30. The numbers of insects on Earth are vast—many times greater than the numbers of people—and insects reproduce with great speed. How can humans defeat insects? Should they?

Grammar Check

Writers may join independent clauses using a semicolon (;). Each clause has a subject and predicate and could stand alone as a sentence. However, the ideas in the clauses are closely related, so they are combined.

The farm was ringing with the clamor of the gong; and they could see the laborers come pouring out of the compound, pointing at the hills and shouting excitedly.

Find two other sentences in the story that use semicolons. Write the sentences, including all punctuation marks. Then write a sentence of your own using a semicolon.

 Writing on Your Own

Write a journal entry Margaret might have written after this experience. Include details about her observations of the locusts and the men fighting them. Express how she feels. Then write a journal entry Richard might have written about the same experience.

 Speaking

Prepare an oral report about a natural disaster you have observed or read about, such as a hurricane or drought. Take notes about details you recall. Look up more facts about the disaster, such as ways people and the land were affected and how long the effects lasted. Organize your notes. Practice delivering your report until you are comfortable with your material. Give your report to the class.

 Media

Locate and listen to a farm news report on radio or TV. Write down the main idea and several interesting facts you learned from at least one story on the report.

 Research

Research to learn about the life cycle and traits of locusts. Find information in library books on insects, encyclopedias, and online articles. Study photographs and diagrams of locusts. Compare the story description of the insects. Do they look as you expected? Prepare a report of your findings.

Anita Desai
1937–

About the Author

Anita Desai was born in 1937 in Delhi, India. Her father was Bengali and her mother was German. She grew up speaking German at home and English and Indian dialects at school and in public. Desai has said that her German heritage causes her to see India as an outsider, while her Indian heritage makes her "feel about India as an Indian." It is not surprising, then, that her writing often explores the lives of outsiders in Indian society. Desai is considered the writer who introduced to India novels with a psychological focus like those of Virginia Woolf.

Desai attended Delhi University. She married and raised several children before beginning her career as a writer. Desai has written a number of novels, short stories, and children's books. She has received many awards and prizes. She lives in Massachusetts and teaches writing at Massachusetts Institute of Technology (MIT). She returns to India for part of each year.

About the Selection

"Games at Twilight" was published in 1978 in the short story collection by the same name. Set in a city in India, it is rich in images that bring to life the sounds, colors, and heat surrounding the children of an Indian family. The story's narrator follows one small boy, Ravi, during a game of hide-and-seek.

Literary Terms An author tells a story from a certain **point of view.** It controls what readers see and understand about characters and events. The narrator of this story is not a character but someone who observes all the characters and reports on them. This kind of story is written in the **third person.** The author also uses a great deal of **imagery,** or word pictures, to help readers see, hear, feel, smell, and taste the surroundings.

Reading on Your Own As you read the story, notice the imagery. Stop to think about how each image involves the senses and what feelings it stirs up. What mood do images of the terrible heat and the helplessness of the children create in this story?

Writing on Your Own Think of a time in childhood when you played a game outdoors with other children. Write a description of the game and how you felt about playing with the others.

Vocabulary Focus In the story, the author describes several tropical plants that may be unfamiliar to you. Learning about them will help you picture the setting and add to the mood of the story. A *bougainvillea* is a woody vine that can grow quite large and is covered with brilliant purple or red clusters of flowers. *Eucalyptus* is a type of evergreen tree or shrub that has stiff, rounded leaves and a strong scent. *Crotons* are plants or shrubs with large leaves that are brightly colored with yellow and pink. *Hibiscus* are plants or trees with glossy leaves and big, showy flowers in various colors.

Think Before You Read Use what you know about children's games to predict how the children feel about winning and losing in this story.

point of view
the position from which the author or storyteller tells the story

third person
a point of view where the narrator is not a character and refers to characters as *he* or *she*

imagery pictures created by words; the use of words that appeal to the five senses

Games at Twilight

As you read, notice which character the narrator follows most closely. What do you learn because the narrator knows this character's thoughts and feelings?

It was still too hot to play outdoors. They had had their tea, they had been washed and had their hair brushed, and after the long day of **confinement** in the house that was not cool but at least a protection from the sun, the children strained to get out. Their faces were red and bloated with the effort, but their mother would not open the door, everything was still curtained and shuttered in a way that **stifled** the children, made them feel that their lungs were stuffed with cotton wool and their noses with dust and if they didn't burst out into the light and see the sun and feel the air, they would choke.

"Please, ma, please," they begged. "We'll play in the **veranda** and porch—we won't go a step out of the porch."

"You will, I know you will, and then—"

"No—we won't, we won't," they wailed so horrendously that she actually let down the bolt of the front door so that they burst out like seeds from a crackling, over-ripe pod into the veranda, with such wild, **maniacal** yells that she retreated to her bath and the shower of talcum powder and the fresh **sari** that were to help her face the summer evening.

Notice the contrast between the children inside the house and outside the house.

confinement captivity	**veranda** roofed open porch	**sari** clothing made of a long piece of cotton or silk worn wound around the body, usually by Hindu women
stifled made breathing hard	**maniacal** crazy	

They faced the afternoon. It was too hot. Too bright. The white walls of the veranda glared **stridently** in the sun. The bougainvillea hung about it, purple and **magenta,** in **livid** balloons. The garden outside was like a tray made of beaten brass, flattened out on the red gravel and the stony soil in all shades of metal—aluminium, tin, copper and brass. No life stirred at this **arid** time of day—the birds still drooped, like dead fruit, in the papery tents of the trees; some squirrels lay limp on the wet earth under the garden tap. The outdoor dog lay stretched as if dead on the veranda mat, his paws and ears and tail all reaching out like dying travellers in search of water. He rolled his eyes at the children—two white marbles rolling in the purple sockets, begging for sympathy—and attempted to lift his tail in a wag but could not. It only twitched and lay still.

Then, perhaps **roused** by the shrieks of the children, a band of parrots suddenly fell out of the eucalyptus tree, tumbled frantically in the still, sizzling air, then sorted themselves out into battle **formation** and streaked away across the white sky.

The children, too, felt released. They too began tumbling, shoving, pushing against each other, frantic to start. Start what? Start their business. The business of the children's day which is—play.

"Let's play hide-and-seek."

"Who'll be It?"

"You be It."

"Why should I? You be—"

"You're the eldest—"

"That doesn't mean—"

The shoves became harder. Some kicked out. The motherly Mira **intervened.** She pulled the boys roughly apart. There was a tearing sound of cloth but it was lost in the heavy panting and angry grumbling and no one paid attention to the small sleeve hanging loosely off a shoulder.

What clues in the story tell you this is told from a third-person point of view?

How does the author link the children to the animals outside? Why do you think she does this?

stridently harshly	**arid** very dry	**formation** arrangement
magenta purplish red	**roused** awakened	
livid bruised		**intervened** came between

The clapping game that Mira organizes is a way to pick who will be It during the game of hide-and-seek.

"Make a circle, make a circle!" she shouted, firmly pulling and pushing till a kind of **vague** circle was formed. "Now clap!" she roared and, clapping, they all chanted in **melancholy** unison: "Dip, dip, dip—my blue ship—" and every now and then one or the other saw he was safe by the way his hands fell at the crucial moment—palm on palm, or back of hand on palm—and dropped out of the circle with a yell and a jump of relief and **jubilation.**

Raghu was It. He started to protest, to cry "You cheated— Mira cheated—Anu cheated—" but it was too late, the others had all already streaked away. There was no one to hear when he called out, "Only in the veranda—the porch—Ma said—Ma *said* to stay in the porch!" No one had stopped to listen, all he saw were their brown legs flashing through the dusty shrubs, scrambling up brick walls, leaping over **compost** heaps and hedges, and then the porch stood empty in the purple shade of the bougainvillea and the garden was as empty as before; even the limp squirrels had whisked away, leaving everything gleaming, brassy and bare.

Only small Manu suddenly reappeared, as if he had dropped out of an invisible cloud or from a bird's claws, and stood for a moment in the centre of the yellow lawn, chewing his finger and near to tears as he heard Raghu shouting, with his head pressed against the veranda wall, "Eighty-three, eighty-five, eighty-nine, ninety . . ." and then made off in a panic, half of him wanting to fly north, the other half **counselling** south. Raghu turned just in time to see the flash of his white shorts and the uncertain **skittering** of his red sandals, and charged after him with such a blood-curdling yell that Manu stumbled over the hosepipe, fell into its rubber coils and lay there weeping, "I won't be It—you have to find them all—all—All!"

Details suggest that the children are stressed and bothered. Notice the contrast between Raghu and Manu.

vague not definite	**compost** decayed plant matter used for fertilizer	**skittering** skipping quickly
melancholy very sad		
jubilation joy	**counselling** advising	

"I know I have to, idiot," Raghu said, **superciliously** kicking him with his toe. "You're dead," he said with satisfaction, licking the beads of perspiration off his upper lip, and then stalked off in search of worthier prey, whistling **spiritedly** so that the hiders should hear and tremble.

Ravi heard the whistling and picked his nose in a panic, trying to find comfort by burrowing the finger deep-deep into that soft tunnel. He felt himself too **exposed,** sitting on an upturned flower pot behind the garage. Where could he burrow? He could run around the garage if he heard Raghu come—around and around and around—but he hadn't much faith in his short legs when matched against Raghu's long, hefty, hairy footballer legs. Ravi had a frightening glimpse of them as Raghu combed the hedge of crotons and hibiscus, trampling delicate ferns underfoot as he did so. Ravi looked about him desperately, swallowing a small ball of snot in his fear.

The garage was locked with a great heavy lock to which the driver had the key in his room, hanging from a nail on the wall under his work-shirt. Ravi had peeped in and seen him still sprawling on his string-cot in his vest and striped underpants, the hair on his chest and the hair in his nose shaking with the **vibrations** of his **phlegm-obstructed** snores. Ravi had wished he were tall enough, big enough to reach the key on the nail, but it was impossible, beyond his reach for years to come. He had **sidled** away and sat **dejectedly** on the flower pot. That at least was cut to his own size.

But next to the garage was another shed with a big green door. Also locked. No one even knew who had the key to the lock. That shed wasn't opened more than once a year when Ma turned out all the old broken bits of furniture and rolls of matting and leaking buckets, and the white ant hills were

> The story focuses on Ravi now. The narrator knows what Ravi is thinking and feeling. What is the effect of this closeness on readers?

superciliously in a way that shows dislike	**exposed** uncovered; unprotected	**sidled** crept away sideways
spiritedly with energy	**vibrations** shaking	**dejectedly** sadly
	phlegm-obstructed blocked by mucus	

broken and swept away and Flit sprayed into the spider webs and rat holes so that the whole operation was like the looting of a poor, ruined and conquered city. The green leaves of the door sagged. They were nearly off their rusty hinges. The hinges were large and made a small gap between the door and the walls—only just large enough for rats, dogs and, possibly, Ravi to slip through.

Ravi had never cared to enter such a dark and depressing **mortuary** of **defunct** household goods seething with such unspeakable and alarming animal life but, as Raghu's whistling grew angrier and sharper and his crashing and storming in the hedge wilder, Ravi suddenly slipped off the flower pot and through the crack and was gone. He chuckled aloud with astonishment at his own **temerity** so that Raghu came out of the hedge, stood silent with his hands on his hips, listening, and finally shouted "I heard you! I'm coming! *Got* you—" and came charging round the garage only to find the upturned flower pot, the yellow dust, the crawling of white ants in a mud-hill against the closed shed door—nothing. Snarling, he bent to pick up a stick and went off, whacking it against the garage and shed walls as if to beat out his prey.

What problem has Ravi solved by going into the shed? What problem does he create by doing so?

mortuary funeral home

defunct no longer used

temerity boldness

Ravi shook, then shivered with delight, with self-congratulation. Also with fear. It was dark, spooky in the shed. It had a muffled smell, as of graves. Ravi had once got locked into the linen cupboard and sat there weeping for half an hour before he was rescued. But at least that had been a familiar place, and even smelt pleasantly of starch, laundry and, **reassuringly,** of his mother. But the shed smelt of rats, ant hills, dust and spider webs. Also of less **definable,** less recognizable horrors. And it was dark. Except for the white-hot cracks along the door, there was no light. The roof was very low. Although Ravi was small, he felt as if he could reach up and touch it with his finger tips. But he didn't stretch. He hunched himself into a ball so as not to bump into anything, touch or feel anything. What might there not be to touch him and feel him as he stood there, trying to see in the dark? Something cold, or slimy—like a snake. Snakes! He leapt up as Raghu whacked the wall with his stick—then, quickly realizing what it was, felt almost relieved to hear Raghu, hear his stick. It made him feel protected.

But Raghu soon moved away. There wasn't a sound once his footsteps had gone around the garage and disappeared. Ravi stood frozen inside the shed. Then he shivered all over. Something had tickled the back of his neck. It took him a while to pick up the courage to lift his hand and explore. It was an insect—perhaps a spider—exploring *him.* He squashed it and wondered how many more creatures were watching him, waiting to reach out and touch him, the stranger.

There was nothing now. After standing in that position—his hand still on his neck, feeling the wet splodge of the squashed spider gradually dry—for minutes, hours, his legs began to tremble with the effort, the inaction. By now he could see enough in the dark to make out the large solid shapes of old wardrobes, broken buckets and bedsteads piled on top of each other around him. He recognized an old bathtub—patches of enamel glimmered at him and at last he lowered himself onto its edge.

> To which senses does the imagery in this paragraph appeal?

> Why does Ravi *feel protected* knowing Raghu is outside the shed?

> Ravi struggles with his fear of being found against his fear of remaining in the shed.

reassuringly in a way that gives confidence or comfort

definable able to be explained

He **contemplated** slipping out of the shed and into the **fray.** He wondered if it would not be better to be captured by Raghu and be returned to the milling crowd as long as he could be in the sun, the light, the free spaces of the garden and the familiarity of his brothers, sisters and cousins. It would be evening soon. Their games would become **legitimate.** The parents would sit out on the lawn on cane basket chairs and watch them as they tore around the garden or gathered in knots to share a loot of mulberries or black, teeth-splitting *jamun* from the garden trees. The gardener would fix the hosepipe to the water tap and water would fall **lavishly** through the air to the ground, soaking the dry yellow grass and the red gravel and arousing the sweet, the **intoxicating** scent of water on dry earth—that loveliest scent in the world. Ravi sniffed for a whiff of it. He half-rose from the bathtub, then heard the despairing scream of one of the girls as Raghu bore down upon her. There was the sound of a crash, and of rolling about in the bushes, the shrubs, then screams and accusing sobs of, "I touched the den—" "You did not—" "I did—" "You liar, you did *not*" and then a fading away and silence again.

Ravi sat back on the harsh edge of the tub, deciding to hold out a bit longer. What fun if they were all found and caught—he alone left unconquered! He had never known that sensation. Nothing more wonderful had ever happened to him than being taken out by an uncle and bought a whole slab of chocolate all to himself, or being flung into the soda-man's pony cart and driven up to the gate by the friendly driver with the red beard and pointed ears. To defeat Raghu—that **hirsute,** hoarse-voiced football champion—and to be the winner in a circle of older, bigger, luckier children—that would be thrilling beyond imagination. He hugged his knees together and smiled to himself almost shyly at the thought of so much victory, such **laurels.**

> Ravi thinks with longing of the comforting things outside the shed. What keeps him inside?

> What goal gives Ravi courage?

contemplated thought about	**lavishly** generously; richly	**hirsute** hairy
fray fight; conflict	**intoxicating** refreshing; revitalizing	**laurels** glory
legitimate permitted		

There he sat smiling, knocking his heels against the bathtub, now and then getting up and going to the door to put his ear to the broad crack and listening for sounds of the game, the pursuer and the pursued, and then returning to his seat with the **dogged** determination of the true winner, a breaker of records, a champion.

It grew darker in the shed as the light at the door grew softer, fuzzier, turned to a kind of crumbling yellow pollen that turned to yellow fur, blue fur, grey fur. Evening. Twilight. The sound of water gushing, falling. The scent of earth receiving water, **slaking** its thirst in great gulps and releasing that green scent of freshness, coolness. Through the crack Ravi saw the long purple shadows of the shed and the garage lying still across the yard. Beyond that, the white walls of the house. The bougainvillea had lost its **lividity,** hung in dark bundles that quaked and twittered and seethed with masses of homing sparrows. The lawn was shut off from his view. Could he hear the children's voices? It seemed to him that he could. It seemed to him that he could hear them chanting, singing, laughing. But what about the game? What had happened? Could it be over? How could it when he was still not found?

It then occurred to him that he could have slipped out long ago, dashed across the yard to the veranda and touched the "den." It was necessary to do that to win. He had forgotten. He had only remembered the part of hiding and trying to **elude** the seeker. He had done that so successfully, his success had **occupied** him so wholly that he had quite forgotten that success had to be **clinched** by that final dash to victory and the ringing cry of "Den!"

With a whimper he burst through the crack, fell on his knees, got up and stumbled on stiff, **benumbed** legs across the shadowy yard, crying heartily by the time he reached the veranda so that when he flung himself at the white pillar and

> Contrast the imagery here with earlier descriptions of the yard and house. How has the arrival of twilight changed the scene?

dogged stubborn	**elude** avoid	**clinched** sealed; made final
slaking quenching	**occupied** kept busy	
lividity angry, swollen look		**benumbed** without feeling

bawled, "Den! Den! Den!" his voice broke with rage and pity at the disgrace of it all and he felt himself flooded with tears and misery.

Out on the lawn, the children stopped chanting. They all turned to stare at him in amazement. Their faces were pale and triangular in the dusk. The trees and bushes around them stood inky and **sepulchral,** spilling long shadows across them. They stared, wondering at his **reappearance,** his passion, his wild animal howling. Their mother rose from her basket chair and came towards him, worried, annoyed, saying, "Stop it, stop it, Ravi. Don't be a baby. Have you hurt yourself?" Seeing him attended to, the children went back to clasping their hands and chanting "The grass is green, the rose is red. . . ."

But Ravi would not let them. He tore himself out of his mother's grasp and pounded across the lawn into their midst, charging at them with his head lowered so that they scattered in surprise. "I won, I won, I won," he bawled, shaking his head so that the big tears flew. "Raghu didn't find me. I won, I won—"

It took them a minute to grasp what he was saying, even who he was. They had quite forgotten him. Raghu had found all the others long ago. There had been a fight about who was to be It next. It had been so fierce that their mother had

> Contrast Ravi's behavior now with his earlier thoughts of victory.

---

sepulchral gloomy; like a tomb   **reappearance** return

---

emerged from her bath and made them change to another game. Then they had played another and another. Broken mulberries from the tree and eaten them. Helped the driver wash the car when their father returned from work. Helped the gardener water the beds till he roared at them and swore he would complain to their parents. The parents had come out, taken up their positions on the cane chairs. They had begun to play again, sing and chant. All this time no one had remembered Ravi. Having disappeared from the scene, he had disappeared from their minds. Clean.

"Don't be a fool," Raghu said roughly, pushing him aside, and even Mira said, "Stop howling, Ravi. If you want to play, you can stand at the end of the line," and she put him there very firmly.

The game proceeded. Two pairs of arms reached up and met in an **arc**. The children trooped under it again and again in a **lugubrious** circle, ducking their heads and **intoning**

> "The grass is green,
> The rose is red;
> Remember me
> When I am dead, dead, dead, dead . . ."

And the arc of thin arms trembled in the twilight, and the heads were bowed so sadly, and their feet tramped to that melancholy **refrain** so mournfully, so helplessly, that Ravi could not bear it. He would not follow them, he would not be included in this **funereal** game. He had wanted victory and triumph—not a funeral. But he had been forgotten, left out and he would not join them now. The **ignominy** of being forgotten—how could he face it? He felt his heart go heavy and ache inside him unbearably. He lay down full length on the damp grass, crushing his face into it, no longer crying, silenced by a terrible sense of his **insignificance**.

The list of things the children have done since playing hide-and-seek shows how long Ravi hid in the shed.

Why does the game seem to Ravi like a funeral?

arc half-circle	**refrain** repeated lines in a song or poem	**ignominy** shame
lugubrious sad		**insignificance** unimportance
intoning chanting	**funereal** gloomy; like a funeral	

Games at Twilight   by Anita Desai

Directions Choose the letter of the best answer or write the answer using complete sentences.

Comprehension: Identifying Facts

1. The children have not been allowed to go outside because _____.
   A they have been bad
   B it is too hot outside
   C they have been sick
   D they are observing a religious holiday

2. What game do the children decide to play?
   A hide-and-seek
   B keep-away
   C football
   D ring around the rosy

3. Why are the children allowed to go out?

4. What is happening outside when they go out?

5. Who is It when playing the game?

6. Where does Ravi hide?

7. Why is he afraid to go inside this place?

8. Why does Ravi decide to stay in his hiding place?

9. What do the other children do while Ravi hides?

10. What does Ravi do when he returns to the group?

Comprehension: Putting Ideas Together

11. Throughout the story, the children's actions with each other are _____.
    A kind and gentle
    B uncertain and shy
    C rough and mean
    D jolly and amusing

12. The thing that controls their activities on this day is _____.
    A heat   C storm
    B sickness   D society

13. In what ways do the children seem like animals?

14. How many children are in the family?

15. What is the relationship of Mira to the other children?

16. What is the relationship of Raghu to the other children?

17. Where does Ravi fit into the family order? How can you tell?

18. How do Ravi's emotions change during his time in the shed?

19. Compare being in the shed with being in the house. What is ironic about Ravi choosing this place to hide?

20. How would you describe Ravi's view of himself?

Understanding Literature: Point of View and Imagery

The point of view of a story controls what we see and understand of the characters and action. The storyteller gives us our perspective on all that happens. Authors use imagery, or word pictures that focus the senses, to make the experiences of characters seem real.

21. Who is the storyteller in "Games at Twilight"?

22. Whom does the storyteller follow most closely?

23. Why is it important to know what Ravi is thinking and feeling?

24. To what senses do most images in the beginning of the story appeal?

25. Reread the paragraphs on pages 609–611, describing what the shed is like. What do these images suggest about the shed?

Critical Thinking

26. In spite of playing games, the children seem upset and fearful. Why do you think this is?

27. Why do you think it is so important to Ravi to win the game of hide-and-seek?

28. How is Raghu like a predator and the other children like his prey?

29. What does this story suggest about the relationships of young brothers and sisters in a family?

Thinking Creatively

30. Do you think it is best to be the oldest, youngest, or middle child in a family? Explain your choice.

After Reading continued on next page

Games at Twilight by Anita Desai

 Grammar Check

Usually, words spoken by characters in a story are set inside quotation marks (" "). In addition, when someone is addressed directly in a sentence, that name is set off by a comma:

"Children, where are you? It's time to come in, Ravi and Manu."

When the noun of direct address appears in the middle of a sentence, it is set off by two commas:

"Please, Mama, let us play a little longer."

Find three sentences of dialogue that use direct address in this story. Write the sentences, using commas and quotation marks correctly. Then write a short dialogue of your own, using direct address.

 Writing on Your Own

Write a one-paragraph summary of this story. Tell about the characters briefly. Paraphrase the most important events and ideas in your own words. Use a Sequence Chain or Concept Map to organize your ideas. (See Appendix A for a description of these graphic organizers.)

 Speaking and Listening

In a small group, discuss your reaction to this story. Do you think the description of children playing games together was true to life? Explain your opinion, giving examples from the story. Listen to other students' ideas without interrupting. Write down your thoughts and questions about what they say.

 Media

Choose a TV program about a family with young children. As you watch, take notes about the way the children act toward each other. Does this interaction seem realistic or unrealistic? Write a review of the show explaining your thinking.

Viewing

Locate photographs that show children playing in groups. Determine what themes, or main ideas, each photograph is showing. For example, a photograph might show competitive spirit, cooperation, or determination. Sort the images by theme. Create a poster with labels for each theme.

BEFORE READING THE SELECTION

from *Omeros*   *by Derek Walcott*

About the Author

Derek Walcott was born in 1930 on the Caribbean island of Saint Lucia, in the Lesser Antilles. Growing up on this island, a former British colony, affected his life and writing. On his mother's side, Walcott's heritage includes former slaves. His father, who was British and an artist, died when Walcott and his twin brother were very young. After attending college on his native island and on Jamaica, Walcott settled in Trinidad in 1953.

Walcott founded the Trinidad Theatre Workshop in 1959. It has produced many of his plays. He has published many books of poetry since 1962, including *Omeros* in 1990. Walcott's writing skillfully joins folk culture, classical literature, and forward-looking ideas and techniques. Often, his work explores his African heritage and personal conflicts that arise from a mixed-race background. In 1992, he received the Nobel Prize for Literature.

About the Selection

Omeros is a long poem that tells a story. It contains seven sections, called books, and each book is divided into chapters. It is written in three-line stanzas similar to those the Italian poet Dante used in his work. The title *Omeros* comes from the Greek pronunciation of Homer, the Greek poet who wrote *The Iliad* and *The Odyssey*. Walcott's poem tells the story of Caribbean fishermen on the island of Saint Lucia. Achille and Hector are friends who both love the beautiful Helen and become rivals for her hand. These character names come from Homer's *Iliad*. However, Walcott redefines the idea of the hero by giving these names to peasants.

Derek Walcott
1930–

Objectives

- To read and understand an excerpt of an epic poem
- To define epic
- To describe the effect of imagery, figurative language, and allusions
- To identify the theme of a poem

Before Reading continued on next page

from *Omeros*   *by Derek Walcott*

epic a long story written in verse

figurative language writing or speech not meant to be understood exactly as it is written

theme the main idea of a literary work

allusion something referring to a historical event, a person, a place, or a work of literature

Literary Terms An **epic** is a very long poem that follows the adventures of a heroic figure. Imagery draws readers in by appealing to the senses and painting word pictures. **Figurative language** adds to these word pictures. This kind of language is not meant to be understood exactly as written. Instead, it helps readers make new connections.

A **theme**, or main idea, of many epics is the greatness of the hero. In *Omeros*, the characters are ordinary men and women of a Caribbean island. They become heroic because of their ability to survive and regain a sense of their identity taken from them by colonial rule. **Allusions,** or references, to classical literature are an important part of Walcott's epic.

Reading on Your Own As you read this excerpt, imagine the characters gathered for the funeral of a friend or husband. Use the imagery to understand the mood. Be aware of the attitude of Achille toward Hector—his friend and rival.

Writing on Your Own What is the purpose of a funeral? What does it mean to the mourners? Write your thoughts as a journal entry.

Vocabulary Focus The epic's main characters are fishermen. This excerpt contains terms that refer to their boats and equipment and the sea. For example, a *gunwale* is the upper edge of a boat's side. A *seine* is a large net with sinkers on one edge and floats on the other. It hangs vertically in the water. When its ends are drawn together, it traps fish inside. A *fathom* is a unit for measuring the depth of water—usually about six feet.

Think Before You Read What do you think Achille will have to say about the dead man, Hector, who was both his friend and rival? What attitude do you expect from Helen, Hector's widow?

FROM
OMEROS

As you read, notice the details that show what Achille admired about his friend Hector. How does Achille introduce their African heritage into his eulogy, or the speech he gives at the funeral?

Achille and Hector are fishermen and friends. Both fall in love with the beautiful Helen, who works as a servant at a farm on Saint Lucia. Helen first chooses Achille, but she believes he cannot support her. When Hector starts up a taxi business, she marries him instead. Achille suffers a sunstroke. In a trance, he is transported to his ancestral village in Africa. There he learns his ancestry and gains a sense of who he is. In this excerpt, Achille mourns for his old friend Hector, who has died.

I

Hector was buried near the sea he had loved once.
Not too far from the shallows where he fought Achille
for a tin and Helen. He did not hear the sea-almond's

moan over the bay when Philoctete blew the shell,
5 nor the one drumbeat of a wave-thud, nor a sail
rattling to rest as its day's work was over,

and its mate, **gauging** depth, bent over the **gunwale**,
then wearily sounding the **fathoms** with an oar,
the same **rite** his shipmates would repeat soon enough

Philoctete is also a fisherman on Saint Lucia.

The character names and many details of this epic are allusions to Homer's epics. Why do authors make such references to famous works?

gauging measuring; estimating

gunwale upper edge of the side of a boat

fathoms units for measuring water depth

rite ritual; custom

10   when it was their turn to lie quiet as Hector,
     lowering a pitch-pine canoe in the earth's **trough,**
     to sleep under the piled conchs, through every weather

     on the violet-wreathed mound. Crouching for his friend
       to hear,
     Achille whispered about their **ancestral** river,
15   and those things he would recognize when he got there,

     his true home, forever and ever and ever,
     forever, *compère.* Then Philoctete limped over
     and rested his hand firmly on a shaking shoulder

     to anchor his sorrow. Seven Seas and Helen
20   did not come nearer. Achille had carried an oar
     to the church and propped it outside with the red tin.

     Now his voice strengthened. He said: "Mate, this is your
       spear,"
     and laid the oar slowly, the same way he had placed
     the parallel oars in the hull of the gommier

25   the day the African **swift** and its shadow raced.
     And this was the prayer that Achille could not utter:
     "The spear that I give you, my friend, is only wood.

     Vexation is past. I know how well you treat her.
     You never know my admiration, when you stood
30   crossing the sun at the bow of the long canoe

     with the plates of your chest like a shield; I would say
     any enemy so was a compliment. 'Cause no
     African ever hurled his wide **seine** at the bay

To sleep under the piled conchs is an example of figurative language. Hector is not sleeping but dead. How does figurative language add to this poem?

Seven Seas is another fisherman.

Achille implies that the oar, which carried Hector through the sea in life, will serve as his protection in the next life.

The *gommier* (line 24), or candle tree, grows up to 100 feet tall and 3 to 5 feet in diameter. Here the word refers to a canoe made from the trunk of a gommier tree.

---

trough trench

ancestral from ancestors; inherited

compère friend or companion (in French)

swift bird that resembles a swallow

vexation anger; irritation

seine large fishing net with weights on one edge to make it hang down in the water

by which he was born with such beauty. You hear me?
    Men
35 did not know you like me. All right. Sleep good.
    Good night."
Achille moved Philoctete's hand, then he saw Helen

standing alone and veiled in the widowing light.
Then he reached down to the grave and lifted the tin
to her. Helen nodded. A wind blew out the sun.

II

40 Pride set in Helen's face after this, like a stone
    bracketed with Hector's name; her lips were **incised**
    by its dates in parenthesis. She seemed more stern,

more ennobled by distance as she slowly crossed
the hot street of the village like a distant sail
45 on the horizon. Grief heightened her. When she smiled

it was with such distance that it was hard to tell
if she had heard your **condolence.** It was the child,
Ma Kilman told them, that made her more beautiful.

How does Achille's speech help you understand the theme of common people heroically overcoming challenges?

The description of Helen that begins in line 40 includes both simile (*like a stone*) and metaphor (*incised/by its dates in parenthesis*) that refer to gravestones. What is the effect of this kind of figurative language?

A Saint Lucia fisher repairing his nets

bracketed attached or fixed to   **incised** chiseled   **condolence** expression of sympathy

AFTER READING THE SELECTION

from *Omeros*   *by Derek Walcott*

Directions Choose the letter of the best answer or write the answer using complete sentences.

Comprehension: Identifying Facts

1. What does Achille whisper to Hector?
   - **A** details about their ancestral home
   - **B** a spell to get Helen back
   - **C** a religious poem
   - **D** an apology

2. What does Achille admire about Hector?

3. What does Achille give Helen?

Comprehension: Putting Ideas Together

4. Details in this passage show that Achille and Hector _____.
   - **A** were close as brothers
   - **B** were arch-enemies
   - **C** were both married to Helen
   - **D** spent much time fishing together on the sea

5. What purpose does the oar most likely serve, in Achille's mind?

6. How does grief affect Helen?

Understanding Literature: Epic, Imagery, and Theme

This excerpt comes from an epic poem, a long story in verse. Its imagery, or word pictures, bring the island of Saint Lucia to life. Its theme, or main idea, relates to the simple dignity and pride of fishermen in their work and their African ancestry.

7. What picture of Hector does Achille paint with his words?

8. What does the description of Helen add to the theme of dignity and pride?

Critical Thinking

9. Helen is described as being "heightened" by grief. What do you think this means?

Thinking Creatively

10. Why do you think people put items into a grave with the dead?

Grammar Check

Adverbs modify verbs, adjectives, or other adverbs by answering the questions *when? where? how?* and *to what degree?*

> *Hector was buried near the sea he had loved* once. (had loved when?)

> Not too *far from the shallows where he fought Achille.* (how far?)

The negatives *not, never, hardly,* and *nowhere* can serve as adverbs too.

> *Seven Seas and Helen/did* not *come* nearer.

Find at least four more adverbs in the selection. Write the adverb, the word it modifies, and the question it answers.

 Writing on Your Own

Write a description of a person who is very proud of something. Include images and comparisons to emphasize and characterize the person's pride. Use concrete nouns, vivid adjectives, and strong verbs to sharpen your writing. Use a Semantic Line graphic organizer to help you think of words to use. (See Appendix A for a description of this graphic organizer.) Vary the length and type of sentences you use to add interest.

 Speaking and Listening

With a partner, take turns reading parts of this selection aloud. Practice reading the lines until you can read them smoothly and with expression. As you listen to your partner, make notes about what you think he or she does well and about ways to improve the reading. With your partner, plan and make a recording of the excerpt for classmates to hear.

 Viewing

Find many Caribbean and African artworks, including paintings, sculptures, and crafts. Takes notes about themes, symbols, and images that you see in several of the artworks and in Walcott's poetry. Write a paragraph explaining some common ideas and visual elements in Caribbean and African art.

 Research

Read about the history of Saint Lucia in an encyclopedia or online article. Learn about its colonial past and its present government, people, and economy. Write an essay telling how you think this place influenced the writing of Derek Walcott.

A metaphor is a figure of speech that makes a comparison without using the words *like* or *as*. Instead, it says or suggests that one thing *is* another. The things compared are often very different but are usually alike in some small, surprising way. For example:

The lake was a sheet of glass burnished by the brilliant sun.

The hours until the bell would ring stretched, an endless desert, before him.

These metaphors compare a lake's surface to glass and the time left in the school day to a desert. Notice that the second example does not use the word *is* or *was*. The comparison is implied.

Metaphors give readers new ways of looking at the subject. The first example emphasizes the smooth surface of the lake and the way sunlight glints off it. The second example suggests that the person feels the school day is torture and the time passes slowly for him.

Doris Lessing uses the following metaphors in "A Mild Attack of Locusts":

Through the hail of insects a man came running.

By midday, the reddish cloud had gone.

The first sentence compares the locusts to hail. It suggests the noise of the hard-shelled insects hitting buildings and trees, the vast number of them, and their destructive power. The second sentence compares the mass of locusts taking off to a cloud. This comparison emphasizes the great size of the horde and connects its power to the power of nature.

Review

1. What is a metaphor?

2. Why do you think a writer uses metaphors?

3. Do you think Lessing's metaphors make the story more interesting? Why or why not?

4. In "Araby," James Joyce uses this metaphor: "The other houses . . . gazed at one another with brown imperturbable faces." What is compared in this metaphor?

5. What do you think Joyce's metaphor adds to his description of the neighborhood?

Writing on Your Own

Write three metaphors of your own describing a place or a public scene. Do not include the words *like* or *as*.

Unit 7 presents writings by authors who live or lived in British dominions—lands that Britain once governed. Most of the writings are set during the 20th century, when these regions were struggling to become independent nations.

The writers covered in this unit write from two points of view. Their works often focus on the experiences and attitudes of their homelands, but they also show the effect of British culture and language. This blend of culture, custom, language, and experience helped give the British dominions their own distinct voices as they gained independence.

Selections

- "Araby" by James Joyce is a short story about a boy who likes a playmate's older sister and how it leads him to a harsh realization about life.

- "Next Term We'll Mash You" by Penelope Lively is a short story revealing a small boy's fears as his parents choose a boarding school for him.

- "A Mild Attack of Locusts" by Doris Lessing is a short story about the overwhelming power of nature and the efforts of African farmers to fight it.

- "Games at Twilight" by Anita Desai is a short story about Indian children playing games in the stifling heat and about the fears and disappointments of one small boy.

- The selection from the epic poem *Omeros* by Derek Walcott describes the funeral of a fisherman and the grief and admiration of his friend and his wife.

Directions Choose the letter of the best answer or write the answer using complete sentences.

Comprehension: Identifying Facts

1. Dominions of Britain had control over _____.
   A going to war
   B their own military
   C their own internal affairs
   D all foreign affairs

2. What happened to the colony of India?

3. What was the last British colony? When did Britain release control of it?

4. Which authors in this unit represent Africa?

5. Which author in this unit has ancestors who were slaves?

Comprehension: Putting Ideas Together

6. Which selection shows a negative view of wealth?
   A "Araby"
   B *Omeros*
   C "A Mild Attack of Locusts"
   D "Next Term We'll Mash You"

7. How are the main characters in "Games at Twilight" and "Next Term We'll Mash You" alike? How are they different?

8. Compare the epiphanies (when a character recognizes a truth) experienced by the main characters in "Araby" and "Games at Twilight."

9. Describe some differences in the writing styles of James Joyce and Penelope Lively.

10. What are two common themes of the selections in this unit?

Understanding Literature: Short Story

A short story is a brief fictional narrative. It contains characters, plot, setting, point of view, and theme. The purpose of a short story is often to reveal the true nature of a character or a situation. It is not simply the reporting of an incident.

11. What do you learn about the true nature of the situation in "Next Term We'll Mash You"?

12. What do you learn besides the main events in "A Mild Attack of Locusts"?

13. Why does *Omeros* not fit into the genre of short story?

14. Which selection in this unit gave you the strongest sense of another country and culture? Explain.

15. Doris Lessing, Anita Desai, and Derek Walcott all spend part of each year living outside their native countries. Why do you think they made this choice?

Critical Thinking

16. What is one way in which *Omeros* reaches into the past?

17. What common concerns do the authors in this unit share?

18. Do the works in this unit seem positive or negative? Explain your response.

19. Which author in this unit do you like best? Tell why.

Thinking Creatively

20. Do you think the experience of childhood is the same or different in different countries of the world? List details from the stories as evidence.

Speak and Listen

Choose a character in one of the unit selections. Make notes about the character's personal qualities and feelings he or she experienced. Write a monologue, a scene in which the character talks to a silent listener. Think about how best to represent this character with your voice, posture, and actions. Gather any props that may help you communicate character. Give your monologue in a small group. Listen to the monologues of others. Write a response telling what you learned about the character.

Writing on Your Own

Write a story in which a child is the main character and he or she learns an important lesson. Include descriptions, dialogue, and actions that reveal the child's character. Be sure your story has a beginning, middle, and end.

Beyond Words

Choose a selection from the unit with a setting that interests you. Make a map showing the location of this country and its geographic features. Add labels that tell facts about the land, climate, and people living there.

Test-Taking Tip

Take more than one evening to study for a major test. Break your study time into short sessions. Spend some time every day reviewing your notes in the week before the test.

Appendix A: Graphic Organizers

Graphic organizers are like maps. They help guide you through literature. They can also help you plan or "map out" your own stories, research, or presentations.

1. Character Analysis Guide

This graphic organizer helps you learn more about a character in a selection.

To use: Choose a character. List four traits of that character. Write down an event from the selection that shows each character trait.

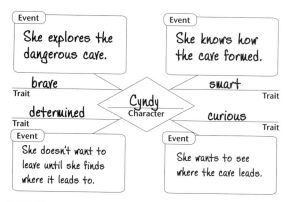

2. Story Map

This graphic organizer helps you summarize a story that you have read or plan your own story.

To use: List the title, setting, and characters. Describe the main problem of the story and the events that explain the problem. Then write how the problem is solved.

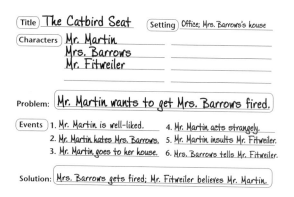

3. Main Idea Graphic (Umbrella)

This graphic organizer helps you determine the main idea of a selection or of a paragraph in the selection.

To use: List the main idea of a selection. Then, write the details that show or support the main idea of the story.

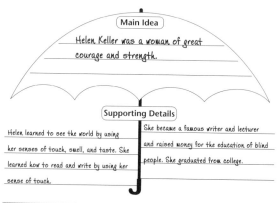

4. Main Idea Graphic (Table)

This graphic organizer is another way to determine the main idea of a selection or of a paragraph in the selection. Just like a table is held up by four strong legs, a main idea is held up or supported by many details.

To use: Write the main idea of a selection or paragraph on the tabletop. Then, write the details that show or support the main idea of the selection or paragraph on the table legs.

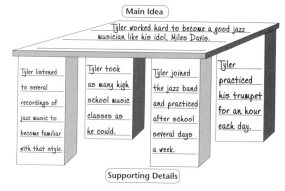

5. Main Idea Graphic (Details)

This graphic organizer is also a way to determine the main idea of a selection or of a paragraph in the selection. If the main idea of a selection or paragraph is not clear, add the details together to find it.

To use: First, list the supporting details of the selection or paragraph. Then, write one sentence that summarizes all the events. That is the main idea of the story.

6. Venn Diagram

This graphic organizer can help you compare and contrast two stories, characters, events, or topics.

To use: List the things that are common to both stories, events, characters, and so on in the "similarities" area between the circles. List the differences on the parts that do not overlap.

What is being compared? _____

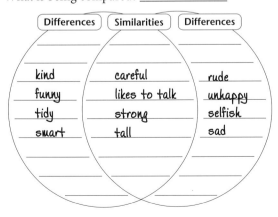

7. Sequence Chain

This graphic organizer outlines a series of events in the order in which they happen. This is helpful when summarizing the plot of a story. This graphic organizer may also help you plan your own story.

To use: Fill in the box at the top with the title of the story. Then, in the boxes below, record the events in the order in which they happen in the story. Write a short sentence in each box and only include the major events of the story.

Sequence Chain for: ___Cinderella___

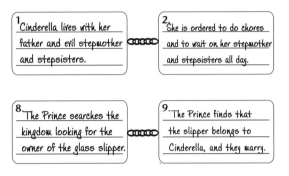

8. Concept Map

This graphic organizer helps you to organize supporting details for a story or research topic.

To use: Write the topic in the center of the graphic organizer. List ideas that support the topic on the lines. Group similar ideas and details together.

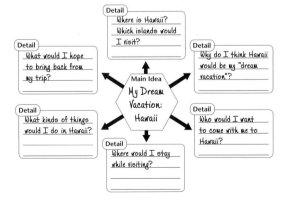

9. Plot Mountain

This graphic organizer helps you organize the events of a story or plot. There are five parts in a story's plot: the exposition, the rising action, the climax, the falling action, and the resolution (or denouement). These parts represent the beginning, middle, and end of the selection.

To use:

- Write the exposition, or how the selection starts, at the left base of the mountain. What is the setting? Who are the characters?
- Then, write the rising action, or the events that lead to the climax, on the left side of the mountain. Start at the base and list the events in time order going up the left side.
- At the top of the mountain, write the climax, or the highest point of interest or suspense. All events in the rising action lead up to this one main event or turning point.
- Write the events that happen after the climax, or falling action, on the right side of the mountain. Start at the top of the mountain, or climax, and put the events in time order going down the right-hand side.
- Finally, write the resolution, or denouement, at the right base of the mountain. The resolution explains how the problem, or conflict, in the story is solved or how the story ends.

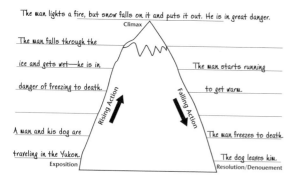

10. Structured Overview

This graphic organizer shows you how a main idea branches out in a selection.

To use: Write the main idea of a selection in the top box. Then, branch out and list events and details that support the main idea. Continue to branch off more boxes as needed to fill in the details of the story.

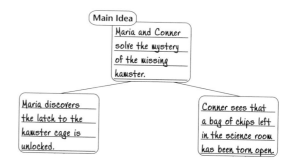

11. Semantic Table

This graphic organizer can help you understand the differences among words that have similar meanings.

To use: Choose a topic. List nouns for that topic in the top row. Put adjectives that describe your topic in the first column. Then, fill in the rest of the grid by checking those adjectives that are appropriate for the nouns. That way, in your writing, you can use words that make sense for your story.

Topic: _____ **Homes**

Adjectives \ Nouns→	apartment	4-bedroom home	cabin
large	—	✓	—
expensive	—	✓	—
quiet	—	✓	✓

12. Prediction Guide

This graphic organizer can be used to predict, or try to figure out, how a selection might end. Before finishing a selection, fill in this guide.

To use: List the time, place, and characters in the selection. Write what the problem, or conflict, is in the story. Then, try to predict possible endings or solutions. Compare your predictions with others.

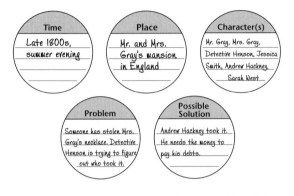

13. Semantic Line

This graphic organizer can help you think of synonyms for words that are used too often in writing.

To use: At the end of each line, write two overused words that mean the opposite. Then, fill in the lines with words of similar meaning. In the example below, the opposite words are *beautiful* and *ugly*. Words that are closer in meaning to beautiful are at the top. Words that are closer in meaning to ugly are at the bottom. The word *plain* falls in the middle.

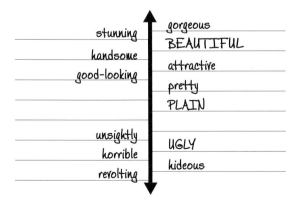

14. KWL Chart

This graphic organizer can help you learn about a topic before you start reading a selection or conducting research.

To use: Before you start reading a selection or conducting research, fill in the organizer. Write the topic on the line. In the first column, write what you already *know (K)* about your topic. Next, list what you *want (W)* to know about your topic in the next column. Then, as you start reading a selection or conducting research, write down what you *learn (L)* in the last column.

Topic: **Mount Everest**

K What I Know	W What I Want to Know	L What I Have Learned
It's a tall mountain in Asia. People may have tried to climb it. It's part of a larger mountain chain. It's one of the most famous mountains in the world.	How tall is it? Is it the tallest? What mountain chain is it part of?	It is the tallest in the world. It is part of the Himalayas. People have climbed it before. Some people have died trying.

Appendix B: Grammar

Parts of Speech

Adjectives

- Adjectives describe nouns and pronouns. They answer *What kind? Which one? How many?* or *How much?* Example: The *new* book costs *five* dollars.

- Comparative adjectives compare two nouns and usually end in *–er*. Example: *newer*

- Superlative adjectives compare three or more nouns and usually end in *–est*. Example: *newest*

Adverbs

- Adverbs modify verbs, adjectives, and other adverbs. They answer *When? How? How often?* and *How long?* Many adverbs end in *–ly*. Example: She laughed *loudly*.

Conjunctions

- Conjunctions connect parts of a sentence.

- Coordinating conjunctions connect two equal parts of a sentence using words like *and, but, nor, or, for, yet, so,* and *as well as*. Example: Do you want milk *or* water?

- Correlative conjunctions are used in pairs and connect equal parts of a sentence. Correlative conjunctions are *both/and, neither/nor, either/or, but/also*. Example: The teenagers had *neither* the time *nor* the money.

- Subordinating conjunctions connect two unequal parts of a sentence using words like *after, although, before, because, since, if, unless, while*. Example: *Since* you are arriving late, we will eat dinner at 7 p.m.

Interjections

- Interjections are words or phrases that show strong feeling, often followed by exclamation points. Examples: Wow! Ouch! Oops!

Nouns

- A noun names a person, place, thing, or idea.

- Proper nouns are names that are capitalized. Examples: Susan, New York

Prepositions

- Prepositions relate nouns and pronouns to other words in a sentence. Examples: above, from, with

Pronouns

- Pronouns replace nouns. Antecedents are the nouns that the pronouns replace. Example: Jorge takes karate lessons, and *he* practices every week.

- Demonstrative pronouns identify particular nouns: *this* hat, *those* shoes

- Indefinite pronouns do not refer to particular nouns. Examples: all, everyone, none

- Interrogative pronouns begin questions. Examples: who, which, what

- Personal pronouns refer to people or things. Examples: I, me, you, it, he, she, we, us, they, him, her, them

- Possessive pronouns show ownership. Examples: my, mine, his, hers, its, our, yours, their, ours, theirs

- Reflexive pronouns follow a verb or preposition and refer to the noun or pronoun that comes before. Examples: myself, themselves, himself, herself

- Relative pronouns introduce a subordinate clause. Examples: who, whom, whose, which, that, what

Verbs

- Verbs show action or express states of being.

- If the verbs are *transitive*, they link the action to something or someone. Example: John *hit* the ball. Action verbs that are *intransitive* do not link the action to something or someone. Example: The ball *flew*.

- Linking verbs connect a subject with a word or words that describe it. Some linking verbs are *am, are, was, were, is,* and *be.* Example: Susan *is* student council president.

Grammar Glossary

Active and Passive Voice

- Active voice is when the subject is *doing* the action. A sentence written in active voice is often shorter and easier to understand. Example: Jane drove the car to school.

- Passive voice is when the subject *receives* the action. A sentence written in passive voice can be awkward. Use a passive sentence only when the doer is unknown or unnecessary. Example: The car was driven by Jane.

Antecedent

- An antecedent is the noun or pronoun that a pronoun refers to in a sentence. Example: *Kevin* ran for Student Council so that *he* could help improve the school. *Kevin* is the antecedent for the pronoun *he.*

Appositives

- An appositive is a noun or pronoun that follows another noun or pronoun. An appositive renames or adds detail about the word. Example: Mr. Smith, *our principal,* is a great leader.

Clauses

- A clause is a group of words that contains a subject and a verb. There are independent and dependent clauses.

- An independent clause can stand alone because it expresses a complete thought. Example: Our dog eats twice a day. She also walks two miles a day. Two independent clauses can also be joined to form one sentence by using a comma and a coordinating conjunction, such as *and, but, nor, or, for, yet, so,* and *as well as.* Example: Our dog eats twice a day, *and* she walks two miles a day.

- A dependent clause cannot stand alone because it does not express a complete thought. Example: Because exercise is good for pets. This is a fragment or incomplete sentence. To fix this, combine a dependent clause with an independent clause. Example: Our dog walks two miles a day because exercise is good for pets.

Complements

- A complement completes the meaning of a verb. There are three types of complements: direct objects, indirect objects, and subject complements.

- A direct object is a word or group of words that receives the action of the verb. Example: Jane set the table. (*The table* is the complement or direct object of the verb *set.*)

- An indirect object is a word or group of words that follow the verb and tell for whom or what the action is done. An indirect object always comes before a direct object in a sentence. Example: Setting the table saved her mother some time. (*Her mother* is the complement or indirect object of the verb *saved.*)

- A subject complement is a word or group of words that further identify the subject of a sentence. A subject complement always follows a linking verb. Example: Buddy is the best dog. (The word *dog* is the complement of the subject *Buddy.*)

Contractions

- A contraction is two words made into one by replacing one or more letters with an apostrophe. Examples: *didn't* (did not), *you're* (you are)

Double Negatives

- A double negative is the use of two negative words, such as *no* or *not*, in a sentence. To fix a double negative, make one word positive. Incorrect: She *did not* get *no* dessert after dinner. Correct: She did not get *any* dessert after dinner.

Fragments

- A fragment is not a complete sentence. It may have a subject and verb, but it does not express a complete thought. Incorrect: The leaves that fell in the yard. Correct: The leaves that fell in the yard needed to be raked.

Gerunds

- A gerund is a verb with an *–ing* ending. It is used as a noun. Example: *Golfing* is fun! Here, *golfing* is a noun and the subject of the sentence.

Infinitives

- An infinitive is the word *to* plus the present tense of a verb. An infinitive can be a noun, adjective, or adverb in a sentence. Example: *To write* was her dream job. Here, *To write* is the infinitive, and it serves as a noun.

Modifiers

- A modifier is a word or group of words that change the meanings of other words in the sentence. Adjectives and adverbs are modifiers.

- A dangling or misplaced modifier is a group of descriptive words that is not near the word it modifies. This confuses the reader. Incorrect: Tucked up in the closet, Sarah found her grandma's photographs. *Tucked up in the closet* modifies Sarah. However, the photographs, not Sarah, are tucked up in the closet! Correct: Sarah found her grandma's photographs tucked up in the closet.

Parallel Structure

- Parallel structure is the use of words to balance ideas that are equally important. Incorrect: In the winter, I love to skate, snowmen, and to ski. Correct: In the winter, I love *to skate, to make* snowmen, and *to ski*.

Phrases

- A phrase is a group of words that does not have both a subject and a verb. Types of phrases include gerund phrases, infinitive phrases, and participial phrases.

- A gerund phrase has a gerund plus any modifiers and complements. The entire phrase serves as a noun. Example: Playing basketball with his friends was Trevor's favorite pastime. *Playing basketball with his friends* is the gerund phrase.

- An infinitive phrase has an infinitive plus any modifiers and complements. The entire phrase serves as a noun, adjective, or adverb in a sentence. Example: My mother liked to bake cookies on the weekend. *To bake cookies on the weekend* is the infinitive phrase.

- A participial phrase has a participle (a verb in its present form *[–ing]* or past form *[–ed or –en]*) plus all of its modifiers and complements. The entire phrase serves as an adjective in a sentence. Example: Wearing the robes of a king, Luis read his lines perfectly during play tryouts. *Wearing the robes of a king* is the participial phrase, and it modifies or describes the subject, Luis.

Plural Nouns

- A plural shows more than one of a particular noun. Use the following rules to create the plural form. Remember that there are exceptions to many spelling rules that you must simply memorize.

- Add *–s* to most singular nouns. Example: table/tables

- Add *–es* to a noun if it ends in *–ch, –sh, –s, –x,* and *–z*. Example: chur<u>ch</u>/churches

- If a noun ends with a vowel and a *–y,* add an *–s* to make the plural. Example: donk<u>ey</u>/donkeys

- If a noun ends with a consonant and a *–y,* drop the *–y* and add an *–ies* to make the plural. Example: pupp<u>y</u>/puppies

- If a noun ends in an *–f* or *–fe,* change the *–f* or *–fe* to a *v* and add *–es*. Example: kni<u>fe</u>/knives

- If a noun ends in an *–o,* sometimes you add *–es* and sometimes you add *–s*. Look in a dictionary to find out. Examples: pota<u>to</u>/potatoes, rad<u>io</u>/radios

Possessives

- A possessive noun shows ownership of an object, action, or idea. A possessive noun ends in *'s*. Example: Susan's book

- A possessive pronoun also shows ownership of an object, action, or idea. Example: his glove

Pronoun–Antecedent Agreement

- Pronoun-antecedent agreement occurs when the pronoun matches the antecedent (the word it refers to) in gender and number.

- To agree in gender:
  –Replace the name of a male person with a masculine pronoun. Example: *Jake* ran down the field, and *he* scored.

  –Replace the name of a female person with a feminine pronoun. Example: *Ana* read "The Most Dangerous Game," and *she* loved it.

  –Replace singular names with *it* or *its*. Example: The *kitten* ran through the room, and *it* pounced on the ball.

  –Replace plural names with *they, them,* or *their*. Example: The *tenth graders* came into the gym, and *they* played volleyball.

- To agree in number:

  –Make the pronoun singular if its antecedent is singular. Example: *Michael* told *himself* that he did the right thing.

  –Make the pronoun plural if its antecedent is plural. Example: The hungry *teenagers* ordered sandwiches for *themselves*.

Run-on Sentences

- A run-on sentence is the combination of two or more sentences without proper punctuation.

- To correct a run-on sentence, you can break it into two or more sentences by using capital letters and periods. Incorrect: The house was built in 1960 it needs new windows. Correct: The house was built in 1960. It needs new windows.

- You can also correct a run-on sentence by adding a comma and a coordinating conjunction to separate the sentences. Correct: The house was built in 1960, *so* it needs new windows.

- Another way to correct a run-on sentence is by adding a semicolon between the sentences. A semicolon should stand alone and should not have a coordinating conjunction after it. Correct: The house was built in 1960; it needs new windows.

Sentence Construction

- A simple sentence has one independent clause that includes a subject and a predicate. Example: The afternoon was warm and sunny.

- A compound sentence has two or more independent clauses joined by a comma and a coordinating conjunction or joined by a semicolon. Example: The afternoon was warm and sunny, so we decided to drive to the beach.

- A complex sentence has one independent clause and one or more dependent clauses. Example: We are going to the beach if you want to come along.

- A compound–complex sentence has two or more independent clauses joined by a comma and a coordinating conjunction. It has at least one dependent clause. Example: Although the morning was cold and damp, the afternoon was warm and sunny, so we decided to drive to the beach.

Sentence Types

- You can use a declarative sentence, an exclamatory sentence, an imperative sentence, or an interrogative sentence in writing.

- A declarative sentence tells us something about a person, place, or thing. This type of sentence ends with a period. Example: Martin Luther King Jr. fought for civil rights.

- An exclamatory sentence shows strong feeling or surprise. This type of sentence ends with an exclamation point. Example: I can't believe the price of gasoline!

- An imperative sentence gives commands. This type of sentence ends with a period. (Note: The subject of an imperative sentence is the implied "you.") Example: Please read chapter two by next Monday.

- An interrogative sentence asks a question. This type of sentence ends with a question mark. Example: Will you join us for dinner?

Subjects and Predicates

- The subject of a sentence names the person or thing doing the action. The subject contains a noun or a pronoun. Example: The students created posters and brochures. The subject of this sentence is *The students*. The predicate of this sentence (see definition below) is *created posters and brochures*.

- The predicate of a sentence tells what the person or thing is doing. The predicate contains a verb. Example: The fans waited for the hockey game to begin. The predicate of this sentence is *waited for the hockey game to begin*. The subject of this sentence is *The fans*.

Punctuation Guidelines

Apostrophe

- Shows ownership (possessive nouns): Kelly's backpack

- Shows plural possessive nouns: The five students' success was due to hard work.

- Shows missing letters in contractions: that's (that is)

Colon

- Introduces a list after a complete sentence: We learned about planets: Mars, Venus, and Jupiter.

- Adds or explains more about a complete sentence: Lunch was one option: pizza.

- Follows the salutation in a formal letter or in a business letter: Dear Mr. Jackson:

- Separates the hour and the minute: 2:15

- Introduces a long quotation: Lincoln wrote: "Four score and seven years ago . . ."

Comma

- Separates three or more items in a series: We planted corn, squash, and tomatoes.

- Joins two independent clauses when used with a coordinating conjunction: Sam and Raul did their homework, and then they left.

- Separates a city and state: Los Angeles, California

- Separates a day and year: October 15, 2006

- Follows the salutation and closing in a friendly letter: Dear Shanice, Love always,

- Follows the closing in a business letter: Sincerely,

- Sets off a restrictive phrase clause: Angela, the youngest runner, won the race.

- Sets off an introductory phrase or clause: Before he started the experiment, Jason put on safety glasses.

Dash

- Sets off an explanation in a sentence: The three poets—Langston Hughes, Robert Frost, and William Carlos Williams—are modernist poets.

- Shows a pause or break in thought: After years away, I returned—and found lots had changed.

Ellipses

- Show that words have been left out of a text: Our dog dove into the lake . . . and swam to shore.

Exclamation Point

- Shows emotion: Our team won!

Hyphen

- Divides a word at the end of a line: We enjoyed the beaches.

- Separates a compound adjective before a noun to make its meaning clearer: much-loved book

- Separates a compound number: thirty-three.

- Separates a fraction when used as an adjective: two-thirds full

Period

- Marks the end of a statement or command: July is the warmest month.

- Follows most abbreviations: Mrs., Dr., Inc., Jr.

Question Mark

- Marks the end of a question: How many eggs are left?

Quotation Marks

- Enclose the exact words of a speaker: He said, "I'll buy that book."

- Enclose the titles of short works: "Dover Beach," "America the Beautiful"

Semicolon

- Separates items in a series when commas are within the items: We went to Sioux Falls, South Dakota; Des Moines, Iowa; and Kansas City, Kansas.

- Joins two independent clauses that are closely related: We went to the movie; they came with us.

Capitalization Guidelines

Capitalize:

- the first word of a sentence: The teacher asked her students to read.

- the first word and any important words in a title: *To Kill a Mockingbird*

- all proper nouns: Marlon Smith, Atlanta, March

- the pronoun *I*

- languages: English, French

- abbreviations: Mrs., Sgt., FDR, EST

Commonly Confused Words

accept, except

- *Accept* (verb) means "to receive." Example: The children will *accept* ice cream.

- *Except* (preposition) means "leaving out." Example: The children enjoyed all flavors *except* strawberry.

affect, effect

- *Affect* (verb) means "to have an effect on." Example: This storm will *affect* our town.

- *Effect* (noun) means "a result or an outcome." Example: The *effect* was a struggling local economy.

its, it's

- *Its* (adjective) is the possessive form of "it." Example: Our hamster liked to run on the wheel inside *its* cage.

- *It's* is a contraction for "it is." Example: *It's* a long time before lunch.

lie, lay

- *Lie* (verb) means "to rest." Example: Jenny had a headache, so she needed to *lie* down.

- *Lay* (verb) means "to place." Example: Jamal went to *lay* his baseball glove on the bench.

lose, loose

- *Lose* (verb) means "to misplace or not find something." Example: I always *lose* my sunglasses when I go to the beach.

- *Loose* (adjective) means "free or without limits." Example: Someone let Sparky *loose* from his leash.

than, then

- *Than* (conjunction) shows a comparison. Example: You are older *than* I am.

- *Then* (adverb) means "at that time." Example: Will turned the doorknob and *then* slowly opened the door.

their, there, they're

- *Their* (pronoun) shows possession. Example: This is *their* house.

- *There* (adverb) means "place." Example: Sit over *there*.

- *They're* is a contraction for "they are." Example: *They're* coming over for dinner.

to, too, two

- *To* (preposition) shows purpose, movement, or connection. Example: We drove *to* the store.

- *Too* (adverb) means "also or more than wanted." Example: I, *too*, felt it was *too* hot to go outside.

- *Two* is a number. Example: Ava has *two* more years of high school.

your, you're

- *Your* (adjective) shows possession and means "belonging to you." Example: Take off *your* hat, please.

- *You're* is a contraction for "you are." Example: *You're* the best artist in the school.

Appendix C: Writing

Types of Writing

Before you can begin the writing process, you need to understand the types, purposes, and formats of different types of writing.

Descriptive Writing

Descriptive writing covers all writing genres. Description can be used to tell a story, to analyze and explain research, or to persuade. Descriptive writing uses images and colorful details to "paint a picture" for the reader.

Five Senses in Descriptive Writing

Consider the five senses in your descriptive writing: sight, smell, touch, sound, and taste. Using your senses to help describe an object, place, or person makes your writing more interesting. Before you begin, ask yourself the following:

- How does something look? Describe the color, size, and/or shape. What is it like?

- What smell or smells are present? Describe any pleasant or unpleasant smells. Compare the smells to other smells you know.

- How does something feel? Think about textures. Also think about emotions or feelings that result from the touching.

- What sounds do you hear? Describe the volume and the pitch. Are the sounds loud and shrill, or quiet and peaceful? What do the sounds remind you of?

- What does something taste like? Compare it to a taste you know, good or bad.

Expository Writing

Expository writing explains and informs through essays, articles, reports, and instructions. Like descriptive writing, it covers all writing genres. The purpose of this type of writing is to give more information about a subject. This can be done in many ways. The two most common formats in the study of literature are the compare and contrast paper and the cause and effect paper.

- Compare and Contrast Paper—This paper shows the similarities and differences of two or more characters, objects, settings, situations, writing styles, problems, or ideas.

- Cause and Effect Paper—This paper explains why certain things happen or how specific actions led to a result. A cause and effect paper can be set up by writing about the result (effect) first, followed by the events that led up to it (causes). Or, the paper can trace the events (causes), in order, that lead up to the result (effect).

Narrative Writing

Narrative writing tells a story. The story can be true (nonfiction) or made up (fiction). Narratives entertain or inform readers about a series of events. Poetry, stories, diaries, letters, biographies, and autobiographies are all types of narrative writing.

Key Elements in Narrative Writing

Think about the type of narrative you want to write and these key elements of your story:

- Characters: Who are the major and minor characters in the story? What do they look like? How do they act?

- Dialogue: What conversations take place among the characters? How does the dialogue show the reader something about the personalities of the characters?

- Setting: Where and when do the events take place? How does the setting affect the plot?

- Plot: What events happen in the story? In what order do the events occur? What is the problem that the main character is struggling with? How is the problem solved?

There are two common ways to set up your narrative paper. You can start at the beginning and tell your story in chronological order, or in the order in which the events happened. Or, you can start at the ending of your story and, through a flashback, tell what events led up to the present time.

Persuasive Writing

Persuasive writing is used when you want to convince your reader that your opinion on a topic is the right one. The goal of this paper is to have your reader agree with what you say. To do this, you need to know your topic well, and you need to give lots of reasons and supporting details. Editorials (opinion writing) in the newspaper, advertisements, and book reviews are all types of persuasive writing.

Key Elements of Persuasive Writing

Choosing a topic that you know well and that you feel strongly about is important for persuasive writing. The feelings or emotions that you have about the topic will come through in your paper and make a stronger argument. Also, be sure that you have a good balance between appealing to the reader's mind (using facts, statistics, experts, and so on) and appealing to the reader's heart (using words that make them feel angry, sad, and so on). Think about these key elements:

- Topic: Is your topic a good one for your audience? Do you know a lot about your topic? Is your topic narrow enough so that you can cover it in a paper?

- Opinion: Is your opinion clear? Do you know enough about the opposite side of your opinion to get rid of those arguments in your paper?

- Reasons: Do you have at least three reasons that explain why you feel the way you do? Are these reasons logical?

- Supporting details or evidence: Do you have facts, statistics, experts, or personal experience that can support each reason?

- Opposing arguments: Can you address the opposite side and get rid of their arguments?

- Conclusion: Can you offer a solution or recommendation to the reader?

- Word choice: Can you find words that set the tone for your opinion? Will these words affect your readers emotionally?

There are two common ways to set up this paper. The first format is a six-paragraph paper: one paragraph for your introduction, three paragraphs for each of your three reasons, one paragraph for the opposing arguments and your responses to them, and one paragraph for your conclusion. Or you can write a five-paragraph paper where you place the opposing arguments and responses to each of your three reasons within the same paragraphs.

Research Report

A research report is an in-depth study of a topic. This type of writing has many uses in all subjects. It involves digging for information in many sources, including books, magazines, newspapers, the Internet, almanacs, encyclopedias, and other places of data. There are many key elements in writing a research report. Choosing a thesis statement, finding support or evidence for that thesis, and citing where you found your information are all important.

There are several uses of a research report in literature. You can explore a writer's life, a particular writing movement, or a certain writer's style. You could also write about a selection.

Business Writing

Business writing has many forms: memos, meeting minutes, brochures, manuals, reports, job applications, contracts, college essays. No matter what the format, the goal of business writing is clear communication. Keep the following key elements in mind when you are doing business writing:

- Format: What type of writing are you doing?

- Purpose: What is the purpose of your writing? Is the purpose clear in your introduction?

- Audience: Are your words and ideas appropriate for your audience?

- Organization: Are your ideas well-organized and easy to follow?

- Style: Are your ideas clearly written and to the point?

The Writing Process

The writing process is a little different for each writer and for each writing assignment. However, the goals of writing never change: Writers want to:

- have a purpose for their writing
- get their readers' attention and keep it
- present their ideas clearly
- choose their words carefully

To meet these goals, writers need to move through a writing process. This process allows them to explore, organize, write, revise, and share their ideas. There are five steps to this writing process: prewriting; drafting; revising; editing and proofreading; and publishing and evaluating.

Use the following steps for any writing assignment:

Step 1: Prewriting

Prewriting is where you explore ideas and decide what to write about. Here are some approaches.

Brainstorming

Brainstorming is fast, fun, and full of ideas. Start by stating a topic. Then write down everything you can think of about that topic. Ask questions about the topic. If you are in a group, have one person write everything down. Think of as many words and ideas as you can in a short time. Don't worry about neatness, spelling, or grammar. When you are finished, group words that are similar. These groups may become your supporting ideas.

Graphic Organizers

Graphic organizers are maps that can lead you through your prewriting. They provide pictures or charts that you fill in. Read the descriptions of these organizers in Appendix A, and choose the ones that will help you organize your ideas.

Outline

An outline can help you organize your information. Write your main ideas next to each Roman numeral. Write your supporting details next to the letters under each Roman numeral. Keep your ideas brief and to the point. Here's an example to follow:

Topic for persuasive paper: Lincoln High School should have a swimming pool.

I. Health benefits for students

    A. Weight control

    B. Good exercise

II. Water safety benefits for students

    A. Learn-to-swim programs

    B. Water safety measures to help others

III. School benefits

    A. Swim team

    B. Added rotation for gym class

IV. Community benefits

    A. More physically fit community members

    B. More jobs for community members

Narrowing Your Topic

Narrowing your topic means to focus your ideas on a specific area. You may be interested in writing about Edgar Allan Poe, but that is a broad topic. What about Poe interests you? Think about your purpose for writing. Is your goal to persuade, to explain, or to compare? Narrowing your scope and knowing your purpose will keep you focused.

Note-Taking and Research

Refer to the "How to Use This Book" section at the beginning of this textbook and Appendix D for help with note-taking and research skills.

Planning Your Voice

Your voice is your special way of using language in your writing. Readers can get to know your personality and thoughts by your sentence structure, word choice, and tone. How will your writing tell what you want to say in your own way? How will it be different from the way others write?

Step 2: Drafting

In the drafting step, you will write your paper. Use your brainstorming notes, outline, and graphic organizers from your prewriting stage as your guide. Your paper will need to include an introduction, a body, and a conclusion.

Introduction

The introduction states your topic and purpose. It includes a *thesis statement*, which is a sentence that tells the main idea of your entire paper. The last line of your introduction is a good place for your thesis statement. That way, your reader has a clear idea of the purpose of your paper before starting to read your points.

Your introduction should make people want to read more. Think about what your audience might like. Try one of these methods:

- asking a question
- sharing a brief story
- describing something
- giving a surprising fact
- using an important quotation

When you begin drafting, just write your introduction. Do not try to make it perfect the first time. You can always change it later.

Body

The body of your paper is made up of several paragraphs. Each paragraph also has a topic sentence, supporting details, and a concluding statement or summary. Remember, too, that each paragraph needs to support your thesis statement in your introduction.

- The topic sentence is usually the first sentence of a paragraph. It lets the reader know what your paragraph is going to be about.

- The supporting details of a paragraph are the sentences that support or tell more about your topic sentence. They can include facts, explanations, examples, statistics, and/or experts' ideas.

- The last sentence of your paragraph is a concluding statement or summary. A concluding statement is a judgment. It is based on the facts that you presented in your paragraph. A summary briefly repeats the main ideas of your paragraph. It repeats your idea or ideas in slightly different words. It does not add new information.

Conclusion

The conclusion ties together the main ideas of the paper. If you asked a question in your introduction, the conclusion answers it. If you outlined a problem, your conclusion offers solutions. The conclusion should not simply restate your thesis and supporting points.

Title of the Paper

Make sure to title your paper. Use a title that is interesting, but relates well to your topic.

Step 3: Revising

Now that you've explored ideas and put them into a draft, it's time to revise. During this step, you will rewrite parts or sections of your paper. All good writing goes through many drafts. To help you make the necessary changes, use the checklists below to review your paper.

Overall Paper

- ☑ Do I have an interesting title that draws readers in?
- ☑ Does the title tell my audience what my paper is about?
- ☑ Do I have an introduction, body, and conclusion?
- ☑ Is my paper the correct length?

Introduction

- ☑ Have I used a method to interest my readers?
- ☑ Do I have a thesis statement that tells the main idea of my paper?
- ☑ Is my thesis statement clearly stated?

Body

- ☑ Do I start every paragraph on a new line?
- ☑ Is the first line of every paragraph indented?
- ☑ Does the first sentence (topic sentence) in every paragraph explain the main idea of the paragraph? Does it attract my readers' attention?
- ☑ Do I include facts, explanations, examples, statistics, and/or experts' ideas that support the topic sentence?
- ☑ Do I need to take out any sentences that do not relate to the topic sentence?
- ☑ Do the paragraphs flow in a logical order? Does each point build on the last one?
- ☑ Do good transition words lead readers from one paragraph to the next?

Conclusion

- ☑ Does the conclusion tie together the main ideas of my paper?
- ☑ Does it offer a solution, make a suggestion, or answer any questions that the readers might have?

Writing Style

- ☑ Do I use words and concepts that my audience understands?
- ☑ Is the tone too formal or informal for my audience?
- ☑ Are my sentences the right length for my audience?
- ☑ Do I have good sentence variety and word choice?

Step 4: Editing and Proofreading

During the editing and proofreading step, check your paper or another student's paper for errors in grammar, punctuation, capitalization, and spelling. Use the following checklists to help guide you. Read and focus on one sentence at a time. Cover up everything but the sentence you are reading. Reading from the end of the paper backward also works for some students. Note changes using the proofreader marks shown on the following page. Check a dictionary or style manual when you're not sure about something.

Grammar

- ☑ Is there a subject and a verb in every sentence?
- ☑ Do the subject and verb agree in every sentence?
- ☑ Is the verb tense logical in every sentence?
- ☑ Is the verb tense consistent in every sentence?
- ☑ Have you used interesting, lively verbs?
- ☑ Do all pronouns have clear antecedents?
- ☑ Can repeated or unnecessary words be left out?
- ☑ Are there any run-on sentences that need to be corrected?
- ☑ Does sentence length vary with long and short sentences?

Punctuation

- ☑ Does every sentence end with the correct punctuation mark?
- ☑ Are all direct quotations punctuated correctly?
- ☑ Do commas separate words in a series?
- ☑ Is there a comma and a coordinating conjunction separating each compound sentence?
- ☑ Is there a comma after an introductory phrase or clause?
- ☑ Are apostrophes used correctly in contractions and possessive nouns?

Capitalization

- ☑ Is the first word of every sentence capitalized?
- ☑ Are all proper nouns and adjectives capitalized?
- ☑ Are the important words in the title of the paper capitalized?

Spelling

- ☑ Are words that sound alike spelled correctly (such as *to*, *too*, and *two*)?
- ☑ Is every plural noun spelled correctly?
- ☑ Are words with *ie* or *ei* spelled correctly?
- ☑ Is the silent *e* dropped before adding an ending that starts with a vowel?
- ☑ Is the consonant doubling rule used correctly?

If the paper was typed, make any necessary changes and run the spell-check and grammar-check programs one more time.

Proofreading Marks

Below are some common proofreading marks. Print out your paper and use these marks to correct errors.

Symbol	Meaning
¶	Start new paragraph
◡	Close up
#	Add a space
∏	Switch words or letters
≡	Capitalize this letter
/	Lowercase this letter
ℯ	Omit space, letter, mark, or word
∧	Insert space, mark, or word
⊙	Insert a period
∧,	Insert a comma
◯ sp	Spell out
. . . . stet	Leave as is (write dots under words)

Step 5: Publishing and Evaluating

Once you have made the final text changes, make sure that the overall format of your paper is correct. Follow the guidelines that were set up by your teacher. Here are some general guidelines that are commonly used.

Readability

- Double space all text.
- Use an easy-to-read font such as Times Roman, Comic Sans, Ariel, or New York.
- Use a 12-point type size.
- Make sure that you have met any word, paragraph, or page count guidelines.

Format

- Make at least a one-inch margin around each page.

- Place the title of the paper, your name, your class period, and the date according to your teacher's guidelines. If you need a title page, make sure that you have a separate page with this information. If you do not need a title page, place your name, class period, and date in the upper right-hand corner of the first page. Center the title below that.

- Check to see if your pages need to be numbered. If so, number them in the upper right-hand corner or according to your teacher's guidelines.

- Label any charts and graphics as needed.

- Check that your title and any subheads are in boldface print.

- Check that your paragraphs are indented.

Citations

- Cite direct quotations, paraphrases, and summaries properly. Refer to the Modern Language Association (MLA) or American Psychological Association (APA) rules.

- Punctuate all citations properly. Refer to MLA or APA rules.

Bibliographies

- Include a list of books and other materials you reviewed during your research. This is a reference list only. Below are examples of how you would list a book, magazine article, and Web site using MLA style:

Book:

Author's Last Name, Author's First Name. *Book Title*. Publisher's City: Publisher's Name, Year.

London, Jack. *The Call of the Wild*. New York: Scholastic, 2001.

Magazine:

Author's Last Name, Author's First Name. "Article Title." *Magazine Title*. Volume Date: Page numbers.

Young, Diane. "At the High End of the River." *Southern Living*. June 2000: 126–131.

Web Site:

Article Title. Date accessed. URL

Circle of Stories. 25 Jan. 2006. <http://www.pbs.org/circleofstories/>

Appendix D: Research

Planning and Writing a Research Report

(↓) *Use the following steps to guide you in writing a research report.*

Step 1: Planning the Report

Choose a subject. Then narrow your topic. You may be interested in the poetry of Robert Frost, but that subject is too broad. Narrow your focus. The graphic organizers in Appendix A may help you narrow your topic and identify supporting details.

Step 2: Finding Useful Information

Go to the library and browse the card catalog for books. Check almanacs, encyclopedias, atlases, and other sources in the reference section. Also review *The Reader's Guide to Periodical Literature* for magazines.

Draw from primary sources. Primary sources are first-hand accounts of information, such as speeches, observations, research results, and interviews. Secondary sources interpret and analyze primary sources.

Use the Internet to further explore your topic. Be careful; some Internet sources are not reliable. Avoid chat rooms, news groups, and personal Web sites. Check the credibility of sites by reviewing the site name and sponsor. Web sites whose URL ends with .org, .gov, and .edu are typically good sources.

Step 3: Logging Information

Use index cards to take notes. Include this information for each source:

- name of author or editor
- title of book or title of article and magazine
- page numbers
- volume numbers
- date of publication
- name of publishing company
- Web site information for Internet sources
- relevant information or direct quotations

Step 4: Getting Organized

Group your cards by similar details and organize them into categories. Find a system that works for you in organizing your cards. You can color-code them, use different-colored index cards for different sections, label them, and so on. Do not use any note cards that do not fit the categories that you have set up. Make conclusions about your research. Write a final topic outline.

Step 5: Writing Your Report

Follow the writing process in Appendix C to write your report. Use your own words to write the ideas you found in your sources (paraphrase). Do not plagiarize—steal and pass off another's words as your own. Write an author's exact words for direct quotations, and name the author or source.

Step 6: Preparing a Bibliography or Works Cited Page

Use the information on your note cards to write a bibliography or works cited page. If you are writing a bibliography, put your note cards in alphabetical order by *title*. If you are writing a works cited page, put your note cards in alphabetical order by *author*.

See *Bibliographies* in Appendix C.

Research Tools

Almanac
An annual publication containing data and tables on politics, religion, education, sports, and more

American Psychological Association (APA) Style
A guide to proper citation to avoid plagiarism in research papers for the social sciences

Atlas
A bound collection of maps of cities, states, regions, and countries including statistics and illustrations

Audio Recording
Recordings of speeches, debates, public proceedings, interviews, etc.

The Chicago Manual of Style
Writing, editing, proofreading, and revising guidelines for the publishing industry

Database
A large collection of data stored electronically and able to be searched

Dictionary
A reference book of words, spellings, pronunciations, meanings, parts of speech, and word origins

Experiment
A series of tests to prove or disprove something

Field Study
Observation, data collection, and interpretation done outside of a laboratory

Glossary
A collection of terms and their meanings

Government Publications
A report of a government action, bill, handbook, or census data usually provided by the Government Printing Office

Grammar Reference
Explanation and examples of parts of speech, sentence structure, and word usage

History
A chronological record that explains past events

Information Services
A stored collection of information organized for easy searching

Internet/World Wide Web
A worldwide network of connected computers that share information

Interview
A dialogue between a subject and a reporter or investigator to gather information

Journal
A type of magazine offering current information on certain subjects such as medicine, the economy, and current events

Microfiche
Historical, printed materials saved to small, thin sheets of film for organization, storage, and use

Modern Language Association (MLA) Handbook
A guide to proper citation to avoid plagiarism in research papers for the humanities

News Source
A newspaper or a radio, television, satellite, or World Wide Web sending of current events and issues presented in a timely manner

Periodical
A magazine, newspaper, or journal

The Reader's Guide to Periodical Literature
A searchable, organized database of magazines, newspapers, and journals used for research

Speech
A public address to inform and to explain

Technical Document
A proposal, instruction manual, training manual, report, chart, table, or other document that provides information

Thesaurus
A book of words and their synonyms, or words that have almost the same meanings

Vertical File
A storage file of original documents or copies of original documents

Appendix E: Speaking

Types of Public Speaking

Public speaking offers a way to inform, to explain, and to entertain. Here are some common types of public speaking:

Debate

A debate is a formal event where two or more people share opposing arguments in response to questions. Often, someone wins by answering questions with solid information.

Descriptive Speech

A descriptive speech uses the five senses of sight, smell, touch, taste, and sound to give vivid details.

Entertaining Speech

An entertaining speech relies on humor through jokes, stories, wit, or making fun of oneself. The humor must be appropriate for the audience and purpose of the speech.

Expository Speech

An expository speech provides more detailed information about a subject. This can be done through classification, analysis, definition, cause and effect, or compare and contrast.

Group Discussion

A group discussion allows the sharing of ideas among three or more people. A group discussion may be impromptu (without being planned) or may include a set topic and list of questions.

Impromptu Speech

An impromptu speech happens at a moment's notice without being planned. The speaker is given a random topic to discuss within a given time period.

Interview

An interview is a dialogue between a subject and a reporter or investigator. An interview draws out information using a question-and-answer format.

Literature Recitation

A literature recitation is the act of presenting a memorized speech, poem, story, or scene in its entire form or with chosen excerpts.

Literature Response

A literature response can serve many purposes. A speaker can compare and contrast plots or characters. An analysis of the work of one author can be presented. Writing style, genre, or period can also be shared.

Narrative

A narrative is a fiction or nonfiction story told with descriptive detail. The speaker also must use voice variation if acting out character dialogue.

Reflective Speech

A reflective speech provides thoughtful analysis of ideas, current events, and processes.

Role Playing

Role playing is when two or more people act out roles to show an idea or practice a character in a story. Role playing can be an effective tool for learning.

Preparing Your Speech

⬇ *Use the following steps to prepare your speech:*

Step 1: Defining Your Purpose

Ask yourself:

- Do I want to inform?

- Do I want to explain something?

- Do I want to entertain?

- Do I want to involve the audience through group discussion, role playing, or debate?

- Do I want to get the audience to act on a subject or an issue?

Step 2: Knowing Your Audience

Ask yourself:

- What information does my audience already know about the topic?

- What questions, concerns, or opinions do they have about the topic?

- How formal or informal does my presentation need to be?

- What words are familiar to my audience? What needs explanation?

- How does my audience prefer to get information? Do they like visuals, audience participation, or lecture?

Step 3: Knowing Your Setting

Ask yourself:

- Who is my audience?

- Is the room large enough to need a microphone and a projector?

- How is the room set up? Am I on stage with a podium or can I interact with the audience?

- Will other noises or activity distract the audience?

Step 4: Narrowing Your Topic

Ask yourself:

- What topic is right for the event? Is it timely? Will it match the mood of the event?

- Is there enough time to share it?

- What topic is right for me to present? Is it something I know and enjoy? Is it something people want to hear from me?

Step 5: Prewriting

Ask yourself:

- What examples, statistics, stories, or descriptions will help me get across my point?

- If telling a story, do I have a sequence of events that includes a beginning, middle, and end?

Step 6: Drafting Your Speech

Your speech will include an introduction, a body, and a conclusion.

The introduction states your topic and purpose. It includes a thesis statement that tells your position. Your introduction should also establish your credibility. Share why you are the right person to give that speech based on your experiences. Lastly, your introduction needs to get people's attention so they want to listen. At the top of the next page are some possible ways to start your speech.

- Ask a question.
- Share a story.
- Describe something.
- Give a surprising fact.
- Share a meaningful quotation.
- Make a memorable, purposeful entrance.

The body of your speech tells more about your main idea and tries to prevent listener misunderstandings. It should include any of the following supporting evidence:

- facts
- details
- explanations
- reasons
- examples
- personal stories or experiences
- experts
- literary devices and images

The conclusion of your speech ties your speech together. If you asked a question in your introduction, the conclusion answers it. If you outlined a problem, your conclusion offers solutions. If you told a story, revisit that story. You may even want to ask your audience to get involved, take action, or become more informed on your topic.

Step 7: Selecting Visuals

Ask yourself:

- Is a visual aid needed for the audience to better understand my topic?
- What visual aids work best for my topic?
- Do I have access to the right technology?

The size of your audience and the setting for your speech will also impact what you select. Remember that a projection screen and overhead speakers are necessary for large groups. If you plan on giving handouts to audience members, have handouts ready for pickup by the entrance of the room. A slide show or a video presentation will need a darkened room. Be sure that you have someone available to help you with the lights.

Practicing and Delivering Your Speech

Giving a speech is about more than simply talking. You want to look comfortable and confident.

Practice how you move, how you sound, and how you work with visuals and the audience.

Know Your Script

Every speaker is afraid of forgetting his or her speech. Each handles this fear in a different way. Choose the device that works for you.

- Memorization: Know your speech by heart. Say it often so you sound natural.
- Word-for-word scripts: Highlight key phrases to keep you on track. Keep the script on a podium, so you are not waving sheets of paper around as you talk. Be careful not to read from your script. The audience wants to see your eyes.
- Outlines: Write a sentence outline of your main points and supporting details that you want to say in a specific way. Transitions and other words can be spoken impromptu (without being planned).

- Key words: Write down key words that will remind you what to say, like "Tell story about the dog."

- Put your entire speech, outline, or key words on note cards to stay on track. They are small and not as obvious as paper. Number them in case they get out of order.

Know Yourself

Your voice and appearance are the two most powerful things you bring to a speech. Practice the following, so you are comfortable, confident, and convincing:

- Body language: Stand tall. Keep your feet shoulder-width apart. Don't cross your arms or bury your hands in your pockets. Use gestures to make a point. For example, hold up two fingers when you say, "My second point is . . ." Try to relax; that way, you will be in better control of your body.

- Eye contact: Look at your audience. Spend a minute or two looking at every side of the room and not just the front row. The audience will feel as if you are talking to them.

- Voice strategies: Clearly pronounce your words. Speak at a comfortable rate and loud enough for everyone to hear you. Vary your volume, rate, and pitch when you are trying to emphasize something. For example, you could say, "I have a secret. . . ." Then, you could lean toward the audience and speak in a loud, clear whisper as if you are telling them a secret. This adds dramatic effect and engages the audience.

- Repetition of key phrases or words: Repetition is one way to help people remember your point. If something is important, say it twice. Use transitions such as, "This is so important it is worth repeating" or "As I said before, we must act now."

Appendix F: Listening

Listening Strategy Checklist

Here are some ways you can ensure that you are a good listener.

Be an Active Listener

- ☑ Complete reading assignments that are due prior to the presentation.
- ☑ Focus on what is being said.
- ☑ Ask for definitions of unfamiliar terms.
- ☑ Ask questions to clarify what you heard.
- ☑ Ask the speaker to recommend other readings or resources.

Be a Critical Listener

- ☑ Identify the thesis or main idea of the speech.
- ☑ Try to predict what the speaker is going to say based on what you already know.
- ☑ Determine the speaker's purpose of the speech.
- ☑ Note supporting facts, statistics, examples, and other details.
- ☑ Determine if supporting detail is relevant, factual, and appropriate.
- ☑ Form your conclusions about the presentation.

Be an Appreciative Listener

- ☑ Relax.
- ☑ Enjoy the listening experience.
- ☑ Welcome the opportunity to laugh and learn.

Be a Thoughtful and Feeling Listener

- ☑ Understand the experiences of the speaker.
- ☑ Value the emotion he or she brings to the subject.
- ☑ Summarize or paraphrase what you believe the speaker just said.
- ☑ Tell the speaker that you understand his or her feelings.

Be an Alert Listener

- ☑ Sit up straight.
- ☑ Sit near the speaker and face the speaker directly.
- ☑ Make eye contact and nod to show you are listening.
- ☑ Open your arms so you are open to receiving information.

Analyze the Speaker

- ☑ Does the speaker have the experiences and knowledge to speak on the topic?
- ☑ Is the speaker prepared?
- ☑ Does the speaker appear confident?
- ☑ Is the speaker's body language appropriate?
- ☑ What do the speaker's tone, volume, and word choices show?

Identify the Details

- ☑ Listen for the tendency of the speaker to favor or oppose something without real cause.
- ☑ Be aware of propaganda—someone forcing an opinion on you.
- ☑ Don't be swayed by the clever way the speaker presents something.
- ☑ After the speech ask about words that you don't know.

Identify Fallacies of Logic

A fallacy is a false idea intended to trick someone. Here are some common fallacies:

- *Ad hominem*: This type of fallacy attacks a person's character, lifestyle, or beliefs. Example: Joe should not be on the school board because he skipped classes in college.

- False causality: This type of fallacy gives a cause–effect relationship that is not logical. This fallacy assumes that something caused something else only because it came before the consequence. Example: Ever since that new family moved into the neighborhood, our kids are getting into trouble.

- Red herring: This type of fallacy uses distractions to take attention away from the main issue. Example: Since more than half of our nation's people are overweight, we should not open a fast-food restaurant in our town.

- Overgeneralization: This type of fallacy uses words such as *every*, *always*, or *never*. Claims do not allow for exceptions to be made. Example: People who make more than a million dollars a year never pay their fair share of taxes.

- Bandwagon effect: This type of fallacy appeals to one's desire to be a part of the crowd. It is based on popular opinion and not on evidence. Example: Anyone who believes that our town is a great place to live should vote for the local tax increase.

Take Notes

- Write down key messages and phrases, not everything that is said.

- Abbreviate words.

- Listen for cues that identify important details, like "Here's an example" or "To illustrate what I mean."

- Draw graphs, charts, and diagrams for future reference.

- Draw arrows, stars, and circles to highlight information or group information.

- Highlight or circle anything that needs to be clarified or explained.

- Use the note-taking strategies explained in "How to Use This Book" at the beginning of this textbook.

Appendix G: Viewing

Visual aids can help communicate information and ideas. The following checklist gives pointers for viewing and interpreting visual aids.

Design Elements

Colors

☑ What colors stand out?

☑ What feelings do they make you think of?

☑ What do they symbolize or represent?

☑ Are colors used realistically or for emphasis?

Shapes

☑ What shapes are created by space or enclosed in lines?

☑ What is important about the shapes? What are they meant to symbolize or represent?

Lines

☑ What direction do the lines lead you?

☑ Which objects are you meant to focus on?

☑ What is the importance of the lines?

☑ Do lines divide or segment areas? Why do you think this is?

Textures

☑ What textures are used?

☑ What emotions or moods are they meant to affect?

Point of View

Point of view shows the artist's feelings toward the subject. Analyze this point of view:

☑ What point of view is the artist taking?

☑ Do you agree with this point of view?

☑ Is the artist successful in communicating this point of view?

Graphics

Line Graphs

Line graphs show changes in numbers over time.

☑ What numbers and time frame are represented?

☑ Does the information represent appropriate changes?

Pie Graphs

Pie graphs represent parts of a whole.

☑ What total number does the pie represent?

☑ Do the numbers represent an appropriate-sized sample?

Bar Graphs

Bar graphs compare amounts.

☑ What amounts are represented?

☑ Are the amounts appropriate?

Charts and Tables

Charts and tables organize information for easy comparison.

☑ What is being presented?

☑ Do columns and rows give equal data to compare and contrast?

Maps

☑ What land formations are shown?

☑ What boundaries are shown?

☑ Are there any keys or symbols on the map? What do they mean?

Appendix H: Media and Technology

Forms of Media

Television, movies, and music are some common forms of media that you know a lot about. Here are some others.

Advertisement

An advertisement selling a product or a service can be placed in a newspaper or magazine, on the Internet, or on television or radio.

Broadcast News

Broadcast news is offered on a 24-hour cycle through nightly newscasts, all-day news channels, and the Internet.

Documentary

A documentary shares information about people's lives, historic events, objects, or places. It is based on facts and evidence.

Internet and World Wide Web

This worldwide computer network offers audio and video clips, news, reference materials, research, and graphics.

Journal

A journal records experiences, current research, or ideas about a topic for a target audience.

Magazine

A magazine includes articles, stories, photos, and graphics of general interest.

Newspaper

A newspaper most often is printed daily or weekly.

Photography

Traditionally, photography has been the art or process of producing images on a film surface using light. Today, digital images are often used.

The Media and You

The media's role is to entertain, to inform, and to advertise. Media can help raise people's awareness about current issues. Media also can give clues about the needs and beliefs of the people.

Use a critical eye and ear to sort through the thousands of messages presented to you daily. Be aware of the media's use of oversimplified ideas about people, decent and acceptable language, and appropriate messages. Consider these questions:

- Who is being shown and why?
- What is being said? Is it based on fact?
- How do I feel about what and how it is said?

Technology and You

Technology can improve communication. Consider the following when selecting technology for research or presentations:

Audio/Sound

Speeches, music, sound effects, and other elements can set a mood or reinforce an idea.

Computers

- Desktop publishing programs offer tools for making newsletters and posters.
- Software programs are available for designing publications, Web sites, databases, and more.
- Word processing programs feature dictionaries, grammar-check and spell-check programs, and templates for memos, reports, letters, and more.

Multimedia

Slide shows, movies, and other electronic media can help the learning process.

Visual Aids

Charts, tables, maps, props, drawings, and graphs provide visual representation of information.

Handbook of Literary Terms

A

Act (akt) a major unit of action in a play (p. 113)

Alliteration (ə lit e rā′ shən) repeating sounds by using words whose beginning sounds are the same (pp. 14, 102, 286, 391)

Allusion (ə lü′ zhən) a reference to a historical event, person, place, or work of literature (pp. 308, 444, 620)

Analogy (ə nal′ ə jē) a figure of speech that uses one thing to stand for another (p. 194)

Anecdote (an′ ik dōt) a short account of an interesting event in someone's life (p. 34)

Antagonist (an tag′ ə nist) a person or thing in the story struggling against the main character (p. 159)

Archetype (är′ kə tīp) detail, plot pattern, character type, or theme found in the literature of many different cultures (p. 5)

Aside (ə sīd′) when a character in a play is heard by the audience but not by the other characters (p. 113)

Assonance (as′ n əns) repeating sounds by using words with the same vowel sounds (p. 159)

Autobiography (ȯ tə bī og′ rə fē) a person's life story, written by that person (p. 45)

B

Ballad (bal′ əd) a simple song that often uses a refrain, sometimes uses rhyme, and is passed from person to person (p. 23)

Biography (bī og′ rə fē) a person's life story told by someone else (p. 242)

Blank verse (blangk vėrs) unrhymed poetry (p. 269)

C

Character (kar′ ik tər) a person or animal in a story, poem, or play (pp. 5, 159, 292, 472, 565)

Characterization (kar ik tər ə zā′ shən) the way a writer develops character qualities and personality traits (pp. 34, 159, 396, 472, 578)

Character trait (kar′ ik tər trāt) a character's way of thinking, behaving, or speaking (pp. 308, 350)

Classical drama (klas′ ə kəl drä′ mə) play that follows the style of ancient Greek and Latin drama (p. 113)

Climax (klī′ maks) the high point of interest or suspense in a story or play, at which a major change occurs (pp. 23, 590)

Column (kol′ əm) an article that appears regularly in a newspaper or magazine (p. 549)

Comedy (kom′ ə dē) a play with a happy ending, intended to amuse its audience (p. 396)

Conceit (kən sēt′) a complex or strained metaphor (p. 131)

Conflict (kon′ flikt) the struggle of the main character against himself or herself, another person, or nature (pp. 159, 292, 590)

Consonance (kon′ sə nəns) the repetition of consonant sounds, usually within the context of several words (p. 444)

Couplet (kup′ lit) a rhyming pair (pp. 34, 108, 215)

a	hat	e	let	ī	ice	ȯ	order	u̇	put	sh	she	ə	a	in about
ā	age	ē	equal	o	hot	oi	oil	ü	rule	th	thin		e	in taken
ä	far	ėr	term	ō	open	ou	out	ch	child	͡TH	then		i	in pencil
â	care	i	it	ȯ	saw	u	cup	ng	long	zh	measure		o	in lemon
													u	in circus

D

Description (di skrip′ shən) a written picture of the characters, events, and settings in a story (pp. 183, 590)

Dialect (dī′ ə lekt) the speech of a particular part of a country or of a certain group of people (pp. 23, 374)

Dialogue (dī′ ə lög) the conversation among characters in a story (pp. 374, 578); the words that characters in a play speak (p. 113)

Diary (dī′ ə rē) a daily record of personal events, thoughts, or private feelings (p. 280)

Diction (dik′ shən) proper choice of words; saying words correctly (p. 501)

Drama (drä′ mə) a story told through the words and actions of characters, written to be performed as well as read; a play (pp. 113, 396)

Dramatic monologue (drə mat′ ik mon′ l òg) a poem in which a character talks to the reader or to a silent second character (p. 350)

E

Epic (ep′ ik) a long story written in verse, usually involving a heroic figure (pp. 5, 620)

Epiphany (i pif′ ə nē) the moment in a story when a character realizes an important truth (p. 565)

Essay (es′ ā) a written work that shows a writer's opinions on some basic or current issue (pp. 63, 96, 249, 449)

Etymology (et ə mol′ ə jē) a history of a word shown by tracing its development from its first use in a language (p. 5)

Exaggeration (eg zaj ə rā′ shən) the use of words to make something seem more than it is (p. 183)

F

Falling action (fò′ ling ak′ shən) the action that occurs after the climax to wind up the story (p. 590)

Fantasy (fan′ tə sē) imaginative fiction that often has strange settings and characters (p. 183)

Farce (färs) writing that uses satire and comedy, with an unlikely plot (p. 396)

Fiction (fik′ shən) writing that is imaginative and designed to entertain; the author creates the events and characters (p. 292)

Figurative language (fig′ yər ə tiv lang′ gwij) writing or speech not meant to be understood exactly as written; writers use figurative language to express ideas in vivid or imaginative ways (pp. 137, 343, 449, 620)

Figure of speech (fig′ yər uv spēch) a word or phrase that has meaning different from the actual meaning, such as idioms, metaphors, and similes (pp. 91, 323, 408, 438)

First person (fèrst pèr′ sən) a point of view where the narrator is also a character, using the pronouns *I* and *we* (pp. 14, 183, 565)

Foil (foil) a character who contrasts with the main character (p. 113); a minor character who shows the traits of a major character through contrast (p. 242)

Free verse (frē vèrs) poetry that does not have a strict rhyming pattern or regular line length and uses actual speech patterns for the rhythms of sound (p. 464)

G

Genre (zhän′ rə) a specific type, or kind, of literature (pp. 137, 308)

H

Historical fiction (hi stôr′ ə kəl fik′ shən) fictional writing that draws on factual events of history (p. 205)

Humor (hyü′ mər) literature created to be funny or to amuse (p. 531)

Hyperbole (hī pèr′ bə lē) extreme exaggeration that shows something is important (pp. 108, 153)

I

Iambic pentameter (ī am′ bik pen tam′ ə tər) five two-beat sounds in a line of poetry where the second syllable is stressed in each pair (pp. 81, 215, 269, 350, 433)

Idiom (id′ ē əm) a phrase that has a different meaning than its words really mean (p. 578)

Imagery (im′ ij rē) pictures created by words; the use of words that appeal to the five senses (pp. 5, 223, 323, 385, 507, 605)

Irony (ī′ rə nē) difference between what is expected to happen in a story and what does happen (pp. 419, 449); the use of words that seem to say one thing but mean the opposite (pp. 183, 323, 449)

J

Journal (jėr′ nl) writing that expresses an author's feelings or first impressions about a subject (pp. 205, 280)

L

Legend (lej′ ənd) a story from folklore featuring characters who actually lived or real events or places (p. 53)

Letter (let′ ər) impressions and feelings written to a specific person (p. 194)

Lyric poetry (lir′ ik pō′ i trē) a short poem that expresses a person's emotions or feelings (p. 408)

M

Main idea (mān ī dē′ ə) the overall, general idea that is set forth in a written work and supported by details (p. 96)

Metaphor (met′ ə fôr) a figure of speech that makes a comparison but does not use *like* or *as* (pp. 108, 194, 328, 444, 590)

Metonymy (mə tä′ nə mē) a figure of speech that replaces the intended word with a related word that is symbolic (p. 194)

Mood

Mood (müd) the feeling that writing creates (pp. 14, 343, 413, 578)

Motive (mō′ tiv) a reason a character does something (p. 486)

N

Narrator (nar′ ā tər) one who tells a story (pp. 14, 565)

Nonfiction (non fik′ shən) writing containing information that is factual; may be presented through detailed descriptions or examples (p. 234); writing about real people and events (p. 549)

Novel (nov′ əl) a long work of fiction (p. 292); fiction that is book-length and has more plot and character details than a short story (p. 362)

O

Onomatopoeia (on ə mat ə pē′ ə) using words that sound like their meaning (p. 286)

P

Paradox (par′ ə doks) a statement that includes opposite meanings but still makes sense (pp. 86, 148, 269)

Parallel structure (par′ ə lel struk′ chər) the phrasing of words to balance ideas that are equally important (p. 126)

Parody (par′ ə dē) an exaggerated look at a situation (p. 108)

Pastoral (pas′ tər əl) dealing with shepherds or country life (p. 102)

Personification (pər son ə fə kā′ shən) giving animals or objects the characteristics or qualities of humans (pp. 108, 223)

Plot (plot) the series of events in a story (pp. 5, 183, 308, 374, 565)

Poetry (pō′ i trē) literature in verse form that usually has rhythm and paints powerful or beautiful impressions with words (pp. 14, 102)

a	hat	e	let	ī	ice	ȯ	order	u̇	put	sh	she		ə	a	in about
ā	age	ē	equal	o	hot	oi	oil	ü	rule	th	thin			e	in taken
ä	far	ėr	term	ō	open	ou	out	ch	child	ᵺ	then			i	in pencil
â	care	i	it	ȯ	saw	u	cup	ng	long	zh	measure			o	in lemon
														u	in circus

Point of view (point uv vyü) the position from which the author or storyteller tells the story (pp. 167, 362, 486, 605)

Prose (prōz) all writing that is not poetry (pp. 242, 280)

Protagonist (prō tag′ ə nist) the main character in a story; also called the hero (pp. 183, 374, 565)

Q

Quatrain (kwot′ rān) group of four lines (p. 23)

R

Refrain (ri frān′) repeated words or phrases that create mood or give importance to something (p. 23)

Repetition (rep ə tish′ ən) using a word, phrase, or image more than once, for emphasis (pp. 137, 464)

Resolution (rez ə lü′ shən) the act of solving the conflict in a story (p. 590)

Rhyme (rīm) words that end with the same or similar sounds (pp. 81, 357)

Rhyme scheme (rīm skēm) the pattern created by the ending sounds of the lines of a poem (p. 433)

Rhythm (riŦH′ əm) a pattern created by the stressed and unstressed syllables in a line of poetry (pp. 81, 223, 343, 433, 520)

Rising action (rī′ zing ak′ shən) the buildup of excitement in a story (p. 590)

Romance (rō mans′) a story about heroes, mysterious settings, or love (pp. 53, 323)

S

Satire (sat′ īr) humorous writing that makes fun of foolishness or evil (pp. 183, 396)

Sequence (sē′ kwəns) the order of events in a literary work (pp. 143, 223)

Setting (set′ ing) the time and place in a story (pp. 531, 565)

Short story (shôrt stôr′ ē) a brief work of prose fiction that includes plot, setting, characters, point of view, and theme (pp. 472, 565)

Simile (sim′ ə lē) a figure of speech in which two things are compared using a phrase that includes the word *like* or *as* (pp. 303, 472, 578)

Sonnet (son′ it) a 14-line poem written in iambic pentameter (pp. 81, 357, 433)

Speech (spēch) a written work meant to be read aloud (p. 513)

Stanza (stan′ zə) a group of lines that forms a unit in a poem (p. 86)

Stream of consciousness (strēm uv kon′ shəs nis) a writing technique that develops the plot by allowing the reader to see how and what the characters are thinking (pp. 472, 565)

Style (stīl) an author's way of writing (pp. 86, 234, 513, 525)

Surprise ending (sər prīz′ en′ ding) an ending in a narrative that has an unusual, unexpected twist and usually makes a strong point (p. 419)

Symbol (sim′ bəl) something that represents something else (pp. 143, 444)

Symbolism (sim′ bə liz əm) the larger meaning of a person, place, or object (p. 544)

T

Theme (thēm) the main idea of a literary work (pp. 5, 96, 249, 444, 620)

Third person (thėrd pėr′ sən) a point of view where the narrator is not a character and refers to characters as *he* or *she* (pp. 45, 486, 605)

Tone (tōn) the attitude an author takes toward a subject (pp. 131, 433)

Tragedy (traj′ ə dē) a play that ends with the suffering or death of one or more of the main characters (p. 113)

V

Voice (vois) the way a writer expresses ideas through style, form, content, and purpose (pp. 86, 234, 513)

Glossary

A

Abase (ə bās′) make lower; put down (p. 379)

Abhor (ab hôr′) hate (p. 315)

Abhorrence (ab hôr′ əns) hate (p. 254)

Ablative absolute (a′ blə tiv ab′ sə lüt) a Latin grammatical term (p. 550)

Aboon (ə bün′) above (p. 26)

Abrogated (ab′ rə gā tid) made invalid (p. 251)

Abstemious (ab stē′ mē əs) not taking much food or drink (p. 245)

Accumulated (ə kyü′ myə lā tid) piled up (p. 309)

Acknowledge (ak nol′ ij) accept as true (p. 492)

Acknowledged (ak nol′ ijd) agreed upon as true (p. 293); recognized (p. 476)

Acrid (ak′ rid) bitter (p. 593)

Adamantine (a də man′ tēn) unbreakable (p. 160)

Adieu (ə dyü′) goodbye (in French) (p. 330)

Adjournment (ə jèrn′ mənt) ending until a later time (p. 515)

Admonish (ad mon′ ish) give friendly advice to (p. 16)

Adulteries (ə dul′ tər ēz) falseness (p. 138)

Affectation (af ek tā′ shən) posing; pretending something one is not (p. 97); artificial behavior (p. 255)

Affections (ə fek′ shənz) frame of mind (p. 120)

Affinity (ə fin′ ə tē) kinship (p. 237)

Affliction['s] (ə flik′ shən[z]) distress (p. 9); sickness, suffering (pp. 116, 161); belonging to the weak or troubled (p. 168)

Affront (ə frunt′) meet (p. 115); insult (p. 553)

Aggregated (ag′ rə gā tid) collected (p. 236)

Aggrieved (ə grēvd′) suffering from a denial of legal rights (p. 58)

Agitate (aj′ ə tāt) stir up (p. 251)

Agitated (aj′ ə tāt id) upset; not calm (p. 366)

Ailment (āl′ mənt) illness (p. 398)

Aimless (ām′ lis) without a goal (p. 450)

Alack (ə lak′) interjection showing sorrow (p. 25)

Alleged (ə lejd′) brought forward as an authority (p. 169)

Allowance (ə lou′ əns) excuse (p. 515)

Allusion (ə lü′ zhən) reference (p. 377)

Altered (ȯl′ tərd) changed (p. 457)

Alternative (ȯl tèr′ nə tiv) choice (p. 457)

Alum (al′ əm) aluminum sulfate (p. 67)

Amble (am′ bəl) walk in an unnatural way (p. 120)

Amends (ə mendz′) repayment (p. 298)

Amiability (ā mē ə bil′ ə tē) friendliness (p. 569)

Amiable (ā′ mē ə bəl) pleasing; admirable (p. 48); friendly (p. 583)

Amorous (am′ ər əs) passionate (p. 155)

Anarchy (an′ ər kē) lawless disorder (p. 445)

Ancestral (an ses′ trəl) from ancestors; inherited (p. 622)

Anemone (ə nem′ ə nē) flowering plant in the buttercup family (p. 281)

Anguish (ang′ gwish) suffering (p. 363); great pain (p. 573)

Angular (ang′ gyə lər) sharp; not smooth (p. 377)

Annals (an′ lz) chronicles (p. 225)

Annihilate (ə nī′ ə lāt) wipe out (p. 569)

Anointest (ə noint′ əst) apply oil or perfume as part of a ritual (p. 127)

Anon (ə non′) soon (p. 56); again (p. 309)

Anticipation (an tis ə pā′ shən) looking ahead (p. 585)

a	hat	e	let	ī	ice	ȯ	order	ü	put	sh	she
ā	age	ē	equal	o	hot	oi	oil	ü	rule	th	thin
ä	far	èr	term	ō	open	ou	out	ch	child	ᴙ	then
â	care	i	it	ȯ	saw	u	cup	ng	long	zh	measure

ə { a in about / e in taken / i in pencil / o in lemon / u in circus }

Anti-climax (an ti klī′ maks) letdown (p. 536)

Apathy (ap′ ə thē) lack of interest or concern (p. 255)

Apostate (ə pos′ tāt) abandoning a previous loyalty (p. 163)

Apostolical (ap ə stol′ i kəl) related to religious authority (p. 238)

Appeased (ə pēzd′) calmed; soothed (p. 539)

Appellation (ap ə lā′ shən) name or title (p. 252)

Apprehension (ap ri hen′ shən) nervousness; fear (p. 532)

Arc (ärk) half-circle (p. 615)

Ardent (ärd′ nt) eager (p. 440)

Arduous (är′ jü əs) difficult; tiring (p. 243)

Argent (är′ jənt) silver or white (p. 217)

Arid (ar′ id) very dry (p. 607)

Array (ə rā′) clothing and possessions (p. 36)

Aspect (as′ pekt) face (p. 304)

Aspirations (as pə rā′ shənz) goals (p. 378)

Aspiring (ə spīr′ ing) seeking to reach a goal (p. 219)

Assay (ə sā′) attempt (p. 92)

Assayed (ə sād′) tried (p. 55)

Assemblies (ə sem′ blēz) gatherings of people (p. 296)

Assertion (ə sėr′ shən) claim (pp. 65, 377)

Astute (ə stüt′) shrewd (p. 477)

Athwart (ə thwôrt′) from side to side; crosswise (p. 287)

Atone (ə tōn′) make up for something (p. 368)

Au pair (ō pâr) foreign person who cares for children in exchange for room and board and a chance to learn the language of employers (p. 580)

Automaton (ȯ tom′ ə ton) robot (p. 364)

Avail (ə vāl′) help (p. 236)

Avowed (ə voud′) swore (p. 353)

Awful (ȯ′ fəl) creating a sense of awe or wonder (p. 510)

B

Bade (bād) told (p. 47)

Baited (bā′ tid) did something to get someone else to react (p. 450)

Baldrick (bȯl′ drik) ornamental belt (p. 39)

Baleful (bāl′ fəl) fearsome (p. 7); evil (p. 161)

Bane (bān) source of ruin (p. 6)

Barb'rous (bär′ brəs) extremely cruel, brutal (p. 168)

Bark (bärk) boat (p. 109)

Barricade (bar ə kād′) block (p. 309)

Base (bās) low (p. 380)

Baser (bās′ ər) lacking higher qualities of mind or spirit (p. 92)

Bawd (bȯd) person who keeps a brothel (p. 119)

Bawn (bȯn) hall (p. 7)

Bays (bāz) outward curved portions of a window (p. 473)

Bazaars (bə zärz′) outdoor markets (p. 450)

Befallen (bi fȯ′ lən) happened to (p. 368)

Beholden (bi hōl′ dən) indebted (p. 57)

Belied (bi līd′) gave a false impression of (p. 109)

Benevolent (bə nev′ ə lənt) kind (p. 315)

Benumbed (bi numd′) without feeling (p. 613)

Bereaved (bi rēvd′) deprived, robbed (p. 169)

Betimes (bi tīmz′) early (p. 409)

Blanch (blanch) grow pale (p. 18)

Blasted (blas′ tid) ruined (p. 120)

Bloke (blōk′) man (p. 550)

Bodice (bo′ dis) top portion of a dress, covering the torso (p. 489)

Bodkin (bod′ kən) dagger (p. 117)

Bone-lappings (bōn la′ pingz) joints and ligaments (p. 7)

Bough (bou) branch (p. 352)

Bounty (boun′ tē) generosity (p. 229)

Bourn (bôrn) border, boundary (p. 118)

Bracketed (brak′ i tid) attached or fixed to (p. 623)

Braid (brād) open (p. 24)

Brawling (brô' ling) fighting (p. 309)

Breach (brēch) a break, rupture, or tear (p. 133); violation, breaking (p. 169)

Brede (brēd) embroidery (p. 331)

Brevity (brev' ə tē) shortness (p. 537)

Brinded (brin' did) streaked with dark hairs (p. 392)

Broo (brü) brew, water in which something has been boiled (p. 29)

Brooch (brōch) decorative pin or pendant (p. 40)

Brooded (brü' did) worried; thought dark thoughts (p. 534)

Brutes (brüts) animals (p. 195)

Bubbled (bub' əld) made into something that lacks firmness or reality (p. 251)

Buff jerkin (buf jėr' kən) leather jacket (p. 185)

Buoyancy (boi' ən sē) optimism; good spirits (p. 516)

Burgess (bėr' jis) town leader (p. 46)

Burnished (bėr' nisht) polished (pp. 39, 476)

Buttery (but' ər ē) pantry (p. 49)

C

Cadence (kād' ns) rhythm; beat (p. 386)

Cadet (kə det') one in training for military service (p. 37)

Callousness (kal' əs nis) coldness (p. 534)

Calumny (kal' əm nē) insults that call one's character into question (p. 119)

Candidly (kan' did lē) truthfully (p. 400)

Canny (kan' ē) clever; careful (p. 7)

Cant (kant) word used by a particular group (p. 238); insincere speech (p. 379)

Capacity (kə pas' ə tē) position; job (p. 537)

Caprice (kə prēs') sudden whim (p. 235); impulsiveness (p. 295)

Cartridges (kär' trij iz) small containers that hold bullets and gunpowder (p. 453)

Cast (cast) covering (p. 118)

Catalogue (kat' l óg) list (p. 516)

Cataract (kat' ə rakt) waterfall (p. 272)

Cataract-like (kat' ə rakt līk) like a waterfall (p. 369)

Cavalry (kav' əl rē) army on horseback (p. 38)

Caverns (kav' ərnz) caves (p. 458)

Ceaseless (sēs' lis) never-ending (p. 597)

Certitude (sėr' tə tüd) certainty; sureness (p. 387)

Chafed (chāft) rubbed raw; became irritated (p. 569)

Chaired (chârd) carried (p. 409)

Chaise and four (shāz ənd fôr) light carriage pulled by four horses (p. 293)

Charge (chärj) run toward something with force (p. 456)

Charitable (char' ə tə bəl) generous (p. 566)

Charity (char' ə tē) goodwill or helpfulness (p. 46)

Chasm (kaz' əm) deep gorge (p. 287)

Chaste (chāst) pure in thought and act; virtuous (pp. 19, 149)

Chasten (chā' sn) punish (p. 273)

Cherub (cher' əb) angel (p. 488)

Chirurgeon (kī rėr' jən) surgeon (p. 209)

Chivalry (shiv' əl rē) the customs of medieval knighthood (p. 36)

Christened (kris' nd) named (or renamed) (p. 401)

Chrysalis (kris' ə lis) cocoon of a butterfly (p. 345)

Cincture (singk' chər) sash (p. 479)

Circumscribed (sėr kəm skrībd') limited (p. 226)

Circumspection (sėr kəm spek' shən) caution (p. 297)

Citadel (sit' ə dəl) walled city (p. 330)

Civilly (siv' əl ē) politely (p. 376)

a	hat	e	let	ī	ice	ó	order	ù	put	sh	she	ə	a in about
ā	age	ē	equal	o	hot	oi	oil	ü	rule	th	thin		e in taken
ä	far	ėr	term	ō	open	ou	out	ch	child	ᴛH	then		i in pencil
â	care	i	it	ȯ	saw	u	cup	ng	long	zh	measure		o in lemon
													u in circus

Clamor (klam′ ər) loud, continuous noise (p. 592)

Clarion (klar′ ē ən) a loud, clear trumpet (p. 224)

Clemency (klem′ ən sē) mercy (p. 314)

Climes (klīmz) climates (p. 304)

Clinched (klincht) sealed; made final (p. 613)

Closely (klōs′ lē) secretly (p. 115)

Clotted (klo′ tid) made thick (p. 599)

Cloy'd (kloid) overfull (p. 330)

Coherent (kō hir′ ənt) consistent; understandable (p. 217)

Colossal (kə los′ əl) huge (p. 324)

Comfy (kum′ fē) comfortable (p. 492)

Commerce (kom′ ərs) interaction (p. 119)

Commiserate (kə miz′ ə rāt) pity; feel compassion for (p. 315)

Commiseration (kə miz ə rā′ shən) sympathy (p. 535)

Commission (kə mish′ ən) fee paid for a service (p. 474); charge; assignment (p. 514)

Commons (kom′ ənz) common people (p. 55)

Compass (kum′ pəs) boundary (p. 210)

Compassion (kəm pash′ ən) pity (p. 49)

Compère (com pâr′) friend or companion (in French) (p. 622)

Comply (kəm plī′) to do as asked (p. 316)

Composed (kəm pōzd′) calmed (p. 533)

Compost (kom′ pōst) decayed plant matter used for fertilizer (p. 608)

Compound (kom′ pound) group of buildings, usually within a wall or fence (p. 592)

Compressed (kəm prest′) pressed together tightly (p. 476)

Compulsion (kəm pul′ shən) force (p. 378)

Conception (kən sep′ shən) beginning of an idea (p. 468)

Concussion (kən kush′ ən) hard blow (p. 311)

Condescend (kon di send′) lower (p. 169); stoop to an undignified level (p. 255)

Condescension (kon di sen′ shən) stooping to a lower level (p. 377); the attitude that one is better than others (p. 582)

Condolence (kən dō′ ləns) expression of sympathy (p. 623)

Conference (kon′ fər əns) formal discussing of views among people (p. 98)

Conferred upon (kən fėrd′ ə pon′) given to (p. 515)

Confessor (kən fes′ ər) priest who hears confessions (p. 46)

Confinement (kən fīn′ mənt) captivity (p. 606)

Confirmation (kon fər mā′ shən) something that proves truth (p. 316)

Confounded (kən foun′ did) frustrated (p. 161); confused (p. 237)

Confute (kən fyüt′) overwhelm in argument (p. 97)

Conjectured (kən jek′ chərd) supposed (p. 184)

Conjecturing (kən jek′ chər ing) wondering; guessing (p. 298)

Conjured (kon′ jərd) called up (p. 551)

Conjurer (kon′ jər ər) magician (p. 455)

Consolation (kon sə lā′ shən) comfort (p. 310)

Conspicuous (kən spik′ yü əs) obvious (p. 256)

Constitution (kon stə tü′ shən) law or custom (p. 253); nature (p. 256)

Constraining (kən strā′ ning) holding back (p. 376)

Consummation (kon sə mā′ shən) completion, end (p. 117)

Contemn (kən tem′) dislike (p. 97)

Contemplated (kon′ təm plā tid) thought about (p. 612)

Contempt (kən tempt′) lack of respect (p. 252)

Contend (kən tend′) debate (p. 98)

Contention (kən ten′ shən) rivalry; competition (p. 163)

Continual (kən tin′ yü əl) constant (p. 508)

Contortion (kən tôr′ shən) twisting of the body (p. 377)

Contracts (kən trakts′) grows smaller (p. 584)

Contrite (kon′ trīt) sorry; regretful (p. 414)

Contrived (kən trīvd′) designed (p. 196)

Contumely (kon′ tyüm lē) insulting behavior (p. 117)